WE HAVE NEVER BEEN WOKE

We Have Never Been Woke

The Cultural Contradictions of a New Elite

Musa al-Gharbi

PRINCETON UNIVERSITY PRESS

PRINCETON AND OXFORD

Published by Princeton University Press
41 William Street, Princeton, New Jersey 08540
99 Banbury Road, Oxford OX2 6JX

press.princeton.edu

Library of Congress Cataloging-in-Publication Data

Names: al-Gharbi, Musa, 1983– author.
Title: We have never been woke : the cultural contradictions of a new elite /
    Musa al-Gharbi.
Description: Princeton : Princeton University Press, [2024] | Includes
    bibliographical references and index.
Identifiers: LCCN 2024006064 (print) | LCCN 2024006065 (ebook) | ISBN
    9780691232607 (hardback) | ISBN 9780691232614 (ebook)
Subjects: LCSH: Social conflict—United States—History—21st century. |
    Social justice—United States—History—21st century. | Equality—United
    States—History—21st century. | Identity politics—United
    States—History—21st century. | Power (Social sciences)—United
    States—History—21st century.
Classification: LCC HN90.S62 A44 2024 (print) | LCC HN90.S62 (ebook) |
    DDC 306.0973—dc23/eng/20240326
LC record available at https://lccn.loc.gov/2024006064
LC ebook record available at https://lccn.loc.gov/2024006065

British Library Cataloging-in-Publication Data is available

Editorial: Eric Crahan, Erik Beranek
Jacket: Katie Osborne
Production: Erin Suydam
Copyeditor: Ashley Moore

This book has been composed in Adobe Text Pro and Gotham

Printed in the United States of America

10 9 8 7 6 5 4 3 2 1

CONTENTS

TABLES

Introduction

Until 2016, I'd spent virtually my entire life in a smallish southern Arizona military town about forty minutes from the U.S.-Mexico border. I started my academic journey at Cochise Community College in Sierra Vista, Arizona. I attended college off and on, working full time throughout, eventually earning a BA and an MA at my local land-grant university. However, I had a hard time finding good work in the town I grew up in. Ultimately, I ended up selling shoes at Dillard's. I was great at it—one of the top salespeople in the store. However, I was passed over for management because I was viewed as overqualified and unlikely to stay, and so I left. In 2016, some thirteen years after graduating high school, I embarked on a PhD in sociology at Columbia University. My program offered a generous graduate stipend—more than I'd ever made doing full-time retail sales or management in Arizona. However, I was also supporting a family of four, and Manhattan is an expensive place to live. Consequently, I continued to work outside jobs while completing my PhD.

Politically, I grew up during the height of neoliberalism. The Cold War ended when I was relatively young. America presided over a unipolar global order, and everything from poverty to AIDS to war itself seemed like it could be solved by the right mix of free markets and technocratic know-how. At the time, Sierra Vista (and Arizona more broadly) skewed decisively "red." However, having come of age in the aftermath of 9/11 and the War on Terror, I ended up going another direction. I cast my first presidential vote for John Kerry in 2004—and not begrudgingly. It's humiliating to admit in retrospect, but I *believed* in John Kerry. At that time, I subscribed to what you might call the "banal liberal" understanding of who is responsible for various social evils: those damn Republicans! If only folks in places like podunk Arizona could be more like the enlightened denizens of New York, I thought, what a beautiful country this could be! What a beautiful world! I had already shed a lot of this in the years that followed—but the vestiges that remained got destroyed soon after I moved to the Upper West Side.

One of the first things that stood out to me is that there's something like a racialized caste system here that everyone takes as natural. You have disposable servants who will clean your house, watch your kids, walk your dogs, deliver prepared meals to you. If you need things from the store, *someone else* can go shopping for you and drop the goods off at your place. People will show up outside your door to drive you wherever at the push of a button. It's mostly minorities and immigrants from particular racial and ethnic backgrounds who fill these roles, while people from *other* racial and ethnic backgrounds are the ones being served. The former earn peanuts for their work, the latter are well off. And this is all basically taken for granted; it is assumed that this is the normal way society operates.

And yet, the way things are in places like New York City or Los Angeles— this is *not* how things are in many other parts of the country. For instance, in other American locales, the person buying a pair of shoes and the person selling them are likely to be the same race—white—and the socioeconomic gaps between the buyer and the seller are likely to be much smaller. Even the most sexist or bigoted rich white person in many other contexts wouldn't be able to exploit women and minorities at the level the typical liberal professional in a city like Seattle, San Francisco, or Chicago does in their day-to-day lives. The infrastructure simply isn't there. Instead, progressive bastions associated with the knowledge economy are the places with well-oiled machines for casually exploiting and discarding the vulnerable, desperate, and disadvantaged. And it's largely Democratic-voting professionals who take advantage of them—even as they conspicuously lament inequality.

If relocating to New York put me on the path to this book, the aftermath of the 2016 election radically accelerated my journey. A few months after I arrived at Columbia University, Donald Trump won the presidency. I did not find this surprising at all. I'd spent most of the election cycle, beginning in the primaries, begging anyone who would listen to take Trump's prospects seriously and respond accordingly.[1] However, most of my peers in Manhattan went into election night confident that we were on the "right side of history," and that the election would probably be a blowout. That is, of course, not what ended up happening. In the days that followed, many Columbia students claimed to be so traumatized by the electoral results that they couldn't do their tests or homework. They needed time off, they insisted. There were a few things that were striking about these demands to me.

First, these are students at an *Ivy League university*—overwhelmingly people from wealthy backgrounds. And even if they didn't come from wealth, they're likely to leave well positioned. After all, Columbia is an elite school (i.e., a school designed to cultivate elites).[2] And this is not a secret. Students choose to attend a school like Columbia instead of their local land-grant university precisely because they aspire to be more elite than most other college graduates (who, as we will see, themselves tend to be far better off than the rest of the population). People from less advantaged backgrounds routinely shed tears of joy when they get into schools like Columbia precisely because they know that they've just received a ticket to a different life. Many from privileged backgrounds respond just as emotionally because admission to a school like Columbia is a critical milestone in reproducing or enhancing their social position.

Hence, even in students' own descriptions about what the impact of the election would be—the poor and vulnerable would be crushed underfoot while elites flourished more than ever—guess what? We're the elites! Realistically speaking, we're the type of people who stood to benefit from someone like Trump in these narratives. We certainly shouldn't be thinking of ourselves as victims, or as the "little guy." But there seemed to be strikingly little recognition of these realities on campus. Instead, many students seemed to view *themselves* as somehow uniquely vulnerable to Trump and his regime, as being especially threatened or harmed. They demanded all manner of accommodations for themselves in order to cope with Trump's victory—and the university eagerly and uncritically obliged.

Meanwhile, there was this whole other constellation of people around the students who seemed to be literally invisible to them. The landscapers, the maintenance workers, the food preparation teams, the security guards. There was no major student movement on their behalf. And these were the people, according to the prevailing narratives, who stood to lose the most from Trump's victory. While those attending classes at Columbia are overwhelmingly wealthy or upwardly mobile, these workers are generally from more humble backgrounds. They are disproportionately immigrants and minorities. Yet the students didn't begin by demanding that *those* people receive a day off, nor by advocating for higher pay and better benefits or protections for *those* people. Instead, they were focused on themselves.

Nor were these ignored laborers—the people with the most at stake in this election (in the students' own narratives)—saying *they* needed time off because they were too traumatized. They weren't painting themselves as victims. Although the classrooms were full of tears in the days that followed, one never saw, say, the janitors making a scene, sobbing uncontrollably about politics as they scrubbed rich kids' messes out of the toilets. They just showed up to work the next day and did their jobs. The juxtaposition was sobering.

And I want to be clear, I'm not picking on Columbia students here. When I left campus, walking around the Upper West Side, or other affluent parts of Manhattan, similar scenes were playing out. The winners of the prevailing order were out on the streets, walking around in a daze like a bomb went off, comforting each other and weeping for the disadvantaged, even as they were chauffeured around and waited on—even more than usual—because they were just too distraught to do anything themselves. And they were able to indulge themselves in this way, of course, because the people who were serving them showed up to work per usual.

New York City was hardly unique in this. Other symbolic economy hubs had similar scenes playing out.[3] And the same drama that I observed at Columbia was unfolding at colleges and universities across the country.[4] This is precisely what I found so troubling, so difficult to shake off: it wasn't about my own school. It was about this broader disjuncture between symbolic economy elites' narratives about the world and the realities on the ground.

These contradictions grew especially pronounced in the wake of the COVID-19 pandemic and the unrest that followed George Floyd's murder. Even as they casually discarded service workers en masse to fend for themselves—and increased their exploitation of those "essential" workers who remained (so that they could stay comfortably ensconced in their homes)—individuals and institutions associated with the symbolic economy aggressively sought to paint themselves as allies for the marginalized and disadvantaged. Billions were donated to groups like Black Lives Matter (BLM); antiracist literature shot to the top of best-seller charts; organizations assigned antibias training and appointed chief diversity officers at an extraordinary pace. Meanwhile, many inequalities continued to grow[5]—indeed, their growth accelerated through much of the pandemic.

Watching this unfold, I couldn't help but be reminded of Jean Baudrillard's argument that "the Gulf War did not take place."[6] Sure, there were bombings, there were soldiers—but to call it a "war" would be misleading. It was a spectacle. And behind that spectacle was a massacre. And when it was over, the status quo remained roughly intact (indeed, that was the purpose of the "war"—to protect the regional status quo). Seeing how events played out in 2020 convinced me that the so-called Great Awokening, likewise, did not take place. Indeed, we have never been woke.

Orwell's Demon

On the Upper West Side of Manhattan, one of the most striking scenes that continued to replay itself throughout the summer of 2020 was that, on many Friday afternoons, demonstrators would gather in the medians on Broadway Boulevard holding up signs declaring "Black Lives Matter" and the like. Although there are plenty of Black people who live and work in the area, the people taking part in these demonstrations were overwhelmingly white—academics and professionals by the looks of them. They would shake their signs as cars drove by, and the cars would occasionally honk as if to signal agreement, and the demonstrators would cheer.

However, on several occasions I observed demonstrators engaging in this ritual literally right in front of—sharing the median with—homeless Black men who didn't even have shoes. They were crowding the benches that homeless people were using, standing amid the bags that contained their few worldly possessions, in order to cheer on BLM. Meanwhile, the Black guys right in front of them seemed to be invisible. They were a piece of scenery akin to a bench—an obstruction the demonstrators had to work around, lest they fall over while waving their BLM signs at passing cars. In order to remove these obstructions, many from the same demographic as the protesters, perhaps including many of the protesters themselves, would ultimately band together to purge most of these homeless people from the Upper West Side.

During the height of the pandemic, many vacant hotels were converted into temporary housing in order to reduce COVID-19's spread within New York City's tightly packed homeless shelters. In an area that voted more than nine to one for Hillary Clinton in the 2016 general election, and that would do the same for Joe Biden in the months that followed, in the midst of a global pandemic, and contemporaneous with a racial justice movement that they wholeheartedly supported *in principle*, Upper West Side liberals rallied together to declare "Not in my backyard" to the unsheltered—and they successfully pushed the city to move the poor somewhere else.[7] And by refusing to host homeless people in their own neighborhoods, Upper West Side liberals ended up pushing these populations into less affluent and less white communities. That is, in order to alleviate risks and inconveniences for themselves, they forced less advantaged people, who were already bearing the brunt of most other pandemic-related risks and disruptions, to *also* deal with any challenges related to hosting large numbers of unsheltered individuals in their communities. And they did all this while evoking social justice discourse—often pretending their primary concern was for homeless people themselves.[8]

Watching scenes like these unfold, I couldn't help but wonder, "Who, exactly, are these street-corner BLM demonstrations *for*? What is the point of it?" After all, there is not really any plausible story in which getting random cars to honk at their signs would lift anyone out of poverty, save anyone from police violence, or get anyone released from prison. There didn't seem to be any connection at all between the cause these demonstrators were claiming to support and the means through which they were choosing to "support" it. There was no relationship between the seriousness of the problems they claimed to be consumed with and the ways they went about advocating for those causes: giddily cheering on the street when people honked at their signs. I found this juxtaposition maddening—especially because contradictions like these seemed to be present virtually everywhere I looked. Once I started seeing them, I couldn't *not* see them. They seemed to lurk over every scene I observed, every interaction I had, every institution I was engaged with, over my own plans and aspirations in life . . .

George Orwell once observed that "writing a book is a horrible, exhausting struggle, like a long bout with some painful illness. One would never undertake such a thing if one were not driven on by some demon whom one can neither resist nor understand."[9] As a result of the experiences I've just described and many other incidents like them, I became increasingly consumed, possessed even, by a handful of interrelated questions:

- Why is it that the people who benefit the most from what sociologists call systemic or institutionalized racism or sexism *also* happen to be the people most conspicuously concerned with "ideological" racism, sexism, and so on (i.e., people saying, thinking, feeling, believing the "wrong" things about gender, sexuality, race, and other "identity" issues)? How can elites whose lifestyles and livelihoods are oriented around the production, maintenance, and exploitation of inequality still view themselves as egalitarians?
- If the social justice discourse and the symbolic "justice-oriented" actions that contemporary elites gravitate toward seem to have little to do with tangibly addressing social problems—if they don't seem to well reflect the will and interests of the people who are supposed to be "helped" by these gestures—what *do* these conspicuous displays

actually accomplish? What *functions* do they serve? Who actually benefits from these behaviors and how?

- Insofar as social justice discourse is co-opted by elites to serve their interests, how, precisely, does social justice ideology come to serve these alternative functions? How aware are participants with respect to the dissonance between their lifestyles, their behaviors, and their professed beliefs? How do elites reconcile these tensions, to the extent that they perceive them at all?

- Why is it that the "winners" in the prevailing order seem so eager to paint themselves as helpless victims, as marginalized, as vulnerable, and as allies of the same? If it is a genuine disadvantage to be a woman, or a minority, or LGBTQ, or disabled, then why are elites so eager to identify themselves as these very things, or to publicly associate themselves with people who can—even to the point of bending the truth in order to accomplish these goals?

- What's the deal with the so-called Great Awokening? There *seems* to have been a rapid and substantial change in norms and discourse, but is there really a "there" there? And if so, what caused it? Why did it happen when it did? Who was affected and how? Is this period of heightened vigilance around "social justice" issues just a phase? Or is it the new normal?

We Have Never Been Woke is my sociological attempt to answer these questions insofar as I am able, by exploring the historical and contemporary connections between social justice discourse, growing inequality, and the rise of a new elite tied to the symbolic economy.

Overview

This book is divided into six chapters. Chapter 1 begins by introducing readers to a constellation of elites I refer to as "symbolic capitalists."

In sociological terms, a *capitalist* is not someone who simply favors capitalism, but rather someone who possesses financial resources (capital) that are used to acquire, exert control over, and extract profits from the means of (material) production. Drawing on Pierre Bourdieu, we can define a *symbolic capitalist* as someone who possesses a high level of symbolic capital and exerts control over, and extracts profits from, the means of symbolic (re) production. If that sounds a little hard to get your head around, don't worry; we'll do a lightning run through Bourdieu's notion of symbolic capital in chapter 1. In the meantime, a less technical way of putting it is that symbolic capitalists are defined first and foremost by how they make a living: nonmanual work associated with the production and manipulation of data, rhetoric, social perceptions and relations, organizational structures and operations, art and entertainment, traditions and innovations, and so forth. Think academics, consultants, journalists, administrators, lawyers, people who work in finance and tech, and so on.

Chapter 1 will argue that what is often referred to as "wokeness" can be fruitfully understood as the ruling ideology of this increasingly dominant elite formation. The genuinely marginalized and disadvantaged in society are not the folks who tend to embrace and propagate these ideas and frameworks. Instead, highly educated and relatively affluent professionals associated with the symbolic economy are most likely to embrace (and enforce) these norms, dispositions, and discourses.

However, symbolic capitalists are not an ideological or political monolith. Many of us are sympathetic to "woke" narratives but do not fully embrace them. Others are explicitly opposed. Some symbolic capitalists (although not many) are even right wing. Chapter 1 will walk through some of these divisions around wokeness to help bring clarity to this highly contested term.

We'll close with a brief exploration of how and why symbolic capitalists associate themselves so strongly with social justice beliefs and causes. As we'll see, the symbolic professions have been legitimized from the outset by appeals to altruism and serving the greater good—especially the vulnerable, marginalized, and disadvantaged in society. This mode of legitimation has given rise to novel forms of status competition among symbolic capitalists.

Chapter 2 will explore how some of these struggles for power and status have played out during the Great Awokening(s). The chapter will synthesize many types of data to illustrate that, since 2010, there have indeed been rapid and dramatic shifts in symbolic capitalists' discourse and expressed beliefs about social justice issues. There have been important changes in our political alignments and behaviors as well. Using these same types of data, however, we can see that the post-2010 Great Awokening is not particularly novel. It's actually a *case* of something.

Since the rise of the symbolic professions, there have been three other Great Awokenings. By comparing and contrasting these episodes, we can gain leverage on questions like, Under what circumstances do these Awokenings come about? When and why do they tend to fade? What, if anything, do they tend to change? Does one Awokening inform the next, and if so, how? And so on. Moreover, because social justice discourse is rendered much more pronounced and salient during these periods, Great Awakenings also provide excellent opportunities to study if and how symbolic capitalists leverage social justice discourse in the service of their own ends—in the past and in the present.

However, one challenge in analyzing wokeness as a means of elite legitimation and competition is that most symbolic capitalists decline to see themselves as elites. Since the onset of the current Great Awakening, most discourse about "social elites" in symbolic capitalist spaces has instead conveniently focused on the top 1 percent of income earners. Chapter 3 will push readers to widen their analytic lens. The chapter will illustrate that, if we want to understand how almost anything happens in society today, symbolic capitalists have to be a core part of the story. Other elites—politicians, plutocrats, multinational corporations, and others—largely act with and through us to accomplish their goals. Symbolic capitalists are among the primary "winners" in the prevailing socioeconomic order. We are some of the main beneficiaries of the inequalities we condemn. Our lifestyles and our social positions are premised heavily on exploitation and exclusion—particularly with respect to women, minorities, and the economically vulnerable. We resent social elites, yet we are social elites.

Chapter 4, meanwhile, will provide a deep dive into how symbolic capitalists understand and engage in politics. Our socioeconomic position and unique cognitive profiles predispose us toward political preferences and modes of political engagement that are far out of step with most other Americans'. Consequently, as symbolic capitalists have grown increasingly influential, and as we've been increasingly consolidated into the Democratic Party, we have profoundly reshaped that party and the U.S. political landscape more broadly—albeit not in the ways we may like to imagine. By the end of the chapter, readers will have a good sense of why it is that symbolic capitalists' approach to social justice focuses so intensely on symbols, rhetoric, and culture war issues instead of the "bread and butter" struggles that other Americans are most concerned about.

Chapter 5 will explore the moral culture of symbolic capitalists. Among contemporary symbolic economy professionals, it is not enough to merely present oneself as an advocate for the vulnerable and the downtrodden—many of us also try to present ourselves as literal embodiments or representatives of historically marginalized and disadvantaged groups. Chapter 5 will explore what's going on here. It will show that, in presenting themselves as racial and ethnic minorities, gender and sexual minorities, neurodivergent, physically disabled, or allies of the same, contemporary elites are trying to harness a novel form of symbolic capital.

There is a widespread perception among symbolic capitalists that Americans who are cisgender, heterosexual, able-bodied, white, and male are responsible for most of the world's problems. Those who belong to historically marginalized and disadvantaged groups, on the other hand, are viewed as particularly moral. They hold special epistemic authority on issues discursively associated with the groups they identify with. They are perceived as more interesting, and perhaps more innovative, than members of historically dominant groups. They are often eligible for special accommodations and opportunities that others covet. In order to lay claim to these benefits, symbolic capitalists have strong incentives to understand and describe themselves as victims, and to associate themselves, directly or indirectly, with minority identity groups. Many stretch the truth to portray themselves this way. Virtually always, these narratives ignore highly relevant but inconvenient realities—including and especially proponents' class positions.

Chapter 6 will highlight some of the ways symbolic capitalists leverage wokeness to obscure unpalatable truths from themselves and others. The chapter will do a dive into the cognitive and behavioral science literatures to illustrate how our sincere commitments to antiracism, feminism, LGBTQ rights, and related causes can actually blind us to the role we play in the social order—including and especially as it relates to exploiting and perpetuating inequalities. It will explore how symbolic capitalists deploy social justice discourse to reinforce their own social position, delegitimize rivals, and deflect blame for social problems onto others.

However, before we dive into any of that, it may be prudent to lay out some of the core assumptions undergirding this text, and some of the literatures the book is in conversation with.

Minority Report

I began my academic career as a philosopher. Many people are drawn to philosophy after encountering work by some great thinker who heroically tackled huge questions and tried to wrestle them to the ground as best they could. These works tend to be thrilling and mind opening—ambitious in their scope and argumentation. But when you become an academic philosopher in the United States, you quickly discover that producing work like this is not something you are practically permitted to do. Your readings will focus narrowly on secular, analytic, Western (white) liberals. The work that gets published tends to be *extremely* narrow in its focus—for example, here's my interpretation of Martha Nussbaum's response to Joseph Raz's critique of John Rawls's *Theory of Justice*. I literally published a paper like that.[10] It's pretty good, as far as these things go. But it's not the kind of work that anyone goes into philosophy to do, I suspect.

Sociology, my current field, is much the same. The discipline started with scholars asking huge questions and producing works that were truly epic in their ambitions (if deeply flawed in some of their assumptions and generalizations). The works themselves were adventurous, with scholars actively building the methodological and theoretical boats they were simultaneously trying to sail in. Today, most work published in the discipline is far narrower in scope, modest in its ambitions, and "safe" in its arguments. Here, too, it's difficult to publish the kind of work that helped establish the field. There are many good reasons for this and some not-so-good reasons. In any case, for my own first book, I decided to go bold. I set out to write the type of text I would love to read. The type of book that might get others excited about sociology and its potential to explain the world around us. For less specialized readers who are eager to get started on that journey, feel free to skip to the beginning of Chapter 1. What follows is a little bit of "inside baseball" to help situate this text for academic audiences.

My education, teaching, and collaborations cut across a range of fields: philosophy, sociology, political science, communications, psychology, journalism. This book draws on research from all these fields and is designed to be accessible and compelling to nonspecialists too. The upside of this ecumenicism is that the book should be relevant and generative for scholars across a range of disciplines. The downside, however, is that it may be difficult for some readers to "place" this work—to figure out what its intended contribution is, and to which scholarly fields. So let me say a little about this at the top.

Methodologically and theoretically, this work draws heavily from an interdisciplinary tradition called science, knowledge, and technology (SKAT). Work in this field tends to be very "meta." SKAT scholars think about cognition, talk about discourse, conduct research on the process of research, analyze others' analyses, theorize about theory, and so on and so forth. The emphasis is less on producing novel empirical studies than on reporting on, contextualizing, synthesizing, and criticizing other research from disparate fields. This integrative work often helps us advance our knowledge (and understand the state of our knowledge) much more powerfully than one-off empirical studies.

This book, to be clear, *will* include lots of original empirical research. It will also bring together academic scholarship from a wide range of fields, research produced by think tanks, and occasionally, primary reporting by journalists. Putting together this mosaic should allow us to see something new and important that we would not have been able to perceive by examining any of the components in isolation.[11] And seeing the world in terms of this big picture can, in turn, change how people subsequently understand and utilize the research drawn on here, or any new pieces of scholarship that others produce that might help us expand the picture further.

Within my home discipline of sociology, this book is most tightly connected to work on the sociology of elites. Most social research attempts to understand and address social problems by focusing on people at the "bottom" of social hierarchies. Sociologists of elites instead turn the scholarly gaze toward people at the top of the social order, studying their lifestyles, behaviors, expressed beliefs, and so on in a similar manner to how others study the poor, the marginalized, and the disadvantaged. This can be a powerful analytic move. However, as sociologist Shamus Khan has emphasized, research in the field has been undermined by a set of persistent blind spots.[12]

Sociologists tend to focus on elites aligned with industries and political causes distant from our own, while the types of elites that we tend to favor, sympathize with, or receive patronage from are often exempted from similar scrutiny. Moreover, when scholars analyze elites, they focus almost exclusively on folks near the pinnacle of the wealth and earnings distribution. However, the sphere of Americans who can be sensibly discussed as "elites" is much larger than that. Hence, a huge swath of elites tends to be more or less "invisible" in the literature. Scholars also tend to discuss elites in homogeneous terms. Demographically, they are presumed to be whites and men. The growing diversity within elite circles is underanalyzed to the extent that it is acknowledged at all. Socioeconomically, elites are often treated as an undifferentiated mass. In reality, there are many different subsets of elites, each relying on different modes of legitimation and tied to very different institutions. There are many differences in values, priorities, and sources of wealth (and, thereby, material interests) within virtually any stratum of elites, giving rise to myriad forms of intraelite competition and conflict. These differences are too often flattened or ignored.

In defiance of these trends, this book widens the analytic lens considerably beyond the millionaires and the billionaires. However, it also focuses narrowly on a specific elite formation: symbolic capitalists. They have a particular history and occupy a special place in the socioeconomic order. They have modes of legitimation, institutional associations, and perceived interests that tend to diverge systematically from other elites. They have idiosyncratic tastes and preferences relative to other elites and congregate in very particular places. And so, rather than just labeling symbolic capitalists "elites" and then talking about elites in generic terms, this book will go into the weeds about symbolic capitalists in particular.

Another core aspiration of this book is to analyze the political economy of the knowledge economy. That is, the text will help readers better understand the political affiliations and ideological commitments of symbolic capitalists, and how these relate to their personal financial prospects and to the evolving position of symbolic capitalists writ large in the broader socioeconomic order—here building on a series of important works charting the growth of the symbolic professions and their influence over society.

The institutional clout of symbolic capitalists began to grow rapidly during the interwar period (that is, the years between World War I and World War II).[13] Shortly after the outbreak of World War II in Europe, American political theorist James Burnham published a milestone book, *The Managerial Revolution*, analyzing the ascendence of this new elite formation. Somewhat to Burnham's consternation,[14] his book sparked a genre of important texts, many of which I'll cite in the pages that follow, charting shifts in the global economy and how they relate to the growing cultural, economic, and political power of professionals who traffic in ideas, symbols, and information. Many early works in this literature adopted a critical take on the rise of these elites, their changing role in society, and the ways symbolic capitalists were, in turn, changing society writ large. Later works in the genre have been more sympathetic or even valorizing. Across the board, these books have been written nearly unanimously by white scholars, overwhelmingly white men.[15] *We Have Never Been Woke* is the first major work in this genre, analyzing the symbolic economy writ large, written by an African American.[16] And in terms of the influences drawn on, the dimensions of social behavior this book will focus on, and so on, it's a very different book from the texts that preceded it.

As an example, few works in this tradition or adjacent literatures attend much to what could be called "identity" issues. Conversations about "elite overproduction," for instance, generally undertheorize the gendered nature of this phenomenon. In previous eras, the elites being overproduced were men. Now, they're largely women. This is a highly consequential change that has important implications for how unrest tied to elite overproduction plays out. Likewise, conversations about "brain drain" rarely delve into the gender dynamics at play. Yet it is disproportionately and increasingly *women* being pulled out of communities around the country and consolidated into knowledge economy hubs (while growing numbers of men are floundering)—generating important consequences for both the communities that highly educated workers are flocking to and the areas they are leaving behind. Although more critical works in the knowledge economy genre have flagged how symbolic capitalists are among the primary "winners" in the prevailing order, few have analyzed the specific ways we profit from and perpetuate gendered or racialized inequalities in particular. Even less attention has been paid in this literature to analyzing how symbolic capitalists leverage social justice discourse in the service of their power struggles, or the extent to which changes in social justice discourse and activism relate to changes in the socioeconomic position of symbolic capitalists. This text will help fill in many of those blanks. In the process, we'll unsettle popular approaches to "identity" as well.

This book takes part in a tradition of Black critique—running from W.E.B. Du Bois through the present—highlighting how liberals exploit social justice advocacy to make *themselves* feel good, but ultimately offer up little more than symbolic gestures and platitudes to redress the material harms they decry (and often exacerbate). Up to now, this corpus of social analysis has been largely disconnected from research on the sociology of elites, the rise of the knowledge economy, or science, knowledge, and technology studies. Moreover, its critiques of symbolic politics have generally been nonreflexive: *white* liberals are subject to intense scrutiny while nonwhites of any persuasion are largely excluded from analysis. For our purposes, this is a problem because an ever-growing share of contemporary symbolic capitalists identify as something other than cisgender heterosexual able-bodied neurotypical white men. And symbolic capitalists are constantly inventing new forms of marginalization and novel ways to lay claim to existing minoritized identities. Consequently, to the extent that elites who identify with some historically marginalized or disadvantaged group are exempted from critique, we will be left with an increasingly impoverished understanding of whom the social order serves and how inequalities reproduce themselves over time. Practically speaking, the only way to get around this problem is to eliminate the exemptions entirely.

Analytic (In)equality

A core objective of this book is to explore contemporary inequality. It may be worth saying a few words at the top about how "inequality" is understood here. Racialized, gendered, and socioeconomic inequalities are often discussed as outcomes. For instance, the Black-white wage gap is viewed as an *outcome* of some other set of factors. However, as sociologist Andrew Abbott argued, inequality is perhaps best understood as a *process*—one sustained largely as a result of how systems and institutions are structured and reproduced, and the ways in which people act or interact within them across time.[17] Systemic racism, for instance, is not a product (outcome) of people holding the "wrong" beliefs or feelings. It is a function of ongoing *behavioral patterns* and (unjust) *allocations* of resources and opportunities that systematically advantage some, and disadvantage others, within particular contexts. It is not "caused" by the past so much as it is actively *maintained* in the present. It persists because it is enacted moment to moment, situation to situation, *today*.

In equally processual terms, Karen and Barbara Fields defined "racism" as the *action* of applying a social, civic, or legal double standard based on someone's (perceived) ancestry.[18] This is roughly the definition that we will adopt here. Mutatis mutandis, many other forms of discrimination will be similarly understood. However, it is critical to note that the Fields' definition of racism was *not* focused on the application of double standards that specifically favor the historically dominant group. Instead, *any* racialized double standard is "racist" on their definition, irrespective of its intent or purported beneficiaries.

Consider the myriad cases where policies and initiatives intended to benefit historically marginalized and disadvantaged groups end up primarily serving elites from those groups, while the people from the target populations who actually *need* help end up benefiting far less, if at all. Here one might think that perhaps we could tweak those programs to better assist those from the target group who are poor, vulnerable, and genuinely disadvantaged, while excluding those who are already relatively well off. But of course, if the main goal is to help those who are in need, it isn't clear why a factor like race would be used as a criterion at all. Insofar as people from the target group are disproportionately disadvantaged, helping people who are disadvantaged would disproportionately improve prospects for the target group. However, to extend benefits *specifically on the basis of race* would be tantamount to denying aid to many desperate and vulnerable people on the basis of *their* race (i.e., because they are not a member of the target minority group); this does not exactly seem like "social justice."

As Karen and Barbara Fields put it, "Racial equality and racial justice are not figures of speech, they are public frauds, political acts with political consequences. Just as a half-truth is not a type of truth but a type of lie, so equality and justice, once modified by racial, become euphemisms for their opposites."[19] Political scientist Adolph Reed Jr. has likewise emphasized that "the proposition that desert on the basis of special injury should be the standard of eligibility for social benefits is . . . the opposite of the socialist principle that everyone in the society is entitled to a reasonable and secure standard of living, consistent with prevailing norms for a decent life."[20]

In this text, efforts to avoid racialized, gendered, and other forms of double standards will be realized in the form of "analytical egalitarianism."[21] The behaviors of whites and racial and ethnic minorities, men and women, and LGBTQ and "cishet" (cisgender, heterosexual) Americans will be discussed in equivalent terms. This is a commitment that is perhaps more radical than it appears to be at first blush.

Often scholars and essayists analyze and discuss the behaviors of people from more and less "privileged" groups in asymmetrical ways. For instance, when racial and ethnic minorities demonstrate a preference to hire, promote, mentor, and otherwise do business with coethnics, this is frequently analyzed in terms of in-group solidarity or building and leveraging social capital, and these behaviors are lauded. When whites engage in the exact same behaviors, they tend to be analyzed in a completely different way—almost exclusively through the lenses of racism and discrimination—and those who engage in such behaviors are pathologized and denounced. Similar tendencies hold for interpreting the behaviors of men as compared with women, LGBTQ versus "straight" actors, and so on: behaviors that are condemned when carried out by the "dominant" group are interpreted differently, and often praised, when carried out by "others." Indeed, even when harmful behaviors by other actors are recognized and condemned, responsibility is often still laid at the feet of the historically dominant group. For instance, hate crimes committed by African Americans are regularly attributed to white supremacy; women's abuse and exploitation of other women (or men) is blamed on the patriarchy.[22] As I've discussed elsewhere at length, while these tendencies may be well intentioned, they are also profoundly condescending—and the tortured explanations they produce tend to obscure far more than they elucidate about why certain phenomena occur, or how social orders persist, and who they serve (or don't).

Critical discussions of "elites" likewise tend to focus primarily on whites and men, especially those who are cisgender and heterosexual. Elites from other groups are often passed over in silence or are explicitly exempted from critique (and even celebrated!). People railing against the "1 percent," for instance, tend to be focused on Jeff Bezos and Elon Musk, not Oprah Winfrey or Jay Z (who are also billionaires). That will not be the case here.

Behaviors, lifestyles, and relationships that are exploitative, condescending, or exclusionary do not somehow become morally noble or neutral when performed by members of historically marginalized or disadvantaged groups. Indeed, it is primarily others *from these same populations* who end up on the receiving end of these elite predations. But it deserves to be emphasized that it would not somehow be "better" if the people condescended to, exploited, and excluded were whites, men, or cisgender heterosexuals instead. The problem is not that the "wrong" people are being preyed on; it's the preying on per se.

In "the Discourse," people often seem less concerned about poverty as such, or exploitation as such, than with the fact that poverty or exploitation disproportionately affects people they strongly sympathize with, to the perceived benefit of those they do *not* sympathize with. That is, people don't seem to be concerned with suffering so much as they hate that the "wrong" people are suffering. This book *will* spend significant time highlighting the plight of women, ethnic and racial minorities, and LGBTQ Americans within the symbolic economy. This is not because the suffering of people from these groups matters more than the suffering of those who are white, men, cisgender, or heterosexual. Rather, the goal is to sharpen the contradiction between symbolic capitalists' expressed positions with respect to feminism, antiracism, and LGBTQ rights and how they behave "in the world."

For now, the key point is that elites who are women, men, nonbinary, cisgender, trans, straight, queer, white, minorities, newly affluent or born so—insofar as they occupy similar positions in similar institutions and live similar lifestyles, engage in similar behaviors, and reside in similar places—will be discussed in the same way. Indeed, as Adolph Reed Jr. explained, elites from historically marginalized and disadvantaged groups do not just share similar material interests and lifestyles with their peers from historically dominant groups, they tend to share similar worldviews as well: "As black and white elites increasingly go through the same schools, live in the same neighborhoods, operate as peers in integrated workplaces, share and interact in the same social spaces and consumption practices and preferences, they increasingly share another common sense not only about frameworks of public policy but also about the proper order of things in general."[23]

As a function of this convergence, the expressed will and interests of elites from historically marginalized and disadvantaged groups are often significantly and demonstrably out of step with most others' in the populations they purport to represent. Nonetheless, said elites often portray advancing their *own* interests as somehow being a "win" for the groups they identify with writ large. As philosopher Olufemi Taiwo points out, these "gains," while comforting to imagine, rarely translate into meaningful uplift for others in the "real world":

> One might think questions of justice ought to be primarily concerned with fixing disparities around health care, working conditions, and basic material and interpersonal security. Yet conversations about justice have come to be shaped by people who have ever more specific practical advice about fixing the distribution of attention and conversational power. . . . Elites from marginalized groups can benefit from this arrangement in ways that are compatible with social progress. But treating group elites' interests as necessarily or even presumptively aligned with full group interests involves a political naiveté we cannot afford. Such treatment of elite interests functions as a racial Reaganomics: a strategy reliant on fantasies about the exchange rate between the attention economy and the material economy. Perhaps the lucky few who get jobs finding the most culturally authentic and cosmetically radical description of the continuing carnage are really winning one for the culture. Then, after we in the chattering class get the clout we deserve and secure the bag, its contents will eventually trickle down to the workers who clean up after our conferences, to slums of the Global South's megacities, to its countryside. But probably not.[24]

Unfortunately, elites from historically dominant *and* historically marginalized groups share an interest in obscuring or ignoring this nonrepresentativeness. Insofar as they affirm their preferred narratives about the world, elites from majority groups have a strong interest in "consecrating" elites of other backgrounds as "authentic" voices for "their people." Elites from historically underrepresented backgrounds have strong material and emotional incentives to understand *themselves* in this way as well. As a result of this overlap, as we will see, elites from historically marginalized and disadvantaged groups end up playing a pivotal role in legitimizing broader elite attempts to enrich themselves and undermine rivals *in the name of social justice*.

Consequently, while we will spend significant time in this text exploring how socioeconomic inequalities are reproduced, racialized, and gendered within institutions, we will *not* spend much time singling out whites, men, cisgender heterosexuals, the able-bodied, and others for unique condemnation. Being an elite from a minority population doesn't negate the fact that one is an elite. Identifying with a historically disadvantaged or marginalized group neither entails nor should be held to imply that one is *personally* marginalized or disadvantaged—especially not in conversations about elites. Elites are, definitionally, *better off* than most.

By virtue of their social position, elites tend to benefit significantly more than others from inequalities, and actively reinforce and perpetuate those inequalities in order to preserve or enhance their elite status. Nonetheless, elites who hail from historically underrepresented populations often conspicuously denounce those same inequalities, attempt to exempt themselves from responsibility for social problems, and try to deflect blame onto others. Of course, this is precisely what elites from historically dominant groups do as well. It's one more thing they share in common. Indeed, it's something they collaborate on, as we will see.

Coda: We Have Never Been Woke

As symbolic capitalists have grown in power and influence, we have dramatically reshaped the symbolic landscapes of the institutions and societies we preside over. Many of these changes have been unambiguously positive. Overt and casual sadism against members of historically marginalized and disadvantaged groups is less common and less tolerated. There is increased awareness of the potential for unjust bias and discrimination even when people do not harbor ill will against members of minority populations. There is greater representation of nonwhites, women, LGBTQ people, and people with mental illnesses and physical disabilities in virtually all cultural domains. There is greater recognition and accommodation of the unique challenges faced by members of these populations. As the work of Michele Lamont has powerfully illustrated,[25] these changes matter. They have been transformational for how beneficiaries understand themselves and the ways they experience the institutions and societies they are embedded in. Myself included.

However, it hasn't all been good news. Lamont's work has also highlighted that, even as identity-based stigma and discrimination have steeply declined in recent decades, socioeconomic inequalities and segregation have increased just as dramatically.[26] And as formal barriers preventing people from flourishing have been dismantled, there is a growing sense that those who are unsuccessful *deserve* their lot. There is diminished solidarity across lines of difference, and a reduced willingness to make redistributive investments that serve *others* instead of oneself or the groups that one personally identifies with.[27] And, as we will see, most of the benefits from the symbolic shifts highlighted by Lamont have accrued to a fairly narrow band of elites who happen to identify with historically marginalized and disadvantaged groups. The most vulnerable, desperate, and impoverished in society have not been able to profit nearly as much. In many respects, their lives have been growing worse—including in the symbolic realm. Meanwhile, heightened demographic inclusion has been accompanied by a growing homogenization of identity, and increased parochialism against divergent perspectives (including and especially with respect to minority group members who reject institutionally dominant narratives on identity issues). Put another way, inclusion tends to be little more than skin deep at most symbolic economy institutions.

The problem, in short, is not that symbolic capitalists are too woke, but that we've never been woke. The problem is not that causes like feminism, antiracism, or LGBTQ rights are "bad." The problem is that, in the name of these very causes, symbolic capitalists regularly engage in behaviors that exploit, perpetuate, exacerbate, reinforce, and mystify inequalities—often to the detriment of the very people we purport to champion. And our sincere commitment to social justice lends an unearned and unfortunate sense of morality to these endeavors. As Pierre Bourdieu put it:

> The blindness of intellectuals to the social forces which rule the intellectual field, and therefore their practices, is what explains that, collectively, often under very radical airs, the intelligentsia almost always contribute to the perpetuation of dominant forces. I am aware that such a blunt statement is shocking because it goes against the image of themselves that intellectuals have fabricated: they like to think of themselves as liberators, as progressive . . . and it is true that they have often taken sides with the dominated . . . [albeit] much less often than they could have and especially much less than they likely believe.[28]

This *belief* in social justice advocacy is critical to underline. The pages that follow will illustrate a profound gulf between symbolic capitalists' rhetoric about various social ills and their lifestyles and behaviors "in the world." They will detail at length the ways symbolic capitalists often leverage social justice discourse in the pursuit of their own ends—often at the expense of the genuinely vulnerable, marginalized, and disadvantaged in society. Some readers may be inclined to interpret these behaviors as evidence that symbolic capitalists are being cynical when they align themselves with social justice causes. That may well be the case in some instances, but that is not the core argument of this book.

As Noam Chomsky explained, most people have a tough time consistently endorsing things they don't believe in. To avoid this, most find pathways toward believing the things they say, even if they didn't believe those things at the outset (and people generally try to avoid issues for which they *cannot* find a way to earnestly toe the preferred line). Indeed, the ability to bring one's own expressed convictions into compliance with the dominant talking points is one of the key attributes many elite institutions seem to filter for:

> It's very hard to live with cognitive dissonance: only a real cynic can believe one thing and say another. So whether it's a totalitarian system or a free system, the people who are most useful to the system of power are the ones who actually believe what they say, and they're the ones who will typically make it through. So take Tom Wicker at the *New York Times*: when you talk to him about this kind of stuff, he gets very irate and says, "Nobody tells *me* what to write." And that's perfectly true, nobody tells *him* what to write—but if he didn't already *know* what to write, he wouldn't be a columnist for the *New York Times*. . . . You think the wrong thoughts, you're just not in the system.[29]

We will discuss this idea in greater detail later on. For now, the key takeaway is that, generally speaking, symbolic capitalists likely believe the things they say. However, most of the time, these sincere beliefs don't meaningfully translate into egalitarian behaviors, relationships, or states of affairs.

It's not particularly revelatory to point out that symbolic capitalists are hypocrites. Everyone's a hypocrite, almost by necessity. Moral principles tend to be austere, categorical, and unchanging while the world we navigate is full of ambiguity, uncertainty, complexity, contingency, and dynamism. All of us are born into circumstances that are not of our own making. As agents, we are fallible in our judgments and limited in our powers. Overcoming our personal limitations requires cooperation and compromise. As a result of these factors, our lives and societies are typically far out of sync with our aspirations. However, this is not to say that the gulf between our professed ideals and our actions doesn't matter. On the contrary, the struggle to bring these realms into closer alignment is a core source of purpose and meaning in our lives. And more concretely, by virtue of the growing wealth and influence symbolic capitalists wield, the extent to which we do (or fail to) act in accordance with our egalitarian ideals is of significant practical importance to virtually everyone else in society—including and especially those who are genuinely vulnerable, marginalized, or disadvantaged.

Here the reader may be wondering, if the purpose of this book is not to condemn symbolic capitalists as hypocrites, insincere or cynical, then what *do* I mean with the declaration that "we have never been woke"?

In *We Have Never Been Modern*, Bruno Latour called for a "symmetrical anthropology," insisting that social researchers study and discuss their own societies and cultures in the same way they analyze "primitive" or "premodern" ones.[30] He then proceeded to illustrate the power of this approach by turning the analytical gaze toward modernity—demonstrating that the narratives "moderns" tell themselves about what makes them unique in fact obscure the nature of the "modern world," making it difficult for its denizens to properly understand and effectively address contemporary social problems.

Just as Latour encouraged readers to turn the anthropological lens toward their own societies and cultures, and then proceeded to model this approach (*as* a "modern") himself, *We Have Never Been Woke* is a work by a symbolic capitalist, about symbolic capitalists, primarily *for* symbolic capitalists— looking at our history, the social order we've created, and the ideologies used to justify that social order. It will demonstrate how symbolic capitalists' preferred narratives about social problems often inhibit our ability to accurately understand and adequately address those problems. We will explore how actions undertaken in the name of social justice often exacerbate the inequalities we condemn, even as our ostensibly egalitarian commitments blind us to this reality.

In *We Have Never Been Modern*, Latour sought to collapse misleading distinctions between subjects and objects or culture and nature in order to perceive the more unified systems of action and meaning that we tend to be immersed in, in practice. This work will likewise seek to bridge the symbolic and material dimensions of conflict and inequality in order to better illuminate the stakes and the contours of contemporary social struggles.

Finally, in the same way that Latour encouraged the development of a symmetrical anthropology, this work seeks to encourage and model reflexivity—a social scientific principle stating that general theories should also apply to the theorists themselves, as well as the institutions they are embedded in, the actors and causes they support, and so on. For instance, if we want to understand systemic inequality, we must include academics, journalists, social justice activists, progressive politicians, dutiful bureaucrats, nonprofit workers, and others "in the model" alongside those whom symbolic capitalists are less sympathetic toward (such as Trump voters or the dreaded "1 percent"). By folding ourselves and our allies into the analytical picture in this way, we can get a much richer understanding of how social problems arise and persist, and what can be done about them.

The picture that emerges will be complicated and messy—it won't be something that lends itself easily to stories about "good guys" and "bad guys."

Nor will it generate some kind of clear social or political program, concluding in a set of action steps or policy proposals. This text is not intended to provide people with clean answers, but rather to unsettle much of what is taken for granted. What to *do* about the problems and dynamics raised here . . . *that* is something we're going to have to figure out together.

1

On Wokeness

Sociologist Pierre Bourdieu grew up in a peripheral region of France, the son of a postal worker and a homemaker. His origins led him to be dismissed and looked down on in many of his early encounters with elite institutions. These encounters inculcated a sense of alienation and resentment toward mainstream elites that persisted throughout Bourdieu's life in spite of his later success. He emerged as a pugilistic public intellectual, and one of the most trenchant analysts of the ways that elites and elite aspirants jockeyed for status, influence, wealth, and power.[1] His work exposed and cataloged the ways elites reproduced and justified their social position (and the inequalities entailed thereby)—often while claiming to be altruistic or pursuing the "greater good." Bourdieu's work plays an important role in shaping the arguments of this book. It will therefore be useful to highlight a few core elements of his thought to set the stage for what follows.

In his 1979 book *Distinction*, Bourdieu introduced the idea of symbolic capital.[2] In contrast with more traditional resources associated with wealth, material assets, and so on, Bourdieu defined symbolic capital as the resources available to someone on the basis of honor, prestige, celebrity, consecration, and recognition. These symbolic aspects of social life are intimately bound up with power and wealth, or with material and political needs and aspirations. According to Bourdieu, the roles people are assigned to on the basis of their symbolic capital (or lack thereof) may actually be more important than more conventional economic forces in determining how power is arranged within a society. And regardless of how inequalities come about,[3] it is primarily through symbolic capital that they are legitimized and maintained.

However, symbolic capital operates much more subtly than other forms of power and wealth. Indeed, when deployed effectively, neither the person wielding this capital nor the people it is exercised on will consciously recognize the power dynamics at play. Instead, interactions, relationships, and states of affairs will seem natural, necessary, inevitable, or in any case *normal* for all parties involved. Even those at the bottom of social hierarchies will often acquiesce or resign themselves to their own domination. As Bourdieu put it, "Symbolic power is that invisible power which can be exercised only with the complicity of those who do not want to know that they are subject to it or even that they themselves exercise it."[4]

In his initial formulation, Bourdieu highlighted three forms of symbolic capital: cultural, academic, and political. Each of these, he argued, could be converted into the others under the right circumstances—and symbolic capital can also be converted into financial capital (indeed, this is precisely how intellectual or cultural elites "make a living").[5] Collectively, these different forms of symbolic capital serve as the basis for defining others as insiders or intruders, experts or amateurs, leaders or brutes, authentic or posers, geniuses or hacks, sincere or cynical, worthy or unworthy, and so forth. I will briefly walk through them here.

Political capital includes the trust, goodwill, relationships, and institutional authority that can be used to mobilize others in the service of particular goals. One's formal title within an organizational hierarchy, one's perceived credibility, reliability, efficacy, experience, and virtue—these are all resources that can be drawn on to convince others to throw their lot in with someone, to trust *their* vision, to run with *their* plan, to pursue *their* priorities.

Academic capital, on the other hand, is about getting others to defer to one's judgment based on special knowledge, intellect, skill, or expertise. Academic capital is mainly derived from one's credentials, degrees, formal training, and such. People most commonly demonstrate their academic capital by drawing attention to their book knowledge (for instance, name-checking scholars or academic texts or deploying academic concepts in communications), appealing to epistemic authority ("I have a PhD in x," or "As an expert on y . . ."), or evoking their association with institutions or professions that are bound up with academic knowledge (e.g., professor, researcher, analyst, specialist, doctor, lawyer, consultant, or journalist).

Finally, cultural capital is about demonstrating oneself as interesting, cool, sophisticated, charismatic, charming, and so on. People reveal their cultural capital through how they talk, how they carry themselves, their dress, their manners, their tastes and expressed opinions—all of which provide strong cues as to one's level of education, socioeconomic background, ideological and political alignments, place of origin, and so forth. Of these three main forms of symbolic capital, it is cultural capital that is the least accessible to nonelites. As Bourdieu emphasized, it is only those with "distance from necessity" who tend to have the luxury of cultivating the "long-lasting dispositions of mind and body" associated with high status.[6]

A core argument of this book is that wokeness has become key a source of cultural capital among contemporary elites—especially among symbolic capitalists. We will spend a lot of time discussing this elite formation in the pages that follow. However, here is a quick definition: symbolic capitalists are professionals who traffic in symbols and rhetoric, images and narratives, data and analysis, ideas and abstraction (as opposed to workers engaged in manual forms of labor tied to physical goods and services). For instance, people who work in fields like education, science, tech, finance, media law, consulting, administration, and public policy are overwhelmingly symbolic capitalists. If you're reading this book, there's a strong chance you're a symbolic capitalist. I am, myself, a symbolic capitalist.

The idiosyncratic understandings of social justice and attendant dispositions and modes of engagement colloquially referred to as "being woke" are popular almost exclusively among people like us. Those who are genuinely vulnerable, marginalized, disadvantaged, or impoverished don't think or talk in these ways. And that's part of the point. Among symbolic capitalists, wokeness has come to serve as a sign that someone is of an elite background or is well educated. Through espousing woke beliefs, symbolic capitalists (and aspirants to the symbolic professions) demonstrate that they are the kind of people who "play ball"—they are aware of, and are willing and able to competently execute, the appropriate scripts for cultural and intellectual elites in response to various cues. That is, wokeness is increasingly a means of identifying who is part of "the club"—and it provides a basis for deeming those who are *not* part of the club unworthy of symbolic capital (i.e., people who fail to embrace elite conceptions of "social justice" are held to be undeserving of honor, fame, prestige, deference, etc.).

This statement, of course, raises a question: What does "wokeness" mean? It's a great question. Let's dive into it.

"Woke"

There was a time when the term "politically correct" was used largely unironically. The phrase has its origin in U.S. Communist circles in the 1930s. At
the time, it was used both in a positive way, to denote someone who was
genuinely committed to "the cause," but also in a negative way, to refer to
someone who was overly zealous, compliant, or dogmatic.[7] The term "politically *in*correct" was initially used in Black Power and New Left movements of
the 1960s and 1970s to describe people who were out of step with the movement orthodoxy ("problematic" in today's parlance). By the 1980s, the term
was most deployed in feminist circles, folded into the sex wars of that era.
One faction used "politically correct" somewhat literally to denote that their
politics were correct. Their opponents associated political correctness with
rigidity and closed-mindedness.[8] Over the course of this decade, political
correctness came to be associated with a certain approach to "culturally left"
politics more broadly—hailed by advocates as a necessary evolution of the
quest for social justice, and criticized by its detractors as being needlessly
alienating and esoteric, and too focused on symbols over substance.[9] At the
time, these struggles were largely *within* the left.

By the 1990s, however, conservatives and their allies had turned "politically correct" into a catchall slur. The term became a way to disparage and
deride leftist thought and, in particular, what conservatives perceived to be
its excesses. To be "politically *in*correct" took on an increasingly positive
valence in the popular culture. Although many of the beliefs and aspirations
associated with the unironic use of "political correctness" continued to resonate, by the mid-1990s, virtually no one would proudly identify themselves
or their behaviors as "P.C." anymore.[10] It took a while before left-aligned activists clearly settled on a replacement term, but eventually they did: "woke."

Much like the term it replaced, "woke" goes back a long way. In 1860,
there emerged a movement of urban, Northern youth committed to abolish-
ing slavery and ensuring workers' rights who called themselves the Wide
Awakes. In the parlance of the times, to be "Wide Awake" was to be alert to
social injustice, and to be committed, *militantly*, to doing something about
it.[11] As former Republican candidate William Seward put it, "The reason
we didn't get an honest President in 1856 was because the old men of the
last generation were not Wide-Awake, and the young men of this generation hadn't got their eyes open. Now the old men are folding their arms and
going to sleep, and the young men throughout the land are Wide Awake."[12]
The initial usage of "Wide Awake," then, was very similar to how the term

"woke" eventually came to be used more than a century later.[13] However, in the leadup to the Civil War, many Wide Awake chapters evolved into actual militias—at which point the term "Wide Awake" took on a second meaning, evoking vigilance to threats against the Union.[14]

After the war, there are references going back to the early twentieth century of African Americans urging peers to "stay woke." In this context, the phrase likewise evoked vigilance: to "stay woke" was to be alert to potential threats; to be wary around whites.[15] The phrase remained a part of Black vernacular in the decades that followed and became increasingly connected to an awareness of social injustices and a commitment to rectifying them. For instance, one article in 1943 observed, "The Negro is coming to 'have faith in organized labor as a force for social justice.' . . . A Negro United Mine Workers official in West Virginia told me in 1940: 'Let me tell you, buddy, waking up is a damn sight harder than going to sleep, but we'll stay woke up longer.'"[16] Drawing on the same metaphors, Martin Luther King Jr. delivered a 1959 talk at Morehouse College entitled "Remaining Awake through a Great Revolution." A version of this speech would also end up serving as the final Sunday sermon he would give.[17]

With respect to popular culture, "woke" had a breakthrough moment in 1962, when the term was prominently featured in a *New York Times* editorial disparaging white attempts to appropriate Black vernacular . . . a column that may have had the ironic effect of leading *more* whites to use the word. In any case, the connections between being woke and social justice advocacy seem to have been well cemented by the 1970s. For instance, in the 1971 play *Garvey Lives!*, a character explains, "I been sleeping all my life. And now that Mr. Garvey done woke me up, I'm gon' stay woke. And I'm gon help him wake up other black folk."[18] Leveraging the term in roughly the same way, a popular 2008 song by Erykah Badu included the refrain, "I stay woke"—and the exhortation to "stay woke" (#StayWoke) became a staple of the social upheavals that began around 2011.[19]

Reflecting this history, Google nGrams show an initial peak for the term "woke" in 1872 ("wide awake" peaked around the same time).[20] Thereafter, there was a fairly consistent decline in use of the term through the early 1970s. However, there was a steady rise in usage from the mid-1970s through the mid-1990s. From 1996 through 2016, the increases became meteoric as "politically correct" became increasingly passé (and "woke" began to be used in its stead). The overall patterns strongly suggest that one phrase is replacing the other: "politically correct" and "political correctness" saw declines as usage of "woke" accelerated. As these two terms seem to serve similar discursive functions, it is likely that these trends were not independent of one another.

Since then, things have played out for "woke" much like they did for "political correctness": within activist circles, the term increasingly gained two meanings. In its initial contemporary usage, the term was used to identify someone who was alert to social injustice and committed to resisting it. Gradually, however, others on the left began to use the term pejoratively to refer to peers who were self-righteous and non-self-aware. "Wokeness" came to be associated in *these* circles with empty symbolic gestures and ideological dogmatism. Eventually, the political Right seized on this intra-Left disagreement and began using "woke" as a catchall for anything associated with the Left that seemed ridiculous or repugnant.[21] And this began to take the luster off the term.

Looking at Google nGrams, we see a decline in the use of "woke" from 2015 through 2017—and a rebound thereafter.[22] This pattern likely reflects the term growing increasingly passé in left-aligned circles, with the subsequent uptick reflecting increased ironic and pejorative uses.[23] An analysis of all mentions of "woke" or "wokeness" in major media outlets on the left and right from 2021 to 2022 found that the terms were overwhelmingly used in pejorative ways in right-wing media, and most mentions in left-aligned media seemed to be responding to GOP anti-woke campaigns.[24] Reflective of these developments, a 2023 poll by *USA Today* and Ipsos found that although most Americans viewed the term "woke" positively in the abstract, a plurality of respondents said they would interpret it as an insult instead of a compliment if someone referred to *them* as "woke."[25]

There is a sense, then, in which this book arrives at an awkward time in "the Discourse": it is now becoming increasingly difficult for people to refer to themselves, their actions, or their behaviors as "woke" unironically (as happened with "politically correct" before)—but no clear successor term has emerged yet. Moreover, a growing number of empirical indicators suggest that the period of "Awokening" that began after 2010 seems to be winding down.[26] And it is likely that when the next period of rapid normative and discursive change around identity issues eventually arises, the term "woke" will no longer be as central to these discussions.

Of course, the current ambivalence in the meaning, usage, and likely future of "wokeness" raises the question of what *I* mean by "woke" as used in this text. Let me start by marking what I do *not* intend: "woke" will not be used as a pejorative or a slur here. Beyond this, and perhaps to the consternation of some readers, I will decline to provide an analytical definition of the term.

As Ludwig Wittgenstein observed,[27] it is difficult to define even a relatively simple word like "red" in a nontautological way, such that someone who had no experience of "red" would be able to tell from the definition alone what "red" means, and go on to identify it well in the world (try teaching a child "red" by providing them nothing but analytic definitions, never once pointing to any concrete phenomenon in the world and designating it "red"). Of course, as tough as it is to define a relatively uncontested term like "red," defining a word like "woke" is much more complex. But as Wittgenstein likewise emphasized, a word does not become meaningless in the absence of a clean analytic definition. In fact, many of the most meaningful words in the English language are difficult to precisely define, as analytic philosophers have been demonstrating for centuries now. Consider "love," "knowledge," "justice," "freedom," "beauty." The fact that these terms cannot be defined cleanly and unobjectionably doesn't imply they're meaningless and should not be used.

In a similar vein, cultural critic Raymond Williams referred to certain terms as "keywords": highly prominent but also much-contested terms for which debates over their meaning are inextricably bound up with the problems they are used to discuss.[28] "Woke" seems to be a contemporary "keyword": insofar as it indicates a certain disposition toward social justice, then how one understands "social justice" will significantly influence how one understands, evaluates, and deploys the term "woke." Like other keywords, "woke" is mobilized by different constellations of social actors toward very different ends—and the struggles over its meaning are tied to broader sociocultural unrest.

For words such as these, Williams argued, to simply choose a definition and run with it is to paper over important tensions. It is to render oneself a partisan in the struggles the word is bound up in—thereby reducing the scope of one's analytic gaze so as to exclude inconvenient realities. For those who would prefer to be chroniclers of, rather than active participants in, the culture wars, their most important task with respect to keywords is to describe their uses and explore how their meanings have evolved over time. Hence, we began with a brief recap of the history of the term "woke" (and the cited references can provide a deeper dive for interested readers). And throughout the rest of the text, the term will frequently appear within quotation marks, precisely to draw attention to its ambivalent and contested uses.

As an alternative to providing an analytic definition, essayist Sam Adler-Bell has argued that the term "woke" is probably best understood not as a set of substantive beliefs but, rather, as a communicative register. On this model, "wokeness" entails invoking "unintuitive and morally burdensome political norms and ideas in a manner which suggests they are self-evident."[29] One tension in this definition, of course, is that it is perfectly possible for, say, a conservative Christian fundamentalist to insist on unintuitive and morally burdensome political norms and ideas while taking these as self-evident. However, it's not clear that we would refer to such a person as "woke." There seems to be something to the idea that "wokeness" may be less about what one believes than about how one articulates and seeks to advance these beliefs. However, it is also the case that not *any* belief could be construed as "woke."

Indeed, there are certain views that seem to be discursively associated with "wokeness" by both critics and sympathizers alike. Ticking through these may be useful to add some texture to our discussions because many who would now be hesitant to self-identify as "woke" may nonetheless continue to identify with some version of these beliefs—and may also view it as reasonable to associate these particular commitments with the term "woke." For instance, trans-inclusive feminism. People across the spectrum would likely find it uncontroversial to assert that someone who is woke is a trans-inclusive feminist—and that someone who is *not* a feminist or is *not* trans-inclusive would generally not be considered "woke." Several other such examples could be proliferated. For instance:

- Identification as an "ally" with respect to antiracism, feminism, LGBTQ rights, and environmentalism—and an understanding of these struggles as deeply interconnected with one another.
- An aesthetic embrace of diversity and inclusion that extends to honoring and accommodating trauma and disability alongside various demographic characteristics.
- A focus on identity, subjectivity, and lived experience—and on validating the expressed identities and lived experiences of oneself and others.
- An embrace of, and emphasis on, self-care and self-affirmation.
- Recognition and explicit acknowledgment of various forms of privilege, alongside a commitment to defer to minoritized populations whenever possible—especially in matters marked as especially salient to historically marginalized or underrepresented populations.
- An embrace of the idea of "unconscious bias," which creates the need to "work" on oneself while also recognizing that many prejudicial impulses can never be fully transcended.

- A tight focus on disparities between groups. In the event they favor the "more privileged" group, they are held as evidence of injustice. For instance, disparities between men and women that favor men are presumptively viewed as evidence of sexism (while those that favor women are unproblematic); disparities between racial and ethnic groups that favor whites specifically are taken as evidence of racism, and so on (if other racial or ethnic groups outperform whites on various measures, this is often ignored; the focus is on whites).
- An approach to identity that is, for lack of a better term, somewhat mystical. For instance, on the one hand race is held as a fiction in need of being abolished and transcended—but on the other hand, it is argued that virtually any social phenomenon should be analyzed and discussed in terms of race, and failure to do this is viewed as an unwillingness to be "real." Race is held to be biologically *un*real but is nonetheless something that people are not permitted to change: "whites" who identify themselves with other races or ethnicities and minorities who attempt to identify themselves as "white" are both viewed as deeply "problematic." People must strive to understand the struggles of people from historically marginalized and disadvantaged groups, although to claim one deeply understands others' experiences, beliefs, or feelings is itself a sign of privilege or lack of self-awareness.[30] Gender and sexuality are understood to be fluid, nonbinary, and socially constructed—yet it is held that people can also essentially be "born" gay or born trans (i.e., "born into the wrong body").[31] Essentializing and stereotyping are held to be wrong, but people are also widely held to have something like "objective interests" on the basis of their race, gender, sexual orientation, and so on. Cultural appropriation is held to be wrong, but cosmopolitanism is also cherished.

Here it bears repeating that the original formulation of the term in activist spaces indicated an orientation toward politics rather than denoting any particular beliefs: to be "woke" was to be aware of social injustice and committed to doing something about it. The more specific associations just described came later, and each association is contestable. That is, neither individually nor collectively are they viewed here as "essential" to being "woke." Indeed, this text eschews any kind of analytical definition (which would set out necessary and sufficient conditions), so it is beyond our scope to propose *anything* as "essential." The list is merely intended to provide some examples of the kinds of phenomena people seem to be talking about when they talk about "wokeness."

It should also be underlined again that "woke" is not intended as a pejorative in this text. The discursive association of the aforementioned ideas with "wokeness" therefore implies nothing about their "rightness" or "wrongness." The observation on the "mystical" nature of beliefs about identity is likewise intended as a description, not a critique. As a Muslim, I don't necessarily view it as a *problem* to hold beliefs with these sorts of deep tensions (see: free will and divine providence, for instance)—however, it *is* important to be aware of, and to wrestle with, apparent contradictions.

Hegemony and False Consensus

In *The Prison Notebooks*, social theorist Antonio Gramsci argued that ideas that help dominant elites maintain or expand their social influence tend to become hegemonic within institutions and are widely promoted by intellectuals (understood broadly to include bureaucrats, technicians, managers, scientists, journalists, clergy, professors, et al.—symbolic capitalists, for short). Symbolic capitalists and the institutions they dominate tend to be the first and primary proponents of ideologies through which elites legitimize their rule. "Wokeness" is no exception.

The Americans most likely to profess beliefs associated with wokeness also tend to be the Americans most likely to become symbolic capitalists: highly educated, relatively affluent white liberals. Within the Democratic coalition, for instance, studies have repeatedly found that those who strongly and consistently identify with far-left political positions are especially likely (as compared with other Democratic Americans) to skew young, white, highly educated, and urban-dwelling and to hail from relatively advantaged backgrounds.[32] These same constituencies are also the most likely to self-identify as antiracists, feminists, or "allies" to the LGBTQ community.[33]

Interestingly, despite how prominent the term has become, data are relatively sparse with respect to which Americans are most likely to self-identify as "woke." At time of writing, I could only locate a single poll, which had 938 respondents and was carried out in 2021 by *The Hill*.[34] While one should be cautious about inferring too much from a single poll, its findings are roughly commensurate with those of studies exploring identification with other "culturally left" labels—albeit with one important exception. The Americans most likely to identify as "woke" are young college graduates who live in cities, have household incomes above $75,000 per year, and vote Democrat.

The one way that "woke" seems to diverge from other "social justice" identities (e.g., "antiracist," "feminist," "environmentalist") is that *nonwhites* were significantly more likely to embrace the term overall. (But it may be that, after controlling for income, education, party identification, and other factors, this relationship would be rendered insignificant or would reverse. That is, *among* symbolic capitalists, it may be that whites and nonwhites identify as "woke" at comparable levels, while in the general population, minorities are more likely to associate with the label. Or it could be that minority elites are especially likely to associate with this term over the other social justice terms, which enjoy wider embrace among whites. Again, it is tough to infer too much from an individual poll where the primary data are not publicly available.)

Here a couple of clarifications are in order. The fact that a belief is most likely to be held by social elites does not entail or imply that all social elites share the same worldview. Likewise, the fact that a position has achieved institutional dominance should not lead one to infer that all (or even most) people in those institutions personally subscribe to the dominant beliefs. That may not be the case. As Nassim Nicholas Taleb argued, a minority perspective (even one held by less than 5 percent of a population) can easily come to define a system or institution if its advocates are highly committed and disciplined while most others are ambivalent, unorganized, disengaged, sympathetic (if not fully onboard), or otherwise unwilling to publicly disagree.[35]

In many instances, people may not agree fully (or at all) with the dominant view, but do not want to be seen as *opposed* to it either. Under such circumstances, people can actually zealously defend or advocate for positions they don't personally subscribe to, and persecute those who dissent therefrom, in order to protect and enhance their social or professional standing.[36] Some will go so far as to rally around the most extreme, absurd, or polarizing positions available precisely to demonstrate how committed they are[37]—even to the point of attaining personal credibility at the expense of the cause itself. For instance, many highly educated white liberals, eager to demonstrate their alignment with causes like Black Lives Matter, aggressively embraced "defunding the police," even though African Americans themselves generally rejected this aspiration. Moreover, striking this position alienated most Americans who were *not* symbolic capitalists from the cause of criminal justice reform. Symbolic capitalists' prominent embrace of "defunding the police" also became an albatross around the neck of Democratic politicians nationwide.[38] However, publicly striking the "right" posture on this issue seemed to matter more to adherents than advancing the stated preferences of

Black people or building and sustaining viable coalitions that could achieve concrete change.

Most typically, however, rather than engaging in moral grandstanding, people simply decline to *publicly* express reservations about or disagreement they may have with institutionally dominant views, generating a misleading impression of widespread assent.[39] As George Orwell put it, "At any given moment there is an orthodoxy, a body of ideas which it is assumed that all right-thinking people will accept without question. It is not exactly forbidden to say this, that or the other, but it is 'not done' to say it, just as in mid-Victorian times it was 'not done' to mention trousers in the presence of a lady."[40] In environments where people are unwilling or unable to speak honestly about particular topics, "preference falsification" grows increasingly common.

Wide gaps between people's rhetoric and behaviors on specific issues are often signs of preference falsification at work. For instance, to return to the example of a "woke" belief that I led with earlier, most in symbolic capitalist spaces would express agreement with—or avoid publicly *dis*agreeing with— the claim that "trans women are women." By this, many seem to be vaguely asserting that trans people should not be subject to formal discrimination or mistreatment, and that their felt identities should be publicly affirmed (for instance, through the use of preferred pronouns, or being permitted to use facilities for the gender they identify with). Yet the behaviors of people who profess that "trans women are women" suggest strongly that most do not *literally* believe that trans women are the same as cisgender women. Proponents who are romantically interested in women typically do not treat these two populations equally *as* women with respect to *their own* dating and marriage decisions—not even remotely.[41] Yet these same people, who overwhelmingly fail to *behave* as though trans and cisgender are equivalent or indistinguishable (that is, who *implicitly* disagree with the idea that "trans women are women"), may nonetheless pillory others who *explicitly* disagree with the proposition that there is no meaningful difference.

We will more deeply explore the gap between symbolic capitalists' rhetoric and practices in dating and mating in later chapters; tensions like these abound. For now, however, the goal is merely to illustrate that people often publicly profess (or avoid disagreeing with) beliefs that are out of step with their actual preferences (as revealed through behaviors)—and to note that, at times, in an apparent bid to avoid confronting or exposing the gap between their own rhetoric and behaviors, people can become especially militant in policing *others* who publicly diverge from the institutionally dominant view.[42]

As a result of these tendencies, symbolic capitalists and the institutions they dominate may seem much more woke than they actually are.[43]

The Symbolic Mainstream

This book will be focused intensively on the Left because symbolic capitalists are overwhelmingly aligned ideologically with the Left and politically with the Democratic Party.[44] Within this coalition, there is a long-standing divide between self-identified "liberals" and "leftists"—a symbolic boundary that is highly and asymmetrically important to the latter[45] (who, as discussed earlier, tend to be the most "privileged" members of the Democratic coalition). For the purposes of this book, however, there is little difference between them.

To be sure, leftists tend to be much more supportive *in principle* of revolutionary change as compared with liberal peers. They likewise tend to be much more critical of capitalism *in principle*. As a function of these commitments, there are slight differences at the ballot box: leftists are more likely to support candidates like Bernie Sanders or Elizabeth Warren in primary elections, while liberals tend to gravitate toward people like Pete Buttigieg or Hillary Clinton. In general elections, leftists are marginally more likely to abstain from voting (due to dissatisfaction with both party nominees) or to support third-party options, such as 2016 Green Party candidate Jill Stein. Typically, however, self-identified leftists "vote blue no matter who" just like their liberal peers.

There also doesn't seem to be any robust difference between how liberal and leftist symbolic capitalists go about their lives. Leftists tend to support "the revolution" in the abstract, but because revolution does not appear to be in the offing anytime soon (certainly not a *leftist* revolution), they largely carry on day to day in much the same fashion as their liberal peers. If anything, under the auspices of claims like, "There is no ethical consumption under capitalism," leftist symbolic capitalists may show even *less* regard for making practical changes in their own lives, institutions, and communities to advance their espoused social justice goals. Individual sacrifices or changes, it is commonly argued, are futile; nothing shy of systemic change is worth aspiring toward.[46] While awaiting this systemic change, leftist symbolic capitalists generally gravitate toward roughly the same kinds of professions and urban environments as their liberal peers. They behave similarly to their liberal peers within institutions, although their rhetoric is generally more cosmetically "radical." Even these differences, however, are beginning to soften. There has been a bit of an ideological convergence between liberals and leftists over the last decade.

For instance, many traditionally class-oriented leftist organizations, from labor unions to the Democratic Socialists of America, have leaned increasingly heavily into "identitarian" conceptions of social justice and woke symbolic politics.[47] In turn, mainstream symbolic capitalists have increasingly embraced these ostensibly class-based organizations. There has been dramatic growth in unionization and union action within the symbolic professions, even as other workers seem to be increasingly alienated from unions (in part due to unions' growing embrace of postmaterialist politics).[48] Membership in the Democratic Socialists of America has exploded, driven heavily by young professionals (although, despite this growth, its membership remains nearly 90 percent white and overwhelmingly male).[49] Indeed, socialism is no longer a unique "leftist" commitment—it's now a standard Democrat position. Since 2010, there has been a 13 percentage-point increase in the share of Democrats who view socialism positively, with two-thirds of contemporary Democrats holding the term in high esteem.[50] Likewise, liberals have increasingly adopted more radical language about transformational change, traditionally associated with various strains of leftism. Banal Democrats like Joe Biden and Kamala Harris, for example, now regularly talk about "systemic" inequalities (a frame that implicitly evokes a need for dramatic system-wide change rather than marginal tweaking and gradual reform).

In short, the ideological distinctions between liberals and leftists have grown increasingly blurry over the last fourteen years. Although there are still noteworthy differences in emphases, priorities, and proposed solutions, contemporary liberals and leftists seem to be broadly united in an "intersectional" concern for both socioeconomic inequality and systemic inequalities along the lines of, say, race, gender, sexuality, or disability status—and in ways that vary systematically from nonliberals and nonleftists.

Federal Election Commission campaign contribution data provide stark insights into how firmly symbolic capitalists have aligned themselves with the Democratic Party in recent cycles. In 2016, roughly nine out of ten political donations from those who work as activists, or in the arts, academia, and journalism were given to Democrats. Similarly, Democrats received around 80 percent of donations from workers involved in research, entertainment, nonprofits, and science. They also received more than two-thirds of donations from those in IT, law, engineering, public relations, or civil service.[51] Among industries that skewed Democratic, the party's highest total contributions came from lawyers and law firms, environmental political action committees, nonprofits, the education sector, the entertainment sector, consulting, and publishing.[52]

Similar patterns held in 2020: roughly three-quarters of all donations by accountants, engineers, executives, entertainers, and physicians went to Democrats, as did more than 80 percent of donations by attorneys, journalists, and tech professionals, and more than 9 out of 10 donations by creatives, teachers, and professors.[53] The occupations and employers with the highest concentrations of individual workers who donated to the Biden-Harris campaign included teachers, professors, and other educators; lawyers; medical and psychiatric professionals; people who work in advertising, communications, and entertainment; consultants; HR professionals and administrators; architects and designers; IT specialists; and engineers.[54] Industries, professions, and fields that provided the highest total contributions to the Democrats included securities and investments, education, lawyers and law firms, health professionals, nonprofits, electronics companies, business services, entertainment, and civil servants.[55] Geographically speaking, Democratic votes in 2020 were tightly clustered in major cities and college towns where symbolic capitalists live and work—and outside those zones, it was largely a sea of "red."[56] Since the 2020 election, this sorting has only grown more pronounced as nonprofessionals have increasingly abandoned symbolic capitalist hubs, even as symbolic capitalists have fled areas where Republicans hold sway.[57]

Symbolic Conservatives

Overall, the symbolic professions favor Democrats at a ratio of about two to one (and growing). However, it should be noted that some symbolic professions *do* lean toward Republicans. For instance, geologists and many types of engineers (mining, petroleum, chemical, mechanical, civil) skew right. Although engineers on the whole favor Democrats, it makes sense that some subfields would defy the prevailing trend—particularly those tightly connected to (generally right-aligned) manufacturing and extractive industries. These specialists are much more likely than other symbolic capitalists to live in Republican states and communities (because the industries they serve are based there). Most employees in banking or lending also skew right, as do most insurance agents. This, too, is intuitive: those working at local branches for banks, insurance companies, and so on will typically be immersed in communities that lean Republican (as, again, most communities in America writ large skew right) and interact heavily with "normies" in their day-to-day lives. Perhaps unsurprisingly, Catholic priests and religious missionaries also skew right (although most other religious workers favor Democrats).[58]

Critically, these right-aligned symbolic capitalists are no *less* symbolic capitalists than their mainstream brethren. Indeed, they largely agree with mainstream symbolic capitalists on many bread-and-butter issues (although they tend to be more dogmatic about free markets, and more skeptical about various redistribution schemes, as compared with mainstream peers). What generally separates these symbolic capitalists from most others is that they are *symbolically* conservative: patriotic, religious, nondisdainful toward U.S. history, culture, and traditions. On the one hand, these are significant differences—ones that align right-leaning symbolic capitalists more closely with most other Americans. As we'll see, those on the symbolic Right often legitimize their power grabs partially on the basis of this affinity, by painting mainstream peers as unrepresentative and out of touch. However, much like their mainstream peers, right-aligned symbolic capitalists also claim to be advocates for the disadvantaged in society, arguing that their approaches to social issues will do a better job of helping people achieve mobility, prosperity, and true fulfillment than those of their political opponents.

On the whole, there is much more uniting than dividing left- and right-aligned symbolic capitalists. Across the board, symbolic capitalists tend to take words, symbols, and ideas *very* seriously (much more than other Americans). The goal of right-aligned symbolic capitalists is generally to defend the symbols, ideas, and cultural artifacts that resonate with *them*—namely, those based in "Judeo-Christianity" or "Western civilization." (Woke ideology is, of course, itself a product of "Western civilization"—no less so, perhaps even more so, than Plato or Jesus. But that's a topic for a later time.) The primary grievance of these symbolic capitalists in the "culture wars" is that the abstractions they cherish are being denigrated, villainized, marginalized, and neglected as a result of their peers' widespread embrace of an alternative symbolic paradigm—one that purports to unsettle the symbolic boundaries between men, women, nature, humanity, and God. Yet they share with mainstream symbolic capitalists a sense that this fight over language, ideas, history, and cultural artifacts is of deep importance—world-historical importance even—to the point where more practical problems that most "normies" confront in their day-to-day lives should take a back seat. Indeed, most of what will be said in later sections detailing symbolic capitalists' postmaterialist approach to politics applies just as much to right-aligned symbolic capitalists as to those in the mainstream.

However, not all right-aligned symbolic capitalists skew *symbolically* right. There is also a subset of urban professionals whose work is tightly connected to money and business who also lean toward the GOP: accountants, financial advisers, brokers, traders, entrepreneurs, chairpersons, and many executives. Like their mainstream peers, these symbolic capitalists tend to skew left on cultural issues.[59] Even though their embrace of feminism, antiracism, gay rights, and environmentalism may be more moderate than many mainstream peers, they certainly do not view themselves as *opposed* to these causes and are keen to avoid being seen by others as opposed to them as well. Indeed, the primary thing separating this block of symbolic capitalists from the mainstream is that they tend to prioritize free markets over cultural liberalism (although they are fairly supportive of both in principle), while most other symbolic capitalists rank these priorities in the opposite way (at least ostensibly). The alliance of this particular subset of symbolic capitalists with social conservatives has always been uneasy, and in the wake of Donald Trump, many of these have outright defected to the other side.[60]

All said, contemporary symbolic capitalists are overwhelmingly and increasingly aligned with the Democratic Party and the "cultural left." However, there *is* a right wing among them. They amount to a relatively small share of symbolic capitalists overall yet exert a disproportionate impact in virtue of being highly organized, well funded, and quite skilled at eliciting strong (outraged) reactions both *from* mainstream symbolic capitalists and *against* mainstream symbolic capitalists—often in alliance with "anti-woke" peers.

The Anti-woke

Sociologist Pierre Bourdieu influentially argued that people often seem to misunderstand the relationship between people's institutional and ideological positions: "It is not, as is usually thought, political stances which determine people's stances on things academic, but their [social] positions in the academic field which inform the stances that they adopt on political issues in general as well as on academic problems."[61]

This dynamic comes through clearly in how people position themselves with respect to "wokeness." Much of the rest of this book will explore how it is those of a particular stratum of society who tend to embrace "woke" symbolism, often mobilizing social justice discourse in the service of their own ends. Other symbolic capitalists, however, are explicitly *anti*-woke. That is, they position themselves in direct antagonism toward institutionally dominant social justice narratives. There seem to be two groups of symbolic capitalists who are drawn to the anti-woke position, and they are structurally analogous to those who most aggressively push "wokeness."

First, there are folks who are highly prolific and institutionally secure. For them, imposing or resisting wokeness seems to be a kind of "flex"—a status demonstration. One faction engages in a dominance display by imposing new ways of talking and thinking on mainstream symbolic capitalists and aligned institutions (that others are expected to conform with or risk ostracism from the "it" crowd). Others, meanwhile, attempt to show everyone how elite they are, how "above it all" they are, by very aggressively and publicly defying the prevailing discursive and normative trends among their peers. These elites among elites form the first core constituency of "woke" and "antiwoke" advocacy.

Then there are folks on the opposite end of the professional spectrum: symbolic capitalists who have *not* been so successful at attaining stable high-income or high-status positions yet. They're often more loosely affiliated with symbolic economy institutions. As a consequence, they have less to lose, and a lot to potentially gain, by causing a ruckus. Those in this latter category of "anti-woke" people are in basically the same condition that typically drives others to participate in Awokening movements (as we'll see)— and their "anti-woke" campaigns seem oriented toward basically the same ends: undermining institutionally dominant elites in the hope of opening up opportunities for themselves. Indeed, moments of Awokening tend to foster anti-woke movements driven by a coalition of already highly successful elites and frustrated *erstwhile* elites who seek to distinguish themselves—to enhance their own status—by conspicuously moving in the opposite direction of most peers.

Although the anti-woke are not conservative, they often align themselves with the political right, be it de facto or intentionally. Sometimes these marriages of convenience lead to outright conversions. For instance, in response to the cultural unrest of the mid-1960s and early 1970s, a cadre of prolific liberals began striking an anti-woke posture. Initially, they insisted that they were *not* conservatives, and bristled at insinuations that they were.[62] Eventually, however, many ended up embracing the identity of "neoconservative" and aligned themselves firmly with the Republican Party or Republican administrations (and were quite influential therein). Political theorist Christian Gonzalez has argued that many contemporary anti-woke figures seem to be on a similar trajectory.[63]

Today, as in the early stages of the neocon movement, anti-wokes purport to *agree* with mainstream symbolic capitalists at the broad level. They typically claim to be lifelong Democrats. They almost uniformly profess to hate Trump, although some go so far as to argue that wokeness is such a "threat" that they reluctantly voted for the GOP candidate in 2016 or 2020, or in any case strongly sympathize with those who did. They insist that they strongly support feminism, LGBTQ rights, environmentalism, racial equality, and so on *in principle*. The problem, in their telling, is that the "woke" crowd is pursuing these goals in the "wrong" way—in ways that are not just ineffective but counterproductive. This, they argue, is what fundamentally motivates their anti-woke crusade: a desire to *better achieve* shared social justice goals.

On race, for instance, they purport to revere Martin Luther King Jr. Tellingly, however, the anti-woke do not themselves organize, lead, or participate in contemporary MLK-style campaigns to address poverty, discrimination, exploitation, and so on. Indeed, they don't seem very preoccupied with tangibly addressing social problems at all—beyond focusing on how *others* are doing it "wrong." In much the same way as the behaviors of "woke" elites suggest an implicit belief that symbolic gestures are necessary and sufficient to fulfill their social justice obligations, the *anti*-woke behave as if condemning, mocking, or deriding wokeness somehow obviates the need for further action on their part in pursuit of the social justice goals they ostensibly endorse. That is, despite endorsing the goals of feminism, antiracism, LGBTQ rights, helping the poor, and so forth—and despite mocking the focus on symbolism and performative gestures among the woke—the anti-woke do not actually seem to be *doing* anything differently from the people they criticize.

This is perhaps because, at bottom, the anti-woke actually subscribe to the same fundamental worldview as those who are woke. They are obsessed with wokeness and view it as dangerous precisely because they *share* the mainstream symbolic capitalist conviction that symbols, rhetoric, and beliefs are very important. Without this shared premise, there wouldn't be much at stake in their struggle. The woke are often criticized as being overly focused on themselves—on their own beliefs, feelings, intentions, and self-presentation. However, the anti-woke are *likewise* obsessed with the woke. They are just as focused on the woke as the woke are on themselves!

All said, despite painting themselves as importantly different from woke symbolic capitalists, in fact, the anti-woke are best understood as a *variation* of their mainstream peers. They're just playing a slightly different status game.[64] Indeed, at bottom it cannot even be said that the anti-woke are genuinely hostile to wokeness—they parasitically feed off moments of Awokening to build and enhance their personal brand. They are dependent on wokeness far *more* than most other symbolic capitalists. They derive their income and status from keeping people engaged on the subject of wokeness, and from making woke ideas seem important and threatening to the status quo. In the process, they actually end up reinforcing the very impressions that their mainstream peers are desperate to impart: that the actions of "woke" symbolic capitalists *are* genuinely radical and influential.

Ultimately, however, they are running on borrowed time, and anti-Wokenings begin to die out after Awokenings wind down. While mainstream symbolic capitalists seem militant and extreme, "normies" are happy to align with anti-woke and conservative symbolic capitalists to bring them into line. However, as symbolic capitalists and their institutions moderate, most other Americans move on to bread-and-butter issues. The only people inclined to focus *persistently* on institutions of cultural production and their outputs tend to be other elites, whose lives and livelihoods are oriented around the same.

In short, behind their claims of difference, the anti-woke generally share the same broad political leanings and expressed goals as mainstream symbolic capitalists (they purport to be Democrats who support civil rights, feminism, LGBTQ pride, and assisting the marginalized, vulnerable, and disadvantaged, among other initiatives), and are just as "hands off" with respect to these goals as the peers they deride. They deploy similar tactics to woke peers, such as selectively centering women and ethnic, religious, and sexual minorities who advance their preferred sociopolitical narratives, and elevating views expressed by those convenient spokespeople as the "truest" representations of the groups to which they belong. Anti-wokes share mainstream symbolic capitalists' worldview with respect to the importance of the symbolic struggles; this is what gives their own campaigns perceived urgency and meaning. Materially speaking, they do similar types of work, and live similar lifestyles in similar places, relative to their woke peers. Consequently, virtually everything that follows applies just as much to the anti-woke as to mainstream symbolic capitalists. For our purposes, there is no significant difference between them.

Wokeness, Faith, Insecurity

Among right-aligned and anti-woke symbolic capitalists, it has become popular to analogize "wokeness" to a new religion—a faith embraced primarily by highly educated and relatively affluent whites who have abandoned mainline Protestantism. In line with this narrative, the most popular term for referring to the period of rapid normative and discursive change that began after 2010 in the United States is "the Great Awokening"—a clear analogy to the "Great Awakenings" of the eighteenth and nineteenth centuries. This comparison is not without its virtues.

There is compelling empirical evidence that highly educated, relatively affluent, religiously unaffiliated white liberals are increasingly leaning on politics to replace religion. Polls and surveys consistently show that nonreligious and irreligious Americans are the most politically involved groups in the country—participating in many political activities at a rate double that of white evangelicals.[65] Progressive politics, in particular, seems to increasingly serve as a means through which highly educated, relatively affluent whites find purpose, transcendence, and community in their lives in the absence of religion (and sometimes directly at the expense of religion).[66] As political scientists David Campbell, Geoffrey Layman, and John Green put it, "All in all, our evidence suggests that secularism is connected to the 'aggressive liberalism' that is ascendant in the contemporary Democratic Party. Secularists are among the most liberal activists in the Democratic camp, they prioritize ideological goals, they blanch at calls for intraparty harmony and compromise, and they zealously oppose compromise with the GOP." Secularists are also, the authors illustrate, predominantly college-educated whites.[67]

Genealogically speaking, the concept of "social justice" in its recognizably "modern" form is itself a religious concept. It was first coined by Catholic theologian Luigi Taparelli in the mid-nineteenth century and was later adapted by Protestants and eventually secularized by symbolic capitalists.[68] Many of the attitudes and dispositions now associated with "wokeness" are derivative of the anti-hierarchical, anti-traditional, and anti-communitarian impulses of American Protestantism—secularizing its emphases on victimhood, guilt, and individual spiritual redemption.[69] Historian René Girard has gone so far as to argue that "all discourses on exclusion, discrimination, racism, etc. will remain superficial as long as they don't address the religious foundations of the problems that besiege our society."[70]

Consider the phenomenon colloquially referred to as "cancel culture." Although most of Girard's work was published before that specific term came into common parlance, drawing on his work, one could theorize "cancellation" as a secularized religious scapegoating ritual. When people are consumed by anger over a problem, but the real object of their anger is untouchable (or is, in fact, themselves), folks have long tried to collectively focus their rage on some other target instead—to purge, ostracize, or inflict immense suffering on someone who is not truly *responsible* for the problem that consumes us, but who comes to be *representative of* that problem in some way.

"It is easier than in the past to observe collective transferences upon a scapegoat because they are no longer sanctioned and concealed by religion," Girard argued, "and yet it is still difficult because the individuals addicted to them do everything they can to conceal their scapegoating from themselves, and as a general rule they succeed. Today, as in the past, to have a scapegoat is to believe one doesn't have any. The phenomenon in question doesn't usually lead any longer to acts of physical violence, but it does lead to a 'psychological' violence that is easy to camouflage. Those accused of participating in hostile transference never fail to protest their good faith, in all sincerity."[71]

A recurrent example: some white woman has an unfortunate encounter with a nonwhite person, and part of the exchange is caught on video and disseminated online. People immediately and intensively research her, reach out to her employer to get her fired, and disseminate her contact information, her social media profiles, her physical address, and the identities of her family and friends online in order to subject her and her loved ones to harassment, ostracism, and humiliation. "Canceling" this woman, of course, will not do anything to end police brutality, mass incarceration, systemic racism, or ethnic strife. It's precisely because people feel helpless to solve *those* problems that they concentrate their ire so intensely on the woman in the video—laying upon her the sins of society and seeking to punish her for these social sins before expunging her from our presence. Although cancelers may feel impotent to eliminate racism, they recognize that they *do* have the capacity to destroy this person who has come to be emblematic of that ill. In seventeenth-century Salem, they burned witches. Today, we cancel Karens. In both cases, Girard would likely argue, the impulse is the same.

Scapegoating is far from the only religious tendency that seems to have taken on a secularized form. Wokeness heavily appropriates religious symbolism and eschatology: there is a discourse of slavery as America's original sin; "whiteness" is described as a primeval and malevolent force responsible for, or implicated in, virtually all the world's ills. There is a gnostic element, with adherents believing that they can see the "real" structures of the world, which others are blind to—along with the sense of superiority that accompanies such beliefs. There is a sense of being on the "right side of history" and, in many circles, an intolerance for doubts or heresy.[72] There is an intense focus on authenticity and sincerity (that is, on the contents of hearts and souls). There are confession rituals. There are martyrs. Former Speaker of the House Nancy Pelosi, for instance, described George Floyd as having "sacrificed his life for justice" (as though he had willfully chosen to die or risk death for the sake of advancing a political cause).[73] One could go on and on.

Critically, however, wokeness does not seem to be symbolic capitalists' only substitute for the Divine. Sociologist Carolyn Chen has compellingly argued that, among a growing number of contemporary professionals, work has itself become a kind of religion—a primary source of transcendence and fulfillment—crowding out more traditional forms of faith, ethics, and civic ties.[74] *Everything* comes to revolve around the market, and the extent to which one can demonstrably enhance the bottom line. Salaries, promotions, bonuses, and so on—these become important not just in the financial sense but because they demonstrate that one is valuable, that one *brings* value to the organization and *is* valued by the organization. To be unable to stick to boundaries or to truly unplug from work, to be chronically exhausted and overextended, this is interpreted as a sign of how indispensable one is. It signals that one serves some important role in a bigger picture. Many workplaces are nearly "total" institutions: meals are often business meals, consumed at the office or with colleagues and clients; "play" often occurs in the context of the workplace or by going out with colleagues or in company retreats. And regardless of where one is, even on vacation, symbolic capitalists are often expected to remain connected to their workplace (for instance, through their smartphones), to be available for calls, texts, and emails as "needed," and to perhaps work on projects a bit in their downtime to get a "jump" on things before returning to the office.

Incidentally, "wokeness" and the professional "calling" share a similar genealogy. As will be discussed in greater detail at the end of this chapter, early symbolic capitalists secularized the "social gospel" movement as a means of legitimizing their nascent professions. As Max Weber famously emphasized, managerial capitalism was itself importantly shaped by religious impulses from the same faith lineage (descended from the Puritans).[75] Historically speaking, the symbolic professions and their social justice–valanced legitimizing narratives arose roughly contemporaneously and were mutually reinforcing. It is quite possible, then, to draw an analogy between wokeness and religion that is substantial and insightful. Unfortunately, that isn't the way these comparisons usually go.

Instead, the arguments typically run something like this: the Puritans were "bad" (they were zealous, oppressive, closed-minded, etc.); wokeness is similar to, and in some respects derived from, Puritanism; it is, therefore, no wonder that wokeness is "bad" (i.e., woke people are zealous, oppressive, and closed-minded like the Puritans were). Some take it a step further, arguing that religion is wholly "bad" (it is irrational and often leads to impositions on others, social strife, and other unfortunate outcomes); wokeness is a new religion; wokeness is, therefore, "bad" in the same ways. As a religious person, I find these "guilt by association" arguments to be grating and borderline bigoted. Reading these polemics, one also gets the consistent impression that authors started by assuming the premise they ostensibly seek to prove (wokeness is bad), with the superficial appeals to religion serving as a post hoc means of justifying a conclusion they were already unwaveringly committed to. More importantly, I think these pejorative comparisons between wokeness and religion miss the essence of Puritanism and therefore fail to comprehend a critical aspect of the post-2010 Great Awokening.

The Puritans believed that God had ordained who would be among the "Elect" and the "Damned" before the beginning of the world. One's fate was cast before birth, and there was nothing anybody could do to change their own destiny or anyone else's. Worse, one could never be certain of whether they were among the Elect or the Damned until after they passed from this world. Until then, all one could do was to *act* as if they were the kind of person who might be saved. They should work hard (engaging in all tasks as if to the glory of God). They should strive to purify their own hearts and minds (and encourage others to do the same). They should eliminate anything that could lead oneself or others astray (efforts that would later extend to ameliorating poverty and other social problems). Critically, none of these efforts had any prospect of changing anyone's eternal fate. They merely helped *reveal* to oneself and others which camp one was likely fated to. Puritans often *did* demonstrate a distinct sense of superiority over those who did not strive to demonstrate their valor—because while they themselves could at least *hold out hope* that they were among the Elect (in virtue of behaving like a member of the Elect), the people who were not even making the effort were almost certainly among the Damned. But even this did not erase their anxiety; it merely allowed them to keep entertaining the prospect that they might be counted among the "good people" in the end. Put another way, Puritans had faith that they would attain salvation but, as Søren Kierkegaard famously emphasized, faith is *not* the same as knowledge. It is instead an "act of freedom, an expression of will" carried out in response to genuine uncertainty.[76] Many focus on the strong faith of the Puritans to the exclusion of the deep insecurity it was responding to.

In the contemporary context, similar dynamics seem to be at play among many "woke" Americans.[77] Wokeness is primarily a phenomenon of symbolic capitalists and, as we will see, Awokenings tend to arise in moments of strong socioeconomic insecurity among them. But even in ordinary times, symbolic capitalists tend to wrestle with anxiety and insecurity. As Weber illustrated, bureaucrats wield impressive power and social prestige. However, the influence and honor they enjoy is never truly *theirs* to possess.[78] Instead, it typically derives from their office. If they are pushed out of their position or institution, their wealth and status tend to vanish precipitously as well. In order to avoid this outcome, Weber argued, bureaucrats try not to alienate anyone with the capacity to strip them of their rank and prestige (even to the point of compromising their integrity or alienating large swaths of the rest of society in order to ingratiate themselves with elite gatekeepers). Critically, bureaucrats are not unusual in these respects. They are representative of symbolic capitalists as a whole.

Cultural and intellectual producers, Bourdieu argued, are economically dominated but symbolically dominant; they are the dominated faction of the dominant class. They are elites, but their elite position is typically contingent on continued patronage from wealthy people or the state—and on association with prestigious institutions such as universities or media outlets (which, themselves, are reliant on patronage from other elites or the government). As a consequence, although they may fancy themselves rebels or speakers of uncomfortable truths—and although they can and often do leverage their clout to push elites or institutions in particular directions—intellectual and cultural elites also tend to know their limits, and generally take care not to cross any lines that would result in their expulsion from corridors of influence.

Granted, today, thanks to platforms like Patreon, YouTube, or Substack, there is a possibility to become a sort of "populist" influencer—to retain a voice and a livelihood independent of mainstream gatekeepers and patronage via crowdfunding (particularly for those who have already built a decent following by means of "playing the game" in elite spaces before "going rogue"). However, those whose livelihoods are contingent on building and maintaining a particular audience can often find themselves "captured" by that audience—delivering more of what their subscribers have shown themselves to like or expect, and avoiding content demonstrated to alienate or otherwise fail to resonate with said audience.[79] And one must also, of course, attend to the rules and norms of the platforms one relies on, to help ensure one's content reaches the largest possible audience, and to protect said content from being removed by the companies that own the platforms.[80]

That is, in virtually all cases, even in the wake of digital technologies and the like, symbolic capitalists achieve and maintain their position by producing information, ideas, art, entertainment, and other things that their benefactors find to be useful, interesting, aesthetically pleasing, or otherwise satisfying—that is, *not* genuinely threatening, challenging, or unpleasant. Mostly, they tell benefactors what they want to hear, show them what they want to see, or otherwise prove themselves useful to people with money or power. Our own livelihoods and social positions depend on our willingness and capacity to "play ball" in this way. Success, however, brings its own anxieties.

Sometimes consciously, often in the background, symbolic capitalists are aware of the dissonance between their legitimizing narratives and their life-styles and behaviors "in the world." All manner of mental gymnastics and displacement are therefore required to allow us to see ourselves as "good" people, as worthy of the station we inhabit in society, as the solution to social problems (rather than being part of the problem), as exceptions to the rule (relative to other "privileged" people), as being on the "right side of his-tory," and so on. These efforts are only, at best, partially successful. We can see this in the social fact that the people most likely to embrace "woke" views—that is, the "winners" in the social order—are also far more likely than most other Americans to suffer from anxiety and depression.[81] Imposter syn-drome is widespread as well, affecting an estimated two-thirds of symbolic capitalists.[82]

The abuse of stimulants like Adderall, common at elite schools, is becom-ing increasingly prevalent in the symbolic professions too. According to data from Quest Diagnostics, the workers who test positive for *non*prescription amphetamines at the highest rates include those employed in education services, public administration, health care, information, professional and technical services, and administrative support (i.e., symbolic capitalists).[83] Prescription use among professionals has spiked over the last decade as well. Many seek out these drugs to enhance their focus and productivity in hypercompetitive environments.[84] However, as criminologist Russil Durrant emphasizes, stimulants also "have the capacity to promote feelings of confi-dence, high self-esteem and power . . . attractive subjective states because of their role in signaling high social status."[85] In either case, the growing abuse of amphetamines among symbolic capitalists seems to be driven by anxieties around whether they can prove to themselves and others that they "deserve" the positions they have or aspire toward.

All said, although symbolic capitalists may view themselves as superior to most other Americans, that doesn't necessarily mean they hold them-selves in particularly high esteem (it's just that everyone else is worse). What might look like arrogance is often overcompensation for profound guilt and insecurity. We aren't just trying to convince *others* that we deserve elite status through our appeals to social justice, meritocracy, and the like. Often, we're trying to convince ourselves as well.

The Banality of Wokeness

Many on the right talk about wokeness in apocalyptic terms, as some kind of extraordinary danger to "the West," democracy, liberalism, truth, and freedom—as corrosive to U.S. society and culture. At the other end of the political spectrum, there are many on the left who hold that elites have been able to "capture" woke ideology because the associated beliefs are uniquely prone to capture and especially useful for dividing "the people" against one another (making them easier to rule). These critics typically suggest class-based organizing as an alternative, as though this approach were somehow immune or more resistant to elite capture. In fact, there have been myriad oppressive, exploitative, and hierarchical regimes that were ushered into power on the back of class conflict, ostensibly to support the working man at the expense of greedy capitalists (Mao Zedong's China, Joseph Stalin's Russia, Pol Pot's Cambodia, the current regime in North Korea, and on and on).

For that matter, consider Occupy Wall Street. As Richard Reeves argued, "The rhetoric of 'We are the 99 percent' has in fact been dangerously self-serving, allowing people with healthy six-figure incomes to convince themselves that they are somehow in the same economic boat as ordinary Americans, and that it is just the so-called super rich who are to blame for inequality."[86] Reeves's research amply shows that declines in social mobility and rising inequality cannot be well explained or addressed by simply focusing on the "1 percent." Yet that is precisely what many symbolic capitalists attempted to do via Occupy: deflect blame onto others using class-based rhetoric, just as they often do with identitarian frameworks. And it was ultimately these same elites who killed the Occupy movement through their insistence on symbolic politics. As Catherine Liu aptly described it,

> The highly educated members of Occupy fetishized the procedural regulation and management of discussion to reach consensus about all collective decisions. Daily meetings or General Assemblies were managed according to a technique called the progressive stack. Its fanatical commitment to proceduralism and administrative strategy suppressed real discussion of priorities or politics and ended up promoting only the integrity of the progressive stack itself. Protecting the stack became more important

than formulating political demands that might have resonated with hundreds of millions of Americans whose lives were being directly destroyed by finance capital. PMC [professional-managerial class]/New Left ideas about mass movements dominated Occupy's dreams of politics and limited the effectiveness of its activism. Demographically and politically, Occupy was squarely a PMC elite formation.[87]

In the wake of Occupy's collapse, one of the movement's self-described "cofounders," Micah White, attempted to cash in on the Occupy "brand" by creating a firm—Boutique Activist Consultancy—that offered, among other things, talks and workshops on activism for $10,000–$75,000.[88] Although the consultancy venture ultimately flopped, White continues to try to advertise "Activist School" classes on his website, emphasizing that he partnered with elite universities like Bard and Princeton to produce the content (which, among other issues, continues to include lectures on activism by Rachel Dolezal!).[89] As the capstone to his post-Occupy journey, White penned a self-promotional editorial in *The Guardian* gushing about being invited to the 2020 World Economic Forum in Davos and speculating about the revolutionary potential of hobnobbing with the millionaires and billionaires therein.[90] In short, class-based activist movements seem to be quite amenable to elite capture as well. Indeed, as philosopher Asad Haider explained, this is a tension that has basically defined Socialist movements from Karl Marx's time through the present . . . and has often been their undoing.[91]

The bottom line is that literally *any* ideology can be "captured" by elites. There was nothing in the Gospels that dictated the particular form of the Holy Roman Empire, nor that rendered Christianity especially useful (relative to other religions) for establishing such an empire. If anything, the message of Jesus stands in direct opposition to such a regime. Similarly, the Qur'an nowhere dictated the structure of the contemporary petrostate monarchy of Saudi Arabia any more than *Das Kapital* determined the character of the Chinese government—either in Mao's time or today. Instead, as Friedrich Nietzsche argued, "There is no set of maxims more important for an historian than this: the actual causes of a thing's origin and its eventual uses, the manner of its incorporation into a system of purposes, are worlds apart; that everything that exists, no matter what its origin, is periodically reinterpreted by those in power in terms of fresh intentions . . . in the course of which the earlier meaning and purpose are necessarily either obscured or lost."[92]

Elites in other social orders justified their status, their behaviors, and the prosecution of their enemies in the name of Christianity, Islam, or communism. Contemporary symbolic capitalists often do so in the name of antiracism, feminism, LGBTQ rights, and so on. But it is not as though we'd be disinclined or somehow unable to legitimize our behaviors or justify power grabs in the absence of "woke" ideology. We would, of course, simply rely on some other framework instead.

However, any ideology used by elites to justify the prevailing order can also be used by opponents to undermine that order. There were Christian arguments against the injustice of the medieval Christian regimes—ultimately leading to the Protestant Reformation and many other dramatic social changes. Many contemporary Muslims rail against the contemporary regime in Saudi Arabia on explicitly Islamic grounds.[93] Contemporary youth in China use Marxism to criticize their ostensibly Communist government for failing the working class.[94] Ideas associated with wokeness can similarly provide us with tools for challenging the order that has been established in its name. In many respects, that is precisely the project of this book.

In short, critics on the left and right, alongside die-hard believers, are united in an erroneous perception that there is something special about "woke" ideology, that the ideas associated with wokeness are somehow especially dangerous or powerful. In truth, there is nothing extraordinary about these ideologies. We can and should talk about wokeness, and explore the relationship between "woke" ideology and the social order, just as we would for any other constellation of beliefs, norms, and dispositions.

Ideals and Interests

Consuming prominent analyses of the post-2010 era, one might gain the impression that wokeness became institutionally dominant because huge numbers of elites and elite aspirants read a bunch of Marx, Theodor Adorno, Michel Foucault, and Kimberlé Crenshaw, were completely convinced by their respective arguments, and are now trying to reshape institutions and society writ large in accordance with the prescriptions of these thinkers, as derived from their texts. In reality, many of the practices associated with wokeness betray, if anything, a *lack* of deep knowledge or engagement with the literatures that are purported to have spawned the dispositions, discourses, and practices in question.

For instance, sociologist Patricia Hill Collins invented the "matrix of oppression" framework illustrating that race, class, gender, and sexual oppression are intimately interrelated and mutually reinforcing. One *could* point to her work as a source of the idea that some groups are uniformly and objectively more oppressed than others on the basis of intersectional advantages and disadvantages, allowing one to add up the different identity categories one belongs to and determine how oppressed one is relative to others—a mode of thought perhaps best captured by the (possibly satirical) "intersectionality score calculator."[95] One *could* argue that Collins's integration of her Matrix of Oppression framework with standpoint epistemology contributed to the widespread notion that people who are most oppressed can understand society most clearly, and therefore those who identify with a greater number of, and more severely oppressed, identity categories should be given more deference and respect as compared with those who can lay claim to fewer and less marginalized identities. The problem with making these attributions, however, is that Collins rejected each of these ideas directly and unequivocally in *Black Feminist Thought* (the text that introduced the Matrix of Oppression framework):

> Rather than emphasizing how a Black woman's standpoint and its accompanying epistemology differ from those of White women, Black men and other collectivities, Black women's experiences serve as one specific social location for examining points of connection among multiple epistemologies. Viewing Black feminist epistemology in this way challenges additive analyses of oppression claiming that . . . oppression can be quantified and compared. . . . The more subordinated the group, the purer the vision available to them. . . . Although it's tempting to claim that Black women are more oppressed than everyone else and therefore have the best standpoint from which to understand the mechanisms, processes and effects of oppression, this is not the case. Instead . . . each group speaks from its own standpoint and shares its own partial, situated knowledge.[96]

Wokeness is clearly *not* a result of people being indoctrinated into social justice activism through a deep reading of primary texts like these. For a better understanding of what's going on, we can turn to the ethnographic research of sociologist Shamus Khan. In *Privilege*, Khan illustrated that a core competency elites develop over the course of their upbringing is how to confidently name-drop works, thinkers, and ideas they know little about—and in ways that create a veneer of sophistication and erudition.[97] References perceived to enhance prestige among peers and institutional gatekeepers are especially likely to be cultivated. Critically, these superficially deep yet substantively shallow modes of speaking about hot topics, big ideas, and influential thinkers are a product of enculturation, not *studying* in any traditional sense, not even when these discourses are adopted in college (as they often are).[98]

Far from being intellectually converted by intensive engagement with academic arguments, symbolic capitalists embrace wokeness largely because it serves their interests to do so. They often encounter these social justice ideas in distorted and simplified form via secondary or tertiary sources. They may genuinely believe in these ideas, as they understand them. However, they generally interpret and mobilize these social justice discourses in ways that serve their interests. It's worth unpacking these claims a bit because they're central to the argument of this book. They're also easy to misunderstand.

To get a handle on the relation between symbolic capitalists' interests and wokeness, we can leverage some theoretical tools from Max Weber. Weber argued that behaviors, discourse, and cognition tend to be goal oriented: we do the things we do, say the things we say, and think the things we think because we want things. And before wanting anything else, we seek to satisfy our material needs. Pretty much everyone desires wealth (sufficient to ensure food, clothing, shelter, etc.), security (broadly construed to include not just physical safety but also the minimization of uncertainty, precarity, and risk), health, sexual satisfaction, and an ability to reproduce. However, the very universality of these materialist desires limits their explanatory value for social theory. Insofar as core material interests are universal and more or less constant, they can't do much to explain social differences or social change. You can only explain variation by appealing to things that vary. Happily for social theorists, Weber argued, not all of our aspirations are oriented toward material ends, and not everything we do can be reduced to materialist motives. People also have *ideal interests* that transcend and can supervene our most primal wants and needs.[99]

In contrast with material interests, ideal interests are mental, social, or spiritual in nature. Desires for status, prestige, deference, or honor are examples of ideal interests. So is the hunger for meaning, purpose, or fulfillment. Or yearning to understand others or to be understood, or to love and be loved in turn. The drives for technical mastery and intellectual or spiritual enlightenment represent ideal interests. Enhancing the social position of the groups or institutions one identifies with is an ideal interest. So is the desire to be "on the right side of history," or the aspiration to build a legacy that survives one's physical death, or the quest to attain spiritual salvation. Weber argued that although ideal interests have a generic component (which is why we can talk about them abstractly), they are much more culturally and historically informed than material interests. Their specific content varies more radically depending on the historical and sociocultural milieu in which one operates and the roles one occupies therein.

Weber emphasized that although they're less critical to survival per se, ideal interests are extremely important to people—especially social elites (who worry less about satisfying their basic material needs). In fact, when material and ideal interests come into conflict, it's regularly the ideal interests that end up dominating—for instance, people often put their own health and safety at risk for a principle or a cause. In other cases, there can be a strong synergy between ideal and material interests. Among symbolic capitalists, for instance, ideal interests like status, prestige, and deference are intimately bound up with our ability to satisfy basic material needs. The pursuit of ideal interests on behalf of ourselves and others is how we put food on the table.

Collectively, Weber asserted, our ideal and material interests often shape which ideologies we are drawn to, and how we interpret and leverage them. Here, too, some clarification can be useful.

Insofar as one's interests are shown to inform one's beliefs, this is often interpreted as a sign that someone is being cynical or insincere. In truth, this is a pretty bad way to think about thinking. Our brains are designed to perceive and interpret the world in ways that enhance our success or further our goals.[100] We readily believe and focus on that which is useful or pleasurable to embrace. We tend to avoid, resist, or abandon information or ideas that are inconvenient or detrimental. There is no contradiction, then, in assuming that a belief or identity claim is sincere *while also* recognizing that material or ideal interests seem to inform the adoption of this identity or belief. Nor is there any contradiction in observing that sincerely held beliefs tend to be deployed instrumentally. Indeed, the more useful a belief or identity *is*, the more sincerely it is likely to be held. Having an interest in striking a particular position does not undermine one's sincerity—it typically enhances it.[101]

It is also critical to emphasize that the relationship between interests and ideas is not unidirectional. At certain points, and under the right circumstances, ideological innovations can dramatically change how people understand and pursue their interests. Ideas and world-images even have the capacity to transform the character and operation of society writ large. Weber's most famous illustration of this latter point was in *The Protestant Ethic and the Spirit of Capitalism.*

Weber began that work by emphasizing that, although capitalism had existed in most societies for most of human history, its growth was often constrained by cultural and religious norms that rendered the accumulation of wealth or the aggressive pursuit of commercial interests unethical for most people. Calvinist theology, however, urged believers to work as if their labors were being performed for God himself, and to be prudent in expending the fruits of their labor. Calvinist-derived interpretations of predestination, meanwhile, led many to believe that people God favored would generally enjoy prosperity in this life as well as the next (as a function of their hard work, discipline, and other positive virtues). These theological beliefs gave Calvinists powerful new ideal interests in pursuing industry and wealth—above and beyond the materialist concerns for comfort and security that all people share.

Critically, while Calvinist theology weakened many Christian taboos against wealth accumulation, it imposed and maintained others. For instance, Calvinist theology insisted that wealth should be acquired by hard work, thrift, and discipline (rather than deception, theft, gambling, etc.). Even those who had accumulated great fortune were expected to continue being industrious for as long as they were able to work. Calvinists were not permitted to use any fortune they amassed to secure additional mates, to eat gluttonously, to drink recklessly, or to acquire ostentatious clothes or homes. That is, they were largely forbidden from using their wealth to satisfy material interests once their basic needs had been met. As a consequence of these taboos, many Calvinists' wealth grew dramatically over time and accumulated across generations. Others then began emulating Calvinists in order to compete with them (and in the hope of enjoying similar prosperity).

In turn, Weber argued, growing numbers of people behaving like Calvinists supercharged and transformed capitalism. Processes and institutions became increasingly rationalized and disciplined. Productivity expectations began to rise. Eventually, it became difficult for those who did *not* behave like Calvinists to sustain themselves. Even people who had no desire to live like Calvinists were compelled nonetheless to embody Calvinist ideals upon pain of destitution. Europe, the United States, and eventually the entire globe were radically transformed by this "elective affinity" between capitalism and Calvinism—despite the fact that Calvinists were a religious minority. At the time Weber was writing, Calvinism was an even weaker force in Western society than it had been when these transformations began, yet everyone continued to be trapped in the "iron cage" of bureaucratic rational capitalism inspired by Calvinist ideology. Today, Calvinism is even more marginal, but rational-legal capitalism has only grown more hegemonic. The social transformations Weber cataloged may have been initiated by an ideology, but they were not ultimately bound by it.

Under the right conditions, then, ideas can not only supervene upon material interests, they can reshape institutions and social dynamics in such a way that their influence continues to be felt even when they are no longer widely believed, discussed, or even recognized in their original form. Specters of these ideas may persist, disconnected from their genesis, while adherents have little sense of their origin (in much the same way that Americans continue to embrace many Calvinist ideas about work with little knowledge of their theological foundations and typically having never read *anything* by John Calvin). Ultimately, the practical ways that ideas function "in the world" are often very different than what their creators may have anticipated or desired. (John Calvin, for instance, did not set out to establish rational-legal capitalism worldwide. Were he alive today, he may even be deeply troubled by the social order that is, in important respects, a product of his work.)

With all this in mind, we can restate a core argument of this book: a set of idiosyncratic ideas about social justice have come to inform how mainstream symbolic capitalists understand and pursue their interests—creating highly novel forms of competition and legitimation. When symbolic capitalists deploy social justice discourse in self-interested ways, sometimes they're pursuing material interests like securing high-paying jobs or eliminating rivals. Other times, however, they're seeking ideal interests, like convincing themselves and others that they're good people who deserve what they have (while their opponents are bad people who deserve to have bad things happen to them). In many cases, they're pursuing material and ideal interests simultaneously. Across the board, symbolic capitalists often pursue their interests by embracing beliefs that seem superficially antithetical to those interests. For instance, white symbolic capitalists regularly align themselves with antiracism, male symbolic capitalists support feminism, and so forth. To understand how symbolic capitalists' bids for status and power became so entangled with woke signaling, we'll have to brush up on some history.

Coda: Birth of the Symbolic Professions

Across the world and over time, elites have attempted to justify their social position in many different ways. Why is it that, of all things, symbolic capitalists justify their elite status through appeals to left-aligned social justice discourse? An adequate answer to that question will require us to travel back to the birth of the symbolic professions.

At the beginning of the twentieth century, factories were being consolidated into larger-scale operations. Businesses were being merged into large national corporations. The people at the helm of these organizations enjoyed immense wealth as compared with everyone else; inequality in the United States approached unprecedented levels. Meanwhile, working conditions for most laborers, and quality of life within cities, were often abysmal. Workers began fighting back: there was a rapid expansion of unionization. Strikes and labor disputes became far more common, often devolving into violence. Then, a series of catastrophes seemed to push socioeconomic conditions to their breaking point: there was a significant recession in 1917, followed by a devastating global pandemic (the 1918 Spanish flu), which triggered a deep economic recession from 1919 through 1921. Rumblings of revolution were in the air.

In 1917, a revolution *did* occur in Russia. The Bolsheviks led an uprising and declared their intent to found a Communist state. Five years later, they emerged victorious from the Russian Civil War and established the Soviet Union with neighboring countries that had launched their own communist revolutions. There were significant fears of a similar uprising taking place in the United States.[102] Inspired by the work of left-anarchist Mikhail Bakunin, aspiring revolutionary Luigi Galleani and his followers carried out a series of high-profile bombings and assassination attempts against prominent business, religious, and political leaders—culminating with the 1920 Wall Street bombing. This two-year campaign of terror triggered the first U.S. "Red Scare"—leading to clampdowns against dissidents, particularly those hailing from populations deemed especially susceptible to the Communist message (such as ethnic, racial, and religious minorities).

Layered on top of these socioeconomic pressures were deep cultural tensions. Hundreds of thousands of immigrants arrived in the United States from China from 1830 through 1880. Between 1880 and 1924, 2.5 million Jewish people sought refuge in America.[103] Tens of millions of other European migrants also arrived between 1880 and 1920—many from predominantly Catholic countries.[104] In the wake of the 1910 Mexican Revolution, migration across America's southern frontier also accelerated rapidly—and increased even further following the onset of Mexico's Cristero War in 1926.[105] Each of these waves was perceived as a threat to the hegemony of white Anglo-Saxon Protestants (WASPs) in America. Collectively, they were understood as an existential crisis. At the dawn of the twentieth century, roughly three-fourths of the populations of many large U.S. cities were immigrants and first-generation Americans.[106]

A wave of laws and policies followed, from 1875 through 1924, restricting immigration from Asia and eastern Europe and enhancing government powers to deport political dissidents (i.e., labor organizers, anarchists, and Communists) and other "undesirables." Immigration was restricted to specific ports of entry, and government agents were assigned to vet aspiring migrants. The U.S. Border Patrol was established to restrict traffic across America's southern frontier. Modern police forces were established in major U.S. cities to keep poor and minority populations "in line," and to ensure that WASPs and WASP-owned businesses were insulated from violence, infrastructure damage, or crime in the event of public disorder.[107] However, ethnic tensions continued to roil many cities.

In addition to the large influx of immigrants into the United States, there was a major wave of internal migration of African Americans from the South to the North (the Great Migration) beginning around 1910—driven by the desire to escape Jim Crow laws, Black codes, and a relatively stagnant southern economy.[108] This movement accelerated after the onset of World War I, as African Americans moved to fill the vacancies caused by the deployment of large numbers of white men to Europe (generally in foundries, factories, slaughterhouses and related lines of work). A resurgent Ku Klux Klan and accelerating racial violence in the South post-1915 further hastened the exodus. Up north, a growing Black middle class launched the New Negro movement, which was focused on developing Black culture and institutions while resisting segregation and racialized violence. Growing numbers of Black Americans began attending college, and their expectations and demands continued to rise—chafing against the bigotry and restrictions that, while less severe, were still quite present in the North.[109]

Women were likewise demanding more say in public decisions and greater opportunities in the professional world. In the United Kingdom, radical feminists carried out a campaign of bombings, arsons, and attempted assassinations and kidnappings from 1912 through the onset of World War I.[110] Women's rights campaigns in the United States were never as militant. However, there were fears that this could change—especially as the nascent Communist regimes made a point of emphasizing parity between the sexes, and as Socialist organizations in the United States sought to build alliances with feminist movements.[111] Meanwhile, many women who served in the war, or occupied vacancies formerly held by men during the war, were disinterested in returning to domestic life once the conflict was over.[112] Middle-class women began pursuing college in significantly higher numbers and increasingly aspired toward professional jobs upon graduation.[113]

Meanwhile, many white men returned from World War I and found themselves unemployed—and often struggling with physical and psychic injuries as well. There was not yet a department of veterans affairs to help disabled veterans, nor were there funds (like the post–World War II GI Bill) to help returning soldiers retrain for alternative jobs.[114] Many returning vets were none too pleased with the demographic and cultural changes that had occurred in America during their absence, nor were they content to allow Blacks, immigrants, and women to continue occupying their former jobs.

Of course, hundreds of thousands of Black men *also* fought in World War I.[115] Although still largely segregated, Black soldiers experienced a level of freedom and respect in Europe that had been unknown to them in the United States. Upon returning home, they were not only disinterested in going back to their former status quo, they were willing to fight for their freedoms and to defend themselves by force from white aggression as needed. These ethnic, racial, and economic tensions ultimately culminated in waves of violence—from the Red Summer of 1919 through the 1921 Tulsa Massacre.[116]

Into this milieu stepped the Progressives. Secularizing the social gospel movement, they promised to help America transcend its divides, redeem its soul, and experience unprecedented peace and prosperity by leveraging science and reason to maximize human flourishing in a way that laissez-faire capitalism never could. They promised a world where robber barons would be restrained by technocrats, where corruption, nepotism, exploitation, and unjust discrimination would be replaced by meritocracy and professionalization. The poor and the unfit would be cared for and gradually eliminated through a combination of aid, education programs, expanded rules and regulations (and intensified enforcement), and eugenics programs. Political partisanship, ethnic and religious conflict, and other forms of tribalistic struggles would be settled by objective and disinterested experts committed to the greater good.[117] Class struggle would be eliminated, not because inequality was vanquished, but because people across the social strata would be made to see that the prosperity and economic dynamism unleashed by free markets could benefit everyone—so long as the wealthy and powerful could be persuaded to entrust a share of their wealth and authority to symbolic capitalists to manage the economy and society writ large.[118] The symbolic professions arose in the service of this project.

Journalism, for instance, was established as a profession with a purported ethos of exposing corruption, waste, fraud, or abuse; holding the powerful to account; speaking on behalf of those whose voices typically went unheard; and educating the public into more capable citizens.[119] At the same time, newspapers sought to maximize their reach by abandoning blatant political partisanship in favor of ostensibly neutral and fact-based reporting.[120] Journalism schools were established at many prominent universities, and expectations and codes of conduct with respect to editing and reporting became far more standardized.[121]

Simultaneously, millionaires (and eventually corporations themselves) were persuaded to demonstrate their magnanimity by creating and supporting nonprofit organizations oriented toward uplifting the needy. It was argued that foundations overseen by successful businessmen, and staffed by experts, could make much better decisions about what the public needed, and could more effectively and efficiently deliver the required goods and services than corrupt, myopic, and partisan career politicians ever could. Therefore, rather than being taxed away, the affluent should be empowered and encouraged to exercise their own judgment about how to leverage some portion of their resources to promote the public good.[122] This was the beginning of "big philanthropy" as we understand it today. The proliferation of these wealthy nonprofits also led to a boom in social workers and advanced the establishment of "social work" as a profession. From the outset, it was a profession primarily staffed by women[123]—serving as an outlet for the growing numbers of highly educated women who were seeking professional employment they deemed "worthy."

Wealthy patrons also invested in postsecondary educational institutions that bore their names. One worth singling out briefly is Johns Hopkins University, established in 1873. Based on the German model of higher education, Johns Hopkins became America's first full-fledged research university—and it transformed the higher education landscape in the United States. Many other research universities were founded in the subsequent decades, often bearing the names of the wealthy philanthropists who bankrolled them. Prestigious private colleges and flagship public universities sought to remake themselves as research institutions as well (today, the formerly dominant "liberal arts college" is the exception rather than the rule). Meanwhile, other elites invested in think tanks to convene scholars and policymakers to come up with actionable solutions for particular social problems, beginning with the Carnegie Endowment for International Peace in 1910.

The rise of research universities, think tanks, and related institutions also allowed for the emergence of a new type of expert: the professional scientist. This new type of scientist was affiliated with knowledge-producing institutions (unlike citizen scientists or industry researchers) and aspired to do basic research, or "pure" science. That is, rather than serving private or state interests, they ostensibly aspired to serve all humankind by deepening our understanding of the world and following the truth wherever it led—without regard for whether their work was immediately useful, profitable, marketable, or palatable.[124]

The *social* sciences were professionalized during this same period.[125] Economics, sociology, psychology, and political science developed their own scholarly canons, established their own methods, and secured their own degree programs with chaired faculty. Graduates were expected to readily find employment in the service of policymakers, nonprofits, or think tanks, or as public intellectuals, as university professors, or in some combination of these options. New information sciences were also born to help organizations effectively manage the growing scale and complexity of their operations. In 1881, the Wharton School at the University of Pennsylvania became the first U.S. business school. In 1908, Harvard Business School was founded, and it became the first institution in the world to offer a master of business administration (MBA) degree.[126] Other programs were established at universities nationwide for accounting, personnel management, and library science—and there was extremely rapid growth in managerial, clerical, and technical jobs in the public, private, and nonprofit sectors.

There was also massive demand in the private sector and at all levels of government for engineers and urban planners (and later architects) to address the profound infrastructural, housing, and technical challenges associated with rapid industrialization (and the radically increasing scale and complexity *of* industry), urbanization, and the unprecedented waves of migration many cities experienced from 1880 through 1924. Engineering programs were established at colleges and universities around the country—although, for a host of interesting reasons, they failed to constitute themselves as a coherent "discipline" along the lines of economics, or as a profession with the level of cultural cachet that doctors or lawyers receive.[127]

Progressives simultaneously spearheaded the proliferation of secondary schools and successfully lobbied for mandatory attendance laws, with the aim of assimilating ("civilizing") ethnic or religious minorities and getting restless youth off the streets.[128] Much as in the expansion of social work, newly created positions in the education field were filled heavily by middle-class women who were seeking professional employment.[129] In order to train the needed army of instructors in how to educate students the "correct" way, teachers' colleges were established around the country (evolved from "normal schools"), and many colleges and universities established departments or schools of education.[130]

Across the board, a key aspect of the growth of these new professions was the adoption of ethical standards and codes. These documents typically defined the professions in question as fundamentally altruistic in nature—ostensibly dedicated *not* to profit or prestige but to the public good. In 1847, the American Medical Association passed its first code of ethics, which enshrined the Hippocratic oath as a cornerstone for the medical profession.

Adjacent and derivative fields (psychiatry, nursing) followed suit. The 1883 Pendleton Civil Service Reform Act established merit-based appointments for work in the civil service and codified that bureaucrats were to orient themselves toward the public good. In 1908, the American Bar Association adopted its Canons of Professional Ethics. The American Society of Newspaper Editors likewise adopted its Canons of Journalism in 1922. In 1940, the American Association of University Professors and the Association of American Colleges and Universities would issue their Statement of Principles on Academic Freedom and Tenure, which called for independence of university faculty on the basis that it freed up professors to better pursue the common good and follow the truth wherever it leads. As I've explored elsewhere,[131] one of the first things professors did with their newfound power over hiring and promotion was attempt to stack departments with allies and purge or marginalize opponents of the dominant faction. They were far from alone in this regard.

From the outset, the movement to define the symbolic professions in terms of altruism was fundamentally rooted in parochialism, elitism, and the pursuit of wealth and power. As sociologist Randall Collins put it, "The altruistic professions, in fact, are among the highest paid, and their 'altruism' gives a further payoff in the form of status and deference. . . . The introduction of stringent ethical standards among professionals has always resulted in an improvement of their economic and social position and a restriction of their ranks."[132] Indeed, Collins's research shows that although the symbolic professions and the credentialing system were ushered in under the auspices of transferring wealth and opportunity from those at the top to those who were needy and desperate, in fact the primary wealth transfer that actually occurred during this period was from the upper class to the upper-middle class.[133] Symbolic capitalists took from the rich and gave . . . primarily to themselves. As sociologist Matthew Desmond has powerfully illustrated, similar realities hold today. Since the 1970s, when changes to the global economic order radically elevated the position of symbolic capitalists in societies worldwide, wealth redistribution in America has been increasingly funneled into compelling other sectors of society to subsidize the lifestyles of the upper-middle class. There has been little benefit for the genuinely marginalized and disadvantaged. "When it comes to poverty reduction," Desmond argues, "we've had fifty years of nothing."[134]

The symbolic professions presented themselves as ethically oriented and *self*-regulating as a means to avoid regulation and supervision by others. Although these institutionally secure and politically insulated workers were, indeed, protected against being compelled to promote *others'* private interests, they were simultaneously freed up to develop and pursue their own group interests—accountable almost exclusively to peers who shared those same interests.[135] In order to justify their positions, increase their compensation, and expand their influence, they sought to take more and more decisions out of the realm of democratic contestation by redefining them as matters of expert judgment. It would be for *them*, the experts, to discern not only what the public *did* want but what it *should* want. *They* would likewise determine the best way to achieve particular goals and officially evaluate progress toward those goals.

Of course, the relatively high pay, prestige, influence, and unaccountability of these professions made it all the more important for Progressives to ensure that the "right" people (i.e. WASPs, especially WASP men) occupied these roles.

Consider, for instance, government bureaucracies, which expanded rapidly during the Progressive Era—particularly after income tax was first authorized in 1913.[136] Following the Pendleton Civil Service Reform Act, "meritocratic" testing was required for all civil servants. For a time, these tests were effective at locking out most minorities and people from "low" socioeconomic backgrounds. However, with much larger numbers of immigrants and minorities now present in America, mandatory secondary school in most locations, and growing numbers of ethnic and racial minorities aspiring to college, the tests grew less effective than they used to be at selecting for well-heeled WASPs.[137] In order to help ensure these jobs ended up being filled by the "right" people, Woodrow Wilson authorized African Americans to be cut from the civil service on the basis of their race and, post-1914, required pictures with job applications to facilitate racial discrimination henceforth.[138] Later, under Franklin D. Roosevelt (and to a lesser extent Harry S. Truman), immigrants and minorities would also be disqualified in various ways from taking advantage of New Deal and Fair Deal job opportunities or benefiting from associated government wealth-building programs.[139]

In the private and nonprofit sectors, various barriers were likewise set up to keep non-WASPs out of the symbolic professions. There were moves to restrict access to journalism jobs to those possessing professional degrees.[140] Teacher certification requirements increased dramatically.[141] New licensing, testing, certification, and degree requirements likewise proliferated for medicine (and derivative fields such as dentistry, pharmacology, nursing, and psychiatry), law, social work, the information professions, and beyond.[142] Scientists (in the natural or social sciences) increasingly required advanced degrees in order to be taken seriously or even officially work *as* scientists. These measures were taken somewhat explicitly to ensure the "right" kinds of people (upper-middle-class WASPs) ended up in these jobs while the "wrong" kinds of people (ethnic and religious minorities) were filtered out. The American Medical Association, the American Bar Association, and many other professional organizations explicitly restricted membership to whites and denied accreditation to most of the schools that arose to train immigrants and minorities in the professions.[143]

Educational institutions got in on the action as well. Colleges and universities increasingly began awarding scholarships and admission on the basis of "merit." However, when too many of the "wrong" people (i.e., Jewish people) started qualifying for meritocratic admission and aid, universities shifted to a "holistic" decision-making process that would allow them to discreetly cut "undesirables" who otherwise qualified on the basis of grades and exam scores.[144] Black people, of course, were already forbidden from attending most white universities (and were kept to very small numbers even in predominantly white universities that allowed "coloreds" to attend). Indeed, all the way until 1973 (in the wake of *Adams v. Richardson*), nineteen states retained overtly segregated higher education systems.[145]

In short, the symbolic professions were designed, fairly explicitly, to be sinecures for WASPs—primarily for men, with some roles set aside for upper-middle-class WASP women. Yet these professions were also legitimized, from the outset, by appealing to social justice discourse. From the beginning, affiliated institutions were starkly elitist and parochial, yet they ostensibly aspired to assist the downtrodden, vulnerable, marginalized, and impoverished.

Today, the symbolic professions—doctors, lawyers, professors, journalists, bureaucrats, nonprofit workers, tech workers—continue to be explicitly legitimized on the basis of their altruism. Many other cultural producers, such as scholars and artists, are expected to display indifference or disdain toward wealth and influence. They are instead supposed to prioritize the pursuit of "truth," "beauty," and related abstractions (with those who conspicuously fail to conform with these expectations derided as "hacks" or "grifters" or otherwise less "authentic" or "pure").[146] Now, as in the past, these claims to altruism and serving higher principles or the public good provide the basis for the high levels of pay, prestige, deference, and autonomy that symbolic capitalists enjoy.

However, this mode of legitimation can also present a vulnerability. Insofar as symbolic capitalists are perceived to be selfish or myopic, as serving elite interests at the expense of the broader public, or as parasitic on society rather than advancing the greater good, their authority and job security can be severely undermined. This mode of legitimation also sets the stage for a unique form of status competition *within* the symbolic professions: those who are perceived to be more effective or committed to promoting the common good and (especially) helping the vulnerable, marginalized, and disadvantaged are generally perceived to be more worthy of prestige, deference, autonomy, and so on. Meanwhile, those who are successfully portrayed as possessing values, priorities, and behaviors that seem unworthy of their profession will often find their jobs and social status in a precarious position. And when times get hard, symbolic capitalists grow even more aggressive in trying to preserve or enhance their social position by demonstrating that their peers and rivals have never been woke.

2

The Great Awokening(s)

Over the past several years, there has been a dramatic shift in discourse and expressed attitudes about prejudice, discrimination, and disrespect. More striking than the intensity and rapidity of the movement was its breadth. Although race was a central axis, discourse and beliefs around immigration status, gender, and sexuality experienced similar and roughly simultaneous transformations.

Documenting these changes, colleagues David Rozado, Jamin Halberstadt, and I analyzed twenty-seven million news articles published in forty-seven media outlets over the past half century. We found that, beginning in the early 2010s, there was a major rise in the use of terms referring to various forms of prejudice and discrimination.[1] Bias and oppression along the lines of race, gender, or sexuality—and even discrimination against religious minorities (Muslims, Jews)—all experienced rapid and simultaneous increases in salience. Similar patterns held for television news broadcasts. Statistical tests suggested that these shifts were not independent of one another but instead seemed to be products of some deeper, underlying change among the people who produce the news.

Academic research followed the same trend. Analyzing thematic patterns since the turn of the century across six of the most expansive scholarship databases, Rozado and I identified a dramatic and simultaneous increase in research studying discrimination along the lines of race, gender identity, sexual orientation, and disability status after 2011.[2] Google nGrams show equivalent changes in published books: there were huge and simultaneous spikes in discussions of racism, xenophobia, sexism, homophobia, transphobia, Islamophobia, anti-Semitism, and related terms that began after 2011 and continued through the end of the dataset (2019).[3]

Artistic outputs moved in a similar direction. As early as 2014, cultural critics began to note that overtly political—and politically and morally uncomplicated—art was beginning to dominate the cultural landscape in symbolic capitalist circles.[4] In the aftermath of Donald Trump's election, this trend seems to have been exacerbated.[5] Diversity, representation, and politics were core themes for museum exhibitions throughout the 2010s.[6] Art education trended in the same direction: statistical analyses of art pedagogy journals showed a significant spike in focus on "identity" issues after 2010 and running through the rest of the decade.[7]

Diversity, representation, and identity became core priorities of the entertainment industry too. With respect to feature films, for instance, roughly 14 percent of major studio films released in 2012 included an LGBTQ character, and only half of those passed the Vito Russo test. By 2020, nearly a quarter (23 percent) included identifiably LGBTQ characters, and nearly all (90 percent) of those movies passed the test.[8] Simultaneously, the percentage of films with nonwhite leads quadrupled over the decade to the point where the percentage of films with white leads now roughly mirrors the percentage of whites in the general population. The diversity of supporting roles also increased radically over this same period. By 2020, nearly 30 percent of films had primarily nonwhite casts. Over this same period, the percentage of movies with female leads likewise doubled and is now approaching parity with the percentage of films with male leads.[9] The number of films passing the Bechdel test radically increased after 2010 as well. Of the thirty highest-grossing films of 2006, only 27 percent passed the test. In the period between 2013 and 2019, 76 percent passed.[10]

Representation in television and streaming shows followed a similar trajectory. The share of regular and recurring LGBTQ actors more than doubled from 2012 to 2020—including a rapidly growing presence in children and family programming. LGBTQ representation also grew more diverse. By 2020, a majority of LGBTQ characters on the small screen were nonwhite.[11] Overall, the share of scripted television shows with nonwhite leads more than doubled from 2012 to 2020, and supporting casts grew radically more diverse as well.[12]

However, entertainment outputs didn't simply grow more diverse, they also grew more overtly political.[13] And it wasn't just the themes that shifted but also the mode of discussion. In the words of cultural critic Molly Fischer, entertainment outputs increasingly adopted "a tone along the lines of an after-school special," despite a dearth of viewers who would be "simultaneously surprised and receptive to such lessons."[14] Those in the entertainment industry who failed to toe the preferred institutional line on cultural and political issues increasingly faced professional sanctions. Content out of step with the preferred narratives grew increasingly difficult to produce.[15]

The advertisements that accompany (and typically subsidize the production of) these cultural outputs simultaneously grew more diverse along the lines of race, gender, and sexuality—and more explicitly political in their themes and content—from 2012 through 2021. The changes were particularly pronounced in advertisements for symbolic economy–aligned industries such as education, technology, telecommunications, nonprofits, and entertainment (TV, music, film), and in ads targeting strong Democrat-voting regions (such as symbolic economy hubs).[16]

Collectively, these changes in symbolic economy outputs happened in tandem with radical attitudinal shifts among the primary producers and consumers of these outputs: highly educated white liberals. After 2011, there were dramatic changes in how highly educated white liberals answered questions related to race and ethnicity.[17] These shifts were not matched among nonliberal or non-Democrat whites, nor among nonwhites of any political or ideological persuasion. By 2020, highly educated white liberals tended to provide more "woke" responses to racial questions than the average Black or Hispanic person; they tended to perceive much more racism against minorities than most minorities, themselves, reported experiencing; they expressed greater support for diversity than most Blacks or Hispanics.[18] White Democrats also became significantly more likely to perceive others in their social circles as "racist," even as nonwhite copartisans moved in the opposite direction (and white non-Democrats were flat).[19] On "feeling thermometer" questions, white liberals shifted so much that they now tend to view all other racial and ethnic groups more favorably than their own. There is no other combination of ideology and race that produces remotely similar results.[20]

Critically, race is not the only axis on which these dramatic trends were apparent. They are visible in questions related to gender and sexuality as well. For instance, from 2010 to 2020 Democrats became 16 percentage points more likely to insist that abortion should be legal under all circumstances. There was more movement in this ten-year span than in the entire preceding time series, going back to 1975.[21] Over this same period, white liberals became much more likely to self-identify as "feminist," and self-identified "feminists" grew much more likely to identify as strong Democrats. Moreover, although white liberals' views on "identity" issues shifted far more than their positions on economic matters, dramatic shifts were apparent in expressed attitudes on poverty as well.[22] As an example, between 2011 and 2017, Republicans grew 1 percentage point less likely to say that the government should do more to help the needy even if it exacerbates the national debt. Democrats shifted 17 percentage points in the opposite direction.[23] On dataset after dataset, question after question, this same pattern emerges: a rapidly growing polarization between highly educated white liberals and virtually everyone else in society from 2011 through 2021.

As symbolic capitalists' attitudes about the social world changed, their emotional states moved in tandem. There was a rapid and asymmetrical increase in Democrats experiencing anxiety, depression, and other forms of negative affect after 2011—including and especially among those who are highly educated, white and identify as liberal—perhaps driven by increased awareness, concern, and discussion about social injustices (and heightened worry about actual or perceived complicity in said injustices or impotence to meaningfully address them).[24]

The political and ideological alignments of highly educated white Americans shifted significantly over this same period too. Since 2010, rapidly growing shares of highly educated whites have aligned themselves with the Democratic Party. And within the Democratic Party, there has been a dramatic rise in the share of highly educated and white voters who identify as "liberal." It is particularly highly educated *white* voters within the Democratic Party who have undergone this ideological shift. Black and Hispanic Democrats with college degrees, for instance, remain far less likely to self-identify as "liberal" than white peers and saw far less movement over the span of time in question.[25] There was also systematic variation along gender lines: the shifts were far more radical and sustained among women than men.[26] Across the board, however, highly educated whites underwent dramatic changes in their political and ideological identification. As an indication of how far they've shifted: in recent polling, college-educated white voters have shown a stronger preference for the Democratic Party than racial or ethnic minority voters. This is unprecedented in the record of polling going back to the mid-1960s.[27]

In addition to shifting how they talk and think about social justice issues, and adjusting their political and ideological alignments, highly educated white liberals also became much more militant in advocating for their preferred social agenda. Highly educated white Democrats, for instance, began to contact elected officials and donate to political campaigns and causes at much higher levels after 2010, and in a way that was not mirrored by nonwhite copartisans.[28] In response, the preferred political party of these constituents shifted dramatically as well. Work by economist Sahil Chinoy shows that there was an aggressive (and asymmetrical) leftward shift in the Democratic Party platform beginning in 2012 and persisting through subsequent cycles.[29]

Here it's worth emphasizing that, although polls and surveys tend to break up the electorate in terms of characteristics like race, income, education, or political and ideological identification instead of identifying them by the work they do, it's probably more precise to think of the shifts as being driven by symbolic capitalists in particular, rather than whites, liberals, or highly educated voters more generically. Much-discussed phenomena like the growing urban-rural divide, the diploma divide, and the gender divide are all proxies for a more fundamental schism between symbolic capitalists (and the communities they congregate in) versus those who are more socioeconomically or culturally distant from the symbolic economy—a schism that has grown significantly wider in recent years.

Symbolic capitalists lie squarely at the intersection of the populations whose ideological and political perspectives have changed most since 2011 (highly educated white liberals). As will be detailed at length in subsequent chapters, symbolic capitalists are overwhelmingly white. This is not just a function of baseline U.S. population characteristics: relative to other American workers, symbolic capitalists are disproportionately likely to be white. They nearly unanimously possess at least a BA. Politically and ideologically, they are overwhelmingly Democratic and liberal. All said, the lion's share of symbolic capitalists are highly educated white liberals, and Americans who happen to be highly educated white liberals are quite likely to be symbolic capitalists. The particular slice of Americans who primarily comprise the symbolic professions underwent idiosyncratic and dramatic political and ideological transformations after 2011, and this significantly and uniquely transformed the outputs and the operations of the symbolic professions over this same time period (relative to other occupations).

In a 2019 essay, *Vox* analyst Matthew Yglesias popularized the term "the Great Awokening" as a shorthand to refer to the rapid shifts in the expressed views of white liberals on identity issues after 2011.[30] This is the term I will use here to collectively refer not just to the shifts in expressed attitudes among symbolic capitalists but also to the simultaneous and likewise dramatic changes in protest activity, ideological and political alignments, and symbolic economy outputs.[31] These trends are often analyzed and discussed in isolation. However, it's likely more revelatory to analyze them as different facets of a single overarching social phenomenon that started in late 2010 and began to decline around 2021.

Point of Origin

One of the most striking aspects of the rapid shift in discourse and norms around "identity" issues is their timing: they don't seem to be a response to anything in particular that happened "in the world" with respect to race, gender, or sexuality at time of onset.

For instance, given that the shifts on race became increasingly pronounced through 2012, one might assume they were straightforwardly a response to the February 26 murder of Trayvon Martin. However, it is harder to explain why we see similar changes in discussion and public attitudes with respect to sexism, homophobia, transphobia, Islamophobia, and anti-Semitism—all at roughly the same time as we observe the spikes related to race.

The shifts with respect to sexism and misogyny were clearly not a response to #MeToo. They preceded the emergence of #MeToo by a few years and may help explain why the movement was able to achieve the impact it did—why it was able to find such a receptive audience when previous efforts to elevate the issues of sexual violence, harassment, and discrimination were less successful gaining traction.

In a similar fashion, changes that were *already underway* leading into 2012 may explain why the murder of Martin—and the subsequent slayings of Eric Garner, Michael Brown, and Tamir Rice—resonated so strongly when previous incidents of state violence against African Americans (including other incidents caught on film) did not. That is, rather than the shift in racial attitudes being a response to, for instance, Black Lives Matter (BLM), instead, *antecedent shifts* among symbolic capitalists may help explain why BLM was able to attain such prominence in 2013, and to rise to such heights in the years that followed.

In light of this timeline, it should go without saying that the ongoing Great Awokening was *not* a response to Trump. Instead, Trump seems to have emerged on the political scene in the context of already-heightened social tension around identity issues, and may have been ushered out of office by the same. Research by my colleagues and I found that the shifts in media discourse and public attitudes continued unabated six months after Joe Biden was sworn into office—underscoring yet again that the shifts were not "about" Trump.[32]

Instead, if we are trying to pinpoint the beginning of the Great Awokening, it seems most accurate to say it began in September 2011, with the emergence of the Occupy Wall Street movement. This claim may be shocking to some readers. In the popular discourse, the Occupy movement is often discussed as being in tension with, or even antithetical to, identitarian approaches to social justice. Some have gone so far as to claim that the Great Awokening was cooked up by superelites and corporations in order to divert attention away from the broad-based and class-focused movement that Occupy Wall Street allegedly represented.[33] In reality, however, Occupy and the identitarian movements that succeeded it are more contiguous than contradictory.

E Pluribus Unum

From the outset, a key mission of symbolic capitalists has been to rein in capitalism run amok (thereby rendering the prevailing order more beneficent, efficient, and stable). Although mainstream symbolic capitalists have consistently aligned themselves with the "Left," in practice their efforts have been largely oriented toward saving capitalism from the capitalists rather than overthrowing the system entirely. In pursuit of this objective, millionaires and billionaires have been a consistent foil for symbolic economy professionals. Superelites whose fortunes are tied to material extraction and production are subject to particular scorn. Across the board, however, symbolic capitalists have consistently condemned superelites as selfish, short-sighted, and insufficiently deferent to people like ourselves.

As sociologist Max Weber emphasized, elites who hold social status in society on the basis of attributes like their knowledge, skills, or institutional rank tend to be resentful and disdainful toward those who enjoy a high social position primarily on the basis of their business success and accumulated wealth. It has always been our strong conviction that society would be vastly improved if people listened to and admired the millionaires and billionaires *less* and valued the perspectives of intellectuals *more*. These sentiments are heightened, Weber argued, when symbolic capitalists find their own status or socioeconomic position threatened or particularly precarious.[34] During these periods, we become much more likely to rail aggressively against capitalism and the superrich—often cloaking our struggles for wealth, status, and power as social justice advocacy—although our passion for revolution tends to rapidly fade once our own objectives are met:

> In truth—let's be honest with ourselves here—this belief in the cause, as subjectively sincere as it may be, is almost always a "moral legitimation" for the desire for power, revenge, booty, and benefits: the materialist

interpretation of history too is no hansom cab to be hailed at will, and it doesn't stop for the agents of revolution! But then, after the emotional revolution, comes the return to traditional everyday life; the hero of the believers, and even the belief itself, disappears or becomes even more effective as a conventional slogan in the political philistine's or functionary's arsenal.[35]

Taking symbolic capitalists' rhetoric at face value during these periods of heightened unrest, it would be easy to mistake us as genuinely populist or egalitarian. However, the methods and constitution of the movements we take part in typically suggest a different story: they tend to be campaigns by and for one faction of elites against another. Occupy Wall Street was no exception.

In reality, Occupy was not class oriented. It was a movement that, if anything, helped *obscure* important class differences and the actual causes of social stratification. As David Autor aptly put it, "The singular focus of the public debate on the 'top 1 percent' of households overlooks the component of earnings inequality that is arguably most consequential for the 'other 99 percent' of citizens: the dramatic growth in the wage premium associated with higher education and cognitive ability."[36] That is, precisely what Occupy helped us *avoid* talking about is how symbolic economy institutions and their employment practices are some of the main drivers of contemporary inequality, and how people like *us* are the primary "winners" in this arrangement. Conveniently for symbolic capitalists, rather than focusing on concrete policies to rectify inequalities, the Occupy movement's approach to social change was intensely academic and, in the name of "inclusivity," was outright hostile to politics per se.[37] Rather than advocating for concrete policies that could tangibly assist the marginalized and disadvantaged in society, or developing some actionable platform that could help promote broad-based prosperity, the movement was primarily focused on villainizing those above symbolic capitalists on the socioeconomic ladder.

Contrary to depictions of Occupy as a broad-based movement, symbolic capitalists were its primary base. For instance, despite the diversity of the city, participants of Occupy demonstrations in New York were overwhelmingly non-Hispanic white. They were nearly uniformly liberal in their political orientations. They were also relatively affluent: roughly three-quarters (72 percent) of participants came from households above the 2011 New York City median. A plurality came from households that brought in over $100,000 per year. Seventy-six percent of participants had a BA degree or higher, and a majority of the rest were currently enrolled in college. Those who had jobs hailed overwhelmingly from the symbolic professions. Only about a quarter of employed participants had blue-collar, retail, or service jobs.[38] Across the rest of the country, the picture was basically the same. Occupy protests were concentrated largely in symbolic economy hubs, and there were low rates of participation across the board for those who were *not* college educated, white, and liberal.[39]

The composition of Occupy was broadly continuous with the "identitarian" movements that followed. For instance, analyzing the post-2016 #Resistance protest movements such as the March for Science, the Women's March, and the March for Racial Justice, sociologist Dana Fisher likewise found that the demonstrators were majority white, disproportionately female, extremely well educated (with more than 70 percent possessing a bachelor's degree, and many others pursuing a college degree), and overwhelmingly left-leaning. Whether we analyze by sheer number of events or by participants, or if we look at attendees per capita, #Resistance protest events were overwhelmingly concentrated in knowledge economy hubs, just like Occupy protests were. The average adult age of the demonstrators was thirty-eight to forty-nine years old. Far from being a project of passionate young people, the #Resistance movement comprised primarily midcareer professionals associated with the symbolic economy.[40] The Occupy crowd, but a half decade later.

Consequently, instead of thinking about Occupy Wall Street and post-2011 identitarian shifts as competitors, it's probably more accurate to view them as different phases in the same Awokening. As the initial (Occupy) movement fizzled out, roughly the same constituencies began mobilizing alternative modes of social justice discourse, largely toward the same ends. Many who spent 2011 shouting "We are the 99 percent" spent 2013 proudly declaring that "Black Lives Matter," identified as part of the #Resistance under Trump, began telling #MeToo stories in 2017, and became "trust the science" stans from 2018 through the COVID-19 pandemic. It's all been part of the same wave of activism among mainstream symbolic capitalists.

Alternative Facts

There have been many alternative theories to explain the rapid cultural shifts and heightened social unrest that began after 2010. One popular narrative attributes the tumult to new digital technologies allowing ordinary people to circumvent elite gatekeepers, coordinate, and share information and ideas in hitherto unprecedented ways.[41] A popular variation on this argument interprets the Great Awakening as a product of women, minorities, LGBTQ Americans, and young people having a greater ability to "talk back" to established authorities as a result of the aforementioned technological shifts alongside changing demographics in the United States. Resistance to "wokeness" is described as backlash against historically marginalized and disadvantaged populations making gains in society. These narratives are comforting to symbolic capitalists. However, they have glaring problems.

Again, the most dramatic shifts in norms, discourse, and political activity occurred among highly educated and relatively affluent white liberals. They were not reflected among poor or working-class people or nonwhites of any political persuasion to anywhere near the same degree. Geographically, wealthy symbolic economy hubs were the main sites of mobilization. Looking at occupations, there have been massive changes to journalistic outputs and the operations of many newsrooms since 2011. There were major shifts in the themes of academic research and teaching. Nonprofit and advocacy organizations experienced constant and explosive conflict over what their priorities should be and how best to advance them.[42] Advertisers, PR firms, and consultants made significant adjustments to their strategies and communications. Art and entertainment outputs underwent massive transformations. New rules, procedures, trainings, and positions proliferated rapidly in HR departments. However, there were no comparable social justice–oriented shifts in how waitresses serve food, how truck drivers deliver freight, how beauticians cut nails, how construction workers build houses, how grocery store clerks ring up food, how plumbers unclog toilets, and so on (excepting some additional rules and training imposed by the aforementioned corporate HR administrators, often to the chagrin of "normie" workers). The Awokening was primarily constrained to the symbolic professions. And within those professions, the shifts were led by the most prestigious institutions (later emulated by others),[43] and conflicts were consistently more pronounced in elite spaces than in less prestigious firms and institutions. These realities are difficult to square with depictions of the Great Awokening as a "bottom-up" movement.

Narratives attributing the Great Awokening to young people are just as problematic. For example, there was a significant uptick in demonstrations at college campuses nationwide that began in 2011 and continued to build over subsequent years.[44] We now know that the unrest unfolding on campuses was not unique to institutions of higher learning. Most other spheres of the symbolic economy were undergoing contemporaneous transformations. The changes were *especially visible* at colleges and universities early on because these are institutions filled with huge numbers of symbolic capitalists and aspirants thereto. That is, they contain exceptionally large concentrations of the elites who were undergoing the shifts. At the time, however, many instead attempted to explain the tumult affecting colleges and universities in terms of the unique characteristics of "kids these days." As the discourse continued, there came to be a particular focus on Gen Z, who, relative to previous cohorts, were held to be especially sensitive to offense, intolerant of resistance or dissent, and politically progressive and engaged, but also overly impatient and idealistic.

However, Gen Z was clearly *not* responsible for the identitarian shifts in mainstream media reporting, published books, academic journal articles, or arts and entertainment programming that kicked off as Occupy was winding down. At the time these shifts began, the *oldest* members of Gen Z were just sixteen years old—they were not producing these cultural outputs, let alone serving as gatekeepers of what gets published or not. These teens and preteens were not the demographic most advertisers, media companies, and publishing houses were trying to reach, nor were they the main constituents that Democratic Party decision makers were trying to appease as they shifted their messaging and priorities (they weren't even old enough to vote, let alone having the discretionary income and autonomy to donate and volunteer for campaigns). Instead, it was millennials and younger members of Gen X who led the Great Awokening—people who were in their twenties through forties at its outset. Consequently, although it may be empirically true that contemporary young people have unique experiences, characteristics, and preferences that set them apart from previous generational cohorts in nontrivial ways, these differences are not particularly relevant for understanding most of the post-2011 social, cultural, and institutional transformations.

Technological changes can't explain the Great Awokening either. Facebook became available to the general public in 2006. Google acquired YouTube in that same year. Twitter began taking off in 2007, contemporaneous with the release of the first iPhone. All said, social networking sites and smartphones existed for years before the Awokening began—and the erstwhile rebels who made effective use of these technologies were often, themselves, highly educated and relatively affluent. They were disaffected elites or elite aspirants rather than "normies." The cofounders of BLM, for instance, all had BA degrees from top-notch universities. Two out of three had advanced degrees on top of their BAs. One could go on and on.

Rather than empowering ordinary people to circumvent elite gatekeepers, it may be that the primary way digital technologies and platforms contributed to social unrest was by making it easier for counterelites to spread their messaging and attain a following. Yet, as Evgeny Morozov powerfully illustrated, the specific technologies and platforms broadly credited with sparking revolutions are also widely used by established authorities to surveil dissidents, suppress resistance, and otherwise preserve the status quo.[45] Put another way, one could just as easily point to the technologies in question to explain why status quos persist instead of why they change.

Perhaps the biggest problem with the technological account, however, is that it implies (1) the post-2011 Great Awokening would not have happened in the absence of the technologies in question and (2) events like this did not happen, and indeed could not have, before these technologies existed (because the shifts are, themselves, products of the new technologies and platforms). Both these implicit premises are demonstrably false.

Not the First, Not the Last

While there is a tendency in some circles to assert that we live in "unprecedented" times, in fact, there have been multiple other Awokenings in the twentieth century that played out quite similarly to the current period of rapid normative and discursive change. We can isolate these periods using many of the same types of metrics we used to substantiate the current one.

For instance, highly educated white voters moved aggressively toward the Democratic Party after 2011. Political scientists Matthew Grossman and David Hopkins showed that there were similar shifts in the political identification of highly educated whites in the late 1980s through the mid-1990s, and in the mid-1960s through the late 1970s.[46] Looking at trends in white racial liberalism from 1954 to 2020, political scientist Zach Goldberg identified three periods of significant attitudinal shifts among white liberals: one that crested in the mid-1960s, one in the early 1990s, and another that had yet to crest as of 2020.[47] Looking at Google nGrams, political scientist Eric Kaufmann found that there were *three* major spikes in literary discussion around racism, sexism, and homophobia: one beginning in the mid-1960s, one in the late 1980s, and another in the early 2010s.[48] Quantitative analysis of academic publications from 1980 to 2018 reveals a dramatic uptick in discussions of "trauma" and other terms related to victimhood starting in the early 1990s, with another spike after 2010.[49]

This is all resonant with what my colleagues and I discovered in analyzing media articles: although our dataset did not go back to the 1960s, we found evidence of a dramatic shift in discourse and public attitudes related to a broad range of "identity" issues that peaked in the early 1990s[50] (in addition to the spike that began after 2011). Sociologist Leslie McCall likewise identified a dramatic spike in media coverage of socioeconomic inequality in the early to mid-1990s.[51] Political scientists Dennis Chong, Jack Citrin, and Morris Levy subsequently illustrated that there was a major spike in media conversation around free speech and equality in the late 1980s through the mid-1990s followed by another spike beginning after 2008 and proceeding through 2021.[52] Moreover, they highlight, major national longitudinal surveys show contemporaneous and rapid declines in tolerance for speech perceived to demean or offend members of historically marginalized and disenfranchised groups during these periods—at least for a certain subset of the population. Explaining their findings in the *New York Times*, Chong noted that "the most pronounced declines [in tolerance for offensive speech] over time have occurred among white, college educated liberals."[53] Writing in 1994, sociologist Steven Brint observed that "episodic surges of reformist activity" seem to "affect middle class professionals" more than anyone else in society.[54]

It is important to underline just how episodic these surges are. As philosopher Oliver Traldi has pointed out, the contemporary debates about identity politics, free speech, and "political correctness" on college campuses played out nearly verbatim in the late 1980s and early 1990s.[55] In a book written at the tail end of the last Awokening, Barbara Ehrenreich describes how responses to student activists in the late 1980s and early 1990s were virtually identical to how "radical" students were portrayed in the 1960s. One excerpt is worth quoting at length, as it underscores how little has changed from the time of the boomers—not just relative to the 1990s but even today (emphases mine):

> Psychiatrist Bruno Bettelheim likened the student rebels to Nazis. Then– liberal professor John Sibler called them "the new Fascisti." Nathan Glazer *compared them not only to Hitler but to Lenin and Stalin.* Daniel Bell described the students at Columbia as "*impelled not to innovation but to destruction.*" Irving Kristol, not yet a conservative, called them "rebels without a cause—and *without hope of accomplishing anything* other than mischief and ruin." Nor did the howls of outrage come only from the liberal center of the political spectrum. . . . Socialist Irving Howe dismissed the student movement as "romantic primitivism," motivated by a "*quasi-religious impulse.*" . . . Edward Sihls described the students as "a uniquely indulged generation." . . . If they were "acting out" it was only

because they had been acted upon—in the wrong way—by their *indulgent parents*.[56]

Sound familiar? Again, this is Ehrenreich writing in 1990 about how student protesters *in the 1960s* were received. She found startling continuity between the culture war narratives and battle lines of the 1960s and the 1990s. It was even more startling to reread this text in the 2020s and observe how little has changed in our cultural scripts over the last sixty years.

All said, few elements of the current Awokening are actually unique to the present. Consider the phenomenon of "cancellation" within left-aligned spaces. Although often discussed in connection with online platforms and smartphones, it's a practice that goes back decades. In the 1960s, for instance, it was called "trashing," but the dynamics were the same, as illustrated powerfully in a 1976 article in *Ms.* magazine by Jo Freeman:

> Trashing has reached epidemic proportions. . . . What is "trashing," this colloquial term that expresses so much, yet explains so little? . . . It is not done to expose disagreements or resolve differences. It is done to disparage and destroy. The means vary. . . . Whatever methods are used, trashing involves a violation of one's integrity, a declaration of one's worthlessness, and an impugning of one's motives. In effect, what is attacked is not one's actions, or one's ideas, but one's self. This attack is accomplished by making you feel that your very existence is inimical to the Movement and that nothing can change this short of ceasing to exist. These feelings are reinforced when you are isolated from your friends as they become convinced that their association with you is similarly inimical to the Movement and to themselves. Any support of you will taint them. Eventually all your colleagues join in a chorus of condemnation which cannot be silenced, and you are reduced to a mere parody of your previous self.[57]

Contemporary tensions around "grievance studies," "words as violence," "victimhood culture," and affirmative action are likewise mostly reruns of debates from the late 1980s and early 1990s—themselves largely rehashes of debates from the late 1960s and early 1970s.[58] "Asymmetrical multiculturalism" (the tendency of white intellectuals to hold their coethnics in contempt while celebrating romanticized views of minorities) is not a product of the post-2010 period either. Instead, as political scientist Eric Kaufmann has shown, this impulse towards "white bashing" first became prominent in the 1920s.[59]

In fact, many elements of the contemporary Awokening date back roughly a century. Looking at mentions of "antiracism" in Google Books, we can see *four* major spikes: one in the early 1930s, one in the late 1960s, one in the late 1980s, and one in the early 2010s. Similarly, with respect to feminism, many have described the current moment as part of the "fourth wave."[60] The third wave was in the late 1980s and early 1990s. The second wave was during the 1960s through the early 1970s. And the *first* wave peaked toward the 1920s and crested through the early 1930s. In many respects, this initial Great Awokening was far more intense than any that followed. It also happens to be the most neglected in contemporary discussions about these periods of rapid sociocultural change, even though it shares almost all the same characteristics of later uprisings.

For instance, writing in 1929, toward the tail end of the first Great Awokening, George Orwell highlighted how the predominant social justice movement of the time, while ostensibly egalitarian, was primarily a product of professionals (the "middle class" in the parlance of the times). Social justice discourse, he argued, was often used by elites as a means of self-enhancement. Their approach to talking and thinking about these issues was alienating to most nonelites, to the detriment of the genuinely marginalized and disadvantaged in society. Orwell's description of the tone and character of this period of heightened "social justice" activism should be immediately familiar to the contemporary reader (emphases mine except where indicated):

> The first thing that must strike any observer is that Socialism in its developed form is a theory confined entirely to the middle class. The typical Socialist is not, as tremulous old ladies imagine, a ferocious-looking working man with greasy overalls and a raucous voice. He is either a youthful snob-Bolshevik who in five years' time will have been converted to Roman Catholicism; or, still *more typically, a prim little man with a white-collar job*, usually a secret teetotaller, and often with vegetarian leanings, with a history of Nonconformity behind him, and, above all, with a social position that he has no intention of forfeiting. . . . Most middle-class Socialists, *while theoretically pining for a classless society, cling like glue to their miserable fragments of social prestige.* . . . Sometimes I look at a Socialist—the intellectual, tract-writing type of Socialist, with his pullover, his fuzzy hair, and his Marxian quotation—and wonder what the devil his motive really *is* (emphasis in original). It is often difficult to believe that it is love of anybody, especially of the working class, from whom he is of all people the furthest removed. . . . When I listen to these people talking, and still more when I read their books, I get the impression that, to them, the whole Socialist movement is no more than a kind of *exciting*

heresy-hunt—a leaping to and fro of frenzied witch-doctors to the beat of tom-toms and the tune of "Fee, fi, fo, fum, I smell the blood of a right-wing deviationist."[61]

It should be emphasized, however, that despite the many similarities between each of these movements, each Awokening has been importantly different from those that preceded and followed in various ways. For instance, the current Awokening is occurring in an age with the internet, smartphones, and social media, all of which do change symbolic exchange in profound ways (even if they aren't the *cause* of the latest Awokening). After the 1960s, anti-war protests were decoupled from subsequent uprisings for reasons that will be explored. LGBTQ rights, while part of the agenda during all periods of Awokening, have grown increasingly pronounced over time. The position of symbolic capitalists in society has evolved with each Awokening too, and as a result, turmoil within the symbolic professions has differential impacts on the rest of society across different historical periods. But for all of these significant differences across cycles—and they are significant—there are also patterns that repeat. By comparing cases and looking at elements that persist across cycles, we can gain insight into why and under what circumstances these movements begin, how and why they fizzle out, what (if any) changes they tend to leave in their wake, and whether (and how) one Awokening informs the next.

Colleges and universities play a central (and ever-growing) role in the symbolic economy. They also contain especially large concentrations of the people who tend to undergo dramatic normative and discursive shifts during Great Awokenings. For these reasons, institutions of higher learning provide nice sites for comparing one episode with another. Moreover, because "kids these days" narratives have been perennially popular[62]—while scholars and journalists are much less consistent about turning the analytical lens toward professionals like themselves—there is a particularly robust media and scholarly record of student protest activity that can help shed light on the timing of these Awokenings and their correlates. As a function of these realities, the walkthrough that follows will be heavily focused on student activism. However, it deserves to be emphasized that students were *not* the primary drivers of these movements.

To be sure, young people broadly embraced social justice movements when they were already underway, serving alternately as foot soldiers and scapegoats for older elites. However, they are rarely the instigators or leaders of these revolts. Consider the quintessential period of student activism, the

1960s. As psychologist Jean Twenge illustrated, the activism and counter-culture movements of that period were *not* driven primarily by baby boomers. Instead, they were led by people from the Silent Generation who were in their mid-twenties through thirties at the time the Awokening took hold.[63] Similar patterns hold across all Awokenings, from Orwell's time through the present. Hence, although we will spend a lot of time discussing student protest movements in the pages that follow, readers should bear in mind that the patterns observed among college students are symptomatic of trends among symbolic capitalists writ large. After briefly walking through these episodes, we'll zoom back out to reinforce this point.

The First Awokening

As the symbolic professions were being consolidated, and their position elevated, educational and certification requirements were increasingly used as barriers to lock out minorities, immigrants, and the poor. Meanwhile, upper-middle-class whites began enrolling in colleges and universities at significantly higher rates. For instance, between 1920 and 1930, the share of Americans with a BA doubled (from 2.3 percent to 4.9 percent); the share possessing an MA tripled (from 0.24 percent to 0.78 percent); the percentage of Americans possessing a PhD quadrupled (from 0.03 percent to 0.12 percent). Moreover, the share of young adults enrolled in higher education institutions in 1930 was nearly 50 percent higher than it was at the outset of the previous decade (rising from 8.9 percent to 12.4 percent of Americans aged nineteen to twenty-one).[64] With the economy booming from 1922 through 1929, graduating cohorts of students flourished and successfully secured the cushy positions that had been set aside for people like them in the symbolic professions. Jobs grew at a rate that easily kept up with the increased production of degree holders.

Then, the Great Depression hit. Suddenly, many who had taken for granted a position among the elite, who had felt more or less entitled to a secure, respected, and well-paying professional job, found themselves facing deeply uncertain futures—especially because layered on top of the economic insecurity were profound geopolitical concerns.

In 1917, the United States issued a draft for all men twenty-one through thirty—and it successfully defended the right to forced conscription in the Supreme Court a year later. That draft campaign was short lived because an armistice was reached between the Allies and Germany in November 1918, bringing an end to World War I. However, now that the government had secured conscription authority, in the event of a subsequent war, it seemed likely that a draft order would be issued from the beginning rather than at the end of fighting (and indeed, it ultimately was—conscription for World War II began in 1940, before the United States had even officially entered the conflict). At the outset of the Great Depression, war seemed to be breaking out in Europe again, and it seemed increasingly likely that America could be pulled into the fray. Consequently, rather than enjoying the secure and comfortable lives they had imagined for themselves, aspiring elites were facing the prospects of downward social mobility (as a result of the Depression) and possible deployment into a war.[65]

The anxiety, frustration, and looming socioeconomic humiliation of elite aspirants quickly curdled into rage against existing elites and the society that failed them. As one college magazine editorial bluntly put it, "Educated for jobs that do not materialize, students will grow resentful towards the existing order and will use the learning they have acquired to overthrow it."[66] At campuses across the country, students increasingly began attaching themselves to various protest movements: some supported the New Negro movement in campaigning for civil rights; other students aligned themselves with feminists who were likewise seeking greater professional opportunities and more social influence; the first gay rights advocacy organizations were also formed at this time;[67] still others took part in Socialist and Communist organizing; and antiwar protests were especially popular.

Of course, there was a certain irony to the radical rhetoric that students increasingly began to espouse given that most were attending university in the first place for the staunchly *in*egalitarian purpose of exploiting the barriers that had been set up to exclude non–white Anglo-Saxon Protestants (WASPs) (and women) from the symbolic professions in order to secure those jobs for themselves. And again, their primary grievance—the explicit impetus for their rebellion—was that the elite futures they felt entitled to were failing to materialize. The core demands of the student protesters were, likewise, largely self-oriented. They wanted more aid from the universities so they could more comfortably pursue their studies. They wanted job guarantees upon graduating, or greater job placement assistance. They wanted greater freedom on campus to do and say what they pleased. They wanted to avoid being drafted into war. These are all quite reasonable things to desire—but they are not exactly altruistic.

In any case, colleges and universities attempted to curb student unrest through censorship, the imposition of new rules, and disciplinary actions against perceived agitators. These efforts generally backfired, reinforcing the sense in many students' minds that the ruling class was corrupt, out of touch, unable to rise to the moment, and in need of replacement (by people like themselves). Student disillusionment had grown so pronounced that, at the time of the 1932 election, large numbers of students supported the Socialist candidate, Norman Thomas, over progressive Franklin D. Roosevelt. Among growing numbers of college students, Roosevelt was derisively viewed as a liberal establishment candidate aiming to *preserve* the system rather than overturn it. They didn't see a big difference in choosing the Democrat or the Republican: either way, the status quo would persist. Because the left-aligned vote was so split between the Socialist and Democratic candidates, FDR lost decisively among the college crowd to sitting Republican president Herbert Hoover. On many campuses, FDR came in below Thomas as well.[68]

By the time FDR ran for reelection in 1936, however, the situation had completely changed. College students and younger college graduates had become one of Roosevelt's strongest constituencies—and they remained so throughout his political career. The irony, of course, is that the students' description of FDR in 1932 was apt. He *was* an establishment candidate. He may have been the *ultimate* establishment politician insofar as his policies and leadership saved liberal capitalism and defanged the appeal of socialism in America (he preserved the establishment better than some of his more moderate opponents likely would have).[69] The political coalition he built set the paradigm for the next half century of Democratic Party politics. That is, he literally *became* the establishment in a deep sense. And all of that was just fine with the students in the end. Contrary to their radical rhetoric, they wanted relatively high-status jobs and socioeconomically comfortable lives far more than they wanted to *actually* overthrow the existing order. And the Roosevelt administration provided what they wanted.

By the time FDR stood for reelection for the first time, the New Deal was well underway. Major expansions of the government bureaucracy provided elite workers with stable, respected, and well-paying positions. The administration made significant investments in science and technology. Social workers and social scientists were deployed to assist with the design and administration of government aid programs.[70] The perceived oversupply of engineers found work planning and guiding the massive infrastructure projects funded by the federal government. And as the economy began turning around, professional jobs in the private and nonprofit sectors began reappearing as well.

By the time the 1960s rolled around, the formerly discontent students were well established in the symbolic professions. They had started and raised families in the post–World War II era of relative peace and prosperity. Civil rights and feminism did not consume their efforts or attention much. Socialism and communism no longer held much purchase with them. The "radicals" of the 1930s became the establishment that protesters would later rebel against in the 1960s and 1970s. In fact, some of the most prominent student protesters of the 1930s evolved into some of the most vocal critics of students in the 1960s.[71]

The Second Awokening

In many respects, universities were much changed in the 1960s as compared with the time of the first Great Awakening. The post–World War II GI Bill covered tuition and provided a generous stipend to returning veterans, many of whose jobs had been filled while they were overseas. Millions took advantage of the opportunity and, because the government was picking up the tab for tuition, they aggressively targeted the most prestigious private schools.[72] The targeted universities, however, were keen to maintain their elite status and to avoid being inundated with students from lower socioeconomic backgrounds who were often ill prepared for academic study, and whose values and culture were out of sync with their "traditional" constituencies. Elite colleges increasingly relied on the SAT to screen candidates, restricting admission to students with the best scores (whom they assumed would be primarily well-off WASPs and a small number of exceptional people from other backgrounds whose presence would genuinely enrich the school).[73] Before long, standardized testing became a near-universal aspect of college admissions. An institutional hierarchy developed based on how "selective" universities were with respect to their admission policies.

Less selective universities eagerly embraced GI Bill recipients and were able to radically expand their faculties and facilities.[74] As World War II vets cycled out of these institutions, they gradually began admitting more women to maintain enrollments. "Coeducation" became the dominant model over the course of the 1960s and 1970s.[75] Simultaneously, in the aftermath of the *Brown v. Board of Education* cases, the Civil Rights Act of 1964, and the "affirmative action" executive orders,[76] colleges began admitting significantly more nonwhite students.

At the time, tuition was inexpensive or free at most institutions of higher learning. The main costs families had to cover were occasional fees, books, school supplies, lodging, and food. These were nontrivial costs, to be sure, but well within the reach of most middle-class families—and many schools had generous support programs to assist those who hailed from more modest means. If one was not trying to attend an elite school, admissions were relatively open. Nonetheless, many who *could have* attended college chose not to, because there wasn't really a need. There were still plenty of good jobs that didn't require a degree, especially for men—and those opportunities grew over the course of the post–World War II boom. Hence, despite admitting many more minorities and working-class students than they used to, colleges and universities were still dominated by upper-middle-class WASPs, including rapidly growing numbers of WASP women. Nonetheless, as the schools diversified, there were increased tensions and clashes related to gender, race, and class.

Some student organizations from the first Great Awokening were still present on campus, such as the Students for a Democratic Society (SDS; formerly the Student League for Industrial Democracy). However, their influence and membership had waned significantly from their heyday. Although SDS leadership theorized universities as key sites of social revolution, there was no student movement to speak of. The SDS's 1962 national conference, convening its eleven chapters nationwide, had a total of fifty-nine registrants.[77] Some new campus groups were formed, most notably the Student Nonviolent Coordinating Committee (SNCC) in 1960. However, SNCC focused its actions primarily *outside* the campus—organizing sit-ins, freedom rides, marches, and voter registration drives in support of the broader civil rights movement. There were occasional localized outbursts focused on campus-specific issues, such as the Berkeley Free Speech Movement of 1964. However, organizers had no ties to the SDS or any other national group and were explicitly hostile toward politics per se. As cultural historian Louis Menand put it, the Berkeley Free Speech Movement "was not a war for social justice. It was a war against the university administration."[78] It was a war that only gained traction once *faculty* got involved, and its effects were largely confined to the University of California system.

Through the early 1960s, on-campus student activism was not particularly pronounced. Most students were focused on getting degrees and securing the still-plentiful opportunities of the post–World War II economy. And then an expansion of the war in Vietnam, and an economic downturn, changed everything.

The 1964 Gulf of Tonkin Resolution granted President Lyndon B. Johnson wide latitude in escalating the conflict in Vietnam. Beginning in March 1965, the United States shifted its focus from supporting and advising South Vietnamese forces to actively trying to crush the Viet Cong via a ground war.

Many more troops began to be deployed into the theater, and by the end of the summer, the United States had doubled its monthly draft calls. Yet, even after the White House eliminated exemptions for married men without children, college students remained exempt from being drafted so long as they remained enrolled full time in good standing. And when drafted, recruits with college degrees tended to get the best assignments (doing less grueling or risky jobs, and farther from the front lines). As a result of these policies, men who were able to gain admission into college and cover its costs began enrolling in much higher numbers—especially following the Higher Education Act of 1965, which expanded student loans available to students.

However, states contemporaneously began cutting the aid *they* provided to students, effectively shifting the responsibility of funding to individual borrowers and the federal government. Schools simultaneously became more selective in their admissions (in order to cope with the large influx of applicants) and began raising their tuition and fees (to capitalize on the increased federal grants and loans provided to students). This rendered it more difficult for many to attend or persist in college.[79] Moreover, the same year the government passed the Higher Education Act, the Johnson administration changed its rules with respect to the draft: college enrollment would no longer provide an automatic deferral. Instead, students would be compelled to take the Selective Service Qualification Test, and colleges would be obligated to rank their pupils in terms of their academic performance. Only those who came in above a particular cutoff would be guaranteed a college exemption. The rest were entered into a new draft pool, and thousands would be called each month.[80] *This* led to the nation-wide student protest movement.

The driver was not the Vietnam War itself, which had been ongoing for roughly a half decade prior with little student resistance. The driver was not the civil rights movement, which had been long ongoing, and indeed had begun to *lose* momentum by this time, as it shifted north (more on this soon). The driver was not women's liberation. Although track for the "second wave" of feminism was already being laid by this point, and momentum being built, there was no major national feminist movement just yet. The driver was not the gay liberation movement, which kicked off *after* 1965 and grew increasingly confrontational, public, and assertive in the years leading up to the Stonewall Uprising.[81] Instead, middle-class students became "radical" precisely when their plans to leave the fighting in Vietnam to minorities and the poor by enrolling in college and waiting things out began to fall through. It was at *that* point that college students suddenly embraced antiwar activism, the Black Power movement, feminism, postcolonial struggles, gay rights, and environmentalism in immense numbers.

Upper-middle-class students and affluent students, for their part, were not terribly worried about the draft itself. They had many options to avoid combat irrespective of their college enrollment or employment status, and they exercised them aggressively. Many families leveraged professional connections to doctors or psychiatrists to gain medical deferments. Others hired attorneys and obtained exemptions for their children via the legal process.[82] Nonetheless, the massive influx of students into college created adverse conditions for elites too. They faced much more intense competition to get admitted into their preferred colleges, not just at the undergraduate level but in graduate school as well (as growing numbers of students tried to maintain their student exemptions as long as possible by pursuing postgraduate degrees). Within colleges, class sizes grew and resources were spread thinner. Worse, the newcomers aggressively targeted the specific courses of study elites had been relying on to secure their own sinecures.[83] And upon graduating, these neophytes aimed for the specific jobs that children of elites had been counting on to provide *themselves* a good life.

The draft provided exemptions for many symbolic professions—doctors, engineers, scientists, teachers, and so on. This may have been designed in part as a hedge to protect children of affluent families from the draft postgraduation, but it ended up radically increasing the levels of competition aspiring symbolic capitalists faced, both at the university level and in the professional realm. And then it started becoming tougher for *anyone* to get a job.

Even before the expansion of the draft and the surge in college enrollments, the post–World War II economy was showing signs of faltering. In the years leading up to widespread student protests, there had been a stall in the growth of symbolic capitalist jobs. The share of professional-managerial jobs in the total economy, which had been growing rapidly from 1952 to 1962, stagnated from 1962 to 1968. The number of professional-managerial jobs per college graduate had been falling consistently since 1958.[84] College graduates were increasingly forced to work outside their field, or in jobs that did not require a degree at all.[85] In 1958, roughly 6 percent of PhDs graduated without specific career prospects; by 1974, that number had risen to 26 percent.[86] Worse, those who got jobs were making considerably less than they used to. It became a "buyer's market" for skilled labor: by 1969, salaries had begun falling for degree holders at all levels and across fields.[87] With the comfortable careers they had been counting on now called into question, upper-middle-class youth joined their middle-class peers in indicting the system. As with the first Awokening, it was a combination of a draft expansion and an economic downturn that seemed to trigger the widespread uprising.

Then came Richard Nixon. Although Nixon expressed admiration for student activists of the previous Great Awakening, he believed young people "these days" were getting it all wrong: "As I look at the 'student revolution' in the U.S.—back in the Thirties, the student rebel had a cause, a belief, a religion. Today the revolt doesn't have that form."[88] This is a common trope. Again, in the 1990s, many of those condemning student activists praised (or themselves participated in) similar movements in the 1960s, when people apparently mobilized the "right" way or for the "right" causes. As we will see, this nostalgia seems to be driven largely by inaccurate narratives participants come to tell about what their own (earlier) student movements accomplished. The uncomfortable reality is that these Awakenings are more alike than most recognize, and in ways that are unpleasant to contemplate.

In any case, Nixon despised 1960s counterculture. More importantly, he believed that domestic unrest undermined America and its leaders on the world stage and emboldened their Cold War enemies. Consequently, Nixon set out to break the student protest movement from the outset of his 1968 campaign—and he believed he could do this by ending the draft. Implicit in this strategy was an assumption that, despite their talk about revolution and social justice, student protesters were, in fact, mostly concerned about avoiding military service. They were attempting to deflect attention away from their selfishness and cowardice (as he saw it) by painting themselves as allies for the marginalized and disadvantaged, but once they no longer had to worry about being deployed, they would just get on with their lives—and leave others to do the same.

Hence, although Nixon disdained the antiwar movement, he campaigned in 1968 pledging to end conscription and bring a dignified end to the conflict in Vietnam. Upon taking office, he promptly ordered investigations of how to transition the U.S. military to an all-volunteer force (and thereby end the specter of the draft indefinitely). He began a drawdown of U.S. soldiers in Vietnam, suspended draft calls during the fall of 1969, and, in December of that year, announced that the United States was formally pursuing an end to the conflict. Young people reacted to these measures just as Nixon anticipated they would: Among recent high school graduates, male enrollment in college rose from 52.3 percent in the year before the Gulf of Tonkin Resolution to a high of 63.2 percent in 1968. By the end of Nixon's first year in office, that number had dropped to 60.1 percent. By the time the transition to an all-volunteer force was completed in 1973, male enrollment had sunk to a lower level than before the draft-induced surge: 50 percent.[89] The people who were attending college primarily to avoid the draft stopped enrolling or dropped out, gradually choking off protest movements' supplies of new recruits (even as the existing activist populations continued to cycle out of college and into their "adult lives").

Protests nonetheless briefly increased in 1970 following Nixon's escalations in Cambodia, and in the wake of national guardsmen opening fire on student protesters at Kent State.[90] However, as Todd Gitlin aptly put it, "the post-Cambodia uprising was the student movement's last hurrah. Activism never recovered from the summer vacation of 1970. During the academic year of 1970–71 there were fewer demonstrations than the year before; in 1971–72, fewer still. . . . Demonstrations declined at the old centers of protest, and press coverage declined precipitously."[91] Polls and surveys show that between 1970 and 1974, there was a major drop in the percentage of students who were interested in politics or activism or who held "radical" views, and a sharp increase in students whose primary goal or objective in school was setting themselves up to find a good job and earn a comfortable salary.[92] Many major student organizations such as SNCC and the SDS began to fall apart due to infighting.

Unfortunately for Nixon, his presidency came to an end around the same time as the protest movements were collapsing. At the time he left office in 1974, the economy was rough. The United States was still recovering from the 1973 OPEC (Organization of Petroleum Exporting Countries) oil crisis, stock market crash, and resultant "stagflation" recession. However, by the following year, the economy began to recover.[93] As enrollments declined, competition eased for professional jobs, and college students turned their focus back to building their careers. The Awokening was not just on the decline, it was over. Writing in 1979, Arthur Levine and Keith Wilson observed,

> The aura of revolution no longer exists. The "Student Movement" of the 1960s is receding into the pages of history and many activists have settled into their own struggles with adult life: Sam Brown is now director of ACTION in Washington, Gary Hart became a U.S. Senator, Eldridge Cleaver found religion, Jerry Rubin announced he was finally growing up at 37, and last we heard, Mario Salvo was getting a PhD in Los Angeles. . . . The student movement of the 1960s collapsed almost as quickly and unexpectedly as it had begun. There is little evidence of 1960s-style student protest on campus today.[94]

The Third Awokening

By most measures (public opinion polls, media trends, Google Books nGrams, levels of student activism, etc.) the Great Awokening of the late 1980s through the early 1990s was significantly smaller than the others. It was shorter as well: the first two Awokenings persisted for more than a decade. The current (fourth) Great Awokening likewise lasted roughly a decade. However, the third Great Awokening lasted for about half the usual cycle—perhaps because the crisis elites faced was less severe, and they were able to be appeased much faster.

In a nutshell, universities, especially state schools, were hit hard by austerity in the 1980s. They responded by raising tuition and reducing student aid. Consequently, aspiring elites were increasingly forced to go into debt, and to take on ever-larger quantities of debt, in order to secure their credentials for professional jobs.[95] However, even these measures were not enough for many universities to remain solvent—especially given declining male attendance in the post-Vietnam period. Schools needed more students who could both meet their "meritocratic" admissions standards and pay tuition in full (or, ideally, pay *more* than the standard tuition). They turned to recruiting, and increasing admissions of, international students.[96] Postgraduation, these foreign-born professional aspirants were often willing to accept significantly lower salaries for "high-skill" work than their American-born competitors. Unsurprisingly, employers came to prefer these candidates on the job market. In many high-skill sectors, most of the new jobs produced began going to foreign-born workers.[97] Native-born students who landed jobs often had to accept lower wages than they would have in the recent past.[98]

Then came a series of exogenous economic shocks. There was the savings and loan financial crisis of 1986–1995. There was a "mini crash" of the stock market in October 1989 that led to a recession followed by anemic growth. The same Republican-led austerity wave that gutted university budgets also led to a decline in the availability of government jobs.[99] Simultaneously, in the late 1980s and early 1990s, corporate consultant firms like McKinsey helped oversee a wave of mergers and restructuring in the corporate world. These institutional transformations resulted in the elimination of enormous numbers of "middle-management" jobs and other formerly secure and well-paying positions, led to the outsourcing of many functions overseas, and encouraged a general emphasis on doing more with less in order to maximize return on investment for corporate shareholders.[100]

It was a bleak picture: aspiring symbolic capitalists had to go into more debt to get professional jobs, for which competition had grown much fiercer. Those who managed to land work had less job security, higher workloads, and lower pay relative to previous years. Indeed, the real earnings of college graduates dropped consistently through the late 1980s. Nonetheless, the divide between college and noncollege incomes grew because everyone else was faring even worse![101] Rather than being a means for upward mobility, their credentials primarily served to guard against downward mobility. Symbolic capitalists (and aspiring symbolic capitalists) responded with a new wave of "radicalism"—ostensibly in the name of racial equality, feminism, gay rights, and environmentalism. Once again, however, the movement died out as the market was able to accommodate the apparent primary concerns of "radicalized" elites.

In 1990, there were major changes to U.S. immigration laws that established quotas on temporary visas for high-skill workers, even as it streamlined the process for these workers to achieve permanent residence.[102] This reduced employer capacity to rely on contingent high-skill laborers whose continued presence in the country was indexed to the whims of their employers (who could overwork, underpay, and otherwise mistreat them—deporting anyone who raised a fuss). There continued to be displacement of native-born workers at the hands of more permanent immigrants, particularly with respect to STEM jobs, but wages for these positions stabilized and began to rise.[103] That is, the native-born workers who remained in these roles generally found themselves in a stronger economic position than they were before the reforms.

There was a contemporaneous increase in jobs requiring a degree, albeit created primarily by "degree inflation" (reclassifying jobs such that they now require a degree when they didn't previously) that deprived people from more humble socioeconomic backgrounds of the few stable and well-paying jobs that remained to them.[104] And as the 1990s rolled on, there was a proliferation of what anthropologist David Graeber called "bullshit jobs"[105] that helped replace some of the white-collar positions that had been cut during the peak season of mergers, acquisitions, and downsizing.

Here, it is important to stress that the social coordination processes through which phenomena like these transpire are not yet well understood. There was an acute overproduction of elites. It began creating social unrest. Employers began to envision new (somewhat extraneous) roles in their organizations and reclassified existing jobs to set them aside for degree holders. However, it is unlikely that many, if any, employers *consciously* changed or created these jobs specifically as a means of addressing elite overproduction and its destabilizing effects. Nonetheless, this is what they did. Beginning in 1993, incomes for BA holders began to take off again. Meanwhile, incomes for most others remained stagnant or declined relative to 1990 levels over the coming decades.[106] This latter fact, however, seemed to be of little consequence to symbolic capitalists. As their own fortunes began to rise, social justice concerns receded into the background.[107] The Awokening died out once again as symbolic capitalists eagerly embraced Bill Clinton, his worldview, and his agenda.

The Fourth Awokening

By the end of the Clinton years, the United States was once again beginning to overproduce elites. Between 2000 and 2019, the American labor market added twenty-two million workers over the age of twenty-five with at least a BA. However, only about ten million jobs were added that required a college degree. There were more than twice as many graduates as there were jobs for graduates.[108] Although the wages for degree-requiring jobs continued to climb (even as nondegree wages stagnated), this was cold comfort for the growing number of graduates who found themselves unemployed or underemployed. This situation reached a breaking point after the 2008 global financial crisis and subsequent Great Recession.

Law degrees, for instance, were long perceived to be a surefire bet for enjoying a comfortable professional life. However, in the wake of the 2008 financial crisis, tens of thousands of young people had the same idea to ride out the recession in college, and to continue into law school specifically, resulting in a bubble that burst in 2010. JD graduates had a difficult time finding jobs in the legal profession and faced unfavorable terms with respect to salary, pay, and working conditions because employers had all the leverage in negotiations.[109]

Likewise, in the wake of the 2008 financial crisis, there was a major shift away from humanities and into STEM fields.[110] However, even before the COVID-19 pandemic, technical majors were producing about three times the number of graduates as there were job openings in the field per year (with the exception of computer science, which was not yet producing enough graduates to fill demand).[111] STEM unemployment rates are low—but this is primarily because graduates typically end up working in jobs outside the fields they got their degrees in. Moreover, the pay, job stability, and working-condition returns that graduates receive on their

STEM education diminished as growing numbers of Americans flocked to these fields.[112]

Government jobs have also long been viewed as a pathway to a secure post with good pay and excellent benefits. However, government jobs at the federal, state, and local levels saw consistent attrition in the period leading up to the latest Great Awokening. Even before the COVID-19 pandemic (and any austerity measures that may follow downstream), federal employment had reached its lowest share of total employment since 1952; state and local governments were down to the levels of the mid- to late 1960s.[113]

Rather than "safe" choices like law, STEM or government, others decided to follow their passions and went into significant debt pursuing elite credentials in journalism and the arts, only to find that there were few jobs to be had—not even for those with graduate degrees from top programs.[114] A decade after the onset of the Great Recession, more than one in four 2008 newsroom jobs had been eliminated.[115] The jobs that remain tend to have much less security, and often lower pay and benefits, relative to decades past. The COVID-19 pandemic led to a new round of significant layoffs, furloughs, and pay cuts at media organizations across the spectrum.[116] Although the situation began to stabilize in 2021,[117] good media jobs remain scarce and extraordinarily competitive.

For those interested in a career in academia, the odds grew especially bleak. According to National Center for Science and Engineering Statistics estimates, 30 percent of those awarded PhDs in 2020 graduated without employment commitments of any kind—not in the private sector, not as postdocs, and not as contingent or tenure-track faculty.[118] Strikingly, this marked a significant improvement over recent years! For PhD students who *did* graduate with jobs, most landed positions outside academia (e.g., for industry, nonprofits, or governments). Moreover, the vast majority of people who were hired as faculty in any capacity were hired on a contingent basis— with much lower pay, benefits, job security, and future prospects as compared with tenured or tenure-track faculty.

In short, symbolic capitalists and aspirants to the symbolic professions were increasingly going into enormous debt, not just to secure a BA, but often to pursue graduate degrees as well. However, they were receiving diminishing returns on these investments and uncertain life prospects.

A 2021 analysis by the Foundation for Research on Equal Opportunity estimated that as many as 16 percent of recent college graduates—particularly those who majored in the "wrong" fields—may actually receive a *negative* return on their college investments (relative to if they had spent that time acquiring vocational certifications or working full time and building a career in a position that does not require a degree).[119] According to 2020 estimates by the Federal Reserve Bank of New York, 41 percent of employed recent college graduates are working in positions that don't require a degree (and again, many jobs that *formally* require a degree don't actually require advanced training in practice; many of these jobs did not require a degree in recent years; and many people who work in jobs that "require" a degree hold credentials in fields unrelated to their jobs).[120] Analytics firm Burning Glass likewise estimated that, as of 2018, 43 percent of recent college grads were underemployed. It projected that two-thirds of these underemployed graduates (or 29 percent of all recent college graduates) would likely remain underemployed five years after graduation—and three-quarters of those who are still underemployed five years out (an estimated 21 percent of all recent college graduates) were likely to remain underemployed a full decade after graduation.[121]

Growing numbers of BA holders exited the symbolic economy altogether and attended community colleges to learn skilled trades.[122] Indeed, the *un*employment rate for degree holders has remained lower than for less educated Americans primarily because graduates have been increasingly snatching up decent jobs that do *not* require a degree when they failed to secure a position that *would*.[123] Of course, this leaves non–degree holders with still fewer prospects—hence the growing socioeconomic divide in recent years between those who possess a degree and those who don't. In many respects, this divide is again being driven more by diminishing prospects for those with *less* education than by growth in prosperity among college graduates. That is, although the return on investment for education seems to be growing in *relative* terms, it may actually be shrinking in *absolute* terms.

All said, nearly half of upper-middle-class children born in the 1980s failed to replicate their class position by age thirty.[124] Most of these downwardly mobile elites were not in real danger of being *poor* (according to U.S. Census Bureau estimates, only 4 percent of degree holders live below the poverty line).[125] Nonetheless, there is often significant frustration at the step down in wealth, security, and status they enjoyed as children and expected to be able to provide for their own families as adults. Once again, these anxieties were channeled into a Great Awokening. Frustrated symbolic capitalists and elite aspirants sought to indict the system that failed them—and also the elites that *did* manage to flourish—by attempting to align themselves with the genuinely marginalized and disadvantaged.

Around 2022, however, evidence began to emerge that the structural conditions that gave rise to the post-2010 Awokening might be easing.[126] Looking at trends in symbolic economy outputs (journalism, books, scholarship), expressed attitudes, "cancel culture" incidents, Democratic Socialists of America membership, symbolic capitalist protest activity, and institutional responses to employee activism, it appears as though the Great Awakening that began in 2010 started to subside at around the same time socioeconomic indicators began to improve.[127] At time of writing, most measures of the Awokening remain significantly elevated relative to their pre-Awokening baselines, but downward trends are clear.

The Next Awokening

Although there are signs that the current Great Awokening may be winding down, the seeds seem to already be sown for the next one. Looking at the Bureau of Labor Statistics projections of which jobs are expected to see the most growth from 2020 to 2030, for example, few of the projected high-growth jobs are likely to pay well or require college degrees.

The twenty occupations listed in the following table are projected to account for nearly half (47 percent) of all new jobs created over the next decade. All other occupations are individually projected to contribute less than 1 percent of all new jobs over the next ten years.

Critically, most of the jobs that are anticipated to grow rapidly over the next ten years pay below the current U.S. median income. Seven out of ten occupations with the highest numbers of projected new jobs require no college degree (although a handful require some specialized postsecondary training and licensing—which college graduates would have to acquire just like everyone else). Literally none of the top twenty occupations require advanced degrees. And most of the jobs outside this list do not currently, and are not anticipated to, require a college degree of any sort either.

Put another way, you know those "hot" fields college recruiters and media folks are talking about? There likely will not be a ton of positions available in absolute terms anytime soon.[128] Moreover, although outsourcing and automation hit blue-collar jobs hardest in previous eras, rapid advances in AI are projected to primarily disrupt highly paid white-collar work in the coming decades.[129] As things currently stand, the "jobs of the future" are going to be relatively low-paid service positions providing various amenities for retirees and college graduates who *did* land cushy professional roles. As for

TABLE 2.1. Occupations Projected to Produce the Largest Numbers of New Jobs, 2020–2030

Occupation	Percentage of all new jobs projected to be created, 2020–2030	College degree typically required (Y/N)	Median annual wage, 2020 (USD)
Home health and personal care aides	9.5	N	27,080
Cooks, restaurant	4.7	N	28,800
Fast-food and counter workers	4.4	N	23,860
Software developers, software quality assurance analysts, and testers	3.4	Y	110,140
Waiters and waitresses	3.4	N	23,740
Registered nurses	2.3	Y	75,330
Hand laborers and freight, stock, and material movers	2.2	N	31,120
General and operations managers	1.9	Y	103,650
First-line supervisors of food preparation and serving workers	1.6	N	34,570
Passenger vehicle drivers (excluding public transit)	1.5	N	32,320
Market research analysts and marketing specialists	1.4	Y	65,810
Bartenders	1.3	N	24,960
Security guards	1.3	N	31,050
Medical and health services managers	1.2	Y	104,280
Cleaners: maids and housekeepers	1.2	N	26,220
Medical assistants	1.1	N	35,850
Cleaners: janitorial and other	1.1	N	29,080
Management analysts	1.0	Y	87,660
Heavy and tractor-trailer truck drivers	1.0	N	47,130
Exercise trainers and group fitness instructors	1.0	N	40,510

Source: U.S. Bureau of Labor Statistics. Data from U.S. Bureau of Labor Statistics 2023d.
Note: Overall, the Bureau of Labor Statistics estimates that roughly 11.8799 million new jobs will be created between 2020 and 2030. The percentage in the first column represents the share of these jobs each occupation is projected to contribute. For context on wages, the overall median annual wage in 2020 was $41,950.

everyone else, they won't need to learn to code, but to learn to care. And they probably won't make much money doing that either.

Of course, the fact that the prospects seem so bleak for non–symbolic economy positions is likely to intensify competition for elite credentials and for jobs within the symbolic professions. As the "losers" in this competition grow increasingly numerous and increasingly frustrated, they will likely seek to co-opt existing social justice movements in order to enhance their own position, and the cycle will begin again.

Having walked through each of the Awokenings, we are now well positioned to identify some threads that run between them. Let's start with what seems to be the main driver of these rebellions: elite overproduction.

Elite Overproduction

In a 2010 issue of *Nature*, ecologist-turned-historian Peter Turchin famously predicted that the forthcoming decade would be defined by social upheavals, with a number of adverse social trends reaching their peak around the year 2020.[130] Characteristics he was observing in the U.S. economy and culture at the time seemed very similar to trends in the lead-up to the Civil War and the periods of unrest in the 1920s and 1970s—that is, the first and second Great Awakenings. In that *Nature* essay, his coauthored book published the previous year, and a follow-up scholarly paper published in 2012, Turchin emphasized "elite overproduction" as a core driver of this historical and predicted instability.[131]

Elite overproduction occurs when a society produces too many people who feel entitled to high status and high incomes relative to the capacity of that society to actually absorb elite aspirants into the power structure. Under these circumstances, growing numbers of frustrated erstwhile elites grow bitter toward the prevailing order and try to form alliances with *genuinely* marginalized populations in order to depose existing elites and install themselves in their stead.

Typically, Turchin argues, these attempted alliances prove unstable because, at the end of the day, elites mostly just want to be elites. Consequently, their interests, worldviews, and priorities tend to be far out of step with those they are ostensibly advocating for, and this becomes increasingly obvious and problematic to all parties over time. Due to these internal tensions, rebellions generally fail to produce revolutions. More typically, existing elites find ways to incorporate and co-opt enough of the alienated elite population to break the uprisings.[132] The newly expanded elites then collaborate to secure their position from others, while offering placating concessions to constituencies that the former counterelites tried to mobilize during their insurrection.[133] However, these concessions are usually designed to ensure that the fundamentals of the political-economic system remain roughly unchanged—an outcome that the newly integrated elites are now just as invested in as the old guard.

As growing numbers of former rebels are co-opted into the establishment and disengage from the struggle, it becomes harder for those elite aspirants whose ambitions remain unfulfilled to continue exerting pressure on institutions or commanding social attention for their chosen causes. Exhausted after years of futile conflict, most elite aspirants who failed to enhance their position before the uprising passed its peak eventually resign themselves to a lower station in life than they'd expected or hoped for.[134] The unrest comes to a close . . . until the next time conditions are ripe.

Diverted Movements

Elite overproduction disposes large numbers of elites and elite aspirants toward indicting both the prevailing order and the more established and successful elites at its helm. However, possessing a motive for carrying out an insurrection doesn't entail the opportunity to effectively launch one.

A key obstacle faced by frustrated elites is that the fortunes of people like themselves tend to rise and fall countercyclically to the rest of the population.[135] Hard times for most people are usually pretty good times for elites, and the "winners" in this arrangement tend to want to keep the good times rolling as long as possible. Conversely, hard times for elites are usually relatively good times for everyone else, leading most other Americans to care even less about elite problems than they otherwise would. Public concern about social justice issues tends to recede into the background during these periods as well,[136] constraining the ability of frustrated elites and elite aspirants to leverage social justice discourse in the service of their own ends.

However, there are occasional moments when the trajectories between elites and nonelites are partially collapsed—when things have been bad and getting worse for ordinary folks for a while and are suddenly fraught for symbolic capitalists too. *These* are moments when Awokenings tend to occur.

Here's how things tend to play out: many who had come to expect secure and well-renumerated work in the symbolic professions instead end up facing uncertain prospects and downward mobility. This anxiety curdles into frustration toward those who *are* enjoying success and apparent security.

However, insofar as they've been enculturated into mainstream symbolic capitalists' preferred modes of talking and thinking about the world (and competing for status and power), they don't lead with lamentations about poor employment prospects for professionals like themselves. Instead, they start by emphasizing how bad things are for everyone else, including and especially the marginalized and disadvantaged. The frustration, humiliation, and anxieties of these elite aspirants are expressed in terms of socialist, feminist, antiracist, or queer critiques of the prevailing order.

During these periods of shared immiseration, precisely because things have been bad and growing worse for most others in society for a while, there is often momentum already building behind various movements to address social problems. Narratives indicting the prevailing order and the people at its helm are already taking off. Perennial campaigns, such as women's rights movements or racial justice movements, which generally fall into abeyance patterns during times of prosperity, begin gaining new traction among a broader swath of society.[137] Elective affinities between the claims and aspirations of these social movements and the ostensibly altruistic claims of the symbolic professions lead many disenfranchised elites to attach themselves to these campaigns in order to reclaim their sense of dignity, agency, and purpose, and to push for desired concessions or social reforms.

However, these newly mobilized symbolic capitalists are rarely content to be mere foot soldiers or subordinates in social movements. They're elite aspirants, after all. And in virtue of their ostensibly superior knowledge and skills, they often see themselves as uniquely well suited to determine the ideal aims and tactics of movements. Despite being latecomers and numerical minorities, these erstwhile elites are often well positioned to dominate campaigns they affix themselves to—frequently to the consternation and at the expense of those who had been "doing the work" before it became a cause célèbre. And as symbolic capitalists become conspicuous faces and voices of social movements, they generally define and pursue the cause in ways that flatter their own sensibilities and serve their personal interests. This is commonly to the detriment of the genuinely marginalized and disadvantaged in society because the preferences and priorities of symbolic capitalists tend to be demonstrably out of sync with those of the people they are ostensibly speaking for and advocating on behalf of.

As a trivial example, consider recent high-profile campaigns to rename schools in honor of those whom contemporary symbolic capitalists find praiseworthy instead of the "problematic" historical figures whose names are currently plastered across buildings nationwide. These campaigns were carried out in the name of racial justice. However, if nonwhites who live in the affected communities had been consulted about *their* top concerns, it would have been clear that the name of the local school would not rank anywhere near the top of their priorities.[138] Although they might not be *opposed* to naming the school in honor of, say, Rosa Parks instead of Jefferson Davis, parents of ethnic and racial minority students who attend these schools would identify many concerns that are more salient with respect to their kids' lives and education than the name on the building. Yet, rather than addressing *those* concerns, or even bothering to find out what *those* concerns are, mainstream symbolic capitalists focus on securing symbolic victories over right-aligned symbolic capitalists—who satisfyingly respond with indignation and outrage at these maneuvers because, again, they share the sense that something "big" is at stake here. And should mainstream symbolic capitalists emerge victorious, we declare the name change some kind of "win" for racial justice and move on to the next culture war battle. Yet little has changed for the families whose kids attend these schools. They face the same struggles as ever. Their life prospects have not been meaningfully changed one way or the other. The concerns that parents and other community members genuinely find pressing remain largely unaddressed.[139]

Likewise, Betty Friedan's 1963 *The Feminine Mystique* has been largely credited with helping launch "second-wave" feminism. The text purported to highlight the plight of "women" in the 1950s—languishing as suburban housewives, struggling to find meaning or fulfillment in their domestic duties, and desperate for fulfillment outside the home. In fact, most women in America have *always* worked—including at the time Friedan was writing.[140] It was a relatively small share of families who could afford to have women stay home without bringing in money or directly supporting business efforts, and who gained prestige from being able to sustain a "kept" wife. It was a very particular slice of America who could afford to enjoy the comfortable suburban existence that Friedan and others described as stifling. As bell hooks put it,

> Some white, middle-class, college-educated women argued that motherhood was a serious obstacle to women's liberation, a trap confining women to the home, keeping them tied to cleaning, cooking, and child care. Others simply identified motherhood and child-rearing as the locus of women's oppression. Had black women voiced their views on motherhood, it would not have been named a serious obstacle to our freedom as women. Racism, lack of jobs, lack of skills or education, and a number of

other issues would have been at the top of the list—but not motherhood. Black women would not have said motherhood prevented us from entering the world of paid work because we have always worked. From slavery to the present day . . . that work gave meager financial compensation and often interfered with or prevented effective parenting. Historically, black women have identified work in the context of family as humanizing labor, work that affirms their identity as women, as human beings showing love and care, the very gestures of humanity white supremacist ideology claimed black people were incapable of expressing.[141]

That is, less privileged women often struggled *to be able* to spend time with their families, and to carve out space to be a wife or a mother instead of just a worker. The dilemmas Friedan described were fundamentally "problems of privilege." And those afflicted were generally quite keen to keep their privilege: Despite railing against suburban life, the women who sympathized with Friedan's critique were generally disinterested in living in the kinds of households or communities these "other" women lived in (nor in having "others" move into their own neighborhoods). Nor did they have any interest in taking on the kinds of jobs these "other" women worked in. They wanted well-compensated and socially respected professional jobs, befitting their social status. And they ultimately achieved that goal by offloading unwanted domestic responsibilities onto *other* women—lower-income women, typically immigrants and women of color. Nonetheless, elite women sought to conflate their own interests with the interests of "women" writ large. The campaign to enhance the position of upper-middle-class women was (and continues to be) carried out in the name of feminism per se.[142]

As a function of divides like these between symbolic capitalists and the rest of society, rather than promoting genuine change, the widespread embrace of various causes by symbolic capitalists often correlates with a leveling-off or decline in progress, increased polarization around the issues being championed, and growing alienation from the affected movements among former supporters.[143]

The More Things Change

Despite their intense focus on social justice issues, Great Awakenings have rarely generated positive outcomes for the genuinely needy or vulnerable. With respect to racial equality, for instance, political scientist Robert

Putnam shows that gains for African Americans began around 1860—that is, before *any* of the Great Awokenings, and indeed, before the Civil War (the war may have been launched to halt those gains). After the war, Black gains proceeded apace through the 1960s. Gaps between Blacks and whites continued to close. There was a steady increase in rights and protections for African Americans, in Black institution building, in Black political power, and in interracial solidarity despite campaigns to halt this progress.[144] There was no apparent impact from the first Great Awokening on any of these trends—for better or worse. Likewise, the civil rights movement notched most of its successes *before* the second Great Awokening began[145]—and stalled out thereafter. That is, the second Great Awokening was not responsible for the civil rights movement and its victories. It may have derailed them. From the mid-1960s through the present, the racial story in America has largely been one of stagnation and declines. Black-white income disparities in 2016 were roughly identical to what they were in 1968.[146] Gaps in wealth and home ownership between Blacks and whites have actually grown *larger* than they were in 1968.[147] Rates of incarceration among African Americans, and racial disparities between Blacks and whites in incarceration rates, while declining, remain higher than they were in 1960.[118]

Critically, as a recent National Bureau of Economic Research paper by economist Erik Hurst and coauthors shows, the growing centrality of the symbolic professions played a central role in halting racial progress.[149] As a result of major changes to the global economic order beginning in the late 1960s, the significance of symbolic hubs, professional and business services, and symbolic capitalists more broadly rose dramatically.[150] In this same period, following the civil rights movement, prejudice-based discrimination in most job markets declined.[151] However, skill- and education-based discrimination increased dramatically, as did the returns on having the "correct" credentials and talents. Because education was (and continues to be) unevenly distributed across racial lines, the practical effects of these new "meritocratic" forms of reward and exclusion have been comparable to overt racial discrimination in many respects. Hence, racialized socioeconomic gaps persist, largely unchanged, even as overtly bigoted attitudes and behaviors have become far less common and increasingly taboo.

According to Putnam, the trajectory of women's equality tells a similar story.[152] At the end of the nineteenth century, women in the United States began making significant gains in terms of rights and protections, and gaps between men and women on a range of dimensions began to close. These patterns did not accelerate as a result of the second Great Awokening, as many perhaps assume. Instead, they *slowed* beginning in the mid-1960s. And on many measures, women have been *losing ground* relative to men since the 1990s (i.e., the third Great Awokening).[153]

Women's progress, however, has not seen the same level of reversals as African Americans'—in large part because well-off whites have a direct stake in women's rights that they generally lack with respect to racial equality. (Roughly half of all white people are women, after all—and even white *men* have a stake in increasing the earnings or prospects of their wives and daughters.) Nonetheless, Putnam argues, feminist gains since the 1960s have primarily benefited upper-class whites, especially professionals. Far from promoting general egalitarianism, increased gender equality in the United States has correlated with growing socioeconomic inequality.[154] More women are graduating college and attaining professional success. They are partnering with others who have equivalent socioeconomic prospects to their own, or higher, and opportunity-hoarding to maximize the chances that their kids will replicate their own elite position. Meanwhile, most nonelites across genders are experiencing stagnation and declines.

Overall, Putnam shows, the century from 1860 through 1960 was defined by steady and broad-based gains in socioeconomic equality, civil rights, trust in social institutions, religious attendance, union membership, and other forms of civic participation. There have been shocking reversals across all of these dimensions since—to the point where America in 2020 eerily resembled the United States of the Gilded Age in many respects. In short, the transition to the symbolic economy in the 1960s—and the ascendance of symbolic capitalists—has been accompanied by stark *declines* in equality, social cohesion, and civic participation. The first Great Awokening did little to enhance the pre-1960 "upswing," and subsequent Awokenings seem to have done even less to halt or reverse the post-1960s declines.

Instead, since the second Great Awokening, protest movements have grown significantly more professionalized and less disruptive, and they're increasingly driven by relatively affluent people rather than the genuinely marginalized or disadvantaged.[155] As we've seen, this trend continues through the present day, with movements like Occupy and the #Resistance protests driven primarily by symbolic capitalists and concentrated in symbolic capitalist hubs. The fact that these movements are, at bottom, by and for elites with little to no benefit for ordinary people is often recognized by the folks whose interests symbolic capitalists purport to represent. For instance, when asked in 2022 whether the most recent "racial reckoning" has led to changes that are improving the lives of Black people, nearly two-thirds (64 percent) of Black respondents answered in the negative. Female, lower-income, and less-educated (i.e., less advantaged) African Americans were especially unlikely to perceive positive changes.[156]

Here the reader may wonder, even if the story seems bleak in looking at laws or socioeconomic statistics, surely the Awokenings are responsible for changing public attitudes, right? There are two key things to note in response to this question. First, it is not clear that changing discourse or attitudes actually *matter* if they don't manifest "in the world" via beneficial changes in behaviors, relationships, policies, or allocations of resources. In any case, it is empirically unclear that the previous Awokenings *did* have any broad-based and long-term effect on public attitudes—let alone any *positive* effects.[157]

For instance, as political scientist James Stimson observed, the Great Awokening of the 1960s–1970s did *not* usher in a liberal age. In fact, it marked the culmination of a long-running leftward trend in public opinion and corresponded with a significant rightward lurch in public attitudes that persisted through the early 1980s: "The liberalism we see of the 1960s is the liberalism that produced the Kennedy administration and then fueled it, in full force at the outset of the civil rights movement. It is not the liberalism of the youth revolt or the anti-Vietnam War protest. These came later, after the political impetus of liberalism was spent."[158]

Attitudes on gender, race, and sexuality, meanwhile, have been on a pretty steady liberalizing trajectory for as far back as public opinion on these questions is available—both across generational cohorts and within them.[159] Rapid changes in expressed attitudes *among white elites*—or bursts in publications of books, media articles, academic essays, and so on corresponding with the Great Awokenings—do not seem to have had any enduring effects on the trend lines of public opinion writ large. Media "agenda setting" can raise the salience of certain issues—for instance, in the midst of each Awokening we see dramatic spikes in the share of Americans who view racial tensions or racism as the most pressing problem facing the United States—however, attitudes like these quickly revert to their antecedent baselines once symbolic capitalists start talking about other things again.[160]

All said, Awokenings seem unrelated to significant changes in law or allocation of resources.[161] They probably aren't responsible for durable and broad-based attitudinal shifts on "culture" issues either.[162] The shifts that were clearly responses to Awokenings tended to fade alongside those Awokenings. Trends that preceded the Awokenings continued on unaffected by them.

Social Justice Sinecures

Although Awokenings do not seem to be responsible for generating major transformations in society writ large, they often *do* produce significant and durable changes within symbolic capitalist institutions. Many of these changes are symbolic in nature—for example, new speech codes and performative gestures to show that one is "up" on social justice. However, other changes are more substantial—for instance, new hiring and recruitment practices that provide new opportunities for aspirants who identify as members of historically marginalized groups, or new deference practices that can enhance the clout of symbolic capitalists who identify with particular groups. Yet, rather than enhancing the position of those who are significantly disadvantaged in society, these opportunities primarily benefit elites from the target populations.[163]

Symbolic capitalist spaces tend to be highly parochial. An especially small share of people from minoritized populations tend to make it into the symbolic professions—generally people who are "privileged" in other ways. As a function of these realities, benefits from changes in symbolic capitalist institutions that occur during Awokenings tend to accrue primarily to those *who are already relatively well off or well positioned.* Illustrative of these realities, the most significant and enduring material legacy of the Great Awokenings has been the proliferation of what I have taken to calling "social justice sinecures": well-renumerated symbolic capitalist jobs explicitly oriented around helping organizations conspicuously conform with the latest fads in social justice signaling (thereby reducing their vulnerability to subsequent attacks by frustrated elites and elite aspirants).

Corporate HR departments and their ever-expanding rules and administrative processes began proliferating after the second Great Awokening.[164] They have leveraged every subsequent Awokening to expand their institutional influence. For instance, post-2011, there has been a rapid enlargement in many symbolic capitalist institutions of bureaucrats and policies aimed at regulating even "sexual conduct that is voluntary, non-harassing, nonviolent, and does not harm others."[165]

The second Awokening likewise corresponded with the birth and proliferation of administrators to curate and manage diversity at postsecondary institutions, elite K–12 schools, and increasingly the private and nonprofit sectors.[166] These positions have also seen major expansions in the aftermath of each Awokening. Their ranks have swelled to the point that, today, many colleges and universities have nearly as many noninstructional staff as they have undergraduate students, and in some cases more.[167]

Diversity specialists typically make about $75,000 per year. Chief diversity officers typically pull in around $120,000, although there are diversity, equity, and inclusion (DEI) administrators at many universities who earn up to $400,000 per year (putting them well into the top 5 percent of all income earners in the United States).[168] Alongside diversity managers, diversity-related training consultants similarly emerged in the aftermath of the second Great Awakening, became a staple of the American institutional landscape following the third Great Awakening, and received incredible sums of money during the current period of elite agitation—particularly in the wake of George Floyd's murder.[169] To help people compete for these positions, universities increasingly see a lucrative opportunity in providing BAs and graduate certification programs in diversity studies.[170]

It's critical to note the gender dynamics at play in the proliferation of these roles. Again, Awokenings happen in the midst of elite overproduction. Since the tail end of the second Great Awakening, a majority of college students and graduates have been female. That is, the elites being overproduced are increasingly women. And the people occupying these new "diversity and inclusion"–oriented positions are *overwhelmingly* women. These positions are serving as new sinecures almost entirely for female aspirants—providing well-paying and relatively prestigious work for women who might otherwise be excluded from the symbolic professions. As cultural critic Mary Harrington observed,

> "Administrative bloat" has been a remarked on feature of higher education for some time. . . . Less remarked on is the sex breakdown of the growing proportion of administrators. A recent diversity and inclusion report by the University of California indicates that women make up more than 70 per cent of non academic staff. . . . And that support system has an increasingly symbiotic relationship with student activism, which over my lifetime has (on both sides of the Atlantic) shifted noticeably away from a focus on material conditions toward something more like the bureaucratic regulation of personal identity and interpersonal interactions. A 2015 look at student protesters across 51 campuses showed the most common demands—alongside greater diversity among faculty—were diversity training and cultural centres. In turn, this focus requires a ballooning staff tasked with managing identities, or variously supporting or disciplining types of relationship. . . . In practice, then, as pursued within universities, one byproduct of student activism is something akin to a "jobs for the girls" scheme, in which a heavily female student body drives

demand for . . . feminized non-academic administrative roles, which in turn helps create an environment geared toward women, and so on. Young alumnae graduating from this ecosystem might be expected to carry its insights out into professional life. And indeed, according to America's Bureau of Labor Statistics, HR (a career whose employees are 71 per cent female, according to one industry report) is one of the fastest growing occupations in the country. Within that field, the fastest growing sub discipline is diversity and inclusion. . . . And a principal task of diversity professionals is increasing the job opportunities available for women, and especially of women engaged in diversity work.[171]

Indeed, not only are these positions overwhelmingly staffed by women, DEI programs are especially likely to be championed, implemented, and protected by female managers (relative to male peers).[172] Relative to comparable symbolic capitalist positions, DEI professionals are especially likely to be non-white as well.[173]

Now, it's not a *bad* thing to provide relatively well-paying and socially prestigious jobs for already-advantaged women and people of color. The world would not be a better place if these professionals were unemployed or underemployed instead. Nonetheless, it is unclear what (if any) *good* is being accomplished by this ever-expanding constellation of social justice sinecures beyond providing practitioners with gainful employment. Many of the programs associated with these DEI roles (such as diversity training) are demonstrably ineffective with respect to their stated goals.[174] The proliferation of diversity bureaucrats has corresponded with a significant *increase* in social inequality and *decreases* in social solidarity, as highlighted in the previous section. Moreover, as we will see, the spaces where these workers exert the greatest influence (i.e., the symbolic professions, symbolic hubs) are among the *most* unequal and parochial in the contemporary United States— and they've been growing *more* exclusionary, hierarchical, and detached from the rest of society over time. The world, in short, does not seem to be a more equitable place due to the ever-growing DEI-industrial complex.

However, as a function of perverse incentive structures within these fields, unfortunate social trends may nonetheless be good for business. A lack of progress or worsening conditions are not typically interpreted as evidence that DEI-oriented positions and programs are unnecessary or unhelpful. Rather, they often serve as a pretext to demand still *more* institutional power and resources for DEI professionals. These maneuvers are accepted because, generally speaking, the proliferation of these positions works well for incumbent elites too. These sinecures divert people who might otherwise be aggressive competitors or underemployed rebels into legitimizing management and institutions instead (hiring these workers, formally complying with their rules and processes, assigning their training programs, etc. shows that an institution "cares" and is "committed" to "doing something" about various forms of inequality and exclusion—including in court as needed). The proliferation of rules and regulators also allows institutions to expand discipline and surveillance over their workforce—and in the name of social justice, no less.[175] To be clear, it is unlikely that employers expand DEI positions with these explicit considerations in mind. However, these seem to be the main institutional functions DEI professionals serve *in practice*, and this may help explain why so many institutions have been eager to expand these positions despite their demonstrated inefficacy at achieving their stated goals.

Theories of Failure

Awokenings tend to be driven by elite overproduction, and they tend to collapse when a sufficient number of frustrated aspirants are integrated into the power structure or come to believe their prospects are improving. But this is not the kind of story we like to tell ourselves about why these social movements occur and why they taper off. Instead, as these periods of unrest begin to wind down, theories of failure are generated—accounts of why "the revolution" didn't succeed as anticipated—typically detailing how the aims and methods of activists should be adjusted to be more successful downstream. Robust debates ensue as to which account best explains what went wrong and what lessons can be learned. The most successful theories of failure end up informing the character of the next Awokening in important ways.

The original theory of revolution that symbolic capitalists gravitated toward was Marxism. Karl Marx's core project was to explain why the liberal revolutions that deposed aristocrats, the church, and monarchs somehow culminated in the exploitative and hierarchical relationships that defined the industrial period. Marx sought to illustrate how the bourgeoisie (roughly, symbolic capitalists and business owners)[176] shifted from being a revolutionary bloc ostensibly committed to widespread freedom and prosperity—advocates for a society where the circumstances of one's birth need not dictate the path of one's life—into a class dedicated to unending capital accumulation at the expense of the rest of society. The bourgeoisie oversaw an age of unprecedented innovation and productivity; they established institutions that operated at an immense scale and were increasingly complex and inter-connected. Vast wealth was created at a rapid pace. Yet very little of this wealth "trickled down" to the workers, whose labor undergirded the whole system. *They* were working harder than ever, under increasingly harsh conditions, while being paid subsistence wages (at best). In the process of articulating how and why the capitalist revolution turned out as it did, Marx also formulated an alternative model of activism: revolutionaries should focus on mobilizing exploited workers against the bourgeoisie; they should emphasize interdependence, collective action, and the common good over individualistic ("bourgeois") conceptions of rights, freedoms, and prosperity.

Communist ideology became increasingly popular in America during the first Great Awokening—at least among symbolic capitalists.[177] For instance, membership and chapters of the Communist National Student League expanded significantly on campuses nationwide. Indeed, the organization ultimately cannibalized rival Socialist organization the Student League for Industrial Democracy at the tail end of the first Awokening.[178] However, Marxism was far less popular among the working class. Labor unions and workers' movements tended to favor alternative forms of socialism (and syndicalism) over Marxism per se.[179] Consequently, it may be worth briefly clarifying how an ideology that centered the working class as the key to social justice could emerge as a revolutionary framework for highly educated professionals in particular—not just in the United States but also in Europe and prerevolutionary Russia and China.[180] Understanding this can provide important insights into how symbolic capitalists select and co-opt ostensibly "radical" frameworks in the service of their own ascendance and hegemony.

Although Marxism is widely associated with a call for "equality of outcomes" today, Marx himself disparaged equality per se as an absurd political goal.[181] Although a core goal of communism was to ensure work and renumeration was allocated to "each according to his ability, each according to his needs,"[182] as Marx repeatedly observed, abilities are not equal! Nor is the level of value that each worker produces. Marx's foundational critique of capitalism was that it was a system in which virtually no one actually got what they deserved. Capitalists produce little but extract "surplus value" from those who *do* produce via their monopoly over the means of production (that is, capitalists get far *more* than they deserve by coercing others into accepting *less* than they deserve). The goal of communism, at bottom, was to reset social relations so that all were *appropriately* rewarded for the value they produced. On Marx's account, inequality would be less dramatic following the communist revolution, but it would not be the case that everyone was *identical* (nor would that even be desirable to Marx). Although "private property" as we understand it today would be abolished, people would still have "individual property."[183] Differences would emerge with respect to that individual property on the basis of different preferences and aspirations, different passions and interests, different capabilities and lines of work, different ways that people choose to leverage individual property, and so forth—and those differences would be morally legitimate. As Marx explains in *The Communist Manifesto*, when "capital is converted into common property, into the property of all members of society, personal property is not therefore transformed into social property. It is only the social character of the property that is changed. It loses its class-character . . . we by no means intend to abolish this personal appropriation of the products of labor . . . all that we want to do away with is the miserable character of this appropriation."[184]

Of course, the latter part of the maxim, "according to his needs," suggests nonmeritocratic redistribution as well. However, it is important to clarify who would be "needy" under communism. In a world where people were compensated according to the value they produce, Marx theorized, there wouldn't necessarily *be* "working poor." And in a world where people were no longer alienated from their labor, there wouldn't be people who chose not to work and tried to live parasitically on society. Marx argued that the desire to be productive, to create, to add value—these are fundamental human drives currently blunted by capitalism and the alienation it produces. Communism, he argued, would set those drives free—leading to radically increased prosperity. People would *want* to work. They would become far *more* productive, far *more* innovative—because they would finally get what they deserve for the value they produce and would be freed from coercive and dispiriting labor relations. Pretty much the only people who would be "needy," then, would be those who literally *cannot* work (i.e., the very old, the severely mentally or physically ill or impaired, orphaned children, victims of natural disasters). And it would not necessarily be the task of *the state* to provide for them. Marx believed that in a world where people's relationships were less exploitative, where society was less self-oriented, and where there was an understanding that all wealth flows fundamentally from the earth itself, which no one actually *owns* (or, better, which we all own in common), people would look out for one another. Marx did not envision a permanent welfare state, perennially seizing and reallocating income according to citizens' apparent needs. Instead, he argued, the state would eventually "wither away."[185]

That is, Marx envisioned a world where hard work, innovation, and ambition are valued and nurtured, where people can be anything they want to be (commensurate with their talents), and where all receive their just rewards for the value they produce. None of this is out of line with mainstream symbolic capitalist ideals. Indeed, as Marx repeatedly emphasized, communism was not orthogonal to capitalism—it was to evolve organically *out of* capitalism, retaining the best aspects of the bourgeoisie revolution while correcting for its excesses and shortcomings. This was part of the appeal among symbolic capitalists.

Marx also described his social vision as more objective, scientific, and rational than others conceived before or since (and more "grounded" as compared with those of "utopian socialists" like Saint-Simon).[186] His patron and frequent collaborator, Friedrich Engels, would go so far as to argue that people who mastered Marxian analysis could gain the same power over the social world that the natural sciences afford us over the material world.[187] This was obviously a seductive proposition for people (like symbolic capitalists) who define themselves in terms of their intellect and erudition. And the revolution itself, on Marx's account, would ultimately be premised on the emergence of people who understand society as it really is (i.e., epistemic elites) and are simultaneously committed to social justice (i.e., moral exemplars) uniting the proletariat and then *leading* them to take control of the state.

Many contemporaries of Marx viewed this latter element as a fatal defect of his thinking. Mikhail Bakunin, for instance, argued it was unreasonable to expect the emergence of some alliance of noble leaders who would seize control over the state and all the nation's wealth, and then redistribute it all fairly, taking nothing extra for themselves, their families, their friends, their own communities, or their allies—and who would then voluntarily dismantle the state and live among their fellow citizens as equals.[188] More likely, those who took control of the state would find justifications to give themselves more than others, find reasons to perpetuate and expand the state indefinitely, and target anyone who challenged these maneuvers as traitors and enemies of the revolution. No one, Bakunin argued, is or could be immune to these temptations: "If you took the most ardent revolutionary, vested him in absolute power, within a year he would be worse than the Tsar himself."[189] Bakunin's arguments have proved highly prescient virtually everywhere people have attempted to establish an ostensibly "Communist" state.

Nonetheless, symbolic capitalists, from the first Great Awokening through today, have imagined themselves as *just* the kind of people whose wisdom and beneficence allow them to transcend the myopia and selfishness of common folk and serve the greater good. We are *just* the kind of people who could avoid being corrupted by wealth or power—which is why, we argue, a larger share of wealth and power should be consolidated in *our* hands as opposed to others'. With this in mind, it is not hard to understand why symbolic capitalists would find Marxism particularly appealing, nor why the working classes may have been wary of it.

Critically, as part of his "scientific" approach to socialism, Marx believed that slavery, patriarchy, and violent conflict were ultimately fated to be outgrown alongside capitalism. Although he lauded these predicted developments, he viewed organized efforts to advance causes like pacifism, feminism, and antiracism per se to be dangerous distractions.[190] On Marx's view, campaigns such as these were tantamount to expending immense energy and resources on treating symptoms at the expense of curing the disease. If the communist revolution was successful, these other forms of exploitative relationships would be abolished alongside capitalism. Meanwhile, to the extent that ameliorative campaigns on these other issues were successful, they could render the status quo more bearable and forestall the "real" revolution. Marx also perceived that a focus on issues like race, gender, and sexuality tended to divide workers against one another, to largely the same effect: delaying the revolution. In order to keep U.S. Socialists united and focused tightly on the issue of class struggle, Marx endorsed the purging of feminists, sexual freedom advocates, pacifists, and antiracists from the American branch of the International Workingmen's Association.[191]

Nonetheless, by the time of the first Awakening, Marx had been dead for some time, and many who embraced his ideas had found ways to reconcile communism with other forms of advocacy. As Orwell lamented at the time of the first Great Awakening, "One sometimes gets the impression that the mere words 'Socialism' and 'Communism' draw towards them with magnetic force every fruit-juice drinker, nudist, sandal-wearer, sex-maniac, Quaker, 'Nature Cure' quack, pacifist and feminist in England."[192] Marxism, in turn, would come to inform and transform many other struggles that Marx deprioritized, such as feminism, antiracism, and anticolonialism. Developments like these are not unusual. As we will see, Awokenings often mobilize ideas in ways, and in the service of ends, that their progenitors neither anticipated nor approved of.

Ultimately, the communist revolutions many were anticipating in the United States and western Europe did not occur as planned (or at all). As the first Awakening came to an end, a theory of failure emerged and eventually rose to prominence: critical theory. The term itself was formally introduced by Max Horkheimer in his 1937 *Traditional and Critical Theory*. That book, and much of his subsequent work, sought to explain why "the revolution" failed to materialize during the first period of Awokening. Rather than seeing successful worker-driven movements toward social liberation (as Marx had predicted), the twentieth century seemed to be defined by the rise of fascism, totalitarianism, and later, globalized capitalism. The divisions between states and markets were increasingly blurred. Workers had not united and risen up against their bosses but instead remained bitterly divided along the lines of race, nationality, religion, and so on. Rather than a unified struggle against capitalists, there was a world war, with workers primarily on the front lines killing each other (and another such war on the horizon). The prospects for meaningful resistance or productive revolution seemed increasingly bleak. "Critical theory" sought to work out where "conventional theory" (more specifically Marxism) went wrong, and to figure out how, and in what sense, its emancipatory project might still be possible.

Critical theorists ended up settling on culture and institutions of cultural production as the most important fronts in the struggle. That is, symbolic capitalists identified *themselves, their* institutions and outputs—*not* the workers, *not* the business owners—as central agents in creating a better world. By winning the culture war, they could create the conditions for "the Revolution" to occur—they could empower "the people" to understand their oppression and rise up to emancipate themselves. As C. Wright Mills put it in his "Letter to the New Left" (a 1960 essay that popularized the idea of a "New Left" in the United States and helped set its agenda),

> We are frequently accused of being "utopian"—in our criticisms and in our proposals; and along with this, of basing our hopes for a New Left politics . . . upon the intelligentsia in its broadest sense. There is truth in these charges. But must we not ask: what now is really meant by utopian? And: Is not our utopianism a major source of our strength? I do not quite understand . . . why they cling so mightily to "the working class" of the advanced capitalist societies as *the* historic agency, or even as the most important agency, in the face of the really historical evidence that now stands against this expectation. . . . Who is it that is getting fed up? Who is it that is getting disgusted with what Marx called "all the old crap"? Who is it that is thinking and acting in radical ways? All over the world—in the bloc, outside the bloc and in between—the answer's the same: it is the young intelligentsia.[193]

Critical theory would ultimately provide the means for the "young intelligentsia" of the 1960s to distinguish itself from its Marxist forebears and articulate a new social vision.

Put another way, although formulated at the end of the first Great Awo-kening, critical theory didn't really have its "moment" until the second Great Awokening. This kind of trajectory is not unusual. Successful theories of fail-ure are usually influential within their domain at the time they are put for-ward, but don't become particularly prominent among symbolic capitalists writ large until the next Awokening, as elites who want to call for "radical" change begin grasping at ways to distinguish their current campaigns from previous (failed) efforts. Again, these frameworks are often interpreted and deployed in ways that the theorists themselves would be uncomfortable with. For instance, although the 1960s New Left associated itself with the aims and methods of critical theory, most of the foundational critical theorists (e.g., Theodor Adorno, Horkheimer, Jürgen Habermas) were highly critical of the New Left and aligned student movements. They did *not* view the "radi-cals" as understanding or applying the insights of critical theory particularly well. They were not particularly optimistic that the activists were poised to radically change society *for the better*.[194] Perhaps with good reason: by the mid-1970s, the second Awokening was sputtering out. It was again clear that the "revolution" would not be occurring anytime soon.

At the tail end of that Awokening, the Combahee River Collective (CRC)—an association of Black lesbian feminist socialists—put forward a new theory of failure to explain why "the Revolution" had not yet arrived. The problem, they argued, is that feminism, racial equality, gay rights, and socialism have typically been pursued as separate, if allied, campaigns. The CRC argued that this approach was doomed to failure. A socialist revolu-tion that was not *simultaneously* a feminist and antiracist revolution would be insufficient to ensure people like *them* experienced liberation (the same held for a feminist revolution that was not simultaneously antiracist and socialist, and so on). Moreover, they explained, the encouragement of altru-ism in many of these movements had a pernicious effect on people who were especially marginalized or oppressed *within* a disadvantaged group. *Their* concerns and perspectives were consistently overlooked, their needs chronically unmet, as they perennially subordinated their own demands for the sake of the "greater good." For instance, it was considered threaten-ing to the cohesion, momentum, and legitimacy of "the cause" to talk about the unsavory racial dynamics of the feminist or gay rights movement, or homophobia and misogyny that often manifested themselves in the Black Power movement. People who sought to address these issues were often told that, while their concerns may be legitimate, they were things that could be attended to after the "main" objective had been achieved. A better path to liberation, the CRC argued, was to embrace "identity politics" (a term they have been credited with coining): "We realize that the only people who care enough about us to work consistently for our liberation are us. Our politics evolve from a healthy love for ourselves, our sisters and our community which allows us to continue our struggle and work. This focusing upon our own oppression is embodied in the concept of identity politics. We believe that the most profound and potentially most radical politics come directly out of our own identity, as opposed to working to end somebody else's oppression."[195]

By working to ensure liberation first and foremost for oneself, and for others like oneself—allying with others if and only insofar as there were overlapping interests—those who face multiple forms of marginalization or oppression would no longer have to choose to fight one form of oppression at the expense of the others. Nor would they have to pursue racial, gender, sexual, and socioeconomic justice as separate domains. By grounding their politics in their own specific identities, and the challenges they personally face, people could form coalitions to address multiple dimensions at once. They could come to more deeply understand (and, in turn, help others understand) how different forms of oppression are interrelated by looking at the concrete ways they intersect in their own lives, and in the lives of their allies. By being forthright about the pursuit of their own interests, allies would no longer need to deceive themselves or others about their true goals and motivations—rendering alliances more effective.

Of course, the idea that focusing on one's own interests can promote the greater good more effectively than "working to end somebody else's oppression"—at least superficially—is not far removed from Adam Smith's famous argument in favor of capitalism: "He intends only his own security . . . he intends only his own gain, and he is in this, as in many other cases, led by an invisible hand to promote an end which was no part of his intention. Nor is it always the worse for the society that it was not part of it. By pursuing his own interest he frequently promotes that of the society more effectually than when he really intends to promote it."[196]

Many certainly seem to have synthesized the CRC's argument with Smith's. Elites, especially those who identify with historically marginalized and disadvantaged groups, increasingly define the relentless pursuit of their own self-interest as a "radical" act. High-end consumption is redefined as an act of "self-care" or "self-affirmation"—as a feminist or antiracist "victory"—because they (elites who are women, nonwhite, LGBTQ, neurodivergent, or disabled) are "worth it" and "deserve it."[197] Likewise, elites from historically disadvantaged groups who accumulate ever more power or influence in their own hands are described as somehow achieving a "win" for those who remain impoverished, marginalized, and vulnerable. As discussed in the introduction to this book, behaviors that would be recognized as exploitative, oppressive, or disrespectful if carried out by people who are white, heterosexual, or male are often interpreted as empowering, righteous, or necessary when carried out by "other" elites and elite aspirants. As CRC founding member Barbara Smith has repeatedly emphasized, this is all very far from what they intended with their statement.[198]

In any case, the CRC's theory of failure was hugely influential for the third Great Awokening—including (perhaps especially) with respect to third-wave feminism. Debates around "identity politics" also took off in the late 1980s and early 1990s, as the CRC's ideas went increasingly mainstream. The waning of the third Awokening, in turn, gave rise to a new theory of failure that has grown especially prominent in the midst of the current period of tumult: critical race theory.

Critical race theory was born from the Critical Legal Studies (CLS) movement. At the time said movement was coming into its own, in the midst of the third Great Awokening, the civil rights movement had stalled out in the face of assassinations, riots, internal tensions, and growing public frustration; Nixon won two landslides, then Ronald Reagan unseated Jimmy Carter in yet another landslide in 1980. The GOP would control the White House for the next twelve years. How could one reconcile the fact that public attitudes had apparently moved so much on race, but racial inequalities remained so pronounced? How could one explain the rightward electoral swing following the successes that did occur in the civil rights movement? Most importantly, how could the cause of Black emancipation proceed in the current landscape, where mass mobilization seemed implausible? Critical race theory sought to answer questions like these.

The pioneers for critical race theory were largely *not* armchair theorists—they were lawyers. The ideas they developed were intended to be put to practical use (and indeed *were* successfully put to use in the courtroom). Their ambition was to use the very legal institutions that were designed to oppress and exploit in order to empower and liberate—to subvert laws written to serve the interests of the powerful in order to instead constrain their influence and undermine the status quo. Rather than focusing on the economic sphere (like the Marxists) or the cultural sphere (like the critical theorists), the CLS movement emphasized the laws and codes as an ideal site of struggle. Rather than mass movements or culture wars, their tools were lawsuits and legislation, or the amendment of contracts, institutional rules, codes of conduct, standard operating procedures, teaching and training materials, and so on.

That is, in their focus and their methods, the CLS movement and critical race theory were quite distinct from "critical theory" per se. Indeed, if you read the movement's foundational texts, beyond occasional references to Antonio Gramsci, there is little "critical theory" present;[199] the authors draw on other, largely unrelated, sources. However, as the frameworks developed by the CLS movement jumped out of the legal sphere and began interacting more directly with third-wave feminism, postcolonial activism, environmental advocacy, the gay rights movement, and queer theory, bridges were increasingly built between critical race theory and critical theory as such . . . and also with many other ideas and causes. Indeed, CLS movement cofounder Kimberlé Crenshaw has lamented how ideas associated with the movement have been taken to some weird places, and used in ways she and her peers did not intend and wouldn't endorse.[200] This is, of course, the perennial joy and terror of putting ideas out into the world and seeing them "catch on": after a point, they take on a life of their own and are no longer "yours" to control.

From our current historical vantage point, it is unclear what theories of failure will emerge and gain prominence as the fourth Awokening winds down—let alone which of these theories future symbolic capitalists will ultimately find useful in their struggles. However, we can be confident that future frustrated elites will try to distinguish their own efforts from the failed campaigns of the past by leaning on a narrative that currently exists or will soon be produced about the limitations of the current Awokening and how they can be transcended downstream. If a preferred theory of failure does not naturally flatter the priorities and worldviews of said elites, it will be reinterpreted so it can serve this purpose.

Culture Wars

In his 1976 *The Coming of Post-industrial Society*, sociologist Daniel Bell highlighted how changes to the global economy were leading to the emergence of a new social order—one driven by a "knowledge economy," dominated by technical elites, and highly stratified on the basis of factors like intellectual acumen and academic credentials.[201] Meanwhile, he argued, the labor and assets of those who traded in material goods and services would become increasingly devalued, leading to growing tensions between the technocrats and everyone else. Exacerbating these tensions, Bell argued, was the widespread embrace among intellectuals of what essayist Lionel Trilling referred to as "adversary culture."

Within the new elite class, people gained status through delegitimizing and denigrating institutions, traditions, values, and ways of life associated with the middle class. This, Bell argued, would lead to further mistrust of and resentment against the new elites—as the "common man" was being marginalized not just within the economy but within the culture as well. Moreover, Bell noted, there were two deep tensions in the cultural project of these new elites.[202] First, adversary culture was itself unmistakably a product of the very bourgeois culture it condemned and was, therefore, unlikely to present a true threat to the prevailing order. Indeed, although these new elites continued to view themselves as outsiders and subversives, they were themselves, increasingly, "the man." This leads to the second core tension: insofar as these new elites were successful in advancing adversary culture, they could ultimately end up destroying the foundations of their own authority (i.e., trust in science, expertise, rationality, meritocracy, universities, the press, etc.). The dynamic Bell described becomes especially clear during Awokenings.

Frustrated erstwhile elites often attempt to delegitimize and displace establishment rivals (to make room for themselves) by indicting symbolic capitalist institutions and successful symbolic capitalists as too cozy with the wealthy and the privileged—and by presenting *themselves* as more authentic or effective champions for minoritized populations and the poor. Incumbents generally respond to these campaigns by trying to show that they are just as committed to eliminating inequalities as their critics or are even *better* allies for the marginalized and disadvantaged. That is, they try to meet or outflank their critics on "social justice" issues—creating a new consensus position among symbolic capitalists that is more symbolically "left" than before the Awokening. This, in turn, creates an opportunity for the opponents of mainstream symbolic capitalists to enhance *their* credibility, notoriety, and influence.

Again, symbolic capitalists are generally much farther to the left on "culture" issues than most Americans—and Awokenings drive them to stake out positions that are even farther out of touch with the rest of their countrymen. And as symbolic capitalists become more aggressive in trying to impose their values and priorities on others—and confronting, denigrating, marginalizing, or sanctioning those who refuse to get with the program—the differences between them and everyone else don't merely grow larger, they also become much more salient. Moreover, during these interelite struggles, symbolic capitalists tend to be very publicly divided among themselves, with a faction of frustrated and aspiring elites explicitly disparaging more established symbolic capitalists and their affiliated institutions, often while they are themselves engaged in discourse and performative displays that strike most "normies" as extreme, unappealing, and ridiculous. Consequently, both established elites and frustrated aspirants often end up mutually discredited in the eyes of much of the public by the time Awokenings have run their course.

Right-aligned symbolic capitalists—anti-wokes and conservatives—often try to exploit and exacerbate both the divisions within mainstream symbolic capitalists and the growing gulf between the mainstream consensus position and the rest of society. They attempt to lump insurgents and incumbents together as corrupt, out of touch, and out of control. Right-aligned symbolic capitalists and their allies paint themselves as populists who will restore order, sanity, and dignity to the country and its institutions—or, that failing, defund, dismantle, and disempower them. What starts out as an intermainstream struggle often devolves into a left-right struggle.[203] Awokenings and culture wars, therefore, tend to travel hand in hand—and dramatic leftward movements within symbolic capitalist institutions are usually followed by "red waves" at the ballot box and beyond. Terms that were once the subject of inter-Left disputes, such as "identity politics," "political correctness," and "woke," are appropriated by the Right as cudgels to attack *everyone* left of center and come to be used in almost exclusively pejorative or ironic ways.

These conservative shifts that follow Awokenings are often uncharitably described as "backlash" against progress. However, readers should recall that, since the 1960s, progress toward egalitarianism has largely stalled out on most fronts—with the relationships between Blacks and whites, rich and poor, roughly the same as they were sixty years ago. There is no meaningful relationship between Awokenings and material gains for marginalized and disadvantaged populations, nor is there a meaningful connection between Awokenings and durable attitudinal changes among the general public. If anything, there has been an *inverse* relationship between Awokenings and material "progress" from the second Awokening forward.

It is actually somewhat intuitive that Awokenings could correspond with a perpetuation or exacerbation of inequalities given that these uprisings are fundamentally "about" frustrated elite aspirants trying to secure superior social positions. But what this means with respect to interpreting the culture wars is that, when Americans shift right in the aftermath of Awokenings, they are generally *not* reacting against material changes that benefit marginalized populations at the expense of the majority group. Those have been few and far between and don't cleanly correlate well with Awokenings in any case. The "backlash" instead seems to be about growing alienation among "normies" from elite culture and elite institutions, whose outputs shift far more during Awokenings than any laws or relative material circumstances between groups.

We see these dynamics clearly in the data on public trust in experts. The General Social Survey began collecting these data in 1973, so we can only see the aftereffects of the second Awokening (not the antecedent baselines) and the most recent two episodes. Looking at trust in the scientific community along ideological lines,[204] we see a few important periods. In the aftermath of the second and third Great Awokenings, we see significant drops in public trust in scientists. Toward the tail end of Awokenings, trust among moderates and liberals tends to recover. However, conservative trust seems to have been more durably shaken after 1986, leading to increased polarization around science: liberals became significantly *more* trusting of scientists after 1994 (as the Awokening was ending), while conservatives continued a more modest decline and moderates joined them.[205] This polarization was exacerbated after 2010, and again starting in 2018. Political scientist Matthew Motta has argued that these latter shifts seem to be a product of the March for Science, wherein large numbers of scientists, engaging *as* scientists, more or less overtly declared themselves to be opposed to Trump and aligned with his political opposition—maneuvers that further increased (already high) trust in scientists among liberals while exacerbating declines among conservatives.[206]

We see the same patterns when we look along partisan (Democrat, Republican, independent) lines instead of ideology: after the late 1980s, there were consistent declines in Republicans' trust in scientists. After 1991, Democrats' trust in the scientific community began to increase, and it continued to rise steadily through 2016. After Trump was elected president, there was a *massive* upward shift in Democratic support for scientists. The share of Democrats expressing "a great deal" of confidence in the scientific community rose by more than 20 percentage points in the next five years.[207] On the other side of the aisle, declines in trust in experts among Republicans began after 1987. From then through the early 1990s, Democrats, independents, and Republicans were all trending together: Americans across the board were growing more skeptical of the scientific community. However, after 1991, Democrats began shifting the other direction, while Republicans persisted on roughly the same steady downward trajectory from 1987 through 2018. After 2018, however, there was an accelerated decline in Republican confidence in the scientific community—7 percentage points over the subsequent three years. Nonetheless, Republican declines in trust in the scientific community were less than half the magnitude of Democratic *increases* over roughly the same span of time.

Across the board, trust in experts tends to decline during Great Awokenings. In their aftermath, however, attitudes tend to polarize. Left-aligned Americans shift from critiquing mainstream symbolic capitalist institutions to trying to bolster their legitimacy. Trust among right-aligned Americans, meanwhile, is often more durably eroded. One regular response to this erosion of trust is to construct alternative (right-valanced) infrastructures for cultural production. These often persist long after Awokenings and anti-Wokenings have run their course and durably undermine the authority and reach of mainstream symbolic capitalists.

For instance, in the aftermath of the second Great Awokening, many on the right concluded that academia was a lost cause and sought to establish an alternative ecosystem for right-aligned intellectual pursuits, beginning with the establishment of the Heritage Foundation (1973) and the Cato Institute (1977).[208] In the wake of the third Great Awokening, there was a perception that a right-aligned intellectual sphere was not enough, and there were moves to establish right-aligned media, beginning with a major push for conservative talk radio and culminating with the 1996 establishment of Fox News.[209] In the midst of the current Awokening, there have been repeated attempts to establish right-aligned social media spaces, from Parler to Truth Social to Elon Musk's "anti-woke" takeover of Twitter and Peter Theil and J. D. Vance's major investments in Rumble.[210]

In each Awokening, the already-large gap between symbolic capitalists and the general public tends to rapidly expand and is made highly salient. This creates a perceived market for alternative institutions of cultural production. Born out of the culture wars, these new institutions tend to have an existential stake in perennially sowing mistrust in mainstream symbolic capitalists and perpetuating the culture wars. They build symbolic capital for themselves, capture audience share, and grow their revenues by depicting mainstream institutions as biased, exclusionary, censorious, and out of touch. To the extent that mainstream symbolic capitalists actually do come to approximate these right-wing caricatures during periods of Awokening, they produce and empower their own gravediggers.

Coda: White Liberals

In a prescient series of essays for *Radical America* in 1977, Barbara and John Ehrenreich defined the professional-managerial class (the term they coined for symbolic capitalists) as "salaried mental workers who do not own the means of production and whose major function in the social division of labor may be described broadly as the reproduction of capitalist culture and capitalist class relations."[211] In layman's terms, the major role they play in society is to keep the capitalist machine running (in the present and in perpetuity), maximize its efficiency and productivity, and justify the inequalities that were required in order to achieve these ends. This posed a bit of a problem for symbolic capitalists, who, as the Ehrenreichs noted, were generally aligned with the New Left. They sympathized with radical feminism, the Black Power movement, environmental activism, the weakening of sexual taboos, socialism, the antiwar movement, and so on. However, they also had bills to pay and, as time went on, families to support—and there were lots of lucrative and new opportunities for those who were willing and able to partake in the globalized knowledge economy.

Toward the end of the second Awokening, the primary way most resolved this tension without nakedly "selling out" was to insist that they would use their new influence within "the machine" to help the disadvantaged. That is, they would be subversive "cogs," who would engage in a "long march through the institutions" and leverage them toward alternative ends.[212] They would learn to uplift those who were suffering, and empower those who were marginalized, through the very systems and institutions that would have otherwise exploited and oppressed them. Notice, however, that in defining their own flourishing within the "system" as a means of increasing their capacity to help the desperate and vulnerable, symbolic capitalists provided themselves with a powerful justification for climbing as high up the ladder as they could and accumulating more and more into their own hands: the more resources they controlled, and the more institutional clout they wielded, the more they would be theoretically able to accomplish on behalf of the needy and vulnerable (and the less capital would be in the hands of the "bad" elites). "Doing well" was redefined as a means of "doing good."

From the outside, it often seemed as though symbolic capitalists were relentlessly engaged in a rat race to enhance their own social position. However, the Ehrenreichs noted, they typically did not think of themselves as being oriented toward such banal ends. Granted, the promised reallocation of the assets and opportunities amassed—ostensibly on behalf of the downtrodden—would likely never come (and indeed, some four decades after the Ehrenreichs published their essays, we're still holding our breath on that). However, symbolic capitalists could nonetheless generate a sense of "progress" toward their egalitarian commitments by pushing their institutions to take *symbolic* actions with respect to empowering women and minorities, validating LGBTQ people, protecting the environment, and so forth.

The second key strategy adopted by the symbolic capitalists to reconcile their "day jobs" with their political beliefs was to try to live in accordance with their New Left values *personally* (that is, to find ways to signal their own individual commitment to feminism, antiracism, environmentalism— including through "just" consumption), and to encourage their peers to do the same. In the process, they turned the campaign for social justice "inward"—into a psychological and even spiritual project. The status quo may persist, largely as a result of their own work no less. However, symbolic capitalists could still think of themselves as virtuous in light of how they carried themselves in the private sphere and by conspicuously demonstrating the purity of their own hearts and minds.

Over the course of their essays, the Ehrenreichs powerfully explain some of the "pull" factors that led symbolic capitalists of the 1970s to disengage from social justice activism. However, there were also "push" factors that led them away from direct action during the second Awokening. Exploring those is perhaps an ideal way to both close out this chapter and transition to the themes of the next.

In the news media of the 1960s (as remains the case today in some respects), racism was depicted as primarily a problem of "backwards" rural and southern areas.[213] However, as civil rights leaders began to see major breakthroughs in the South, they decided that their work was not yet done. At the invitation of the Coordinating Council of Community Organizations, a Chicago-based civil rights body, Martin Luther King Jr. and the Southern Christian Leadership Conference (SCLC) launched a campaign against the de facto segregation in northern schools, neighborhoods, and workplaces in 1965. They began by trying to move Black families into predominantly white neighborhoods in Chicago. Rather than being welcomed with open arms by enlightened urban northerners, they were violently resisted at every turn. Here, it is worth quoting King at length:

> Bottles and bricks were thrown at us; we were often beaten. Some of the people who had been brutalized in Selma and who were present at the Capitol ceremonies in Montgomery led marchers in the suburbs of Chicago amid a rain of rocks and bottles, among burning automobiles, to the thunder of jeering thousands, many of them waving Nazi flags. Swastikas bloomed in Chicago parks like misbegotten weeds. Our marchers were met by a hailstorm of bricks, bottles, and firecrackers. "White power" became the racist catcall, punctuated by the vilest of obscenities. . . . I've been in many demonstrations all across the South, but I can

say that I had never seen, even in Mississippi, mobs as hostile and as hate-filled as in Chicago. When we had our open housing marches many of our white liberal friends cried out in horror and dismay: "You are creating hatred and hostility in the white communities in which you are marching. You are only developing a white backlash." They failed to realize that the hatred and the hostilities were already latently or subconsciously present. Our marches merely brought them to the surface. . . . We were the social physicians of Chicago revealing that there was a terrible cancer. . . . We were the social psychiatrists, bringing out things that were in the subconscious all along. . . . As long as the struggle was down in Alabama and Mississippi, they could look afar and think about it and say how terrible people are. When they discovered brotherhood had to be a reality in Chicago and that brotherhood extended to next door, then those latent hostilities came out.[214]

As King explained in his 1967 address to the American Psychological Association, this vicious reception among the people who were supposed to be "allies"—among those who had been cheering the civil rights movement *elsewhere*—this stalling-out of progress in the section of the country that was supposed to be *easier* than the South led to deep rage in the Black community.[215] The SCLC's message of nonviolence, forbearance, faith in humanity, and interracial cooperation increasingly rang hollow. Riots broke out. Increased repression followed. Black militias gained in prominence, encouraging African Americans to defend themselves against white aggression.[216] Black nationalist movements grew.

As scenes of unrest played out in *northern* streets (rather than comfortably far away in the South), media coverage of King and civil rights demonstrations grew overwhelmingly hostile.[217] Despite previously holding King up as a national hero, the Johnson administration cut off contact and access altogether when King began to criticize the Vietnam War. In 1967, with President Johnson's blessing, the FBI launched a new campaign, COINTELPRO–BLACK HATE, seeking to "disrupt, misdirect, discredit, or otherwise neutralize the activities" of King, the SCLC, and many other civil rights organizations and activists.[218] Public opinion quickly soured as well: at the time he was assassinated, King had a 75 percent *dis*approval rating according to polls.[219]

Seeing the establishment turn so rapidly on a person who had bent over backward to accommodate them—who had consistently extended the benefit of the doubt to whites and encouraged others to do the same—the sense grew in Black organizing spaces that white liberals could not be trusted. They may even be worse than right-wing opponents, many argued. Reactionary conservatives, for instance, would directly tell you how they felt and what they were after. You could plan around that; you could work with that (even if what they had to say was often horrifying or offensive). It was much harder to deal with people who pretended to be on board but were unwilling to make meaningful sacrifices and constantly deflected blame for social problems onto others. It was much more difficult to work with people who wouldn't resist the movement per se, but instead try to hijack it to suit their own interests. It was far tougher to tolerate someone who would not only lie to others, but who couldn't seem to be honest with themselves about what they were trying to accomplish and what their ideal endgame was. As *Ebony* magazine editor Lerone Bennett Jr. explained at the time,

> White friends of the American Negro claim, with some justification, that Negros attack them with more heat than they attack declared enemies. . . . Oppressed people learn early that the problem of life is not the problem of evil but the problem of good. For this reason, they focus their fire on the bona fides of avowed friends. . . . The white liberal is a man who finds himself defined as a white man, as an oppressor in short, and retreats in horror at that designation. But—and this is essential—he retreats only halfway, disavowing the title without giving up the privileges, tearing out, as it were, the table of contents and keeping the book. The fundamental trait of the white liberal is his desire to differentiate himself psychologically from white Americans on the issue of race. He wants to think, and he wants others to think, he is a man of brotherhood. . . . What characterizes the white liberal, above all, is his inability to live the words he mouths . . . he joins groups and assumes postures that permit him and others to believe something is being done. The key word here is *believe*.[220]

King grew increasingly disillusioned as well, arguing toward the end of his life that "Negros have proceeded from a premise that equality means what it says, and they have taken white America at their word when they talked of it as an objective. But most whites in America in 1967, including many persons of goodwill, proceed from a premise that equality is a loose expression for improvement. White America is not even psychologically organized to close the gap—essentially, it seeks only to make it less painful and less obvious but in most respects to retain it. Most abrasions between Negros and white liberals arise from this fact."[221]

The year before King uttered these words, SNCC issued a position paper arguing, "More and more we see black people in this country being used as a tool of the white liberal establishment. Liberal whites have not begun to address themselves to the real problem of black people in this country. . . . Previous solutions to black problems in this country have been made in the interests of those whites dealing with these problems and not in the best interests of black people in the country. Whites can only subvert our true search and struggles for self-determination, self-identification, and liberation in this country."[222] Ultimately, SNCC would vote to expel whites from the organization entirely. Reporting on the purge in *New Republic*, journalist Andrew Kopkind noted at the time, "What galls SNCC people most is the way white radicals seem to have treated SNCC as some kind of psychotherapy, as a way to work out problems of alienation and boredom and personal inadequacy."[223]

James Baldwin would find himself frustrated by the same. In 1972, he observed that even when white liberals tried to engage critiques by frustrated African Americans, they seemed to convince themselves (and tried to convince their interlocutors) that *other* white liberals were the problem. They sought to maintain themselves as an exception and aligned themselves fervently with Black Power and civil rights as a kind of indulgence (in the Catholic sense) for their *ongoing* sins: "It seemed very clear to me that [white liberals] were lying about their motives and were being blackmailed by their guilt . . . struggling to hold on to what they had acquired. For, intellectual activity, according to me, is and must be, disinterested. The truth is a two-edged sword—and if one is not willing to be pierced by the sword, even to the extreme of dying on it, then all of one's intellectual activity is a masturbatory delusion and a wicked and dangerous fraud."[224]

Baldwin, like King, began his public career as a firm believer in the possibility of racial reconciliation. While unflinching in discussing the horrors of the past and present, he was optimistic that the future could be better than the past. And he was beloved by white liberals for these characteristics. However, witnessing the growing infighting within the Black community, seeing the public turn against the civil rights struggle, and particularly in the wake of King's assassination—Baldwin's work increasingly reflected frustration and disillusionment. His trademark "critical patriotism" became less evident. As a consequence, his perspective grew increasingly out of step with his (symbolic capitalist) primary readers in the post–second Awokening era, who wanted to pat themselves on the back for the gains made in the civil rights era, hagiographize King (who was broadly despised at the time of his death), pretend King's mission had been more or less accomplished, and get back to business.[225]

Of course, some Black leaders never grew alienated from white liberals because they never trusted them to begin with. For instance, in 1963, before the second Great Awokening was even fully underway, Malcolm X declared,

> In this deceitful American game of power politics, the Negros (i.e. the race problem, the integration and civil rights issues) are nothing but tools, used by one group of whites called Liberals against another group of whites called Conservatives, either to get into power or to remain in power. . . . The white liberal differs from the white conservative only in one way: the liberal is more deceitful than the conservative. The liberal is more hypocritical than the conservative. Both want power, but the white liberal is the one who has perfected the art of posing as the Negro's friend and benefactor; and by winning the friendship, allegiance, and support of the Negro, the white liberal is able to use the Negro as a pawn or a tool in this political "football game" that is constantly raging between white liberals and white conservatives. Politically the American Negro is nothing but a football.[226]

Baynard Rustin, however, argued that the focus on white liberals' sincerity or consistency was ultimately a dead end, as were attempts to try to carve out special considerations for members of historically marginalized and disadvantaged groups.

> I believe that the Negro's struggle for equality in America is essentially revolutionary. While most Negroes—in their hearts—unquestionably seek only to enjoy the fruits of American society as it now exists, their quest cannot objectively be satisfied within the framework of existing political and economic relations. . . . "Preferential treatment" cannot help them. . . . Sharing with many moderates a recognition of the magnitude of the obstacles to freedom, [many] survey the American scene and find no forces prepared to move toward radical solutions. From this they conclude that the only viable strategy is shock; above all, the hypocrisy of white liberals must be exposed. These spokesmen are often described as the radicals of the movement, but they are really its moralists. They seek to change white hearts—by traumatizing them. Frequently abetted by white self-flagellants, they may gleefully applaud (though not really agreeing with) Malcolm X because, while they admit

he has no program, they think he can frighten white people into doing the right thing. To believe this, of course, you must be convinced, even if unconsciously, that at the core of the white man's heart lies a buried affection for Negroes—a proposition one may be permitted to doubt. But in any case, hearts are not relevant to the issue; neither racial affinities nor racial hostilities are rooted there. It is institutions—social, political, and economic institutions—which are the ultimate molders of collective sentiments. Let these institutions be reconstructed today, and let the ineluctable gradualism of history govern the formation of a new psychology."[227]

We're now sixty years after Rustin penned those words, and his warnings about the futility of focusing on the hearts and minds of white liberals seem to have been quite prescient. Symbolic capitalists' rhetoric and expressed attitudes have grown markedly more progressive during each period of heightened concern about social justice. Institutions and allocations of resources, however, remain highly inegalitarian. Since the dawn of the twentieth century, symbolic capitalists have undergone four Great Awokenings. In practice, however, we have never been woke.

3

Symbolic Domination

Who are the elites? In contemporary America, it seems no one wants to adopt this label. The people who administer institutions claim to be helpless cogs in a system and country that are beyond redemption.[1] Those who pull in healthy six- and seven-figure incomes define themselves in opposition to "the wealthy," whom they describe as greedy, materialistic, ostentatious, privileged, and so on (unlike themselves).[2] Multimillionaires typically view themselves as "middle class."[3] The "hidden curriculum" of elite boarding schools now emphasizes ease over properness, prioritizes direct and plain-spoken modes of communication over demonstration of one's sophistication, and portrays overt displays of wealth as gauche.[4] The overwhelming majority of contemporary American billionaires (a rapidly growing share of whom are associated with symbolic economy industries) define themselves as "self-made."[5] They dress in casual clothes and prioritize "inconspicuous consumption."[6] They express a deep commitment to charity and solving social problems.

Taking these self-presentations at face value, it almost seems as though no one is running the place, no one is truly interested in wealth and status, and those who enjoy various privileges would gladly renounce them if only they could. The social position that socioeconomic and cultural elites occupy is portrayed as almost an accidental and burdensome effect of their massive talent—not anything they consciously and ruthlessly strove to achieve or aggressively work to maintain. None of these socioeconomic and cultural elites view themselves as responsible for social problems. However, virtually all assert that many issues can be resolved by giving more power and autonomy to people like themselves.

In his best-selling *Winners Take All*, Anand Giridharadas powerfully illustrates how the superrich use philanthropy as a means of shaping society in accordance with their own interests and preferences under the auspices of helping *others*—often exacerbating the very problems they claim to be trying to solve.[7] It's a great book, but in some respects its focus is too narrow. After all, millionaires and billionaires are hardly capable of creating, enforcing, managing, and perpetuating society and culture all on their own. Instead, symbolic capitalists are indispensable to the workings of contemporary capitalism writ large. It's difficult to understand how any systemic process works without accounting for people like us.[8]

For instance, it is symbolic capitalists who enable the mystification Giridharadas describes, wherein the actors who create or exacerbate social problems come to be held up as the solution to those very problems.[9] *We* are the people running the nonprofits and PR firms through which superelites attempt to launder their reputations. We are also the ones managing the financial firms through which they launder their money and avoid taxation. Likewise, *we* are typically the ones designing and implementing corporate and governmental policies that exploit, impoverish, mislead, and oppress. People "higher up" might set the agenda, but *we're* the ones who actually make things happen. And for those who have a grievance with an organization or institution, it is *we* who must be reckoned with to get their problems addressed. For instance, a citizen struggling to secure federal government benefits can't take up their problem directly with the president of the United States. Instead, they're forced to engage with functionaries of whichever agency oversees the program in question. And these bureaucrats often have wide latitude in how they respond to issues brought before them—and thereby exert significant arbitrary power over other people's lives.[10]

Moreover, although symbolic capitalists broadly defer to superelites, it is also the case that the wealthy and powerful regularly defer to us. As sociologist C. Wright Mills put it in his 1956 *The Power Elite* (a book exploring the interrelationships between corporate, military, and political leaders), "The power elite are not solitary rulers. Advisers and consultants, spokesmen and opinion-makers are often the captains of their higher thought and decisions."[11] Indeed, a core sociopolitical issue of our time is that decision-making in the political sphere, the private sector, the nonprofit world, and beyond is increasingly informed and constrained by unelected, minimally accountable, largely nontransparent experts and administrators—often at the expense of constituents who are sociologically distant from mainstream symbolic capitalists.[12]

To be sure, much of what symbolic capitalists design, implement, oversee, sustain, and justify is on behalf of superelites, directly or indirectly. But that's far from the whole story. Symbolic capitalists serve wealth, but we also have significant agency and power. We shape the system in accordance with our own tastes and desires, independent of, and sometimes in conflict with, the preferences and priorities of superelites. As Pierre Bourdieu noted, this freedom is necessary for us to effectively mystify social processes and legitimize inequalities. Absent autonomy, our outputs would seem like blatant propaganda rather than "objective" descriptions and rulings. We would seem like mere toadies for rich and powerful interests rather than disinterested observers, arbiters, and advisers. Distance between symbolic capitalists and the superelites, however, enables us to "serve external demands under the guise of independence and neutrality."[13] That is, not only is it the case that we do have significant freedom, superelites are actually somewhat compelled to respect this independence in order to protect our capacity to effectively advance their own interests and goals (through us).

What's more, even when superelites try to outright dominate us, they often lose. Here, the Ford Foundation is an instructive case. The nonprofit was created by auto magnate Henry Ford and his son Edsel with a mission of supporting hospitals, museums, and basic science in the Detroit metro region and beyond. However, during the second Great Awokening, administrators decided to focus the organization intensely on "social justice" issues instead—funding controversial research, projects, and activism on antiracism, feminism, and anticapitalism—against the protests of Henry Ford II. When Ford tried to push the foundation back toward its original mandate, he was largely ignored. Eventually, recognizing that the bureaucrats now exerted more control over the institution than he did, Ford resigned in protest of what his family's nonprofit had become. In his resignation letter he noted, "The foundation is a creature of capitalism, a statement that, I'm sure, would be shocking to many professional staff people in the field of philanthropy. It is hard to discern recognition of this fact in anything the foundation does. It is even more difficult to find an understanding of this in many of the institutions, particularly the universities, that are the beneficiaries of the foundation's grant programs."[14] In subsequent interviews, he expressed regret at having declined to break up the organization when he had the chance, and said he hoped the foundation would go bankrupt in the near future, putting an end to its pernicious work (as he saw it).[15] This was not to be. Instead, some forty years after Henry Ford II's resignation, his son Henry III would eventually be invited to rejoin the foundation—albeit only after explicitly embracing the foundation's new initiatives to address systemic inequalities.[16] The Fords went to war with symbolic capitalists in their own family foundation. The symbolic capitalists won.

In short, symbolic capitalists do not just passively receive or mindlessly execute the dictates of superelites. And contrary to our own frequent self-depictions, we do not stand outside society—nor are we passive, neutral, or helpless observers of the prevailing order. We are active participants. Just like the "1 percent," we attempt to shape society in accordance with *our own* will and interests. We facilitate the operation of the prevailing order, ensure its continued viability, and implement reforms. As this chapter will explore, we are also among the primary beneficiaries of contemporary inequalities. And yet, no less than the superelites described in Giridharadas's book, symbolic capitalists dress up our attempts to consolidate power behind high-minded rhetoric about empowering the marginalized and vulnerable. Much like the millionaires and billionaires, we also play a major role in fomenting the very problems that we present ourselves as the solution to. However, symbolic capitalists generally have a hard time truly understanding ourselves as elites. This chapter is designed to help readers get over that mental block.

Empire of Signs

If you want to understand whom a social order serves, or who benefits most from systemic inequalities (and at whose expense), the starting point of analysis should be to look at who is flourishing in society and who is falling behind. By almost any measure, symbolic capitalists are the primary "winners" in the prevailing order. It is hard for us to recognize this fact because, since the onset of the latest Great Awokening, discussions of inequality have overwhelmingly focused on the top 1 percent.[17]

More realistically, however, if the goal is to understand whose interests are being served by a social order—to see how it is formed, reproduced, and sustained—we should look not just at the top 1 percent of society but the upper *quintile* (i.e., those whose incomes fall into the top 20 percent) at minimum.[18] As Richard Reeves's research robustly illustrates, "opportunity hoarding" by those in the upper quintile has been the primary driver of rising inequality and stagnating social mobility in recent decades.[19] In their efforts to preserve their socioeconomic position, and help their children advance further up the ladder (or at least avoid sliding "down"), upper-middle-class families have effectively "captured" key sources of symbolic and financial capital, and zealously defend their hold on them. Because this "new American aristocracy" is overwhelmingly white,[20] this hoarding of wealth and opportunity has not only exacerbated inequality but has reinforced its racialization as well. It has been estimated that the Black-white income gap would have closed by roughly 30 percent over the last fifty years were it not for these consolidations.[21]

According to estimates by the U.S. Federal Reserve, at the end of 2022 the top 1 percent of income earners controlled about 26 percent of wealth in the United States. To be sure, this is a *radically* disproportionate share—a share that has grown dramatically since the late 1980s. However, it's also the case that the vast majority of wealth in America remains unaccounted for when we focus on the 1 percent. Meanwhile, the other 19 percent of the upper quintile also controlled a hugely disproportionate share (45 percent) of all U.S. wealth. By looking at those in the top 20 percent of incomes, then, we can account for 71 percent—that is, the overwhelming majority—of all wealth in America.[22]

In 2022, the upper quintile included those with a total *household* income of $153,001 or higher per year.[23] When we look at how household incomes vary by education level, we can get a clearer sense of who forms this top quintile.

All said, roughly 40 percent of American households have a primary bread-winner who possesses at least a BA. They form more than 71 percent of all U.S. households that earn more than $155,000 per year. The median income for households with a degree holder is $118,300 per year (mean: $155,300). Meanwhile, 60 percent of households are *not* supported by someone who possesses a BA or more. *Their* median income is less than half that of their more educated peers: $56,778 (mean: $76,508).

A similar story holds for the distribution of *wealth*. According to estimates by the Federal Reserve, the 41 percent of households supported by someone possessing a degree ended 2022 controlling 72 percent of all wealth in the United States. The majority of American households, which are unsupported by a degree holder, are left to divide the remaining 28 percent of U.S. wealth.[24] Since 1989, the wealth of families headed by a college degree holder has increased by 83 percent. Others saw much smaller gains or, in the case of people who lack high school diplomas, marked declines. Consequently, the wealth gap between more and less educated households has widened considerably in recent decades. In 1989, households headed up by a person with "some college" had nearly half as much wealth as degree-holding families. By 2021, they had only thirty cents for every dollar owned by degree-holding

TABLE 3.1. Educational Attainment and Household Income

Highest level of educational attainment for householder	Median household income, 2022 (USD)	Mean household income, 2022 (USD)	Percentage of total U.S. households, 2022	Percent of U.S. top-quintile households
Less than high school	34,847	53,428	8	2
High school or equivalent	51,470	70,300	25	10
Some college, no degree	64,150	85,450	16	10
AA degree	74,920	95,740	11	8
BA degree	108,800	141,700	24	38
MA degree	128,000	165,500	12	24
PhD degree	151,400	203,000	2	6
Professional degree (MD, JD, etc.)	157,800	209,100	2	4

Source: Data from U.S. Census Bureau: Household Income in 2022 (All Races).

households (while households headed up by someone with only a high school diploma possessed only twenty cents for every dollar, and those who lacked high school diplomas had just ten cents for every dollar).[25]

These wide gaps in household income and wealth along the lines of education have a few core causes. The kinds of jobs degree holders get (generally in the symbolic professions) tend to pay significantly better than most. However, Americans with a college degree are also more likely to be married, and they're more likely than other married couples to have a dual-career configuration—often with *both* partners bringing in above-average incomes.[26] In virtue of having multiple streams of solid income, they are much more capable of converting a decent share of their household income into wealth (stocks, property, bonds, etc.). That is, a college education does not just help *oneself* earn substantially more, it also renders someone much more likely to secure a partner with strong earning capacity[27]—thereby increasing both parties' ability to accumulate wealth. However, because symbolic capitalists tend to belong to dual-breadwinner households, families often reach the upper quintile without either partner *individually* meeting or exceeding a six-figure income, leading many to erroneously assume they are not elites.

Another way we can get at this question is to look at the average incomes of different categories of workers. Writing in 1994, sociologist Steven Brint demonstrated that the share of highly educated professionals whose compensation approached the top of the economic distribution had grown dramatically over time. In 1940, roughly 45 percent of highly educated professionals had top-quintile incomes. By 1960, it was a majority (51.2 percent). By 1980, 60 percent had top-fifth incomes.[28] Since then, the divides between symbolic capitalists and everyone else have only grown more pronounced. According to Richard Florida's estimates, contemporary symbolic capitalists (the "Creative Class" in his verbiage) make significantly more money than all other laborers. They make so much more, in fact, that they set the curve for incomes in the United States writ large: Creative Class professionals earn significantly above-average incomes while all other categories of workers tend to earn below-average wages. As of 2017, we earned roughly double the incomes of those in the next-closest income category (Working Class).

Florida published the first edition of *The Rise of the Creative Class* in 2002. Since that time, the share of Americans twenty-five and older who possess a college degree has increased by nearly 6 percentage points. However, the percentage of U.S. workers in the Creative Class has remained relatively stagnant (and even contracted a bit since 2010). As a function of these trends, competition for Creative Class jobs has intensified. Meanwhile, the stakes of securing a Creative Class job (as opposed to some other type of work) have grown.

Even as their share of the workforce held stable, the average wages and salaries for Creative Class workers rose 69 percent between 1999 and 2017. For contrast, there is a growing unmet demand for service workers, and their share of the workforce increased significantly (5 percentage points) between 1999 and 2017. Yet their pay increased significantly less than Creative Class workers over this same period (59 percent). All other categories of workers have seen even smaller increases since the turn of the century.

These patterns are difficult to reconcile with traditional supply-and-demand dynamics. In principle, a growing glut of qualified workers for a shrinking or stagnant set of jobs should lead to a suppression of wages (it becomes a "buyer's market" for labor). Meanwhile, a growing number of positions and undersupply of workers should lead to significant increases in pay relative to other industries (because the "sellers" of labor have many options and are in a strong bargaining position). If the world conformed to the model, we would expect to see anemic wage growth among the Creative Class, especially as compared with the Service Class. The patterns we actually observe seem to be a product of cartel-like behaviors among the Creative Class to ensure that their wages, job security, and working conditions remain superior to most others' *despite* elite overproduction[29]—even as they

TABLE 3.2. The Creative Class

Employment class	Average annual individual wages and salaries, 1999 (USD)	Share of U.S. workforce, 1999	Average annual individual wages and salaries, 2010 (USD)	Share of U.S. workforce, 2010	Average annual individual wages and salaries, 2017 (USD)	Share of U.S. workforce, 2017
Creative Class	48,752	30	70,714	33	82,233	30
Working Class	27,799	26	36,991	21	41,776	21
Service Class	22,059	43	29,188	47	34,979	48
Agriculture	18,000	< 1	24,324	< 1	25,200	< 1
U.S. full-time workers	31,571	100	44,410	100	50,634	100

Sources: Florida 2002, 2019a, 2019c. Data from the U.S. Bureau of Labor Statistics Occupational and Employment Survey.

artificially suppress compensation for workers who provide the services they consume. More on this soon.

In the meantime, it should be emphasized that even these data, striking as they are, fail to fully capture the difference between symbolic capitalists and other workers. This is because, in addition to our generous wages and salaries, symbolic capitalists tend to enjoy significantly better benefits, perks, and working conditions compared with other workers, which can make a huge difference with respect to quality of life.[30] We also enjoy much higher social status than virtually everyone else. Across geographic and temporal contexts, status seems to be awarded primarily on the basis of perceived competence or virtue.[31] In the contemporary world, across cultural and gender lines, the most status-enhancing things people can do include attending a prestigious university; obtaining a college degree; coming across as intelligent, creative, or knowledgeable; holding a well-paying job; and serving in executive capacities or roles.[32] As a consequence of broadly shared tendencies to award status along these dimensions, even people from low-status backgrounds tend to become high status (relative to "normies") once they become symbolic capitalists.

However, the symbolic professions are not just a means through which elites secure their own social position (and lock "others" out)—they are also used by elites to transfer accrued symbolic capital across generations. In recent decades, the children of symbolic capitalists have increasingly adopted professions similar to their parents. For instance, the child of an anthropologist may become a sociologist, or a curator at a museum. Someone whose parents work in advertising may end up as a journalist, lobbyist, or graphic designer instead. By continuing in their parents' professions, or choosing a closely associated one, children of symbolic capitalists are able to draw from the accumulated knowledge and connections of their parents, helping them acquire a well-paying job and rise through organizational ranks at a more rapid speed.[33] Comparative studies looking at the United States and other advanced economies have found that the symbolic professions have become a central means for reproducing inequalities across generations—exerting perhaps a greater influence than class per se on transferring advantages and shaping life chances.[34]

We see a similar story at the macro level. Symbolic exchange has largely displaced physical production at the center of economic activity. Although most employees in the United States continue to work in the productive economy (at a ratio of nearly two to one), symbolic industries are approaching the lion's share of GDP. Finance, insurance, and real estate (FIRE) is the largest industry sector by "value added" overall, despite the fact that this sector does not *produce* anything—it mostly extracts rents on assets and phenomena that already exist or are theorized to be produced downstream. After FIRE comes professional and business services. Manufacturing comes in at a somewhat distant third.

What's more, symbolic economy firms largely own the rest of the economy and often dictate how it operates. One study found that a small number of transnational corporations (1,318 out of more than 43,000 total) directly controlled more than 20 percent of all global revenues. These firms also collectively owned (via shares) a majority of the world's largest "real" economy firms, representing an additional 60 percent of the global economy. A small subgroup of this elite set, 147 companies (mostly in FIRE), controlled 40 percent of the entire network—a network that, again, directly and indirectly governed roughly 80 percent of the global economy.[35] However, even data like these, in many respects, understate the centrality of symbolic economy in contemporary life.

As philosopher Roberto Unger explains, it is insufficient to simply look at which economic sectors control the highest share of GDP or employ the largest number of workers in a country or control most company stock. To determine which mode of production is "dominant," we must also consider which has the greatest capacity to reshape how people in a society live, how we relate to one another, and how we do work in all other sectors.[36] Following the "agricultural revolution," farming clearly played this role. It led

TABLE 3.3. The Symbolic Economy versus the Productive Economy

Industry sector	Value added by industry as a percentage of GDP (2021 averaged)	Percentage of American workers in major industry sectors, 2021
Manufacturing	10.7	7.8
Health care and social assistance	7.5	12.7
Wholesale trade	6.2	3.6
Retail trade	6.0	9.7
Construction	4.1	4.7
Transportation and warehousing	3.0	3.9
Accommodation and food services	2.9	8.9
Utilities	1.6	0.3
Mining and extraction	1.4	0.3
Agriculture, forestry, fishing, hunting	0.9	1.4
Total	44.3	53.3
Finance, insurance, real estate (FIRE)	21.0	5.6
Professional and business services	13.0	13.4
Information	5.6	1.8
Educational services	1.2	2.3
Arts, entertainment, recreation	0.9	1.3
Total	41.7	24.4

Sources: U.S. Bureau of Labor Statistics; U.S. Bureau of Economic Analysis.
Note: This chart excludes the government industry sector because they are not easily categorized in either camp. On the one hand, government bureaucrats tend to be highly paid symbolic capitalists. However, the government sector also includes vast numbers of police officers, bus drivers, and others who provide physical goods and services—and who are often compensated at much lower levels than bureaucrats. The "other services" industry sector was similarly excluded due to concerns of ambiguity. As a consequence, the columns do not sum to 100 percent.

typically small nomadic bands of hunters and foragers to form much larger, sedentary, and increasingly hierarchical communities.[37] Following the Industrial Revolution, the manufacture of physical goods displaced agriculture as the dominant mode of production, radically transforming where and how people lived, and recasting power relations yet again.[38] And today, Unger argues, it is the "knowledge economy" (or in my verbiage, the "symbolic economy") that plays this role.

Previous modes of production, such as agriculture and manufacturing, have themselves been completely reshaped by the knowledge sector (giving rise, for instance, to "smart" manufacturing and "smart" farming), even as their relative social prestige has been diminished. Rather than the growing and harvesting seasons—or the Monday-through-Friday, nine-to-five factory workdays—it is the knowledge economy that sets the pace of contemporary life. Its modes of organization increasingly pervade all other economic sectors, and indeed society writ large: constant connection and exchange, unending data collection and surveillance, algorithmic curation of options, personalized products or services, "on-demand" availability, and so on. Virtually everything, from state governance to entertainment to sexual relations, is increasingly inflected with these logics.

An implication of Unger's argument is that professionals associated with the symbolic economy exert immense influence over the shape, character, and trajectory of society—far more than their (relatively high) incomes, wealth, or status might suggest.

Inequalities in Context

The amount of money symbolic capitalists take home every year is higher than for virtually anyone else in society. The only competitive nonsymbolic occupational group is "health-care practitioners and technicians"— and those who compose one of the largest and best-compensated sets of actors within this group, physicians, are perhaps best understood as symbolic capitalists too (in contrast with, say, surgeons or others who more directly intervene on physical bodies).[39] That said, there is wide variation in pay *among* symbolic capitalists depending on the specific work they do. Jobs in finance, for instance, tend to be compensated much more highly than those in education.

There are also profound inequalities within the symbolic professions along the lines of gender and race. Female-skewed symbolic occupational groups tend to be less well compensated than those that favor men. In fact, the gender pay gap is actually wider among workers who possess a college degree than for those without.[40] Moreover, despite the rhetorical focus on diversity, equity, and inclusion in these spaces, the symbolic professions skew overwhelmingly and disproportionately white—much more so than nonsymbolic occupational groups. Within the symbolic professions, Black and Hispanic professionals also tend to earn significantly less than other occupational peers.

TABLE 3.4. Comparing Occupational Pay, Demographics, and Share of Total Workforce

Minor occupation group	Average salary, 2020 (USD)	Percentage of total workforce, 2020	Percentage of occupation employees: Non-Hispanic white, 2020	Percent of occupation employees: Male, 2020
Management, business, and financial	94,769	15	71	54
Computers, engineering, and science	89,942	6	64	73
Health-care practitioners and technicians	83,339	6	67	24
Education, legal, community service, arts, media	56,625	11	70	34
Protective services	54,903	2	59	76
Installation, maintenance, and repair	51,735	3	67	96
Sales and related	51,468	10	65	47
Military	50,074	< 1	62	86
Construction and extraction	47,919	5	56	96
Production	42,620	6	56	70
Office and administrative support	38,864	11	62	25
Transportation and material moving	37,401	8	53	79
Farming, fishing, and forestry	28,164	< 1	41	72
Health-care support	27,300	3	46	14
Building and grounds cleaning and maintenance	27,288	4	44	59
Personal care and service	23,339	3	57	25
Food preparation and serving	19,637	6	52	45
OVERALL	55,954	100	62	52

Source: Data USA. Data from U.S. Census Bureau and American Community Survey Public Use Microdata Sample 5-Year Estimate.

It is critical to put these facts in perspective, however. Although Black professionals earn on average eighty-one cents for every dollar earned by white professionals, the gap between Black people who are professionals and those who aren't is larger still (African Americans who do not belong to these occupations earn only sixty-seven cents for every dollar earned by Black professionals). That is, Black professionals may experience systemic disadvantage compared with white professional peers, but this does not erase the reality that they are elites compared with most other Black people and, indeed, most other Americans writ large. To the extent that Black

TABLE 3.5. Median Weekly Earnings by Race/Ethnicity and Occupation, 2017–2019 (USD)

Professional affiliation	White	Black	Hispanic	Asian American and Pacific Islander
Management occupations	1,527	1,175	1,153	1,730
Business and financial operations occupations	1,304	1,135	1,058	1,442
Computer and mathematical science occupations	1,404	1,138	1,233	1,605
Architecture and engineering occupations	1,676	1,595	1,579	1,730
Life, physical, and social science occupations	1,410	1,268	1,363	1,553
Community and social service occupations	942	865	881	983
Legal occupations	2,001	1,689	1,680	1,952
Education, training, and library occupations	1,036	923	961	1,059
Arts, design, entertainment, sports, and media occupations	1,057	933	899	1,165
Health-care practitioner and technical occupations	1,251	1,117	1,199	1,466
Average for U.S. professionals	1,288	1,045	1,080	1,498
Average for U.S. workforce overall	965	702	673	1,042

Source: V. Wilson, Miller, & Kassa 2021. Data from Economic Policy Institute Current Population Survey Extracts, Version 1.0.15.

professionals cast themselves as poor or marginalized because they earn less than other *elites*, they are misrepresenting (and likely misunderstanding) social reality.

Likewise, within the symbolic professions there is a growing bifurcation allowing some symbolic capitalists to enjoy still *higher* incomes and social status by exploiting other symbolic capitalists. At the upper end of the spectrum are professionals engaged in the most creative and nonroutine labor. They enjoy an especially high degree of autonomy, flexibility, and authority. They are compensated well, with great benefits and secure employment. They tend to possess advanced degrees. At the lower end of the spectrum, the work is more about executing someone else's vision and doing the tasks that higher-ranking symbolic capitalists find tedious or otherwise unpleasant. This work tends to be much more routine in nature (rendering some of these jobs vulnerable to loss via outsourcing or automation). These positions are also more likely to be contingent or unstable, with workers drawn on as a reserve labor pool by multiple organizations or actors in order to complete particular tasks. Their labor is generally not compensated nearly as well. Although these positions tend to require fewer (and less prestigious) credentials, even at the low end of the spectrum most symbolic capitalists possess at least a BA.

Once again, there is systematic variation with respect to who persists in which camp: whites, men, people from relatively affluent backgrounds, and graduates of elite schools are especially likely to occupy more prolific positions and in more prestigious institutions—and they tend to spend far less time in the lower rungs of organizational hierarchies compared with peers who are women, minorities, or from less privileged backgrounds. In virtue of these facts, one might be tempted to interpret many who fall into the less prestigious group of symbolic capitalists as nonelites. This would be a mistake.

As sociologist Shamus Khan has explained, there is a sense in which income or wealth is an incomplete measure for marking out elites.[41] Symbolic capitalists' dominance over knowledge production, cultural curation, institutional bureaucracies, and (through these) the political sphere often affords us far more sway over society than most other Americans. As society has been reoriented around the symbolic economy, the people who traffic in data, ideas, knowledge, and representations have been growing, and continue to grow, ever more influential—even when they're not pulling in above-average incomes (although, typically, they are).

Indeed, even though their pay and benefits are low relative to peers in more permanent and prestigious roles, symbolic capitalists on the low end of the spectrum still tend to earn about as much as or more than they would if they pursued work outside the symbolic professions.[42] They tend to enjoy much better working conditions than most other workers as well (even if their working conditions tend to be significantly worse than many other symbolic capitalists). Some from this "lower" tier of symbolic capitalists earn well into the six figures doing contracting, consulting, and other contingent labor, and *choose* to do this kind of work in order to enjoy greater employment flexibility (and are often empowered to do so because they are partnered with someone who retains the "traditional" employment benefits they are walking away from).[43]

As a concrete example from my own neck of the woods, consider the plight of contingent faculty members. Full-time non–tenure line faculty tend to bring in less than half as much money per year as full tenured professors. Nonetheless, 2022 American Association of University Professors estimates show that full-time instructors, lecturers, and unranked faculty take home between $66,000 and $73,000 per year on average.[44] For context, according to U.S. Bureau of Labor Statistics estimates, the median salary of full-time year-round workers in 2022 was roughly $60,000. In fact, full-time contingent faculty members don't just earn more than most other workers, they *individually* collect roughly the same income as the median *household* in America. Without a doubt, contingent faculty are exploited relative to tenured and tenure-track professors. However, it is also critical to bear in mind that the challenges they face generally pale in comparison to the kinds of problems that exploited nonsymbolic workers have to deal with.

Moreover, irrespective of salaries, benefits, and the like, symbolic capitalists tend to enjoy *much* higher levels of social prestige from their work relative to other laborers.[45] Indeed, many who inhabit relatively low-paid roles within the symbolic professions persist in part because they prioritize symbolic capital over financial capital: they would prefer to be a freelance writer or a part-time contingent faculty member (earning an average of $3,874 per course section)[46] rather than work as a manager at the Cheesecake Factory, or a flight attendant, or a truck driver, or a postal worker—even if they could make a bit more money, with more stable income and better benefits, doing these other jobs instead. And symbolic capitalists often have the ability to make that choice due to other advantages they possess over others.

The people who occupy the *really* low-paid positions within the symbolic professions (working for free or nearly so) are often able to persist in these roles while living in expensive cities (rather than relocating to somewhere more affordable but less glamorous and doing something else with their lives) because they are supported in part or in full by families or partners who tend to be relatively affluent, or because they have a nest egg of their own. Symbolic capitalists generally try to "stick it out" in these positions *not* because they lack other options but rather because they view even the unglamorous and poorly compensated work they're doing as more valuable or meaningful than pursuing other forms of employment that might pay more in the short to medium term—and because they view these contingent jobs as stepping stones to positions with especially high pay, benefits, and social prestige.[47]

In the meantime, the lack of compensation helps reduce the number of competitors for higher-pay, higher-status positions by weeding out most of those who are *not* from elite backgrounds early in the process (because most nonelites are unable to sustain themselves for long on little to no pay). Working in these relatively lowly positions also helps elite aspirants feel as though they have "earned" any eventual high-paying posts they might secure. As a consequence, if they are able to outlast the other competitors and successfully make the leap to the higher echelons, they demonstrate little sympathy or solidarity with those occupying the positions they used to hold. Instead, they often assert that others need to "prove" themselves in the same ways that *they* did—by being subjected to the same kinds of pressures and degradations that *they* had to endure. Exploiting others and being exploited are thereby recast as a virtue game—as a means of revealing the most driven, the most skilled, and the most tenacious players (rather than serving as a means of filtering out and, in the meantime, taking advantage of women, minorities, and people from more humble socioeconomic backgrounds).[48]

None of this is to suggest that exploitation within the symbolic professions is trivial or unproblematic. Rather, the point is to illustrate that even those symbolic capitalists who *are* exploited are not really in the "same boat" as most other workers[49]—and what's more, they generally don't want to be (Awokenings, again, are driven by frustration among certain symbolic capitalists that they are not as elite as they feel they "should" be). More importantly, irrespective of where they fall within the symbolic professions, and irrespective of their ancestry, gender, sexuality, and other identity characteristics, symbolic capitalists' lifestyles tend to be premised heavily on the precarious and poorly compensated labor of *non*–symbolic capitalists— especially those who are immigrants, minorities, or women.

Disposable Labor(ers)

Compared with other Americans, symbolic capitalists possess idiosyncratic tastes and unusual lifestyles. These preferences and expectations are generally fulfilled by exploiting desperate and vulnerable people, whose poverty and precarity are prerequisites for the elite lifestyles we enjoy.

For instance, although significant inequalities remain between the genders, highly educated women of middle- and upper-class backgrounds have achieved significant gains in the professional sector. In some circles, this is portrayed as a great victory for feminism. And yet, this change has *not* come about due to some major change in gender roles—for instance, because men have taken on a reciprocally larger share of domestic responsibilities. Generally speaking, they have not.[50]

Within highly educated households, for instance, wives continue to perform significantly more domestic work than husbands. Highly educated mothers also engage in much more intensive parenting compared with either their husbands or less educated mothers.[51] Elite couples typically try to reconcile their traditionally gendered relationship patterns with the progressive gender ideologies they explicitly subscribe to by justifying divisions of labor in instrumental and gender-neutral ways. As one study put it, insofar as highly educated couples "understand the [domestic labor allocation] processes as gender-neutral, they can write off gendered outcomes as the incidental result of necessary compromises made among competing values."[52] The fact that women do the overwhelming majority of the domestic and caregiving work in symbolic capitalist households is recast by *both* parties as a mere coincidence—just the way things "happen to work out" situation to situation, day after day.

Of course, the persistence of this gendered division of labor raises an obvious question: Given that there has *not* been a major shift in gender roles or domestic responsibilities within elite households, how have highly educated women been able to make such significant gains in the professional sphere? Largely by offloading domestic responsibilities onto *other* women—poorer women, typically women of color, disproportionately immigrants.[53] Within a growing number of symbolic capitalist households, "other" women are tending to children while the parents are at work or socializing. Likewise, "other" women are preparing and serving meals, cleaning the home, caring for the sick and elderly, tending to pets, and so on. Symbolic capitalist families have typically been able to profit from having two salaries *despite* purchasing increasing quantities of domestic labor by paying these "other" women below-market (often nonlivable) wages for their services.[54]

Within symbolic capitalist households, even sex is being increasingly outsourced to "other" women. Contemporary American adults report having less sex with their partners than previous cohorts—a trend that is especially pronounced among highly educated and married couples.[55] Yet there has been a simultaneous increase in demand for prostitution, particularly in symbolic economy hubs, facilitated by online platforms that allow relatively well-off urbanites to procure sex on demand—to shop for sexual services the same way they shop for dining options, and to rate providers much like restaurants are reviewed on Yelp.[56] Those who regularly connect to sex workers through internet sites like the Erotic Review ("hobbyists") are disproportionately white, married, highly educated, and financially well off. More than 84 percent earn above the median national income in the United States; about 43 percent make $120,000 per year or more; 79 percent have a BA or higher, and 41 percent possess graduate degrees. More than 84 percent are white.[57] Sex workers, on the other hand, are primarily cis and trans women of color (and often immigrants)[58]—although clients are willing to pay more for providers who are white. Here, too, there is a strong premium on degrees:

highly educated sex workers tend to earn much more money for less work and are treated significantly better by their (highly educated) clients as compared with those who lack college education.[59]

More banal forms of shopping have also been transformed by symbolic capitalists' reliance on "disposable labor." As a function of their relatively high incomes and geographic concentrations, symbolic capitalists generally have more shopping options available to them than virtually anyone else in the United States. Nonetheless, relatively well-off urban residents are *much* more likely than anyone else in America to buy things online rather than in-store.[60] However, they still want to get their hands on desired merchandise within a time period that rivals in-store shopping—the same day or, at most, a couple of days. And they want all of this without significantly increased expense—at least, without additional expense *to themselves*. Instead, the costs for fulfilling these preferences are typically transferred to *others*, whose exploitation plays a central role in providing elites with the immediate gratification they demand.

With respect to online retail purchases, orders are translated into parcels that arrive at one's doorstep thanks to tens of thousands of warehouse workers who toil under immense strain and deplorable conditions. At Amazon, the largest online retailer in the United States by far, individual movements and productivity for fulfillment center employees are constantly and relentlessly tracked. Failure to hit the always-intense quotas can lead to one being written up or terminated. This disciplinary process is often automatic—carried out by machines, with little option to appeal and little regard for any extenuating circumstances.[61] If you don't hit your targets, you are punished. Your peers are quite possibly punished alongside you (by being denied team-based performance incentives). Journalists have documented how the resultant desperation leads many workers to skip eating, to urinate in trash cans, or to hold their waste until they develop urinary tract infections[62] because the windows workers are provided for breaks are impossibly short, and the quotas seem otherwise impossible to reach. The intense pressure many employees feel to hit their targets leads to unsafe behaviors: rates of serious injuries at Amazon warehouses are nearly twice as high as in the industry overall.[63]

Critically, Amazon's exploitative labor practices do not end at the warehouse doors. Once the fulfillment centers have packaged the orders, parcels are transported to metropolitan hubs by undercompensated truckers.[64] They ultimately arrive at one's home by means of post office workers and delivery contractors who are overburdened by the sheer quantity of packages to be distributed (paired with their employers' desires to keep staffing as low as possible).[65] Like warehouse workers, Amazon's drivers are constantly surveilled by AI systems and given unreasonable quotas—and they face abrupt termination if they fail to reach them.[66] And just like fulfillment center employees, drivers are punished for bathroom breaks, leading people to regularly urinate in their vehicles.[67] Worse, many feel pressured to drive recklessly in order to hit their quotas. This has resulted in unnecessary injuries and deaths to bystanders throughout the country.[68] Injury rates to drivers are also extreme, with nearly one in five (18 percent) reporting harm in 2021. This is more than double the injury rates of non-Amazon package deliverers.[69]

Many of the vendors Amazon lures to its platforms also end up as its victims. The company often draws small businesses into participating in its Amazon Marketplace under the auspices of supporting local vendors and expanding the reach of small businesses. In reality, the company often kills participating businesses, apparently quite willfully. Through various fees, Amazon typically takes more than a third of all revenues from transactions done on their platforms—in many cases, taking most or all of the *profit* companies stand to receive from transactions.[70] Many small businesses often end up *losing* money on orders placed through Amazon as a result of the company's high commissions and fees. Hence, even when vendors actually *do* reach more customers through the Amazon Marketplace, they often end up making substantially less money overall. Worse, should businesses deliver a product that proves profitable and popular despite these obstacles, Amazon often creates its own version of that good, copied very closely (typically labeled as an Amazon Basics product, but sometimes sold under private-label brands like Rivet or Goodthreads), sold at a much lower cost, and made to appear higher in search results.[71] This often forces businesses to lower their prices even further to compete, or else increase contributions to Amazon in order to improve their search rankings. These moves by Amazon tend to simultaneously reduce vendors' sales volume and their profit margins, often driving them out of business altogether. And the closures of these small businesses often bring myriad adverse side effects for the communities they were embedded in.

Critically, killing off small businesses is a feature and not a bug of Amazon's approach. From the outset, the company has operated by selling goods at an unprofitably low price (often below the manufacturer's suggested retail price) in order to drive competitors out of business and capture their customers. The Amazon Marketplace likewise seems oriented around pressuring or enticing small businesses around the country to convert their customers into Amazon customers and then cutting local businesses out of the picture entirely once it has captured their clients (and, in many cases, emulated their most successful products), so that Amazon can take an even higher cut of all transactions and become the direct supplier for those products (and anything else customers might need).[72]

The company's brutal approach to labor is also quite intentional. It is not lost on managers or corporate executives that most workers cannot maintain the intensity Amazon demands of them for very long. The employee turnover rate at Amazon is nearly double that of the rest of the retail and logistics field. This is not an accident: founder Jeff Bezos (in)famously described an entrenched workforce as a "march to mediocrity."[73] His company willfully pushes manual laborers to the point of burnout and then casts them aside when they're all used up.[74] Amazon understands that this approach is not sustainable in the long run. The goal has always been to lay off most of their human workforce outright once they were able to replace them with machines.[75] After all, machines don't need breaks or overtime or benefits. They can't lawyer up or organize. There's no public outcry or government investigations or civil suits if the company breaks one of its machines.

In the meantime, all of the exploitation just described is the cost of saving symbolic capitalists some trips to the store (or even to multiple websites)— and to spare us the indignity of waiting a reasonable amount of time to receive online orders. "Everything" is available on one site, the prices are low, and the shipping is fast and "free" because *others* are paying high costs to make this a reality. And we *love* Amazon for its willingness to exploit these others on our behalf. According to one striking study by the Baker Center at Georgetown University, Democrats (America's "left-wing" party) place more "institutional confidence" in Amazon than in any other company or institution in America. Faith in Amazon is higher than in colleges and universities, nonprofit institutions, the press, religious institutions, any branch (executive, legislative, judicial) of government at any level (local, state, federal), labor unions, the military, law enforcement—you name it.[76]

The runaway success of Amazon has led many to imitate its business model to provide not just goods but also services to symbolic capitalists—taking advantage of urban elites' high disposable incomes, our inclination to have everything "on demand," and our apparent indifference to the treatment of workers and small businesses that satisfy our desires.

For instance, symbolic capitalists are especially inclined toward eating from restaurants. A growing share of residences in symbolic economy hubs don't even have kitchens because renters often don't use them and, increasingly, don't really know how to cook at all.[77] However, for large and growing numbers of symbolic capitalists, it is not enough to simply have others prepare food for us—we often insist that meals are rapidly delivered to our homes as well (as it is apparently too much for us to pick up the food ourselves, let alone actually dining *at* the restaurants we order from). Unsurprisingly, the cities with the highest per capita spending on food delivery are all major symbolic economy hubs: New York City, San Francisco, Boston, Los Angeles, and Miami[78]—with the average consumer expenditures per year driven heavily by outsize spending among professionals within these cities.

Within symbolic economy hubs, food deliveries are overwhelmingly and increasingly orchestrated through third-party platforms such as DoorDash, Grubhub, and Uber Eats (rather than customers ordering directly from the restaurants they wish to eat from). These apps are convenient for symbolic capitalists, allowing us to scroll menus and order food from myriad establishments on a single site. Like Amazon, they afford us the convenience of one-stop shopping from our smartphones. However, also like Amazon, the use of these platforms is often devastating for local businesses.

Restaurants have always operated on slim margins: even for a healthy restaurant, only about 10 percent of revenues will generally be left over as "profits" (after subtracting rent, supplies, labor, utilities, and other necessary expenses). Because companies like DoorDash often take 30 percent or more of all revenue for orders placed through their apps, establishments typically end up fulfilling these orders *at a loss*.[79] However, because customers prefer the use of these apps, and competitors are allowing customers to order through these apps, many businesses feel as though they have little choice except to follow suit in order to avoid losing customers who occasionally make *profitable* orders as well (for instance, by dining in-restaurant, or calling in and picking up orders themselves). Indeed, even when restaurants explicitly decline to do business with delivery apps, they are often simply added without consent (a move platforms make in order to avoid having to negotiate more favorable terms with local businesses).[80]

Critically, it's not just the restaurants that are shortchanged. Only a tiny fraction of the money raised by the delivery companies goes to the people making the deliveries. One study found that DoorDash deliverers took home an average of $1.75 per hour after taxes and operating expenses were factored in—and they actually *lost* money on roughly a third of their deliveries (i.e., they incurred more expenses to deliver the food than they received in wages, commissions, and tips for the delivery).[81] Even in relatively lucrative markets like New York City, app-based food deliverers average roughly $12 per hour in gross compensation—far below the general state minimum wage of $15 per hour. After deducting the considerable expenses incurred to do their jobs, they earn on average $7.87 for each hour worked—significantly below the *pre*-tip minimum wage for tip-eligible food service workers in New York ($8.65).[82] The picture is little better for those who deliver groceries (rather than prepared food from restaurants) through platforms like Instacart.

Across the board, delivering food for third-party apps is grueling, high-pressure work. Deliverers are exposed daily to road hazards and the elements. Indeed, customers become *especially* likely to lean on these apps when it is dangerous or miserable to go out. This was true during the COVID-19 pandemic, when professionals chose to keep *themselves* safe by exposing "others" (largely poor people and minorities) to risk in order to procure things on their behalf. This was also true in 2021's Hurricane Ida, when food delivery workers in Manhattan were forced to navigate historic flood conditions in order to allow professionals to enjoy take-out food during the storm (professionals who often tipped poorly, to boot).[83] It is likewise true during blizzards and heat waves, and all manner of other terrible conditions.

On top of this, much like Amazon, food delivery apps provide workers with extremely tight windows to complete deliveries, and deprioritize or drop couriers who do not hit their windows, often pushing workers to navigate cities in an unsafe way in order to keep working. According to 2020 U.S. Bureau of Labor Statistics estimates, couriers and express delivery workers hold one of the most dangerous jobs in America, with rates of occupational illness and injury that are 2.6 times higher than the average for workers overall.[84] And because those who deliver for these "gig" companies rarely receive benefits, should workers get sick or injured, they typically have to pay out of pocket for any care they receive, and earn no compensation while they are out of commission.[85] Hence many work even when they are unwell because they don't really have a choice—a decision that often puts them at higher risk for even *more* severe illness or injury down the line.

Within urban areas, the people filling these jobs are disproportionately immigrants and minorities. According to an estimate presented in the *New York Times*, roughly 80 percent of delivery app workers in New York City are undocumented immigrants (primarily from Central America, Africa, and Asia).[86] Studies in San Francisco, Boston, and other major cities have produced similar findings to the *Times'* reporting on New York City: while the workers fulfilling orders are widely represented as "side-hustlers" attempting to earn some "extra" money in their downtime via casual work arrangements, in fact most orders are being fulfilled by people working full time as deliverers. This reality is partially concealed in company data because workers are typically forced to work with multiple platforms (e.g., DoorDash, Uber Eats, *and* Grubhub) in order to make ends meet, and they often fail to reach full-time hours with any of them *individually*. Moreover, these studies have found that the app-based delivery workforce has shifted dramatically toward minorities and, especially, immigrants over time—and the pay and autonomy for these jobs have declined significantly as the workforce has grown more diverse.[87]

In a nutshell, orders placed via food apps commonly generate losses for the restaurants fulfilling the orders, sometimes driving them under. Deliveries tend to be made by vulnerable and marginalized individuals working heavy hours, under difficult conditions, with low compensation and few benefits or protections.[88]

Similar realities hold with respect to delivering *people*. What are Uber and Lyft drivers, for instance? They are chauffeurs for people who cannot deign to drive themselves around, take public transportation, or even exert the minimal effort of hailing a cab.[89] They provide members of the new elite with an experience formerly available only to the rich: having someone available at their beck and call to transport them privately wherever they want to go, whenever they want to go there. How has this service been rendered affordable to white-collar professionals? Rideshare companies outsource expenses like insurance, gas, vehicle acquisition, and maintenance to the drivers themselves,[90] provide few benefits, and offer such low compensation that contractors typically have to work well over full time just to make ends meet if this is their only "gig."[91] Companies try to portray this last fact as unproblematic by claiming that most drivers are just working for them part time in order to supplement other income (consequently, their wages and benefits don't *need* to be livable). This narrative, while technically factual, also fails to tell the truth.

Within symbolic economy hubs, while most *drivers* "on the books" may be part time, a majority of *rides* are actually provided by the subset of drivers who work more than thirty-two hours per week.[92] Critically, this is just looking at data *within* individual companies. But as with food couriers, many who may be categorized as "part time" on one particular app *are* in fact driving full time—just splitting their assignments over multiple apps (typically driving for both Uber *and* Lyft). That is, the actual full-time driver workforce these companies rely on—and the share of rides provided by full-timers— is likely much higher than can be observed by looking at the companies individually. As these are data that *external* researchers have been able to glean from public reports and empirical investigations, it is safe to assume that none of these facts are lost on company executives. Yet they continue to publicly (and deceptively) profess that their services are provided by casual workers side-hustling to earn some spare change in their free time: students looking for some pocket money, housewives with some free time while the kids are at school, bored retirees, and so on. In reality, as with food delivery apps, rideshare drivers (especially the full-timers) are disproportionately minorities, especially immigrants, and people of humble socioeconomic means—often struggling to keep a roof over their head, working long hours with few benefits or workplace protections, and living in precarity.

Nonetheless, it is also the case that many others *do* drive part time—drawn in by (unrepresentative and often inaccurate) stories of people making tidy sums of money for doing very little work and putting in just a few hours here and there in their free time. Most of these more casual workers do not last long (months at the most), as it quickly becomes clear that the only way to really make any money from these apps is to reorient one's life around them— and again, even people who spend all day every day driving for rideshare companies tend to barely scrape by. As a consequence, the "churn" for rideshare companies tends to be extraordinarily high—even relative to other service work.[93] This constant turnover has two somewhat contradictory effects. First, it renders long-term and full-time drivers even *more* critical to companies in order to ensure a consistent and positive customer experience: were it not for the fact that most rides are provided by durable full-timers, rideshares would be extremely unreliable, unpredictable, and undesirable for most (rides would be perennially delivered by neophytes with unstable availability, little commitment to the job, and inadequate knowledge or experience to efficiently navigate the city). At the same time, however, the constant inflow of new recruits hoping for a quick buck helps to perennially suppress the wages of full-timers by artificially inflating the apparent "supply" of drivers.

Yet, despite providing little pay, benefits, or protections for their workers, rideshare enterprises have consistently operated at a loss—propped up by vulture capitalists who quite explicitly plan on radically jacking up fares as soon as taxis have been effectively killed off, or else laying off all their human "contractors" once self-driving car technology sufficiently advances—whichever comes first (again, cribbing the Amazon model).[94] Unfortunately for these companies, taxis have proved more resilient than many projected. Meanwhile, the pursuit of self-driving cars has proved to be more protracted, demanding, and expensive than many anticipated.[95] And now that companies like Uber and Lyft have gone public, raising billions in their initial public offerings, they have a fiduciary duty to shareholders to provide consistent returns on investment. In order to meet these obligations (and get "in the black"), Uber and Lyft have been forced to significantly increase their fares[96] (which have always been artificially low, even after accounting for poor driver compensation). Yet the revenue generated by these rate hikes is being directed almost entirely toward paying out dividends to the aforementioned shareholders— *not* the drivers through whom this wealth is derived. Stock prices have plummeted despite these maneuvers, as it is becoming increasingly obvious to investors that their profit model is not sustainable (and never was). And it's not just rideshares: food delivery apps[97] and other "urban millennial lifestyle" services are experiencing similar crises for roughly the same reasons.[98]

For their part, customers often seem blissfully unaware of these tensions. Indeed, beyond their low fares (provided largely by imposing expenses on drivers) and ease of use, perhaps the most valuable service these companies provide to clients is that, in serving as a middleman between the customers and exploited workers, they eliminate any sense of responsibility for laborers among those who consume their services. With respect to drivers, for instance, chauffeurs tended to be direct *employees* of a family or a company— and they typically got paid regardless of whether their clients needed to be driven around much on a given day or not. If there was a problem with the vehicle, the employer was typically obliged to help remedy the situation if they wanted to get driven around. Rideshare customers, however, get all the benefits of having a chauffeur without any of the social obligations. If professionals don't have anywhere to go, drivers get nothing. If their cars break down, it is up to *drivers* to remedy the situation, out of their own pockets. If said drivers can't pay their bills as a result of either of these factors, that isn't the client's problem. It isn't anyone's problem but their own.

Symbolic capitalists love intermediaries like Uber, Grubhub, and Amazon precisely because they carry out the requisite exploitation to enable symbolic capitalists' idiosyncratic preferences and lifestyles, but they also help create a "distance" between symbolic capitalists and the workers exploited on their behalf. Clients are rarely forced to understand or confront the actual costs of the cheap and disposable labor they rely on. *We* simply experience goods and services being delivered according to our preferences in a fast, frictionless, and affordable manner (thanks to the magic of the internet, according to popular mythology). And we often punish workers when they fail to help us maintain our preferred illusions.

For example, as we will see, symbolic capitalists tend to prioritize physical fitness—dedicating significantly more money and time toward health and wellness than any other segment of American society. Yoga and spin classes are especially popular, but many engage in other forms of guided exercise too. Sessions tend to be offered at all hours to cater to client schedules. Classes are usually small in size or altogether private, and are regularly carried out in well-appointed studios or in the client's home (sometimes remotely). The people leading these lessons are often struggling to get by—receiving low pay, few benefits, inconsistent hours, and highly unpredictable and insecure employment conditions. There are significant disparities along racial and gender lines in terms of how much clients and companies are willing to pay these workers, and whom they are willing to retain as permanent or full-time staff. Yet fitness professionals (fitpros) typically go to great lengths to hide their struggles. Clients attend these sessions to escape the "real world" rather than confront it—and they expect sessions to be all about *themselves*, their own needs, their own progress, and so on. As historian Natalia Petrzela put it, "Looking like you're living your best life—even if you woke up at 4 A.M. in the Bronx to teach a 6:30 A.M. class in TriBeCa on knees that are shot because otherwise you won't get paid and have no insurance—is an important part of the job. Indeed, many fitpros feel a responsibility to maintain that fantasy beyond the studio via social media. Interrupting that embodied ideal by pointing out labor conditions rather than panting inspirational exhortations is in itself a considerable professional peril. . . . Fitness instructors are as successful as the image of leisure and wellbeing they project."[99] Those who fail to provide elites with the sense of escape they are looking for tend to quickly find themselves without clients or income.

And it's not just the services symbolic capitalists consume that tend to be especially exploitative, but often the goods we prefer as well. Consider restaurants offering the "organic," "fair trade," "free range," or otherwise "ethically sourced" products we tend to gravitate toward: given the high cost of the ingredients themselves, establishments often try to keep their prices relatively affordable (for professionals, at least) by paying subpar wages to "back of the house" workers who, disproportionately, tend to be immigrants and minorities.[100] Meanwhile, the "front of the house" workers at these higher-end restaurants (where someone can actually make solid money from waiting tables) are much more likely to be white.[101] Women and minorities, who form the overwhelming majority of waiters, servers, and hostesses, tend to be more heavily concentrated in less lucrative restaurants, where they often earn less than the minimum wage (even after tips) and struggle to survive. Across the board, because their livelihood is contingent on the whims of their patrons, these workers are often forced to endure racism, sexism, harassment, and other forms of demeaning and degrading behaviors from customers—with a smile on their face—in order to make a living.[102]

Similar dynamics hold with respect to the "urban manufacturing" of high-quality, small-batch, specialized (or "artisanal") goods sold in trendy, high-end, or boutique stores—increasingly popular among symbolic capitalists. Such goods are regularly described as "American made"—a label that perhaps leads many to assume that they were constructed by well-paid craftspeople who are doing this work out of their passion for the product. Often this perception is reinforced by the progressive values the companies producing these goods purportedly aspire to, and the apparently middle-class workers who often work the "front" of the stores. In reality, making these more specialized items at a rate and price that symbolic capitalists find acceptable generally leads vendors to rely on urban sweatshops, typically staffed by undocumented workers who receive subpar wages, with no benefits, and who work under horrible conditions.[103]

Across the board, industries that cater to more high-end clientele tend to have significantly higher wage inequality.[104] The "front of the house" people whom elites engage with directly are often compensated and treated relatively well (reinforcing the illusion that the products in question are ethical), while less visible workers experience subpar pay and working conditions. Moreover, in areas where wealth is being concentrated in America today, minorities (and especially immigrants) are especially likely to do domestic work, food service, retail, construction, janitorial, groundskeeping, security, and maintenance jobs—providing the infrastructure and services that empower (disproportionately white) symbolic capitalists to do *their* work and live *their* lives in relative comfort and ease.[105]

Symbolic capitalists actively seek out cities with "diversity" and "amenities." The "diverse" workers who provide these amenities often live precarious lives—facing down high costs of living, uncertain employment, long hours, low (and inconsistent) wages, few benefits, poor schools, pollution, and fear of crime *and* law enforcement. Their marginalization, vulnerability, and desperation allow symbolic capitalists to extract labor and services from them at an extremely low cost. And once their purpose has been served, these workers are casually cast aside.

Symbolic Hubs

In the 1970s and 1980s, as the symbolic economy was coming into its own, there was a widespread and growing perception that America's great cities were dying. As a result of automation and outsourcing, manufacturing jobs began disappearing at a fast rate. In the wake of this dedustrialization, many U.S. cities faced high levels of unemployment. Drug use, especially crack cocaine, was on the rise. Violent crime and property crimes were as well. Pollution was out of control. White people, especially well-off professionals, increasingly moved to the suburbs and exurbs. Many companies relocated their headquarters in turn. And without professionals patronizing local businesses, still more workers soon found themselves unemployed. All of this resulted in a lower municipal tax base—prompting cuts to city services and infrastructure projects. Urban decay accelerated, driving still more residents who were capable of leaving to flee. Cities seemed to be in a death spiral.[106]

However, although the 1970s were a rough time for many urban institutions and constituencies, they turned out to be a transformative period for colleges and universities and their role in American society. Institutions of higher learning were able to acquire property at extremely low prices, secure immense tax breaks, and extract many other important concessions from the cities they were embedded in (and state and federal governments besides). As the shift to the symbolic economy grew increasingly pronounced, colleges and universities positioned themselves as keys to urban renewal. The result, as urbanist Davarian Baldwin explained, was the rise of UniverCities.[107]

In many urban areas, colleges and universities have carved out semiautonomous zones. They are the primary landlords in these areas (and often in the city as a whole), allowing them to set rents in ways that drive out existing residents—at times partnering with the actual government to seize private property from others under the auspices of eminent domain. They close many roads to public traffic. They lock others out via walls, gates, and doors that require university credentials to access—privatizing many formerly public spaces. They have their own private security forces that exert jurisdiction over not only the university itself but the entire area under its domain—empowered to surveille, harass, detain, and at times commit violence against others as they see fit (students, staff, and the public alike), with even less transparency and accountability than regular cops.[108] Within these areas, and sometimes in the city writ large, colleges and universities are also the largest employers—allowing them to dictate prices for various goods and services, set wage ceilings for the rest of the city for various types of work, bust unions, and snuff out competition. In short, within these fiefdoms, the vast majority of the population lives in university-owned buildings, works for the university or one of its contractors, gets health care from the university health system, is policed by campus security, and is bound not just by state, local, and federal laws but often by a host of additional university-imposed rules and norms—upon penalty of being expelled from the UniverCity (with all that entails for their lives and livelihoods).

There is a clear hierarchy of how different people are valued within UniverCities. Students (the "paying customers") are at the top, followed by university faculty and administrators. Most others are essentially third-class citizens. Granted, the students cycle in and out of the community every few years while these "others" remain—because the city is actually their *home*. Nonetheless, denizens of UniverCities are perpetually subordinated to the whims of twentysomethings who are just "passing through"— twentysomethings whose demographic characteristics, values, and priorities are often sharply at odds with those of the more durable residents.

UniverCities, and the broader metropolitan areas they are embedded in, form the backbone of the symbolic economy. They serve as central hubs for research, collaboration, and exchange. For historically and geographically contingent reasons, specialized differences have emerged between these symbolic hubs. For instance, Chicago became a key hub for commodities, New York City for finance, Los Angeles for movie and television production, Nashville for music, Boston for technology, and Washington, DC, for lobbying and policymaking—with "circuits" of exchange connecting cities with similar or complementary specializations across the country and around the world.[109] Alongside these specialized economic differences arose systematic variations in culture among symbolic capitalists. Seattle, San Francisco, Austin, Atlanta, Miami, and Boston all have very different vibes with respect to architecture, clothing, food offerings, prominent forms of art and entertainment, and so on.

That said, there are a number of characteristics that tend to unite cities that emerge as key focal points of the symbolic economy—responding to tastes and preferences common to virtually all symbolic capitalists. For example, as Richard Florida's research shows, symbolic capitalists generally demand amenities like beautiful parks, bike paths, diverse and high-quality restaurants, convenient and reliable transit options, and so forth.[110] They gravitate toward cities with a vibrant cultural (art, music, nightlife) scene. And they aggressively purge anyone who isn't "their kind of people."

Since 1970, cities have grown increasingly segregated along the lines of race, wealth, employment, and education status. Whites, the affluent, the employed, and the college educated have been concentrated heavily into particular regions of cities, while racial and ethnic minorities, the poor, the less educated, and the unemployed or underemployed are concentrated in others. This sorting has been especially pronounced within symbolic hubs and is driven heavily by symbolic capitalists.[111]

Although relatively affluent, highly educated white liberals are among the strongest proponents of affordable housing *in principle*, they often adopt a "not in my backyard" position with regard to their own communities. Studies have consistently found that as cities trend increasingly left, denizens tend to choke off new housing development.[112] This significantly increases costs of living and drives out poorer residents—contributing greatly to racial segregation and the consolidation of minorities into areas of "concentrated disadvantage" (increasingly in suburbs and exurbs, creating significant commutes for people who do service work, while reducing their access to critical resources).[113] Lower-income and minority residents are gradually replaced by highly educated, Democratic-voting, relatively affluent (disproportionately white) professionals.[114] Yet symbolic capitalists' fairly blatant maneuvers to preserve or increase the value of their own property (thereby building their wealth), and to restrict the neighborhood to the "right" kind of people, are often framed in anticapitalist terms—as "ordinary joes" banding together against ruthless real estate developers who want to destroy the "character" of their neighborhoods.[115] Actions that dislocate the poor and further disadvantage minorities for the sake of affluent professionals are described as if they were socialist revolts.

As the work of Richard Florida and others has emphasized, symbolic capitalists tend to cluster in places that are perceived to be liberal, tolerant, and diverse. In reality, however, most symbolic capitalists have fairly homogeneous social networks: their lovers, close friends, and coworkers tend to be the same race or ethnicity as themselves, and generally share similar educational and class backgrounds too.[116] Although symbolic hubs tend to be extremely diverse, interactions among people of different classes are rare and fleeting (occurring primarily in the context of lower-class people selling goods or providing services to professionals).[117] Beyond these interactions, symbolic capitalists tend to live in different neighborhoods, send their kids to different schools (even when they live in the same neighborhood), attend different places of worship (if at all), shop in different stores, and engage in different modes of recreation.

Yet, although they do not necessarily *engage* in a meaningful way with people different from themselves, symbolic capitalists nevertheless like to *see* diversity when they are traversing the city. They want to have the *option* of forming relationships with a diverse cadre of people, even if they don't often exercise that option—indeed, even as their own behaviors actively undermine that possibility. They love diversity and inclusion in principle, but generally not at the expense of their property values or aesthetic preferences. As a function of these contradictory responses to diversity, life often becomes quite precarious for those who live at the frontier of symbolic capitalists' domains.

Higher-income people who are drawn to "frontier" spaces between the wealthy and the poor tend to be symbolic capitalists (typically young professionals or artists), and they lean overwhelmingly "blue" in terms of their politics.[118] Despite the leanings, as symbolic capitalists begin to colonize an area, policing tends to grow much more frequent and aggressive—even for small crimes.[119] Calls placed to 311 also rapidly increase, largely due to new white residents complaining about minorities being too loud or unruly. Studies have found that these calls by new white residents are especially likely to result in arrests (compared with 311 calls by others). Lower-income nonwhites are the overwhelming majority of those arrested.[120] In a similar vein, an investigation by the Center for American Progress found that a plurality of 911 calls in major symbolic economy hubs are for nonemergency, low-priority incidents.[121] Most commonly, callers are attempting to sic armed police on those who are homeless, mentally unwell, or under the influence of drugs or alcohol. Often, however, callers end up reporting someone for simply "walking while Black" or "driving while Black."

These same residents happen to be the prime urban constituencies for services like Nextdoor or the ironically named Citizen and Neighbors apps— used to surveille, report, and discuss "suspicious" individuals and activities in one's community. Those flagged as "suspicious" in gentrifying areas are overwhelmingly people of color—often just doing their jobs (i.e., delivering packages, reading meters) or passing through their own neighborhoods.[122] And when even these efforts prove insufficient to establish the kind of order gentrifiers prefer, many pool their money to retain private security firms to patrol their neighborhoods as well.[123]

It deserves to be emphasized: these are "liberal" metro areas we're talking about here—symbolic economy hubs. Indeed, those calling the police on people of color for things like taking shelter from the rain, failing to wave at a white passerby while leaving their Airbnb, sitting in their own car waiting for yoga class to start, accidentally brushing up against a white person in a store, selling water on the street, or barbequing in a public park—the people who regularly seek out law enforcement for things like loud music, loitering, "suspected" criminal activity, or domestic disturbances—tend to be relatively well off, highly educated, liberal, white denizens who are eager to "clean up" or "protect" their adopted neighborhood.[124] In *practice*, what they are often doing is using police to punish people of color who are insufficiently deferent to their own demands or preferences or who simply violate their aesthetic sensibilities (such as homeless people).[125] However, their ostensibly antiracist convictions seem to make it difficult for symbolic capitalists to "see" their own behaviors this way. After all, they often moved into these neighborhoods in the first place because they are "historic," "cultured," or "diverse."[126] That is, although symbolic capitalists tend to define themselves in terms of open-mindedness, tolerance, and an embrace of diversity, how these values are expressed "in the world" is often much different from what their rhetoric might suggest.

Sex and Symbolic Capital

Symbolic capitalists nearly unanimously possess college degrees as preconditions for their jobs. In the United States, 81 percent of college-educated breadwinners who happen to be married are partnered with someone who also possesses at least a BA. Degree holders whose parents also graduated college are still more likely to marry a fellow degree holder: 86 percent of married degree holders with college-educated parents are partnered with someone who has a degree.[127] This "assortative mating" is a significant driver of inequalities between more and less educated households. According to one estimate, inequality in the United States would be reduced by at least a fifth if assortative mating on education was scaled back to 1960s levels.[128]

The gender dynamics underlying these patterns are complex. On the one hand, these trends have been driven primarily by preferences among women. To this day in the United States, just as in other historical and cultural contexts, women overwhelmingly prefer men who earn more than they do. This preference is even more pronounced among highly educated women.[129] Indeed, when highly educated and professionally successful women earn more than their husbands, they often feel embarrassment and resentment toward their spouses and become significantly more likely to initiate divorce (in the contemporary United States, divorces are overwhelmingly initiated by women).[130]

However, this preference to "marry up" (or at least "marry equal") puts many educated women in a bind because even as women have become increasingly educated, are increasingly employed, and are earning more than they have in the past, the opposite trends are taking root for men. Male college graduation rates have been relatively stagnant, and men are growing *less* likely to be employed, to live independently, and so on.[131] These trends, which were already severe, have been greatly exacerbated by the COVID-19 pandemic.[132] Indeed, in many symbolic economy hubs, especially New York, Los Angeles, and Washington, DC, young women are now making more than young men on average—a pattern driven by disparities in education between the sexes (and the heightened importance of education for earnings in these locales).[133] Consequently, insofar as they desire a partner who earns as much as or more than themselves, highly educated or professionally successful heterosexual women are forced to compete ever more intensely with one another for an ever-diminishing pool of acceptable guys.

The big "winners" in this arrangement are elite men. Even as growing numbers of nonelite men find themselves increasingly "unmarriageable" (even undatable), men who are well educated, affluent, or upwardly mobile are having more sex than ever.[134] The decline of men overall gives *them* even more power to dictate the terms for sex and relationships.[135] In contexts with significant gender imbalances, as the ratios skew more intensely female, men become less likely to commit to relationships. Women, meanwhile, grow less confident, more sexually permissive, and more concerned with conforming to the apparent preferences of desirable male partners.[136]

And what do elite men want? Across the board, men tend to prefer women who earn less than them and are comparably or less educated.[137] This reality may help explain why, in contexts where opportunities for women approach parity with those for men, gender differences in career choices actually *increase* rather than decrease:[138] were elite women to fully capitalize on the opportunities available to them, their dating and marriage prospects may be greatly diminished. That is, in a world where women aggressively pursued the highest-earning jobs they could obtain, elite men would likely continue to gravitate toward those women who had comparably *less* education or income than themselves—rendering it difficult for high-earning women to secure a high-earning male partner, or perhaps any stable male partner at all (as, again, relationships where women outearn men tend to be less durable). Indeed, research has found that men in the highest income category are 57 percentage points more likely to marry than men in the lowest income category. For women, income has a mild *inverse* correlation with probability of marriage. And while the highest-income married men have a much lower probability of divorce compared with those in the lowest income category—and are similarly more likely to get remarried in the event of divorce (typically to someone younger)—for women, the situation is reversed. The highest-earning married women are *more likely* to undergo divorce than the lowest-earning married women, and the effects of income on probability of remarriage are empirically uncertain.[139]

To be clear, it is unlikely that many elite women *consciously* decide to choose a suboptimally earning career path in order to avoid being punished on the dating and marriage market. These kinds of social coordination processes play out more subtly than that and, truthfully, are not yet well understood.[140] Moreover, there are many other factors that likely play a large role in decisions to "opt out" of certain high-paying careers as well—including hostile work environments in many male-dominated symbolic capitalist spaces. However, from a behavioral perspective, it is nonetheless clearly the case that this tendency among many women (to choose courses of study and careers that are well compensated but not the *highest* earning) does help heterosexual men *and* women find acceptable high-earning partners. And when they are able to successfully form unions, the household income for *both* partners is radically enhanced compared with a world where elite women chose to maximize their individual earnings but were unable to find an acceptable partner or were forced to more aggressively "marry down" because elite men preferred to do the same.

Beyond income and education considerations, highly educated and wealthy men also tend to be far more concerned than most about their partners being attractive and physically fit.[141] It is perhaps not a coincidence that highly educated Americans, especially highly educated *women*, spend significantly larger shares of their leisure time engaged in physical exercise than most others, are much more conscious about their diets, and are more likely to pursue elective cosmetic medical procedures[142]—even as they encourage *others* (i.e., potential competitors) to look however they want and enjoy whatever body type they happen to have. Likewise, women who live in metro areas with high levels of socioeconomic inequality (such as symbolic economy hubs) tend to spend much more money on clothes and at beauty salons compared with other women, and they're much more likely to post sexualized pictures of themselves online.[143] Across many lines of research, the picture is clear: the types of women who take part in the symbolic professions seem to be engaged in much more aggressive aesthetic intrasex competition than comparably positioned men or less elite women.

Yet with respect to physical appearance, important filtering has often taken place even before college: those who are perceived to be physically attractive tend to get better grades and treatment throughout their K–12 journey and are much more likely to go to college, to persist through college to graduation, and to attain relatively high-paying positions postgraduation.[144] How much more likely? Sociologists have found that the magnitude of earning disparities between more and less attractive people rival the size of race gaps in earnings.[145]

Indeed, attractiveness is itself an important source of symbolic capital. Those viewed as more physically attractive than average also tend to be perceived by others as being especially intelligent, authoritative, trustworthy, and competent (the so-called halo effect)—and they view *themselves* as especially talented, moral, and hardworking too (and are more confident and extroverted, on average, as a result).[146] Given that symbolic capitalists trade largely on how people perceive them and who they are connected to, and because attractiveness significantly enhances social perceptions and facilitates relationship building, it is no wonder that highly attractive people tend to cluster in the symbolic professions (where returns on the halo effect tend to be especially pronounced). Nor should it be surprising that symbolic capitalists seem to be especially attentive to physical appearance.[147] However, the intense competition among elite women to secure acceptable male partners seems to exacerbate these trends (helping to explain why the differences between symbolic capitalists and everyone else on all the dimensions just explored tend to be especially pronounced among *women*).

"Woke" ideologies play an interesting role in reinforcing these gender dynamics. For instance, women who self-identify as "feminists" (who, as we have previously explored, are especially likely to be highly educated, relatively affluent whites) exhibit much stronger preferences for premium beauty products as compared with nonfeminist women. The practical purpose and effect of these investments is to help elite women stand out relative to female rivals—both in professions where looks matter for symbolic capital and in dating and mating markets that heavily favor elite men. Yet these investments are often justified in the name of female empowerment.[148]

In *American Hookup*, sociologist Lisa Wade similarly details how college-educated women often try to reconcile their personal desires, political beliefs, and the stark realities they are faced with on the dating market by essentially defining "hookup culture" in feminist terms.[149] They try to convince themselves that it is empowering for women to emulate the purported male ideal of casual, emotion-free, commitment-free sex. And for some, perhaps it is. Yet, Wade's research showed, most women actually found this arrangement to be unsatisfying and coercive. Many felt they *had* to be willing to "hook up" in order to be considered a viable dating option at all (at least, for the kind of men they were interested in). Those who wanted to "take things slow" found themselves consistently passed over in favor of those willing to "put out." When relationships were initiated, they tended to turn primarily around sex. Women often found themselves unable to signal desire for more depth or commitment, lest they be perceived as "clingy" (and be subsequently abandoned in favor of someone who was more willing to engage "without strings"). Even in purely physical terms, the women in Wade's study rarely achieved orgasms during sexual encounters because, in a dating market so heavily tilted in favor of elite men, successful males often felt little obligation to reciprocate sexual favors or ensure encounters were *mutually* satisfying.

And yet, on dating apps, elite men regularly portray themselves as committed feminists, antiracists, and anticapitalists in order to lure college-educated women. There's even a term for it: woke fishing.[150] On its face, it may seem absurd for *any* online daters to paint themselves as social justice revolutionaries given that, across genders, the people who use these apps tend to be elites. U.S. Tinder users, for instance, skew urban, upper socio-economic status, and highly educated.[151] But in fact, and perhaps counter-intuitively, this strategy may work because precisely what a "radical" profile signals to potential mates *is* one's elite status. Again, "woke" discourse is deployed primarily by highly educated elites affiliated with the symbolic professions. It can therefore serve as a means for symbolic capitalists to identify others like themselves. On most dating apps, where the vast majority of users tend to be men, and the overwhelming majority of these men are undesirable to most female users, filtering for "woke" profiles may be a good heuristic for helping elite women identify partners who can meet or exceed their own earning potential.

Here again, I am describing how woke dating profiles seem to function *in practice*, not necessarily by design. That is, women likely do not *consciously* seek out woke profiles as a means of identifying high–socioeconomic status men, and elite men may not *consciously* present themselves as socially progressive as a means of signaling their high social status. However, such profiles do clearly indicate socioeconomic status: nonelite men generally would not have the ability to produce a convincingly woke dating profile, nor see it as an advantage for them to do so. And highly educated women, who are the most concerned with securing a high-earning mate, *do* use signaled political affiliations to identify compatible partners. Indeed, empirical studies have found that it is primarily upper–socioeconomic status and highly educated users who are prone to disclose their political leanings in dating profiles, and who gravitate toward political affiliation as a means of selecting matches.[152]

In any case, it is clear that many women are finding it increasingly difficult to find an acceptable male partner, and that these shortages are particularly acute among college-educated women (and also, statistically, African American women).[153] According to research by the American Enterprise Institute's Survey Center on American Life, nearly half (45 percent) of single women with a college degree say "not being able to find someone who meets their expectations" is a major reason they're single (with an additional 28 percent describing this as a minor reason they remain unpartnered). For contrast, only one-third of college-educated men, 28 percent of non-BA women, and less than a fifth of non-BA men view this as a major obstacle to forming a relationship.[154]

Faced with a shortage of men who earn as much as, or more than, themselves, a growing share of highly educated or high-earning women are deferring or opting out of marriage altogether rather than "marrying down."[155] While unsuccessful men are being pulled into "incel" culture, growing numbers of *successful* women are identifying as "femcels" and resigning themselves to indefinite celibacy,[156] or else freezing their eggs to extend their "biological clock" while they hold out hope for an acceptable mate.[157] Still others are expanding their sexual horizons.

According to Gallup, the share of Americans who identify as LGBTQ increased by 60 percent from 2012 through 2020 (rising from 3.5 percent up to 5.6 percent).[158] The trends were driven almost entirely by *women* (who shifted toward LGBTQ identity at three times the rate of male peers). Moreover, they occurred almost exclusively among millennials and Gen Z—that is, the age groups that are forced to contend with the lopsided dating market just described. In terms of education, the shifts were most pronounced among college grads, for whom the rate of conversion was roughly 50 percent higher than for those who have not obtained at least a BA (non–college grads became roughly 1 percentage point more likely to identify as LGBTQ between 2012 and 2017; for college graduates it was 1.5 percentage points). In terms of race or ethnicity, minorities gravitated toward LGBTQ identity at a faster pace than non-Hispanic whites. And the shifts overwhelmingly entailed women from these categories (liberal, highly educated, under forty) coming to define themselves as "bisexual" (rather than, say, as lesbian or trans).

Using data from the General Social Survey, sociologists D'Lane Compton and Tristan Bridges identified virtually the exact same patterns.[159] Between

2008 and 2018, there was a 72 percent increase in the number of Americans who identified as lesbian, gay, or bisexual (rising from 2.9 percent of respondents up to 5 percent). They found that these shifts were driven virtually entirely by women, and particularly by the subgroups of women facing the most acute shortages of marriageable men: racial and ethnic minorities (especially Black women), women under thirty-five, and those who are college educated. And like Gallup, they found that the changes were almost exclusively a product of more women from these categories coming to identify as bisexual; the number of Americans identifying as lesbian or gay was essentially flat between 2008 and 2018.

From a sociological standpoint, it is highly significant that the changes in sexual orientation are overwhelmingly driven by women—and the particular subset of women who face acute shortages of eligible men. It likewise telling that the shifts mostly entail these women coming to identify as bisexual. According to Pew estimates, roughly nine out of ten partnered people who identify as bisexual are currently in a relationship with someone of the opposite sex.[160] Among 2018–2021 General Social Survey respondents, most women under thirty who identify as bisexual report *exclusively* male sexual partners over the last five years.[161]

Collectively, data like these suggest that many of the women newly identifying as bisexual still primarily desire to settle down with an opposite-sex partner—and the increased apparent openness to same-sex relationships is driven largely by a dearth of acceptable males. Put another way, the observed shifts in sexual orientation in the United States may have less to do with changing values, aspirations, and preferences, and more to do with upwardly mobile young women trying to cope with a highly competitive and increasingly bleak heterosexual dating and marriage market. This is emphatically *not* to suggest that the growing numbers of bisexual women are being insincere in their sexual identification. The claim is merely that, although these women may be genuinely sexually attracted to people of both genders, statistically speaking, they do not seem to be *equally* interested in males and females. In *practice*, they strongly favor males. At the macro level, these shifts in sexual identification may not have occurred to the same extent (if at all) in a world where the heterosexual dating and marriage market was less off-kilter.

The good news is that female symbolic capitalists open to partnering with other women can generally find numerous high-quality dating and marriage options in symbolic economy hubs and in the symbolic professions. As Richard Florida's data show, although symbolic capitalists are overwhelmingly cisgender and heterosexual, they tend to cluster in cities that are especially

LGBTQ friendly and possess a vibrant "gay scene."[162] LGBTQ people, in turn, are particularly likely to settle in cities that have a robust "creative class," and to work in the symbolic professions themselves.[163]

In terms of household prosperity, lesbians tend to earn more than heterosexual women.[164] And much like their cisgender and heterosexual peers, *married* LGBTQ Americans tend to be more educated and prosperous than most others in the United States. In fact, on average, lesbian and gay married couples enjoy significantly higher household income than their heterosexual married counterparts.[165] Recent research likewise suggests that children raised by married same-sex couples tend to outperform most others in terms of educational attainment.[166]

All said, male or female, straight or queer, symbolic capitalists are more likely than most to settle into long-term, committed, and monogamous relationships—typically with other people who are also highly educated and high earning.[167] And they leverage those relationships to enhance the social position of their households relative to everyone else. Indeed, although symbolic capitalists are the Americans most likely to disparage "traditional families," they are also among the most likely to have hailed from "traditional families" themselves, and to establish "traditional families" of their own.[168] And not for nothing: family structure, sequencing, and stability can make a huge socioeconomic difference in one's own life trajectory and earning prospects—and for those of one's children as well.[169] Symbolic capitalists "bristle at restrictions on sexuality, insistence on marriage or the stigmatization of single parents. Their secret, however, is that they encourage their children to simultaneously combine public tolerance with private discipline, and their children then overwhelmingly choose to raise their own children within two-parent families."[170]

In light of these realities, it's striking that symbolic capitalists so regularly and conspicuously denigrate *to others* the very strategies they use to ensure their own socioeconomic prosperity—and typically in the name of social justice, no less! Social psychologist Rob Henderson referred to positions like these as "luxury beliefs":[171] it is easy to encourage everyone to be satisfied with their appearance insofar as one happens to be physically fit and conventionally attractive oneself. It is easy to declare it unnecessary to find a "breadwinner" when one happens to be earning far more than most Americans and is well positioned to find a partner who can do the same. It is easy to describe traditional families as unnecessary and outmoded when one has already reaped the benefits of growing up in a traditional family structure and is well on the way to producing a traditional family oneself. However, were the less privileged to internalize and live in accordance with these espoused beliefs, it would generally be to their detriment. It would render them less competitive. It would hinder their social mobility. Luxury beliefs, in a nutshell, entail striking cosmetically "radical" postures on social issues that help elites signal and reinforce their social position, often at others' expense. Nonelites would be well advised to ignore what symbolic capitalists *say* and look at what we *do* instead. Those interested in understanding contemporary inequality would be well served by adopting the same strategy.

Coda: Rich, White, and Blue

Across the board, with few exceptions, those who lack at least a BA tend to be outright excluded from the symbolic professions. Within the symbolic economy, the possession of a degree (and where it is from) shapes which voices are deemed worth listening to or taking seriously; which candidates for a position are worth considering; and who has access to institutions of cultural or political influence as bureaucrats, politicians, teachers, journalists, researchers, artists and entertainers, and so on. Indeed, even religious leaders are increasingly expected to be "credentialed." Consequently, those who tend to be systematically excluded from colleges and universities will tend to be even more dramatically underrepresented in the symbolic professions and possess relatively low symbolic capital overall.

There are dramatic disparities in educational attainment in the United States along the lines of race, gender, and class. For instance, a white American is twice as likely to have a PhD as a Black American, and nearly four times more likely to hold a PhD than a Hispanic American. U.S. men are 33 percent more likely to possess a PhD than U.S. women, and 27 percent more likely to possess a professional degree (JD, MD, etc.), despite women significantly outpacing men for AA, BA, and MA credentials. As a function of these disparities, jobs that require a BA will exclude 83 percent of African Americans right out of the gate (and an even higher share of Hispanics). A job that requires an MA will exclude 95 percent of Hispanic Americans. When a preference for elite schools is added in, the disparities grow even more pronounced.[172]

Nonetheless, as a growing share of the U.S. public began to attain college degrees, the educational requirements for symbolic economy jobs increased—as did employer preferences for credentials from elite colleges and universities.[173] Consequently, the symbolic professions tend to be highly

TABLE 3.6. Postsecondary Completion Rates, Highest Attainment by Race/Ethnicity and Sex, Americans Twenty-Five Years and Older, 2021

Self-identification	AA	BA	MA	PhD	Professional
Asian (alone)	6.7	33.7	19.6	5.4	2.3
Male	9.5	22.8	9.5	2.4	1.8
Non-Hispanic white (alone)	11.1	26.0	11.8	2.3	1.8
U.S. average (total population)	10.5	23.5	10.7	2.1	1.5
Female	11.3	24.1	11.9	1.8	1.3
Black (alone)	10.6	17.2	8.6	1.3	1.0
Hispanic (any)	9.0	14.5	4.8	0.6	0.7

Source: U.S. Census Bureau.

unrepresentative of America as a whole. To illustrate just how out of step they tend to be, consider the demographic breakdown of the professoriate.[174]

Disaggregating these data by institutional rank reveals even deeper disparities: tenured professors are especially likely to be white and male. Black, Hispanic, Indigenous, and female scholars, meanwhile, are especially likely to occupy part-time and contingent faculty positions, with much lower pay, benefits, job security, institutional authority, and academic freedom.[175] They also tend to be concentrated into less prestigious and lower-paying schools (including two-year colleges),[176] and in fields where faculty are not compensated as well.[177] Put another way, even as more nonwhites are aspiring to become professors, a growing share of aspirants are being dumped into a disposable labor pool, with systematic variance along the lines of race, gender, ideological leanings, and socioeconomic or regional background with regard to who gets sorted where.[178] The growing stratification of academic faculty roles in recent decades is striking because, over this same period, the professoriate has also grown far more politically progressive. In 1969, liberal professors outnumbered conservatives by 1.7 to 1. By 2019, it was 6.9 to 1. Moreover, the ideological constitution of schools is correlated strongly with prestige: the more elite a school is, the more homogenously liberal it tends to be.[179]

For a host of reasons, it would be difficult to include the socioeconomic backgrounds and the community types (rural, urban, suburban) that faculty were typically raised in within this same breakdown. However, an ambitious recent study exploring the socioeconomic backgrounds of faculty

TABLE 3.7. How the American Professoriate Compares with the Broader U.S. Population: Full-Time Professors at Four-Year Colleges and Universities

Self-identification	Percentage of U.S. professoriate	Percentage of U.S. population	Percentage over- or underrepresented in professoriate (relative to general population)
Non-Christian faith	13	4	+225
Politically "left"	62	24	+158
Asian and Pacific Islander	11	6	+83
LGBTQ	8	5	+60
Religiously unaffiliated	31	20	+55
White	69	60	+15
Man	52	49	+6
Woman	48	51	−6
Politically "moderate"	29	35	−20
Christian	53	76	−30
Black	6	13	−54
Hispanic	6	18	−67
Politically "right"	9	37	−76

Sources: Data on the professoriate from the National Center for Education Statistics and the Higher Education Research Institute. Baseline data on U.S. adults from same-year estimates by the U.S. Census Bureau and Gallup.

members found that nearly nine in ten professors seem to have grown up in urban areas; on average they enjoyed household incomes that were 23.7 percent higher than the national average at the time of their childhoods. More than three out of four grew up in houses their parents owned (also higher than national averages during their childhoods). Most faculty had at least one parent with an advanced degree; nearly three-quarters had a parent with at least a BA. Moreover, the authors found, those raised by one or more parent with a PhD were significantly more likely to land a *tenure-track* position at an elite school as compared with faculty whose parents did not have terminal degrees.[180] Across the board, the overwhelming majority of tenured and tenure-track faculty hail from a small number of elite schools, which themselves cater primarily to students from well-off families.[181]

In short, tenured and tenure-track college professors represent a very narrow geographic and socioeconomic slice of society. They are highly unrepresentative of the rest of the country demographically and ideologically as well. However, the professoriate is *not* an outlier relative to the other symbolic professions.

Take journalism as an example: more than nine out of ten contemporary journalists have a BA or higher (as compared with fewer than six in ten journalists in 1971).[182] Ubiquitous degree requirements for journalism jobs tightly constrain the field—de facto excluding the overwhelming majority of African Americans, Hispanics, people from rural backgrounds, low-income, and working-class Americans from taking part in the journalistic enterprise. Other industry factors intensify this exclusion.

Over the last few decades, media organizations have been consolidated into the hands of a small number of companies. In 1983, roughly 90 percent of all media were controlled by fifty companies. By 2012, that stat had been reduced to six companies.[183] Even local newspapers and television conglomerates are increasingly being bought up by huge conglomerates.[184] There have been massive layoffs of journalists nationwide, and a huge and growing share of the media jobs that remain have been centered in a small number of coastal metropolitan hubs.[185] These consolidations have led to a significant decline in coverage of local issues (and the issues locals care about).[186] People in "flyover country" therefore not only are left with few outlets to influence the *national* discourse but also have less capability to make their voices heard even at the state or local level. Instead, local and state news has largely been replaced with nationalized and centralized news, contributing to the "nationalization of politics" in turn.[187]

Media organizations have contemporaneously become more politically parochial. Although the profession has long skewed left, in 1971 roughly 25.7 percent of U.S. journalists identified as Republican; this was a figure not much lower than the general population at the time (28 percent). By 2022, however, only 3.4 percent of journalists identified with the GOP. Republicans have gone from being outnumbered 1.4 to 1 within the journalism profession to being outnumbered by more than 10 to 1.[188] And this is just in terms of *formal* partisan affiliation. Although a majority of journalists identify as "independent," polls show they tend to donate to or vote for Democrats at far higher rates than their explicit identification might suggest.[189]

Moving beyond the narrow partisan political divide, the values and priorities of journalists tend to be far out of step with those of most other Americans. For instance, 76 percent of Americans believe that journalists should strive to cover all sides of an issue with equanimity; only 44 percent of journalists share this sentiment.[190] Likewise, a recent study by the Media Insight Project found that journalists also tend to emphasize social criticism over focusing on solutions or things that are going right or working well. They tend to reactively side with rebels and minority populations in conflicts at the expense of more dominant groups. Only about 20 percent of the public aligns with journalists in terms of values and priorities like these—primarily, highly educated liberals. What's more, the Media Insight Project found that the wide moral chasm between journalists and the rest of the public is widely recognized by laypeople, and it significantly undermines their trust in journalistic outputs.[191] Nonetheless, journalists tend to labor under the mistaken impression that their values and politics are broadly aligned with "the people."[192]

Beyond being consolidated along the lines of geography, ideology, and education, the journalistic profession has also increasingly become a profession by and for the affluent. As communication scholar Christopher Martin demonstrated, around the same time that the Democratic Party shifted away from the working class (in the late 1960s), journalists did as well. Working-class issues and working-class readers were largely abandoned in favor of more "upscale" and "sophisticated" audiences; labor was cast aside in favor of consumer and business interests.[193] However, the changes were not just in the stories produced and how they were covered—there were roughly contemporaneous shifts in the socioeconomic backgrounds of journalists themselves.

Much like university faculty, a hugely disproportionate (and growing) share of contemporary media interns, reporters, and editors hail from a small number of highly selective schools—a reality that is especially pronounced at "prestige" media institutions. Indeed, outlets like the *New York Times*, *Wall Street Journal*, and *New Republic* tend to have higher shares of graduates from elite schools than *Fortune* 500 CEOs, the U.S. Congress, or federal judges. They have shares of elite school graduates comparable to that of the *Forbes* Billionaires list.[194]

Similar to academia, newsrooms have come to increasingly rely on poorly compensated (or altogether uncompensated) labor. Freelancers are typically paid little to nothing because the pool of people desperate to have their work published *anywhere* (especially prestige media outlets) has grown so large.[195] Many are convinced they *must* give away content for free, in order to build a portfolio that would allow them to charge for content later (or to have a chance at being hired as a staff writer somewhere). Moreover, interning is now viewed as an almost necessary rite of passage to land a secure and well-compensated media job—especially if one aspires to work at a prestige media outlet. But of course, it is a very particular type of young person who can work long and flexible hours without getting paid (or barely getting paid), yet still survive in the expensive cities that media organizations are located in: people who come from wealthy backgrounds. Indeed, much like journalists themselves, interns at flagship news organizations tend to hail overwhelmingly from highly selective schools that cater primarily to the well-off.[196] Consequently, journalism's increased reliance on freelancers and interns has reinforced and accelerated its transformation into a profession of privilege.

This is a problem, of course, because journalism was founded *as* a profession under the auspices of holding elites to account. This becomes much more difficult to do in a world where the rich, the powerful, and the famous are also journalists' family, friends, lovers, and mentors; when they have convergent socioeconomic and political interests; when they share similar backgrounds, life experiences, tastes, and worldviews (all of which clash dramatically with those of the hoi polloi). It has become *especially* difficult to hold to account the new class of symbolic capitalist millionaires and billionaires who directly underwrite many contemporary journalistic enterprises and also *in*directly fund news organizations via "sponsored content" (advertisements made to look like regular news stories) purchased by the nonprofit and advocacy organizations these superelites control.[197] Not only do journalists broadly sympathize with these new oligarchs and their social and political agendas, they also want to keep the checks coming. These ties and incentives can influence coverage in all sorts of subtle, often unconscious, ways—irrespective of how sincerely committed the affected journalists might be to independence, rigor, and other purported values of the profession.[198]

With respect to race and ethnicity, much like academia, the media industry writ large skews significantly whiter than the general population. Flagship publications tend to be even worse with respect to racial and ethnic diversity than most other journalistic outlets. And as unrepresentative as journalists are relative to the general U.S. population, they are even more out of sync with the demographics of the cities that media outlets tend to be based in. These dynamics grow even more pronounced as one moves "up" the organizational ladder: editors and executives are significantly more likely than journalists themselves to be non-Hispanic whites. Likewise, journalistic editorial and executive positions continue to be dominated by men.[199] At the very highest level, of the people who direct the six newspapers with the largest

TABLE 3.8. Demographics of Selected Occupations by Percentage of Total Workforce, 2022

Occupation	Percentage women	Percentage white	Percentage Black	Percentage Asian	Percentage Hispanic
U.S. workforce overall	46.8	77.0	12.6	6.7	18.5
News analysts, reporters, and journalists	48.4	79.8	13.1	3.0	8.8
Writers and authors	57.3	87.7	6.7	4.5	7.3
Technical writers	65.1	87.6	0.0	9.5	9.2
Editors	66.0	91.5	2.6	3.5	3.0
Graphic designers	53.7	82.0	6.3	7.7	12.9
Photographers	47.8	83.3	8.4	3.7	15.8
Artists and related workers	49.2	83.9	6.1	5.7	14.5
Public relations and fundraising managers	64.3	87.4	8.9	2.9	7.5
Public relations specialists	67.0	81.4	12.2	2.4	11.9
Promoters, agents, managers for public figures, performers, entertainers, or events	42.7	68.2	19.0	8.1	17.9
Advertising and promotions managers	49.7	80.3	13.8	4.4	8.9
Marketing managers	58.9	83.9	6.8	7.5	11.4
Advertising sales agents	52.1	85.6	7.8	5.4	9.9

Source: U.S. Bureau of Labor Statistics. Readers should note that the Bureau of Labor Statistics does not currently separate out Hispanic from non-Hispanic whites. Hence, racial and ethnic statistics typically sum to more than 100 percent. Full dataset available in U.S. Bureau of Labor Statistics 2023b.

circulations, the three major broadcast networks, the three big cable news channels, and the websites with the most monthly visitors, 80 percent are non-Hispanic whites and 73 percent are male.[200]

Although the lack of diversity in many U.S. newsrooms is often explained as a "pipeline problem," it is also the case that minority graduates in communications or journalism are not being hired when they hit the job market. An investigation by *Columbia Journalism Review* found that graduating minority students in journalism or communications were significantly (17 percentage points) less likely to land a media job as compared with white graduates.[201] A big part of the story seems to be that minority graduates are less likely to possess credentials from elite schools (which many institutions prefer). They're also less likely to be able to afford to do unpaid internships and are less connected to elite networks (through which many affluent whites find jobs). In short, the growing educational and socioeconomic elitism within U.S. media reinforces disparities along racial and ethnic lines as well.

Nonetheless, a 2022 Pew Research poll found that nearly half of U.S. journalists believe news organizations do a good job "giving voice to the unrepresented." Less than a quarter of the broader public agreed.[202] This is another of many cases where laymen seem to have a better handle on the situation than practitioners. As communications scholar Nikki Usher memorably argued, news media is increasingly becoming an industry by and for the "rich, white and blue."[203] Yet these trends are hardly limited to the journalistic sphere. They are pronounced in the arts and entertainment industries more broadly.

Although these industries lean overwhelmingly Democrat, with few exceptions, they also skew disproportionately white. Those calling the shots in these industries are *especially* likely to be white and male. For instance, on its face, the motion picture and film industry seems close to parity with the broader U.S. population in terms of race and ethnicity—although women are heavily underrepresented. However, looking at producers and directors, a different picture emerges. Women are a little better represented, minorities less so. According to 2022 U.S. Bureau of Labor Statistics estimates, producers and directors are 83 percent white, 3 percent Asian, and 9 percent Hispanic (with African Americans near parity at 12 percent). As revealed in the previous table, the demographics of writers and authors are even more skewed in favor of whites.

That is, the minorities who work in the film and television industry are largely consolidated into positions where they work to execute *other* (white) people's visions. They work in positions where they have less agency, and also less pay and prestige, than white decision makers. Similar realities hold across gender lines: women make up 44 percent of producers and directors overall. However, for the top 250 movies of 2020, less than 23 percent of the writers, directors, producers, executive producers, editors, and cinematographers were women. For the top 100 films, it was 21 percent.[204] Pretty much the same story holds for broadcast and streaming television programming.[205] Across the board, to the extent that women are directors or producers, it is typically for smaller-budget and less widely distributed or publicized works. At the highest level, a 2020 *New York Times* investigation highlighted that among the people who run the top twenty-five TV

TABLE 3.9. Demographics of Selected Industries by Percentage of Total Workforce, 2022

Occupation	Percentage women	Percentage white	Percentage Black	Percentage Asian	Percentage Hispanic
U.S. workforce overall	46.8	77.0	12.6	6.7	18.5
Newspaper publishers	46.0	81.8	10.2	3.7	7.3
Periodical, book, and directory publishers	55.8	83.1	4.7	6.2	7.2
Libraries and archives	77.5	82.0	7.5	8.1	7.7
Performing arts companies	46.3	77.8	12.1	7.8	13.1
Independent artists, writers, and performers	46.2	85.7	8.6	3.4	11.2
Museums, art galleries, historical sites	48.5	87.5	7.0	2.0	11.1
Motion picture and video industries	31.0	77.5	11.9	6.7	14.0
Software publishing (including video games)	31.1	75.6	5.6	14.4	6.7
Broadcasting (except internet)	38.8	82.4	10.7	3.0	13.1
Internet publishing and broadcasting	39.6	63.7	10.0	22.5	9.7

Source: U.S. Bureau of Labor Statistics. Readers should note that the Bureau of Labor Statistics does not separate out Hispanic from non-Hispanic whites, so racial and ethnic statistics typically sum to more than 100 percent. Full dataset available in U.S. Bureau of Labor Statistics 2023c.

networks and Hollywood studios, 60 percent were men, and 88 percent were non-Hispanic whites.[206]

Irrespective of their gender or race, people who work in the entertainment industry tend to be from wealthy backgrounds. Like journalism, the film and entertainment industry increasingly relies on workers who get paid little to nothing in the hope of getting a foot in the door to becoming a writer, editor, producer, director, agent, or executive. The only people who can afford to live in the expensive cities where these productions take place, and work more than full time on erratic schedules (which interfere with taking a second job), and for little to no money, tend to be people who hail from affluent backgrounds and receive financial support from others with significant discretionary income.[207] Much like superfluous degree requirements, the extremely low (or nonexistent) pay in the initial career stages of many symbolic professions serves as a filtering mechanism to exclude people from the "wrong" backgrounds from being able to secure the coveted industry jobs that are *very* well paid, secure, and vested with significant prestige, autonomy, and influence.

A recent study looking at U.S. "creatives"—artists, musicians, actors, and other performers, writers, filmmakers, and so on—found that they tend to be highly educated, skew disproportionately white, and hail from relatively affluent backgrounds (with their wealthy families subsidizing their artistic lifestyles and endeavors, as creatives tend to earn inconsistent income, and less money than other symbolic capitalists, while living in very expensive cities).[208] Those who prove able to sustain themselves as artists, to persist in the arts over time or work across genres, are especially likely to hail from these backgrounds.[209] Geographically speaking, creatives overwhelmingly tend to have grown up in symbolic economy hubs.

Within those hubs, it used to be the case that creatives would cluster in lower-income areas within cities, often beautifying them and fostering a vibrant cultural scene—making their adopted neighborhoods more appealing to other symbolic capitalists (and thereby serving as a vanguard for gentrification). While this still happens in some places, today it is more common for creatives to operate in neighborhoods that either have long been affluent or are *already* gentrified.[210] That is, creatives swoop in *after* the long-standing poor and minority residents have been largely displaced, and often work directly with cities, developers, advertisers, and incoming businesses (i.e., "the man") to give recently gentrified areas a more "edgy" feel through relatively sterile forms of graffiti, public installations, interior decorations, and so on.[211] Likewise, creatives are often given space to open galleries or studios and put on shows or classes in order to make an area seem more "cultured" *after* its preexisting culture has been largely cleansed (a phenomenon colloquially known as "artwashing").[212]

Because creatives are often surrounded by extremely rich people, many mistakenly assume they are not, themselves, elites. However, as Richard Florida explained, "even though the vast majority of creatives are not truly wealthy, they are relatively advantaged relative to most urbanites and most Americans. This becomes clear when we take into account the amount of money that artists and cultural creatives have left over after paying for housing."[213] The typical creative in New York, Los Angeles, or San Francisco, he showed, tends to have nearly three times as much discretionary income as the typical service worker in those same cities. "Empirically speaking," he continued, "their aggregate economic situation puts them closer to the company of a more advantaged urban elite, and a world away from that of the less advantaged service class."[214]

Alternatively, consider the tech industry. Mirroring trends among media organizations, a small number of tech institutions have been gobbling up all competitors, killing competition, stifling innovation, and, increasingly, engaging in cartel-like behaviors.[215] Moreover, much like being a professor or a journalist, being a successful inventor today is heavily contingent on being relatively affluent and well connected.

A study of 1.2 million U.S. inventors since 1980 found that they tend to come from the top income quintile—and one's likelihood of becoming an inventor increases exponentially when one's family income surpasses the top 10 percent, and again at the top 5 percent. Inventors, like artists, tend to hail from symbolic economy hubs. Much like how tenure-track academics reproduce across generations, a child is especially likely to grow up to be a successful inventor if their parents were inventors too—largely because they have much greater access to key social networks and nonpublic knowledge. Critically, all of this holds even while controlling for popular measures of innate ability. People from the high end of intellectual acumen (as measured by standardized test scores) are unlikely to become inventors if they happen to hail from lower socioeconomic backgrounds. Likewise, independent of raw ability, one's prospects as an inventor also tend to be much lower if one happens to be female, Black, Hispanic, or a product or resident of "flyover country." People who are nonmale, nonwhite, and from nonurban and non-affluent backgrounds are even less likely to become *highly cited or highly paid* inventors—irrespective of their measured aptitudes (if they manage to become an inventor at all).[216]

Like academia or the media and entertainment industries, the tech industry skews overwhelmingly left politically.[217] In 2018, for instance, 95 percent of political donations $200 or higher went to Democrats from workers at Facebook, Salesforce, Alphabet/Google, Lyft, Stripe, Apple, Airbnb, Twitter, and Netflix. Additionally, roughly nine out of ten donations in excess of $200 from employees at Amazon, Microsoft, PayPal, eBay, and Tesla also went to Democrats. The major tech company workforce that is furthest to the right, Oracle, still had more than two-thirds of its employees' political donations go to the Democratic Party.[218] However, these workers don't just support Democrats in general, they strongly favor the candidates who are furthest to the left. An analysis by the *Financial Times* found that, during the 2020 Democratic primary election, the overwhelming majority of tech workers favored Bernie Sanders and Elizabeth Warren. All other candidates combined (including the eventual winner, Joe Biden) garnered less support than either of these two individually.[219]

Yet despite this tight alignment with America's primary left-wing party (and its most left-aligned candidates), the tech industry is also roughly 70 percent male, and it is notorious for its culture of casual sexism and sexual harassment.[220] The field's well-earned reputation for gender discrimination and misogyny reinforces the demographic skew, as most women are disinclined to pursue courses of study and lines of work that will probably embed them in a hostile work environment.[221]

The racial picture is just as bad. Only about 5 percent of all tech employees are Black or Hispanic. Given that roughly 30 percent of America is Black or Hispanic according to U.S. Census estimates, this underrepresentation is extreme—and is roughly double what would be expected if the "pipeline" (i.e., the dearth of Black or Hispanic college graduates in relevant fields) was the main issue.[222] Instead, in tech, as in journalism, a big part of the problem is that formally qualified Black and Hispanic candidates simply aren't getting hired. For those who *do* land jobs, Black and Hispanic tech employees also tend to earn much less than their white peers.[223] On average, Hispanics in tech earn about 25 percent less than non-Hispanic whites. African Americans earn 30 percent less.

The racial pay gap is significantly larger than the gender pay gap in the industry. Women in tech earn on average about 18 percent less than men. *This* gap is typically explained in terms of the fact that women are more likely to take time off to raise children, which interrupts their career trajectories. Moreover, because they are more likely to prioritize their families over their jobs relative to men, women are often less willing to work an extreme number of hours per week, especially unconventional hours, which puts them at a competitive disadvantage with respect to male colleagues who more fully embrace "crunch culture."[224] These explanations don't seem to well explain the racial wage gaps, which hold even among Black and Hispanic *men* as compared with white and Asian peers—and which have been *growing* even as the gender pay gaps have been shrinking.

Similar realities hold across the symbolic professions (e.g., finance, law, consulting). They tend to skew overwhelmingly liberal while also being extremely parochial, hierarchical, and exploitative. Although they profess to champion the marginalized and disadvantaged, symbolic economy institutions are composed primarily of people from highly educated, relatively affluent, urban-dwelling families. Notwithstanding intense institutional preoccupations with diversity, equity, and inclusion, symbolic professions tend to be far less diverse than most other American workplaces. Systematic inequalities along the lines of race and gender are quite pronounced, not just in symbolic capitalists' workplaces but also in their communities and in their tastes and lifestyles. Our intense rhetorical focus on the millionaires and billionaires should not distract from the reality that symbolic capitalists are among the primary "winners" in the prevailing order. We're some of the main beneficiaries of the inequalities we condemn. And we have never been woke.

4

Postmaterialist Politics

As symbolic capitalists have been increasingly consolidated into a relatively small number of specialized urban hubs, capital has followed them. In the contemporary United States, wealth has been concentrated heavily in urban, coastal regions, particularly the West Coast (Seattle through San Diego), and the Northeast Corridor running from Boston through New York to Washington, DC, plus a handful of other major cities such as Chicago, Miami, Atlanta, Minneapolis, Austin, and Boulder.[1] These metropolitan regions serve as hubs for the most lucrative and essential industries in today's economy: finance, consulting, law, technology, and medicine.[2] Perhaps unsurprisingly, college graduates from around the country are increasingly flocking to these cities as well—creating a "brain drain" for much of the rest of the country.[3]

The states hosting this nexus of social and financial capital tend to be solidly "blue." Within those states, districts containing major metropolitan centers where symbolic capitalists tend to work and live trend even further left—and have been growing even bluer in recent cycles as a result of symbolic capitalists' tightening alignment with the Democratic Party. To give some perspective of how much has changed: in 1993, the richest 20 percent of congressional districts were represented by Republicans over Democrats at a ratio of less than two to one. Today, they tilt *Democrat* by nearly five to one.[4] The socioeconomic profiles of Democratic primary voters have shifted significantly as well. Counties with higher concentrations of lower- and working-class Americans are today a much smaller portion of Democratic primary voters than they were in 2008, while counties with large concentrations of affluent

households comprise an ever-growing share.[5] This has important consequences for the types of candidates that succeed in primary elections, the
language those candidates use, the issues they center, what the party platform
ends up looking like, and, ultimately, who is drawn to the party and their
candidates in national elections (and who is alienated therefrom).[6]

Likewise, in the wake of *Citizens United v. FEC*, there was much hand-
wringing among Democrats about "dark money" and its potential to warp
policymaking to serve the hidden agendas of millionaires and billionaires.
Almost the entire conversation on this topic was focused on the political
Right.[7] Yet, in the decade following *Citizens United*, Democrats were the primary recipients of dark money from elites—and the disparities between the
parties have continued to grow. In 2020, for instance, Joe Biden raised more
than six times as much money from anonymous donors than Donald Trump.
Perhaps unsurprisingly, as Democrats emerged as the main beneficiaries of
dark money, financial transparency became a much smaller priority on the
left. "Social justice" arguments *against* financial disclosure have even been
developed and deployed by progressives to protect and legitimize discreet
access to the pocketbooks of billionaires and their foundations.[8]

At a more local level, U.S. cities associated with the symbolic economy
are not just places where vast and ever-growing sums of wealth are consolidated; they are perhaps more uniformly "liberal" than they have ever
been, and tend to be starkly segregated along political lines.[9] According to
estimates by Ryan Enos and his collaborators, roughly 38 percent of contemporary Democrats live in "political bubbles" (where less than a quarter
of one's neighbors belong to the nondominant political party)—largely as a
result of how politically homogeneous most major cities have become: "The
most extreme political isolation is found among Democrats living in high-
density urban areas, with the most isolated 10% of Democrats in the United
States expected to have 93% or more of encounters in their residential
environment with other Democrats. . . . In major urban areas, Democrat
exposure to Republicans is extremely low, especially in the dense urban cores.
Notably, a large plurality of Democrat voters live in these areas and the very
low levels of exposure extend even to the medium-density suburbs of these
major areas and to minor urban areas."[10]

Now, given the current concentrations of financial and cultural capital into
these areas—which are controlled by Democrats to an extent that approaches
one-party rule—it is actually well within the power of mainstream symbolic
capitalists and their copartisans to significantly upend the distribution
of wealth and opportunity in the United States purely through how they

allocate their own resources, manage the organizations and institutions they are embedded in, and leverage city and state governments that Democrats firmly control. And yet, the regions symbolic capitalists dominate also happen to be the most unequal places in the United States—with an ever-growing share of denizens classifying as either extremely well off or impoverished.[11] Although these metropolitan centers are more diverse than ever, they remain heavily segregated along racial and ethnic lines.[12] As economist Tyler Cowen put it,

> The data show that the rich and well educated are keener to live together, in tight bunches and groups, than are the less well educated. Democrats cluster themselves more tightly than do Republicans. . . . And if we look at professions? Well, the so-called creative class is more clustered than the working class. Ironically, it's these groups—the wealthy, the well-educated, and the creative class—who often complain about inequality and American segregation with the greatest fervor. The self-selection process is running its course, and how people are voting with their feet often differs from what's coming out of their mouths.[13]

Granted, the cities symbolic capitalists gravitate toward *do* tend to have significantly higher taxes, largely to fund more generous social safety nets, infrastructure projects, and government services. However, these state and local tax revenues tend to be extracted at significantly higher rates from people in the *lower* quintiles of the income distribution.[14] It is the poor and middle classes who disproportionately fund the more generous social safety nets in these states and municipalities. Meanwhile, upper-middle-class and wealthy taxpayers tend to be much more aggressive in using charitable donations and other deductions and loopholes to reduce their tax liability—in the process, drastically reducing government revenues, and thereby undermining state-led efforts to assist the disadvantaged.[15]

Yet despite being more likely to claim deductions, and despite having more discretionary income at their disposal than most, the relatively well off in symbolic economy hubs tend to be *less* likely to make charitable donations than other Americans. They also generally give a smaller share of their income to charity and tend to focus the donations they do provide on causes *other than* helping the poor or mitigating inequality. Studies consistently show that the Americans who are most likely to give, and who dedicate the largest share of their income to charity, are actually those from the lower socioeconomic quintiles and those who live in rural, suburban, or "red" districts—particularly those who identify as religious or conservative.[16] These are also the donors whose charity is most directly oriented toward addressing poverty and human suffering. In contrast, wealthier, more educated, urban donors (who trend left) are more likely to dedicate resources to causes like environmental protection or animal rights, or to organizations like the ACLU or Amnesty International.[17] Very few donations by these donors are aimed at underserved communities.[18] Instead, the largest charitable contributions consistently go to universities, especially elite private schools, and museums or the arts—that is, to institutions that these elites (and their families) are, themselves, among the most likely to utilize.[19] Indeed, even when they invest in ostensibly public spaces like parks, said elites often work to tightly restrict access thereafter—particularly with respect to minorities and the poor.[20]

A bitter irony underlying this stinginess is that it is precisely the "coerced philanthropy" of the poor and working classes that allows symbolic capitalists to enjoy the lifestyles they take for granted. As discussed in the previous chapter, it is their desperation and exploitation that subsidize our ability to rely on cheap, disposable labor to run our errands, care for our loved ones, cart us around on demand, produce boutique goods and services at an "affordable" price, and so on. As Barbara Ehrenreich powerfully emphasized,

> When someone works for less pay than she can live on—when, for example, she goes hungry so that you can eat more cheaply and conveniently—then she has made a great sacrifice for you, she has made you a gift of some part of her abilities, her health and her life. The "working poor," as they are approvingly termed, are in fact the major philanthropists of our society. They neglect their own children so that the children of others will be cared for; they live in substandard housing so that other homes will be shiny and perfect; they endure privation so that inflation will be low and stock prices high. To be a member of the working poor is to be an anonymous donor, a nameless benefactor, to everyone else. As Gail, one of my restaurant coworkers put it, "you give and you give."[21]

To illustrate the tensions at play, consider the case of California: the state has been a Democratic bastion for decades. It is, by far, America's most populous state[22] and also the most "culturally diverse."[23] California includes some of the nation's best universities, and it serves as a key hub for tech, entertainment, media, and more. With respect to real GDP, it is far and away the richest state in the union.[24] Many in the state are personally rich as well: roughly one out of every twelve Californians is a millionaire. Yet the state also has the highest poverty rate in the nation.[25] Many of its metropolitan areas host vast encampments of homeless people due to a lack of affordable residential options—yet the overwhelmingly liberal denizens of these cities nonetheless aggressively resist the construction of shelters or multifamily housing. In the same election cycle that Democrat Joe Biden carried the state by more than 29 percentage points in his quest for the White House, Californians *also* decisively voted to prevent gig workers from being counted as employees—thereby disqualifying them from the benefits and protections most other laborers enjoy.[26] Noting contradictions like these, Ezra Klein observed, "There is a danger—not just in California, but everywhere—that politics becomes an aesthetic rather than a program . . . where the symbols of progressivism are often preferred to the sacrifices and risks those ideals demand. California, as the biggest state in the nation, and one where Democrats hold total control of the government, carries a special burden. If progressivism cannot work here, why should the country believe it can work anywhere else?"[27]

A similar story could be told of New York. It has also long been a Democratic stronghold. In terms of ideological self-identification, its residents are among the most liberal in America.[28] The state boasts some of the most prestigious private and public higher education institutions in the nation, including two Ivy League universities. New York City serves as a key hub for banking and finance—not just for America but for the world. It is also, perhaps, the single most important city for media and publishing in the United States. New York State's economy is the third largest in the nation (measured in terms of real GDP). The state has the fourth-largest population in the United States as well. Roughly one out of every thirteen New York State residents is a millionaire.[29] Yet New York also has the second-highest level of income inequality in the country.[30] Hence, despite its immense wealth, alongside California, the state has one of the highest poverty rates in America. Although New York is one of the most diverse states in the union, it also has the ignoble honor of possessing the most racially and ethnically segregated school systems in the entire United States.[31]

As *New York Times* economic analyst Binyamin Appelbaum put it, "Blue states are the problem: Blue states are where the housing crisis is located. Blue states are where the disparities in education funding are the most dramatic. Blue states are the places where tens of thousands of homeless people are living on the streets. Blue states are the places where economic inequality is increasing most quickly in this country."[32] Despite Democrats describing Republican efforts to restrict the ballot as "Jim Crow 2.0," blue northeastern states also happen to have some of the heaviest voting restrictions in the country.[33]

As bad as these contradictions may look at the state level, they are far, far worse when one drills into the specific cities symbolic capitalists are congregated in. They tend to be far richer and more diverse than the rest of the state and skew far more liberal than the rest of the state—yet they also tend to contain much higher levels of poverty, segregation, inequality, and exploitation than other parts of the state. Indeed, on all counts, these metropolitan areas tend to drive the overall trends for the states they are embedded in. Put another way, despite how blue these symbolic economy hubs are, and despite how vocally preoccupied symbolic capitalists are with various forms of inequality, wealth continues to be concentrated into the hands of elites in these regions at a far higher clip than it is being reallocated to the disadvantaged.

In order to understand these dynamics, it is necessary to go beyond understanding symbolic capitalists in generic terms, for instance as "liberals" or "Democrats." This chapter will illustrate that symbolic capitalists are not just different from other people in terms of our professions and social position; we also tend to be very different from the broader public in terms of our ideological and psychological tendencies. As a result of the interplay between our unique social position and cognitive profiles, symbolic capitalists are predisposed toward a peculiar style of politics and tend to have a political agenda that does not easily fit in the traditional left-right American spectrum. As symbolic capitalists became increasingly influential in the U.S. economy and culture, both parties actively tried to court them. Ultimately, they ended up aligning with the Democrats. In the process, they profoundly changed the Democratic Party and, indeed, the U.S. political landscape writ large.

Sophisticated Accumulation

Many alternative names for symbolic capitalists refer to them as a class: the professional-managerial class, the new class, the creative class, the aspirational class, Class X. On the one hand, this is sensible, as these elites have convergent interests, especially around issues like intellectual property laws, public trust in education, science and expertise, or continued investments in science, technology, research, and the arts. They concentrate in the same urban hubs. They broadly share certain ideological and cultural dispositions. However, at best, they could be understood as a class *in statu nascendi*—that is, a class still in the process of being formed. This process has been consistently undermined, most notably by changes in the economy that have created growing inequalities within and between the symbolic professions—generating often-intense internal struggles over resources and prestige, claims and counterclaims for authority and jurisdiction, and so on. Great Awokenings are largely manifestations of these internal tensions.

What's more, as scholars of this elite constellation have long observed, symbolic capitalists tend not to think of *themselves* as a class. Consequently, they do not organize themselves *as* a class in pursuit of shared interests in the way that earlier generations of elites have done. As Shamus Khan explains,

> The culturally important shift in the elite identity has been from being a "class" to a collection of individuals—the best and brightest. That is, rather than identifying as a group which is constituted through a set of institutions (families, schools, clubs, a shared cultural-historical legacy, etc.), today's elites consider themselves as constituted by their individual talents. . . . While they certainly know that their individual traits, capacities, skills, talents and qualities are cultivated, they suggest that this cultivation is done through hard work, and access is granted through capacity rather than birthright. If I were to talk about elite culture today, then, I would talk about a culture of "individual self-cultivation."[34]

To the extent that symbolic capitalists identify with groups, it is generally in the service of enhancing their individual position. Costly sacrifices on behalf of other people or collectives are rare in symbolic capitalist spaces. Although our language often makes appeals to solidaristic altruism, symbolic capitalists primarily deploy political discourse (broadly construed) for the purposes of individual enhancement and personal expression. These bids tend to focus on things like representation, symbols, distinctions (between people and across and within groups), various forms of etiquette and decorum, deference practices, and nomenclature because precisely what symbolic capitalists are primarily concerned about—the main thing they are struggling over—is social status. And their desire for symbolic capital tends to be insatiable.

Generally speaking, there are diminishing returns for financial capital. After a certain point, the happiness or empowerment people receive from additional material assets begins to taper off, as does the ambition to increase one's wealth. There is loss aversion (most are hesitant to move *down* from their current position), but the desire to accumulate still *more* begins to cool. Indeed, contrary to earlier narratives defining humankind as the profit-maximizing *homo economicus*, it turns out that most people are happy being whatever they perceive to be average, or a little better than average, with respect to wealth. That is, it is possible for people to feel more or less satisfied and secure with respect to *financial* capital. This is much less the case for symbolic capital. Instead, research shows that as people approach the point where they become less concerned with materialistic forms of capital, their desire for symbolic capital begins to accelerate rapidly.[35] Millionaires and billionaires create charities and invest in institutions essentially to convert excess financial capital into symbolic capital.[36] Those few who continue to aggressively chase wealth despite being rich often do so because they view their wealth *as a sign* of social status and they're trying to surpass peers who possess more than they do.[37] That is, after a point, even the pursuit of financial capital stops being "about" the money; it's used as a placeholder for symbolic capital.

There seems to be no point after which the desire for *symbolic* capital levels off. The returns don't diminish either. Instead, the more status one has, the more intense one's desire becomes for still *more* symbolic capital.[38] As sociologist Cecilia Ridgeway put it, "The desire for status is never really satisfied because it can never really be possessed by the individual once and for all. Since it is esteem given by others, it can always, at least theoretically, be taken away."[39] This possibility is a source of significant anxiety among symbolic capitalists because many aspects of our social standing are also nontransparent and outside our control. As Jeff Bezos helpfully put it, "Your brand is what people say about you when you're not in the room."[40]

Moreover, because status is intrinsically *relative*—that is, it is fundamentally "about" being better or worse (higher or lower) than others—status competition much more closely approximates a zero-sum game. It is difficult for someone or something to rise in status without others *losing* attention, recognition, deference, and so on relative to what they once enjoyed. Materially speaking, it is theoretically possible for everyone in a society (indeed, everyone in the world) to have sufficient resources to live secure and comfortable lives. It is more or less definitionally impossible to ensure that everyone enjoys a high level of symbolic capital. A world where everyone had the same status would be a world where no one and nothing really held *any* status.[41]

As a function of these realities, those whose lives and livelihoods are oriented around symbolic capital tend to feel as though their position is precarious, irrespective of the financial assets at their disposal. More than most, they are constantly comparing themselves to others, and competing against others, to affirm, enhance, or protect their status[42]—including and especially through symbolic political engagement.

A Tempest in a Teapot

Symbolic capitalists tend to be supportive of egalitarian causes. However, we generally concentrate our efforts on the symbolic realm—how people talk and think, what they say and feel—rather than the reallocation of power and resources. This symbolic engagement, in practice, is often sterile. We primarily engage others who already agree with us. Our "social justice"–oriented engagement also tends to circulate nearly exclusively among other elites, with little impact on the genuinely impoverished and marginalized in society.

As an example, many academics aspire to improve the world through their research. Others go so far as to style themselves "radicals" and erstwhile revolutionaries. Yet quantitative analyses suggest that 82 percent of articles in the humanities—and roughly a third of all articles published in the social sciences—are never cited, not even once. As bad as these numbers seem, they would actually look much worse if self-citations were excluded from consideration. It has been estimated that roughly half of all journal articles are never read by *anyone* other than the articles' authors, editors, and reviewers.[43] And very few of the academic works that *do* enjoy solid readership or citations actually manage to break out of the Ivory Tower. They mostly circulate among other intellectuals. White papers and policy briefs often do a bit better in terms of readership. However, they still tend to be consumed nearly exclusively within policymaking, nonprofit, and elite activist spaces. Vanishingly little scholarly work of any kind, produced by academics *or* think tanks, is read (let alone utilized) by those who are not symbolic capitalists. Most of it is barely read at all.

The picture is not much better for books. In 2022, for instance, the bestselling nonfiction title (a self-help book called *Atomic Habits*) sold 1.2 million copies. The number two bestseller, *The Body Keeps Score*, sold roughly half as many units (637,000). For context, there are roughly 258 million adults (eighteen years and older) in the United States. This means the absolute bestselling nonfiction title in the U.S. reached less than 0.5 percent of American adults, and the runner-up reached roughly 0.25 percent. Even the number one fiction book, *It Ends with Us*, only sold enough units to reach roughly 1 percent of American adults.[44] For university presses, the numbers tend to be much lower. The typical monograph sells less than 500 copies. More trade-oriented academic press books tend to move around 5,000 units at the high end.[45] At the pinnacle of the academic publishing world, Thomas Piketty's *Capital in the 21st Century* has sold more than 2.5 million copies worldwide since 2013. As impressive as that sounds, it amounts to only 1 percent of the current U.S. adult population—and this statistic counts all units sold over the last *decade*, many in international markets.

And of course, as it relates to impact, many who buy books never read them (there's even a Japanese word for this practice, *tsundoku*). Even those who start to read titles regularly fail to finish them. E-reader-based estimates by mathematician Jordan Ellenberg suggest that the overall book completion rate for American readers may be as low as 3 percent—with Piketty's bestselling *Capital* being among the least likely to be finished once started.[46] With only around 1 percent of the population buying even the best-selling titles in a given year, and only a small fraction of purchasers actually reading those texts to completion (if at all), even the most successful titles typically reach a miniscule share of the public and have a negligible effect on the social world.

News media circulation and consumption also tend to be confined to a relatively narrow slice of the population. Looking at circulation and subscriptions, even the nation's top newspapers each only reach 1–2 percent of U.S. households.[47] Pew Research estimates the total circulation of all U.S. newspapers combined was roughly 20.9 million copies per day in 2020 (the latest year available at time of writing).[48] The U.S. Census estimated there to be roughly 128.5 million households in the United States that year.[49] Even if we assume that households never buy more than one periodical, these data suggest only 16 percent of U.S. households are reached on a given day by *any* paper. In reality, however, there is significant overlap between readers of most major newspapers and magazines (i.e., many people who regularly read the *New York Times* also read the *New Yorker* or the *Washington Post*), so the total share of Americans who consume this content is smaller still. And it's not a representative cross-section of the country either. Instead, Americans who *pay* for news are especially likely to be white, to possess a college degree, to self-identify as liberal, and to have a household income in excess of $150,000 per year.[50]

Should we expand to look at digital news consumption across various platforms, most Americans do not even view one single article in a typical month from the outlet with the widest online reach, CNN. Nor are most of those who *do* consume at least one article regular or repeat viewers: average users, themselves a minority among Americans in virtue of engaging with this content at all, spend twenty-two minutes per month (roughly forty-four seconds per day) on CNN digital platforms. The audience and engagement for all other news websites tend to be significantly smaller. Even the largest runners-up tend to reach less than a third of Americans in any given month, even once, on *any* platform, counting everything they publish, anywhere.[51]

Television broadcasts tell a similar tale: evening network TV news programs (ABC, CBS, NBC, PBS) collectively reach about 10 percent of Americans in a typical night. For the cable news networks (Fox, CNN, MSNBC), even the most popular prime-time newscasts are viewed by less than 1 percent of Americans. According to estimates by political scientist Markus Prior, only about 10–15 percent of voting-age Americans watch even ten minutes of news per day from CNN, MSNBC, *or* Fox News (combined).[52] Most Americans do not even watch an hour of cable news over the course of an entire *month*. Even the age bracket that consumes the *most* television news, Americans fifty-five years or older, only watch roughly ninety minutes per day including all channels.[53]

Across its various platforms, Americans who consume content from NPR are overwhelmingly white, affluent, urban, college educated, and Democrat aligned.[54] Likewise, the minority of Americans who listen to podcasts vary systematically from the broader population. For one thing, they tend to skew towards the younger side of the age distribution. Yet, in spite of their relative youth, most podcast listeners possess college degrees; more than one in three possess graduate education as well.[55] The median household income for podcast listeners in 2020 was $82,641 (well above the 2020 median U.S. household income of $67,521). Those who listen to podcasts about news, history, science, technology, business, or society and culture are especially likely to be white or Asian, to be "heavy" podcast listeners (who consume podcast content at least ten times per month), and to be well off (median incomes for listeners in these categories tend to be above $90,000 per year).[56]

Frequent social media users tend to look a lot like heavy podcast streamers: young, highly educated, and relatively affluent. For virtually all social networks, those with college degrees, with incomes over $75,000, or who live in urban areas are the most likely to use social media—and they tend to engage with these platforms *much* more frequently than other users. On the whole, those who use social media at all, for any purpose, tend to use it lightly. Most users check in once per day or less. In contrast, roughly 40 percent of those who are urban, are college graduates, or earn at least $75,000 per year say they are "almost always" online. Among users under fifty from these demographics, it is well over a majority.[57]

Critically, most content that is shared on social media receives few views and even fewer engagements. The median YouTube video, for instance, receives 0 likes, 0 comments, and only 40 views.[58] And across social media platforms, views and engagement of posts have been steadily plummeting, even for large accounts with social media managers and paid campaigns.[59] In short, it is a small subset of Americans who use social media regularly and an even smaller share who produce or engage with content when they *do* log on. Users who share or interact with *political* content are even more niche.

Among Americans who use social media at all, the overwhelming majority (70 percent) rarely, if ever, post or share content about political or social issues—especially if their views tilt right of center—most commonly out of fear that they will be maligned or attacked for their views, or that their posts will otherwise be used against them.[60] Most instead leverage the platforms primarily for entertainment and to connect with family, friends, and others in their local community.[61] Research has found that the type of people who *do* use social media for political purposes tend to be very different from most others in terms of their dispositions both online and off. They are especially likely to be aggressive and status hungry. They tend to enjoy offending others but are also more easily offended themselves.[62] The more intensely the user base of a site is dominated by symbolic capitalists, the more prevalent users like these seem to be.

For instance, data collected prior to Elon Musk's acquisition show that, compared with other networks, Twitter (now "X") users tend to be *especially* young, educated, urban, and left-skewed. Only about 22 percent of Americans were on Twitter at all (32 percent of Democrats and 17 percent of Republicans)[63]—and just one-quarter of these users (roughly 6 percent of the broader U.S. public) produce 97 percent of the content on the site.[64] Only about 10 percent of users ("power users") log on daily or almost daily. They are responsible for 90 percent of all tweets and generate more than half of Twitter's global revenue.[65] Since Musk's acquisition, the platform has only grown more niche. The daily active user base declined by roughly 13 percent, and the remaining power users account for 72 percent of all time spent on the app.[66]

Even before Musk purchased it, Twitter was an incredibly political site. According to 2019 Pew Research estimates, roughly one out of every three tweets were political in nature—and it is a very specific subgroup of users who posted this political content. Roughly 70 percent of all U.S. political tweets were produced by college graduates. Along gender lines, 70 percent of political tweets were produced by women. Along political lines, 85 percent of political tweets were produced by Democrats. Ideologically, most political content on Twitter was produced and shared by people who trend toward the extreme ends of the American spectrum.[67] With respect to age, 78 percent of political tweets were produced by users who are fifty-plus years old. Put another way, it is older, female, highly educated, ideologically extreme, and Democratic users who dominated the political discussion on

Twitter prior to Musk's takeover.[68] The discourse on the site was (in)famous for being especially vitriolic, with disputes often devolving into mobbings and cancellation attempts. However, the platform was *not* toxic as a result of democratization—that is, a cacophony of "unsophisticated" people being able to say whatever they want. Quite the reverse: highly educated users seem to produce and amplify most of the politically polarizing content on the site and drive most of its unfortunate dynamics.[69]

In contrast, about 40 percent of Americans use Instagram. Of the major social networks, it tilts the farthest left, and it is also heavily skewed toward females. Content on the platform tends to be positive, however, and largely apolitical. To the extent that people post political content at all, it's typically images intended to affirm a particular position or promote a cause, or else show the user and their friends taking part in a political event (e.g., attending a rally or march).[70]

Facebook is the only traditional social networking platform used by a majority of Americans—although only about a third in the United States say they regularly get *news* from the site. Those who follow political news on Facebook are especially prone to "liking" ideologically homogeneous pages across different categories. However, most Facebook users are not particularly polarized or political.[71] Female Facebook users are especially unlikely to engage with political content or get into online arguments with strangers about controversial topics (this is likely, again, because female Facebook users are significantly more likely to be "normies" than are participants on Twitter or other sites).[72]

All said, it is a relatively small segment of the population that is "very online" with respect to social media, or that regularly consumes journalistic media in virtually *any* format (TV, online, print, podcasts)—let alone engaging with research by think tanks, nonprofits, activists, or academics. Mostly, it's people like us. Virtually the entire political and cultural melodrama carried out in academia, policymaking spaces, media outlets, and social networking sites is carried out *among* symbolic capitalists. The views and priorities of most others are simply unrepresented in these spaces. And for their part, most of those who are *not* symbolic capitalists are not particularly interested in the highly idiosyncratic struggles we invest so much of ourselves into.

The Curse of Knowledge

Symbolic capitalists broadly recognize that our political views and sensibilities are different from those of most other Americans. Our preferred narrative to explain these gaps is to appeal to our "superior" knowledge, intelligence, and credentials. While the beliefs and preferences of *others* may be driven by prejudices, emotions, superstition, dogma, and ignorance, the positions of well-educated or highly intelligent voters are believed to be shaped by logic and "the facts." *We* make decisions based on a careful consideration of the issues; *we* would readily change our minds if the facts were not "on our side," or as the relevant circumstances evolved.

The faith that education produces just these kinds of citizens has been baked into the project of modern universities from the outset.[73] And symbolic capitalists believe themselves to be proof of the project's success. As Elizabeth Currid-Halkett put it, "The unifying characteristic shared by members of this new elite cultural formation is their acquisition and valuing of knowledge. . . . They use knowledge to attain a higher social, environmental, and cultural awareness. The process by which they obtain knowledge and subsequently form values is what reveals social position."[74]

Highly educated people tend to associate primarily with others like themselves.[75] Even *among* the highly educated, those with high levels of academic performance tend to cluster together—and gradually abandon social ties with those of lower GPAs.[76] College graduates often look down on those with fewer (or worse) credentials than themselves. One series of studies looking at college grads in the United States and western European countries found that people who graduated from college viewed less educated people more unfavorably than they did any other reference group. They were also less supportive of programs to help less educated people compared to other potential recipients. And while they often expressed some sense of shame or regret for prejudices expressed against other groups, they were unabashed in their bias against those less educated than themselves.[77] In light of the ways educational attainment varies systematically along the lines of race, gender, and class, these forms of education-based prejudice often exacerbate and reinforce other forms of bias and discrimination against the "losers" in the prevailing order, left-valanced ideological commitments notwithstanding.[78]

Moreover, mainstream symbolic capitalists tend to interpret deviance from, or resistance to, our own preferences and priorities in terms of pathologies (racism, xenophobia, sexism, homophobia, authoritarianism, reactionary closed-mindedness, ideological zealotry, and dogmatism) or deficits (lack of information or education; lack of cognitive sophistication or capability; lack of imagination, empathy, or perspective). This is not hyperbole; it is quite literally the case.

Entire lines of scholarly research and journalistic reporting are oriented around determining which pathology or deficit best explains why people deviate from the preferred positions of symbolic capitalists.[79] Huge industries have sprung up trying to exploit big data, predictive modeling, and advances in the cognitive and behavioral sciences in order to "nudge" people into behaving in ways that symbolic capitalists think they "should."[80] Government and nonprofit programs are full of restrictions and requirements that convey that others cannot be trusted to make responsible decisions on their own. Inconvenient social movements are typically explained in terms of some noxious counterelite (e.g., Trump, the Koch brothers, Fox News) "brainwashing" and "duping" an easily manipulated public into pursuing the "wrong" ends.[81] A whole government-industrial complex has sprung up ostensibly oriented around combatting "misinformation" and "disinformation," allowing elite tech and media companies, academics, and Democratic politicians to conveniently label anyone and anything that threatens their business model, subverts their epistemic authority, or circumvents their gatekeeping efforts as inherently "dangerous"—not just dangerous for their own pocketbooks and power but harmful to America writ large (and therefore in need of being surveilled and suppressed).[82] Empirical research has found that the kinds of people who buy into alarmist narratives about misinformation, disinformation, "fake news," and so on are especially likely to view others as epistemologically vulnerable (i.e., gullible, stupid, ignorant, irrational) compared with people like themselves.[83]

In short, a sense of intellectual elitism tends to haunt symbolic capitalists—extending into perceptions of the presumed superiority of our political commitments, and the processes by which those commitments were forged. But how well placed is this confidence? Although there is not a lot of work on this question focused on professions per se, there *is* a robust literature on the political psychology and cognition of people with high IQ scores, high GPAs, and high levels of education. We can use this research as a proxy for understanding symbolic capitalists (because we tend to have high education levels, good grades, and above-average test scores). It turns out, the kinds of people who gravitate toward the symbolic professions *do* tend to vary systematically from most other people . . . albeit not in the ways we like to think.

For instance, as compared with other constituents, highly educated voters are much more likely to donate to political causes and to have flexible work schedules that facilitate their higher rates of voting, protesting, and other political activities.[84] Yet, although these constituents tend to be more politically engaged on average, their political involvement is also much *less* likely to be oriented toward pragmatic ends. Instead, Americans with high levels of education gravitate toward "political hobbyism" and "expressive voting"—that is, engaging in political research, discourse, and other activities for the purposes of self-aggrandizement, entertainment, validation of one's identity, and so forth instead of trying to realize concrete and practical goals.[85]

In virtue of these tendencies, highly educated people tend to follow political horse races much more closely than the general public, and are often much better versed in contemporary political gossip, drama, or scandals. Yet we tend to be little more informed than most with respect to more substantive facts—often lacking even rudimentary knowledge about core civic institutions and processes.[86] And we tend to be *less* self-aware than most with respect to our own biases and ignorance.[87] As social psychologist Keith Stanovich put it, "If you are a person of high intelligence, if you are highly educated, and if you are strongly committed to an ideological viewpoint, you will be highly likely to think you have thought your way to your viewpoint. And you will be even less likely than the average person to realize that you have derived your beliefs from the social groups you belong to and because they fit with your temperament and your innate psychological propensities."[88]

In fact, highly educated Americans tend to be less aware of *our own sociopolitical preferences* than most—typically describing ourselves as more left-wing than we actually seem to be. Studies consistently find that highly educated and cognitively sophisticated voters tend to gravitate toward a marriage of cultural liberalism and economic conservatism.[89] However, we regularly understand *ourselves* as down-the-line leftists. As economist James Rockey put it, "How does education affect ideology? It would seem that the better educated, if anything, are less accurate in how they perceive their ideology. Higher levels of education are associated with being less likely to believe oneself to be right-wing, whilst simultaneously associated with being in favour of increased inequality."[90]

Likewise, highly educated Americans tend to express less animus toward minority groups in polling and surveys. However, this posture may be a function of the fact that, precisely in virtue of being elites, our material interests, ambitions, and life prospects do not appear to be threatened by people from historically marginalized and disadvantaged groups. Far from it. As we have seen, our lifestyles and social position are largely predicated on exploiting people from those same populations. However, research has found that when highly educated people *do* come to sense that their own interests or prospects are undermined or threatened by competition with racial or ethnic minorities, they often become significantly more hostile toward the groups in question.[91]

More generally, although cognitively sophisticated people are more likely than most to endorse racial equality in principle, they seem to be no more likely than others to support policies that would undermine relative advantages they *personally* enjoy—and their cognitive sophistication is part of what may allow them to justify this gap to themselves and others.[92] High levels of creativity have likewise been found to be connected with higher levels of unethical behavior—in part because highly creative individuals excel at rationalizing harmful actions to others *and* themselves.[93]

In addition to our poor *self*-awareness with respect to how committed to egalitarianism we actually are, highly educated Americans tend to be much worse at gauging other people too—typically assuming others are more extreme or dogmatic than they actually seem to be.[94] This is perhaps a product of the reality that, as compared with the general public, the kinds of people who become symbolic capitalists (highly educated, cognitively sophisticated, academically high performing) tend to themselves be more ideological in their thinking, more dogmatic in their views, and more extreme in their ideological leanings than everybody else[95]—and the process of attaining a college education seems to drive people even further in the direction of moral absolutism.[96] A recent National Bureau of Economic Research study found that the Americans most prone to zero-sum thinking included people who lived in cities, those who have especially low or high levels of income, people who identify as strong Democrats, and those who possess postgraduate degrees.[97]

Humans' mental capabilities seem to have evolved in large part to help us cooperate with in-group members in competition against "others."[98] That is, our cognitive capacities are fundamentally geared toward group building and coalitional struggles. We tend to reason in ways that help us acquire and maintain social status and belonging. It should not be surprising, then, that those who are cognitively sophisticated tend to be *more* prone to tribalism than most.

For instance, highly educated Americans are much more likely than others to know what positions they "should" hold in virtue of their partisan or ideological identities, and we're more likely to align our beliefs to systematically accord with those identities.[99] We are more likely to form positions on issues we didn't previously have strong opinions about by looking to partisan cues—and to modify our existing positions to bring them into line with new messaging from party leaders.[100] Politically sophisticated Americans are also more likely to systematically accord their political beliefs and preferences to their religion, race, gender, or sexuality—conforming themselves with what they "should" think or say on the basis of their identity characteristics (while other in-group peers tend to have much more heterogeneous sets of views and dispositions).[101] That is, in a literal sense, the kind of people who gravitate toward the symbolic professions strive to be "politically correct" in their views. Perhaps, then, it should not be surprising that people tend to grow *more* politically polarized as their knowledge, numeracy, or reflectiveness increases.[102] They also tend to grow more intolerant of moral and political disagreement.

Although highly educated and cognitively sophisticated Americans are less likely to express racially prejudicial attitudes on surveys, we tend to be far *more* prejudicial than most against those whose ideological views diverge from our own.[103] The kinds of people who become symbolic capitalists are also more likely than other Americans to report self-censoring, and to support censoring others, on the basis of their political views.[104] We are also much more prone to overreact to small shocks, challenges, or slights.[105]

Moreover, those who are highly educated, intelligent, or rhetorically skilled are significantly *less* likely than most others to revise their beliefs or adjust their positions when confronted with evidence or arguments that contradict their preferred narratives or preexisting beliefs.[106] Precisely in virtue of knowing more about the world or being better at arguing, we are better equipped to punch holes in data or narratives that undermine our priors, come up with excuses to "stick to our guns" irrespective of the facts,[107] or else interpret threatening information in a way that flatters our existing worldview.[108] And we typically do just that.

In a decades-long set of ambitious experiments and forecasting tournaments, psychologist Philip Tetlock has demonstrated that—as a result of their inclinations toward epistemic arrogance and ideological rigidity—experts are often *worse* than laymen at anticipating how events are likely to play out . . . *especially* with respect to their areas of expertise.[109] Likewise, experts have been shown to perform a bit worse than laymen at predicting the likely effects of behavioral science interventions.[110] Comparative and longitudinal studies have found that highly educated political leaders perform no better than less educated ones, and may even be a bit worse in some respects.[111]

In short, far from being independent thinkers who come to their positions on issues through a careful deliberation of "the facts," who change their minds readily in accordance with "the facts," and who make wise decisions by deferring to "the facts," symbolic capitalists are instead more likely than most to be dogmatic ideologues or partisan conformists. Yet it is difficult for us to recognize these tendencies in ourselves due to our larger "bias blind spots" and increased capabilities for motivated reasoning.

In light of these realities, it seems unlikely that the consolidation of symbolic capitalists into a single political party would bode well for the messaging, priorities, and policies of that party or, indeed, U.S. politics and civic society writ large. In fact, rather than growing more rational, civil, or moderate as a result of our influence, American politics have grown much more extreme, tribal, unequal, and unstable as symbolic capitalists have risen in power within the Democratic Party and the U.S. political system as a whole.

Consequences of Consolidation

Two decades ago, sociologists Jeff Manza and Clem Brooks observed, "Professionals have moved from being the most Republican class in the 1950s, to the second most Democratic class by the late 1980s and the most Democratic class in 1996."[112] This consolidation has only grown more pronounced in the intervening years. And as symbolic capitalists have been consolidated into the Democratic Party, they've grown increasingly progressive, particularly on "cultural" issues (sexuality, race, gender, environmentalism), and especially relative to blue-collar workers.[113]

As the partisan and ideological alignment of symbolic capitalists has shifted, so has the narrative about what the partisan diploma divide "means." When professionals and highly educated Americans skewed Republican, Democrats held this up as proof that the GOP was controlled by elites while *they* were the party of "the people." Now that the pendulum has swung the other direction, the narrative is that the Democratic Party appeals to the educated and professionals because their policies are simply more rational, informed, and effective. As Stephen Colbert put it, "Reality has a well-known liberal bias."[114] The GOP, meanwhile, is depicted as the party of ignorant and regressive zealots.

The truth is much more complex and, for many, perhaps disturbing: symbolic capitalists follow political horse races more carefully, yes, but we still tend to be pretty ignorant about the basics of government and how things actually work (and are, perhaps, less aware of our ignorance than most). Worse, certain biases and blind spots that are common to all people may be even more pronounced with us. Far from being more reasonable and pragmatic than other Americans, precisely because we are largely insulated from the actual *consequences* of political decision-making, symbolic capitalists often approach politics as either a sport or a holy war. After all, the government programs on the table for being cut or painfully restructured aren't usually ones that *we* directly rely on; it is generally not *our* jobs being automated or outsourced;

our neighborhoods are not being hollowed out by economic forces, ravaged by drugs, or plagued with crime and blight; it's not *our* children getting caught up in the criminal justice system, deployed into a war, or staring down especially grim life prospects. "Those people" and their problems are largely abstractions for us—little more concrete than the principles we are trying to score points for, or the hypothetical future generations for whom our symbolic advocacy, we assert, will somehow pay off.

Reflective of these realities, the increasing dominance of symbolic capitalists over the Democratic Party has had a range of profound impacts on the contemporary U.S. political landscape.

First, symbolic capitalists' prominence within the Democratic Party has contributed to a growing disconnect between the economic priorities of the party relative to most others in the United States, especially working-class Americans. This is because, as sociologist Shamus Khan has shown, the economics of elites tend to operate "counter-cyclically" to the rest of society. Developments that tend to be good for elites are often bad for everyone else, and vice versa.[115] As an example, symbolic capitalists tend to be far more supportive of immigration, globalization, automation, and AI than most Americans because they make our lives more convenient and significantly lower the costs of the premium goods and services we are inclined toward.[116] Those in the symbolic professions primarily see upsides with respect to these phenomena because our lifestyles and livelihoods are much less at risk (we instead capture a disproportionate share of any resultant GDP increases),[117] and because our culture and values are being affirmed (e.g., our embrace of demographic diversity, cultural cosmopolitanism, or scientific progress) rather than threatened thereby. Others experience these developments quite differently.

Likewise, most in the United States skew "operationally" left (i.e., favoring robust social safety nets, government benefits, and infrastructure investment via progressive taxation) but trend more conservative on culture and symbolism[118] (i.e., they are fond of patriotism, religiosity, national security, and public order). Although they are sympathetic to many left-aligned policies, they tend to prefer policies and messages that are universal and appeal to superordinate identities and common goals over ones oriented around specific identity groups (e.g., LGBTQ people, women, Hispanics, or Muslims).[119] They tend to be alienated by "political correctness" and prefer candidates and messages that are direct, concise, and plainspoken.

Symbolic capitalists tend to be virtually the opposite of the rest of society: we skew culturally and symbolically left but favor free markets. As statistician

Andrew Gelman showed, elites in the Republican Party tend to be significantly more liberal culturally and symbolically than the rest of the GOP, yet more dogmatic about free markets. Meanwhile, Democratic-aligned elites tend to skew significantly farther left on cultural and symbolic issues than most Democrats, but tend to be much warmer on markets.[120] The primary difference between Democratic and Republican elites seems to lie in how they rank free markets relative to cultural liberalism: those who prioritize the former have tended to align with the Republicans; those who prioritize the latter have consistently aligned with the Democrats. (Hence, Republican elites tend to be more economically and culturally aligned with the Right relative to Democratic elites, while Democratic elites tend to be more economically and culturally aligned with the Left relative to GOP elites. But across the board, elites in both parties tend to be more right-aligned economically and left-aligned culturally relative to their respective party bases.)

Our prescriptions for addressing unfortunate market externalities vary systematically from everyone else's too. Highly educated Americans, for example, tend to prioritize redistributive policies to address inequalities (taxes and transfers) over predistributive approaches (e.g., high wages, robust benefits, and job protections that render reallocation less necessary). Most other Americans' preferences skew in the opposite direction.[121] Due to divergences like these between elites and everyone else, as the Democratic Party has drawn itself closer to symbolic capitalists, it has grown increasingly divorced from the concerns and priorities of most other Americans.

For our part, as symbolic capitalists have grown increasingly dominant politically and economically, we've likewise grown increasingly out of touch with the values and perspectives of ordinary Americans.

When elites comprise a relatively small share of the population, they are forced to engage with, and consider, the broader public. For instance, in a world where less than 3 percent of Americans possess a college degree, as was the case in 1920,[122] it would be impossible for degree holders to simply ignore everyone else. They wouldn't even be able to keep food on the table if they concerned themselves only with the highly educated. It would be much harder for such a small voting bloc to control a major political party, orient entire cities around their whims, and dictate the flow of the broader economy in the United States and beyond. They would be largely unable to simply exert their will over others with minimal compromise or regard.

Today, however, more than one in three Americans have degrees. They're increasingly consolidated alongside the wealthy into a small number of hubs, with tight networks of institutions that reinforce one another (such as academia, the mainstream media, advocacy organizations, and left-aligned foundations). Under these circumstances, degree holders no longer need to engage much with the rest of the country. Symbolic capitalist enterprises can likewise easily sustain themselves by focusing only on superelites, other symbolic capitalists, and the communities and institutions they inhabit in the United States and around the world. Academics, journalists, entertainment companies, and other cultural producers can focus exclusively on the culture, values, and priorities of symbolic capitalists and their superelite patrons with little concern (or even outright disdain) for being accessible, compelling, or useful to others. A political party can be flush with funds, and viable electorally, by aggressively pursuing the interests of symbolic capitalists and their cities at the expense of most others.

For example, voters with a BA or higher have formed an outright majority of the electorate in Massachusetts, New York, Colorado, and Maryland. Many other states hosting symbolic economy hubs are trending in the same direction.[123] Studies have found that the effect of educational attainment on Democratic partisanship grows stronger as the share of degree holders in a county increases:[124] as symbolic capitalists grow less accountable or connected to "normies," they align more homogeneously with the Democratic Party.

The rise of a new major donor class has exacerbated these divides. As David Callahan notes, the transition to the symbolic economy has led to the rise of a new constellation of millionaires and billionaires who retain most of the wealthy's traditional aversion to regulation, taxes, trade protectionism, and labor unions (and the aversion to focusing on issues like poverty and class per se) but who skew far left on issues like environmentalism, gender, sexuality, race, immigration, criminal justice reform, and aggressively leveraging the state to address perceived social problems.[125] These new millionaires and billionaires (and their families) comprise a growing share of the superelite. Critically, these new symbolic economy oligarchs are not just to the left of the median voter on cultural issues, they are frequently to the left of Democratic *activists*.[126] And these superelites have poured immense sums of money into nonprofit organizations, political campaigns, journalistic organizations, and institutions of higher learning to move symbolic capitalists and their preferred political party further in their preferred direction. Quite successfully. As economist Thomas Piketty demonstrates, the new "Brahmin Left" has more or less fully "captured" the contemporary Democratic Party and its agenda.[127]

In response, those who feel unrepresented by symbolic capitalists and our social order (including growing numbers of minority voters) have shifted toward the GOP.[128] As Richard Florida demonstrated, creative-class workers have moved aggressively toward the Democrats in recent decades and are now by far the most staunchly Democratic labor group. Although service-class workers still lean left, they have been drifting consistently toward the Republicans since 2008. Meanwhile, working-class voters are now decisively Republican, and they have been shifting still further right over time.[129]

This is, in part, because the reorientation of the party around symbolic capitalists has changed not merely the substance of Democratic politics but also the *style*. For instance, as compared with other voters, symbolic capitalists tend to be much more impressed by charts, plans, and data, and gravitate toward "policy wonks" (who often hold limited appeal in a general election).[130] Because our lives are oriented around the production and manipulation of symbols, we also place a lot of stock in things like representation, symbolic actions, performative demonstrations, "proper" rhetoric, semantic distinctions, and so on—what Democratic strategist James Carville derisively described as "faculty lounge politics."[131] In its bid to attract and mobilize symbolic capitalists, the Democratic Party has increasingly adopted this kind of "academic" messaging.

Indeed, even when the party wants to speak to nonelite audiences, these efforts are often hampered by the fact that the people developing the messaging tend to be highly educated ideologues from relatively affluent backgrounds who often possess inaccurate ideas of what will resonate with their intended audience. And even when the message itself is solid, the people *delivering* the intended message—from sympathetic media figures to social media advocates and door-to-door canvassers—all tend to be highly educated, relatively affluent, and ideologically extreme. And they tend to describe the party, its platform, and its candidates in ways that reflect *their own* personal values and priorities, often speaking "off script" in ways that alienate potential voters.[132] That is, Democrats end up delivering "faculty lounge politics," even though party leaders would rather not, because the party apparatus, from top to bottom, is increasingly dominated by symbolic capitalists.

The Republican Party, meanwhile, has largely abandoned the realm of "ideas" altogether.[133] When both parties were actively trying to court the symbolic capitalist vote, the struggle between the parties was defined in terms of principles and competing positive visions of what the United States is or could be. Political polarization increased dramatically during this period, with the dividing lines between the parties cast primarily in ideological terms.[134] This is no longer the case. Contemporary polarization does not seem to be driven by deep philosophical divides, nor by differences on "the issues," nor by incompatible understandings of "the facts."[135] Instead, the conflict between Democrats and Republicans has been largely reduced to a matter of identity: what kind of people Democrats and Republicans are perceived to be, and how constituents feel about "those people."[136] Democrats and Republicans alike hold increasingly negative, and often inaccurate, views about members of the opposite political party.[137] Moreover, it is *negative* partisanship that increasingly drives voting behavior: partisans are often not particularly fond of their own political party or candidates, but they are deeply committed to keeping power out of the hands of "those people" in the rival camp.[138]

However, partisan politics is far from the only arena in American life that has been transformed by symbolic capitalists' growing social influence and our idiosyncratic cognitive and behavioral dispositions. Myriad other social institutions have also been bent to our will, with profound sociopolitical implications beyond the perennial tug-of-war between Democrats and Republicans. For example, there seems to be an inverse correlation between "postmaterialism" and economic growth.[139] As symbolic capitalists increasingly set the sociocultural agenda, economies tend to stagnate. Economic stagnation, in turn, has been shown to exacerbate many of the adverse conditions plaguing contemporary U.S. civic culture, such as calcifying inequalities and declining social mobility, growing tribalism and intolerance, heightened mistrust of institutions, rising antidemocratic impulses, and increased myopic or zero-sum thinking.[140]

This relative lack of economic dynamism within the symbolic economy may be driven in large part by the reality that, contrary to our self-image, symbolic capitalists actually tend to be rather hostile toward innovation and nonconformance.

Disciplined Minds

Consider the dynamics that often define symbolic capitalist spaces: bubbles and crashes, virality and death spirals, "blowing up" and "getting canceled," and so on. Underlying all of these phenomena is the widespread inclination to copy others in one's network, immediately and reactively. These are *not* phenomena one would expect to observe in contexts defined by those who painstakingly seek out "the facts," exercise healthy skepticism, independently arrive at conclusions, and comfortably defy the crowd.

Nonetheless, symbolic capitalists broadly imagine themselves as people who think outside the box and color outside the lines. We see ourselves as visionaries and "disrupters." Our workplaces tend to be less structured, and our jobs more flexible, than most; we tend to have much less direct supervision. According to some narratives, these characteristics define our professions because we're simply not amenable to limitations, structure, and supervision: we're just too free-spirited and open-minded to allow ourselves to be managed like "other" workers.[141]

Since the 1970s, a growing share of Americans have joined the symbolic professions, with the level of credentials ever rising for those who take part. Symbolic capitalists and their outputs exert ever more influence over U.S. society and culture. Governments and the private sector are dumping enormous sums of resources into science, technology, and research and development. In a world where symbolic capitalists' self-narratives were accurate—where our high levels of education, our intellects, and our unique psychological profiles drove us toward nonconformance and originality—one might expect that we would today be living in a period of unprecedented innovation and growth.

Instead, both innovation and scientific discoveries have slowed significantly, corresponding with the rise of the symbolic economy and the growing influence of symbolic capitalists.[142] Total factor productivity has seen similar stagnation since the turn of the century.[143] Despite more money being dumped into science and technology, and more and more Americans taking part in research and development, the societal returns on these labor and financial investments have been consistently *decreasing*.[144] Papers and patents have become *less* disruptive across most scientific fields and draw on increasingly narrow portions of existing knowledge.[145] New ideas no longer fuel economic growth as they did in previous eras.[146] In short, the reality of scientific, technological, and economic dynamism under the reign of symbolic capitalists seems to be the opposite of what our preferred narratives might predict.

Some have attempted to explain these unfortunate trends in terms of changes to intellectual property and antitrust laws that have allowed powerful actors to "capture" markets and stifle competition.[147] Others posit that perhaps the "big" discoveries in many sectors have already been made and it is simply unreasonable to expect that the kinds of revolutions in science, technology, productivity, and standards of living that defined previous eras would persist or be repeated.[148] Still others argue that the sheer size of many scientific fields, and the number of papers that are constantly being churned out, impede the rise of new ideas: unsure of what is reliable or worthwhile, unable to keep tabs on new findings and scholars, and in the midst of a replication crisis, scientists increasingly cluster conservatively around the same subjects and cite the same canonical papers from the same already-established researchers—allowing them to feel as though their own work is premised on a secure foundation (and assuring peer reviewers and potential funders of the same).[149]

All of these narratives likely explain part of what's going on here. However, changes in research and development priorities, and how funds are allocated, are likely a core piece of the puzzle too.[150] Before the 1980s, scientific research was largely conducted by industry scientists at industry labs or conducted by academics supported by industry and in close collaboration with industry scientists. These efforts were oriented largely toward practical ends, such as improving the efficiency, productivity, and reliability of enterprises, and developing new or improved goods and services. Other transformative innovations, such as communications satellites and the internet, were developed directly by government scientists, often in collaboration with industry. After the 1980s, however, many corporations ended up closing or scaling back their labs. Scientific research began to be carried out primarily at universities, by academics rather than government or industry professionals. This research was increasingly funded by foundations and the federal government, often oriented toward addressing huge and borderline intractable social challenges rather than discrete practical problems. There was a greater emphasis on "basic" (rather than "applied") research as well.[151]

This matters because, with some exceptions, scientific and technological revolutions have rarely occurred as a result of top-down planning. Revolutionary discoveries have often been stumbled upon by practitioners, amateurs, or outsiders of a field. They've been the products of accidents, improvisation, or tinkering. These breakthroughs are then explained, refined, built on, and operationalized by systematizers—the scholars, the specialists, the experts, and others.[152] Those in the latter group are generally *not* people who think outside the box; they are the people who build boxes and inhabit them; and once they've settled on a paradigm, they often strongly resist change.[153] Rather than taking intellectual risks, scholars are generally oriented toward producing work that will be easily and widely embraced by peers (thereby maximizing the likelihood of publication, citation, and grant funding); such work tends to affirm rather than challenge the prevailing consensus.[154]

Consequently, in a world where virtually the only people "doing" science are symbolic capitalists embedded within institutions of higher learning, and where there is diminishing exchange between these scholars and everyone else, one would expect to see exactly what we *do* see: a slowing of innovation.

We see similar patterns unfolding with entrepreneurship, likewise corresponding to the changing role of educational institutions and credentials in the symbolic economy. Launching a successful business has been historically associated with two factors: coming from a privileged background and having a propensity toward risk-taking and rebellion.[155] However, in the contemporary context, postsecondary education, especially elite education, has become increasingly important for building social and symbolic capital, the cultivation of which significantly enhances one's prospects of launching a *successful* business, should one make the attempt.[156] The problem is, the kinds of people who tend to enjoy and excel at school are generally *not* particularly original thinkers or bold decision makers.[157] Elite university graduates, for instance, tend to pursue the same kinds of elite jobs at the same elite firms,[158] or else attempt the same kinds of startups in the same fields, making the same kinds of marginal variations on already-existing products or services.[159] Far from being especially prone to disruption or innovation, degree holders have grown increasingly *unlikely* to start their own businesses—instead flocking to safer and relatively high-salary positions within established firms.[160] Indeed, although growing shares of Americans possess college degrees, the share of *entrepreneurs* with a BA or higher fell by more than half between 1985 and 2014. Consequently, rather than seeing a blossoming in entrepreneurship corresponding with the rise of the symbolic economy, entrepreneurship rates in the United States have consistently *declined* since the 1970s.

Pop culture has followed the same basic trajectory as science and enterprise. It has become a conversational meme that just about everything these days seems to be a reboot, a remake, a spinoff, or a sequel. Psychologist Adam Mastroianni has empirically demonstrated that this widespread perception does, in fact, seem to map onto reality. Looking at movies, music, TV shows, and video games, he illustrates that an ever-growing share of the outputs that dominate the cultural landscape are just retoolings or continuations of existing hit franchises in the same medium.[161] Simultaneously, a smaller and smaller share of cultural producers are claiming ever-larger pieces of the pie, with a higher rate of their outputs becoming major successes, and "charting" for much longer, while the prospects for someone or something genuinely novel to "break through" have been rapidly diminishing. Indeed, old outputs from established figures are increasingly eclipsing even successful works by new cultural producers, even as successful new works are growing increasingly similar to one another.[162] That is, rather than seeing unprecedented diversity and churn as a result of shifting demographics, globalization, advances in communications technologies, and a proliferation of platforms, instead there is growing homogenization and hegemony in pop culture. Or as Mastroianni put it, "Pop culture has become an oligarchy."[163] It is likely not a coincidence that over this same period of time, a rapidly growing share of cultural "creatives"—from visual artists to musicians, actors, novelists, and journalists—are people who possess BA and graduate degrees (in an ever-narrowing range of fields, from an ever-narrowing range of prestigious institutions), with rates of credential inflation that far exceed those of the broader U.S. population.[164]

Insofar as college degrees are used to gatekeep access to the symbolic professions, symbolic capitalists will never be particularly prone toward "disruption." As Noam Chomsky pointed out decades ago, colleges and universities (and consequently the symbolic professions) are overwhelmingly composed of the kind of people who showed up to school every day and on time; who did not have bad disciplinary records but *did* have the right kinds of extracurriculars; who turned in their assignments on time and according to the specified instructions; who mastered regurgitating the information that the teachers provided precisely, and in a form that said teachers found aesthetically pleasing; who craved approval from their teachers and other authority figures; who take pride in their grades, believing that their academic records say something meaningful about themselves; who do well on standardized tests—again, often believing that their high scores say something meaningful about themselves; and who are willing to virtually indefinitely delay gratification.[165] *This* is how one ends up with sterling attendance and disciplinary records, a high GPA, and the glowing letters of recommendation that help get one into a selective college. These same dispositions allow one to flourish as a college student and, later, in the symbolic professions.[166]

As economist Bryan Caplan demonstrated at length,[167] the main signal our college degrees send to employers is that we are the kind of people who are willing to endure drudgery, degradation, and busy work (such as is required to obtain a college degree); we are the kind of people who see things through to completion (which is why a degree, even an associate's degree, will give you a bigger boost on the job market than several years of schooling without a degree); we are the kind of people who will follow the rules, who will complete tasks on time and according to specifications, and so on. In other words, the credentials we are so proud of do *not* demonstrate that we are creative thinkers or independent spirits. Quite the opposite: they show people that we are capable and conscientious conformists. And it actually makes sense that the symbolic economy would be organized to select for these traits.

For the most part, it is not the job of symbolic capitalists to question authority, but to build it, to apply it, and to defend it. This is just as true of journalists, scholars, spokespeople for causes or organizations, artists, and "thought leaders" as it is for scientists, government representatives, clergy, and the like. People, movements, and organizations flourish in the symbolic economy by proving themselves useful or interesting to those they are seeking support and deference from—*not* by being threatening. As Jeff Schmidt put it in his provocative *Disciplined Minds* (a book whose publication cost him his position at the magazine *Physics Today*),[168]

> Professionals are licensed to think on the job, but they are obedient thinkers. All professional work is in part creative. However, individuals are selected to do professional work not because they are more creative than others, but because they can be trusted to make sure every detail of what they create is politically correct for their employers' points of view. . . . Employers will hire dull but politically disciplined individuals over those displaying any amount of politically undisciplined creativity. Just as professionals engage in playpen creativity, innovating within the safe confines of an assigned ideology, so too they engage in playpen critical thinking. . . . Professionals generally avoid the risk inherent in real critical thinking and cannot be properly called critical thinkers. They are simply ideologically-disciplined thinkers.[169]

That is, in contrast with our self-narratives about why we enjoy such flexible job structures and light supervision, the true reason symbolic capitalists are not heavily managed is not that we *can't* be. It's because we don't need to be. We manage ourselves. We discipline ourselves (and often our peers as well). We strive not just to conform with but to exceed expectations. While other types of employees regularly have uncompensated labor, long hours, and unpleasant schedules coerced out of them,[170] symbolic capitalists *willingly* work overtime, even uncompensated. We willingly allow our jobs to encroach on our private time and personal lives, and to crowd out other priorities. We make ourselves available around the clock. We see it as a virtue, and humblebrag about how much time we put in and how productive, busy, and exhausted we are.[171] As philosopher Matthew Stewart put it:

> The extra hours . . . are performative. They are not there to get something done, but to prove a point. The obvious part of the point is to manifest the unconditional, strip-me-naked-and-tie-me-to-the-grindstone level of commitment that an employer with access to streams of gusher money may demand in exchange for sharing those market rents with you in particular as opposed to the next fanatical overachiever on the list. It's the less obvious part of the point—the one intended to convince oneself—that is more concerning. This is the part that involves saying—and believing— that "this Kool-Aid tastes great!"[172]

In 2021, journalist Sarah Jaffe published a treatise, *Work Won't Love You Back*.[173] It's a great book, but the fact that a text like hers would even need to be written (with symbolic capitalists as its target audience) is itself tragic—a testament to how fully many of us have internalized the prevailing institutional logic of our employers. Indeed, although only one in three workers without a college degree views their jobs or careers as central to their overall identity, a majority (53 percent) of postgraduate degree holders (and four in ten BA holders) feel this way.[174]

Nonetheless, symbolic capitalists like to think of ourselves as subversives and nonconformists. Businesses have been able to exploit this desire in order to gain access to our talents and relatively high disposable incomes. Beginning in the 1970s, as symbolic capitalists were growing increasingly prominent within the economy, companies began aggressively aligning themselves with rebellion and counterculture. Advertisements began suggesting that buying *their* goods and services (as compared with those of their competitors)—or working at *their* company—was a bold and rebellious act, a challenge to the status quo, and the sign of an independent thinker.[175] Subsequent advertising would be blatantly anticonsumerist, leaning into irony, self-consciousness, and even self-deprecation. Such ads appeal to symbolic capitalists' sense that we're savvy, self-aware, and nonconformist: if we *do* go on to buy their product or service, it's because that's what we were going to do anyway, *not* because we've been manipulated. After all, we see right through the ads (not hard, as the ads render *themselves* transparent).[176]

More recently, particularly during the Trump years, the trend has been toward "woke-washing" or "commodity activism." Companies have been highlighting their charitable giving, and even taking "bold" stances on culture-war issues—signaling toward antiracism, feminism, LGBTQ rights, environmentalism, and so on—as a way of selling more of their products and services, staving off potential criticism, and enhancing their public standing with people like us.[177] Although these campaigns often alienate people who are *not* symbolic capitalists, companies are willing to take that hit because we have more disposable income (and are projected to control an even higher share of wealth down the line)—and we reside in mass markets to boot.[178] These "woke capitalism" campaigns have often paid off handsomely: it seems as though symbolic capitalists (literally) buy into these gestures, despite many of these companies' atrocious track records and ongoing disreputable behaviors with respect to their employees, contractors, or supply chains; their egregious tax avoidance; their environmental harm; and so on.[179]

And why wouldn't we buy into it? The truth is, these companies are "radical" in the same way that *we're* radical: in terms of what is professed (and *not* what we do or how we live). The "nonconformity" these companies advocate may be calculated, sterile, and almost purely aesthetic—but that is exactly the kind of "nonconformity" that we ourselves engage in. At bottom, they want the same things from their "activism" that we do: to be seen as good, and maybe even do some good, but without making meaningful sacrifices or changes to how we go about our business (maybe even *enhancing* our position in the process). This parity is, of course, a product of the fact that "they" actually *are* "us." At the corporate level, it is overwhelmingly symbolic capitalists who run things; it is also symbolic capitalists who work in advertising firms, producing these strategies for appealing to other symbolic capitalists.

Indeed, part of what these campaigns are "about" is brands selling themselves not just to potential customers or investors but also to current and potential high-value employees. While most workers in the United States would rather their employer stay out of politics, symbolic capitalists express a preference for employers to take (the "correct") public stances on social justice issues—and we gravitate toward employers who do this.[180]

In order to recruit and retain what they perceive as the "best" talent while appealing to one of the most lucrative customer bases worldwide, business leaders and corporations try to demonstrate that they share symbolic capitalists' values and politics.[181] And in a deep sense, it must be said, they do.

Coda: "Woke" Capitalism

Symbolic capitalists tend to be *highly* concerned with disparities between demographic groups. We react to perceived incidents of bigotry, harassment, or discrimination with extreme intolerance. We are the Americans most likely to self-identify as antiracists, feminists, or "allies" for people from historically marginalized or disadvantaged populations. We are the primary producers and consumers of content on antiracism, feminism, and the like—be it in mainstream media outlets, academic journals, or beyond. Many of us view these commitments as fundamentally anticapitalist in nature. However, there is a profound sense in which capitalism and "identitarian" approaches to social justice complement each other well.

As Karl Marx noted, the free market doesn't care about, and is indeed hostile toward, tradition, strong kinship ties, community, rootedness, and noninstrumental moral commitments. Capitalism requires the "constant revolutionizing of production, uninterrupted disturbance of all social conditions, everlasting uncertainty and agitation. . . . All fixed, fast-frozen relations, with their train of ancient and venerable prejudices and opinions, are swept away, all new-formed ones become antiquated before they can ossify. All that is solid melts into air, all that is holy is profaned."[182] Identitarians tend to likewise disdain tradition, rootedness, and noninstrumental or unchosen relations and commitments—often describing these as obstacles to personal autonomy and self-realization.[183]

Moreover, as Walter Benn Michaels and Adolph Reed Jr. powerfully argued, a tight focus on inequalities between identity groups is perfectly compatible with high levels of inequality per se:

> The implication of proportionality as the metric of social justice is that the society would be just if 1 percent of the population controlled 90 percent of the resources so long as 13 percent of the 1 percent were black, 14 percent were Hispanic, half were women, etc. . . . It's the fixation on disproportionality that tells us the increasing wealth of the one percent would be OK if only there [were] more black, brown, and LGBTQIA+ billionaires. And the fact that antiracism and antidiscrimination of all kinds would validate rather than undermine the stratification of wealth in American society is completely visible to those who currently possess that wealth— all the rich people eager to embark on a course of moral purification (antiracist training) but with no interest whatsoever in a politics (social-democratic redistribution) that would alter the material conditions that make them rich.[184]

Indeed, although symbolic capitalists tend to view themselves as egalitarians, it is a very particular conception of equality that we tend to be most preoccupied by.

In *The Sacred Project of American Sociology*, Christian Smith argues that sociologists view it as their mission to promote "the emancipation, equality, and moral affirmation of all human beings as autonomous, self-directing, individual agents, (who should be) out to live their lives as they personally so desire—by constructing their own favored identities, entering and exiting relationships as they choose, and equally enjoying the gratification of experiential, material, and bodily pleasures."[185] In this conception of social justice, everyone "deserves to be morally affirmed by everyone else in their society. . . . Unacceptable, therefore, is any form of real or symbolic lack of acceptance, exclusion, or moral judgment against another. Every identity and lifestyle must not only be tolerated but positively validated, affirmed, and included."[186]

Although sociologists pursue this mission in profession-specific ways (e.g., through empirical studies), the moral worldview Smith lays out seems common to symbolic capitalists across the board: people should be able to do whatever they want, to *be* whomever they want, provided they have the requisite skills, drive, resources, and so forth to pull it off. For instance, all things equal, women should be able to work in all the same jobs as men, be treated the same way, and enjoy the same compensation and expectations while bringing their "whole selves" to work. The same holds for Blacks as compared with whites, queer employees as compared with straight employees, and so on. However, insofar as all things are *not* equal, inclusivity often takes a back seat.

As a nice encapsulation of these realities, many student clubs at Yale are explicitly oriented around social justice but are also highly competitive to get into. There's no mission-centric reason that membership in social justice clubs would need to be organized this way. In fact, Yale has repeatedly asked the clubs to stop rejecting people from these organizations on the basis of credentialism (in no small part because students from less advantaged backgrounds end up being especially likely to be excluded from these "social justice" groups when membership is decided in this way). However, the student organizations continue to be highly parochial—even by Yale standards—and in defiance of administration preferences. As one student observed, colleagues seem to derive their sense of purpose and self-worth through being ranked against their peers and turning everything—even social justice advocacy—into a competition.[187] They view inclusion as an imperative for everyone who "deserves" to be part of the group. For everyone else, however, exclusion is not only acceptable, it is viewed as natural and appropriate—even in social justice advocacy.

In short, symbolic capitalists tend to advocate for a form of social justice that jives well with, and indeed enhances, meritocracy. The objective is to eliminate barriers against immigrants, women, LGBTQ people, and racial and ethnic minorities so the "best and the brightest" can rise to the top. But notice, this language about "rising to the top" implies a hierarchy, *not* egalitarianism. The goal, at bottom, isn't to make everyone equal. It's to ensure that *in*equalities are based on the "correct" (meritocratic) attributes. Of course, many capitalist enterprises have a strong interest in the same. The phenomenon derisively referred to as "woke capitalism" is an expression of overlaps like these (an "elective affinity" in Weberian terms).

The embrace and pursuit of mainstream symbolic capitalists' values, language, and priorities is in the direct financial interest of many companies. In the words of Jamie Dimon, current CEO of JPMorgan Chase and former chairman of the influential corporate lobbying group Business Roundtable, "I'm not woke. And I think people are mistaking the stakeholder capitalism thing for being woke. . . . What we give a shit about is serving customers, earning their respect, earning their repeat business. . . . Any senator or congressman who says that's woke, they're not thinking clearly because I want to win in the marketplace. I want the best employees, I want happy employees."[188] The point, in a nutshell, is not to change the world. It's to make more money.

Consider the intense corporate focus on diversity, equity, and inclusion. To be sure, there are PR and legal aspects to this phenomenon. However, there are also direct material incentives at play. As UBS Wealth Management chief economist Paul Donovan has illustrated at length, identity-based bias, prejudice, and exclusion tend to be quite expensive for multinational corporations.[189] In the hypercompetitive global arenas that many companies are operating in, the pursuit of profit maximization often aligns cleanly with the pursuit of greater diversity and inclusion. It increases the efficiency of capitalist enterprises to avoid losing access to talent, partnerships, or customers due to "irrational" discrimination. Properly managed, diversity provides a range of competitive advantages with respect to innovation, problem solving, forecasting, knowledge production, and quality control.[190] Indeed, economists estimate that 20–40 percent of all economic growth in the United States since the 1960s has been due simply to improved allocation of talent— particularly the opening of more opportunities to highly talented women and minorities at the expense of less skilled, less "hungry," and less innovative white men (who had largely taken their positions for granted prior, but are now "hungry" as well due to increased competition, which only enhances corporate profits further).[191]

It should therefore not be surprising that, as Kimberlé Crenshaw put it, "every corporation worth its salt is saying something about structural racism and anti-blackness, and that stuff is even outdistancing what candidates in the Democratic Party were actually saying."[192] And it's not just words or high-profile donations to organizations like Black Lives Matter. Multinational corporations have also leveraged their political clout to resist and overturn laws perceived to disadvantage immigrants, racial minorities, and LGBTQ Americans.[193] This should not be mistaken for altruism or mere cynical gesturing—it is in the perceived material interests of many symbolic economy institutions to become more diverse and inclusive and to resist external impediments to their ambitions in this regard.

But of course, this approach to social justice is also quite limited, with commitments extending only insofar as they actually *do* enhance the "bottom line." Interventions are designed to minimize costs and risks, and to maximize profits and opportunities, for those taking part in "benevolent" acts—often at the expense of the people and causes being championed. Meanwhile, approaches to "social justice" projected to significantly disrupt operations, threaten the business model, or undermine profitability are generally avoided or actively resisted—even if they would likely be far more effective at "moving the meter" on various social problems. Consequently, the marriage of identitarianism and capitalism has had a range of somewhat contradictory effects on U.S. society and culture.

As Enzo Rossi and Olufemi Taiwo recently highlighted, on one side of the ledger, most barriers that *formally* excluded women and minorities from elite spaces have been dismantled over the last half century. This represents a real and significant change to the prevailing order. However, they argue, while it is important to recognize this progress, it is also critical to acknowledge its benefits as quite limited—extending mostly to a small cadre of minority elites.[194] These measures have helped *elites* from historically marginalized and disadvantaged groups *preserve or enhance their elite social position*, but they have not greatly expanded the share of minorities who can climb up the ladder (let alone reducing or altogether dismantling the hierarchies implied by the "ladder" metaphor). In fact, a *smaller* share of Black and Hispanic students attend elite colleges today as compared with the 1980s.[195] The percentage of African Americans who make it into the top income quintile is basically the same today as it was in 1960.[196] Most African Americans who are born poor stay poor throughout their lives, and poverty much more frequently persists across generations for African Americans than for people of other ethnic or racial backgrounds.[197] Meanwhile, most children of middle-class Black families are likely to experience *downward* mobility over their life course, with little wealth accumulating across generations.[198]

At the institutional level, despite the aforementioned incentives for greater diversity and inclusion, systematic inequalities often persist because employees have *personal* interests and preferences that often supervene (in social science parlance, this would be described as a "principle-agent problem"). Elite incumbents and aspirants from historically dominant groups may sympathize with competitors from historically marginalized and disadvantaged populations, but they are also keen to preserve or enhance their own status, security, wealth, and future prospects (and those of their lovers, friends, family members, etc.—who tend to share similar backgrounds). As conveyed through their behaviors (their "revealed preferences"), securing these latter objectives is much more important to most than advancing diversity, equity, or inclusion in their organizations. And insofar as already-advantaged incumbents are trying their best to outcompete aspirants from less advantaged backgrounds, all else equal, the incumbent is likely to win. Under these conditions, inequalities can replicate systematically and virtually indefinitely, even when literally *everyone* supports diversity, equity, and inclusion per se.

And within most symbolic capitalist spaces virtually everyone does support these ideals *in principle*. We support feminism. We support antiracism. We support LGBTQ rights. We support the environment. We don't just support these causes in America, we support them worldwide. In our hearts, in our minds, in our rhetoric, we support them. But less so in our behaviors and in our relations with others—especially if it'll cost us. In this, individual symbolic capitalists tend to operate roughly identically to the organizations we dominate. And Jamie Dimon is right: we have never been woke.

5

Totemic Capital(ism)

From the outset, the high pay, prestige, and autonomy symbolic capitalists enjoy have been justified by claims that we serve the common good and, especially, the most vulnerable, marginalized, and disadvantaged in society. These narratives continue to serve as a core means of legitimation. Increasingly, however, cultural elites are not content to portray themselves as merely advocating for, or representing the interests of, the marginalized and disadvantaged in society. It is becoming increasingly common for symbolic capitalists to assert that they directly embody vulnerable and stigmatized populations. They portray themselves as champions of those victimized by society even as they count themselves among the victimized. This is a mode of legitimation that was previously unique to Black civil rights activists in the segregated South and others occupying similar roles—that is, people who suffered real oppression, who were pushing for concrete changes, who had real followings because they were part of actual movements that they were appointed as spokespeople of. Today, applicants to McKinsey & Co. make similar claims in the service of landing a six-figure job after they graduate from an Ivy.

How did we get here? How did it become appealing for cultural elites to not merely present themselves as concerned with the plight of the less fortunate but to represent themselves *as* the less fortunate? Anthropologists Didier Fassin and Richard Rechtman chronicled the rise of this novel form of status (and eventual status competition) in their landmark text, *The Empire of Trauma: An Inquiry into the Condition of Victimhood*.[1] The following is their story in a nutshell.

Although the notion of psychological trauma goes back to the late nine-teenth century (particularly via the work of Jean-Martin Charcot, Sigmund Freud, and Pierre Janet), even as late as World War II, trauma was not taken very seriously. Many argued that appeals to "trauma" were merely a means for soldiers to excuse their weak constitutions (unlike the "real men" who could hold themselves together in war). It was widely believed that soldiers were exaggerating their symptoms to get sent home from the field or avoid returning thereto. This widespread dismissal spurred a decades-long cam-paign among practitioners treating those soldiers, alongside veteran advo-cacy groups, to privilege testimony and subjective experience—to not only take these seriously but to place them, in some senses, *above meaningful scrutiny or reproach.*

Nonetheless, the concept of trauma was not widely embraced until the Vietnam War. Most intellectuals and academics were against the war. Psy-chologists and psychiatrists, many of whom had been formerly hesitant or skeptical of the "trauma" framework, increasingly sought to ground their opposition to Vietnam in their domain of expertise—by arguing that the con-flict was *traumatizing* America's young men en masse. The image of the psychologically damaged veteran became an important component of anti-war advocacy—and posttraumatic stress disorder was formally added to the *Diagnostic and Statistical Manual of Mental Disorders III* shortly after the U.S. withdrawal from the theater.

From there, the concept was gradually expanded beyond soldiers to include civilian survivors of war and terrorism, then police officers and other first responders, then victims of crimes including (especially) sexual assault[2] and, eventually, those who had lived through natural disasters or other catastrophes. Gradually, to be a "victim" or a "survivor" took on less of a negative connotation—and eventually became something like a source of pride or honor. The 9/11 attacks, and the subsequent wars in Iraq and Afghanistan (and the valorization, even sacralization, of those who were killed or wounded therein), played a pivotal role in this transition.

In the years that followed, scientific advances would both reflect and enhance these changing notions of victimhood. Brain scans and other forms of research purported to demonstrate that "trauma" could literally and durably change one's body and mind.[3] To be "traumatized" expanded from being an experience many undergo (and hopefully, eventually transcend) into being *a type of person that one becomes,* more or less indefinitely. Put another way, "trauma" became naturalized as a basis for identity claims.

Ultimately, a new mode of status competition seems to have emerged from these shifts. For instance, to be pitied by others used to be humiliating, and to be "victimized" by others was a source of shame. People were encouraged to directly (personally) confront those who wronged them. If they were unwilling or unable to stand up to aggressors, they were supposed to be stoic; to be proudly defiant; to not let those who harmed them see them broken. Respect was accorded to those who demonstrated themselves as capable and powerful, who were resilient to suffering and hardship, who were brave in the face of risk and danger, who were collected and confident in response to challenges and uncertainty. These values still prevail in much of the world, and indeed in many U.S. subcultures. However, sociologists Bradley Campbell and Jason Manning argue, a different moral culture has taken hold among contemporary symbolic capitalists—a "victimhood culture."[4]

Victimhood cultures, they argue, operate by a different set of rules and norms as compared to moral cultures oriented around "honor" or "dignity." For instance, rather than directly confronting or negotiating with adversaries (settling things "between ourselves"), the norm in a victimhood culture would be to appeal to third parties to adjudicate conflicts, intervene on one's behalf, or offer support and validation. In order to enlist these third parties, harm is discussed in hyperbolic ways. People attempt to paint themselves as weak, vulnerable, helpless, or damaged—especially relative to their adversaries. The wrongs done to oneself are tied to historical and ongoing injustices affecting others. An awkward racially inflected comment, for instance, is not described as an isolated remark made by a particular person within a specific context—instead, the comment is tied to America's history of slavery or Jim Crow, or contemporary tragedies like the murder of George Floyd. Localized or otherwise trivial incidents are recast as fronts in cosmic struggles that others have a perceived stake in.

In a victimhood culture, extending the benefit of the doubt, laying the burden of proof on accusers, and insisting on due process or withholding judgment are often seen as impediments to justice and affronts against victims, whose accounts and interpretations of events should be sacrosanct. Immense pressure is levied on institutional decision makers for swift and decisive action in response to allegations. There is a consistent focus on "safety" (construed extremely broadly) and on aversion to risk. This often leads to censorship and invasive surveillance and management techniques, as decision makers strive not only to mitigate and (as needed) rectify conflict, offense, or harm but to prevent them outright.

The incentives in a victimhood culture push participants to be extremely sensitive even to minor or unintentional missteps by others, and to interpret ambiguous words, deeds, and situations uncharitably. This is how one maximizes opportunities to enhance one's own moral standing. As essayist Ben Hickman put it, "Pejoratives like 'snowflake' miss the point of such politics. This isn't a discourse of oversensitivity, but of hardheaded pragmatism. It hasn't led people to fragility; it has led them to the most brutal instrumentalism in which no experience is lost as an occasion to bolster one's brand and work one's way up whatever institutional ladder."[5]

Within a victimhood culture, challenging a purported victim's claims or failing to comply with their demands is often recast as a form of abuse—a type of revictimization.[6] To extend compassion, sympathy, curiosity, or understanding toward accused wrongdoers—to press for nuance, caution, and proportionality, or to highlight complexities, ambiguities, and uncertainties—is to risk moral pollution. Even the acts of refraining from judgment, trying to stay out of conflicts, or avoiding taking sides can look extremely suspect.

Put another way, within a victimhood culture there are both "pull" factors (a desire to bolster one's reputation) and "push" factors (a desire to avoid having one's image tarnished or called into question) that operate simultaneously, creating powerful incentives for people to rush to conclusions, conspicuously align themselves with the "right" side of conflicts, demand harsh punishment for perceived violations, absolve "victims" of any responsibility for creating or resolving unfortunate situations, and to acquiesce to "victims" demands with little resistance whenever possible. Because symbolic capitalists' livelihoods are literally predicated on their social standing and their social connections, both the push and the pull factors would impress themselves more heavily on us than on most others. We have much more to gain, and potentially much more to lose, in struggles around victimhood and allyship.

We will explore the manifestations and implications of "victimhood culture" among symbolic capitalists in great detail in the sections that follow. However, before getting into that, it seems important to pause and note that the transition to a victimhood culture within American symbolic capitalist spaces happened at a moment when there was a significant change in the demographic constitution *of* those spaces. As we have seen, the socioeconomic and racial compositions of the symbolic professions, while marginally more diverse, have remained distressingly persistent. However, the *gender* composition of these professions has changed radically. Overall, women are a decisive and growing majority of contemporary symbolic capitalists, and also of college graduates (i.e., future symbolic capitalists). And although institutional inequalities persist *within* those professions (e.g., men remain significantly more likely to be in executive positions), this too is beginning to change. The feminization of the symbolic professions is significant in light of the robust and ever-expanding lines of research in moral and social psychology demonstrating that, in the United States and across cultural contexts, men and women tend to engage in very different forms of conflict, competition, and status seeking.[7]

For instance, although people across sexual lines tend to be highly committed to getting others to conform with their own preferences, expectations, and interests, women tend to be more concerned with ensuring people conform *for the right reasons.* They want others to comply out of love, admiration, or respect—that is, because others hold them in high esteem. They also want people who conform to explicitly validate that conforming is right and good—especially if they had been previously noncompliant or disagreeable. Men are comparably less concerned about *why* people comply. They are, consequently, much more comfortable with bribes and stark coercion to get people to do what they want. Put simply, men tend to be relatively more interested in power, while women prioritize status.[8] Women also tend to be much more sensitive to differences in status than men, and more resentful toward those with higher status than themselves.[9]

Moreover, as compared with men, women are much more likely to avoid direct confrontation with rivals or aggressors. Instead, they typically seek to enlist allies in order to *collectively* ostracize, defame, or humiliate opponents—or else try to rely on formal processes and procedures, and involve institutional intermediaries, in order to address perceived harms—especially in conflicts with those more powerful than themselves.[10] Across cultural contexts, women tend to be more averse to risk, threats, and harm (against themselves or others) as compared with men. They also tend to be *much* more supportive of various forms of censorship, exclusion, surveillance, and related measures in order to proactively ward off the prospect of harm or preemptively neutralize potential threats.[11]

Of course, as detailed earlier, virtually all of these dispositions are similarly associated with "victimhood culture." It seems likely that the cultural and demographic processes described earlier were mutually reinforcing: the feminization of the symbolic professions may have hastened the adoption of a new moral culture and vice versa (although more empirical research on the relationship between these trends would be quite welcome!).

One final thing to bear in mind before moving on is that the question of whether victimhood culture is "better" or "worse" than moral cultures based on honor or dignity is not really a scientific question. It is a subjective and normative evaluation. Practically speaking, any moral culture would have trade-offs for various actors and in various contexts (indeed, new moral cultures seem to arise and "catch on" precisely in response to perceived shortcomings with the dominant paradigm among rising elites). Consequently, whether (and to what extent) victimhood culture is perceived as "good" or "bad" would likely depend on a range of factors, including *whom* we're talking about, what they value, what they're trying to accomplish, and where they fall in a given social or institutional order. This chapter will attempt to more or less sidestep questions like these. The goal in this chapter is to instead provide thick descriptions and empirical analyses of how that culture functions in practice among contemporary symbolic capitalists. We'll start with some observations on how victimhood culture influences status competition.

Victimhood as Status

Let us begin with two stories.

On January 29, 2019, actor Jussie Smollett claimed to be the victim of a hate crime. According to his report to police, two white men wearing Make America Great Again (MAGA) gear were aimlessly roaming through Chicago at two o'clock in the morning in minus-thirty-degree weather, carrying nooses and bleach, when they stumbled upon Smollett, who just so happened to desire a Subway sandwich at two o'clock in the morning and decided to walk to get his meal in below-freezing weather rather than using a delivery service, driving, or hiring a car. In his telling, despite the darkness and the weather (which would require people to be bundled up pretty well), these MAGA whites immediately recognized Smollett as the star of *Empire*—a Fox drama about a hip-hop mogul and his family. They also happened to be up on their Hollywood trivia enough to know that Smollett was gay. They immediately decided to attack him on the basis of his race and sexuality, deploying the nooses and bleach they just happened to be carrying when they encountered him, all while yelling political slogans associated with the Donald Trump campaign. But then, despite outnumbering him and getting the drop on him, Smollett claimed to have heroically fought off his assailants, forcing them to flee, and was miraculously left with only mild scrapes and bruises related to the altercation.

Although virtually every part of his story seemed implausible, even ridiculous, many celebrities and political figures immediately rushed to signal that *they* believed Smollett. Indeed, the fact that the story was so absurd on its face created an opportunity for status competition. It provided a chance for people to distinguish themselves by demonstrating just how committed they were to trusting purported victims relative to their peers.[12] And so, despite the rather obvious problems with Smollett's narrative, many immediately rushed to condemn the ostensibly racist and homophobic attack against him, exerted major pressure on the authorities to identify and punish the perpetrators, and viciously targeted those who expressed skepticism about the actor's claims. Then-presidential hopefuls Joe Biden and Kamala Harris both condemned the incident, with the latter describing it as a "modern day lynching." Black Lives Matter and CNN anchor Don Lemon played especially important roles in elevating the story and disparaging those who doubted Smollett or even those who simply declined to "speak up."[13]

Over the course of the police investigation that followed, it would turn out that the men who "assaulted" Smollett were not only Black (rather than white MAGA supporters, as initially claimed), but they were extras on Smollett's show. Moreover, they regularly ran personal errands for the actor as a side gig. Upon being apprehended, the "assailants" testified that they carried out the fake attack both on Smollett's orders and according to his specifications. Investigators would show that Smollett had wired money to the men before the event and had been in regular communication with them both before and after—with text messages and videographic evidence strongly suggesting they were planning the attack together in the days prior and coordinating on the day of.[14] Smollett was tried and convicted of five crimes related to faking a hate crime. According to investigators, the apparent aim of the hoax was to increase attention for *Empire*, while enhancing Smollett's own public profile, putting him in a position to secure a higher salary in forthcoming negotiations, and generally expanding the suite of opportunities available to the actor downstream.

Although outright hoaxes of this nature seem to be somewhat rare, scholars *have* identified a common set of motives that seem to drive such behaviors when they occur. People generally fabricate victimization in order to get positive attention from others (or ward off negative attention), to feel special, and to secure additional care, assistance, or compensation from others.[15] The Smollett case seems to provide a textbook example of a victimization hoax. The next story is a bit more complicated, and for that reason, perhaps more instructive of certain themes of this chapter.

On December 18, 2018, actress Amber Heard published an essay in the *Washington Post* describing herself as a survivor of sexual violence and domestic abuse, and positioning herself as an advocate for other survivors. Explicitly aligning herself with the #MeToo movement, Heard claimed firsthand experience with the adverse consequences women often face for resisting or exposing the bad behavior of powerful men. Although not explicitly mentioned, the article strongly alluded to her ex-husband, actor Johnny Depp, as the source of victimization she described. The article received significant news coverage and Heard was widely praised for her bravery in coming forward. The day after Heard's article came out, she was announced as an ACLU Artist Ambassador for women's rights. Two days after that, the blockbuster film *Aquaman* was released, with Heard starring in a lead role. The op-ed and the movie fed off each other, each elevating the prominence of the other, to Heard's benefit. She was having "a moment."

Yet, unfortunately (for everyone, in the end), as Heard's star was rising in the wake of the op-ed, Depp was dropped from numerous high-profile projects, including the blockbuster Harry Potter prequel series Fantastic Beasts and a forthcoming Pirates of the Caribbean film—all due to his alleged abuse of Heard. Suffering tens of millions of dollars in purported losses, and insisting that Heard had misrepresented their relationship, Depp sued his ex for defamation. He claimed that the prevailing narrative had the whole thing backward and, in fact, *Heard* had consistently physically and mentally abused *him*. And he successfully convinced a jury of his account of events— winning $10 million in compensatory damages, with an additional $5 million in punitive damages (while Heard won only $2 million in compensatory damages in her countersuit out of a requested $100 million).[16]

Over the course of the trial, it was revealed that the timing of the events leading to Heard's "moment" was not coincidental. In exchange for Heard's pledging $3.5 million to the ACLU (less than half of which ended up getting paid), the nonprofit awarded Heard with the title of Artist Ambassador for women's rights, more or less composed her viral op-ed, helped place it in the *Washington Post*, and promoted it thereafter. Correspondence and testimony released during the trial revealed that, at Heard's insistence, they carefully timed the publication of the op-ed, and the subsequent press release regarding her ambassadorship for women's rights, to correspond with the release of *Aquaman*—in order to build up (and capitalize on) buzz for Heard in the lead-up to the film's debut.[17]

Both Smollett and Heard's stories involve elites leveraging claims of victimhood in order to enhance their projects, their public profile, and their downstream opportunities. Both actors recognized that being perceived as a target of racism, homophobia, or misogynistic abuse could be career enhancing under the right circumstances. However, of the two, Heard's case is perhaps more illuminating because, while Smollett's claimed victimhood was proved to be fraudulent, it seems plausible that Heard actually *was* abused. Indeed, in a previous trial in the United Kingdom, the presiding judge ruled that Heard's accusations were sufficiently credible to dismiss Depp's accusations of libel.[18] Yet recognizing Heard as a potential victim of abuse does not preclude us from *also* recognizing that she clearly saw it as advantageous to her professional career to leverage the surge in public outrage over sexual harassment, assault, and discrimination in order to direct greater public attention *toward herself personally and to her completely unrelated upcoming projects.* The potential for career enhancement seemed to be a nontrivial factor both in her decision to get involved with the ACLU and in her attempt to publicly align herself with #MeToo.

Typically, there is a bifurcation in discourse on these issues. Accusers are cast either as genuine victims seeking the justice they deserve or as shrewd opportunists looking to literally capitalize on others' sympathy for social justice movements. In reality, both are often true at the same time. Within symbolic capitalist spaces, many who seem to sincerely perceive themselves as victims *also* look for ways they can trade on that victimhood in order to enhance their social position. It is often hard for people to recognize this, and even harder to talk about it, because we tend to see victims as ethically superior to others, as being "above" distasteful motives and unsavory behaviors. However, being victimized, or coming to understand oneself *as* a victim, tends to produce a broad range of effects on people—many of them unfortunate.

For instance, research has found that people who understand themselves as victims often demonstrate less concern for the hardships of others; they feel more entitled to selfish behavior; they grow more vicious against rivals—not just against the people who victimized them but against anyone who stands in the way of their goals or aspirations. Yet even as they grow more likely to engage in *im*moral behaviors—and often victimize others who did them no wrong—they also gain a sense of moral superiority relative to everyone else.[19]

Many of the pernicious effects of victimization are heightened when *others* recognize and validate one's sense of victimhood. Bad behaviors are enabled by the fact that people tend to cut others slack if they are recognized as having been victimized. Indeed, it seems to be cognitively difficult for most to simultaneously recognize someone as both a victim *and* a perpetrator of unjust harm (although people seem to regularly occupy both roles "in the world").[20] Consequently, those who view themselves as victims, and especially those who are recognized by others as victims, often exist in a state of moral exception. The more frequently they evoke their victimhood, the more ethically dubious behaviors they feel entitled to engage in—confident that they will not be held responsible, morally or practically, for their actions.

Far from victimization having an ennobling effect, rendering people more worthy of power and judicious in its use, history is replete with examples of formerly subaltern groups taking power and proving themselves to be every bit as oppressive or depraved as the people they overthrew. This should not be surprising as, again, identification with victimhood often renders people more self-oriented and more hostile toward perceived rivals than they were before (rather than encouraging them to be more tolerant, empathetic, or altruistic). Increased affluence and influence have likewise been shown to render people more selfish and aggressive while undermining empathy and attentiveness toward others. Power tends to exacerbate intolerance and feelings of contempt toward those who obstruct one's interests or diverge from one's preferences. It renders people less concerned about the potential downsides of their actions and less aware of others' perspectives.[21] That is, rather than working against one another (with victimhood rendering people more ethical in their use of power, or power helping to blunt some of the pernicious effects of victimhood), the adverse consequences of victimhood and elite status may be synergistic and mutually reinforcing. People with a strong sense of victimization may be especially *ill suited* for being in positions of power; power may have an exceptionally corrupting influence on people who see themselves as victims.

Yet unfortunately, and perhaps counterintuitively, in the contemporary United States, social status and a sense of victimhood seem to travel hand in hand, with each reinforcing the other. For instance, those who are genuinely marginalized and disadvantaged in society are much less likely to perceive or describe themselves as victims of identity-based bias and discrimination than highly educated and relatively affluent liberals.[22] And there's a reason for that. Although virtually no one wants to be genuinely victimized by others, many status seekers are nonetheless interested in *presenting themselves* as victims and being *perceived* as victims—especially in contexts where "victimhood culture" prevails (such as most symbolic capitalist spaces). Some go so far as to reorient their whole identity around having been victimized in order to enjoy the benefits that come with perceived victimization indefinitely. Others find creative ways to capitalize on victimhood they didn't personally experience at all.

Stigmata

Only *certain types* of victimization tend to be honored in a victimhood culture. First, in order to reap the benefits associated with being recognized as a victim, one's victimhood has to be a product of malevolent actions *by others*. That is, one cannot merely be a victim of circumstance—there must be someone who can be blamed (and, ideally, punished) for one's victimized status.[23] Second, one's victimization should appear to be a result of factors outside one's control. Poverty, for instance, is often a product of exploitation and oppression by others. However, it is also widely perceived as something that is at least somewhat within one's control. It is a state that people are viewed as being at least partially responsible for bringing on themselves.[24] It is also a situation that people can conceivably escape. The most compelling forms of victimhood are tied to immutable elements of a person's *being* rather than changeable aspects of their present circumstances. As Richard Rorty explained,

> Leftists have helped to put together such academic disciplines as women's history, black history, gay studies, Hispanic-American studies, and migrant studies. This has led Stefan Collini to remark that in the United States . . . the term "cultural studies" means "victim studies." Collini's choice of phrase has been resented, but he was making a good point: namely, that such programs were created not out of the sort of curiosity about diverse forms of human life which gave rise to cultural anthropology, but rather . . . to help victims of socially acceptable forms of sadism by making such sadism no longer acceptable. . . . Nobody is setting up a program in unemployed studies, homeless studies or trailer-park studies because the unemployed, the homeless and residents of trailer parks are not "other" in the relevant sense. To be other in this sense you must bear an ineradicable stigma, one which makes you a victim of socially accepted sadism rather than merely economic selfishness.[25]

Women, racial and ethnic minorities, sexual minorities, those with disabilities, trauma survivors, certain persecuted religious minorities—these are identities that are especially respected in symbolic capitalists' victimhood culture. Being poor, or coming from poverty, can enhance one's moral standing if one *also* bears some other marginalized identity. However, there is very little sympathy for impoverished "cishet" whites. Indeed, they are often viewed as being not just responsible for their own suffering but deserving of it—and their struggles, frustrations, and concerns are widely mocked or dismissed.[26]

Moreover, although conservatives tend to be consistent in their judgments about victimization and discrimination (viewing America as generally fair and perceiving virtually all "isms" and "phobias" as blown out of proportion), among liberals there is a clear hierarchy of perceived victimization: Blacks and Hispanics at the top, followed by LGBTQ people, followed by Muslims, then Asians and Jews.[27]

These dynamics create strong incentives for individuals and organizations associated with the symbolic professions to align themselves with a particular subset of victimhood-enhancing identities—often by exploiting the vagueness inherent in many social distinctions.

Consider the term "people of color" (POC), or its fashionable cousin BIPOC (in the United Kingdom, they use BAME):[28] Elite institutions are fond of claiming that some large portion of their members are POC. The elite private New York City K–12 school Horace Mann, for instance, proclaims that 46 percent of attendees "identify as students of color."[29] This sounds quite impressive on its face. However, the school's 2022–2023 IRS filings provide striking context to this claim.[30] In fact, less than 13 percent of its students are African American, Indigenous American, or Hispanic. Put another way, roughly 87 percent of its students are white, part white,[31] or Asian American. Collapsing these distinctions into a simple binary of POC versus whites allows the school to imply that it has large numbers of students from populations that are otherwise *underrepresented* in elite spaces. In fact, it does not. Fully half of the minority students at the school are Asian—and Asian Americans tend to be overrepresented in elite institutions like Horace Mann.

Of course, it is also the case that Asian Americans have faced a long history of discrimination in the United States, from the Chinese Exclusion Acts to the internment of Japanese Americans during World War II; to racial zoning, redlining, and persecution that contributed to the rise of "Chinatowns" and "Japantowns" in many American cities; to episodes of racialized violence and lynchings.[32] Asian Americans have been subjected to offensive caricatures and stereotypes that persist to this day. They continue to be subject to occasional hate crimes and other forms of racialized animus.[33] Asian Americans have to work around de facto quotas at elite colleges and universities, and often struggle to break into the very top positions at institutions and firms (the so-called bamboo ceiling).[34] Nonetheless, by most measures, from educational attainment to income, wealth, and social mobility, most Asian racial and ethnic populations tend to do better than most other racial or ethnic minorities in the United States—and indeed significantly outperform whites on average too.[35]

This is a phenomenon that is in no way restricted to Asian Americans. For instance, the same patterns hold true for Middle Easterners (Jews, Arabs, Persians, Turks). There is a long and ignoble history of anti-Semitism and Islamophobia dating back to the very beginning of the United States; hate crimes persist against people of Middle Eastern backgrounds, especially those perceived to be Muslims or Jews. Since 9/11, Muslims have also been subject to heavy and often extraconstitutional surveillance and persecution by law enforcement and national security agencies.[36] Nonetheless, Jews, Persians, Turks, and most Arab subgroups enjoy significantly higher levels of average household income and educational attainment than other Americans. Even populations that are largely marginalized, exploited, and dispossessed throughout the Middle East, such as Palestinians, tend to have higher levels of educational attainment than most other Americans and household incomes roughly equivalent to the national average.[37]

The fact that many Asian and Middle Eastern subpopulations enjoy comparable or higher levels of prosperity as compared with mainstream whites does not negate the other challenges they may continue to face in virtue of their race, ethnicity, religion, or other factors—nor is it to suggest that they should not identify as POC. The point is merely to recognize that within symbolic capitalist spaces, identifying as a POC "does work" for those who so identify. It allows people who hail from ethnic subpopulations that are statistically more likely than most to succeed—who are statistically *overrepresented* in elite spaces—to nonetheless present themselves as underdogs (and implicitly as nonelites).

Likewise, studies have found that a majority of those who identify as "Black" at selective schools—and, by proxy, those who are prominent or hold more lucrative positions within the symbolic professions—seem to be Afro-Caribbean, African, or multiracial (typically, half-white).[38] This is significant because Blacks from immigrant backgrounds often grow up in ethnic enclaves with communities that possess a relatively strong sense of identity, reciprocity, and trust. They tend to go to better schools and grow up in safer neighborhoods than nonimmigrant Blacks. They are also much more likely to grow up in two-parent households and with highly educated parents.[39] Similarly, multiracial Black Americans are much more likely to grow up in wealthier neighborhoods, attend better schools, and be raised by highly educated parents in a two-parent household.[40] Both groups tend to have significantly more diverse social networks as compared with nonimmigrant monoracial Blacks. They also tend to fare significantly better in terms of life outcomes. Indeed, the most populous Afro-Caribbean and African immigrant subgroups in America tend to enjoy median household incomes that are equivalent or superior to overall U.S. averages. Statistically speaking, then, people from such backgrounds have not "beaten the odds" insofar as they also secure above-average levels of income or educational attainment—the odds were literally in their favor! This is in sharp contrast with nonimmigrant monoracial Black Americans, for whom socioeconomic outcomes like median household income or educational attainment tend to fall significantly *below* U.S. averages.[41]

Irrespective of ethnic background, Black students at highly selective colleges and universities tend to be from relatively well-off households.[42] Also independent of ethnic background, lighter skin tone is strongly correlated with socioeconomic success among Black Americans.[43] Those with lighter skin are significantly less prone to experience hostile prejudice and discrimination among whites or to be subjected to disciplinary and law enforcement measures.[44] They are more likely to be integrated into predominantly white social networks and institutions, and have more options in the dating and marriage market.[45] They are more likely to be viewed as competent and intelligent, and are hired and promoted at higher rates.[46] That is, lighter-skinned Black folks do not experience anywhere near the same racial stigma as darker-skinned peers.

All said, Black people in elite spaces tend to be fairer skinned, from relatively well-off backgrounds (especially as compared with most other African Americans), or of immigrant or multiracial backgrounds. Yet elites from these categories often actively and willfully collapse these distinctions into the simple label "Black," in part because it advantages us to do so. It allows us to implicitly portray ourselves as significantly marginalized or disadvantaged even though we are not subject to the same constraints, risks, or prejudices that most other Black people have to face, and despite the fact that we were granted many advantages that the typical Black person in America does not enjoy. This conflation allows elites to pretend as though a "win" for us is somehow also a "win" for those who are more dramatically marginalized or disadvantaged—when in fact, there is little relation between our fates. Indeed, Blacks have long been the most socioeconomically polarized racial group in America (although we were recently edged out by Asian Americans in this regard).[47] There is very little "trickling down" or "lifting up" happening, rhetorical solidarity notwithstanding. Instead, upper-middle-class African Americans have often advanced themselves in ways that concentrate disadvantage for other Black people.[48]

Now, this is not to say immigrants, multiracial people, or fair-skinned people cannot or should not identify as "Black" (I am a biracial person who so identifies; more on that soon)—nor is it to suggest that multiracial, immigrant, light-skinned, or relatively well-off Blacks face no challenges on the basis of their race. The goal is merely to point out that (1) the challenges we face are much less severe than those that monoracial nonimmigrant Black people (i.e., most Black people) face, and (2) Black identification "does work" for elites who lay claim to that identity. It conceals the privileges we typically bear (especially as compared with most other Black people, but even as compared with Americans overall in many cases) and provides us with many additional benefits, to be discussed shortly.

In a similar fashion, we can observe that identifying as LGBTQ seems to "do work" for the growing numbers of elites who identify as queer, bisexual, or nonbinary but who partner overwhelmingly or even exclusively with people of the opposite biological sex. Before the current Awokening, there was a fairly tight correspondence between nonheterosexual identity and nonheterosexual behavior: people who identified as something other than cisgender heterosexuals tended to have sex lives that reflected that identity. This is much less the case today. The share of Americans under thirty who identify as lesbian, gay, bisexual, or queer is now nearly twice the share of Americans who report having actually engaged in nonstraight sexual encounters—and the gap has continued to grow.[49] In fact, young bisexual Americans today seem to be having *more* heterosexual encounters than peers who identify as cisgender heterosexuals.[50] The growing divergence between sexual orientations and behaviors seems to be particularly pronounced among highly educated and left-identifying young women.

There has been a spike in "trans" identification among highly educated and relatively affluent young women in recent years as well.[51] However, a 2023 survey by the *Washington Post* and the Kaiser Family Foundation[52]—the largest of its kind to date—found that the overwhelming majority of contemporary Americans who identify as trans do not behave or present themselves much differently than cisgender lesbian, gay, and bisexual Americans. For instance, only a third of trans identifiers have pursued hormones, gender-affirming surgeries, or counseling for gender transition. Roughly the same share identify with the gender most commonly associated with the opposite biological sex. Likewise, only 30 percent of trans identifiers "always" try to present as a gender different from their biological sex, and just 24 percent have sought to actually change their name on government documents. As for the other two-thirds of trans identifiers, they claim to be "gender nonconforming" or "nonbinary" rather than associating with the opposite gender. They are much less consistent in presenting themselves in a manner incongruent with norms of others who share their biological sex (typically engaging in these activities only "some of the time" or "not at all"). For this two-thirds of respondents, the primary way they seem to express their trans identity is by requesting that others refer to them with less conventional pronouns or adopting chosen names (which they typically do not try to codify in formal documents). In short, as a larger share of highly educated and relatively affluent young women have begun identifying as trans, the meaning of the term has been expanded significantly—now encompassing large numbers of people whose self-presentation and lifestyle choices are not significantly different from those of cisgender same-sex peers. They embrace the label of being "trans" but largely avoid the challenges faced by the one-third of coidentifiers who consistently and overtly present themselves in a manner incongruent with their biological sex, engage in nonreversible body modification, and/or attempt to permanently adjust their legal classifications to render them congruent with the gender they identify with.

Here, the point is not to suggest that growing numbers of bisexual or trans identifiers are not *really* LGBTQ or should not identify as such. Readers should simply accept these identity claims at face value for the purpose of this analysis. However, while *granting* these self-identifications as likely sincere reflections of their feelings, we can nonetheless observe that the "revealed preferences" of growing shares of LGBTQ Americans (as expressed in their dating and mating behaviors, self-presentation, etc.) are largely identical to those of "cishet"–identifying peers. Consequently, in contexts where LGBTQ identification did *not* convey advantages—or especially if it provided *dis*advantages—it may be that many of these people would not have come to identify the same way. However, for the world in which we actually live, and in social arenas symbolic capitalists operate in more specifically, undefined terms like "queer"[53] or umbrella terms like LGBTQ often function much like BIPOC (and derivatives thereof), allowing people from populations that are *not* heavily disadvantaged to rhetorically lump themselves in with those who *are* in order to enhance their personal claims to victimization (and undermine perceptions of privilege).

In reality, collectively speaking, LGBTQ Americans are more likely to be at the tail ends of *both* sides of the socioeconomic spectrum. As compared with cisgender heterosexuals, LGBTQ Americans are more likely to be high school dropouts *and* college grads. They are more likely to struggle with homelessness, poverty, food insecurity, trauma, or violence *and* to be wealthy. Less educated bisexual women, trans Americans who identify with the gender opposite their biological sex, or overtly gender nonconforming individuals are particularly likely to fall into these former categories as compared with cisgender lesbian or gay Americans (whose overall poverty rates are about the same as their cisgender straight peers). Sexual minorities who are also racial and ethnic minorities, or who live in rural areas, tend to be more vulnerable to adversity as well.[54] Meanwhile, highly educated or white cisgender lesbian, gay, and bisexual Americans, especially those who live in urban areas, are more likely to skew toward the *upper* end of the socioeconomic distribution. Nonetheless, identifying with the umbrella term (LGBTQ) allows those who are relatively advantaged to portray themselves as the opposite—often by appealing to statistics that are driven heavily by adverse outcomes among those who are quite sociologically distant from themselves.

The more elite the space, the more pronounced these tendencies become. For instance, polls and surveys estimate roughly one in five Gen Z adults identify as something other than heterosexual (two-thirds of these identify as "bi"—and again, most people who identify as bi seem to partner overwhelmingly or exclusively with members of the opposite sex). At Yale and Harvard, these numbers are much higher: 29 percent of students identify as LGBTQ. At Princeton, it's 35 percent. At Brown, it's 38 percent. These identification patterns have been closely tied to the Great Awokening (and the struggles for power and status entailed thereby). At Brown and Yale, the number of students who identify as LGBTQ has doubled over the last decade. At Harvard, they've tripled.[55]

Comparable analyses could be made of the rapidly growing number of elites who identify as "disabled" (whom we will turn to shortly). Across the board, accepting identity claims as sincere does not negate, and should not distract from, the reality that association with these "stigmatized" identities seems to be perceived as an advantage in symbolic capitalist spaces—leading elites to actively seek out and proudly broadcast labels that have often been thrust on others *in*voluntarily in other contexts. Nor should it prevent us from recognizing that elite struggles for status on the basis of perceived victimhood typically have nothing to do with helping the genuinely marginalized or disadvantaged in society.

Different Boats

For elites who cannot directly claim affiliation with the "right" kind of stigmatized identity, engaging in the culture wars often allows them to experience something like "victimhood by proxy": progressive whites are keen to broadcast their status as "allies" and tell stories about how their unyielding commitments to social justice put them at odds with "other" whites. Insofar as they manage to alienate themselves from white peers (or even family members) on the basis of social justice advocacy, they often portray themselves as being "in the same boat" as minorities. For instance, receiving pushback from whites for their approach to antiracism allows them to paint themselves as *fellow victims* of racism. Constantly "struggling" with (other) whites about racial issues makes them feel like they understand the experience of being a minority. People are often strikingly explicit in making associations like these.[56]

However, it's not just elites from the dominant group who get in on this action. Again, minority elites often describe themselves as being "in the same boat" as the genuinely marginalized and disadvantaged. They depict their intraelite struggles and competitions as somehow being "of a kind" with the challenges more desperate or vulnerable members of their group face or have historically struggled to overcome. The truth is, however, that these elites tend to be in very different "boats" from most others in the groups they purport to represent. Consider the case of African Americans. Over the past seventy years Black people at the upper end of the income distribution have seen significant gains in their earnings relative to similarly advantaged whites. However, the Black-white income gap for everyone else has expanded since the mid-1970s to the point where disparities between *nonelite* Black men and white men are comparable to what they were before the civil rights movement.[57] Yet, as sociologist William Julius Wilson observed, Black elites are often uncomfortable discussing these realities.

In 1978 Wilson published a book demonstrating that, although civil rights law and affirmative action significantly improved the prospects of upper-middle-class and wealthy Black people, there seemed to be little to no measurable socioeconomic benefit to working-class and poor Blacks. Symbolic capitalists' response to these findings was quite telling. Wilson notes, "In the early discussions of *The Declining Significance of Race*, critics were so preoccupied with what I had to say about the improving conditions of the black middle class that they virtually ignored my more important arguments about the deteriorating conditions of the black underclass. The view was often expressed that since all blacks are suffering, there is no need to single out the black poor."[58] Some intellectuals, Wilson noted, went so far as to suggest that it's actually people like *themselves*, Black professionals, who suffer the most from racism today.

In truth, the "hardships" faced by elites from minority populations are not comparable to the difficulties nonelites have to reckon with. It does little to serve the interests of *non*elite minorities to collapse these experiences together (if anything, it trivializes the struggles of the genuinely disadvantaged). This conflation is, instead, carried out nearly exclusively by elites, for their own benefit, often to help them seem less "elite" than they actually are.[59] Sometimes, people from relatively affluent backgrounds who identify as members of historically marginalized and disadvantaged groups go so far as to try passing off others' extreme experiences with identity-based victimization as their own.[60]

Far from using their elite position to meaningfully help genuinely disadvantaged members of the groups they claim affiliation with, symbolic capitalists typically attempt to leverage *collective* identities in the service of their *individual* benefit. Discussions turn on what *I* am entitled to on the basis of *my* identity claims. These claims are, themselves, predicated on pitting women *against* men, Blacks *against* whites, LGBTQ Americans *against* cisgender heterosexuals, wherein one party bears collective guilt, and the other collective entitlements, on the basis of past or ongoing victimization. Even historically marginalized and disadvantaged groups are often competitively set against one another, with exchanges often devolving into a form of "oppression Olympics." Who had it worse historically—Blacks, homosexuals, or women? Who has it worse today? How many stigmatized identities can I claim compared with you?

In order to understand how these status competitions play out within symbolic capitalist spaces, it'll be helpful to build up some theoretical scaffolding by introducing a new concept: totemic capital.

Totemic Capital

In chapter 1, we walked through three different forms of symbolic capital, as formulated by Pierre Bourdieu: academic capital, cultural capital, and political capital. These are intended to be *general* forms of symbolic capital that explain dynamics across societies and cultures. To these, let us add another form of symbolic capital that is more unique to contemporary Western "victimhood cultures": totemic capital.[61]

In sociological terms, a totem is a sacred symbol that represents a people; it marks an essence they are uniquely bonded to; it connects their past with the present; it links the fates of totem bearers and endows them with distinct social proprieties.[62] If we understand labels like "Black," "LGBTQ," "disabled," "woman," and so on as serving a function akin to totems in contemporary victimhood culture,[63] then we can define "totemic capital" as *the epistemic and moral authority afforded to an individual on the basis of bearing one or more of these totems*—that is, on the basis of claimed or perceived membership in a historically marginalized or disadvantaged group.

Individuals from populations that have been persecuted, exploited, oppressed, or excluded are often held to possess special knowledge or insight that others do not have access to.[64] They are also perceived as more truthful and "authentic" than others—especially with respect to issues discursively marked as salient for their group. For instance, lesbian, gay, and bisexual people are held to understand sexuality better, and speak more honestly on the topic, than "straight" people. Those who are female or transgender are assumed to understand gender better, and to speak more authentically on gender issues, than "cishet" men. Ethnic and religious minorities are held to speak with unique authority on matters discursively associated with their group (i.e., Black people on policing, Hispanics on immigration, Muslims on terrorism—notice there are often troubling implicit assumptions that seem to be built into these deference practices). People with more humble socioeconomic roots are purported to speak more truthfully on issues like poverty or inequality than those who come from more privileged backgrounds.

Likewise, there is abundant research suggesting that diverse *teams* are more innovative, less biased, and better at problem-solving as compared with groups that are more homogeneous.[65] This research has often been (mis)translated into a perception that diverse *individuals* are inherently more creative and objective than others. "Diverse individual," of course, is a contradiction in terms. However, people seem to use this construction to nonspecifically refer to someone who is nonwhite, nonmale, noncisgender or heterosexual, nonneurotypical, disabled, and so forth. The perception is that those who can be defined as "other" in some sense may be especially well suited for the kind of work symbolic capitalists do, or they'll add especially high value to organizations.

Related to these perceptions of heightened insight, honesty, and authenticity, totem bearers are held to be *morally* superior to others as well.[66] Many argue that placing people from historically marginalized and disadvantaged groups in positions of power will render institutions more ethical. People from historically marginalized and disadvantaged groups are held up as being more worthy of power—and are presumed to be more judicious and beneficent in the ways they exercise power. Summarizing the mentality prevalent in many symbolic capitalist spaces, Richard Rorty argued, "The cultural Left has a vision of an America in which . . . members of previously victimized groups . . . have somehow come into possession of more foresight and imagination than the selfish suburbanites. These formerly oppressed and newly powerful people are expected to be as angelic as the straight white males were diabolical."[67]

Cultural elites try to exploit these assumptions through the cultivation and expenditure of totemic capital.[68] People attempt to leverage totemic capital by making claims introduced by phrases like, "As a [insert totemic identification here], I think/feel/desire . . . ," under the implicit expectation that their *personal* thoughts, feelings, or desires will be given more weight than they otherwise would in virtue of their affiliation with a historically marginalized or disadvantaged group.[69]

Others attempt to exert totemic capital by suggesting that some slight to them *personally* is actually a slight against their group—tied to the history of oppression, exploitation, or marginalization against "people like them"—or else suggesting that some kind of boon to them *personally* is actually a great "win" for "people like them" more broadly.

Other times, claims are made in the form, "[Insert totemic identification here] people think/feel/want . . . ," where the assertion of what the people in question desire, believe, and so on is derived *not* from cited and robust empirical evidence but apparently from some quasi-mystical connection that unites other group members to one another—allowing the claimant's *own* thoughts, feelings, preferences, and experiences to be held up as representative of "their people" as a whole (without a need to empirically investigate and substantiate how most others in the group think, feel, or desire with respect to the issue at hand).

Critically, like other forms of symbolic capital, totemic capital is context dependent. For instance, Black people are *not* discursively held to possess a special understanding of physics in virtue of their racial identity. Hence, presenting oneself as a representative of Black people would not tend to enhance one's epistemic authority with respect to discussing physics, except perhaps to the extent that conversations about the field touched on matters of race, inequality, and so on. Indeed, a Black physicist may experience less epistemic authority than white peers in most circumstances[70]—especially to the extent that they are perceived to have been hired or promoted on the basis of racial preferences.[71] However, totem bearers in fields such as journalism, social science, the humanities, activism, and policymaking often *do* wield particular moral and epistemic authority—especially on topics coded as salient for the groups they are purporting to represent.[72]

It is also critical to bear in mind that totemic capital, like other forms of symbolic capital, may or may not enhance one's *socioeconomic* status. Again, as discussed throughout this text, there continues to be systematic variance along the lines of race and gender with respect to pay and career advancement in many fields. However, symbolic capitalists are often quite willing to trade wealth for symbolic capital—especially if they are already relatively well off (or hail from relatively advantaged backgrounds). As a recent study in the *American Sociological Review* put it, jobs that increase one's moral standing with others or one's moral self-image often "function as a luxury good, which higher-paid workers are more willing to trade for as the urgency of pecuniary income recedes."[73]

That said, possessing totemic capital can and often does help symbolic capitalists gain access to direct material benefits—typically provided by state, corporate, or nonprofit institutions eager to symbolically rectify historical wrongs against various groups by bestowing honors and benefits on contemporary totem bearers. This can take the form of special funding opportunities (scholarships, fellowships, grants that are explicitly or implicitly restricted to totem bearers); special hiring, promotion, or mentoring initiatives set aside for totem bearers; preferences in publication (that is, all else equal, preferring scholarship, journalism, editorials, or other contributions on various topics from people who hail from particular groups—especially with respect to issues discursively coded as salient for those groups); and beyond.

Collectively, these symbolic and material benefits create a temptation for many to lay claim to totems through deceptive means. Ironically, but also intuitively, people who work on social justice issues seem to be especially inclined to attempt to misleadingly appropriate totems—at least in part to expand the reach and impact of their "justice-oriented" work.

(Mis)appropriating Totems

In 2008, Margaret Seltzer (better known as Margaret B. Jones) made headlines when her critically acclaimed "memoir" *Love and Consequences* was found to be a fraud. Seltzer had purported to be half–Native American, a foster child, a former "gang-banger," and much more. In fact, she had grown up in an affluent suburb of Los Angeles, was raised by her birth parents, attended private schools, and had no known Native American ancestry. When her fraud was exposed, she explained that she made up this fake background largely to "put a voice to people who people don't listen to. . . . I just felt that there was good that I could do and there was no other way that someone would listen to it. . . . I thought I had an opportunity to make people understand the conditions that people live in and the reasons people make the choices from the choices they don't have."[74]

In 2017, BethAnn McLaughlin, then an assistant professor of neuroscience at Vanderbilt University, was denied tenure. In her telling, this outcome was a result of her having testified in a sexual harassment investigation at Vanderbilt (although she ultimately recanted the accusations made against her colleague in court).[75] Soon thereafter, she launched an organization, MeTooSTEM, oriented around addressing sexual discrimination, harassment, and assault in the physical sciences. Roughly simultaneously, McLaughlin created an online persona, Sciencing_Bi, purporting to be a bisexual, Hopi anthropology professor at Arizona State University (ASU) who had been sexually victimized by Harvard University archaeologist Gary Urton.[76] Over the years that followed, Sciencing_Bi accrued a nontrivial following in academic and activist Twitter circles—and aggressively supported and helped raise awareness and money for MeTooSTEM and McLaughlin's tenure decision appeal case. She also zealously defended McLaughlin from growing criticism of how she ran MeTooSTEM—including against charges that she serially mistreated minority staff members. The charade ended in 2020 when McLaughlin attempted to protest colleges remaining open during the COVID-19 pandemic by having Sciencing_Bi contract and "die" from the novel coronavirus after being "forced" by her university to teach in person. Announcing the "death" of her "friend," McLaughlin made a point of emphasizing racial and gender disparities within academia and racialized health disparities with respect to the COVID-19 pandemic. She underlined Sciencing_Bi's commitment to MeTooSTEM and its cause, urging others to donate and join the fight in her memory. The outpouring of grief and outrage was widespread and intense . . . which ultimately led ASU to investigate the matter and announce that, in fact, *none* of its faculty had died from COVID-19, nor were ASU faculty obliged to teach in person at the time Sciencing_Bi was purported to have perished.[77] It quickly became apparent that McLaughlin had created this alternative persona—of someone who was a woman, a sexual minority, a racial minority, and a sexual assault survivor—in order to harness the moral authority ascribed to these populations for the sake of bolstering the credibility of herself, her chosen causes, and her nascent organization.

McLaughlin and Seltzer are far from alone in these respects. Prominent community organizer and activist Satchuel Cole and former NAACP chapter head Rachel Dolezal were both whites who pretended to be Black.[78] Natasha Lycia Ora Bannan, senior counsel at the LatinoJustice Puerto Rican Legal Defense and Education Fund, honored as the first "Latina" president of the National Lawyers Guild, was revealed to be of Irish, Italian, and Russian ancestry—although she pretended to be Colombian and Puerto Rican.[79]

Raquel Saraswati, Chief Diversity Officer of the American Friends Service Committee, claimed to be of Latina, South Asian, and Arab descent. In truth, she is a white American of British, German and Italian ancestry.[80] Many scholars who work on racial issues, and are known as advocates for social justice, have likewise been revealed as lying about their ancestry in recent years. For instance, activist-scholars Jessica "La Bombalera" Krug, Kelly Kean Sharp, Andrea Lee Smith, and CV Vitolo-Haddad were roughly contemporaneously exposed as mainstream white people pretending to be Black, Latina, or Native American.[81] "Food sovereignty" activist Elizabeth Hoover followed soon thereafter.[82]

Although women seem most likely to engage in these particular forms of appropriation, men occasionally get in on the action as well. In 2011, for instance, a popular lesbian Syrian blogger, Amina Arraf (better known as "Gay Girl in Damascus"), was revealed to be Tom MacMaster, a white American PhD candidate studying medieval history at the University of Edinburgh.[83] MacMaster claims to have initially adopted the persona in order to engage with people about the Middle East, Islam, gender, and sexuality without the suspicion and social distance he often experienced engaging on these topics as a white, American, cisgender, heterosexual, Christian male. As Amina, he recognized that he could voice a range of opinions that would be received completely differently if they had come from MacMaster, and people would interact with him in a less guarded way. Writing as "Gay Girl in Damascus," MacMaster publicly advocated for feminism and gay rights in the Muslim world and called for regime change in Syria. But as Amina grew more pro- lific, MacMaster began to feel as though his hoax was getting out of hand. He tried to "disappear" his persona by ceasing all writing and alleging from a separate account that Amina had been abducted by the Assad regime and likely would not be heard from again. Rather than allowing for a clean exit, MacMaster's claim sparked a global outcry for Amina's release, with the U.S. Department of State even becoming involved. At that point, MacMaster came clean. In his confession, like Margaret Seltzer, MacMaster claimed to have "created an important voice for issues that I feel strongly about."[84] He con- tinued, "I only hope that people pay as much attention to the people of the Middle East and their struggles in this year of revolutions. The events there are being shaped by the people living them on a daily basis. I have only tried to illuminate them for a western audience."[85]

Across the board, these actors were engaged in social justice–oriented work. In all cases, they could have done the same work *as* white people—but they recognized that their work would not be received and interpreted the same way were it not for the ruse. It would be unlikely to have the same impact. It would be unlikely to be as well respected. They wanted the moral and epistemic authority that comes with being a totem bearer.[86] They also wanted to exploit, and most of them *did* exploit, opportunities set aside for people who can lay claim to these identities—from scholarships and fellowships to admissions, hiring, promotion, and publication preferences and beyond.[87]

As with Seltzer's, the pseudo-biographies these actors composed about their lives were often extreme and implausible. They often presented themselves (in terms of how they dressed, how they talked, how they carried themselves) in ways that would be understood as offensive caricatures if performed by a white actor in a movie, or a white comedian in a set. And not content with carrying out these exaggerated performances themselves, they were often quite militant in policing "people of color" in their networks for being insufficiently "woke," "authentic," or "committed"—and were especially hard on (other) white liberals. Andrea Lee Smith, for instance, recently resigned from her position at the University of California, Riverside, in order to avoid an investigation into dubious claims she made about her ancestry.[88] However, prior to her own behaviors falling under scrutiny (and perhaps as a means to forestall that), she went so far as to publish a paper denouncing white feminist scholars for appropriating Indigenous aesthetics and practices, or outright pretending to be Native American, in order to disassociate from their whiteness.[89]

The extremism and militancy of Smith, Krug, Dolezal, and others only seemed to enhance their appeal within symbolic capitalist circles. Indeed, Touré Reed has argued that the most troubling aspect of stories like these is not the fraud itself but that these "minstrel acts" are so consistently and enthusiastically embraced by other symbolic capitalists.[90] He continues (emphasis his), "Some white liberals expect black and brown people to 'perform' in ways that comport with their well-meaning, usually underclass-informed, and fundamentally racist expectations of black people. . . . However offensive Krug's act is . . . the *demand* for her performance is *even more* offensive. Indeed, the *demand* for the product Krug was selling merits far more attention than she does." Seltzer and others like her delivered exactly what mainstream symbolic capitalists were hungry for, and they were often rewarded for it. They knew their audience well, because people like themselves (highly educated, relatively affluent, urban-dwelling, liberal whites) *are* the primary audience for "woke" literature, journalism, scholarship, and so forth.

Certain elements of contemporary "victimhood culture" facilitated their ruses: the insistence on accepting identity claims uncritically and nonjudgmentally, the taboo against doubting (let alone demanding evidence for) victimization claims, the more general tendency to place subjective interpretations and experience largely above scrutiny. While intended to serve the genuinely vulnerable, these norms enable—and the rewards of possessing totemic capital create the incentives for—performances like those of Sharp, Vitolo-Haddad, and who knows how many others (there is some evidence that these behaviors may be fairly widespread).[91]

However, as humanities professor Jason England observes, another major contributing factor is that marginalized identities have become standardized and commodified in symbolic capitalist spaces. The preferred scripts are well known—and it isn't just whites like Krug, Dolezal, and Seltzer who attempt to enhance their position by playing to these scripts, often appropriating experiences that are not their own. Elites of color regularly do the same:

> There is no singular, authentic way to be Black. But while Black intellectuals are quick to assert that Blackness is not monolithic, I've observed many of them do so in a duplicitous, self-serving way, as a rationalization that justifies a class monopoly on Black perspective. Regardless of lived experience, many feel they are entitled to speak on the entirety of Black experience. The reality is some of them have such little respect for the lived experiences of Black people (unless they can usurp them) that they couldn't possibly identify an interloper like Krug if they tried; they're running a similar con. . . . 37 percent of Black American households have a net worth of zero or worse; Black households have a median worth of one-tenth of their white counterparts. In my time among the educational "elite," I've crossed paths with very few people who can speak directly to that experience. That doesn't stop them from speaking authoritatively *about* it and even co-opting it.[92]

Indeed, although working-class and poor African Americans are widely depicted in pop culture, most of the Black people creating these depictions are themselves from relatively well-off backgrounds. They are often immigrants or biracial as well (rather than native-born "monoracial" Blacks).[93] In virtue of these background characteristics, these "representatives" typically grew up in communities and homes very different from those of most other African Americans. Their social networks, education levels, and professions are uncharacteristic of most other African Americans. Their material interests and worldviews are often demonstrably out of step with most other African Americans too.

Actors representing working-class and poor Black folks on-screen, for instance, are often people from relatively well-off backgrounds—with prominent roles often going to Black people of recent African origin or actors from the United Kingdom.[94] Collectively, these creatives produce imagery of working-class or poor Blacks primarily by consuming and remixing representations produced by *other* elites of color (and often white elites as well)—presented in ways that appeal to white elites, who are typically the primary patrons and consumers of this content. Mutatis mutandis, the same realities hold among scholars and journalists who claim to represent Black America: they tend not to be particularly representative in truth.[95]

Again, the point is not to say or suggest that *only* nonimmigrant and monoracial Blacks from moderate to humble means can speak to "the Black experience." The point is, this population comprises the overwhelming majority of Black people in the United States and is the primary focus of depictions of Black people, yet they're virtually absent from the actual creative process—and is even further removed from the wealth generated through the appropriation of their culture and purported life experiences.[96] As Bertrand Cooper powerfully argued, "Were [George] Floyd still alive, or somehow reborn, he would not be hired to work within any of the institutions which now produce popular culture in his honor because he never obtained a bachelor's degree. No matter how much Michael Brown or Breonna Taylor might have impacted a living Floyd, he would not be eligible to work at *The Atlantic*, at the *New York Times*, at HBO, or at Netflix."[97] Instead, Black *elites* trade on the struggles and experiences of lower- to moderate-income nonimmigrant and monoracial Black people—enhancing their own credibility and life prospects by purporting to speak on behalf of these others.

Similar realities hold in arenas like academia, journalism, and the nonprofit world. Symbolic capitalists within these spaces often strike "radical" positions on sociocultural topics, or make idiosyncratic demands, often in the name of some historically marginalized or disadvantaged group they claim affiliation with, even though most in the populations they are purporting to represent expressly reject the positions they are advocating for (e.g., "open borders," "defund the police," anti-Americanism). This relationship between nonrepresentativeness and extremism is not incidental. In general, the less connected people are to most others in the groups they claim affiliation with, the more likely they become to endorse radical action in the name of said groups.[98] If their radicalism fosters blowback against others in their group, or if the policies they advocate for would be deleterious to most others in their group, these elite "spokespeople" aren't the ones paying the price. And they do not regularly encounter, nor are they typically accountable to, those who *do* have to live with the consequences.

In a similar vein, nonrepresentative elites regularly enhance their own position by exploiting programs designed to lift people out of poverty or provide opportunities to descendants of those disenfranchised by slavery and segregation. A radically disproportionate share of Black people capitalizing on affirmative action policies at colleges and universities (and downstream in the symbolic economy) are of immigrant or multiracial background.[99] These beneficiaries also tend to be already affluent compared with most other Black Americans. These patterns are especially pronounced at elite schools (and by proxy, elite symbolic professional institutions). Critically, this "elite capture" is hardly unique to Black people. Across ethnicities, comparative studies in the United States and abroad have found that affirmative action programs tend to primarily benefit already financially well-off members of the target groups.[100] Similar patterns hold across gender lines as well: efforts to enhance the position of "women" in recent decades have likewise mostly benefited white professionals. Indeed, some scholars have argued that relatively affluent white women have perhaps benefited more than any other population from affirmative action policies in the United States.[101]

The Totemic Mystique

In addition to enhancing one's moral and epistemic authority, totemic capital intersects with, and often enhances, what Bourdieu called cultural capital.[102] Compared with cishet, able-bodied whites, totem bearers are often perceived as far more "cool," "exotic," and interesting. This creates additional incentives for many to dishonestly lay claim to totems.

For instance, there is a phenomenon among contemporary social media influencers and celebrities called "Blackfishing," wherein whites (often without *explicitly* claiming to be minorities) present themselves as non-white or racially ambiguous by aggressively tanning or otherwise darkening their skin, imitating the fashion of prominent African Americans or Latinas, and styling their makeup and hair (often dyed or curled) in ways that obscure their natural features and suggest an alternative ethnic background—sometimes adjusting the way they carry themselves or talk as well. Here the desire is not to capitalize on moral or epistemic authority but to exploit perceptions of (fair-skinned) minorities as "hip" and aesthetically appealing. However, as with the previously discussed attempts to (mis)appropriate totemic capital, there are often pecuniary interests at stake too. For influencers or celebrities, perceptions that one is "exotic" or otherwise especially unique, compelling, or attractive are often translated into cash and other material benefits.[103] By presenting themselves as non-white, Blackfishers capture opportunities that may have otherwise gone to people from historically underrepresented and disadvantaged groups (likely other elites from those populations, but still).

Perhaps the most prominent recent example of totemic misappropriation in an apparent bid to enhance *cultural* capital is Elizabeth Warren. Beginning in the mid-1980s, as she was aspiring to move from the University of Texas to the Ivy League, Warren began identifying herself as Native American on professional documents. In 1986 she declared her race as "American Indian" on her registration card for the State Bar of Texas. From 1986 to 1995 she listed herself as "Native American" in the Association of American Law Schools *Directory of Law Teachers*. She landed a job at the University of Pennsylvania shortly after she began professionally identifying as Native American. The leap from the University of Texas to the Ivy League UPenn was quite the step up. Warren subsequently insisted that the University of Pennsylvania list her as a Native American—and it was happy to do so, touting her appointment in minority equity reports to show it was making progress on hiring and retaining "diverse" faculty. In 1995, Warren was awarded a named chair at Harvard University Law School and secured the largest salary of any faculty member at the whole school outside of university administration. Harvard now insists that Warren's "Native American" ancestry made no impact in its hiring decisions. Yet the university immediately held up the recruitment of Warren, a "Native American woman," to push back against claims that the faculty was insufficiently diverse. Warren was also celebrated as Harvard Law's "first woman of color" in a 1997 *Fordham Law Review* article and beyond.[104]

Now, it *could* be a coincidence that Warren decided to change how she ethnically identified herself in professional circles just around the time she was looking to land a job at a more elite institution. And it is *possible* that universities did not consider her purported ancestry at all in their hiring and promotion decisions, despite subsequently highlighting that very ancestry themselves immediately upon her appointment. But all this seems to strain credulity. In fact, Warren is far from the only legal professional to have engaged in maneuvers like these. A 2011 investigation by the American Bar Association found there were roughly ten times as many association-accredited law school graduates who identified as Native American in their college and professional documents as there were Native American lawyers identified by the U.S. Census. Digging deeper into the sources of this discrepancy, the bar association concluded that a distressingly high number of those who *professionally* identified as Native American seemed to have no substantive ties to any specific Indigenous tribe or culture, no apparent ancestor on the Dawes Rolls, and so on—just like Warren.[105]

Critically, unlike the others discussed at the outset of this section, Warren was *not* someone whose scholarly and political work was oriented around her professed ethnic identity. She did *not* lay claim to this identity in order to enhance her moral or epistemic authority on issues pertaining to that identity (her scholarship was not oriented around "Native American issues" per se). Insofar as she leveraged her "Native American" identity professionally, it seems to have been to help her stand out to prospective employers; it was a play for "cultural capital" more than anything. After she landed the job at Harvard, there was little more *professional* incentive to identify as Native American: she was the highest-paid professor at the most prestigious university. There was nowhere further to climb in academia, not even in theory (at which point, curiously, she stopped identifying herself as Native American in the Association of American Law Schools *Directory of Law Teachers*). To the extent that she continued to identify herself as Native American to others after that point, she would have been driven almost entirely by nonmaterial motives.

And it is not just whites who are driven by such motives—racial and ethnic minorities have also been known to adopt more "exotic" nonwhite identities in order to present themselves as more interesting. A prominent recent case involves H. G. Carrillo, who built a public persona and a highly regarded corpus of work around his "Afro-Cuban" identity. After his death, it was discovered that he had been born and raised in Detroit and had no Hispanic or Latino heritage.[106] Critically, as a gay Black man, Carrillo already had access to powerful sources of totemic capital. He could have written equally compelling, beautiful, and influential books about growing up Black and gay in Detroit, enjoying the same levels of moral and epistemic authority when speaking on these issues. He could have benefited from many of the same preferences in hiring, promotion, and so on without the pretense to being Afro-Cuban. The claim to this other identity, and all the pseudo-biographical claims that undergirded it, seems to have been primarily about cultural capital—appearing more sophisticated and interesting as compared with other Black folk; feeling special and being perceived as special.

Similar realities hold for "Apache" icon Sacheen Littlefeather, who was posthumously exposed as having no known Native American ancestry. Her family was of Mexican American background. When Littlefeather's genealogy was traced back for several generations, she seemed to have no connection to *any* indigenous tribe, let alone the specific tribes she claimed to belong to. Nor was there any family lore about being of native ancestry in her childhood (which could lead to her claims being an honest mistake). Instead, it seems that Littlefeather took a different name as she was trying to break into the film and modeling industries, and contemporaneously produced a fictionalized background and childhood to render herself more compelling to reporters and institutional gatekeepers in the entertainment industry. In principle, Littlefeather could have identified with the nascent Chicano movement to help distinguish herself from other aspiring models and actresses at the time. But as her sister explained, "you're not gonna be a Mexican-American princess. You're gonna be an American Indian princess. It was more prestigious to be an American Indian than it was to be Hispanic in her mind."[107]

The Wrong Bodies

In response to the widespread and apparently growing prevalence of "ethnic fraud" within elite spaces, Native American advocacy groups and others have issued calls for more formal verification and institutional policing of identity claims made within professional contexts. However, officials have often pushed back, explicitly appealing to institutional acceptance of transgender identity as a model for dealing with identity claims writ large. One university official declared, "It would be a big step backward for institutions to begin verifying or certifying employees' self-identified race or ethnicity. . . . If someone self-identifies their gender, we do not make them prove it—we take them at their word. . . . In today's diverse workplace, we understand that every employee deserves to be treated equally, with respect, and included regardless of what anyone perceives their race, ethnicity, gender or any other protected classification to be."[108]

Leaning into this analogy, growing numbers of whites who assume alternative ethnic identities have taken to insisting that they aren't engaged in fraud or appropriation, but rather, they're "transracial." Proponents insist they are not attempting to deny who they really are but rather to embrace their "true" selves (which are misaligned with the racial or ethnic group they were "born into").[109] Some have undergone radical cosmetic surgeries in order to bring their bodies into harmony with (what they understand to be) the phenotypical tendencies of the groups they identify with.[110] Across the board, advocates for transracialism insist that those who adopt alternative racial or ethnic cultural identities should be recognized and validated—both institutionally and interpersonally—rather than being stigmatized or punished for embracing "who they truly are." After all, their narrative goes, although not everyone falls cleanly into the binary, sex is biologically "real" to a degree that race is not. If it is possible to transgress or transcend one's given sex—to include members of a more historically "privileged" group (men) identifying as members of a historically disadvantaged group (women)—then it seems plausible that other social identities ascribed to people can also fail to match their "true" identity, and these other social categories can also be changed or subverted to allow folks to better align how others perceive and treat them with their own self-identity.

For many whites who attempt by various means to deny or escape their whiteness—especially those who are highly educated and relatively afflu-ent (among whom these tendencies seem to be most prevalent and most extreme)—the refusal to identify with their "given" race or ethnicity often seems to be a result of what psychologists call "splitting." Insofar as many associate whiteness with all manner of negative traits (arrogant, exploitative, manipulative, chauvinistic), then to the extent that they do not see *themselves* as these things, many feel strong internal pressure to disassociate from white-ness.[111] And insofar as "people of color" are perceived as embodying various positive traits (insightful, empathetic, noble, "real," etc.), then to the extent that people see themselves as possessing these attributes, which they view as uncharacteristic of whites, they become more likely to identify as "some-thing else" instead (with myriad contextual factors informing the specific alternatives that they end up latching onto).[112]

The problem for those who feel this pull is that, at present, most who accept the possibility for someone to be transgender reject the possibility of transracialism.[113] Nonetheless, the growing acceptance of "transgender" as a viable social category has led to an increase in people attempting to migrate across other social distinctions as well—and many who attempt these boundary crossings describe themselves as "trans." Race is not the only new dimension on which such claims are being made.

For instance, there are people who are *not* disabled who nonetheless "identify" as such—even to the point of seeking out surgeries to handicap themselves (or else, directly engaging in self-harm) in order to bring their physical bodies into line with their expressed identity. At present, "transable-ism" remains rare, and the data provisional. However, the available empirical evidence suggests this identification is especially prevalent among those who are highly educated, white, and male (i.e., highly "privileged" individuals).[114]

We will soon explore in greater detail how symbolic capitalists attempt to leverage disabilities they purport to have into totemic capital. However, to briefly summarize before moving on: within victimhood cultures, formerly stigmatized identities can become sources of "totemic capital." Symbolic economy elites lay claim to totemic capital in order to enhance their moral and epistemic authority, to take advantage of material opportunities reserved for totem bearers, or to augment their cultural capital and perceived self-worth. Totemic capital can also be leveraged to enhance perceptions of merit. It is to this topic we now turn.

Backward in Heels

In 2019, the College Board announced plans to include an "adversity score" alongside all test-takers' regular SAT scores. This new metric was to be based on environmental factors—the schools test-takers attended, the neighborhoods they lived in, and so on—in order to approximate the barriers and disadvantages different students might have had to overcome in the run-up to their test. Adversity scores, it was argued, would allow colleges and universities to better contextualize a student's overall SAT performance: should two candidates have nearly identical SAT scores but significantly different adversity scores, the implication was that colleges should choose the student who had overcome more life challenges. In some cases, perhaps colleges may even prefer candidates with somewhat lower (but still acceptable) SAT scores who possessed high adversity scores. Through measures like these, it was implied, colleges and universities (especially elite ones) could do a better job of identifying and providing opportunities to talented people from disadvantaged backgrounds.

In the wake of severe pushback, the College Board adjusted the program, and it now provides a much broader range of data to admissions officers rather than a single adversity score.[115] However, the basic intuition behind the initiative seems to be widely shared: if two people achieved the same level of performance, but one of them went to worse schools, had fewer resources, and faced more severe life challenges, then the accomplishments of the latter student would seem to "mean" more. It is more of an achievement for an underprivileged aspirant to ace the exam as compared with someone who went to an excellent school, likely had extensive test preparation, lived in a household conducive to learning and growing, and so on. Perhaps a more straightforward way of phrasing the psychology at work is that *perceived disadvantage enhances perceptions of merit*. In an ostensibly meritocratic system—where prestige, opportunities, and compensation are supposed to be afforded on the grounds of merit—people therefore have a strong incentive to present themselves as disadvantaged.

Many symbolic capitalists recognize that they hail from relatively affluent backgrounds. What's more, they recognize that *others* who were presented with similar advantages may enjoy their current social position in large part as a result of those accrued advantages (i.e., "privilege") rather than merit. Not their own friends, lovers, and so on, of course, but *others* . . . especially peers they dislike. Nonetheless, elites regularly argue that they achieved *their own* positions primarily through hard work and determination. And when their preferred self-image is threatened, they eagerly produce stories about the struggles they've had to overcome (often with significant exaggerations or omissions) in order to portray their ascendance as far from inevitable—a product of grit and labor rather than unearned advantages.[116]

Of course, if symbolic capitalists reflected on these stories, they'd recognize that virtually every single one of their peers would readily produce comparable accounts of striving in the face of adversity—and to take them all at face value, we would have to assume that accrued advantage doesn't really matter much at all . . . a reality that most symbolic capitalists themselves explicitly recognize as false. However, legitimizing narratives are virtually never reflexive in this way because that would undermine the whole point.

Far from acknowledging the dubious nature of their "bootstrapping" accounts, affluent students at elite universities regularly complain about how "broke" they are.[117] Some take "poverty cosplaying" a step further and exploit the fact that they don't *personally* earn income or own assets in order to take advantage of programs intended for the poor.[118] Elite families are increasingly declaring their children as financially and legally independent (although they continue to support them in practice) in order to allow said children to claim they technically have no financial resources, thereby qualifying them to attend college for free and even receive financial support through programs intended to sponsor students of genuinely humble origins (readers should keep this in mind as elite institutions brag about the large numbers of Pell-eligible students they are now enrolling).[119] Even after graduation, wealthy professionals often conspicuously lament how they are "living paycheck to paycheck" in order to sustain their (elite) lifestyles.[120] In a recent *Bloomberg* survey of Americans earning $175,000 per year or more (i.e., the top 10 percent of income earners), a full quarter of respondents described themselves as "poor" or "just getting by."[121]

Even billionaires get in on the action. For instance, stories about the rise of Amazon regularly talk about how the enterprise was run out of Jeff Bezos's parents' garage in the early days. Less discussed is that the enterprise got off the ground because his parents donated more than a quarter of a million dollars that they had just lying around in order to support Jeff's dream (with his siblings kicking in tens of thousands more). The "garage" in question also happened to be well equipped with data servers and other key infrastructure purchased by said parents. Similar realities hold for Mark Zuckerberg, Elon Musk, and Bill Gates, who all had the luxury to drop out of college to pursue their startup dreams in part because their wealthy and well-connected parents provided large quantities of seed money, paid their cost-of-living expenses in the expensive cities they chose to reside in, and leveraged their own extensive connections in order to help ensure their children's ventures flourished.[122] Now, given the extraordinary return these billionaires ultimately delivered on their initial investments—which far exceed those of other entrepreneurs from similarly (or more) wealthy and connected families—there would seem to be little need to pretend (or insinuate) to have come from modest origins. And yet, even *extremely* wealthy and successful people often do just that.

Precisely because virtually *anyone* can (and virtually *everyone* does) produce stories of overcoming material challenges and hardships, the mileage people can get from accounts of socioeconomic struggle are fairly limited. Such accounts may marginally reduce perceptions of privilege, but they do little to actually *enhance* perceptions of merit. Far more effective is to lay claim to a type of disadvantage that most others cannot.

Historically, it was assumed that when women accomplished the same feats as men, it was a testimony to their extraordinary merit. One of the most common analogies was that a woman had to be able to do all the same things as a man but "backward in heels" in order to break through the "glass ceiling," overcome misogyny, and beat men "at their own game." Today, womanhood does not enhance meritocratic perceptions in quite the same way—at least not in symbolic capitalist spaces. After all, a decisive and growing majority of college graduates and symbolic capitalists are women. Although gendered inequalities remain quite prevalent within the symbolic professions, the totemic value of "womanhood" has been significantly reduced therein. Being a woman can enhance other forms of perceived marginality (e.g., accomplishing feats as a *"woman* of color" is more celebrated than doing so as a "person of color" or as a "woman" independently). However, those lacking additional sources of totemic capital beyond womanhood (i.e., "cishet," able-bodied white women) are today often described as quite "privileged."

Likewise, within symbolic capitalist spaces, "trauma" has evolved into a basis for identity claims and status competition. Politicians leverage purported traumatic experiences in order to enhance their credibility and neutralize criticism; college applicants paint lurid (often embellished) stories of striving in the face of trauma in order to enhance their prospects of acceptance; entertainers and social media influencers engage in similar behaviors to build their audiences and drive engagement; various forms of banal mistreatment, inconvenience, or offense are recast as "traumatizing" in a bid to get people to care more than they otherwise would.[123] However, precisely because trauma claims have become so ubiquitous, their power has likewise been reduced in many respects.[124] As cultural critic Yasmin Nair aptly put it, "If everything is trauma then nothing is."[125]

In light of the diminishing returns on appeals to trauma, poverty, or gender, elites seem to be increasingly leaning into disability claims as a means of obscuring their privilege and enhancing perceptions of their merit.

Differently (En)abled

There is a long tradition within white Anglo-Saxon Protestant circles of claiming to be afflicted with disorders that, ultimately, signaled one's elite status. For instance, in the late nineteenth century through the early twentieth century, many elites claimed to suffer from "neurasthenia"—an anxiety disorder that was held to flow from the combination of being exceptionally gifted and being born into a world insufficiently suited to utilize one's talents.[126] Neurasthenics were people who were, in a sense, too imaginative, too intelligent, too principled, too sensitive, too conscientious for their own good; they were too extraordinary in a society that was increasingly focused on standardization and mass production. In order to accommodate the unique burden they were held to bear, neurasthenics were broadly exempted from the obligations and expectations laid on others.

Precisely because many prominent elites claimed to be neurasthenics, and because the traits associated with neurasthenia were desirable—to be afflicted with neurasthenia was a sign that one was especially diligent, bright, creative, and so on—people increasingly began *actively seeking out* neurasthenic diagnoses.[127] As a result of its appeal, neurasthenia eventually jumped out of elite circles. Middle-class, and eventually even working-class, people began claiming to be neurasthenics. At that point, the affliction became dramatically less fashionable among elites, and eventually disappeared from the "West" more or less entirely. Today, neurasthenia is understood as a "culturally bound disorder," largely constrained to former British colonies.[128]

In its place, elites have begun claiming new forms of "neurodivergence." Today, some claim to be simply too honest, blunt, or direct "for their own good" and profess to be literally incapable of "reading the room" or holding their tongue. Others claim to be excessively focused, detail oriented, or precise; or too realistic, perceptive, or grounded; or too rational, logical, or dispassionate; or, at the other end of the spectrum, too passionate, creative, or ambitious. As with neurasthenia, the "disorders" just described (which contemporary elites gravitate toward) are generally products not of *deficits* but of having "too much" of some desirable trait, to the point where it crowds out certain social skills. Said disorders are held to render people especially well suited for jobs that just so happen to be high paying and high prestige (for instance, in the engineering, tech, and finance sectors) and ill suited for "human-centered" work (that happens to be less well compensated or prestigious). Those afflicted with these new forms of neurodivergence are also partially exempted from conventions, expectations, and rules that govern everyone else. As a result, as with neurasthenia, there is a strong set of incentives for contemporary elites to identify themselves with these new forms of neurodivergence. And when such incentives are present, diagnoses tend to spike.

In the Vietnam War era, elites leveraged their connections to doctors and psychiatrists to get their children designated as "disabled" and therefore exempt from the draft. There was another wave of such efforts in the wake of the Americans with Disabilities Act (ADA). Directly and indirectly, the ADA created life-changing accommodations in society for the genuinely disadvantaged. However, it also provided profound material incentives for aspiring elites to identify as "disabled." Through the ADA, federal incentive structures were created for companies that employ Americans with disabilities—leading to a hiring preference for those could be classified as disabled. A similar story held with respect to university admissions. Meanwhile, new laws and norms allowed people with disabilities to receive significant accommodations at work, at school, and in other competitive arenas. In an apparent bid to take advantage of these accommodations and gatekeeper preferences, there was a rapid uptick in Americans claiming to be disabled following the 1990 passage of the ADA—particularly among the affluent.[129]

Wealthy parents began "diagnosis shopping" in order to get their kids classified as possessing some kind of qualifying disability and to thereby secure said children advantages in entrance exams for elite high schools and (especially) the SATs.[130] The share of students taking standardized tests with accommodations has increased more than fivefold as compared with 1987 levels—driven largely by affluent students and students at affluent schools.[131] In many wealthy enclaves, nearly one in five contemporary students has a "504 plan" (a federal disability designation that entitles people to certain accommodations); this is several times higher than the national average of 2.7 percent.[132] At colleges and universities, the number of students with accommodations nearly doubled over the course of the Great Awokening—as competition for elite roles intensified—driven primarily by students attending the most selective higher education institutions.[133] At elite colleges and universities today, as many as one in four students formally identify as disabled[134] (and enjoy various accommodations in their courses on this basis).

As elites have come to increasingly identify themselves as disabled, the public "conversation" about disability has also been gentrified. It has become somewhat passé to focus on those who are genuinely and severely debilitated by their conditions. Instead, the focus has shifted to celebrating and advancing the interests of high-functioning, high-achieving, photogenic elites who claim to possess these same conditions.[135] Many objectively privileged but disabled-identifying young people are becoming online influencers, racking up huge social media audiences and getting sponsorship or advertising deals on the basis of their purported disabilities. As one content creator put it, "There absolutely is a concerted effort to really capitalize on mental illness and particularly on young women's mental illness. It's a very marketable commodity right now."[136]

In addition to the rapid expansion of elites claiming "neurodivergence," alongside the gentrification of mental health discourse to focus on these elites, there has been an expansion of claims to *physical* disabilities too. The range of health challenges that qualify as a physical "disability" has also expanded significantly. For instance, people can now qualify as disabled in virtue of ailments like celiac disease, irritable bowel syndrome, or diabetes. This is striking because, while these diseases certainly *can* be debilitating in extreme cases, symptoms are typically mild. While often somewhat inconvenient, these conditions are relatively easy to manage for most. Indeed, those who have these same conditions but who work outside the symbolic professions would be unlikely to identify themselves as disabled. Despite the fact that these (non-symbolic) workers will tend to do much more physically intensive work (and often have less access to quality health care too), they would not view these physical conditions as significant handicaps—and would be generally *dis*inclined to describe themselves as physically impaired. Outside the symbolic economy, it is not status conferring to identify oneself in this way (often, it is quite the opposite). However, within a victimhood culture, it is not only status enhancing to identify as disabled, but often opportunity enhancing as well.

Indeed, within symbolic capitalist spaces, it is in the interests of virtually all parties to embrace an expansive definition of "disability." Institutions can garner government subsidies and perks, as well as PR benefits (with respect to how inclusive and supportive they are), by increasing the number of people categorized as disabled within their organization. By expanding the pool of conditions considered a disability, they can secure recruits whose productivity is *not* meaningfully impeded by any mental or physical conditions but who still "count" as disabled for the purposes of state recordkeeping and public relations. Meanwhile, the preferences in terms of hiring, promotion, accommodations, aid, admissions, and so on incentivize prospective recruits to identify as disabled even if they aren't meaningfully impaired by their "disability." Hence, despite the fact that symbolic capitalists tend to be among the most physically fit and cognitively sophisticated people in America, we are also extraordinarily likely to present ourselves as disabled.

Here again, it should be stressed, the goal of this section is *not* to argue that people are being disingenuous in their identification (although, for the record, there is strong evidence that "malingering" regularly occurs among the college educated and is relatively easy to get away with).[137] The core objective is to highlight how the act of identifying as disabled is informed by material incentives, status competition, and other personal motives—factors independent of medical realities or "authenticity"—which can supervene on whether and how people pursue medical diagnoses, how people perform on diagnostic tests, and how any diagnosed conditions are operationalized in the professional sphere, in interpersonal interactions, with respect to one's public persona, and beyond.

Critically, the same factors that influence decisions to seek out diagnoses can influence the diagnoses themselves.[138] Earlier in this chapter, we explored how the widespread acceptance of "trauma" among psychologists and psychiatrists was significantly informed by activist campaigns, and the political objectives of mental health professionals themselves, above and beyond "objective facts." The trauma construct is far from being unique in this regard. Analogous stories could be told about the emergence of the dominant paradigms for schizophrenia, bipolar disorder, depression, autism, ADHD, dissociative identity disorder, and myriad other conditions.[139] Just as psychologists attempted to mobilize their profession in support of the antiwar movement in the late 1960s and early 1970s, they have likewise attempted to lend credence to Progressive Era social reform initiatives, civil rights activism, the War on Terror, contemporary social justice activism, and much else besides.[140] In short, both the acts of seeking *and* issuing diagnoses are, always have been, and always will be informed by much more than "objective" empirical facts.

The Rich Get Richer

Racial and ethnic minority elites are widely presumed to have had to over-come significant bias, discrimination, and perhaps privation (given that many people associate nonwhiteness with poverty) in order to achieve the same feats as white peers. LGBTQ symbolic capitalists are presumed to have had to overcome significant homophobia, transphobia, and heteronormative expectations in order to embrace who they truly are and achieve professional success. Those who lay claim to various forms of disability and trauma are held to have triumphed over social stigma, pernicious stereotypes, and the difficulties of navigating infrastructures and institutions "not built for them" in order to flourish in the sphere of competition. Although meritocracy and "identity politics" are often discussed as being in tension, in practice they are often mutually reinforcing. Leveraging totemic capital, many attempt to paint themselves as more meritocratic than their résumés or CVs might convey, because all their accomplishments are held to have been achieved in a competition rigged against them. To the extent claimants meet or exceed the scores, credentials, or achievements of more "privileged" peers, this is held to be due to exceptional raw talent, perseverance, courage, and so on.

However, effectively leveraging these perceptions in the service of one's own interests requires skill in spinning a compelling narrative. The ideal story presents dire obstacles or bleak prospects that the narrator was faced with in virtue of their background or identity. It then describes how—as a result of their grit, ingenuity, hard work, and perhaps a little luck—they were able to "beat the odds." In spite of this success, the ideal narratives go, aspirants still "keep it real" and aspire to "pay it forward" downstream. One irony, as sociologist Lauren Rivera noted in her landmark study of hiring at elite firms, is that the people best positioned to spin compelling narratives of this nature tend to be those who hail from relatively advantaged backgrounds.[141]

People who were or are *genuinely* underprivileged, abused, or stigmatized often try to conceal these facts rather than broadcast them. And even to the extent that they are aware that it would be advantageous to spin a story about their social mobility, and are willing to do so (often, they think it would be harmful or shameful to talk about what they've been through), people from genuinely disadvantaged backgrounds are generally less effective at producing the kinds of accounts that resonate with elites, as compared with people from more advantaged backgrounds. For instance, people from less advantaged backgrounds are more likely to attribute social mobility to lucky breaks, help from others, or broader social changes instead of spinning a heroic and individualistic tale of success. Consequently, their stories do not tend to resonate as well with institutional gatekeepers as compared with the narratives of more privileged people who, precisely as a result of their cultural capital, *know* they should spin a harrowing "bootstrapping" account of confronting and transcending structural barriers and identity-based bias or discrimination.

A recent study analyzing college admissions essays found that students from families with household incomes of over $100,000 per year were significantly more likely to tell stories about overcoming challenges related to physical disability, mental health, or discrimination and harassment on the basis of their race, gender, or sexuality than students from lower-income backgrounds.[142] That is, the people most likely to tell dramatic stories of overcoming totemic adversity—and the people best positioned to profit from these stories—are people who are already well off. Rather than helping give needy people a leg up, a preference for tales of striving in the face of adversity tend to stack the deck in favor of *elites*[143]—and not just the elites who can *directly* lay claim to totemic capital. Consider the following factors.

The symbolic professions tend to be far less diverse than other sectors of the American workforce (and the higher "up" one goes in terms of institutional prestige or internal institutional hierarchies, the less diverse they tend to get). Nonetheless, institutions dominated by symbolic capitalists tend to be highly preoccupied with diversity, equity, and inclusion. Even as employers remain insistent on hiring people who have advanced credentials from top schools—preferences that filter out nearly all applicants from less advantaged backgrounds—they often make significant efforts to identify and recruit people who possess the right credentials *and* can lay claim to totemic capital (in practice, typically recruiting people from minority populations who hail from relatively affluent families). Indeed, even when their organizational workforce and (especially) leadership are not particularly diverse—and for most symbolic economy institutions they will not be—institutions nonetheless tend to heavily feature the "diverse" people they *do* have in externally oriented communications.[144]

Why do they do this? Because a perceived *lack* of diversity raises uncomfortable questions about an organization's leadership and culture: Is it an "old boys' club," nepotistically hiring and promoting on the basis of candidates' backgrounds or connections? Or is it a place that recruits, retains, and rewards talent, hiring the "best of the best" without regard to extraneous factors (like candidates' race, gender, sexuality, etc.)? Paradoxically, the prioritization of hiring and promoting at least *some* people partially on the basis of their underrepresented backgrounds sends a signal that the organization *does not* make decisions on the basis of employees' demographic characteristics. Through expressed commitments to diversity, equity, and inclusion, and by showcasing (often exaggerating) the diversity that exists within an organization, firms trumpet that they are fair, open-minded, and meritocratic. This can help an organization shield itself from criticism (or lawsuits), attract the "best" talent (who, in practice, will typically end up being other liberal whites from relatively advantaged backgrounds), or lure clients and investors (who are likewise eager to demonstrate themselves as institutions that do business with "diverse" firms, for many of the same reasons).

Similar dynamics play out at the individual level. The presence of people from historically marginalized and disadvantaged groups within one's organizations or social circles provides assurance to dominant-group elites about the legitimacy of their own social position. If these "others" secured their place as a result of their talents and accomplishments, it makes it easier for members of institutionally dominant groups to perceive *themselves* as occupying *their* positions for the same reasons—because the organizations and social groups they belong to reward excellence rather than unearned advantage. Indeed, even if these "others" are perceived to have been selected primarily on the basis of their race, gender, or sexuality—that is, in an ostensibly *non-*"meritocratic" way—this only reinforces the perception among majority-group members that *their own* position is fundamentally deserved. It allows them to believe that they got where they are *despite* the fact that the field is allegedly tilted toward minorities. Rather than seeing themselves as privileged, dominant-group members can come to view themselves as disadvantaged and *especially* meritocratic (for succeeding in a competition rigged in favor of minorities).[145]

In short, not only does totemic capital directly enhance perceptions of merit with respect to the people who lay claim to it, the expenditure of this capital can also indirectly enhance perceptions of merit for the organizations one is affiliated with, and for one's majority-group peers.

He Who Lives by the Sword . . .

In the introduction to this text, I highlighted that this was, perhaps, the first in its genre authored by an African American. Notice what I did in those passages: by talking about how I'm coming at this topic with a different set of life experiences, drawing from a different set of influences, I sought to enhance my epistemic authority. I promised a type of analysis that my uniformly white predecessors had not just failed to deliver to date but perhaps *could not* have delivered even if they wanted to. Meanwhile, placing myself within a Black tradition of critique that runs from W.E.B. Du Bois through the present lent my arguments a different moral authority than if I had instead emphasized the (likewise profound) influence of, say, Friedrich Nietzsche and Michel Foucault on my work. Emphasizing my Blackness and the influence of Black scholarship on this text also helped neutralize in advance certain forms of tedious criticism or suspicion that a non-Black author might have had to contend with. That is, I began this book by leveraging totemic capital in order to push readers to listen to me in a different way than they otherwise might.

In the process of making these moves, I also collapsed my more complex ethnic background into a simpler identification: Black. My father is a Black descendent of American slaves (ADOS). My mother, however, is white. Of course, I can offer justifications for why I typically identify simply as "Black" rather than as "biracial" or "mixed." People in my position are always able to offer compelling narratives for why the identity claim that is most advantageous for them to adopt is also the most "authentic." As Bourdieu put it, "Being professionals of discourse and explication . . . intellectuals have a much greater than average capacity to transform their spontaneous sociology, their self-interested vision of the social world, into the appearance of a scientific sociology."[146] And it isn't that the justifications typically offered are untrue per se—they typically are factual, strictly speaking. However, they also tend to paint a conveniently incomplete picture.

The omitted reality in my case, and in the case of most other "Black" symbolic capitalists, is that although, statistically speaking, it is unambiguously an advantage to *be* a multiracial or immigrant Black person in the United States (as compared with being a nonimmigrant, monoracial Black American, as we've explored in this chapter), it is nonetheless more useful in most contexts to *identify* simply as Black than to be more specific about one's background. An implicit awareness of these realities is certainly a factor in our identification. If it were more useful to identify explicitly as "biracial," I suspect my intuitions about the most "authentic" means of self-identification would likely pull in a different direction, as would the intuitions of similarly positioned peers.

As things stand, not only would it be less useful to me personally to identify as anything other than Black in most contexts, these alternative identifications would be less useful for the institutions I belong to as well (rendering me less useful to these organizations, likely lowering my socioeconomic prospects as a result). Universities, for instance, *know* that although affirmative action was created to help monoracial nonimmigrant Blacks overcome the effects of slavery and Jim Crow, in practice, the primary beneficiaries are mixed-race, immigrant, or wealthy Black people. Nonetheless, they willfully obscure this reality when talking about the number of Black students enrolled in their programs. Employers perform the same sleight of hand. It is no secret that the overwhelming majority of people making strong claims on behalf of the Black community in elite media, elite academia, and elite cultural spaces more broadly are from biracial, immigrant, or highly affluent backgrounds—rendering these self-appointed spokespeople not particularly representative of the populations they purport to represent. But although this reality is not particularly well hidden, it's also not something that anyone is supposed to talk about. Indeed, it's something that most try to avoid even *thinking* about—self included in most circumstances.

As Bourdieu emphasized, attempts to leverage symbolic capital are most effective when neither party consciously analyzes what is happening in an exchange and claims seems natural (even inevitable) to the symbolically dominated and the symbolically dominant alike. Totemic capital is no exception. To scrutinize or discuss its operation, especially in relation to oneself, is deeply uncomfortable. It is also a necessary exercise if one hopes to understand power dynamics in the symbolic economy and the ends to which social justice discourse is deployed.

Coda: Accounting for Taste

In previous periods, elites attempted to demonstrate their status—to distinguish themselves from the "common people"—in large part through their knowledge and engagement with "high culture."[147] These efforts grew more strident with the emergence of mass culture and the "culture industry" circa World War II. However, by the 1960s, an ascendant cohort of symbolic capitalists sought to distinguish themselves from their predecessors, and ingratiate themselves with the public, by condemning elite denigration of pop culture as reactionary and closed-minded. As Adam Kirsch put it, "People like humanities professors, arts administrators, and museum curators, whose identity and livelihood depended on the prestige of 'seriousness,' quickly saw that it was now possible to give up the ungrateful mission of telling the public to like things it didn't like. Instead, they could tell the public why it was right not to like them."[148]

Ultimately, boomer symbolic capitalists turned the narratives of their forebears inside out. "High culture" came to be understood as comprising dated, ethically regressive, pretentious, and comparatively boring works—typically composed by repressed white men. Ever since, aspiring elites have prided themselves on being culturally omnivorous. As Shamus Khan put it, "They no longer define themselves by what they exclude, but rather their power now comes from including everything. What marks elites as elites is not a singular point of view or purpose but their capacity to pick, choose, combine and consume a wide gamut of the social strata."[149]

With respect to movies, for instance, they like the dramas, but also romcoms, action films, and the occasional slasher. For contemporary music, they like hip-hop, pop, and rock ("anything but country").[150] But there's a catch: it is a very select group of artists and works that symbolic capitalists tend to gravitate toward in each genre. With respect to TV comedies, for example, *The Office* is "consecrated" while *Two and a Half Men* is gauche. *The Ellen DeGeneres Show* was consecrated; *Dr. Phil* was decidedly not. New Bo Burnham comedy specials are worth a watch; new Jeff Dunham specials are beneath contempt. The Foo Fighters are all right; Nickelback is an embarrassment. New Jordan Peele productions are met with great excitement, while works by Tyler Perry are largely ignored.[151] Symbolic capitalists are expected to know what belongs in each bucket, and to reliably identify with consecrated works in whatever genre is up for discussion (and cast aspersions at the sorts of people who actually like the *genuinely* low-brow stuff).

Insofar as they are able to keep up, this strategy allows symbolic capitalists to enjoy the best of all worlds: they still get to demonstrate refinement in taste relative to the hoi polloi. Yet, in virtue of embracing pop culture, they can simultaneously present themselves as being, in many respects, superior to other elites: more cosmopolitan, more inclusive, more open-minded, more "real."

Works by ethnic and racial minorities play an especially important role in this status game. Studies have found that by identifying themselves with consecrated minority creatives and their work, (disproportionately white) symbolic capitalists come to feel more "authentic" themselves and seem more "authentic" to their (predominantly white) peers. These effects are even more pronounced when elites associate themselves with work produced by people of color from less advantaged socioeconomic backgrounds (works associated with whites of low socioeconomic status, meanwhile, tend to be avoided).[152]

However, many of the creatives from whom this "authenticity" is derived are often torn when they find themselves consecrated. On the one hand, they start to get much more positive attention from critics, journalists, and others. They start winning prestigious awards, they start getting invited to hobnob with movers and shakers, and they make a lot more money than they used to. However, their audience also changes dramatically, as (overwhelmingly white) professionals become their primary constituency. And what these professionals want, more than anything, is pornographic descriptions of privation, risk, strife, and suffering. As novelist Kat Rosenfield put it, "Audiences want to read about pain and suffering, abuse and exploitation. You're supposed to feel bad for the people who had written these books, while also feeling good about how bad you felt."[153]

Complementing these stories of privation and adversity, symbolic capitalists hunger for triumphant tales of how people came from "the bottom" and rose to the top but still "keep it real." They want to hear "authentic" voices affirming their preferred narratives on social and political issues (even when, indeed especially when, most others from the totemic group in question do not share symbolic capitalists' commitments on these matters).

Of course, the task of determining who is an "authentic" voice for a marginalized community is itself a fraught enterprise. As Adolph Reed Jr. noted, "Assigning authenticity requires 'finding' the pulse of the community. Actually . . . it requires *designating* the pulse—thus whites determine black legitimacy, as they have since Booker T. Washington's day at the turn of the century."[154] And in the contemporary context, it seems as though the chief criteria deployed for determining authenticity are (1) the extent to which artists are focused on their "lived experience" and (2) the extent to which artists are say things symbolic capitalists want to hear. When these two priorities come into conflict, it is the latter that typically triumphs. Indeed, whether artist is perceived as being "true" to their lived experience is in large part determined by the extent to which they conform with mainstream symbolic capitalists' preferences and expectations.[155] So long as they meet this essential criterion, "authentic" voices can often produce work that is actually *bad* and have it nonetheless praised as "necessary." Cultural critic Lauren Oyler observed, "When applied to bad art with good politics, 'necessary' allows the audience to avoid engaging with a work in aesthetic terms."[156]

Because the work produced by consecrated voices is often cosmetically radical or subversive—often highly critical of the United States, or various symbolic capitalist institutions, or white people, or men, or cisgender heterosexuals, or socioeconomic elites or liberals—it can be easy to fall under the illusion that consecrated creatives are producing genuinely edgy work or speaking uncomfortable truths to power. In reality, they're typically producing exactly what their primary audience wants. In their never-ending quest for "authenticity," many symbolic elites who are white, male, cisgender, heterosexual, and so on actively seek out content like this. They eat it up enthusiastically. The more brutal, the better. As essayist Sam Kriss aptly described it, "This stuff is *masochism*, pleasure-seeking, full of erotic charge—and as Freud saw, the masochist's desire is always primary and prior; it's always the submissive partner who's in charge of any relationship. Masochism is a technology of power. . . . When non-white people get involved in these discourses, they're always at the mercy of their white audiences, the ones for whom they perform, the ones they titillate and entertain. A system for subjecting liberation movements to the fickle desires of the white bourgeoisie. Call it what it is. This is *white supremacy*."[157]

Put simply, symbolic economy elites often *do* defer to consecrated voices from historically marginalized and disadvantaged populations. Consecrated intellectuals and creatives really *do* influence how elites think and talk about the world. They largely "set the agenda" for what the most pressing issues for their group are perceived to be; their modes of analyzing and talking about issues are rapidly and widely adopted by mainstream symbolic capitalists; their outputs are widely disseminated and used by everyone from corporations to K–12 public schools; they are given progressively larger platforms the more compelling and useful they prove themselves to be for mainstream symbolic capitalists. The higher they rise, the more mainstream elites aggressively defend them from challenges by dissenters, the more they get softball questions in increasingly fawning interviews and profiles, and the more money they make. They may accumulate a growing list of haters, particularly among those aligned with the Right, but they become largely untouchable nonetheless—at least, so long as they keep telling elites what they want to hear.

However, these deference practices also conceal power realities. Maintaining one's status *as* a consecrated voice is generally contingent on affirming the prejudices and ideals of dominant-group elites. Should consecrated minority voices produce content that is *genuinely* challenging or threatening for mainstream symbolic capitalists—something that is actually unpleasant for them to engage with, something that powerfully calls into question rather than affirming their preferred values and narratives, something that threatens their interests—the offending intellectuals and creatives will often find themselves suddenly facing harsh criticism from the people who used to praise them and, sooner rather than later, widespread neglect from mainstream symbolic capitalists. Frustrated elites generally respond to unacceptable deviance not by rethinking their own positions but by consecrating and subsequently deferring to someone else instead—someone perceived to be more congenial to producing the kinds of narratives they want to hear. And there is always some ambitious "diverse" person waiting in the wings to do just that.

These realities are not lost on consecrated cultural elites. It is precisely this implicit threat that led celebrated novelist Chimamanda Ngozi Adichie to rail against those

> who claim to love literature—the messy stories of our humanity—but are also monomaniacally obsessed with whatever is the prevailing ideological orthodoxy . . . who ask you to "educate" yourself . . . while not being able to intelligently defend their own ideological positions, because by "educate," they actually mean "parrot what I say, flatten all nuance, wish away complexity." People who do not recognize that what they call a sophisticated take is really a simplistic mix of abstraction and orthodoxy—sophistication in this case being a showing-off of how au fait they are on the current version of ideological orthodoxy. . . . What matters is not goodness but the appearance of goodness.[158]

It is these same dynamics within symbolic capitalist spaces that consecrated rapper Vince Staples is pointing to when he asks, "Who the activist and who the Devil's advocate? Or do it matter?"[159] Struggling with the effects of consecration, he laments, "All these white folks chanting when I asked 'em where my niggas at? Goin' crazy. Got me goin' crazy. I can't get with that."[160] These uncomfortable realities of being consecrated likewise led Dave Chappelle to abandon his multi-million-dollar television contract, largely drop out of public view, and move far away from symbolic capitalists (to a small town in Ohio). As he put it to *Time* magazine, "I want to make sure I'm dancing and not shuffling."[161]

In his 2017 book *We Were Eight Years in Power*, Ta-Nehisi Coates reflected, "A question—from other black writers and readers and a voice inside me now began to hover over my work—Why do white people like what I write? The question would eventually overshadow the work, or maybe it would just feel like it did. . . . How do you defy a power that insists on claiming you?"[162] Elsewhere, Coates lamented how those who find themselves consecrated no longer have the ability to think and speak freely. Instead, "you become a symbol. And that has kind of happened to me in my career. And I don't know what to do about that. I'm the guy who, I guess, white people read to show they know something. . . . How do you get back to learning and exploring when you get success?"[163] Wrestling with this tension ultimately led Coates to resign from his post at *The Atlantic* in favor of a faculty position at flagship HBCU Howard University.

In short, mainstream symbolic capitalists' move away from "high culture" alongside their passionate embrace of works produced by members of historically marginalized and disadvantaged groups were framed as egalitarianism in action. However, orthogonal to any aspiration to uplift hitherto underappreciated voices and perspectives, sincere though it might have been, these moves were also clearly a gambit by aspiring elites to delegitimize establishment rivals and enhance their own image—efforts sustained through the constant appropriation and policing of others' "authenticity." The explicit politics of deference often serve to mask the actual power dynamics at play. Consecrated intellectuals and creatives are not the ones steering the ship—their affluent, highly educated, white, liberal audiences are. And they have never been woke. And neither have we.

6

Mystification of Social Processes

Imagine that you are (like me) four inches taller than the national average for one's sex. This would give you many benefits relative to others who were average height or below-average height. For instance, tall people tend to have a competitive advantage in many sports and tend to perform better at cognitive tasks as well; they are preferred in the dating market; they tend to live longer and earn more money.[1] These dramatic advantages are completely unearned. People don't meritocratically "deserve" their height (or lack thereof). It is a function of genes, early childhood nutrition, and other factors beyond one's control. Nonetheless, someone taller than the national average would tend to enjoy significant "privilege" as a result of their height, while anyone shorter than average would often face significant (also undeserved) *dis*advantages relative to most others.

However, it would not necessarily be the case that all tall people would gain the *same* advantage for their extra inches. In fact, the amount of "privilege" one had in virtue of height could vary dramatically depending on local context. For instance, if you were four inches taller than the national average but you lived in a community where virtually everyone else was *also* roughly four inches taller than the national average, you would not gain much from your height. You would *not* have a competitive advantage over others in your community in terms of sports, dating, employment, and so on. It may be the case that if some people of below-average height moved into your community, you (and everyone else) would have a competitive advantage over *them*. And in a community where virtually everybody is taller than the national average, it is certainly better to be taller than the average oneself than to *not* be taller than the national average. Indeed, it would be especially bad to be *shorter* than the national average in such a context. But none of this changes the reality that, in your day-to-day life, being four inches taller than the national average would provide you with few advantages over others in your community. Relative to your circumstances, you would not be "above-average" height, you would be average. How would one get the most utility out of being four inches taller than the national average? By living in a community where most others were average or (even better) shorter than average. So it goes with other unearned advantages.

As with height, the premium a person would receive from "whiteness" is relational and context dependent. The whites who have the most capacity to benefit from and exploit their racial privilege—who actually possess the most racial privilege—are those who live in areas with large populations of racial and ethnic minorities to exert that privilege *over*. Racial privilege is also intersectional: just as racial disadvantage is compounded by poverty, white privilege is enhanced by relative wealth. Among the people with the most racial privilege, then, would be upper-socioeconomic-status or upwardly mobile whites who live in areas with large concentrations of significantly less well-off minorities and immigrants—people like the typical symbolic capitalist.

Within symbolic capitalist spaces, it has become fashionable to "call out" others for their privilege, to insist that others recognize and "check" their racial privilege, to ritualistically acknowledge one's own privilege, and to denounce anyone who refuses to follow suit as "racist." Critically, however, the people engaged in these rituals typically make it a point of insisting that *all* whites share the same privilege, that *all* whites are complicit in white supremacy, and so on. These kinds of universalizing narratives are convenient for elites—they allow a white professional in a city like Atlanta to pretend as though they are basically in the "same boat" as a low-income white person who lives in the heart of Appalachia and works part time at the local convenience store—as though they both benefit from their race in the same way. In truth, not only do urban, relatively affluent whites possess more racial privilege than others, but, as we have seen, they also tend to leverage that privilege at a rate, and on a scale, that dwarfs any racialized advantage enjoyed by lower-socioeconomic-status, less educated, nonurban whites (who are more likely to identify as Republican or conservative and dismiss the racial privilege narrative). Nonetheless, these "others" come to be viewed as "the problem" for racial justice in the United States because, unlike symbolic capitalists, they refuse to *acknowledge* the "privilege" they are purported to have been born with. Rather than focusing on who concretely benefits from racialization in America and how, "privilege" talk is instrumentalized in ways that shift attention to who has the "correct" beliefs, feelings, and public posture.

Critically, universalized "privilege" talk not only functions to obscure who benefits most from racialized inequality, it also serves as a means of legitimizing socioeconomic inequalities and blaming the poor for their own misfortune. For instance, studies have found that educating people about "white privilege" does very little to change anyone's attitudes or behaviors toward African Americans or other minorities. Instead, the training primarily leads white elites to hold poorer whites in even lower esteem—it convinces them that struggling whites deserve their suffering and are unworthy of help (apparently, for failing to make good use of their "privilege").[2] The plurality of poor folks in America, who just so happen to be white, are conveniently recast as "privileged' people who are owed nothing by the rest of society (who, indeed, despite their poverty, may *still* have more than they "deserve"). This is, of course, a very convenient position for elites to hold: no need to reallocate their money downward to "those people." Practically speaking, they'll just squander any advantages they're provided. And they're morally unworthy of assistance as well.

In short, the tendency among symbolic capitalists to emphasize racial privilege as common to *all* whites obscures how relatively affluent, urban whites *uniquely* benefit from racialized inequalities. This way of seeing the world also renders it more acceptable to marginalize, subordinate, and exploit the poor, so long as they happen to be white (as a plurality of poor people in the United States are). Although intended as an *explanation* of social processes, "privilege" discourse often serves to "mystify" and legitimize inequalities in practice. The concept of "privilege" is not unique in these respects. This chapter will illustrate how symbolic capitalists regularly deploy social justice in ways that obscure unflattering power relations and social dynamics—from both others and ourselves.

Noblesse Oblige

In early nineteenth-century Europe, elites widely embraced "noblesse oblige": aristocrats demonstrated that they were (morally) worthy of their social status by conspicuously recognizing that they *were* privileged, and then pledging to use that privilege for the benefit of all—especially the less fortunate.[3] Now, the fact that there have been *formal aristocracies* where virtually all elites recognized and publicly professed their privilege should perhaps serve as a kind of reductio ad absurdum proof against the idea that awareness and confessions of privilege have anything to do with actually mitigating inequalities. Nonetheless, a version of the practice persists to this day.

Contemporary elites demonstrate their worthiness—that they are the kind of people who belong among the Google, *New York Times*, and Ivy League crowd—by rhetorically (purely rhetorically) disassociating from their privilege. Conspicuous antiracism, feminism, and so on have become status markers among urban, highly educated elites—a signal to institutional gatekeepers that one deserves to be in the company of other "enlightened" souls.[4] Today, as in the past, these professions of privilege are almost exclusively carried out by elites, and are virtually never accompanied by any costly attempts to actually shed their privilege.

Instead, these confessions end up being a type of "flex." Elites are literally and fairly directly broadcasting their elite status—often describing in great detail how they don't have to play by the same rules as "other" people (i.e., *I* don't have to worry about cops suspecting me of criminal activity while *I'm* shopping). And yet, the braggadocio element is apparently nullified by the speaker's claim to detest this state of affairs—even if they aren't doing much to change it and, indeed, even if they continue to actively exploit it. This blatant inconsistency is itself part of the status display. As Michael Shellenberger put it, "Hypocrisy is the ultimate power move. It is a way of demonstrating that one plays by a different set of rules from the ones adhered to by common people. Hypocrisy demonstrates how unaccountable one is to conventional morality. Such displays work because, unlike wealth, status is inherently subjective. The more of it you are perceived to have, the more of it you actually have."[5]

Understanding social justice discourse as a means through which elites signal their elite status can help recontextualize a number of other contemporary social phenomena. Consider, for instance, the debates that have been raging around "critical race theory" (CRT) in K–12 schools. Interlocutors argue over whether CRT is an appropriate label for these frameworks,[6] and whether the material being pushed on students is pedagogically "good"—but actually, on the most fundamental aspects, there is broad agreement among the warring sides. One faction alleges that (what they call) "critical race theory" is dangerous propaganda that needs to be banned from the classroom. The other side *agrees* that these ideas are genuinely subversive, which is precisely why they insist on pushing them—to equip the next generation to fight for "social justice" and so on[7] (meanwhile, their opponents are held to be resistant to these ideas out of their desire to preserve white supremacy). Lost in the discussion is an important bit of context that renders the entire melodrama around the "revolutionary" nature of these frameworks somewhat absurd: the class dimension.

The K–12 schools that most aggressively began pushing the content in question—the schools where the initial blowups happened and the most vicious fights persist at time of writing—are elite private institutions like Horace Mann and Dalton in New York City, or Harvard-Westlake in Los Angeles.[8] These are schools where families pay tuition of tens of thousands of dollars per student per year in order to signal to institutional gatekeepers that their child is "Harvard material."

The *public* school districts where blowups occur have also tended to be affluent. For instance, one of the earliest and most vociferous struggles took place in Loudon County, Virginia. The median household income for families in this school district is roughly $168,000 (that is, more than $100,000 per year *on top of* the median national household income).[9] In this district, 70 percent of parents have a BA degree or higher (roughly twice the baseline for the general population). Eighty-two percent of families in this district are homeowners—and they often spend enormous sums of money to live where their children can be zoned into Loudon County schools, which are likewise feeders into elite colleges and universities.

According to an analysis by NBC News,[10] similar early blowups around CRT in public schools occurred in Tredyffrin/Easttown School District, Pennsylvania (median household income $206,000; 82 percent of families are homeowners; 89 percent of parents possess at least a BA); Carmel Clay Schools, Indiana (median household income $154,000, 86 percent of families are homeowners, 80 percent of parents possess at least a BA); School Administrative District 51, Maine (median household income $147,000; 92 percent of families are homeowners; 75 percent of parents possess at least a BA); Scottsdale Unified School District, Arizona (median household income $122,000; 66 percent of families are homeowners; 63 percent of parents possess a BA or higher); Newport-Mesa Unified School District, California (median household income $101,000, 46 percent of parents possess a BA); and many other districts around the country where household incomes, homeownership rates, and parental education levels are significantly above the U.S. norm.

It is critical to observe, moreover, that parents dissatisfied with the curriculum at these affluent schools nonetheless overwhelmingly keep their children enrolled.[11] This is likely because they recognize that the credentials being conferred (and from where) matter much more for their child's life trajectory than the specific material being taught. If they must choose between an elite school with a "woke" curriculum and a school for normal kids where these kinds of themes are more muted, this is generally an easy choice. And this *is* basically the choice elite parents are faced with. Even if they could get their kids into a comparable alternative school, it would typically do little good. Virtually all peer institutions seem to be pushing the same woke curriculum.[12] It's worth taking a moment to reflect on why that is.

First and foremost, it is critical to remember that these are elite schools. That is, they are schools *for* elites. Their primary purpose is to help ensure that rich people's children (1) end up attending prestigious universities like Harvard, (2) go on to be wealthy and successful themselves (i.e., reproduce their class position), and (3) feel like they "earned" their social station. This is literally what parents are paying for[13]—and it's not a secret. That is, the very purpose of these schools is to generate inequality—to give children of elites a leg up on everyone else—and to legitimize this inequality on "meritocratic" grounds (the "superior" K–12 education these students receive compared with everyone else provides justification for elite colleges and universities to prefer students from wealthy families; subsequently, the superior education these students receive at elite colleges allows employers to likewise favor children from wealthy backgrounds under the auspices of merit).[14] In light of these facts, it may seem absurd that elite schools dedicate so much time, money, and energy pushing woke ideology onto their students. At least, it seems absurd until these modes of talking and thinking are recognized *as a means of* elite signaling.

Given that the goal of these schools is to place students at elite institutions like Harvard, and Harvard and peer institutions are increasingly presenting themselves as "social justice oriented" (and selecting for students who present themselves in the same way), if these schools were *not* teaching kids how to talk and think in woke terms, they would likely be doing their students a disservice in terms of their life prospects. Parents would be wasting tens of thousands of dollars per year to send their kids to these schools (or to live in a place where they are zoned into these schools). If aspirants seem overtly anti-woke or unwoke in their admissions essays and materials (*especially* if they are "cishet" white men), their chances of getting into the Ivy League or any other prestigious school are severely diminished. Likewise, after college, if said children want to fit in at virtually *any* symbolic capitalist–dominated institution today, *especially* the elite ones, they'll generally need to present themselves as woke or "woke compliant." To be conspicuously nonwoke or anti-woke is to risk becoming a pariah among one's peers (and often among institutional gatekeepers as well). It doesn't *always* work out this way, but it's a common outcome—and a risk many are unwilling to take.

In short, if affluent parents want their kids to be elites, said children need to be fluent in elite discourse. And let's be frank here: the ideas and frameworks associated with what opponents label "CRT" are demonstrably *not* the language of the disadvantaged and the dispossessed. These aren't the discourses of the ghetto, the trailer park, the hollowed-out suburb, the postindustrial town, or the global slum. Instead, they're ideas embraced primarily by highly educated and relatively well-off whites, reflecting an unholy mélange of the therapeutic language of psychology and medicine, the interventionism of journalists and activists, the tedious technicality of law and bureaucracy, and the pseudo-radical Gnosticism of the modern humanities. It is symbolic capitalist discourse, through and through. Consequently, it is not the "wretched of the earth" who endorse and try to proliferate these ideas. Mostly, it's the well-to-do. As social psychologist Rob Henderson aptly put it,

> When someone uses the phrase "cultural appropriation," what they are really saying is "I was educated at a top college." . . . Only the affluent can afford to learn strange vocabulary because ordinary people have real problems to worry about. The chief purpose of luxury beliefs is to indicate evidence of the believer's social class and education. . . . When an affluent person advocates for drug legalization, or anti-vaccination policies, or open borders, or loose sexual norms, or uses the term "white privilege," they are engaging in a status display. They are trying to tell you, "I am a member of the upper class."[15]

Reflecting on his own experience at elite K–12 schools Grace Church, Dalton, and Harvard, journalist Matthew Yglesias likewise observed,

> I am quite fluent in why we don't characterize non-white people as "minorities" anymore, and even why affirmatively characterizing them as "people of color" is in favor rather than saying "non-white," which tends to center whiteness. I know what it means to "center" something. I know that URM stands for under-represented minorities, and that we tend not to spell it out because "minorities" is out of favor. I also know what URM means (not Asians) and how URM is distinguished from BIPOC. I don't talk about "third-world" countries. I know these things in large part for the same reason I know how to tie a bow tie. . . . These elite

institutions and codes of manners are not egalitarian, not just because manners are insufficient but because their purpose is to be inegalitarian. Changing "field" into "practicum" doesn't include more people—it's a new means of excluding people whose information is out of date.[16]

But of course, it would be mortifying for people on all sides of this argument to recognize that what they are actually fighting over is how future generations of elites understand, describe, and legitimize their social position.[17] One side instead pretends as though CRT-associated ideas represent the "authentic" will and interests of most "people of color." The other side pretends as though an embrace of these ideas will somehow harm their children. In reality, mastering these frameworks will enhance students' social status and professional flourishing. And *this* is why elite schools are pushing it.

As for the genuinely marginalized and disadvantaged, they aren't even part of the conversation in any meaningful way, and there is little at stake for *them* in these struggles.[18] In fact, there's a sense in which there's little at stake for elites either: the debates, activism, legislation, and so on are likely to have no bearing on how things play out in the end. Irrespective of parents' preferences or lawmakers' choices, the vast majority of elite aspirants will conform with what elite educational institutions seem to expect of them.

On that front, Hannah Mendlowitz, senior assistant director of admissions and director of recruitment at Yale, recently declared, "For students who come to Yale, we expect them to be versed in issues of social justice. We encourage them to be vocal when they see an opportunity for change in our institution and in the world."[19] Secret societies at Yale, such as Skull and Bones, have adopted a similar posture despite being among the most elite and parochial groups at one of the most elite and parochial institutions in the world. As journalist (and Yale alumni) Rose Horowitch put it,[20] contemporary "secret societies affirmatively select for students who are the first in their family to attend college, who come from a low-income background, or who are part of a minority group. This has created something of a diversity arms race. . . . The Bones class of 2021 had 'people from all kinds of backgrounds,' one member of the class told me—but no conservatives. (Unless you count centrists as conservatives, which some members do.) Like Yale's student body overall, members of secret societies mostly range from far left to left of center."

Yet, as political theorist Leif Weatherby emphasized, despite the ideological hegemony and aggressive social justice signaling present at elite schools like Yale and Harvard, they aren't exactly "pumping out community organizers and beret-wearing literary critics."[21] The most enrolled degree programs at

Harvard are consistently economics, computer science, and government. And upon graduation, Weatherby continues, "a whopping 57 percent of Harvard grads go into finance, consulting or technology; the top landing spots are Google, McKinsey and Goldman Sachs."[22] Here, too, however, fluency in social justice discourse is expected. These firms are (in)famously strong champions of diversity, equity, and inclusion (DEI), environmental, social and governance (ESG) investing, and related frameworks—and they seek out employees who ostensibly share these commitments (or, at the very least, are not overtly opposed).

So long as Ivy League schools and other elite organizations continue to present themselves as "social justice oriented" and select people on the basis of their "social justice" bona fides in this way, elite aspirants will present themselves as deeply fluent in, and committed to, social justice too— irrespective of whether K–12 schools provide training on how to do this or not.[23] But if it's any consolation to wealthy parents, their children's likely embrace of woke ideas and discourse is unlikely to prevent them from reproducing their social position. Quite the opposite: in practice, wokeness often serves as a *sign* of one's elite status and a reinforcer of the same.

Class Canceled

Within a victimhood culture, one of the very worst charges that could be leveled against someone—especially against a person who lacks totemic capital (which can be leveraged to partially insulate oneself against such accusations)—is that they are themselves victimizers, or that they harbor animus toward victimized populations. Symbolic capitalists and affiliated institutions often ritualistically describe *themselves* as racist, sexist, and so on in a paradoxical bid to demonstrate their virtue. However, to have *others* brand one as a bigot, and to be treated as a bigot, is a form of symbolic death: those perceived by *others* to be appropriately labeled with terms like "racist" or "sexist" are held as being unworthy of having their perspectives or priorities taken seriously; they are unworthy of working in the symbolic professions (indeed, their employer risks moral pollution if it does not cut ties, and colleagues risk moral pollution if they come to the defense of the besieged); they are unworthy of being part of the social networks of enlightened people; their work becomes viewed as "contaminated" (and therefore worthy of suspicion, neglect, or censorship). In short, accusations of bigotry or identity-based abuse are powerful weapons. They not only have the capacity to vanquish enemies, but also enhance the relative status of those who wield them. This has incentivized "concept creep" with respect to who counts as a bigot and in virtue of what.[24]

In the past, for instance, "racism" primarily denoted overt discrimination, bigotry, or racial animus. Incidents of this nature are far less common today, and far less accepted, than they were in previous decades.[25] This is unambiguously great news. However, as a function of the immense symbolic capital potentially at stake when accusations of racism are made, and the diminishing opportunities to leverage that capital by "calling out" obvious cases of racism, the sphere of what counts as "racist" has been ever expanding—to the point where it is now possible to qualify as "racist" on the basis of things like microaggressions and implicit attitudes. Critically, it is relatively well-off, highly educated, liberal *whites* who tend to be among the most zealous in identifying and prosecuting these new forms of "racism." Indeed, despite expressed aspirations to center the perspectives of the marginalized and disadvantaged, and to honor *their* priorities and preferences, white elites play an outsize role in setting the agenda for contemporary antiracism (far more so than nonelite racial and ethnic minorities).

In principle, this state of affairs *could* be defended on the grounds that relatively well-off and highly educated liberal whites—precisely in virtue of their college education and higher rates of consumption of "woke" content in the media, online, and so on—perhaps understand the reality and dynamics of racism better than the average Black or Hispanic person. However, given that many of their preferred approaches to "antiracism" are not just demonstrably ineffective but outright counterproductive, I wouldn't recommend that anyone try to take a stand on *that* hill.[26] More realistically, it seems like many whites, in their eagerness to present themselves as advocates for people of color and the cause of antiracism, neglect to actually *listen* to ordinary Black or brown folks about what *they* find offensive or harmful, or what *their* racial priorities are.[27] Instead of seeking out the perspectives of nonelites, white symbolic capitalists, typically in partnership with "consecrated" elites of color, end up defining "racism" in ways that are congenial to their own preferences and priorities. Rather than actually dismantling "white supremacy" or meaningfully empowering people of color, the "good whites" and their allies instead consolidate various forms of capital in their own hands.

Under the auspices of promoting social justice, many symbolic capitalist spaces have become "hotbeds of craven snitches" where elites weaponize resources established to protect and support those who are *genuinely* marginalized, disadvantaged, vulnerable, or victimized in order to settle personal vendettas, gain the upper hand in institutional power struggles, or purge political and ideological opponents.[28] The same anonymity protections and impersonal processes intended to help shield actual victims from bias and retaliation are regularly exploited by bad actors to get revenge on exes, sabotage rivals, and enhance one's own personal standing.[29]

Defenders of what has come to be referred to as "cancel culture" often attempt to portray the phenomenon as folks from less advantaged backgrounds holding the "privileged" to account. In fact, the people engaged in these practices are typically themselves elites or aspiring elites. Again, symbolic capitalists tend to be among the most sensitive and most easily offended sectors of U.S. society. It is people like us who tend to be "very online," who focus intensely on race, gender, sexuality, and politics, and who take part in online mobbings. It is *elites* who are raised from a young age to understand and learn how administrative systems and processes work, allowing them to know which levers to pull to get people fired or disciplined, even on false or exaggerated charges, while minimizing repercussions or blowback for themselves. It is *elites* who feel comfortable folding authorities and third parties into their personal disputes, believing that these institutions, processes, and professionals exist to serve *their* interests (not wrongly), and that the system will typically work to their advantage (not wrongly). It is people from elite backgrounds who simply expect institutions and their representatives to accommodate their personal preferences, priorities, and perspectives—and who will demand to "speak to the manager" when they don't, and who know *how* to "speak to the manager" to get what they want. These kinds of knowledge, dispositions, and behaviors toward institutions are part of the "hidden curriculum" of elite childhoods, elite education, and elite culture.[30] Consequently, while there are many cases of elites "canceling" working-class people,[31] there are *not* many cases of nonelites successfully canceling elites. Even in the cases of "punching up," what is characterized as "holding the privileged to account" is generally an instance in which some faction of elites has managed to purge or inflict damage on someone even better positioned than themselves. Much like cricket or lacrosse in the United States, cancellation is primarily an elite sport.

For their part, people from less elite backgrounds are generally less knowledgeable about how to work "the system." They often try to avoid folding authorities into their problems, because they tend to believe that doing so would make their problems worse (not wrongly). Indeed, when people from less elite backgrounds try to leverage "accountability" resources, they are much less likely to get the result they wanted. Rather than the accused being held to account, the accusers often face retaliation and other forms of blowback that, precisely in virtue of their more tenuous position, people from less elite backgrounds are typically least capable of weathering. Likewise, when they find themselves *targets* of cancellation campaigns, it is people from less advantaged backgrounds who are least equipped to defend themselves, and who tend to face the direst consequences. For example, sociologists Frank Dobbin and Alexandra Kalev have found that when companies institute "grievance systems" to investigate and prosecute incidents of bias, racial and ethnic minorities tend to be the most adversely effected. Asian and African American men, alongside Black and Hispanic women, become far more likely to get pushed out of management roles when these policies are implemented. Meanwhile, white women are among the least affected, and white men tend not to be affected at all.[32]

Similar realities hold for censorship. In contemporary symbolic capitalist spaces, censorious tendencies are frequently justified under the auspices of protecting vulnerable and underrepresented populations from offensive or hateful speech. In reality, however, speech restrictions generally end up enhancing the position of the already powerful *at the expense* of the genuinely marginalized and disadvantaged. Hate speech laws, for instance, have consistently been turned by ruling parties against their political and ideological opponents. They have been regularly used to justify surveillance and censorship of government dissidents and advocates for civil rights and civil liberties. This was true in the civil rights era (indeed, many free speech protections currently under assault by mainstream symbolic capitalists were established in the 1960s to protect civil rights activism from censorship campaigns). This was true with respect to campaigns for feminism and gay rights. It remains the case today[33]—not just in the United States but around the world.[34]

Academic research and audits by media outlets and government agencies consistently find that measures to restrict hate speech online tend to disproportionately silence racial and ethnic minorities, gender and sexual minorities, social justice activists, and political dissenters.[35] Outcomes like these are not unusual "bugs" in otherwise beneficent and well-conceived systems. They are reflections of how censorious practices typically play out: they are almost invariably and necessarily designed and enforced by people with power, typically deployed against those with less power.

To draw an example from my own profession, a majority of faculty fired for political speech tend to be politically aligned with the Left. Female and minority faculty tend to be especially vulnerable to being fired for political speech because they are significantly less likely to be tenured and are much more likely to teach at public schools that are beholden to state legislatures and often politically appointed trustees and governing boards.[36] Indeed, although whites, men, and tenure-line professors are the most commonly targeted in "cancellation" attempts, contingent faculty, women, and Hispanics are significantly more likely to be fired when they find themselves targeted for political speech.[37] Rules that make it easier to fire professors for speech deemed "offensive" tend to disproportionately harm women, people of color, and other institutionally vulnerable scholars.

Similar realities hold for other forms of social sanction for insufficiently "woke" views. In general, immigrants and racial and ethnic minorities tend to be more religious and more culturally and symbolically conservative than whites—as are people of more modest socioeconomic backgrounds compared to social elites. Consequently, inculcating an environment that is hostile to more "traditional" values and worldviews, although typically carried out in the name of diversity and inclusion, will often have the perverse effect of excluding, alienating, or creating a more precarious situation for those who are already underrepresented and marginalized in elite spaces. When we try to understand why it is that so many "people of color," or people from low-income, immigrant backgrounds or otherwise "nontraditional" backgrounds, feel as though they don't "belong" in symbolic capitalist spaces—whether we're talking about elite K–12 schools, or colleges and universities, or professional settings—this is likely a big, and underexplored, part of the story. Rather than being *insufficiently* progressive, these institutions may instead be too homogeneous and extreme in their ideological bearings. They may be too fiercely oriented around the idiosyncratic (ostensibly emancipatory) belief systems of white elites and too oriented around serving *their* agendas.

Invalidating Inconvenient Perspectives

Symbolic capitalists portray ourselves as advocates for (or representatives of) the marginalized and disadvantaged. In practice, however, we often show blatant disregard for the perspectives of those we claim to champion.

Consider the widespread use of "BIPOC" (Black, Indigenous, people of color). The term purports to center the experiences of Black and Indigenous Americans when discussing racial and ethnic minorities in the United States. However, it is a label that resonates primarily with relatively affluent whites. A poll conducted for the *New York Times*, for instance, found that "more than twice as many white Democrats said they felt 'very favorably' toward 'BIPOC' as Americans who identify as any of the nonwhite racial categories it encompasses."[38] The small share of nonwhites who do use the term are typically elites. As we have seen, umbrella terms like these can be quite useful to people like us. For others, not so much.

"Latinx" provides another prominent example of this phenomenon. Within symbolic capitalist circles, the term is increasingly regarded as *the* correct way to refer to people of Hispanic or Latino origin. Its use has grown increasingly pronounced in outputs by nonprofits, think tanks and advocacy groups, academics, journalists, and the Democratic Party. Yet a 2020 survey by Pew Research found that only 3 percent of Hispanics use the term. A strong majority of Hispanic and Latino respondents (roughly two-thirds) were outright opposed to having it serve as the main pan-ethnic term for people like themselves.[39] A subsequent study by Politico found that the term was not just undesirable but outright offensive for two out of every five U.S. Hispanics. One out of five said they are disturbed "a lot" by use of the term. Put another way, more than ten times as many Hispanics are troubled by the use of the term as are validated by it. The Politico report goes on to emphasize that 30 percent of Hispanic and Latino respondents claimed they would be less likely to support a candidate, organization, or cause if the term "Latinx" was deployed in association with it.[40] Democratic congressman Ruben Gallego, head of the Congressional Hispanic Caucus campaign arm, has emphasized that his staff is not allowed to use the term in any official communications, because it signals a disconnect from, or a blatant disregard for, the culture and values of most U.S. Hispanics and Latinos.[41] Yet this has done little to reduce its appeal among mainstream symbolic capitalists.

In an interview with the *New Yorker*, one Latinx-identifying symbolic capitalist described detractors of the term as the "weakest link toward true progress, reciprocity and inclusivity." "For that," he continued, "you are dismissed. Vamoose. Begone. Get to steppin'. Corran camino. And take your shitty misogynistic, homophobic, and transphobic family members with you."[42] As a reminder, 65 percent of U.S. Hispanics and Latinos expressly reject the term as an appropriate label for people like them, and 40 percent found use of the term to be actually offensive. That's a lot of people being "dismissed" on behalf of the 3 percent of Hispanics and Latinos—nearly exclusively symbolic economy professionals and aspirants—who actually identify with "Latinx."

Although superficially oriented toward social justice, symbolic innovations like these are often mobilized as a means for elites—white elites aided and abetted by minority-group peers—to signal their superiority, devalue the perspectives and priorities of nonelites, and disregard objections from the people they are ostensibly advocating for with respect to justice claims made in their name. As philosopher Alain Badiou effectively put it,

> Our suspicions are first aroused when we see that the self-declared apostles of ethics and of the "right to difference" are clearly horrified by any vigorously-sustained difference. . . . [The] celebrated "other" is acceptable only if he is a good other—which is to say what, exactly, if not the same as us? Respect for differences? Of course! But on the condition that the different be parliamentary-democratic, pro free-market economics, in favor of freedom of opinion, feminism, and the environment. . . . It might well be that ethical ideology, detached from the religious teachings which at least conferred upon it the fullness of a "revealed" identity, is simply the final imperative of a conquering civilization: "Become like me and I will respect your difference."[43]

Those who defy symbolic capitalists' preferences and priorities are deemed unworthy of being taken seriously. Opponents of "Latinx"—including (perhaps especially) if they are Hispanic or Latino—are cast as homophobic, misogynistic, and transphobic and therefore worthy of being "dismissed." Increasingly, racial and ethnic minorities who reject symbolic capitalists' preferred narratives on race, or who vote for the "wrong" political candidate, are branded as "multiracially white" or "politically white"—that is, they cease to be minorities at all.[44] As then–Democratic presidential hopeful Joe Biden memorably put it, "If you have a problem figuring out whether you're voting for me or Trump, then you ain't black."[45] Through methods like these, it becomes easy for symbolic capitalists to maintain that they promote the will and interests of racial and ethnic minority groups: dissenters are simply redefined as nonminorities.

Likewise, when women express objections to mainstream symbolic capitalists' approaches to feminism, this opposition is often described as arising from internalized misogyny. Should they vote for Republicans or simply fail to vote for Democrats, it is because they have commitments to white supremacy that override their commitment to their gender; they are more "white" than "female."[46]

Through maneuvers like these, mainstream symbolic capitalists assure ourselves that the only people who are "truly" Black or Hispanic or women or disabled or LGBTQ (or the only people appropriately influenced by those identities)—the only voices we have to view as credible or authentic, or have to take seriously or defer to—are those who affirm our own interests, values, and worldviews.

Critique or Alibi?

In contemporary discussions of inequality, "systemic," "institutional," or "structural" interpretations of racism and sexism have become all the rage.[47] On the one hand, this is both understandable and laudable. Looking at social structures, how institutions operate or how systems function *in concrete terms* can provide powerful insights into how inequalities arise, are sustained, and reproduce over time. However, when these ideas are mobilized in less concrete ways, an appeal to "systems," "structures," and "institutions" can serve as a means to mystify rather than illuminate social processes. These frameworks can be, and regularly are, deployed by elites in order to absolve them of responsibility for social problems and to legitimize inaction to address those problems. They are evoked in hand-wavy ways to avoid getting into specifics (because the specifics are uncomfortable).[48]

For instance, many who insist on talking about inequalities as "systemic" decline to think through, in concrete terms, their own place in the system and the roles they personally play in the social order—let alone engaging in similar considerations of their peers, their loved ones, or the institutions they affiliate with and support. Hence, many rail against "systemic" inequality while persisting in the belief that the *losers* in the symbolic economy (i.e., Americans in "flyover country," nonelite and downwardly mobile whites, and workers connected to productive and extractive industries) are the primary perpetuators and beneficiaries of systemic inequalities. Conversely, as explored throughout this work, contemporary symbolic capitalists are often explicit in counting *themselves* among the marginalized and disadvantaged. Such assertions are more or less completely devoid of serious consideration of social structures or institutional operations—they *must* be.

In a similar vein, elites who identify with historically marginalized or disadvantaged groups regularly pretend as though a "win" for them personally is a "win" for the groups they identify with. In making these assertions, precisely what contemporary elites are failing to consider are the social structures that prevent gains for people like them from "trickling down" in any meaningful way. When elites enrich themselves, empower themselves, or pamper themselves, it does little to assist the genuinely marginalized, vulnerable, impoverished, or disadvantaged. A truly "structural" analysis of inequality would make this clear and would thereby preclude many of the "totemic capital" bids symbolic capitalists routinely make. Yet many who are keen to evoke "systems," "structures," and "institutions" in abstract ways persistently decline to consider the extent to which their personal fortunes—to say nothing of their values, priorities, and worldviews—actually *are* (or, more likely, are not) meaningfully connected to most others in the groups they identify with.

Moreover, the largely abstract focus on social structure conveniently elides considerations of individual agency. In truth, structure and agency are deeply intertwined: as a result of social structure, we all make decisions under constraint. Some have many more constraints than others—particularly those who have little financial or symbolic capital. The flip side, however, is that others have far *more* agency than everyone else, and their decisions or behaviors often exert a disproportionate impact on the possibilities available to others. Symbolic capitalists, again, must be counted among this latter group. We are in a much stronger position than most to influence the prevailing order. We often exercise our agency in pernicious ways when we could do otherwise. Evoking "the system" is often a way of obscuring this fact. By claiming to be mere cogs in the machine, helplessly bound by the prevailing order just like everyone else, contemporary elites implicitly absolve themselves of any unique responsibility for social problems (or any unique obligation to make sacrifices or changes to address those problems).

In a similar fashion, many contemporary symbolic capitalists evoke "history" as a chief cause of contemporary injustices. However, "history" doesn't *do* anything. The tendency of many symbolic capitalists to analyze contemporary injustices in historical terms often obscures how and why certain elements of the past continue into the present. Discussing the persistence of race ideology, historian Barbara Fields explained, "Nothing handed down from the past could keep race alive if we did not constantly reinvent and re-ritualize it to fit our own terrain. If race lives on today, it can do so only because we continue to create and re-create it in our social life, continue to verify it, and thus continue to need a social vocabulary that will allow us to make sense, not of what our ancestors did then, but of what we ourselves choose to do now."[49]

Present-day racial inequalities are not some inevitable by-product of America's history of slavery, Jim Crow, and so on. They are instead reflections of people today, here and now, taking actions that systematically favor certain people over others. Consider racialized differences in home appraisals: studies consistently find that real estate agents value the same home much differently depending on the race of the seller.[50] This tendency is not a mere product of "history." In fact, far from being a holdover of the past, racial gaps in property appraisal have grown dramatically since the 1980s.[51] Large cities across the United States were more segregated in 2019 than they were in 1990.[52] Obviously, these *recent* trends are not going to be well explained by appeals to slavery, Jim Crow, historical redlining, and so forth. The growing gaps are instead overwhelmingly a function of *contemporary* practices. Although appeals to America's racist and sexist history are often portrayed as some kind of critique of the social order, instead they often serve as an alibi: it's not *we* who are to blame, but those terrible people in the past (who are all conveniently dead and therefore unable to be held to account).

"Historical," "structural," "systemic," or "institutional" narratives also tend to present an overly mechanical and deterministic picture of the world. In truth, events are often quite contingent. Societies and institutions are highly dynamic. As sociologist Andrew Abbott emphasized, it is actually a much harder puzzle to explain continuity than change.[53] Change happens all the time. It is literally inevitable. People cycle in and out of institutions, geographic areas, relationships, and life altogether. Individuals learn and grow. The physical environment is constantly evolving. New ideas, practices, and technologies are constantly being developed. Resources are constantly being extracted, transformed, and shifted around. Money is constantly changing hands. Actors external to a particular society or institution are constantly attempting to shape the world in the service of their own ends, influencing the possibilities and incentives for others. Structural or cultural persistence in the face of this constant churn and, especially, across generations and cultural contexts doesn't just "happen." It's an accomplishment.

When we analyze how systems and institutions operate in concrete terms rather than just waving our hands at "the system," "history," or related abstractions, we can see that inequalities within institutions tend to be produced and sustained by everyday practices in local contexts rather than by forces outside one's control.[54] Likewise, it is in discrete behaviors and interactions among actual people in concrete places at particular points in time that abstractions like "race" or "gender" or "class" or "sexuality" express themselves "in the world." To the extent that the macro forces and abstract notions that sociologists focus on exist *at all*, it is only through people enacting them in local contexts.[55] And agents typically have many degrees of freedom with respect to if and how they enact a social order. However, cosmetically radical narratives about "systems," "structures," and "history" are often mobilized by symbolic capitalists to absolve us of responsibility for the choices we make— through hyperbolically deterministic narratives on the one hand, and unduly pessimistic analyses on the other.

According to some prominent accounts, America is fundamentally racist, and it always has been. "Progress" has been largely mythological. Injustices are so deeply entrenched and pervasive that nothing short of revolution can rectify the situation. Smaller ameliorative measures may even be counter-productive insofar as they make a bad situation more tolerable, thereby fore-stalling the dramatic change that needs to happen.[56] However, revolution does not seem to be on the horizon in the foreseeable future, nor is there an obvious path from the current status quo to a (leftist) revolution. Hence, it seems as though the only thing that the clear-eyed can do is carry on as usual (albeit with occasional pangs of guilt) and regularly condemn the system we profit from even as we continue to actively exploit it. Arguments like these are superficially radical yet functionally conservative. They allow adherents to feel self-righteous, and to present themselves as deeply committed to sub-stantial change (especially as compared with those focused on incremental and piecemeal reforms, whom they often mock), while neutralizing any apparent obligation to *do* anything (beyond saying, thinking, or feeling the "right" things). Although the people advancing these arguments often evoke "systems" and "structures," precisely what their pessimism allows them to avoid is any hard thinking about concrete changes that could be made to the system in order to ameliorate social problems—let alone working through specific processes, mechanisms, and consensus-building campaigns that would allow these changes to be successfully implemented. That is, precisely what these pessimists are *not* doing is thinking in genuinely systemic or struc-tural terms.

This pessimism also tends to be applied in a highly selective manner. For instance, an individual's vote virtually never changes the outcome of an elec-tion, certainly not at the national level. Any particular individual participating in a protest, writing a letter to one's representatives, or engaging in political discourse online or in other public forums is similarly unlikely to, themselves, influence or overturn the prevailing order in any meaningful way.[57] However, symbolic capitalists don't tend to assert, "If it doesn't bring about revolu-tion, it's not worth doing," when we engage in expressive politics. We don't shrink before the apparent futility of our actions when engaging in cosmic warfare over symbols, rhetoric, or partisan struggles (i.e., when we're doing things that are satisfying or useful for *us*). Instead, the "drop in the bucket" argument gets conveniently trotted out when we're challenged to take incon-venient actions or make costly sacrifices in pursuit of our expressed ideals.

Across the board, narratives and ideological frameworks presented as "radical" critiques of the social order are regularly deployed as implicit jus-tifications for contemporary inequality-reproducing behaviors and adverse states of affairs. However, symbolic capitalists are often blind to these realities precisely in virtue of our sincere commitments to "social justice" (in the abstract).

Doing Bad, Feeling Good

Imagine two incidents of theft.

In the first case, a bandit takes something valuable from someone else. Deprived of this important source of wealth, the victim and his family live a life of relative destitution, even as the thief and *his* family flourish, with nary a thought about the crime that served as the basis of their wealth, nor the fate of those they stole from. Eventually the perpetrator and his family forget about the theft altogether and come to view their wealth as legitimate.

In the second case, a bandit also takes something precious from someone else, likewise leaving the victim and his family in a state of relative destitution, even as the robber and his family prosper. But in the second case, the bandit constantly acknowledges that his own prosperity was achieved at the victim's expense. He explicitly and repeatedly recognizes the state of privation that the victim and his family live in as a result of the crime. He publicly praises the victim at every turn. Yet he nonetheless declines to return the stolen resources. Instead, he continues to actively leverage the seized assets in order to build his own wealth, but incessantly laments the poor state of the victim and his family, and the horror of the crime that was done to them, and insists that *someone* really ought to do something to help "those people" out.

The second scenario describes the practice of land acknowledgments, which have grown increasingly popular in symbolic capitalist spaces in recent years (while the first scenario depicts how the people who *do* make land acknowledgments describe those who *don't*; I'll leave it to the reader to decide which is worse).

One stated purpose of land acknowledgments is to show respect to those who have been dispossessed. But of course, precisely as a function of that very dispossession, there are almost never people from the affected tribes "in the room" to receive these acknowledgments—particularly in symbolic capitalist spaces (where this practice is most pronounced).[58] Instead, these acknowledgments typically consist of non-Indigenous people virtue signaling *exclusively* to other non-Indigenous people, who nod along approvingly, leading all in attendance to feel good about how enlightened they are . . . and then everyone gets on with business as usual. And of course, even in the exceedingly rare instance that an Indigenous American elite *did* happen to be "in the room," and felt "seen" as a result of a land acknowledgment, this would do precious little to address the more practical challenges *non*elite Indigenous Americans are struggling with.

In a world where 100 percent of symbolic capitalists engaged in this ritual—where every single entertainer made a land acknowledgment before accepting an award; where every single academic made a land acknowledgment before presenting on any topic; where every concert of any type was prefaced by a land acknowledgment; where every corporate, nonprofit, or government meeting began with a land acknowledgment—in itself, this would do absolutely nothing to change material conditions for Indigenous peoples in the United States. Precisely what these acknowledgments lack, what they are more or less designed to elide, is any detail on concrete steps that can, should, or will be taken in order to make restitution—any specific details on what the acknowledger will sacrifice or *do* in order to make things right. The acknowledgment *is* the action. And after making the acknowledgment, people tend to immediately change the topic and get on with whatever they are gathered for.[59]

Of course, it is not just individuals who carry out these land acknowledgments, but often institutions as well. For instance, growing numbers of colleges and universities feature land acknowledgments on their websites. These statements explicitly recognize particular tribes as the "rightful" custodians of the land that higher education institutions occupy, yet they typically offer nothing beyond symbolic gestures to restore the land to the named tribes or to compensate them for its continued use. It would be well within any university's capacities to, for instance, guarantee admission, void tuition, and provide aid to all confirmed members of the named tribes. This would leverage the university to directly aid the dispossessed without significant disruption to university operations or finances. However, most schools who issue land acknowledgments do not even take basic steps like these.[60] If they were more ambitious or dedicated, universities could pay rent to named tribes for continued occupation of "their" land or else provide dividends on their endowments to confirmed members of named tribes, allowing them to share in the wealth generated by the continued occupation of "their" land. Yet most universities seem to have little appetite to render themselves more *literally* accountable for the debts they claim to owe. Again, the symbolic gesture is made to stand in for any *actual* restitution—much like individual confessions of "privilege." Institutional lamentations about racism typically function the same way.

In the aftermath of George Floyd's murder, for instance, Princeton University president Christopher L. Eisgruber issued a strongly worded statement highlighting that the university, "for most of its history, intentionally and systematically excluded people of color, women, Jews, and other minorities." He continued, "Racism and the damage it does to people of color . . . persist at Princeton as in our society, sometimes by conscious intention but more often through unexamined assumptions and stereotypes, ignorance or insensitivity, and the systemic legacy of past decisions and policies. Race-based inequities in America's health care, policing, education, and employment systems affect profoundly the lives of our staff, students, and faculty of color. Racist assumptions from the past also remain embedded in structures of the University itself." The president went on to describe how programs intended to bridge the divide between the university and the community it is embedded in, which are common at virtually all peer institutions (in his own words), continue to be absent at Princeton.[61]

Responding to these confessions, the Department of Education, under then-president Donald Trump and then–secretary of education Betsy DeVos, decided to open a civil rights investigation into Princeton University. The university president himself, they argued, defined it as an institution where students, staff, and faculty of color continue to struggle compared with their white peers, and where intentional and unintentional racism are fairly ubiquitous and baked into institutional structures and policies. Given that the school itself seemed to be acknowledging, indeed broadcasting, that various forms of racialized discrimination frequently occur at Princeton, DeVos argued that there were ample grounds for investigation into whether the university may be in violation of the Civil Rights Acts (and, therefore, be obligated to return tens of millions of dollars in federal funding it has received, contingent upon complying with these laws).[62] This Department of Education investigation was widely lambasted as "trolling" by an administration that had, itself, shown a highly inconsistent level of commitment to civil rights (to put it mildly). And it definitely *was* that. However, the kernel of truth behind this stunt was that if President Eisgruber's account of Princeton University was taken at face value, it seems like far more radical changes should be underway than the measures outlined in the president's letter: creating and modifying committees, dedicating relatively small amounts (given Princeton's resources) of additional funding lines for certain subsets of students and faculty, providing additional (demonstrably ineffective) anti-bias training, renaming some buildings, and so on.[63] None of these measures seem properly scaled to the problems outlined in the letter—to say nothing of making any kind of recompense for Princeton's similarly publicized and immaculately documented ties to slavery.[64]

Princeton is far from alone in these respects.[65] Many other individuals and institutions in the public, private, and nonprofit spheres have issued and continue to issue similar statements implicating themselves in historical and ongoing social injustices. Few are prepared to be *treated* as if what they are saying is literally true. That is, many symbolic capitalists and affiliated institutions profess to be afflicted by racism, to be complicit in racism, and so forth—none expect or would countenance being widely viewed and described by *others* as "racist," or to being socially, commercially, or legally penalized for their "racism." The confessions seem to be a kind of inoculation against *those* outcomes: it is people and institutions that *decline* to associate themselves with implicit or systemic prejudice and discrimination that are viewed as immoral. By declaring oneself part of the problem, one comes to be viewed as part of the solution (even if they never take meaningful action to actually *fix* the problem).[66] Worse, insofar as institutions and individuals are successful in painting themselves as part of the solution, this often increases their propensity and capacity to contribute to the problem.

For example, after a company issues strong statements on DEI, imposes DEI training, hires a "diverse" staff member, or otherwise claims "progress" toward egalitarian goals, organizational leaders and employees often treat minority employees *worse* and take their complaints *less* seriously. Minority employees, meanwhile, often feel *less* comfortable protesting unfair treatment after these symbolic gestures—leading persistent problems to go unaddressed. As a consequence of these dual effects (on majority- and minority-group members, respectively), strong DEI gestures by organizations are often followed by *increased* minority turnover.[67] Nonetheless, engaging in DEI gestures often shields organizations from civil or criminal liability for any subsequent mistreatment or underrepresentation within their organization because courts often have a difficult time accepting that a company that makes strong symbolic gestures toward diversity and inclusion would subsequently engage in discriminatory behavior.[68] Company endorsement of meritocracy tends to have the same effect: it renders people more likely to engage in bias and nepotism even as it convinces them that their decision-making is fair.[69]

Many more examples like these could be proliferated. The basic dynamic at play is that an institution engaging in egalitarian discourse often blinds people to inegalitarian or pernicious behaviors that said organization, its leaders, or its employees are involved in. Alternatively, these gestures can allow people to witness or engage in behaviors they might even *recognize* as problematic—but without viewing themselves, their colleagues, or their organization as "bad." This is not just something that occurs within and among organizations; it also plays out at the interpersonal level and in our everyday lives. Four closely related cognitive processes seem to be at work in situations like these: moral credentialing, moral licensing, moral cleansing, and moral disengagement.

Moral credentialing is a phenomenon where people become more likely to act in inegalitarian ways, and (critically) become *convinced that their actions are nonbiased*, after affirming their commitment to egalitarianism or engaging in behaviors they interpret as egalitarian. For instance, studies have shown that when white people publicly affirm their commitment to antiracism, they often become more likely to subsequently favor other whites in decisions like hiring and promotion, even as they grow more confident that race played no role in their decision-making. When men identify with feminism, they regularly grow more likely to favor other men in their decision-making, but also grow more confident that their judgments were nonbiased.[70] People are especially likely to seek or to brandish their "moral credentials" in the face of actual or anticipated questioning of their behaviors. That is, if we have done, or are about to do, something that might be viewed as controversial or "sketchy," we often try to remind ourselves and others about what good people we are—and this often *does* change how the behaviors in question are subsequently interpreted.[71]

At times, however, conspicuously aligning ourselves with social justice causes can not only blind us to the immorality of our actions, it can even lead us to feel entitled to do things we *recognize* as immoral, and to view these behaviors as acceptable *for us* to engage in, at that moment, under those circumstances. This is called "moral licensing." In virtue of prosocial actions people have performed or plan to perform (or even upon contemplating bad actions one refrained from taking), people can feel it is acceptable to personally take liberties they would ordinarily condemn in others.[72] They can exempt themselves from the moral standards they apply to everyone else, confident that the good actions they have performed, or will perform (or *other* bad actions they have taken or will refrain from taking), will basically "even things out" ethically, result in a net positive, or at least fail to harm their reputation.[73] As with moral credentialing, people are often strategic about moral licensing: when we want to violate a rule or norm that others are bound by, we often seek out and brandish evidence of our exemplary moral character, painting ourselves as worthy of a bit of indulgence (or of leniency in judgment at the very least).[74]

This is not just something individuals do. It occurs at the institutional level as well. Indeed, corporate leaders are often quite explicit about engaging in moral licensing. For example, consulting firm McKinsey & Co. emphasizes that environmental, social, and governance investing is necessary for companies to "maintain their social license" in the face of externalities that multinational corporations impose on governments, workers, communities, and ecosystems worldwide.[75] BlackRock CEO and cofounder Larry Fink has likewise emphasized that, insofar as companies fail to portray themselves as oriented toward some higher cause than maximizing profits, they will "ultimately lose the license to operate from key stakeholders" and provide subpar returns to investors as a result.[76] Behaviors recognized as "greenwashing," "pinkwashing," "diversity washing," and "rainbow washing," are generally clumsy attempts at moral licensing. Insofar as these institutional commitments instead come off as "sincere" or "authentic" (whatever it might mean for an institution to be sincere), the organization can be considered to have successfully engaged in moral licensing.

Sometimes, however, we engage in behaviors that we (and others) recognize as wrong, and we can't make these perceptions go away by simply emphasizing how moral we are. Other times, we come to see ourselves (or are viewed by others) as complicit in the immoral behaviors of institutions or other stakeholders we're associated with. In other cases, we find ourselves unwilling or unable to do what we think we should in morally freighted situations—creating harm not through something we did but by something we failed to do (or failed to do effectively). In situations like these, where our self-image and reputation are compromised or at risk, we often engage in rituals of moral cleansing—behaviors that help restore the sense that we're "on the side of the angels." And it turns out that one of the most effective ways we can come to feel good about ourselves in the aftermath of a moral failing is to point out bad behaviors in *others*. Research shows that condemning and (especially) sanctioning others for wrongdoing can reduce one's guilt over committing the same offense and helps assure oneself and others that they are different from "those people" being condemned (even if one is, in fact, engaged in similar or worse behaviors).[77] Sometimes we can be so effective at cleansing our guilt that we grow more self-righteous than we were before our moral failing. In these instances, moral cleansing can provide us with moral credentials or licenses. That is, moral cleansing doesn't just eliminate our shame, it can actually enable future bad conduct, this time carried out with a clear conscience.

However, should moral credentialing, licensing, and cleansing collectively fail at preserving our sense self-image and reputation, we often resort to moral disengagement instead: redefining situations in ways that neutralize their moral stakes. Sometimes we do this by downplaying the risks or costs imposed on others by our actions or by insisting that any negative eventualities were caused by circumstances beyond our own control, thereby minimizing our own perceived role in others' misfortune. Other times, we tell ourselves that difficulties imposed on others serve some worthy goal or "greater good." In other cases, we recast the people who were harmed so that they no longer fall into our sphere of moral concern, or even seem to deserve misfortune.[78] For instance, this chapter highlighted how symbolic capitalists often define minorities who espouse inconvenient views as "compromised" in some way, allowing us to simply disregard their perspectives despite our expressed commitments to epistemic and moral deference toward people from historically marginalized and disadvantaged groups. This is moral disengagement in action.

Critically, there are peer effects for each of these phenomena as well: when we observe others "like us"—people and institutions we identify with— making egalitarian pronouncements or gestures, or taking prosocial actions, we become more likely to see those people *and ourselves* as egalitarians. Simultaneously, we become more likely to interpret subsequent inegalitarian behaviors from peers *or ourselves* as fundamentally fair or otherwise acceptable.[79] When individuals or institutions we identify with present themselves as moral exemplars, we feel more entitled to exempt ourselves from the standards we would normally apply to others.[80] Meanwhile, being confronted with evidence that people "like us" are responsible for unjust harm to others often leads to "competitive victimhood"—that is, claiming that harmful behaviors people "like us" visited on others are justified or should be excused in light of wrongs that people "like us" have previously experienced.[81] In other cases, guilt over harm caused by people "like us" fuels moral outrage against third-party scapegoats; subsequent retributive actions against these scapegoats tends to cleanse our own guilt or shame.[82] Or, all else failing, we find ways to collectively write off concern about those harmed by the pursuit of our own group interests. For instance, symbolic capitalists regularly portray the "losers" in the symbolic economy as unworthy of moral consideration because they're racist, or sexist, or transphobic, or ignorant, or support "fascists" like Donald Trump. If "those people" are marginalized, good. They should be. If they're suffering, who cares?

One disturbing implication of these cognitive tendencies is that, in contexts where people and institutions go around denouncing racism, sexism, or inequality to one another constantly—painting themselves as staunch advocates for social justice and condemning those who are "backwards" or "regressive"—it would become almost impossible for folks embedded in those circles to see the role that they play in perpetuating systemic inequalities. And in part for this reason, these same people would promote various forms of inequality all the more while feeling incredibly self-righteous about their egalitarianism.

That is, in environments where antiracism, feminism, and other egalitarian frameworks are widely and very publicly embraced, it can become *easier* for people to act in racist, sexist, or otherwise discriminatory ways while convinced that their behaviors are fair—and to have those actions actually perceived as fair by others who share the same ideological and political leanings, or who belong to the same social or institutional groups. In contexts like these, each conspicuous gesture toward social justice would blind oneself *and* one's peers to important details about how various forms of inequality, exploitation, and exclusion are produced and maintained—and generate both opportunities and temptations for oneself *and* one's peers to behave in ways they might otherwise be able to recognize as immoral.[83]

For an example of how dynamics like these can play out in action, consider the case of Morris Dees, an attorney who was almost single-handedly responsible for bankrupting the Ku Klux Klan. He subsequently founded an organization with other attorneys and activists to identify and combat hate groups in the South and in America writ large. Unfortunately, this organization, the Southern Poverty Law Center, became fairly notorious for its institutional culture. The people promoted to high-level positions were overwhelmingly other whites, especially men. Women and minorities in the organization frequently had their contributions minimized, stolen, or overlooked. There was an extremely hostile working atmosphere, with sexualized and racialized remarks and "jokes" regularly aimed at women and minorities. This all culminated in 2019 with a massive reorganization of the center (to include Dees's ouster) and a sweeping investigation into its organizational practices and culture.[84]

Here, we can see moral licensing and credentialing at work. Dees and his allies overwhelmingly hired and promoted other whites and men, sure. But not because of race, right? It's just the way it shook out. After all, they defunded the Klan. They spent all day, every day *fighting* racism. How can their decisions possibly have been race based? Similarly, Dees and his allies felt free to take liberties with their remarks in the workplace. Sure, they regularly made racist comments directed at minority colleagues, but those are *jokes*. They are obviously not racist themselves, right? Again, they spent all day, every day *fighting* racists. Activists and scholars who work on these issues may be especially susceptible to this kind of thinking.

Alternatively, consider the case of Harvey Weinstein. The Hollywood mogul was a liberal darling and a celebrated philanthropist known for supporting the careers of women within his organizations and boosting feminist works and causes.[85] He was also a serial rapist and sexual harasser who threatened, intimidated, and tried to pay off women who might expose his misdeeds. Despite these attempts at suppression, more than ninety women ultimately came forward with accounts of having been harassed or assaulted by Weinstein over the years.[86] At time of writing, he is currently incarcerated after having been convicted of multiple sex crimes. And yet, in a postconviction interview with the *New York Post*, Weinstein audaciously lamented that all his great work for women seems to have been forgotten "because of what happened."[87] Notice the verbiage here: not what *he did*, but rather *what happened*. This is moral licensing and credentialing in peak form. To the extent that Weinstein even recognizes he did anything wrong, he feels it was ultimately outweighed by the good he's done for women, and he laments that others cannot recognize this obvious (in his mind) truth. He sees *himself* as the main victim of the entire ordeal.

Many more cases like these could be proliferated.[88] However, the examples of Weinstein and Dees clearly illustrate how people can engage in egregious and persistent forms of abuse, misconduct, and exploitation while remaining convinced that they are morally praiseworthy—and often convincing others of the same.

Critically, although moral credentialing, licensing, cleansing, and disengagement are *general* cognitive and behavioral tendencies, symbolic capitalists may be especially susceptible to these forms of self-serving moral reasoning. As discussed throughout this text, the kinds of people who become symbolic capitalists (those who are highly educated, cognitively sophisticated, etc.) tend to be particularly prone to, and effective at, motivated reasoning in general. Symbolic capitalists are also far more likely than other Americans to explicitly identify with antiracism, feminism, LGBTQ advocacy, environmentalism, and related social justice causes (and to be associated with institutions that are likewise conspicuously committed to these causes). However, even as we paint ourselves as egalitarians, symbolic capitalists' lifestyles and social positions are largely premised on exploitation, exclusion, and condescension. Taken together, symbolic capitalists have especially powerful means, far more frequent opportunities, and a pronounced need to produce moral credentials and moral licenses or engage in moral cleansing rituals or moral disengagement.

Coda: Babies and Bathwater

We are now approaching the end of our time together. Over the course of this text, we have seen that the attitudes and dispositions associated with "wokeness" are primarily embraced by symbolic capitalists. Wokeness does not seem to be associated with egalitarian behaviors in any meaningful sense. Instead, "social justice" discourse seems to be mobilized by contemporary elites to help legitimize and obscure inequalities, to signal and reinforce their elite status, or to tear down rivals—often at the expense of those who are genuinely vulnerable, marginalized, and disadvantaged in society. What, then, should we make of the ideologies and modes of analysis associated with wokeness? Can they be useful guides for understanding and discussing the social world? Or are they fundamentally dangerous, misleading, or irredeemably corrupted? Is the main issue that symbolic capitalists tend to leverage social justice discourse in unfortunate ways? Or is it that symbolic capitalists have been led astray by wokeness into pursuing social justice in a counterproductive manner? Put simply, is the problem wokeness or are we, ourselves, the problem? Confronting these questions head-on is perhaps the most fitting way to close out this final chapter.

For starters, the fact that symbolic capitalists are increasingly more "woke" than most members of historically marginalized and disadvantaged groups neither entails nor implies that the beliefs commonly associated with "wokeness" are false. Just as it is wrong when symbolic capitalists dismiss the views of "normies" under the presumption that their views are ill considered or ill informed (because they have fewer credentials), it is no better to dismiss a view as false simply because it is embraced by social elites. More broadly, people aren't stupid or crazy to find these ideas compelling. They became popular for a reason. In part, for sure, because they were useful in elite power struggles. But they also helped expose and address significant shortcomings in how others were seeking to understand and mitigate social problems at the time.[89] It was precisely because they were analytically powerful and morally compelling that many sought to mobilize them in other arenas.

Theories are, however, fundamentally about ignoring certain data to see other things more clearly.[90] Consequently, any theoretical approach that elucidates some important aspect of society will generally obscure other phenomena. It will handle some things well and explain other things poorly. Moreover, all theories are products of particular times and places, responding to particular needs and circumstances—and any theoretical approach may need to be refined and updated, or even eventually cast aside, as the "problem space" evolves.[91] This is all to say that even powerful theories have their limits. A recognition of these limits does not diminish their power. On the contrary, it can help us deploy these ideas in cases where they are most effective and avoid applying them to cases where they are not particularly useful.

Many views associated with wokeness seem to be straightforwardly correct, even if they are often taken to excess. For instance, a key insight of the "discursive turn" in social research is that how concepts are defined, and by whom, reveals a lot about power relations within a society or culture. These definitions are not merely *reflections* of social dynamics. At scale and over time, they can impose their own independent sociopolitical influence: they can help legitimize or delegitimize individuals, groups, and their actions; they can render some things more easily comprehensible and others less so; they can push certain things outside the realm of polite discussion and introduce new elements into the language game. This is a genuine contribution to understanding the world.

That said, today many symbolic capitalists seem to attribute *too much* power to symbols, rhetoric, and representation. Many assert, in the absence of robust empirical evidence, that small slights can cause enormous (often underspecified) harm. Under the auspices of preventing these harms, they argue it is legitimate, even necessary, to aggressively police other people's words, tone, body language, and so forth. As we have seen, people from nontraditional and underrepresented backgrounds are among the most likely to find themselves silenced and sanctioned in these campaigns, both because they are less likely to possess the cultural capital to say the "correct" things in the "correct" ways at the "correct" time and because their deviance is perceived as especially threatening (insofar as this heterodoxy undermines claims made by dominant elites ostensibly on behalf of historically marginalized and disadvantaged groups).

Overstating the power of language likewise leads symbolic capitalists to conclude that their symbolic gestures toward antiracism, feminism, and so forth mark significant contributions to addressing social problems when, in fact, they change virtually nothing about the allocation of wealth or power in society, and there is not really a plausible account for how they could. Campaigns to sterilize language, for instance, will never lift anyone out of poverty. Referring to homeless people as "unsheltered individuals," or prisoners as "justice-involved persons," or poor people as "individuals of limited means," and so on are discursive maneuvers that often obscure the brutal realities that others must confront in their day-to-day lives. If the intent of these language shifts is to avoid stigma, the reality is that these populations are still heavily stigmatized despite shifting discourse.

As we have seen, the Americans who are most preoccupied with linguistic hygiene actively avoid personally interacting with the poor, convicted criminals, drug addicts, and others through strategies ranging from personal network choices to where they choose to live (and send their kids to school); their reduced use of public transportation; the zoning restrictions they typically support; their heightened use of police, personal security, and surveillance services against folks who violate their aesthetic sensibilities or behavioral preferences; and beyond. More broadly, gentrifying the discourse about the "wretched of the earth" doesn't make their problems go away. If anything, it renders elites more complacent when we talk about the plight of "those people." On this the empirical research is quite clear:[92] euphemisms render people more comfortable with immoral behaviors and unjust states of affairs. This is one of the main reasons we rely on euphemisms at all.

Critically, however, pointing out unfortunate consequences of symbolic capitalists' approach to language and social justice does not invalidate the idea that language matters. In fact, it powerfully illustrates that how we choose to talk and think about society, alongside the ways we try to influence others' thoughts and discourse, actually *can* have important social consequences—for better and for worse.

The core idea behind intersectionality likewise seems both important and fairly uncontroversial: there are emergent effects, interaction effects, that are greater than, or different from, the effects of two phenomena studied independently. Indeed, Kimberlé Crenshaw's 1989 landmark legal paper, "Demarginalizing the Intersection of Race and Sex," paralleled a movement that had been advanced by statisticians since the mid-1970s—namely, to think in more sophisticated ways about how various "independent" variables interact with one another, and how that might systematically change the effects of these factors on some dependent variable.[93] These effects are very easy to observe in the world. Let's just stick with Crenshaw's pioneering example of the intersection between gender and race.

Black men are far more likely to be victims of homicide or to be incarcerated than Black women or whites across gender.[94] Black women are at near parity with white women with respect to many socioeconomic indicators, yet stark divides remain between Black and white men.[95] Black men lag far behind Black women or whites across genders in terms of educational attainment and intergenerational social mobility.[96] And yet, Black men tend to have higher median earnings than Black women. This is all fundamentally consistent with the idea of intersectionality: the interaction of gender and race produces results not derivable from looking at either factor independently. However, and this is critical, the interaction effects of race and gender cannot be determined a priori because they do not trend in the same direction across all dependent variables. In many important respects Black women are significantly better off than Black men. In other respects, the opposite is true. In general, however, Black women and Black men tend to have very different life experiences, challenges, and prospects—both as compared with one another and as compared with white men and women. The only version of intersectionality that would be refuted by the foregoing examples would be analyses that run something like this:

With respect to a given outcome,

women < men

Black < white

∴ Black women < Black men.

That kind of thinking would tend to do a bad job predicting or explaining most social phenomena—as would any approach wherein people simply tally up their different forms of perceived intersectional disadvantage as though they can be simply stacked on top of one another (e.g., "As a Latinx, bisexual, neurodivergent woman my perspective is more valid, and my needs more important, than yours—a white, cisgender, gay, neurotypical man"). Indeed, as we have seen, those who make the most strident claims of intersectional disadvantage tend to be socioeconomic and cultural elites (it is almost *exclusively* symbolic capitalists who engage in this kind of discourse)—and claimants' class position is virtually never part of their intersectional calculations. However, the fact that many engage in these kinds of self-serving and facile analyses does *not* mean intersectionality itself is wrong or should be discarded. The essential elements of the concept seem straightforwardly true and useful for social analysis.

In a similar vein, this chapter spent significant time exploring how appeals to "systemic" or "institutionalized" racism or sexism are often used to mystify social processes rather than illuminate them. However, the idea of systemic disadvantage seems straightforwardly correct: historical inequalities, paired with the ways systems and institutions are arranged in the present, can lead to situations where certain people face significant disadvantages while others are strongly advantaged. As a product of historical contingencies, these advantages and disadvantages can systematically track along the lines of race or gender or other identity dimensions—producing a situation where people from historically marginalized and disadvantaged groups can have a difficult time flourishing relative to people from more historically advantaged groups—even in the absence of formal discrimination or deeply felt bigotry. A recognition of this fact can help, for instance, illustrate some of the core limitations of the "level playing field" approach to addressing inequality.

Some kids grow up in stable two-parent homes, in safe communities with good schools, and with parents who have the money, skills, connections, and bandwidth to help them develop and leverage their human capital (for instance, by supporting cultural enrichment activities and extracurriculars, or through additional investments in health and nutrition). They are thereby well positioned to flourish on "meritocratic" grounds.[97] Most others lack these advantages. Some grow up in homes and communities that actively *undermine* their capacity to develop knowledge, skills, and experience that are valued in the symbolic economy. As a function of how events have played out in the United States up to now, there is a heavy skew along certain demographic lines with respect to who possesses these (dis)advantages and who does not. Consequently, although various natural capabilities and personality traits may be evenly distributed across groups, existing inequalities *between* groups would nonetheless tend to reproduce themselves—even in competitions that were rendered genuinely open and procedurally fair, and even in the absence of identity-based apprehension or animus.[98] These are important insights that can flow from studying inequalities in systemic terms.

Meanwhile, critical race theory, postcolonial theory, feminist standpoint epistemology, and queer theory have been extremely valuable in demonstrating ways positionality matters to knowledge production and highlighting the political dimensions of knowledge production. That said, it's absolutely the case that advocates of these frameworks often fail to take their own starting premises to their logical conclusions. Taking positionality seriously should lead folks to interrogate the extent to which their own ostensibly emancipatory politics (and especially the homogeneity of these convictions within a field) may undermine their ability to understand certain phenomena, lead them to ignore key perspectives and inconvenient facts in the pursuit of their preferred narratives and policies, and drive them to pursue courses of action that do not, in fact, empower or serve the people they are supposed to be empowering or serving, nor reflect others' own values and perceived interests.[99] Indeed, taking these ideas to their logical endpoint should lead more people aligned with the Left to question the extent to which their own "emancipatory politics" may, in fact, be a product of their own elite position, and may primarily serve *elite* ends rather than uplifting the genuinely marginalized and disadvantaged. The fact so many instead use these frameworks in nonreflexive ways—to reinforce their own sense of moral and intellectual superiority or confirm their prejudices about "those people" who do not profess, believe, or feel the "correct" things—neither entails nor implies that these modes of analysis cannot be put to more productive use.

Similarly, elites of color (and the white elites who look to them as spokespeople for the groups they ostensibly "represent") often fail to recognize or account for the reality that they likely vary in systematic ways from most others in the groups they identify with, and this may undermine their ability to effectively channel the preferences, priorities, and perceived interests of most others in the groups they identify with and purportedly represent—let alone capturing the rich diversity of life experiences, and perspectives on shared experiences, within these populations. That is, when elites wonder what, say, African Americans think about an issue, their first instinct is not to go and talk to a bunch of ordinary Black folk, nor to conduct a large-sample and representative study to solicit the views of African Americans in the community or nationwide. Instead, they turn to "consecrated" Black intellectuals to see what *they* have to say, as though those opinions indicate anything at all about how most other Black people think or feel. In practice, by turning to these consecrated representatives, elites are seeking out confirmatory narratives under the guise of searching for truth.

Pointing this out, however, does not invalidate the idea of "epistemic deference." In fact, it makes a more rigorous point that it is not enough to have *elites* of all genders, races, creeds, and sexualities sitting around the table. It is also absolutely critical to find ways of folding in the perspectives of nonelites—including and especially when they are inconvenient for our preferred narratives and policies.[100] History in the United States and abroad is replete with examples of grievous harm caused by well-intentioned technocrats and ideologues who failed to sufficiently consult and collaborate with the populations whose interests they were ostensibly seeking to advance.[101] This should be at the forefront of symbolic capitalists' minds as they are seeking to understand and address social problems—at least, insofar as they are primarily concerned with helping the marginalized and disadvantaged (instead of themselves).

To put it simply, the fact that symbolic capitalists have never been woke reveals a lot about *us*. It says much less, however, about the frameworks and ideas that we appropriate (and often deform) in our power struggles.

Conclusion

In the introduction to this text, I ticked through a series of questions that have consumed my thoughts for the last several years: Why is it that the "winners" in the prevailing order seem so eager to associate themselves with the marginalized and disadvantaged in society? What functions does "social justice" discourse serve among contemporary elites? How do symbolic capitalists reconcile their egalitarian rhetoric with the reality that their lifestyles and social positions are premised on the reproduction and exploitation of various forms of inequality (to the extent they are aware of this at all)? What caused the "Great Awokening"? We are now in a strong position to gain leverage on these questions.

As a function of the circumstances under which they arose, the symbolic professions have been legitimized from the outset by the claim that they are fundamentally altruistic. We hold ourselves as worthy of our high pay and prestige because we serve the greater good. We rein in the wealth and power of those at the top of the social order for the benefit of the least among us. Put another way, our elite status (which requires others to occupy a subordinate position) has always been, paradoxically, tied to egalitarianism.

This mode of legitimation gave rise to unique modes of status competition among symbolic capitalists. We can increase our status and, often, their socioeconomic prospects by portraying themselves as allies and advocates for the marginalized and disadvantage. On the flip side, those who are successfully branded as racist, sexist, homophobic, or otherwise insufficiently committed to egalitarian goals can be thereby rendered unworthy of status, platforms, or institutional affiliations.

Over time, as the internal constitution and macrosocial position of the symbolic professions continued to evolve, a unique moral culture took hold among symbolic capitalists and the institutions we dominate. Rather than merely championing the interests of the poor, vulnerable, and oppressed in society, we increasingly claim to *literally* embody and *directly* represent the interests of the marginalized and disadvantaged. We regularly count ourselves among them. Contemporary symbolic economy elites attempt to portray themselves as racial and ethnic minorities, gender and sexual minorities, neurodivergent, or physically disabled. They do this because, within symbolic capitalists' dominant moral culture, people who can lay claim to formerly stigmatized identities are perceived to have special moral and epistemic authority, unique cultural cachet, and access to exclusive opportunities and accommodations (intended as reparations for historical wrongs).

These are general patterns of discourse and behavior among symbolic capitalists. When times get tough for us, however, these modes of status competition and moral righteousness get radically intensified. Symbolic capitalists grow much more aggressive in mobilizing social justice discourse to paint themselves as worthy of power and wealth—and to declare their adversaries and rivals as undeserving of the same. This is what Great Awokenings are fundamentally "about": frustrated erstwhile elites condemning the social order that failed them and jockeying to secure the position they feel they "deserve."

Critically, none of this entails that symbolic capitalists are cynical or insincere in their professed commitments to social justice. We tend to be true believers. However, these beliefs are rarely translated into behavioral changes or reallocations of material resources in part because symbolic capitalists tend to hold political priorities, and embrace modes of political engagement, that diverge substantially from those of most other Americans and encourage an idiosyncratic approach to social justice advocacy.

Our lives and livelihoods are oriented around words, numbers, ideas, and other abstractions. As a consequence, we tend to take symbols very seriously. Because we traffic in cultural, political, academic, and totemic capital, we are highly attentive to status differences. We prioritize enhancing others' symbolic standing over improving their material conditions in part because, for us, the former is genuinely a means to the latter (to a degree that is less true for folks outside the symbolic professions). Moreover, the people who gravitate toward the symbolic professions and flourish therein tend to be especially ideological, conformist, and extreme relative to most other Americans.

And in virtue of where and how we live, we tend to be disconnected from the conditions and priorities of most "normies."

As a function of these tendencies, as symbolic capitalists have been consolidated into the Democratic Party, we have completely changed the party. Its messaging and priorities have shifted dramatically. The party's base has evolved in turn. Growing numbers of poor, working-class, and nonwhite voters are growing alienated from the Democratic Party and have been migrating to the GOP. It is difficult for symbolic capitalists to understand these trends because, again, we believe that we represent the will and interests of the marginalized and disadvantaged, while our opponents serve elite interests (and are driven by racism, sexism, authoritarianism, and ignorance).

However, in reality symbolic capitalists are, themselves, among the primary beneficiaries of contemporary inequalities. And we don't just passively benefit. We actively exploit, exacerbate, and reinforce the very stratification that we are pledged to abolish. Indeed, for almost any action we condemn by superelites, multinational corporations, and corrupt politicians, it's people like us who actually make it happen. Yet our sincere commitments to social justice often blind us to the role we play in contributing to social problems. They provide us with moral licenses that allow us to justify inegalitarian behaviors to ourselves and others. They empower us to scapegoat others for social problems.

This is not to say that symbolic capitalists are completely unaware of the dissonance between our rhetoric and our lifestyles, behaviors, or social position. We are often self-critical. However, we also believe that we're more worthy of being elites than just about anyone else. Power, wealth, and resources are better in our hands than most others'. While we might not "deserve" everything we have in some metaphysical sense, we nonetheless view ourselves as good stewards of the "privileges" we've been given. Indeed, the very fact that we *are* self-critical is held up as proof of our essential goodness, fairness, and rationality. Again, cognitive sophistication renders symbolic capitalists especially good at producing these kinds of rationalizations to ourselves and others.

That's the argument of the book in a nutshell. Of course, there's much more that could be said on all these topics. For instance, the book tightly focused on "identity" issues (race, gender, sexuality) at the expense of other elements of symbolic capitalists' ideology, such as environmentalism. However, similar dynamics hold for this issue as well.

The Americans most likely to identify as "strong environmentalists" are the same people who are most likely to identify as "antiracists," "feminists," or "allies" for LGBTQ folks: highly educated white liberals.[1] Those who engage in climate *activism* are mostly female (61 percent) and almost entirely white (93 percent). More than nine out of ten climate activists have at least a BA, and more than a third possess a terminal degree.[2]

Much like other social justice causes, environmentalism is regularly used as a means to feel morally and intellectually superior to others, engage in moral licensing, and mystify social processes.[3] Environmentalism is likewise tied to power and authority claims (i.e., if you don't behave in the ways I find palatable, profess the things that I believe, vote for the people I support, or otherwise comply with my own tastes, priorities, and preferences, then we'll all be underwater in ten years). Likely in virtue of their perceived usefulness in struggles over status and power, expressed concern about environmental issues rose rapidly and unilaterally among highly educated white liberals after 2010 (much like concern about racism, sexism, homophobia, etc.). However, as the broader Great Awokening began to fade after 2020, concern about environmental issues followed suit, as did climate catastrophist narratives in mainstream media.[4] The post-2010 period was not unique in these regards. Environmental activism played a key role in each of the previous Great Awokenings too. Yet, in spite of our strong environmentalist leanings, symbolic capitalists are among the primary beneficiaries of the environmental devastation they conspicuously condemn.[5] Moreover, we can observe the same paradoxes between rhetoric and behaviors with respect to environmentalism that we see with other aspects of mainstream symbolic capitalist ideology.[6]

In a world where word count was not a concern, it may have been fruitful and illuminating to do deeper dives into additional topics like these. Alternatively, it may have been productive to zoom out beyond the United States.

Sans Frontières

This book was fairly epic in scale, but also tightly focused on the United States. We looked rather narrowly at American history and American politics. I drew on studies of the United States, using samples from the U.S. population, and so forth. There were practical considerations at play in the choice of sample, from the availability of research, to my personal level of familiarity with the context in question, to language barriers, to considerations of reader interest and accessibility. There are also theoretical reasons why a focus on the United States makes sense: due to the centrality of the United States to the broader global order, developments in America exert a huge influence over much of the rest of the world, for better and for worse. However, it should be noted that many of the same historical developments and con-temporary dynamics that we explored in the context of the United States have analogues across other Western, highly educated, industrialized, rich, and democratic (WEIRD) countries and beyond.

For instance, this text explored how a narrow slice of the population produces and consumes most symbolic economy outputs. Politically, geo-graphically, socioeconomically, and in terms of race, gender, and sexuality, they diverge in systematic ways from the rest of society. Orian Brook, Dave O'Brien, and Mark Taylor have detailed at length how roughly the same con-solidations, exclusions, and institutional inequalities manifest in the UK cul-ture industries.[7] Christophe Guilluy has illustrated similar trends in France.[8]

The same political consolidations observed in the United States among symbolic capitalists and within symbolic economy hubs are also present in the United Kingdom, in France, and across western (and much of eastern) Europe: left-aligned parties are increasingly captured by symbolic capitalists even as working-class, rural, ethnic or racial, and religious minority voters, and those whose work is tied to physical goods and services, are increasingly drifting toward the right.[9] Moreover, there are growing cultural and insti-tutional ties forming between symbolic capitalists, their institutions, and symbolic hubs *across* countries, even as *within* countries symbolic capitalists are growing increasingly distant from their fellow countrymen.[10]

"Victimhood culture" is increasingly prevalent among symbolic capital-ists across these geographical contexts too. In Australia, for instance, grow-ing numbers of highly educated whites are claiming to be aboriginal in order to leverage the benefits of totemic capital—leading to new requirements in many institutions to verify claims to minority background (rather than rely-ing on self-identification, which has exploded).[11] "Race shifting" is likewise growing increasingly prominent among whites in Canada.[12] In one striking recent high-profile case, the scientific director of the Canadian Institutes of Health Research's Institute of Indigenous Peoples' Health, who is also a professor of epidemiology at the University of Saskatchewan, was found to be lying about her ancestry and life history. In TED talks and other public forums, she claimed to have grown up in poverty, and to have experienced racism her whole life as a result of her Métis background. In fact, she has no known Indigenous ancestors; investigators traced her family's history on both sides through their arrival in North America. She also did not grow up in poverty as she claimed but, rather, was raised in an upper-middle-class household.[13] Contrary to her previous narratives, she did not experience rac-ism growing up either, as no one thought she was Indigenous, and indeed, she didn't start identifying as such until her twenties. Cases like these are far from isolated incidents, not just in America, but across WEIRD countries.

The Great Awokening was not restricted to the United States either.[14] High-income democracies across the board saw roughly contemporaneous shifts in attitudes on "identity" issues such as race, gender, and sexuality beginning around 2011.[15] There were dramatic shifts in media discussion of prejudice and discrimination across a broad spectrum of countries after 2010.[16] Over this period, the same movements broke out worldwide among symbolic capitalists and in symbolic capitalist hubs. In 2011, Occupy movements proliferated worldwide.[17] In 2015, symbolic capitalists across the globe were declaring, "Je suis Charlie," in the aftermath of the Charlie Hebdo massacre.[18] Symbolic capitalists worldwide mourned Brexit and the election of Donald Trump together. The 2017 Women's March and March for Science had analogues in symbolic hubs around the world as well.[19] In the aftermath of George Floyd's murder in 2020, there were major demonstrations evoking Black Lives Matter, even in contexts with few Black people, such as Seoul and Hong Kong.[20]

That said, the post-2010 Great Awokening did not seem to be as intense or protracted in many European contexts as it was in the United States. This is likely, in part, because the employment prospects and social status of symbolic capitalists are much more precarious in America, and the potential upsides of securing a good position are much higher as well.[21] It is much easier to become extraordinarily wealthy in the United States as a symbolic capitalist, and also to end up struggling to maintain one's elite status. In many European contexts, on the other hand, elite overproduction tends to be much better managed, and symbolic capitalist jobs tend to be comfortably compensated and more stable and secure—albeit often with lower renumeration as compared with equivalent posts in the United States at the high end. That is, there is less "at stake" in these moments of crisis in other countries (as compared with the United States), and this probably affects the intensity of Great Awokenings across contexts.

Critically, it's not just Awokenings that have manifested in diverse geographical and cultural milieus—anti-wokenings have proliferated as well.[22] In France, for instance, leaders across the spectrum have condemned the growing influence of "American-imported" ideas about social justice that are not relevant to France's own history and culture. "Anti-wokisme" alliances are being formed to push back against these "dangerous" ideas that threaten to "tear France apart."[23] There is a certain irony here because, as François Cusset has aptly shown, many of the intellectual strands that define contemporary "wokeness" were themselves derived from poorly translated and often misinterpreted works of French theory that were transformed through integration with American identity politics, market ideology, and pop culture influences.[24]

This is all to say, the influence here is not monodirectional, with America as the prime mover and others simply adapting and reacting to us. Rather, what happens in America is influenced by socioeconomic, political, and cultural developments abroad (to include changes to the global order that allowed for the rise of a transnational symbolic economy), and what happens in the United States reciprocally affects how events play out in many other contexts. While practical considerations compelled me to keep the book tightly focused on the United States, many of the findings, arguments, and trends observed have analogues in other WEIRD countries and beyond.

Tentative Answers, New Questions

A source of perennial exhilaration and anxiety for social scientists is that, in the process of answering one set of questions, new and related questions begin to percolate and eventually start to consume you anew. The work, therefore, is never done.

This book was focused tightly on symbolic capitalists, our changing role in society, and the ways we mobilize social justice discourse in our struggles for status, wealth, and power. This approach yielded many important insights about contemporary U.S. society. However, with this foundation in place, still more could be learned by turning the analytic lens from the "winners" in the prevailing order toward those who perceive themselves to be the "losers." For example, the following are some questions that were raised in the course of this investigation but could not be answered herein:

- Symbolic capitalists often expropriate blame for social problems onto those unrepresented in symbolic capitalist spaces—branding our opponents as sexist, racist, authoritarian, ignorant, and so on. This is in part a means of symbolic domination. However, isn't there truth in these narratives as well? Isn't it *actually the case* that many of the people aligned against symbolic capitalists express racist, sexist, homophobic, and transphobic views? Don't they regularly align themselves in opposition to movements oriented around feminism, antiracism, LGBTQ rights, and related causes?

Don't they vote for authoritarian candidates? Aren't they hostile toward key social institutions?

- To the extent that symbolic capitalists' narratives about their opponents have an empirical basis, isn't it *good* that said opponents are marginalized? For all the profound problems with symbolic capitalists and their social order, wouldn't it be far worse if their opponents had more influence over American society?
- How and to what extent do changing gender dynamics within the symbolic economy relate to the growing political and cultural polarization observed between men and women in the United States?
- Why are growing numbers of working-class, racial and ethnic minority, and religious minority voters "voting against their interests" (as we tend to see it) and aligning with the political Right?
- How can we explain the apparent contemporary surge in ethnic and religious nationalist movements that is happening even as the political Right is becoming more diverse, and even as polls and surveys show consistent declines in expressed racism, sexism, homophobia, and so on among voters aligned with the GOP?
- Practically speaking, what, if anything, might be done to escape the sociopolitical and cultural doom loop we seem to be trapped in?

On the whole, this deep dive into the history, culture, and political economy of symbolic capitalists sharpened my conviction that growing inequality, the rise of Trump (and Trumpian politicians and social movements), the "crisis of expertise," and rising tensions around "identity politics" are all part of the same basic story. They're fronts in an overarching struggle between symbolic capitalists and those who feel unrepresented in their social order. Again, this is a struggle that is playing out not just in the United States but, mutatis mutandis, within many other countries as well. This conflict between symbolic capitalists and "the unrepresented" will likely dominate my scholarly attention in the months and years to come.

Beyond Belief

This is the part of the conclusion where readers would typically be presented with a list of advice or policies to mitigate the problems described throughout the text. However, as I emphasized at the outset, *We Have Never Been Woke* is not that type of book. Its project is to describe rather than prescribe. It is beyond my capacity to provide definitive answers about the good life, the good society, and how to get there. These are questions that we'll have to figure out together.

If anything, this book could be considered an exercise in negative epistemology: whatever "social justice" looks like, it does not seem to be well reflected in symbolic capitalist institutions. Whatever the "good life" looks like, symbolic capitalists don't seem to be living it. Whatever "moral virtue" is, we don't seem to embody it in any particularly exceptional way. Whatever the core problems ailing society are perceived to be, we can be confident that the solution is not to just continue what we've been doing, but more or harder or with greater sincerity. Not only are we not "there" yet with respect to social justice, but it isn't clear we're anywhere close to being on the right track. As symbolic capitalists have grown in wealth and power, and as we've grown more overtly and unanimously "woke," various forms of inequality have been expanding instead of shrinking. Rather than growth and innovation, we see stagnation and declines. Rather than increased efficacy and legitimacy in our institutions, we're seeing increasing dysfunction and mistrust. There are no easy solutions or quick fixes available to upend these dynamics, as far as I can tell. And so, in lieu of the typical set of policy prescriptions and life advice, allow me to close with a final methodological point about studying human values instead.

Throughout this text I have insisted that symbolic capitalists are likely being sincere when they espouse social justice commitments. However, just because an expressed conviction is *sincere* doesn't mean it's particularly *important*. One advantage of drawing this distinction is that determining whether something is important (or a priority) for someone does not require scholars to take anyone's word. One's priorities are manifested through action.

Put another way, you don't observe what is important to someone by what they *say* but rather by what they *do*, and by how they structure their lives. If something is valuable to a person, truly central to their being, they make room for it. They make sacrifices for it. It reshapes one's other (more peripheral) commitments, and one's behaviors, relationships, and life plans.[25] On the other hand, if an expressed commitment does *not* meaningfully change how one operates, this is a sign that said commitment is not very important—certainly not relative to other commitments that *do* seem to set one's agenda. Across the board, where and how people invest their resources, and what they are willing to risk or give up in order to achieve or attain something, provides far richer insight into what people care about than the narratives people try to spin about themselves (to include the responses people offer to polls and surveys).[26]

Analyzing symbolic capitalists in these terms, perhaps we really do want the poor to be uplifted. We want the oppressed to be liberated. We want the marginalized to be integrated. However, we'd prefer to find a way to achieve these goals without having to sacrifice anything personally or change anything about our own lives and aspirations. Symbolic capitalists simultaneously desire to be social climbers *and* egalitarians. We want to mitigate inequalities while *also* preserving or enhancing our elite position (and ensuring our children can reproduce or exceed our position). These drives are in fundamental tension. This tension has defined the symbolic professions from the outset. Both commitments are sincere. However, they do not seem to carry equal importance. Instead, the pursuit of social justice seems to be subordinate to the pursuit of affluence and influence—with the latter often subverting the former. This is an outcome that's quite predictable.

In the book of Matthew (chapter 6), Jesus of Nazareth warns people against performative displays of righteousness. Trying to gain status from charity or virtue often undermines our ability to actually do good. Likewise, Jesus argued, it is impossible to devote one's life to wealth *and* morality. The pursuit of one will invariably come at the expense of the other, likely sooner rather than later. Ultimately, Jesus argued, people have to choose what's really important to them—and it's a choice they make with their actions, not their words. You know the tree by its fruit.

Twenty-one centuries later, philosopher G. A. Cohen likewise challenged self-identified leftists and liberals to explain, "If you're an egalitarian, how come you're so rich?"[27] Symbolic capitalists generally insist you can be both. Illustrating the prevailing mentality in the pages of *The Independent*, one writer declared, "As a proud champagne socialist, I know that having money doesn't have to stop you believing in equality."[28] And of course, she's perfectly right. But then again, *believing* in equality is not a political act. Nor does it *change* anything in the world—least of all for the genuinely marginalized and disadvantaged. The problem isn't that there aren't enough people who "believe" in equality—it's that there isn't sufficient will *among* believers to translate their feelings into concrete realities "in the world."

As political theorist Teresa Bejan emphasized,[29] at bottom, equality is not something to be believed in but rather something to be enacted. It's not a cause to be supported in the abstract. It's something we *do*.

ACKNOWLEDGMENTS

As this is my first book, there are many people to thank for helping this text come to fruition—many more than this space will allow. Off the top, of course, I'd like to thank my editors, Meagan Levinson and Eric Crahan, alongside the rest of the Princeton University Press team, whose vision and labor on behalf of this work will prove instrumental to any success it enjoys. Thanks as well to the anonymous reviewers whose tough but fair feedback made the work much stronger, and to John Donohue, Ashley Moore, and the team at Westchester Publishing Services, who helped refine the manuscript into its final form.

Thanks to my agent, Andrew Stuart, who helped me develop my vision into a highly compelling pitch, then arranged and oversaw an auction for the rights to the book, negotiated a great contract with Princeton, and generally guided me through the process.

This work owes an unquantifiable debt to my advisers, Peter Bearman, Shamus Khan (who is now at Princeton), and Andreas Wimmer. Your criticism, encouragement, and patience; your important scholarship; the model you set *as* scholars, mentors, and colleagues . . . I can genuinely say this work would never have been conceived, let alone developed into what it is, without your guidance and support.

It's likewise important to recognize Jon Haidt and Steve Teles for the support and mentorship they provided at various stages of my PhD process.

Profound gratitude is also extended to Fabio Rojas, who helped mentor me throughout my studies and also served as a reader for the book, which served as my PhD dissertation. Michele Lamont rounded out my dissertation committee and provided very critical feedback that strengthened the work significantly.

Thanks also to Marion Fourcade, Rogers Brubaker, Anouar Majid, John Tomasi, Amna Khalid, Jeffrey Snyder, and the late Jeffrey Friedman for your feedback on earlier versions of this book.

A huge shout-out is due to my frequent collaborator, David Rozado, who has done important work both with me and independently to help empirically measure the Great Awokening. The two of us had to put some collaborative projects on hold for longer than initially planned in order for me to complete this book, so I thank you for your patience and look forward to what we'll do next.

The imprint of Columbia University's sociology department is strong in this book. In particular, I would like to celebrate some of the scholars whose work was particularly influential on my own, most of whom are cited within these pages: Saskia Sassen, Gil Eyal, Diane Vaughn, and the late Todd Gitlin. My peers Sandra Portocarrero, Kate Khanna, and Greer Mellon have also been especially great to think with on these topics, and they're doing excellent research, some cited here, on similar topics and themes.

I am grateful to the Stavros Niarchos Foundation Agora Institute at Johns Hopkins University for hosting me as a visiting fellow in fall 2021 as I worked on this book. I would also like to thank the students who enrolled in the class I taught at Johns Hopkins exploring the themes of this book, entitled Inequality and the Knowledge Economy. Kashif Charania, Tim Do, Richard Kim, Faith McCarthy, Matthew Mullner, Winston Pais, and Qinyuan Wu: your feedback and questions were extremely helpful and generative as I was composing the initial draft of this work.

A Mellon-Sawyer Fellowship on Trust and Mistrust of Experts through INCITE and the American Assembly at Columbia University, a Daniel Bell Research Fellowship by Heterodox Academy, and a sabbatical grant from the Institute for Humane Studies allowed me to take additional time off from teaching during grad school to finish the manuscript and take it through the process with Princeton.

My path to Columbia University was long and a bit bizarre. I would never have made it here without the assistance and mentorship of Jonathan Weinberg, Marga Reimer, and Joseph Tolliver in the University of Arizona Department of Philosophy, and Maha Nasser and Leila Hudson in the School of Middle Eastern and North African Studies. A still more profound thanks is due to my first academic mentor, who helped me see myself *as* a scholar and set me on the path from community college to eventually the Ivy League: Myron Jaworsky, professor emeritus of the humanities at Cochise College.

I must also express immense gratitude to my family, starting with Donna and John, who raised me along with my twin brother (peace be upon him); my father, Ray, and the Everette clan (too many of us to name without going way over the maximum word count!); the Sowids; and the Hamilton and Fox families. It truly takes a village.

Fatima, my wife, thank you for your patience, for your support, for being my sounding board and my inspiration. There is no way I'd have written this book, pursued a PhD, striven for the Ivy League, or accomplished almost anything else I've done in recent years were it not for your fateful decision to hitch yourself to what was, at the time, my very rickety wagon.

To my kids, Ezra and Nura: I hope when you're old enough, you'll enjoy this book. It took a lot out of all of us to get this text to press. Your faith in me and love for me help keep me going and striving to be better. I hope the text and any success it might enjoy can serve as a sufficient monument to the effort and sacrifices we *all* put in to make this thing happen.

To my nieces, Faith and Theresa, I hope the publication of this text can inspire you to follow your own dreams, and to let your own voice be heard.

And finally, I must express gratitude to God. May this work and all my work advance the truth and serve His will.

NOTES

Introduction

1. E.g., al-Gharbi 2016c.

2. Gutkin 2019.

3. E.g., S. Malone & Ingram 2016.

4. Soave 2016.

5. Iacurci 2021.

6. Baudrillard 1995.

7. Evershed 2021.

8. N. Stewart 2020; Tadepalli 2020. This response to homeless individuals is not unique. Studies have likewise found that affluent, highly educated white liberals tend to be strongly in favor of accepting and resettling refugees in the United States, albeit in neighborhoods and communities other than their own. See Ferwerda et al. 2017.

9. Orwell 2005, p. 10.

10. Al-Gharbi 2016b.

11. See N. Cartwright 2021 for more on this point.

12. See S. Khan 2012b; Khan 2016; Cousin, Khan, & Mears 2018.

13. For interested readers, Denning & Tworek 2023 provides many excellent essays on the interwar period and the rise of the symbolic capitalists therein.

14. Burnham grew increasingly critical of narratives around the "new class," arguing that unless and until superelites and political decision makers are drawn from this group, allied with them, or meaningfully beholden to them, we must look to superelites and politicians first and foremost to understand why things are the way they are. An intense focus on the new class could serve to blind people to how power actually operates in society. See Lind 2021 for more on this point.

As we will see, the world has changed significantly since Burnham launched his critique. For instance, contemporary superelites are increasingly drawn from symbolic capitalists. Symbolic capitalists dominate one of the two political parties in America. Politicians and the superrich alike are increasingly dependent on (and constrained by) symbolic capitalists to exercise their power. It is now critical to focus on this novel elite formation (alongside "traditional" elites) to understand contemporary social and cultural dynamics.

15. Some of the most influential works in the genre are James Burnham, *The Managerial Revolution* (1941); Christopher Jencks & David Riseman, *The Academic Revolution* (1968); Daniel Bell, *The Coming of a Post-industrial Society* (1976); Barbara Ehrenreich & John Ehrenreich, "The New Left: A Case Study in Professional-Managerial Class Radicalism" (1977); Alvin Gouldner, *The Future of Intellectuals and the Rise of the New Class* (1979); Paul Fussell, *Class* (1984); Robert Reich, *The Work of Nations* (1992); Steven Brint, *In an Age of Experts* (1994); Christopher Lasch, *The Revolt of the Elites* (1996); David Brooks, *Bobos in Paradise* (2000); and Richard Florida, *The Rise of the Creative Class* (2002).

16. One partial predecessor in this genre written by a Black scholar may be Thomas Sowell's *Intellectuals and Society*. However, Sowell didn't much explore the history of the symbolic

professions or shifts in the social position of symbolic workers over time. He was more focused on analyzing the present. Sowell also placed his own book in a very different genre from the one kicked off by Burnham. He placed *Intellectuals and Society* in conversation with Richard Posner's *Public Intellectuals*, Paul Johnson's *Intellectuals*, and Mark Lilla's *The Reckless Mind*—polemics highlighting the moral and epistemological shortcomings of intellectuals (broadly construed) and the unfortunate roles they have often played in public life (Sowell 2009, pp. v–vi).

17. A. Abbott 2016, pp. 233–252.

18. K. Fields & Fields 2012. See p. 17 for their initial presentation of this definition.

19. K. Fields & Fields 2012, p. 159.

20. A. Reed 2022.

21. For a deeper dive into analytical egalitarianism, see Levy & Peart 2008.

22. E.g., Gutkin 2021.

23. A. Reed 2018, p. 111.

24. Taiwo 2020a.

25. E.g., Lamont 2018.

26. Lamont 2023, p. 35.

27. Bloemraad et al. 2019.

28. Wacquant & Bourdieu 1989, p. 18.

29. Chomsky 2002, p. 112.

30. Latour 1993.

Chapter 1. On Wokeness

1. See S. Khan 2021a for a concise and accessible presentation of Bourdieu's background and impact, including his extension of the term "capital" to the symbolic realm.

2. Bourdieu 1987.

3. Bourdieu is sometimes criticized for focusing too much on social positioning and symbolic domination but not enough on labor and exploitation (e.g., Seim & McCarthy 2023). One way that this book diverges from Bourdieu's work is in its focus on how symbolic domination operates in the service of exploitation. This text will highlight how symbolic capitalists' lifestyles and livelihoods are importantly predicated on extracting labor from vulnerable and desperate people at unsustainably low rates. It will illustrate how exclusion is central to symbolic capitalists' preservation of our own elite positions. It will explore the relationship between social justice discourse and the socioeconomic exclusion and exploitation of "normies." The central focus on this text is an elite formation defined by a specific mode of production. That is, in many respects, this text seeks to reconnect Bourdieu's important insights on symbolic struggles with more traditional materialist concerns over exploitation and production.

4. Bourdieu 1993b, p. 164.

5. For elaboration on how and under what circumstances symbolic capitalists convert one form of symbolic capital into another, see Pret, Shaw, & Dodd 2016.

6. See Bourdieu 1987, pp. 53–56, and Bourdieu 1986, pp. 17–19.

7. Battistella 2019.

8. R. Perry 1992.

9. S. Hall 1994.

10. C. Gibson 2016.

11. The Wide Awakes were perhaps the first paramilitary appendage to a U.S. political campaign. Much like Republican militias of today, they often showed up at speeches and voting sites, ostensibly to ensure the integrity of these proceedings. They dressed in militaristic uniforms and marched in formations through cities bearing torches, and sometimes weapons, to raise awareness for their cause. Tired of compromises and half measures, they were explicit in calls for more direct confrontation with their political opponents (the South). Eventually they began forming militias

and engaging in paramilitary operations that helped escalate and foment the burgeoning conflict between Democrats and Republicans. Many of these militias were ultimately folded into the Union army when the Civil War broke out (see, e.g., Galusha Anderson 1908).

12. Grinspan 2009, pp. 365–366.

13. Wills 2020. *Pace* Wills, it should be noted that one important difference between the Wide Awakes of the 1860s and contemporary wokeness is that the former was a working-class movement, which the intellectual class largely derided and dismissed. Wokeness, meanwhile, is largely a phenomenon of the intelligentsia that seems to hold little appeal with working-class Americans. There is a further difference with respect to attitudes on censorship. The Wide Awakes rallied around the cause of "Free Speech, Free Soil, Free Men." In the contemporary context, wokeness is often associated with campaigns to *restrict* speech, ostensibly to protect others from "harm." That is to say, contemporary wokeness is not a straightforward revival or continuation of the 1860s Wide Awake movement. In many respects, the composition, aims, and methods of the two movements are completely different.

Nonetheless, the term "Wide Awake" was deployed similarly to the contemporary term "woke"—including and especially as it relates to denoting a certain moral and epistemological superiority to those who are *not* "Awake" or "woke" (who are, instead, asleep, complacent, unaware, or blind). Moreover, both "Wide Awake" and "woke" are terms widely associated with militancy and young people. And in different ways, the cause of Black liberation featured prominently in both movements.

Interestingly, the Wide Awakes were primarily German first- and second-generation Americans. This is noteworthy because while Germans would simply be regarded as "white" today, at the time, they were a widely disparaged ethnic group, viewed with extreme suspicion by Anglo-Saxons, and subject to regular and fairly severe marginalization and persecution (see Moench 2018 for more on this point). That is, the Wide Awakes were largely not a case of "whites" aligning themselves with Blacks out of benevolence—but rather, they were a movement led by working-class members of a persecuted and marginalized ethnic group, aligning themselves with an even more exploited population, out of an apparent sense that neither group would truly be free or respected unless they attacked American racism at the root. This is another sense in which the Wide Awakes seem to have anticipated strains of thinking that would later come to be associated with wokeness: the idea that different forms of degradation and exploitation are not independent but rather part of the same system of oppression.

14. The Wide Awakes played an important role in precipitating the Civil War. The formation of Northern militias espousing extreme political positions and warlike rhetoric led to people on the other side forming youth groups, and eventually militias of their own. As historian Jon Grinspan put it, "South Carolina fire-eaters began to organize 'Minute Men' militias, not out of empty paranoia, but 'as an offset to the Wide Awakes of the North.' The creation of the Minute Men is often mentioned as a major stepping-stone on the road to disunion, but few historians note that they were a direct response to the Wide Awakes. The link between secession and the movement is even stronger than previously realized. . . . The first Americans to secede did so with the Wide Awake movement on their minds, an emblem of the flawed union they were fleeing" (2009, p. 377).

15. McWhorter 2021.

16. Redding 1943, p. 43.

17. See King 2005 for the original; King 2000 for his final sermon.

18. Zimmer 2017.

19. Romano 2020.

20. For those interested in exploring these trends on nGrams, I would recommend zooming in more closely on particular ranges (e.g., 1980–1996) rather than focusing on the entire time series, in order to more clearly see trend lines during periods when shifts are happening. I would also recommend reducing the smoothing to 0 or 1 (I worked with 1 for the purposes of this analysis).

21. A best-selling "dictionary and handbook" of political correctness produced in the early 1990s makes it clear that the pejorative use of "political correctness" marks out roughly the same constellation of ideas and political dispositions that are now discursively associated with "wokeness." See Beard & Cerf 1993. For a contemporaneous book intended to push back against right-wing narratives about political correctness, but which likewise powerfully illustrates that contemporary debates about wokeness seem to be referring to the same cultural phenomenon, with roughly the same sociopolitical battle lines, see J. Wilson 1995.

22. Google Trends show a similar pattern. U.S. search interest in the term "woke" increased steadily from 2004 (when the record begins) through 2012. However, there was a significant increase in public interest in the term beginning in January 2013 and plateauing from May 2017 through January 2021. A significant spike in search interest followed, persisting through March 2023 and declining thereafter. It is likely that this latter uptick in search interest reflects an increase in ironic and pejorative use (while the 2023 decline is tied to increasing numbers of Americans growing bored with both wokeness and anti-wokeness).

"Wokeness," meanwhile, has more or less always had a pejorative connotation. That term saw an initial spike in March 2004 followed by a sharp decline that persisted through November 2015. Beginning in December 2015, there was a slow and steady build in interest through January 2020. There was a significant spike beginning in February 2020 and peaking in April 2021—although at the time of writing, search interest remains significantly higher than pre-2020 baselines.

"Political correctness," on the other hand, experienced a consistent (if noisy) decline in search interest from the beginning of the time series through December 2012. From January 2013 through May 2015, however, the term saw consistent, albeit slight, upticks in interest. Interest increased dramatically beginning in June 2015, followed by a decline after November 2016—indicating that the spike in interest was tied to the 2016 election cycle. Since then, interest in the term has reached recorded lows. The 2020 election had virtually no impact on the trend, likely because the alternative pejorative ("woke") was, by then, more fully embraced by right-aligned political actors and media.

23. A similar pattern can be observed in Google nGram trends for "political correctness" and "politically correct": there was a decline followed by an uptick to previous levels, likely corresponding to increased negative uses, culminating in a more durable decline as a new term (in this case, "woke") came to replace "politically correct" within the left.

24. Rozado 2023a.

25. Interestingly, although poll respondents viewed "woke" positively in the abstract, there was strong opposition in the same poll to many ideas commonly associated with "wokeness." For instance, most respondents opposed teaching critical race theory in schools, allowing people to identify as something other than male or female on government documents, or using gender-neutral pronouns to refer to people. In short, Americans do not view "woke" negatively, but they are not woke themselves. See Newall, Rollason, & Feldman 2023.

26. Al-Gharbi 2023e.

27. Wittgenstein 2009.

28. R. Williams 1985.

29. Adler-Bell 2022c.

30. Tilton 2024.

31. See Khan 2015b.

32. J. Weeden & Kurzban 2014; Hawkins et al. 2018; Doherty et al. 2021.

33. E.g., McCabe 2005; Fingerhut 2011; S. Perry, Frantz, & Grubbs 2021.

34. Schulte 2021.

35. See especially Taleb 2018, bk. 3, chap. 2 (pp. 67–92).

36. Willer, Kuwabara, & Macy 2009.

37. S. Alexander 2014.

38. Blake 2021; Goldberg 2022b.

39. Noelle-Neumann 1993.

40. Orwell 1972.

41. E.g., Blair & Hoskin 2019. The study found that even among the small minority of people who expressed openness to dating a trans person, respondents frequently gravitated toward partners incongruent with their own sexual identity. For instance, gay men preferred trans women over trans men, and lesbians tended to prefer trans men over trans women.

That is, despite professing to recognize trans men *as* men, women whose sexual identity is oriented around exclusive attraction to other *women* were nonetheless open to dating trans men, and were relatively less interested in trans women (despite ostensibly recognizing trans women *as* women, and defining themselves in terms of attraction to other women). And similar realities hold for gay men: despite defining themselves in terms of their attraction to other men, and explicitly recognizing trans men as men, and trans women as women, gay men tend to nonetheless prefer trans women over trans men. In both cases, people seem to be prioritizing the physical anatomy of prospective partners over their expressed gender identity—insofar as they are open to dating trans partners at all.

In short, the tension between what people profess and how they behave with respect to claims that "trans women are women" (or "trans men are men") is not just common among cisgender heterosexuals. It manifests regularly among lesbian and gay Americans as well.

42. Tosi & Warmke 2020.

43. As a result of the widespread tendency to explicitly or implicitly falsify one's preferences for the sake of social and professional gain, ideologies that "everyone" seems to believe in can quite suddenly fall out of fashion because the institutional elites driving these narratives are deposed, or because formerly ambivalent actors decide to voice their objections, leading others who have long disagreed to speak up as well. That is, institutionally dominant views are often prone to sudden collapse because few are truly committed to begin with. For more on these dynamics, see Kuran 1997.

44. E.g., Bonica 2013.

45. Alto et al. 2022.

46. E.g., Carrington, Zwick, & Neville (2016) argue that not only are individual behaviors unable to truly "solve" the social problems, those calling on people to "walk their talk" are actually, *themselves*, part of the problem. Calling attention to the gap between people's rhetoric and behavior is equally problematic (because it reinforces the idea that something short of total systemic change can resolve core social issues, even as the focus on hypocrisy or aporia diverts attention away from bringing about revolutionary change). Myriad additional examples could be produced that make similar arguments in academic journals, left-aligned media outlets, and beyond. It is a relatively common position among self-identified leftists.

47. E.g., Szetela 2021; Ungar-Sargon 2022.

48. For more on the rapid wave of unionization efforts in the symbolic capitalist sectors, see L. Becker 2016; Baum & Kilkenny 2021; Fu 2021; Harnett 2021; Ding 2022. For more on the simultaneous stagnation and decline of unions among the working class, see T. Johnston 2022; Peck 2022.

49. Heyward 2017.

50. J. Jones 2021b.

51. Verdant Labs 2017.

52. OpenSecrets 2021. Selected cycle: 2016. See also *The Economist* 2019.

53. Bonica 2023.

54. Gu 2020.

55. OpenSecrets 2021. Selected cycle: 2020.

56. Thorson, Haseman, & Procell 2020; see especially the map prefaced by the header "Land Doesn't Vote. People Do." See also Mahtesian & Alexander 2023.

57. Noah 2023.

58. Verdant Labs 2017.

59. Benjamin 2018.

60. E.g., Rubinstein & Paybarah 2020.

61. Bourdieu 1990, pp. xvii–xviii.

62. Vaisse 2009.

63. C. Gonzalez 2019b.

64. For a self-critical, self-reflective essay on this point by an anti-woke essayist, see Hanania 2022a.

65. Burge 2023.

66. According to Pew Research estimates, although most Americans say politics provides little to no meaning to their lives, the kinds of people most likely to become symbolic capitalists are significant outliers:

- Sixty-one percent of college grads find "a great deal" or "some" fulfillment or meaning in supporting a social or political cause. Among those without a degree (those with some college or with high school or less alike), majorities describe their level of meaning or fulfillment from politics as "not much" or "none."
- Likewise, 63 percent of those who identified as "liberal" professed to finding meaning or fulfillment through politics. "Conservatives" were split 50/50.
- Those with incomes over $75,000 were also more likely than most to find meaning in politics, especially with respect to finding a "great deal" of meaning therein.

See van Kessel et al. 2018, p. 8.

67. D. Campbell, Layman, & Green 2020. See pp. 159–160 for the quote featured in the text. See p. 164 for a data table demonstrating that nonreligious secularists are most likely to be college-educated whites. Conversely, college-educated white Democrats are far more likely to be nonreligious secularists than anything else. The book also highlights that highly educated white liberals are especially likely to stop attending religious services, or abandon their faith altogether, when religion seems to clash with their preferred political narratives. That is, many highly educated white liberals have been more or less directly substituting politics for religion in recent years.

68. Behr 2019.

69. P. Gottfried 2004.

70. Girard 2001, p. 160.

71. Girard 2001, p. 157.

72. See al-Gharbi 2020b for an extended treatment of this analogy.

73. Clizza 2021.

74. C. Chen 2022. Within this ecosystem, career coaches increasingly adopt the strategies and narratives of religious revivalists and play a somewhat similar role—see Sheehan 2022.

75. Weber 2001.

76. For more on these points, see C. Evans 2022.

77. For a noteworthy exception to this tendency, see Bottum 2014.

78. E.g., Weber 2020, pp. 43–116.

79. There is not yet much academic research on the phenomenon of audience capture. However, it is a topic of great discussion among influencers—e.g., Gurwinder 2022.

80. Patreon, Etsy, PayPal, and YouTube are known for deplatforming and demonitizing users who violate mainstream symbolic capitalists' and advertisers' moral, aesthetic, and political sensibilities—often with little warning or opportunity for appeal; see, e.g., J. Alexander 2018; Wright 2022.

81. For a deep dive into the empirical literature on this point, with links to dozens of peer-reviewed studies and meta-analyses, see al-Gharbi 2023c.

82. Martins 2023.

83. Quest Diagnostics 2023, table 5.

84. E.g. Schwarz 2015.

85. Durrant 2024.

86. Reeves 2017c.

87. Liu 2021, p. 25.

88. Rensin 2017.

89. See M. White, n.d. For an example of a course with this program that continues to feature Rachel Dolezal (whom we'll discuss later), see Activist School, n.d.

90. Gupta 2020.

91. Haider 2020.

92. Nietzsche 1956, p. 209.

93. E.g., Garcia 2020.

94. Y. Yang 2019.

95. Available here: https://intersectionalityscore.com/.

96. P. Collins 2000, p. 270.

97. E.g., S. Khan 2021b, pp. 167–172.

98. See al-Gharbi 2023f for more on this point.

99. For an excellent review of Weber's writings on the distinction between material and ideal interests (and how they are often misunderstood), see Lizardo & Stoltz 2018.

100. For a good roundup of the literature on this point, see B. Benson 2016.

101. For a nice roundup of the empirical literature on these points, see D. Williams 2022.

102. Lipset & Marks 2000.

103. E. Goldstein 2008.

104. Zeitz 2015.

105. J. Young 2015.

106. C. Hirschman & Mogford 2009.

107. Mitrani 2014.

108. Gregory 2005.

109. Wolters 1975.

110. S. Webb 2014.

111. Jancar-Webster 1978; O. Campbell 2018.

112. Gavin 1997.

113. Kalagher 2014.

114. For more on the struggles returning World War I vets faced upon returning home, and the pivotal role their discontent played in American politics in subsequent decades, see Stoller 2019, chap. 3.

115. Barbeau & Henri 1996.

116. Boskin 1976.

117. McGerr 2005.

118. Stormquist 2006.

119. Hillstrom 2010. However, *pace* Hillstrom, it is important to note that much of the "corruption" muckrakers chose to focus on involved exposing unions, businesses, or other institutions dominated by religious or ethnic minorities, which often operated on rules and standards that were commonplace in the contexts they hailed from, but which WASPs derided as "bad business." That is, despite its practitioners' self-narratives, muckraking was not always about holding the powerful to account. It was also, often, about reinforcing preferred WASP narratives about "those people" and reinforcing WASPs' social position. As Randall Collins put it, "In the political sphere, 'reform' meant an effort, under the name of 'good government,' to destroy the power of Catholic political machines and return urban political power to the more genteel Anglo elites" (2019, p. 133).

120. There were strong financial incentives to maximize newspaper reach related to the increased availability and importance of ad revenue.

Industrialization significantly expanded the supply of manufactured goods available to U.S. consumers, and the rapid urbanization of America gave rise to mass markets. Meanwhile, social scientists, inspired by Sigmund Freud, alleged they could use advertising to "sublimate" people's primal urges into a desire to consume clients' specific goods and services. N. W. Ayer & Sons was established in 1869 in Philadelphia as the first full-service ad agency. By 1900, advertising had become a robust profession, and a key source of revenue for media organizations. In order to maximally exploit the potential revenues from advertising, and to capture the largest share possible of mass markets, news organizations increasingly strove to prevent alienating potential advertisers or their customers through their coverage. This was the origin of journalists' now-hallowed ideal of objectivity. See Ewen 2001; Kaplan 2002.

As a side note, the emergence of mass markets and mass communication channels also allowed for the emergence of mass culture. For instance, the film industry took off in America during the 1920s. Then, as now, Progressives strove mightily to regulate the industry in the service of promoting their favored moral and cultural narratives. See Rosenbloom 1987 for more on this history.

121. Folkerts 2014.

122. Giridharadas 2018, pp. 156–164.

123. Although most social workers have always been women, the field has consistently been defined by men in many critical respects. Hence, the typical description of social work as a "female-dominated profession" is somewhat misleading. The profession was always composed predominantly of women, but they were not often able to truly "call the shots." See McPhail 2004.

124. Lucier 2009.

125. For more on the history of the information professions and the establishment of the field of psychiatry, see A. Abbott 1988, chaps. 8, 10.

126. For more on the creation of business schools and their relation to the Progressive movement and the creation of the other symbolic professions, see Khurana 2010.

127. For a deeper exploration of the frustrated rise of engineering as a profession, see R. Collins 2019, pp. 211–227.

128. R. Collins 2019, chap. 5. As social scientist Agustina Paglayan shows when looking at different geographical contexts across time, periods of high social unrest and conflict seem to heighten elite anxiety about the masses and their character. An expansion of public education systems generally follows. Although these expansions are often portrayed as a concession or beneficent gift to the lower classes, the primary goal of these expansions seems to be inculcating obedience, stunting future rebellion, and ensuring the long-term solvency of the prevailing order. There is no meaningful or consistent link between public education expansion and genuine social democratization. See Paglayan 2022.

129. Sedlak & Schlossman 1986.

130. Labaree 2008.

131. Al-Gharbi 2020c.

132. R. Collins 2019, pp. 180–181.

133. R. Collins 2019, pp. 244–251.

134. Desmond 2023, p. 26.

135. Nelson 1982.

136. Holcombe 1996; Novak 2019.

137. As civil service exams failed to screen out "undesirables," the tests were refined to help them better select for the "right people"—at least, until 1981. In *Luevano v. Campbell*, the plaintiff successfully argued that the required civil service test seemed to have an especially pernicious effect on the job prospects of African Americans and Hispanics. Thereafter, tests were largely eliminated and the remaining exams were significantly changed. See Ban & Ingraham 1988.

138. Matthews 2015.

139. Katznelson 2006.

140. Asher 1994.

141. LaBue 1960

142. R. Collins 2019, pp. 120–253; Rothwell 2019.

143. See Auerbach 1977 and Madara 2021 for histories of exclusion in the American Bar Association and the American Medical Association, respectively.

144. E.g., Karabel 2006, pp. 99–109.

145. Al-Gharbi 2021a.

146. E.g., Bourdieu 1993a, 1996.

Chapter 2. The Great Awokening(s)

1. Rozado, al-Gharbi, & Halberstadt 2021b.

2. Rozado 2022; al-Gharbi 2023b.

3. For readers wanting to replicate these results, I would recommend running the graphs separately to get a clear sense of each line, with a smoothing of 0, and graphing the period of 2000–2019 (when the data end, at time of writing).

4. E.g., Perl 2014.

5. Swanson 2017; Morris 2018.

6. Jansen 2019.

7. Khawaji 2022.

8. Townsend et al. 2021a. For readers who are unfamiliar, the Vito Russo test (a version of the Bechdel test) contains three criteria: the film must include a character that is identifiably LGBTQ; that character cannot be primarily defined by their gender or sexual identity; and the character must be tied to the plot in a substantial way (such that changing or removing the character would make a nontrivial impact on the story).

9. Hunt & Ramon 2021a.

10. Appel & Gnambs 2022. To pass the Bechdel test, a movie must have at least two (named) female characters who talk to one another (that is, who do not engage exclusively with men), and whose conversations are about something other than a man.

11. Compare Kane et al. 2013 and Townsend et al. 2021b.

12. Hunt & Ramon 2021b.

13. E.g., E. Lee 2021.

14. M. Fischer 2018.

15. E.g., Kiefer & Savodnik 2022; Rosenfield 2022.

16. E.g., Nolke 2018; McLaughlin & Blake 2022; Schoenmueller, Netzer, & Stahl 2022.

17. Englehardt 2019, pp. 78–112; Englehardt 2023.

18. Kaufmann 2019; al-Gharbi 2020h.

19. Goldberg 2020.

20. Goldberg 2022a, pp. 102–105.

21. Gallup 2023. From 1975 to 2010, Democrats became 14 percentage points more likely to say abortion should be legal under all circumstances. From 2010 to 2020, the shift was 16 points.

At time of writing, the time series on these graphs goes through 2022, and the shifts among Democrats have grown even more pronounced. However, I chose to stop the analysis in the main text at 2020 to illustrate that the trend was dramatic even before the U.S. Supreme Court took up the *Dobbs v. Jackson Women's Health Organization* case. The changes were not a response to *Dobbs*.

Also of note, this data series shows another dramatic shift in attitudes among Democrats from the mid-1980s through the early 1990s (there was a shift of more than 17 percentage points in Democrats endorsing the idea that abortion should be legal under all circumstances from 1988 to 1995), corresponding with the previous Great Awokening. *That* shift in attitudes regressed to pre-Awokening levels after the Awokening had run its course.

22. Edsall 2023, pp. 180–188, 385–392.

23. Doherty et al. 2017, p. 7.

24. Al-Gharbi 2023c.

25. Galston 2019; Doherty et al. 2020; Gilberstadt & Daniller 2020.

26. D. Cox 2022.

27. E.g., N. Cohn 2022.

28. Goldberg 2023. See figs. 14, 15 (pp. 19–20).

29. Chinoy 2019; Yglesias & Singh 2022.

30. Yglesias 2019.

31. Although I will not be using his specific language here, nor explicitly referencing him elsewhere in this chapter, it should be noted that Pierre Bourdieu offered up an important theory of rapid normative and discursive changes ("symbolic revolutions") and the conditions under which they occur. While importantly different from my own argument in terms of emphases, measurements, and conclusions, Bourdieu's analysis is broadly compatible with the narrative presented here and, indeed, helped inform my thinking on these matters. See Fowler 2020 for an accessible and concise overview of Bourdieu on symbolic revolutions.

32. For more on these points, see Rozado, al-Gharbi, & Halberstadt 2021a.

33. E.g., Ramaswamy 2021.

34. E.g., Weber 1958, pp. 192–194.

35. Weber 2020, pp. 110–111.

36. Autor 2014, p. 843.

37. E.g., Ehrenberg 2017.

38. R. Milkman, Luce, & Lewis 2013.

39. E.g., Silver 2011.

40. See Fisher 2019, pp. 45–46, for information on the demographics of Resistance protesters. Data on the geographical distribution of events are available from Count Love, whose database includes more than twenty-seven thousand protest events and more than thirteen million attendees from 2017 to 2021: https://countlove.org/statistics.html.

With respect to shifts on ideological lean, Gallup's Lydia Saad (2017) likewise found that "older Democrats have shifted much more strongly toward social liberalism than have younger Democrats."

41. E.g., Gurri 2018.

42. Grim 2022; M. Mitchell 2022.

43. E.g., al-Gharbi 2019b; Rozado, al-Gharbi, & Halberstadt 2021b.

44. Buckley 2012.

45. Morozov 2011.

46. Grossman & Hopkins 2022, fig. 1 (p. 7).

47. Goldberg 2022a, figs. 4.14, 4.15.

48. Kaufmann 2021, fig. 5.

49. Vylomova, Murphy, & Haslam 2019, fig. 2 (p. 31).

50. Rozado, al-Gharbi, & Halberstadt 2021b.

51. McCall 2013.

52. Chong, Citrin, & Levy 2022.

53. Edsall 2023, p. 386.

54. Brint 1994, p. 105.

55. Traldi 2018.

56. Excerpted from Ehrenreich 2020, pp. 65–66, 71–72.

57. J. Freeman 1976.

58. See al-Gharbi 2019b, 2020c for more on these points.

59. Kaufmann 2004.

60. E.g., Abrahams 2017.

61. Excerpts from Orwell 1958, pp. 173, 175, 178, 221.

62. Protzko & Schooler 2019.

63. Twenge 2023, pp. 38–39.

64. R. Collins 2019, p. 5.

65. Eagan 1982.

66. Robert Cohen 1993, p. 259.

67. The first recorded gay rights organization in the United States, the Society for Human Rights, was founded in Chicago in 1924. Although the organization was itself short lived, gay activism and gay culture flourished during the period of the first Awokening—especially in urban areas and social circles where symbolic capitalists had a heavy presence. See Heap 2009 and Chauncey 2019 for deeper explorations of LGBTQ culture in the United States during this period.

68. Robert Cohen 1993, pp. 74–79.

69. Lipset & Marks 2000.

70. Blanpied 2009.

71. E.g., Robert Cohen 1993, p. 321.

72. See Olson 1973, p. 609.

73. See Lemann 2000, pp. 58–69.

74. Greenberg 2004.

75. Goldin & Katz 2011.

76. Most relevant for our purposes here are Executive Order 10925 (issued by President John F. Kennedy in 1961) and Executive Order 11246 (issued by President Lyndon B. Johnson in 1965).

77. Menand 2022, p. 698.

78. Menand 2022, p. 701.

79. Thelin 2021.

80. Hatt 2016.

81. Mattson 2019.

82. Rutenberg 2019.

83. E.g., Singer 1989.

84. R. Freeman 1976, p. 17.

85. R. Freeman 1976, p. 19.

86. R. Freeman 1976, p. 92.

87. R. Freeman 1976, p. 11.

88. See Reeves 2002, pp. 50–51, for the quote excerpted here and its context.

89. National Center for Education Statistics 2007.

90. C. Klein 2020.

91. Gitlin 1993, p. 411.

92. R. Freeman 1976, p. 44.

93. Koshet 1976.

94. A. Levine & Wilson 1979, pp. 627–628.

95. Lazeron 1998; J. Mitchell 2019.

96. Bound et al. 2021.

97. Hanson & Liu 2018.

98. Borjas 2005.

99. Nasar 1991.

100. Baumol, Blinder, & Wolff 2003; Markovits 2020.

101. Vobejda 1989.

102. Leiden & Neal 1990.

103. Ransom & Winters 2021.

104. Fuller et al. 2017.

105. Graeber defined "bullshit jobs" as employment where people were "basically paid to do nothing, in positions to make them identify with the perspectives and sensibilities of the ruling class (managers, administrators, etc.)—and particularly its financial avatars"—while fostering a "simmering resentment against anyone whose work has clear and undeniable social value" (2019, p. 245). People who work in artistic and cultural fields, economics, accounting, IT, or finance,

insurance, and marketing are especially likely to recognize their jobs as "socially useless." See Dur & van Lent 2018, table S4.

106. See Carnevale, Smith, & Strohl 2010, p. 4.

107. For an extended treatment of the collapse of the third Great Awokening as people who led it embraced professional success, see Lott 2006.

108. Cass & Oyeniran 2022.

109. Wolf 2021.

110. B. Schmidt 2018.

111. Lohr 2017.

112. Skrentny 2023.

113. J. Fox 2018.

114. Korn & DeBarros 2021; Korn & Fuller 2021.

115. Walker 2021.

116. Tracy 2020.

117. S. Fischer 2021.

118. Falkenheim et al. 2021. There was significant variation in job attainment by major. Those with PhDs who specialized in mathematics and computer science, or psychology and social science, were especially likely to secure jobs postgraduation. Those who attained degrees in the arts and humanities were especially *unlikely* to find work: more than 40 percent graduated with no employment commitments.

119. P. Cooper 2021.

120. Reeden 2020.

121. Taska et al. 2018. Black and Hispanic college graduates are especially likely to experience "vertical mismatch" between their qualifications and their jobs. See Y. Lu & Li 2021.

122. At time of writing, as many as one in twelve current community college students have previously earned a BA or higher elsewhere. See Marcus 2020.

123. Horowitz 2018.

124. Streib 2020.

125. Creamer et al. 2022, fig. 2 (p. 4).

126. There are some signs that elite overproduction pressures seem to be easing as well; see Molla 2022.

127. Al-Gharbi 2023e. See especially the revised and expanded version available on my website, which has several informative charts and graphs that could not be included in the initial publication.

128. The apparently high growth rates in many fields often reflects jobs rising from an extremely low number of positions in absolute terms to a *still* very low number of positions in absolute terms. For instance, some of the above-average-paying jobs with the "hottest" projected growth are wind turbine technicians, solar photovalic installers, and wood model makers. Out of these options, even the job with the highest number of positions today, solar photovalic installers, only has roughly 11,500 positions at present—a number that is projected to rise to about 18,000 by 2030. The growth rate looks impressive, but the total number of jobs remains small. And the current above-average pay for these jobs may decline significantly if people *do* decide to train for them in large numbers over the next decade. More data on the fastest-growing jobs by growth rate are available in U.S. Bureau of Labor Statistics 2023a.

129. M. Webb 2020.

130. Turchin 2010.

131. Turchin & Nefedov 2009; Turchin 2012. For Turchin's assessment of how well his model held up a decade later—looking at the United States and western European countries—see Turchin & Korotayev 2020.

132. Should they manage to secure a good position for themselves, "radicals" are eventually forced to reckon with the reality that the social positions and lifestyles they enjoy or aspire

to are contingent on the exploitation or perpetuation of various inequalities. They come to realize that meaningfully addressing the social problems they purport to be consumed with could only happen at great cost to people like themselves and their loved ones. They are made to confront the massive trade-offs and uncertainties that typically accompany any dramatic social change. In response, their enthusiasm for addressing highly moralized social problems begins to rapidly wane, and attention directed toward those issues in public forums declines in tandem. See Downs 1972.

133. Turchin argues that while having too few positions for aspiring elites causes instability, having too many elites can become a problem too. Growing numbers of elites attempting to influence the political system or struggling with one another for status (which is, again, more of a zero-sum game) can lead to many different forms of dysfunction. Moreover, a large elite class is usually only possible if there is an even larger class of workers at the bottom, with a growing gulf between the two and a shrinking middle class. Eventually, this will culminate in bottom-up rebellions that severely destabilize and, at times, destroy the system. That is, expanding the elite is a short-term solution for a crisis of elite overproduction. Over the long term, the only way to prevent the adverse outcomes of elite overproduction is to aggressively limit the (re)production of elites. See, e.g., Turchin 2023.

134. See Turchin 2023 for more on this cycle.

135. S. Khan 2015a.

136. E.g., Kenworthy & Owens 2012.

137. See V. Taylor 1989 for more on movement abeyance and revival.

138. A recent major Pew survey of African Americans found that the top concerns Black people expressed about the communities they live in include violence and crime, economic stagnation and decline, housing issues, and infrastructure. Racism and culture-related issues were at the bottom of the list, with only 3 percent of respondents listing these as their most pressing concerns. See K. Cox & Tamir 2022, p. 63.

139. For a particularly striking example of these tendencies in action, see Jeffery 2022.

140. Chiswick & Robinson 2021.

141. hooks 2000, p. 133.

142. A long-standing critique of professionally oriented feminism is that a large share of women don't actually *want* to work. Consequently, a feminism focused on pushing women into the workplace and empowering them therein is one that misses (and often denigrates) the desires, needs, and priorities of many, many women in the United States (and an even larger share of women in other contexts). For instance, a 2019 survey by Gallup found that, if they had the financial option to do so, roughly four in ten American women would prefer to be homemakers. A *majority* of women with children felt this way, as did more than one in three women who did *not* have children. Most women who did not currently have jobs would not seek out employment if they had an option not to. See Brenan 2019.

143. See DeBoer 2021a for some theories on why an embrace of symbolic capitalists is often a kiss of death for movements. In addition to those theories, it should be noted that studies have repeatedly identified dealing with white activists within organizations as a core reason for "burnout" among activists of color. Dealing with white liberals in the course of advocacy (that is, among people who were not activists in the organization but were the targets of outreach) was another key driver of burnout. See, e.g., Gorski 2019a; 2019b; Gorski & Erakat 2019. Finally, Han, McKenna, & Oyakawa (2021) show that successful social movements tend to center and empower local stakeholders, while those dominated, defined, and (micro)managed by "outsiders" are significantly more likely to fail.

144. See Putnam 2020, chap. 6.

145. Gains for Hispanics and Latinos similarly *preceded* the second Great Awokening. For instance, the 1947 case *Mendez v. Westminster* banned racial segregation against Hispanic and Latinos. The 1954 case *Hernandez v. Texas* codified that Hispanics and other ethnic and racial

minorities were covered by the Fourteenth Amendment just like African Americans. This allowed them to likewise benefit from the Civil Rights Acts that followed a decade later. Also before the second Great Awokening, Larry Itliong, Cesar Chavez, and Dolores Huerta founded organizations that would be merged into the United Farm Workers in 1966 (although each achieved most of the victories for which they are known today before the formation of the United Farm Workers).

146. Manduca 2018.

147. F. Harris & Curtis 2018.

148. In 1960, the ratio of Black to white prisoners was 5.01:1. In 2018, it was 5.6:1. The overall rate of incarceration among African Americans was 1,313 per 100,000 in 1960. In 2018, it was 1,501 per 100,000. See Drake 2013; Gramlich 2020.

149. Hurst, Rubinstein, & Shimizu 2021.

150. Sassen 2018.

151. Although Hurst and coauthors argue that "taste-based" discrimination has declined markedly since 1960, other studies suggest that progress may have stalled out on this front as well—at least for African Americans. For instance, a 2017 meta-analysis of field studies measuring racial discrimination found no evidence of decline in hiring discrimination against Blacks since 1990. However, there was evidence of modest declines in bias against Hispanics. Other studies have shown even more dramatic declines in discrimination against Asian Americans. See Hilger 2016; Quillian et al. 2017.

152. See Putnam 2020, chap. 7.

153. For an exploration of how the 1990s *set back* feminism in many important respects, see Yarrow 2018.

154. Keister, Thebaud, & Yavorsky 2022.

155. McAdam et al. 2005.

156. K. Cox & Edwards 2022, p. 17.

157. People tend to significantly overestimate the extent to which attitudes have shifted on many issues—largely because they assume people were far more racist, misogynistic, or homophobic in the past than the empirical record actually reflects. That is, our narratives about how much more "enlightened" we are today are largely a product of misunderstanding and misrepresenting history. Mastroianni & Dana 2022.

158. Stimson 2015, pp. 72–73.

159. Atkinson et al. 2021; Hout 2021. It should be emphasized that the liberalizing trends for each of these topics likely predate their measurement in polls. Typically, pollsters begin asking about a given topic after it becomes clear that some kind of movement may already be underway. As Stimson explains, "We don't get to witness the full process because the period before social change and the period after the new consensus produce no measures. Only when the controversy is 'live' do survey organizations produce questions about it. That means what's left is . . . the time of steadily growing support for equality." See Stimson 2015, pp. 29–30.

160. For an illustration of this dynamic in practice—increased salience of racial issues during Great Awokenings followed by returns to antecedent baselines—see Kaufmann 2021, fig. 1. In general, media tend to reflect rather than shape public perceptions about policy issues or social trends. See Hopkins, Kim, & Kim 2017; Wlezein & Soroka 2023.

161. For more on how protest movements, media coverage, broad shifts in public opinion, and even electoral outcomes seem to matter much less with respect to major policy changes than most seem to think, see Grossman 2014. According to Grossman's account, cross-partisan elite governing networks seem to be the primary drivers of policy change—and they pursue a policy agenda largely independent of the aforementioned struggles in the public sphere because they, themselves, are largely unaccountable (and invisible) to the public. Occasionally, public events are leveraged to help accelerate progress on goals that are already being pursued. However, the goals themselves are rarely shaped, or even meaningfully influenced, by the churn of the public sphere.

162. As Stephen Vaisey and coauthors have extensively demonstrated, attitudes on most issues seem to be settled before adulthood and do not change much from year to year. And when significant shifts do occur, they tend to be short lived—most revert to a position approximating their antecedent baselines within a few years. Views on race, gender, and sexuality tend to be especially stable over time and seem particularly unresponsive to cultural fads and current events. See Vaisey & Lizardo 2016; Kiley & Vaisey 2020; Vaisey & Kiley 2021.

163. A viral report by Bloomberg News claimed that, in the aftermath of the 2020 "racial reckoning," S&P 100 companies gave 94 percent of new jobs to people of color. This report turned out to be premised on a major and straightforward statistical error. When the data were properly contextualized, there seemed to be few changes to the workforce at these companies beyond what would be expected from typical annual turnover paired with shifting demographics of the available labor pool (with Black people seeing far smaller shifts than all other nonwhite groups). The explicit social justice commitments made by employers in the aftermath of George Floyd's murder seem to have had little to no discernable effect on companies' overall hiring practices—although there *was* a 2 percentage-point increase in the share of nonwhites occupying professional, management, and executive roles (primarily to the benefit of Asian candidates). See J. Green et al. 2023; Rosiak 2023.

164. Dobbin 2011.

165. Gerson & Suk 2016, p. 882.

166. Johnson 2020.

167. *Chronicle of Higher Education* 2021a.

168. Schoffstall 2022.

169. See Lasch-Quinn 2002 for a definitive history of the idea of diversity training and the eventual rise of diversity consultants. See M. Gonzalez 2023 for more on the rise of DEI positions in the aftermath of George Floyd's murder—and the subsequent contraction in these positions as the post-2010 Great Awokening began to wind down.

170. Pennock 2023; Wong 2023.

171. M. Harrington 2022.

172. Dobbin & Kalev 2021, p. 287.

173. E.g., Wingfield et al. 2021, p. 7.

174. See al-Gharbi 2020e for a comprehensive review of literature on the (in)efficacy of diversity-related training relative to its stated goals.

175. For more on how contemporary HR practices, carried out under the auspices of social justice, exemplify Foucauldian notions of discipline and surveillance, see Gary Anderson & Grinberg 1998; Sewell & Barker 2006; Villadsen 2007.

176. In *Capital*, Marx divided the bourgeoisie into two core blocs: functional capitalists and rentier capitalists. The former term referred to professionals, managers, and administrators—the people who run things but don't own things. The latter term referred to people who own businesses, resources, and so on but don't directly manage most of the decisions for the enterprises and assets under their domain (they have people for that: the functional capitalists). Marx noted there are often tensions, sometimes outright conflict, between these different blocs of elites—although typically the former works to advance the will and interests of the latter. Across the board, they share an interest (and collaborate) in exploiting and oppressing the working class—and in siphoning "surplus value" produced by the working class "upwards" to people like themselves. See Marx 1993, pp. 493–514.

177. Before the 1917 Russian Revolution, Marx was somewhat obscure in the United States. The Russian Revolution elevated Marx's ideas just before symbolic capitalists began looking for a revolutionary framework for indicting the existing order. See Magness & Makovi 2022.

178. Robert Cohen 1993.

179. Marxists and Communists exerted only a marginal influence even within the Socialist Party of America for most of its history—eventually leading the Communist faction to form a separate political party (see, e.g., Zumoff 2020). This splinter party largely failed to convert U.S.

workers or to successfully institutionalize itself in a durable or stable way. Nonetheless, the Communist movement gained significant traction among American *students and intellectuals* during the first Great Awokening.

180. For more on students in prerevolutionary Russia, see Kassow 1989; for more on students in prerevolutionary China, see Lutz 1971. College students subsequently played a central role in driving Mao Zedong's Cultural Revolution as well—see Dikotter 2016 for more on this history.

Likewise, even after the fall of the Soviet Union, university-educated Russians remained two to three times more supportive of the (then banned) Communist Party of the Soviet Union relative to high school graduates. White-collar professionals remained two to three times more supportive of Communist ideology relative to farm laborers and semiskilled workers. See Pereira & Pereira 2003.

Around the world and across time, Marxism seems to hold sway primarily over *symbolic capitalists* rather than the workers who were expected to drive the revolution.

181. Marx perhaps most forcefully deconstructs the ideal of equality as a political goal in his 1875 "Critique of the Gotha Programme." Marx & Engels 1978, pp. 525–541.

182. Marx & Engels 1978, p. 531.

183. For more on this point, see *Capital*, vol. 1 (Marx & Engels 1978, pp. 294–438). Chap. 32 is perhaps especially pertinent.

184. Marx 1978, p. 485.

185. Rogers 2017.

186. Leopold 2018.

187. See Marx 2015, p. 14.

188. E.g., Bakunin 1987, pp. 177–189.

189. Guerin 1970, pp. 25–26.

190. Although Marx supported the emancipation of slaves (as a blow to U.S. capitalists) and was critical of colonialism, he was also known to make comments that would today be understood as blatantly racist with respect to Black people, Jews, Slavs, Chinese, Bedouins, and other groups. Marx believed that Europeans were innately superior to these others (and some European subgroups were superior to other European subgroups). He believed that superior races were endowed with qualities that booster their productivity, innovation, and development—allowing them to lead the way for the rest of humanity. Inferior races, on the other hand, held everyone else back (and would perhaps eventually be extinguished for this reason). These views were not incidental to Marx's thinking; they were deeply integrated into his theory of history and his broader social thought. See van Ree 2019 for more on these points.

191. For a deep dive into this dispute, its buildup, and its aftermath, see Messer-Kruse 2009.

192. Orwell 1958, p. 174.

193. Mills 1960. For more on this essay and the pivotal role it played in galvanizing and defining the American New Left, see Geary 2008.

194. Renaud 2021, p. 241: Herbert Marcuse was more or less the only noteworthy affiliate of the Frankfurt School to expressly identify with the New Left. See also Steinmetz-Jenkins 2022.

195. Combahee River Collective 1977.

196. Adam Smith 2003, p. 572.

197. G'Sell 2022.

198. E.g., Taiwo 2020b; Panovka & Barrow 2023.

199. For a great collection of foundational texts of critical race theory, see Crenshaw et al. 1996.

200. E.g., T. Bartlett 2017; Crenshaw 2017.

201. D. Bell 1976.

202. D. Bell 1972.

203. A study looking at trends in political sectarianism from 1980 to 2020 found dramatic polarization in in-group versus out-group affect after 1986 and 2010—that is, corresponding to the third and fourth Great Awokenings. See Finkel et al. 2020.

204. Often when people discuss these data they talk about conservative and liberal polarization around "science." However, there hasn't been much polarization around *science*. Conservatives continue to strongly support science as an enterprise. However, they have growing mistrust *of the people who make claims* in the name of science. This is an important distinction. See Mann & Schleifer 2020.

205. See Gauchat 2012, fig. 1 for the trends among liberals, moderates, and conservatives from 1974 to 2010. Critically, Gauchat does not analyze the trends among conservatives and liberals symmetrically. Moreover, his analysis is focused primarily on comparing 1974 baselines with 2010 results (rather than doing a deep dive into the intervening patterns). However, by drilling into the longitudinal data in fig. 1, we can see that there are roughly three phases in how ideologues related to one another with respect to trust in scientists. In the first phase, from the mid-1970s through the early 1980s, there is rough parity between liberals and conservatives, with conservatives perhaps a little higher in trust. Over the 1980s through the mid-1990s, there are declines in trust across the board, albeit steeper for conservatives than liberals or moderates. However, in 1994, liberals and conservatives were still quite close to one another, and moderates were the extreme outlier in terms of (low) trust. Then, from 1994 through 2010 we see polarization in attitudes between liberals and conservatives—and this polarization is largely *symmetrical* (i.e., conservatives were not just becoming less trusting of scientists, liberals were also becoming significantly more trusting of scientists). A subsequent analysis extending the data through 2018 found that symmetric polarization between conservatives and liberals persisted through the 2010s. See J. Lee 2021.

206. Motta 2018. A subsequent report by *Nature* likewise found that the journal's endorsement of Joe Biden during the 2020 election dramatically undermined trust in the reliability of its articles among those who encountered the endorsement—particularly among Republicans. See Zhang 2023.

207. Potts 2022. See the interactive graph to explore these trends, visualizing data from the General Social Survey (1973–2020).

208. Al-Gharbi 2021b.

209. Tompkins 2021.

210. Hagey 2021; M. Binder 2022.

211. Ehrenreich & Ehrenreich 1977a, 1977b.

212. Al-Gharbi 2019b.

213. The contradictions that the Southern Christian Leadership Conference's northern campaign exposed ran very deep. For instance, throughout most of the nineteenth century it was common for white northerners to decry the "barbaric" South even while they *actively* promoted, prolonged, and profited from slavery. See A. Farrow, Lang, & Frank 2006.

214. Carson 2001, pp. 305–306.

215. King 1968.

216. The first "open carry" movement in the United States was executed *not* by right-aligned whites but by the Black Panthers. For more on this history and its relevance to contemporary social debates, see al-Gharbi 2016a.

217. Taibbi 2018.

218. Weiner 2012, p. 271.

219. James Cobb 2018.

220. L. Bennett 1964, pp. 75, 76, 77, 79. Emphasis in original.

221. King 2010, p. 8.

222. SNCC Vine City Project 1966, p. 4.

223. Lasch-Quinn 2002, p. 54.

224. J. Baldwin 1998, pp. 371–372.

225. Vogel 2018.

226. X 2020, p. 133.

227. Rustin 1965.

Chapter 3. Symbolic Domination

1. Lasch 1996.

2. Sherman 2017.

3. Seventy-two percent of Americans worth more than $5 million view themselves as "middle class" or "upper-middle class." Among those who "only" have $1 million in assets, the number shoots up to 84 percent (with a plurality of respondents defining themselves as simply "middle class," not even "upper-middle class"). See R. Frank 2015.

4. S. Khan 2021b.

5. O'Donnell 2022; Sanchez-Mora 2022.

6. Currid-Halkett 2018; Wagner 2023.

7. Giridharadas 2018.

8. Gouldner 1979.

9. Drezner 2017.

10. E.g., Watkins-Hayes 2009.

11. Mills 2000, p. 4.

12. Eyal 2019.

13. Bourdieu & Passeron 1990, p. 178.

14. H. MacDonald 1996.

15. Weymouth 1978.

16. Daniels & Wyllie 2019.

17. E.g., D. Hirschman 2021, fig. 4.

18. Analysts should look at the top 20 percent "at minimum" because the goal is to simultaneously capture the rich *and* the upper-middle class. However, there are a few different ways to calculate who belongs to the upper-middle class.

As opposed to looking at the top quintile, one popular alternative classification for the upper-middle class includes all households with incomes at least five times the U.S. poverty threshold, adjusted for household size. The U.S. Census Bureau set the 2020 poverty thresholds at $13,171 for an individual and $26,496 for a family of four. A person living alone earning $65,855 or higher would therefore be upper-middle class or wealthy, as would a four-person household that collectively brings in at least $132,480 per year.

Using *this* definition, we see that the size of the upper-middle class has been growing rapidly since the 1960s. Around 6 percent of the United States earned five times the poverty threshold in 1967. By 1981, 18 percent of Americans were upper-middle class; by 2002, 29 percent of Americans were upper-middle class; by 2016, 34 percent, of Americans climbed into this category (although a larger share of Americans has also fallen into the "low-income" category since 1981). See Rose 2020.

Critically, on this conception, the share of Americans in the upper-middle class is roughly identical to the share of Americans who currently possess at least a bachelor's degree. And not for nothing: irrespective of which model one uses, it is overwhelmingly college-degree holders who form the upper-middle class.

19. Reeves 2017a.

20. M. Stewart 2018.

21. Manduca 2018.

22. U.S. Federal Reserve 2023. Chart: Wealth by Income Percentile.

23. See Guzman & Kollar 2023, pp. 6–7, for a breakdown of the household income cutoffs for each quintile.

24. U.S. Federal Reserve 2023. Chart: Wealth by Education.

25. Hernandez-Kent & Ricketts 2022.

26. K. Parker & Stepler 2017; Leonce 2020.

27. Chiappori, Salanic, & Weiss 2017.

28. Brint 1994, p. 122.

29. See K. Weeden 2002 for more on how this process unfolds.

30. E.g., Boar & Lashkari 2021.

31. Grosz et al., forthcoming.

32. Buss et al. 2020.

33. A study by economist Matthew Staiger found that roughly 29 percent of Americans work at the same employer as their parents as they are launching their careers. Individuals with high-earning parents were especially likely to work for their parents' firms. They also received a larger wage premium as a result of nepotism. The nepotism premium was also higher in "skilled service" industries than elsewhere. See Staiger 2022.

34. Jonsson et al. 2009; K. Weeden & Grusky 2012.

35. Vitali, Glattfelder, & Battiston 2011.

36. Unger 2019.

37. J. Scott 2017.

38. Polanyi 2001.

39. Physicians are so unbound to particular physical locations or the necessity to interact directly with patients' bodies that many switched to remote work during the COVID-19 pandemic. As a heuristic, if someone is generally able and permitted to do their job from home, they are probably a symbolic capitalist. It is a narrow range of workers who are empowered to do their jobs remotely—and those workers are almost entirely symbolic capitalists. See DeSilver 2020; Cantor et al. 2021; Rothwell & Crabtree 2021.

Political alignments provide another way to illustrate how physicians are perhaps best understood as symbolic capitalists. Consider the political differences between physicians and surgeons. Both have similar types and levels of training and education; they bring home generous incomes; they work in the same general field (health and medicine), and often in the same buildings; and they share similar socioeconomic and demographic backgrounds on average. And yet, politically speaking, physicians skew decisively Democrat, while surgeons lean overwhelmingly Republican. What's the difference? Well, one key difference is that physicians are more or less symbolic capitalists. Their primary job is to interpret data and charts, to diagnose, to give advice, and to prescribe medications and courses of treatment. Other hospital workers collect and process samples and data from patients' bodies and directly administer interventions when needed—typically *not* physicians. Surgeons, however, are primarily defined in terms of the physical interventions they make on patients' bodies.

Interestingly, this divide in medicine between people who actually intervene on physical bodies and those who diagnose, analyze, and prescribe is a deep rift that goes back to the very foundation of the medical professions. Surgeons (along with dentists et al.) were seen as "lower," precisely in virtue of their physical interventions on bodies; these practitioners resented physicians in turn. It should not be surprising, then, that while the political alignments of physicians roughly parallel those of mainstream symbolic capitalists (i.e., with the Democratic Party), surgeons, dentists, and related professionals overwhelmingly align themselves with their political adversaries. For more on this long-standing divide between physicians and surgeons, see A. Abbott 1988, e.g., p. 77; R. Collins 2019, pp. 184–185. For a resource on the contemporary political divide between physicians and surgeons, see Verdant Labs 2017.

40. Jennifer Day 2019.

41. S. Khan 2012b.

42. In 2022, the median income for full-time year-round U.S. workers was $60,070 (see Guzman & Kollar 2023, fig. 4). Critically, this is an average that *includes* the symbolic professions; an average that excluded symbolic capitalists would be lower still. That is, even "low-paid" symbolic capitalists tend to earn decent money relative to the typical American for comparable hours of work. The incomes of less prestigious symbolic capitalists are primarily "low" *relative to other elites*.

43. Dill 2022.

44. AAUP 2023, Survey Report Table 1 (All AAUP Categories Combined). Same-year National Center for Education Statistics (NCES) estimates of full-time non–tenure line faculty salaries are roughly equivalent to those of the AAUP: https://nces.ed.gov/ipeds/TrendGenerator /app/build-table/5/50?rid=1&cid=161.

45. B. Hughes et al. 2022.

46. AAUP 2023, Survey Report Table 15.

47. Frenette & Ocejo 2018.

48. For more on how managers most aggressively exploit professionals they perceive as highly dedicated, but also interpret willingness to be exploited as a sign of loyalty and dedication (relevant for deciding who to promote, etc.), see Stanley, Neck & Neck 2023.

49. Likewise, as sociologist Julia Ticona aptly demonstrates, although symbolic capitalists and manual laborers both increasingly do "precarious labor," there are *vast* differences in what "precarious labor" actually means in each of these contexts. Despite superficial similarities (and persistent attempts by symbolic capitalists to lump themselves in with the genuinely disadvantaged), elite "precarious labor" is not even remotely analogous to nonelite "precarious labor." See Ticona 2022.

50. Sociological research suggests that contemporary U.S. men do more domestic labor than men did in the 1960s. However, men tend to significantly overestimate their contributions and continue to do significantly less than women. There has not been a radical change in gender roles in the United States—neither in general, nor among highly educated professional couples in particular. See P. England 2010; Yavorsky, Kamp-Dush, & Schoppe-Sullivan 2015; Brenan 2020.

51. Dotti-Sani & Treas 2016.

52. Daminger 2020, p. 806.

53. Sassen 2009.

54. Wolfe et al. 2020.

55. Twenge, Sherman, & Wells 2017.

56. Cunningham & Kendall 2011; Chan, Mojumder, & Ghose 2019.

57. Monto & Milrod 2014.

58. Dank et al. 2014; Robbins 2014. During the COVID-19 pandemic, many "hobbyists" shifted to virtual sex work via platforms like OnlyFans. While these platforms are often portrayed as an easy way for people (especially women) to make large amounts of money side-hustling, reality typically fails to match this rhetoric. The vast majority of performers seem to make little to no money (less than minimum wage when the time spent planning, setting up, executing, editing, and distributing videos is factored in). Many actually operate at a loss (i.e., they spend more on outfits, equipment, etc. in a month than they recoup in "donations"). Others who actually *do* build up a solid audience often end up getting conned into exploitative contracts. See Hollands 2020; G. Friedman 2021; Steadman 2021. As we will see, the realities faced by OnlyFans performers are broadly contiguous with those of other forms of disposable labor that symbolic capitalists consume.

59. Cunningham & Kendall 2016.

60. Columbus 2018; DePillis 2018; Haag & Hu 2019.

61. Lecher 2019.

62. Godlewski 2018; W. Evans 2019.

63. Palmer 2021.

64. Premack 2019.

65. B. O'Connor 2018; Hayley Peterson 2018.

66. Soper 2021.

67. Hollister 2021.

68. Gurley 2021.

69. Strategic Organizing Center 2022.

70. S. Mitchell 2021.

71. Miranda 2018; Mattioli 2020.

72. MacGillis 2021.

73. Kantor, Weise, & Ashford 2021.

74. The demographic patterns associated with Amazon's labor practices are striking. Blacks and Hispanics are dramatically underrepresented in Amazon's white-collar workforce but occupy most of the company's manual labor jobs. Women are underrepresented at all levels of the company but are *drastically* underrepresented in the white-collar workforce. That is, the workers who are willfully exploited and discarded by Amazon tend to be Black or Hispanic, while Amazon's white-collar workforce, who reap windfalls from this labor and are treated much better, are overwhelmingly white (and to a lesser degree Asian) and male. See Greene 2015; Kantor, Weise, & Ashford 2021.

75. Unfortunately for Amazon, its progress toward automation is not keeping pace with the clip at which it is burning through workers. According to a leaked internal memo, the company is on pace to exhaust its entire available labor pool in many locales within the next few years (and in some places within the next year). However, they now estimate that they won't be able to fully automate key positions for another decade. See Bose 2019; Dastin 2019; Del Rey 2022.

76. Yglesias 2018. There are also deep (and growing) social and institutional ties between Amazon and the Democratic Party. See Adler-Bell 2022a.

77. Mahdawi 2018b; Magner 2019.

78. Patton 2019.

79. Maureen Tkacik, 2020.

80. In fact, according to a *Wall Street Journal* analysis, the overwhelming majority of "partners" listed on these sites are included nonconsensually—often in ways that cause harm to their business. These practices are now the subject of a series of class-action lawsuits against food delivery firms, with state and local governments considering legislation to limit the practice as well. Forman 2020; Littman 2021.

81. Moe Tkacik, 2020.

82. Dzieza 2021.

83. Aponte 2021.

84. See U.S. Bureau of Labor Statistics 2021b.

85. Fickenscher 2021.

86. Marcos 2021.

87. C. Benner et al. 2020; Schor 2020.

88. Zipperer et al. 2022.

89. Beyond taxis, public transportation systems (buses, subways, etc.) have taken a hit from the growth of rideshare companies too, leading to cuts in staffing, routes, and maintenance and increased fares—with the costs falling disproportionately on lower-income and minority residents. See Hill 2018.

90. N. Robinson 2018.

91. A 2018 analysis by the Economic Policy Institute found that after expenses, Uber drivers earned on average about $9.21 per hour. While this was higher than the federal minimum wage, it was significantly lower than state minimum wages in areas where Uber is most prolific. Someone working full time at that rate to support a family would fall well below the 2018 federal poverty threshold of $25,100 per year—even without considering heightened cost of living in the cities where Uber is most prominent. See Mishel 2018.

92. Sonnemaker 2020.

93. Akhtar 2019.

94. Horan 2019; Siddiqui & Bensinger 2019.

95. Despite unanticipated obstacles to developing and implementing self-driving cars, rideshare companies have not abandoned hope of one day eliminating their human drivers. Although Uber and Lyft both sold off their internal operations to develop and test these technologies, Lyft

has recently entered into a partnership with Ford Motors and Argo AI to pilot self-driving rides at a large scale in Miami and Austin over the next couple of years. See Subin 2021.

96. Bensinger 2021.

97. Much like rideshares, the business models for delivery apps also tend to be premised on unrealistic projections, and these companies have likewise struggled to become profitable despite how poorly they compensate their workers and the restaurants they "partner" with. Alongside rideshare apps, delivery apps have been forced to significantly raise the artificially low fees they charged consumers for their services—although as with rideshare companies, most of this money seems to be directed to paying off investors and shareholders rather than better supporting their workers or restaurant partners. See Roose 2021.

98. S. O'Connor 2022; Thompson 2022a.

99. Petrzela 2019.

100. Jayaraman 2014.

101. Dixon 2018.

102. Jayaraman 2016.

103. Sassen 2018, pp. 256–257; Morse 2020.

104. Wilmers 2017.

105. Harvey 2012.

106. Hendrix 2017; Sharkey 2018.

107. D. Baldwin 2021.

108. Reaves 2015; Russell-Brown & Miller 2022.

109. Sassen 2018.

110. Florida 2019c.

111. Trounstine 2021. Other studies have found that strong progressives and strong Trump voters tend to express very different views on diversity, but do not *behave* differently with respect to housing and integration. Both demonstrate an especially pronounced desire for social homophily. See Kaufmann 2023.

112. M. Khan 2011.

113. Rigsby 2016; Reeves 2017b; Le Gales & Pierson 2019.

114. Sorens 2018.

115. Wilkinson 2021.

116. D. Cox et al. 2020.

117. Nilforoshan et al. 2023.

118. McKinnish, Walsh, & White 2010. See Edsall 2018 for a roundup of additional studies on this point.

119. E. Sharp 2014; Laniyonu 2018.

120. Legewie & Schaeffer 2016; Stolper 2019.

121. Irwin & Pearl 2020.

122. Levin 2015; Haskins 2019; Silverman 2021.

123. Hogan 2021; Schemmel 2021.

124. See al-Gharbi 2020a for links to the specific incidents alluded to here.

125. Weaver 2018.

126. Hyra 2017.

127. Fry 2022a.

128. Greenwood et al. 2014.

129. Qian 2016; Buss & Schmitt 2019.

130. Bryne & Barling 2017; Rosenfeld 2017; G. Parker et al. 2022.

131. For competing (albeit perhaps reconcilable) perspectives on what is driving these trends, see Hoff-Sommers 2015; Zimbardo & Coulombe 2016; Plank 2021; Power 2022; Reeves 2022. Differential racial dynamics on male declines are also stark. For instance, according to Chetty et al. 2020, contemporary Black-white income gaps seem to be driven almost entirely

by the extraordinary rates of adverse life outcomes among Black *boys and men*. Again, this also has important implications for the marriage and dating prospects of Black *women*, especially as non-Black men in symbolic capitalist circles tend to avoid Black women as dating and marriage partners (relative to females of other races and ethnicities), as will be explored shortly.

132. Belkin 2021.

133. Fry 2022b.

134. Crispin 2018; Rasanen 2023.

135. Strikingly, as men grow in status and wealth, their dating and mating options (and intra-relationship power) tend to significantly improve. Yet despite greater voluntary sexual compliance from more socially desirable partners, men often grow more likely to engage in sexual deception, infidelity, and nonconsensual sexual behaviors (harassment, assault, rape) as their prospects rise—largely due to an increased sense of impunity and entitlement, and a growing desire to dominate others. See Buss 2021.

136. Birger 2015; Reynolds et al. 2023.

137. Greitemeyer 2007.

138. Stoet & Geary 2018.

139. Hopcroft 2021.

140. Although the specific mechanisms through which women are led to select well-paying but suboptimal career paths to maximize their chances on the marriage market are not yet well understood, there is strong evidence from both statistical analyses and experiments that women do seem to avoid maximizing their career success for the sake of preserving their dating and mating prospects. See Bertrand, Kamenica, & Pan 2015; Bursztyn, Fujiwara, & Pallais 2017.

141. Fales 2016.

142. For more on diets and exercise, see Le et al. 2013; Scholes & Bann 2018. With respect to cosmetic procedures, highly educated professional white women who live on the coasts are disproportionately likely (compared with other white women and compared with other demographic groups) to pursue breast augmentation, rhinoplasty, blepharoplasty, abdominoplasty, and minimally invasive procedures (such as Botox, laser hair removal, or fillers). See Schlessinger, Schlessinger, & Schlessinger 2010; American Society of Plastic Surgeons 2021, pp. 22, 24.

143. Mulder 2018.

144. Gordon, Crosnoe, & Wang 2014.

145. Monk, Esposito, & Lee 2021.

146. Judge, Hurst, & Simon 2009.

147. Sociologist Elizabeth Currid-Halkett has found that denizens of symbolic capital hubs tend to spend significantly more on clothes, shoes, and personal care services than most other Americans. Historian Natalia Petrzela has shown that "fitness" culture was in many respects a byproduct of the rise of symbolic professions, and broadly reflects their culture of discipline, hard work, meritocracy, and so on. See Currid-Halkett 2018, chap. 6 (particularly pp. 169–181); Petrzela 2020.

148. Harrold, Miller, & Perkins 2023.

149. Wade 2018.

150. Serena Smith 2020; Petrarca 2021. Alongside "woke fishing," there is the increasingly common phenomenon of the "woke misogynist": men who present themselves as exceptionally "woke" on gender issues even as they treat women exceptionally terribly in interpersonal relationships (see Aronwitz 2017). As we will discuss in more detail in later chapters, the tendency among some men to publicly present themselves as "feminist" on the one hand and the tendency to treat women terribly in personal interactions on the other hand are behavioral patterns that may not be independent of one another. They may actually be mutually enhancing.

151. M. Iqbal 2021.

152. Klofstad, McDermott, & Hatemi 2012. There are strong asymmetries along the lines of party and gender: women and Democrats (and *especially* female Democrats) are far less willing

to date someone who supports the other party than those who are Republican or men; e.g., N. Rothschild 2021.

153. Sawhill & Venator 2015; Lichter, Price, & Swigert 2019. As challenging as it seems to be for non-college-educated Black women or non-Black college-educated women to find an acceptable partner, the effects are especially pronounced among college-educated Black women. In many elite spaces, eligible Black men are quite rare. Moreover, analyses of dating website data show that non-Black men seem to actively avoid Black women as potential romantic partners—irrespective of these women's education, socioeconomic status, and so on. See Rudder 2015, pp. 105–124.

It deserves to be emphasized: the men who demonstrate this antipathy toward Black women on dating apps tend to be symbolic capitalists (again, they are among the primary users of dating apps writ large), who tend to identify as politically progressive and antiracist. As Amia Srinivasan (2018) aptly put it, "No one is obligated to desire anyone else, . . . no one has a right to be desired, but also . . . who is desired and who isn't is a political question, a question usually answered by more general patterns of domination and exclusion."

154. D. Cox 2023.

155. Ge, Isaac, & Miller 2019; Shenav 2021.

156. Cernik 2021.

157. Inhorn 2023.

158. Newport 2018; J. Jones 2021a.

159. D. Compton & Bridges 2019.

160. A. Brown 2019.

161. Kaufmann 2022.

162. Florida 2019c, pp. 237–245. Moreover, although the competition for partners is far more intense, highly educated and professionally successful heterosexual women also stand a better chance of finding an acceptable partner in a symbolic hub than virtually anywhere else. See J. Compton & Pollak 2007.

163. Tilcsik, Anteby, & Knight 2015; Danielle Taylor 2019.

164. Klawitter 2015.

165. Barroso & Fry 2021.

166. Mazrekaj, De Witte, & Cabus 2020.

167. W. Wang 2015; K. Parker & Stepler 2017.

168. By "traditional family" I am referring to a situation in which children are produced within the confines of a marriage and raised by their genetic parents (or adopted parents), whose marriage persists throughout the children's youth. Symbolic capitalists are much more likely to be raised in circumstances like these, and to raise their own children in the same. Even in the event of divorce, which is less likely among symbolic capitalists, children generally still end up being raised in stable two-parent homes, as their guardians tend to remarry, and the subsequent marriages tend to "stick" (as opposed to less educated households, where parents more often go through a sequence of ill-fated marriages or cohabitation relationships while their children are growing up). See K. Parker et al. 2015; Finkel 2019; Reeves & Pulliam 2020.

169. Kearney 2023. There is a growing body of literature that indicates that family structure is especially influential on young *men*: those who were not raised by their biological mother and father are several times more likely to drop out of school, engage in criminal behaviors, and experience many other adverse outcomes. These negative effects are much less pronounced among young women. See Reeves 2022.

170. Cahn & Carbone 2011, pp. 3–4.

171. Henderson 2019a, 2022.

172. Chetty et al. 2017. Black and Hispanic students and students of lower socioeconomic status are especially likely to attend for profit colleges and land-grant state universities rather than elite private schools that symbolic economy employers often prefer.

173. E.g., Brint & Yoshikawa 2017; Wermund 2017.

174. Notes on the data for table 3.7:

- Data on the gender, racial, and ethnic composition of U.S. faculty are derived from NCES estimates of 2021 employees (https://nces.ed.gov/ipeds/TrendGenerator/app/build-table/5/51?rid=162&cid=165), the latest year available at time of writing. To ensure apples-to-apples comparisons, estimates of the demographic characteristics of the broader U.S. public are derived from same-year NCES estimates (https://nces.ed.gov/programs/digest/d21/tables/dt21_101.20.asp).

- Data on the sexual orientation of faculty members are provided by the Higher Education Research Institute, looking at faculty from the 2016–2017 academic year (the latest HERI faculty survey report published at time of writing): Stolzenberg et al. 2019. Estimates of the sexual orientations of U.S. adults more broadly derived from same-year estimates by Gallup (J. Jones 2021a). Data on the political ideologies of faculty are from 2019 HERI data, presented in Oswal 2021, table 1. Estimates of baseline ideological identifications among U.S. adults based on same-year estimates by Gallup (Saad 2020).

- The most reliable source for religious identification of U.S. faculty was from Gross & Simmons 2009. Estimates for the broader population were derived from the same-year American Religious Identification Survey (Kosmin & Keysar 2009). Critically, as discussed in chapter 1, symbolic capitalists have secularized over the last decade at a far higher rate than the general public. As a consequence, this table is likely to significantly *under*estimate the current religious gaps between professors and the U.S. public.

175. For a deep dive into disparities within the professoriate, and the primary causes of these disparities, see al-Gharbi 2023d.

176. Myers 2016.

177. Li & Koedel 2017; Silbert & Dube 2021.

178. Al-Gharbi 2020g; Zhang, Ehrenberg, & Liu 2021.

179. Oswal 2021.

180. Morgan et al. 2022.

181. Chetty et al. 2017; Wapman et al. 2022.

182. Willnat, Weaver, & Wilhoit 2017, chap. 3. Even as journalists became much more likely to possess a degree than in years past, the range of courses they study, and the range of institutions journalists graduate from, has grown more constrained. Today a majority of journalists possess degrees in journalism or communications—that is, they have little substantive knowledge or expertise other than how to write. This was not the case in previous periods.

183. J. Stewart 2014.

184. Matsa 2017; Abernathy 2018, pp. 30–45.

185. Shafer & Doherty 2017; Walker 2021.

186. GDELT Project 2018; Grieco 2019.

187. Hopkins 2018. The nationalization of politics may contribute to growing political extremism as well: nationalized media tends to be far more ideologically extreme than local media. See Hassell, Miles, & Reuning 2021.

188. Willnat, Weaver, & Wilhoit 2022, p. 11.

189. For more on the long line of research showing journalists tilt toward Democrats in voting even more than in their expressed affiliation, see Noyes 2004.

190. Forman-Katz & Jurkowitz 2022.

191. Rosentiel et al. 2021.

192. Furnas & LaPira 2024.

193. Martin 2019.

194. Wai & Perina 2018.

195. McCready 2016.

196. Amiri et al. 2019.

197. R. Benson & Pickard 2017; Schwab 2020. As political scientist Daniel Drezner (2017) observed, conflicts of interest like these have become endemic to the "ideas industry" writ large.

198. For a good exploration of how corruption can play out—including (perhaps especially) among the highly principled and well intentioned—see Lessing 2018, pp. 139–149.

199. The American Society of News Editors' 2019 Newspaper Diversity Study provides a tool that allows users to explore the composition of newsrooms along the lines of race and gender, compared with the U.S. public and the communities they are embedded in, for both staff and leadership (American Society of News Editors, n.d.).

A recent analysis by Axios shows that radio newsroom employees tend to be even less diverse than newspaper companies. Television newsrooms are a bit better, although still far from reflecting the general population. See S. Chen & Contreras 2021.

200. D. Lu et al. 2021. This same report found that literally *all* of the people at the top of the "Big Five" publishing houses and the ten most read magazines in the United States are white. Seventy-three percent of this group was male also.

201. Alex Williams 2015.

202. J. Gottfried et al. 2022.

203. Usher 2021.

204. Lauzen 2021b.

205. Lauzen 2021a.

206. J. Lu et al. 2020.

207. Gallagher 2019; Perman 2019.

208. Borowiecki & Dahl 2021; Topaz et al. 2022.

209. Frenette, Martin, & Tepper 2018.

210. Grodach, Foster, & Murdoch 2018.

211. Sodd 2016; Ehrenhalt 2018; Ritchie 2019.

212. O'Sullivan 2014; Gamerman 2020.

213. Florida 2017, p. 37.

214. Florida 2017, p. 38.

215. Wu & Thompson 2019; Douek 2020; Ghaffary & Del Rey 2020; Rivero 2021.

216. A. Bell et al. 2019.

217. Tech entrepreneurs tend to skew left on most issues but staunchly oppose government regulation or oversight, especially of their specific industries. See Bacon 2018.

218. Molla 2018.

219. Lee, Burn-Murdoch, & Kantor 2020.

220. E.g., Zetlin 2016; K. Benner 2017; Kapin 2020.

221. Folke & Rickne 2022.

222. Weise & Guynn 2014.

223. Gruman 2020.

224. Goldin 2014; C. Miller 2017.

Chapter 4. Postmaterialist Politics

1. Stebbins 2018; Manduca 2019; Burrows 2020.

2. A. Yang 2018.

3. Dougherty et al. 2018; Florida 2019b.

4. Korte 2021.

5. M. Thomas 2022.

6. Zacher 2023.

7. E.g., Mayer 2017.

8. Rachel Cohen 2021.

9. Badger, Quealy, & Katz 2021.

10. J. Brown & Enos 2021; Wezerek, Enos, & Brown 2021. Notably, Enos and his coauthors found that twice as many Democrats as Republicans live in political bubbles.

11. Galka 2017; Sassen 2018, pp. 235–272.

12. Aaron Williams & Emamdjomeh 2018.

13. Cowen 2017, p.57.

14. J. Cohn 2012; P. Cohen 2015; McCann 2021.

15. Not only are the relatively well off much more likely to itemize charitable deductions, but in virtue of their falling into higher tax brackets, government revenues are drained much more by write-offs from these taxpayers than those from the lower and middle classes. According to an analysis by the Tax Policy Center (2018, p. 262), each dollar in charitable donations from the bottom 60 percent of the income distribution reduced the federal government's income by less than four cents. However, the cost to the government of every charitable dollar increases rapidly in the upper quintiles. At the pinnacle of the distribution, each "philanthropic" dollar from someone in the top 1 percent of earners reduced government funds by thirty-two cents. The Tax Policy Center estimates that charitable donations cost the federal government around $44 billion in tax revenues for 2018 alone, overwhelmingly via deductions from people making $100,000 per year or more. And of course, state governments also take a hit insofar as they allow charitable deductions on their taxes too (most do). See Tax Policy Center 2018; Williamson 2019.

16. Piff et al. 2010; Cote et al. 2015; Zinsmeister 2016; Davis et al. 2017.

17. Callahan 2018.

18. Out of the one thousand largest charitable foundations in the United States, the overwhelming majority (90 percent) dedicate less than half of their grant dollars to directly assisting underserved communities. Overall, underserved communities receive less than one-third of all charitable foundation funding. See Schlegal 2016.

Perhaps the most striking aspect of these statistics is the broad and inclusive definition of "underserved communities" utilized in the study: domestic workers, economically disadvantaged people, immigrants and refugees, incarcerated and formerly incarcerated people, LGBTQ people, people of color, people with disabilities, people with HIV/AIDS, sex workers, women and girls, or victims of crime and abuse (Schlegal 2016, appendix A). All of these groups *combined* receive less than a third of all U.S. charitable foundation funding—and the vast majority of American charitable foundations dedicate less than half of their grants to helping *any* of these groups, individually or collectively.

19. Stern 2013.

20. E. Jaffe 2014; Toloudi 2016.

21. Ehrenreich 2021, p. 221.

22. U.S. Census Bureau 2020a.

23. McCann 2023.

24. U.S. Bureau of Economic Analysis 2021.

25. L. Fox 2020. The Supplemental Poverty Measure includes government subsidies people receive as income but also deducts from said income things like housing, food, and utilities (and geographical fluctuations of these). It is a more comprehensive estimate of an individual's financial standing than the standard poverty measure. See L. Fox 2020, p. 2, for elaboration.

After California (17.2 percent poverty rate), the five states with the highest percentages of people in poverty, according to the Supplemental Poverty Measure, were Washington, DC (16.7 percent); Louisiana (16.2 percent); Florida (15.4 percent); Mississippi (15.2 percent); and New York (14.4 percent). See appendix table 5 of the report (L. Fox 2020, pp. 29–30) for the complete list.

What is striking is that unlike Mississippi or Louisiana, California, Florida, New York, and Washington, DC, are some of the richest states in terms of real GDP: New York is ranked number three and Florida number four. The GDP for Washington, DC, is more complex, as much of the revenue generated in the broader DC area is counted in the stats for Maryland and Virginia. Each of these symbolic hubs, however, has an extraordinarily high rate of poverty despite immense wealth (and, excepting Florida, an overwhelmingly blue voting base).

26. Paul & Wong 2020. Note: similar legislation is being developed in other decisively blue knowledge economy hubs like Massachusetts and New York. See Press 2021.

27. E. Klein 2021.

28. J. Jones 2019.

29. Uttaro 2020.

30. U.S. Census Bureau 2020b.

31. Kucsera & Orfield 2014.

32. J. Harris & Appelbaum 2021.

33. Berman 2021.

34. S. Khan 2012a, pp. 480–481.

35. As individuals become more financially secure, they grow increasingly concerned about symbolic capital. At the macro level, as societies become more affluent, they tend to gravitate toward "postmaterialist" values and priorities. See Inglehart 2018.

36. Callahan 2018.

37. Pinsker 2018.

38. C. Anderson, Hildreth, & Sharps 2020; Z. Wang, Jetten, & Steffens 2020.

39. Ridgeway 2019, p. 60.

40. Avery & Greenwald 2023, p. 148.

41. In small, relatively egalitarian societies, people often had nonidentical—but reciprocal and complementary—rights and duties, roles, and responsibilities. This allowed everyone to enjoy roughly similar levels of status *overall*, even if there were inequalities in particular domains. However, it is difficult to scale this model up beyond a certain size.

Moreover, even in roughly egalitarian societies, there was generally a strong distinction made between societal "insiders" and those who were "outsiders"—wherein the former enjoyed much higher status than the latter (who were generally exempt from enjoying the same privileges and protections that insiders enjoyed).

That is, societies that were *internally* egalitarian tended to be premised on treating "others" as lesser. This is how they built and maintained their *collective* status and identity. See Bowles & Gintis 2013.

The moral: status is pretty much always achieved at someone else's expense.

42. Most people do not strive to be "high" status—and some actively avoid high-status positions in order to avoid the costs typically entailed with occupying those roles. In fact, many are content with being "low" in status in society as a whole, so long as they feel accepted and included within their local context and are able to "get by" all right in terms of their material needs. See Leary, Jongman-Sereno, & Diebels 2014, p. 168. However, for those whose aspirations, lives, and livelihoods *are* oriented around symbolic capital, satisfaction and security often prove elusive—and transient when attained—frequently giving rise to anxiety, restlessness, and resentment.

43. Shema 2012; Eveleth 2014; Remler 2014.

44. Ogunwole et al. 2021; Millot 2023.

45. Schonfeld 2016.

46. Ellenberg 2014.

47. Fiorina 2016; Doctor 2017.

48. Pew Research Center 2023.

49. U.S. Census Bureau 2023.

50. L. Owen 2022.

51. Doctor 2016; Glancey 2021.

52. Prior 2013; Pew Research Center 2021.

53. Allen et al. 2020.

54. Cava 2022.

55. Richter 2018.

56. Nielsen 2021.

57. Auxier & Anderson 2021; Perrin & Atske 2021.

58. McGrady et al. 2023.

59. Freehan 2021; Al-Qudsi 2023.

60. McClain 2021.

61. Knight Foundation & Gallup 2022.

62. Bor & Petersen 2021; Mamakos & Finkel 2023.

63. Wojcik & Hughes 2019.

64. McClain et al. 2021.

65. Dang 2022.

66. Kantrowitz 2023.

67. A. Hughes 2019.

68. Bestvater et al. 2022, p. 17.

69. Hebbelstrup, Osmundsen, & Petersen 2022.

70. Einwohner & Rochford 2019.

71. Praet et al. 2021.

72. Y.-C. Wang, Burke, & Kraut 2013; Park et al. 2016; Gramlich 2021.

73. Knights 2010; Wellmon 2016; U.S. National Archives & Records Administration 2021.

74. Currid-Halkett 2018, p. 18.

75. McPherson, Smith-Lovin, & Cook 2001; Smith, McPherson, & Smith-Lovin 2014.

76. Smirnov & Turner 2017.

77. Kuppens et al. 2018.

78. Tannock 2008.

79. E.g., al-Gharbi 2018b.

80. E.g., Morozov 2013.

81. Mercier 2020.

82. Bernstein 2021; B. Smith 2021; Adler-Bell 2022b; Yglesias 2022b.

83. Altay & Acerbi 2023.

84. A. Hughes 2017; Fisher et al. 2019; Hansen & Tyner 2019.

85. Superti 2015; C. Johnston, Lavine, & Federico 2017; Hersh 2020.

86. Somin 2016.

87. Atir, Rosennzweig, & Dunning 2015.

88. Stanovich 2021, p. 96.

89. E.g., Malka, Lelkes, & Soto 2017.

90. Rockey 2014, p. 12.

91. Manstead 2018. Likewise, Natasha Warikoo's *The Diversity Bargain* documents how aspiring symbolic capitalists from institutionally dominant groups are typically eager to support diversity and inclusion in self-interested and instrumental ways—to enhance their own reputations, to bolster their creativity, and so on. However, they tend to sour on diversity quickly when it doesn't clearly advance their own preexisting aims, commitments, and priorities—and especially when it seems to threaten them. See Warikoo 2016.

92. Wodtke 2016. Relatedly, see Glasford 2022.

93. Storme, Celik, & Myszkowski 2021. Creatives are also more likely to behave unethically in part because they tend to feel entitled—and are often institutionally empowered—to behave according to a different set of rules from "normies." See Vincent & Kouchaki 2015.

94. Yudkin, Hawkins, & Dixon 2019.

95. RePass 2008; Kinder & Kalmoe 2017. See also Hawkins et al. 2018.

96. Brocic & Miles 2021.

97. Chinoy et al. 2023, fig. 3.

98. Whiten & Byrne 1997; Clark & Winegard 2020.

99. Baldassarri & Gelman 2008; Doherty et al. 2016.

100. Bakker, Lelkes, & Malka 2020; P. Jones 2020.

101. P. Jones 2023.

102. Kahan et al. 2012, 2017; Kahan 2013; Kahan & Corbin 2016.

103. Henry & Napier 2017; Ganzach & Schul 2021.

104. Al-Gharbi 2019a; J. Gibson & Sutherland 2021.

105. Karpinski et al. 2018; al-Gharbi 2023c.

106. Hatemi & McDermott 2016; Flynn, Nyhan, & Reifler 2017.

107. Taber & Lodge 2006; Robson 2019; Rekker 2021.

108. Joslyn & Haider-Markel 2014; Drummond & Fischhoff 2017; Guay & Johnston 2021.

109. Tetlock 2006. See also Tetlock & Gardner 2016.

110. See K. Milkman et al. 2021, p. 482. Although participants across the board tended to be bad at predicting the effects of behavioral science interventions, lay respondents tended to be far more accurate in their predictions than academics in the field or behavioral science practitioners.

111. Carnes & Lupu 2016.

112. Manza & Brooks 1999, p. 5.

113. Professionals and managers didn't just shift on "culture issues." They also shifted left on economics (i.e., confidence in business vs. labor unions, wealth redistribution, government spending on poverty)—although they continue to lean more right on pocketbook matters than blue-collar voters. In any case, precisely as a function of the growing *convergence* between blue-collar workers and professionals on economic issues, it seems clear that cultural issues are driving the *polarization* observed between these groups. See Brint, Curran, & Mahutga 2022.

114. Goodman 2006.

115. S. Khan 2015a.

116. Mansfield & Mutz 2009; Aaron Smith & Anderson 2017; B. Zhang & Dafoe 2019; Younis 2020.

117. Carr 2017.

118. Ellis & Stimson 2012; Drutman 2017.

119. J. Abbott et al. 2021.

120. Gelman 2009. See also B. Page, Bartels, & Seawright 2013.

121. Kuziemko, Marx, & Naidu 2023.

122. R. Collins 2019, p. 5.

123. N. Cohn 2021.

124. Zingher 2022.

125. Callahan 2010.

126. Yglesias 2022a.

127. Piketty 2021.

128. Al-Gharbi 2020d.

129. Florida 2018.

130. Yglesias 2020.

131. Illing 2021.

132. Enos & Hersh 2015; Ward 2021.

133. Interestingly, while messaging from the Republican Party itself has moved away from academic language, right-aligned symbolic capitalist spaces nonetheless seem to be growing *more* academic alongside their mainstream peers. Of course, they are largely drawing on very different intellectual traditions. These days, right-aligned symbolic capitalists seem to be doing deep cuts into nationalist, fascist, and otherwise nonliberal thought. However, strikingly, right-wing symbolic capitalists are increasingly putting these works into conversation with left-aligned scholars like Antonio Gramsci and Michel Foucault! See Baskin 2019; Beiner 2021; A. White 2021.

134. Fiorina 2017.

135. Rauch 2019.

136. Mason 2018.

137. Finkel et al. 2020.

138. Abramowitz & Webster 2018.

139. Kafka & Kostis 2021.

140. B. Friedman 2006; Burgess et al. 2021.

141. E.g., Florida 2019c.

142. Cauwels & Sornette 2022.

143. Dourado 2020.

144. Ip 2016.

145. M. Park, Leahey, & Funk 2023.

146. Bhattacharya & Packalen 2020.

147. Lindsey & Teles 2017.

148. Horgan 2015; Robert Gordon 2017; S. Alexander 2018; Bloom et al. 2020.

149. Chu & Evans 2021.

150. Arora et al. 2019.

151. Arora et al. 2020.

152. Feyerabend 2010; Taleb 2016a (see pp. 187–200, 217–238); Taleb 2016b (see pp. 165–189).

153. Kuhn 1996; Azoulay, Fons-Rosen, & Graff Zivin 2019.

154. Foster, Rzhetsky, & Evans 2015; Rzhetsky 2015; S. MacDonald 2023.

155. R. Levine & Rubinstein 2017. These attributes among entrepreneurs are connected to one another: coming from a wealthy, highly educated, and well-connected family helps render risky behavior profitable and decreases the chances of risks proving ruinous. See al-Gharbi 2016d.

156. Guo & Leung 2021.

157. Barker 2017.

158. E.g., A. Binder, Davis, & Bloom 2015.

159. Cowen 2015.

160. Naude 2019. Indeed, contrary to our national mythology, America's rich are far *less* likely than most others in the world to have generated their wealth through entrepreneurship. See al-Gharbi 2016d for more on this.

161. Mastroianni 2022.

162. Gioia 2022; Thompson 2022b.

163. Mastroianni 2022.

164. See Borowiecki & Dahl 2021; B. Cooper 2021.

165. Chomsky 2002; see pp. 111–115, 233–242.

166. Longitudinal measures of creativity in the United States show stagnation and decline in creativity corresponding with the rise of the symbolic economy, with particularly significant declines since 1990. See K. Kim 2011.

167. Caplan 2018.

168. National Writers Union 2006.

169. J. Schmidt 2001, pp. 40–41.

170. Golden 2015; Huizar 2019; 32BJ SEIU et al. 2019.

171. Lufkin 2021.

172. M. Stewart 2021, pp. 130–131.

173. S. Jaffe 2021. See also Nietfeld 2021.

174. Horowitz & Parker 2023. This report finds that workers with higher levels of education are also far more likely than others to do work-related tasks in their downtime.

175. T. Frank 1997; Anne Moore 2007.

176. Corner 2013.

177. Mukherjee & Banet-Weiser 2012; Mahdawi 2018a; Savage 2020.

178. Abad-Santos 2018; Coaston 2018.

179. Holder 2017; N. Iqbal 2019; E. Stewart 2021.

180. Cass 2021; Roth et al. 2021.

181. Hersh & Shah 2023a, 2023b.

182. Marx & Engels 1978, p. 476.

183. The aforementioned points of overlap between capitalism and identitarianism on the *left* have long been a cause of hostility toward free market capitalism on the right. The "fusionist" project (which sought to unite conservatives, libertarians, and anticommunist liberals under the Republican banner) has always been unstable, precisely because many on the right have recognized that unrestrained capitalism is anathema to the very idea of "conservatism." See Ahmari et al. 2019; C. Gonzalez 2019a.

184. Benn Michaels & Reed 2020.

185. C. Smith 2014, pp. 7–8.

186. C. Smith 2014, pp. 13–14.

187. Shin 2023.

188. Franklin 2022.

189. Donovan 2020.

190. E.g., S. Page 2019.

191. Hsieh et al. 2019.

192. Ember 2020.

193. Fan 2019; Wuest 2022.

194. Rossi & Taiwo 2020.

195. Ashkenas, Park, & Pearce 2017.

196. Reeves & Joo 2017.

197. Rodrigue & Reeves 2015; Winship et al. 2021.

198. Chetty et al. 2020; Moss et al. 2020.

Chapter 5. Totemic Capital(ism)

1. Fassin & Rechtman 2009.

2. Simon 2009.

3. Scheeringa 2022.

4. B. Campbell & Manning 2014, 2018.

5. Hickman 2022. Reinforcing Hickman's argument, research finds that people who score high on "Dark Triad" traits (narcissism, Machiavellianism, psychopathy) are especially likely to paint themselves as virtuous victims or portray themselves as champions of the same: e.g., Ok et al. 2021; Bertrams & Krispenz 2023.

6. Schulman 2016.

7. Political scientist Richard Hanania has provocatively argued that many men who hyperbolically compare proponents of "wokeness" to Adolf Hitler, Joseph Stalin, Mao Zedong, and others seem to *wish* they were being confronted by actual totalitarians, because that would be easier than acknowledging the real challenge they face: the feminization of institutions they belong to, and increased intersex competition (which men are increasingly losing). See Hanania 2022b.

8. Hays 2013.

9. Benenson 2022.

10. Benenson & Markovits 2023.

11. For good roundups of the literature on these topics, see Benenson & Markovits 2014; Liesen 2017; Clark & Winegard 2022; Edsall 2022.

12. For more on how a willful embrace of patently false and facially absurd claims often serves as a way of signaling in-group commitment or moral virtue, see Tosi & Warmke 2020; Storr 2021; Henderson 2022.

13. N. Saad 2021.

14. Rumore & Brinson 2019; BBC 2022.

15. S. Newman 2017; Kay 2018; Reilly 2019.

16. Moghe 2022.

17. L. Bazelon 2022; Donaldson & Bennett 2022.

18. Syal 2022.

19. See Kaufman 2020 for a good summary of the empirical research on these points.

20. Gray & Wegner 2009.

21. For some good roundups of the literature on this topic, see MacLellan 2016; Piff & Robinson 2016; Useem 2017; Pike & Galinsky 2020.

22. For a survey of the empirical literature on this point, see al-Gharbi 2023c, specifically the section "Did the 'Great Awakening' Significantly Exacerbate Psychological Distress in Liberals?"

23. Jordan & Kouchaki 2021.

24. Perhaps counterintuitively, the tendency to blame the poor for their poverty may be especially prevalent among people who have, themselves, achieved upward social mobility. Rather than sympathizing with others who are struggling like they used to, many assume that others must be failing to advance like they did because they are too lazy, unambitious, cowardly, weak, and so on. If their own social mobility was earned, then others' relative stagnation or declines must be earned as well. See Koo, Piff, & Shariff 2022.

25. Rorty 1999, pp. 79–80.

26. Isenberg 2017.

27. For more on this point, see al-Gharbi 2024.

28. For unfamiliar readers, BIPOC is an attempt to center those perceived to be the most disadvantaged racial and ethnic groups upfront—Black and Indigenous Americans—followed by other "people of color."

BAME is roughly the same as BIPOC, configured for the U.K. context. It stands for "Black, Asian, and minority ethnic." In 2022, the U.K. national government, the British Broadcasting Company, and others declared that they will no longer use this umbrella term, precisely because it obscures more than it elucidates about who is disadvantaged in the United Kingdom and how. It is also a term that the people it is supposed to empower largely reject themselves (see Race Disparity Unit 2022). Similar realities hold for BIPOC (and POC), but in American symbolic capitalist spaces, these umbrella terms are still going strong.

29. E.g., Horace Mann School, n.d.

30. Demographic data for all New York City nonpublic schools are available in New York State Education Department 2023, with archives that go back to the year 2000.

31. Roughly three out of every four Americans who identify as "multiracial" have a white parent. Those hailing from highly educated families are still more likely to have a white parent. People who are multiracial in this way tend to have socioeconomic profiles and outcomes that are much closer to whites' than to the profiles of others in the minority group they also identify with. Their social networks, residential patterns, and lifestyles are likewise often much closer to those of whites than to those of most members of their other ethnic identification. See Alba 2020, 2021.

32. For a deep dive into the history of American imperialism against Asians abroad, and the marginalization and exploitation of Asians within the United States, see al-Gharbi 2022.

33. Yam 2021. Other research has found that declines in anti-Asian prejudice have been the primary factor behind their extraordinary upward mobility compared with other groups. See Hilger 2016.

34. Kang 2019; Lu, Nisbett, & Morris 2020.

35. Critically, although most Asian subpopulations earn more than non-Hispanic whites and enjoy higher levels of educational attainment, there are exceptions. Overall, income inequality in the United States is more pronounced among Asian Americans than among any other racial or ethnic group. Likewise, although many Asian American subpopulations are more likely than

most to attain high levels of education, Asian Americans who do *not* obtain at least a BA tend to do worse on average than comparably educated whites. See Sakamoto & Kim 2013; C. Kim & Sakamoto 2014; Kochhar & Cilluffo 2018.

36. Al-Gharbi 2020f.

37. Much as with Asian Americans, there are some systematic exceptions to Middle Easterners outperforming whites. Although most Middle Eastern subpopulations have rates of educational attainment that are equivalent to or above the national average, U.S. Census Bureau data reveal that a few have median household incomes that fall significantly below average—most notably Moroccans, Iraqis, and Afghans.

38. Massey et al. (2007) estimate that 30–40 percent of "Black" students at private schools are of immigrant backgrounds—overwhelmingly from African or Afro-Caribbean countries. The more selective the school, the higher the concentration of Black immigrants. At Ivy League schools, for instance, they estimate 40 percent of all Black students come from an immigrant background. Additionally, about 16 percent of the nonimmigrant Black students at these schools (roughly 10 percent of all Black college students in the United States) are mixed race.

Espenshade & Radford (2009) estimate that only about 41 percent of Black students at private universities are "Descendants"—defined as people who belong to the fourth or higher immigrant generation and who are not multiracial (p. 105). Moreover, they find that universities have come to increasingly favor immigrant background and mixed-race Blacks—whom they label "Vanguards"—over time. In the 1980s, 40 percent of Black students were Vanguards; by 1993, 49 percent were. By 1998, 58 percent of Black students were Vanguards (pp. 149–150). Today, the ratio is likely higher still—in part due to the fact that both the multiracial Black and immigrant populations are growing among the Black population, and in part because there does not seem to be a significant change in the other factors driving this concentration.

According to Pew estimates, 13 percent of America's Black population are Hispanic or mixed race (with 87 percent monoracial). Twenty-one percent are first- or second-generation Americans (with 79 percent third generation or higher). In short, Vanguards are highly overrepresented at colleges and universities. Descendants, who are roughly seven out of ten Black people in America, are significantly underrepresented.

Critically, this is just looking at college attendance. There are likely further disparities in graduation rates as well. Black students tend to drop out of college at significantly higher rates than virtually any other block of students. Just 40 percent of Black students—only a third of Black *men* who start college—graduate with a BA within six years (de Brey et al. 2019, p. 138). The same factors that contribute to Vanguards attending college at significantly higher rates than Descendants likely help them graduate at significantly higher rates as well. Hence the percentage of Blacks *possessing a degree* (and, consequently, participating in the symbolic professions) is likely significantly more heavily skewed in favor of immigrant and multiracial Blacks than the enrollment rates (which are already heavily tilted).

Across the board, lighter skin tone is strongly related to socioeconomic success for Black Americans. See Massey et al. 2007; Espenshade & Radford 2009; Tamir 2021; Tamir & Anderson 2022.

39. Logan & Deane 2003; K. Thomas 2011.

40. Alba 2021.

41. For instance, according to 2019 U.S. Census Bureau American Community Survey estimates, the median household income in the 2021 survey was $69,717. Black Americans overall had household incomes of around $46,774. However, many Black immigrant populations tended to be around or above the U.S. median (i.e., they had household incomes roughly 49 percent larger than the typical Black household—or more). A nonexhaustive list of these subgroups includes South Africans, Kenyans, Nigerians, Tanzanians, Ghanaians, Guyanese, West Indians, Trinidadians and Tobagonians, Barbadians, and Jamaicans.

These groups also tended to have education rates at or significantly above the national average. This, too, is in sharp contrast with broader trends among Black Americans. The overall share of African Americans who possess a degree is significantly lower than the national average (about

10 full percentage points lower)—and this is a statistic that *includes* immigrant and multiracial Blacks.

In short, there are vast differences in socioeconomic and educational outcomes between immigrant and mixed-race Blacks as compared with nonimmigrant monoracial Blacks.

42. W. Bowen & Bok 2000. Blacks at highly selective schools who do not themselves come from relatively affluent or highly educated socioeconomic backgrounds are typically what sociologist Anthony Jack calls the "privileged poor": students who, despite modest means, managed to secure admission into elite K–12 schools (supported by student aid throughout). See Jack 2019.

43. Similar patterns hold for Hispanics and other racial and ethnic groups as well: those with lighter skin tone enjoy better treatment, perceptions, and socioeconomic outcomes than darker-skinned coethnics. See Gonzalez-Barrera 2019; Monk 2021.

44. Hannon, DeFina, & Bruch 2013; M. Bennett & Plaut 2018; Monk 2019.

45. M. Hunter 2007; Gardner 2020.

46. For good roundups of research on this point, see Hannon 2015; Bagalini 2020.

47. Kochhar & Cilluffo 2018.

48. Cashin 2021.

49. Kaufmann 2022. See also Mittleman 2023.

50. Wolfinger 2023.

51. Historically, most seeking to transition from one gender to another have been males seeking to become women. Since the mid-2000s, this pattern has reversed. Among young people especially, the growth in trans identification is led overwhelmingly by biological females. This growth has also been driven much more heavily by whites than other groups. See Zucker 2017; Lagos 2022.

In terms of socioeconomic background, the *New York Times* reports, "Most of the young people today who come to [gender] clinics for treatment are affluent and white, live in progressive metropolitan areas and have health insurance." However, it should be emphasized that these latter patterns may result in part from the fact that people who live in other places, and hail from other backgrounds, simply have less access to gender-affirming care. See E. Bazelon 2022.

52. Kirzinger et al. 2023.

53. Analyzing the rapid rise of apparently straight people self-identifying as "queer," journalist Katie Herzog (2020) argued that the meaning of the term seems to have "expanded to include basically anyone who has anything other than penis-in-vagina missionary-position sex. 'Queer' has become less and less a descriptor of who you sleep with than a way of signaling one's political ideology."

54. In addition to the sources cited in the "Sex and Symbolic Capital" section of chapter 3, see Morton et al. 2018; Badgett, Choi, & Wilson 2019.

55. J. Jones 2023; Schlott 2023.

56. Hughey 2012a.

57. Bayer & Charles 2018.

58. W. Wilson 1981, p. 126.

59. When people are made to confront the ways they benefit from inequalities, they often attempt to associate themselves with marginal identities and paint themselves as victims of bias or oppression. See Riana Brown & Craig 2020.

60. E.g., C. Malone 2023; Nair 2023.

61. Some, perhaps most notably legal scholar Nancy Leong, have attempted to capture the idea of "totemic capital" under the rubric of "identity capitalism." However, "identity capital" is already a term in wide use in the corporate and nonprofit sphere, with a significantly different meaning from the one intended by Leong (her book is focused on the same phenomenon explored in this section: how elites exploit identification with marginalized groups in order to shore up their own elite position). "Totemic capital" is a phrase that is not yet in use. It is also, in my view, a more apt description for the phenomenon under consideration. Nonetheless, readers are encouraged to see Leong 2021 for her analysis of "identity capitalism."

62. Durkheim 2008.

63. It was relatively recently, in the mid-twentieth century, that race, gender, class, religion, sexuality, and so on came to be widely understood and discussed as the same "type" of thing—social identities—which intersect *within individuals* in unique ways and serve as the basis for our *personal* identities (and later as a basis for legal protections, affirmative action policies, political organization, etc.). See Moran 2015; Appiah 2018.

In short, the use of these labels *as* totems arose roughly contemporaneously with the rise of "victimhood culture" and the ascendance of the symbolic economy. These phenomena have been deeply intertwined from the outset.

64. Merton 1972.

65. S. Page 2019.

66. For a large set of studies ($N = 9,676$) demonstrating the tendency to perceive victims as more ethical than others, see Jordan & Kouchaki 2021.

67. Rorty 1999, p. 104.

68. For case studies of how nonwhite symbolic workers attempt to cultivate and leverage these perceptions in order to enhance their own perceived expertise, see Portocarrero 2023; Portocarrero, forthcoming.

69. In some cases people are not content to merely represent their own particular racial or ethnic group but even attempt to speak for "people of color" as a whole. For a good deconstruction of this phenomenon, see E. Patel 2019.

70. See S. Khan 2021a for elaboration on this point.

71. Leslie, Mayer, & Kravitz 2014. See also Heilman & Welle 2006.

72. E.g., Thai, Lizzio-Wilson, & Selvanathan 2021; Torrez, Dupree, & Kraus 2024.

73. Wilmers & Zhang 2022, p. 416.

74. Rich 2008.

75. Schneider 2020.

76. Wadman & Gibbons 2020.

77. See Bromwich & Marcus 2020, and the bevy of articles linked to in the section of that article following the heading "My Actions Are Inexcusable," for substantiation of and elaboration on these details.

78. T. Evans & Contreras 2020.

79. Vasquez 2021.

80. Speri 2023.

81. Viren 2021.

82. Agoyo 2022.

83. For more on this story, see K. Young 2017, pp. 140–147.

84. MacMaster 2011.

85. MacMaster 2011. In his "apology," MacMaster audaciously went on to argue that the fact so many fell for his ruse and preferred to listen to him over these "other" voices "only confirmed [his] feelings regarding the often superficial coverage of the Middle East and the pervasiveness of new forms of liberal Orientalism." That is, the *real* villain of the story, in his telling, was not MacMaster himself but the people whom he tricked into caring and talking about Amina instead of other, actually existing, Middle Easterners.

86. There have been occasional instances where people adopt minority personas not to advocate for social justice issues but to push back against them. For instance, University of New Hampshire chemistry professor Craig Chapman pretended to be an immigrant woman of color. Writing as "the Science Femme," he frequently got into heated arguments with nonwhite academics and railed against diversity, equity, and inclusion initiatives; liberals; and more—quickly building a large following on social media before his real identity was exposed. However, cases like Chapman's are exceptions that prove the rule. He sought to engage as a woman of color to wield totemic capital on the same types of social justice topics, just coming from the other

side. He pursued this alternative identity for the same reason as Seltzer and McMaster: he knew his claims would carry more weight in virtue of coming from a totem bearer. His critiques of "wokeness" would be more difficult to simply dismiss as "racist" or "sexist" if offered up by an immigrant woman of color. His arguments would, instead, have to be reckoned with seriously. See Weill 2020 for more on this story.

87. Although hoaxers typically pretend to be Black, Native American, or Hispanic (i.e., the most disadvantaged racial and ethnic groups in America) in order to maximize their totemic capital, there are occasional cases of people pretending to be Asian instead. For instance, a celebrated Japanese poet, Araki Yasusada, turned out to be Highland Community College professor Kent Johnson. Likewise, a "female" Chinese poet, Yi-Fen Chou, had "her" work accepted into the 2015 Best American Poetry anthology series. However, it turned out Yi-Fen was actually Michael Hudson, a white librarian from Fort Wayne, Indiana. When Hudson's ruse was exposed, he was unabashed about the fact that he fabricated the identity in order to change how his work was received. He detailed how the same poem that had been rejected more than forty times from different outlets when written under his own name was quickly accepted and widely celebrated when held to come from Yi-Fen. See Hsu 2015 for more on these stories.

88. V. Patel 2023.

89. Andrea Smith 1993.

90. T. Reed 2020.

91. A recent survey by *Intelligent* found that more than 40 percent of whites under forty-five who applied to or attended colleges and universities claim to have misrepresented their race or ethnicity on their college application materials. The most common lineage they claimed was Native American. These tendencies may be especially pronounced at elite schools, where competition for admission is at its fiercest. For instance, many of the parents involved in the "Varsity Blues" scandal were instructed to falsely describe their children as Black or Hispanic on application materials in order to enhance their prospects of admission.

Unfortunately, whether or not people commit ethnic fraud in application materials is not (yet) a question that is widely asked in survey research—this is the only poll I could find on the topic, and it would be a mistake to overinterpret a single poll. However, the results at least suggest that there may be many, many Jessica Krugs, Kelly Kean Sharps, and Andrea Smiths out there who may have lied on their college application materials and then continued to build careers by lying about their ancestry.

This does not seem to be a practice exclusive to whites. The perception that falsely identifying as Black, Hispanic or Indigenous might enhance one's admissions prospects seems to be widespread among Asian Americans too (who are statistically disadvantaged in applications relative to other racial or ethnic groups, controlling for GPAs, test scores, and other "performance" indicators). There is at least one prominent case of an Indian American who (successfully) pretended to be Black in order to get accepted into medical school.

See Chokal-Ingram & Hansen 2016; N. Anderson 2018; Korn & Levitz 2019; *Intelligent* 2021.

92. J. England 2020.

93. B. Cooper 2021.

94. Antonio Moore 2018.

95. Setting questions of statistical representativeness aside, public opinion polling suggests that most Black people in America do not personally view those most likely to become representatives of "Black" culture as characteristic of "people like themselves" either. For instance, a recent Pew Research study found that only 17 percent of African Americans viewed themselves as sharing "everything or most things in common" with foreign-born Black people. See K. Cox & Tamir 2022, p. 27.

96. Jackson 2019.

97. B. Cooper 2021.

98. Jimenez-Moya et al. 2015. In a similar vein, a hugely disproportionate share of Western-ers who join groups like ISIS are new converts or former "secular Muslims." They often don't have deep ties to local Muslim communities and religious institutions. They often don't have a history of attending religious services and don't possess a deep knowledge of Islam. It is precisely this distance from *actual* Muslim communities and living Islamic traditions that facilitates their extremism (in the name of Islam). See al-Gharbi 2014.

99. Leong 2007; K. Brown 2014; Antman & Duncan 2015.

100. Sowell 2005.

101. Massie 2016. Urofsky 2020, pp. 127, 347, 377–378, provides additional context as to why and how white women may have been able to benefit more than others from affirmative action policies.

102. Totemic capital tends to enhance cultural capital to the extent that totem bearers present themselves in a manner, and deploy their identity in a fashion, that affirms rather than genuinely challenges or threatens the values, preferences, and priorities of the dominant group. See A. Cartwright 2022.

103. Cherid 2021.

104. Genealogical studies tracing Warren's maternal ancestry all the way back to the Revolu-tionary War found no evidence of any Native American heritage (she claimed to be part Cherokee on her mother's side). She has no ancestor listed on the Dawes Rolls. She was not adopted into any clan by a clan mother. Consequently, Warren is not Cherokee—not even a little. Prominent Indigenous Americans have repeatedly bristled at Warren's claims to being Cherokee. Family members have consistently and publicly pushed back against Warren's ancestry claims and her characterizations of "family lore." Nonetheless, goaded by Trump, Warren attempted to "prove" her ancestry through a DNA test. This was an absurd bid because a DNA test cannot actually establish someone as "part Cherokee." In any case, the results of the test showed that Warren possessed roughly the same levels of "Indigenous DNA" as the typical American white. See al-Gharbi 2018b.

105. Clarke 2015, p. 805.

106. Mejia 2021.

107. Keeler 2022.

108. Brubaker 2018, pp. 63–64.

109. Tuvel 2021.

110. E.g., Grasso 2017; L. Brown 2021.

111. Dai et al. 2021.

112. See Hartz 2020; Lewis 2021.

113. Brubaker 2018.

114. A. Taylor 2019; Blom, Hennekam, & Denys 2012.

115. T. Peck 2019.

116. Stories of striving in the face of adversity are especially likely to be produced in response to evidence or perceptions that one might have been "privileged." See Phillips & Lowery 2015, 2018, 2020.

117. Dashan 2019.

118. One particularly egregious example: in New York City, young "creatives" with rich parents exploited the fact that they don't earn much (if any) income *personally* to help their families acquire property at extremely discounted rates, exploiting programs intended to build wealth for the poor. The abuses have grown so rampant that today it is *only* the children of wealthy families who are able to use the program at all—the rich have completely priced out the intended beneficiaries. A program intended to help the poor has become nothing more than a means for wealthy families to further build their wealth. Yet the program persists. See Melby 2021.

119. Conti 2019. Likewise, elite universities increasingly strive to inflate their numbers of "first-gen" students by defining the term to include not only those who are the first in their family to attend college at all (the normal meaning of the term) but also those who are the first in their

family to attend an *elite* school. The University of Pennsylvania, for instance, could count someone as "first gen" if their parents were both professors who had degrees from the City University of New York rather than a school like Columbia. UPenn (and likely some peer institutions as well) also allows people to "identify" as "middle class" and even "low income" on their documents irrespective of their actual wealth—tied exclusively to where students *feel* they fall relative to their (likely wealthy) community peers. See University of Pennsylvania, n.d.

The University of California, Los Angeles, meanwhile, allows students to classify themselves as "first gen" if they are the first in their family to attain a degree from a *U.S.-based* university. The child of a doctor and a lawyer—one of whom graduated from Oxford University, the other from Cambridge—would be counted as a "first-gen" student at UCLA. Small wonder, then, that the university is able to claim that 30 percent of its students are "first gen." See UCLA Undergraduate Admission, n.d.

Through tactics like these, elite universities can inflate the apparent diversity of their student body, and exaggerate the extent to which they are serving genuinely disadvantaged students, while still drawing their students primarily from the already advantaged. See T. Bartlett 2022.

120. Peterson 2017; B. Bartlett 2020.

121. Ballentine & Wells 2023.

122. Holloway 2021. Indeed, studies have found that most successful entrepreneurial enterprises were started by people from affluent families. See al-Gharbi 2016d for more on this point.

123. J. Bennett 2022.

124. As an interesting parallel to this point, Google Books nGrams show that the use of "trauma" in English-language publications accelerated rapidly beginning in 1969 (corresponding to widespread protests against the Vietnam War) and continued to rise through 2014—after which point its usage began to level off, perhaps indicating that the term had reached a point of saturation.

125. Nair 2021.

126. Beran 2021.

127. Beck 2016.

128. Ayonrinde 2020. Neurasthenia also caught on in Japan, where its trajectory was equally instructive: During the Meiji Restoration period, many Japanese elites were very focused on learning from and emulating "the West." Neurasthenia, then a disorder among Western elites, came to be widely adopted by elites in Japan as well. It became a class marker in Japan as it was in the West. Because it was framed as a "problem of excess" rather than of deficit, huge numbers of Japanese people began claiming to be neurasthenic. Frustrated Japanese psychiatrists began reframing the disorder not as one caused by an *excess* of purity, ambition, creativity, and so on but rather as a product of people with weak mental constitutions. Diagnoses rapidly plummeted. See Watters 2011, pp. 203–207.

129. Grigorenko & Lockery 2002, pp. 180–183.

130. Tapper, Morris, & Setrakian 2006; Quealy & Shapiro 2019.

131. See Freedman 2003 for 1987 baselines. See Belkin, Levitz, & Korn 2019 for contemporary numbers.

132. D. Goldstein & Patel 2019.

133. Weis & Bittner 2022.

134. Belkin 2018. According to estimates by the *Chronicle of Higher Education*, at more than one out of five private nonprofit four-year colleges and universities, at least 10 percent of students formally identify as "disabled." Among the types of schools lower-income students and minority students are especially likely to attend (for-profit schools, public two-year schools), fewer than one in twenty-five had disabled populations above this threshold. Roughly nine out of ten of *these* schools had disabled populations of 3 percent or less. See *Chronicle of Higher Education* 2021b.

135. DeBoer 2022a.

136. T. Hunter 2022.

137. E.g., Musso & Gouvier 2012; Grant et al. 2020.

138. Families eager for a confirmed diagnosis in order to attain accommodations and so on often turn to medical or psychiatric professionals with whom they have friendship, familial, or other strong ties. These doctors regularly recognize nonmedical incentives that seem to be driving patients to seek a diagnosis. However, they often view providing these families with the diagnoses they're shopping for as a beneficent act that causes little harm. That is, doctors are often positively predisposed toward telling families what they seem to want to hear. Of course, in addition to their desire to help families out, there are often financial incentives at play for doctors as well (not the least being a recognition that if they deny patients their preferred diagnosis, their clients will probably keep seeking alternative opinions until they get what they want and may subsequently move their other business to more compliant doctors instead). See Schwarz 2013; Lewak 2018; Johnson & Keifer 2019.

139. Eyal 2013; A. Harrington 2019; Romeo 2021; DeBoer 2022b.

140. Daryl Scott 1997; Raz 2013; Stampnitzsky 2013; S. Alexander 2019.

141. Rivera 2016; see esp. pp. 156–161.

142. Ashok 2021; Gebre-Medhin et al. 2022.

143. In the aftermath of the racial uprisings that followed George Floyd's murder, MIT and many other schools eliminated standardized testing requirements in the hope that the move would enhance the racial, ethnic, and socioeconomic diversity of the student body. The move had the opposite effect. In the absence of standardized testing, schools relied more heavily on extra-curricular activities, volunteer work, recommendation letters, and student essays—all of which tend to favor already-advantaged applicants even more than standardized tests. Consequently, the admitted classes grew less diverse on a number of dimensions. In response to this outcome, the school decided to reinstate its standardized testing requirement beginning in the 2022–2023 application cycle. Two years later, Dartmouth followed suit for the same reasons. See Schmill 2022; Leonhardt 2024.

144. Leong 2021.

145. E.g., Portocarrero & Carter 2022.

146. Wacquant & Bourdieu 1989, p. 4.

147. "Conspicuous consumption" has long been a means through which elites attempted to demonstrate their status. In some senses, mastering high culture was itself a form of conspicuous consumption—a sign that one did not have to work for survival and, therefore, had the time and resources to pursue "higher" ends. As material goods became increasingly cheap and abundant, material forms of "conspicuous consumption" failed to provide the same status return on invest-ment. Knowledge and culture became even more important in status games than they already were. See Currid-Halkett 2018 for more on this.

148. Kirsch 2021.

149. S. Khan 2021b, p. 151.

150. Highly educated elites are "cultural omnivores" with one important exception: forms of art linked to (and embraced by) low-status whites. See Hubbs 2014.

151. Childress et al. 2021.

152. Hahl, Zuckerman, & Kim 2017.

153. Rosenfield 2023.

154. A. Reed 2000, p. 73.

155. Rosenfield 2019.

156. Oyler 2018.

157. Kriss 2020.

158. Adichie 2021.

159. Staples 2016.

160. Staples 2015.

161. S. Robinson 2005.

162. Coates 2017, p. 118.

163. E. Klein 2016.

Chapter 6. Mystification of Social Processes

1. Samaras 2007; Olds 2016; Pinsker 2016; Harinam 2021; Amin & Fletcher 2022.

2. Cooley et al. 2019.

3. Deneen 2018.

4. Salam 2018.

5. Shellenberger 2019.

6. With respect to this debate, on the one hand, many people on the left assert that much of what is called CRT has an extremely tenuous relationship to the legal theories advanced by Kimberlé Crenshaw and others. As discussed earlier in this text, they are right about that. However, many of those who advance the unpopular ideas and approaches that are currently being derided understand and explicitly describe *themselves* as operationalizing "critical race theory" in the classroom, the boardroom, and so on. This is also very straightforwardly true (as explored in that same section). They publish papers with titles that include phrases like "a critical race approach" and so forth. It strains credulity that people who insist on defining CRT exclusively in terms of the original legal theories of the 1980s are somehow unaware that derivatives of said theories are now common outside the legal field—to include in pedagogical spaces. Indeed, as we have previously explored, many of the founders of CRT have themselves acknowledged (sometimes praised, sometimes lamented) this fact. Consequently, it seems bizarre and not entirely honest for progressives to deny that versions of CRT have indeed made their way into many American classrooms.

Of course, the opponents of CRT are often attempting to willfully mislead as well. There is a campaign underway to basically name *anything* found to be unpopular as "CRT"—without any regard for whether the label fits. This is a strategy that one of the pioneers of the anti-CRT movement has made quite explicit: "We have successfully frozen their brand—'critical race theory'—into the public conversation and are steadily driving up negative perceptions. We will eventually turn it toxic, as we put all of the various cultural insanities under that brand category. The goal is to have the public read something crazy in the newspaper and immediately think 'critical race theory.' We have decodified the term and will recodify it to annex the entire range of cultural constructions that are unpopular with Americans" (Rufo 2021).

And when pressed, each side points to the other side's fundamental dishonesty to justify their own. See Gutkin 2021 for a deeper dive into these dynamics and their unfortunate consequences for understanding important social phenomena and effectively intervening in the social world.

7. There seems to be a group of right-aligned billionaires funding *both* sides of this culture war through various channels. See M. Thomas 2021.

8. E.g., Powell 2021b; B. Weiss 2021.

9. These data are from the National Center for Education Statistics. Readers can search statistics for Loudon County and all of the other districts mentioned here (or any other district they'd like) in National Center for Education Statistics, n.d.

10. Kingkade & Chiwaya 2021.

11. Although parents often try to keep their children enrolled despite protesting "woke" curricula, elite schools sometimes retaliate against dissenting parents (and attempt to dissuade others from joining them) by expelling students on the basis of their parents' (anti)activism. This mode of silencing is effective because expulsion does not just prevent affected students from attending the elite school they are already in, it often more or less disqualifies them from admission into peer institutions as well. Many elite parents are therefore forced to choose between having to send their children to their zoned *public* school or biting their tongue about "wokeness." Most choose the latter. The culture wars matter far less to them than their kids getting into Brown. See R. Sharp 2021; Woodhouse 2022.

12. Sibarium 2021.

13. LaPorte 2021.

14. For more on this point, see al-Gharbi 2023a.

15. Henderson 2019b.

16. Yglesias 2023.

17. Philosopher Liam Kofi Bright (2023) powerfully described the broader debates around "wokeness" as a "white psychodrama" in which nonwhite elites, if they play their cards right, can assume lucrative supporting roles.

18. One ironic outcome of the campaign to ban CRT in schools is that growing numbers of less selective schools will likely begin to adopt these curricula. Institutions tend to emulate others that are successful or prestigious. If schools that successfully place kids at Harvard are pushing CRT, then other schools will begin doing the same. That is, by exposing and drawing attention to the specific "social justice" curricula at elite schools, upset parents have likely increased the chances that nonelite schools will adopt the same curricula—thereby enhancing the reach of the very ideas and pedagogical practices they are ostensibly trying to fight.

19. Mendlowitz 2018.

20. Horowitch 2024.

21. Weatherby 2024.

22. Weatherby 2024.

23. In fact, it is often elite students themselves who are demanding that their schools provide CRT-related instruction. In making these demands, students are not calling for something they think will harm their prospects or undermine their ambitions in any way. Kids at these schools tend to be ambitious social climbers. Implicitly, they seem to recognize the utility of this training for their own aspirations—including but not limited to applying to highly selective colleges and universities or landing elite jobs.

24. For more on the notion of "concept creep" for terms like "racism," "sexism," "trauma," and "violence," see Haslam et al. 2020.

25. Bonilla-Silva 2017.

26. The internalization of worldviews associated with highly educated white liberals seems to have a pernicious effect on the subjective well-being and social flourishing of nonwhites (and, indeed, likely whites as well). See al-Gharbi 2023c for a review of empirical literature on this point.

27. Hughey 2012b.

28. Kipnis 2022.

29. For some striking examples, see Bolonik 2019; Soave 2019; Viren 2020; Grim 2022; Herzog 2022; N. Malone 2022; S. Weiss 2022.

30. Lareau 2011; S. Khan 2021b.

31. E.g., Mounk 2020; Powell 2021a.

32. Dobbin & Kalev 2016.

33. Nielson 2018; Strossen 2018.

34. DeBoer 2021b.

35. Angwin & Grassegger 2017; Davidson, Bhattacharya, & Weber 2019; Sap et al. 2019; Biddle 2021; FRA 2022.

36. Al-Gharbi & Haidt 2017; Storey 2018.

37. Al-Gharbi 2023g.

38. Harmon 2021. Similar realities hold for identification with pan-ethnic umbrella terms for specific subsets of racial groups, like "Asian American and Pacific Islander." It's primarily highly educated and relatively affluent liberal nonwhites who embrace these labels. See al-Gharbi 2022 for more on this point.

39. Noe-Bustamante, Mora, & Hugo-Lopez 2020.

40. Caputo & Rodriguez 2021.

41. Contreras 2022.

42. Mochkofsky 2020.

43. Badiou 2013, pp. 24–25.

44. E.g., Coates 2018; Beltran 2021. Nonwhite mainstream symbolic capitalists may be especially likely to brand coethnic dissenters as white in order to protect the authority of people like themselves to present their own views and priorities as representative of the group writ large. In so doing, of course, they also help advance the political objectives of the highly educated white liberals who "consecrate" cultural producers as "authentic" representatives of the groups they identify with. Minority-group heretics are especially threatening to dominant-group elites because they severely undermine dominant-group members' claims that they are acting on behalf of the marginalized and disadvantaged. Moreover, it is difficult to dismiss them by simply, say, calling them "racist." Having other, more compliant minority-group elites instead brand these dissidents as "white," "white-adjacent," or "race traitors" helps dominant-group elites preserve and enhance their status as well.

45. Herndon & Glueck 2020.

46. E.g., L. Anderson 2016.

47. Analyzing trends in academic databases such as JSTOR, Web of Science, Google Scholar, EBSCO Essentials, and Scopus, one can observe a dramatic increase in discussions of "systemic," "institutional," and "structural" inequality after 2012, with a particularly dramatic spike from 2018 to 2022.

48. Wacquant 2022.

49. B. Fields 1990, p. 118.

50. Johns & Chavez 2021.

51. Howell & Korver-Glenn 2021.

52. Menendian, Gambhir, & Gailes 2021.

53. A. Abbott 2016. See esp. pp. 198–232 for more on this point.

54. Amis, Mair, & Munir 2020.

55. Goffman 1983.

56. For several prominent examples of these narratives in action, see Levitz 2023.

57. Brennan & Freiman 2022.

58. According to U.S. Census estimates, Indigenous Americans form roughly 2 percent of the U.S. population, and only 15 percent of Native Americans over the age of twenty-five have a BA or advanced degree. Put another way, less than 0.3 percent of Americans are college-educated Indigenous Americans—that is, the type of Indigenous American who would be deemed "qualified" to participate in the symbolic professions.

59. Sobo, Lambert, & Lambert 2021. See also Tuck & Yang 2012.

60. At time of writing, a handful of states have tuition waivers for qualifying members of Native American tribes: Maine, Massachusetts, Minnesota, Michigan, Montana, Nevada, and North Dakota. Maine also guarantees a scholarship covering room and board, although the others do not. A larger number of other states charge in-state (rather than out-of-state) tuition rates to members of qualifying tribes, including Arizona, Nebraska, Oregon, New Mexico, Colorado, California, Iowa, Oklahoma, Utah, and Washington. Idaho offers reduced tuition. A handful of other colleges and universities provide similar benefits irrespective of broader state policies.

However, most states and institutions have not even taken the step of providing in-state tuition rates, let alone waiving tuition altogether, guaranteeing acceptance, or providing room and board for accepted Indigenous Americans to offset the (typically significant) nontuition attendance costs—despite the fact that it would not be particularly difficult or costly for them to do so. Nonetheless, even institutions that happen to provide *none* of these benefits still issue land acknowledgments. See, e.g., Watkins 2020.

61. Eisgruber 2020.

62. Hess 2020.

63. Within universities, many individual departments also issued statements similar to President Eisgruber's. Here, too, the types of actions stakeholders committed to in these statements seemed improperly scaled to the depth and severity of the problems they were purported to

address. Although many scholars who issued these statements explicitly embraced "systemic" and "institutional" understandings of inequality, the proposals advanced typically did not reflect serious consideration of how systems and institutions might plausibly be reformed or transformed to achieve signatories' desired ends. For more on this point, see N. Brown, Tormos-Aponte, & Wong 2024.

64. The Princeton Theological Seminary agreed to pay $27 million in "reparations" (in the form of scholarships and other initiatives) to make amends for its historical ties to slavery. One important thing to recognize about this move is that it is designed to keep Princeton's money "in house" (that is, the seminary is "paying" the earmarked funds mostly to itself. Rather than actually giving money away, it is simply declining to collect money from selected students). The initiative is also relatively modest in scope, considering the resources available to Princeton. Indeed, only one school within the university—the theological seminary—has even committed to going *this* far.

For contrast, Georgetown University, whose endowment is one-fifteenth the size of Princeton's, established a university-wide program to raise hundreds of millions of dollars *per year* in reparations (via tuition) to be paid directly to contemporary descendants of Georgetown's 272 documented former slaves. See Schuessler 2017; DiCorpo 2019; Shanahan 2019.

65. As these things go, Princeton's statement and institutional commitments were more robust than most. However, this is an extremely low bar to clear. For a brief defense by President Eisgruber on the issue of symbolic gestures, see E. Green 2021.

Pace Eisgruber's thoughtful defense, in my own estimation, the costs involved with the kind of social justice signaling described in this section—in terms of warping elites' understandings of how social inequalities are produced and maintained (thereby distorting political discourse, social policy, and much else besides)—radically outweigh the purported benefits of these symbolic gestures for the relatively few elites (and elite aspirants) from underrepresented backgrounds who happen to be present at Ivy League schools. To the extent that embracing or participating in these gestures provides elites of all backgrounds, including elites of color, with moral licenses and moral credentials for continued inegalitarian behaviors, they probably do more harm than good on balance with respect to those who are genuinely vulnerable, marginalized, and disadvantaged.

66. E.g., Baker et al. 2023.

67. For several peer-reviewed studies on these points, see al-Gharbi 2020e, in the section "Training Can Increase Biased Behavior, Minority Turnover."

68. Quintanilla & Kaiser 2016.

69. Castilla & Benard 2010.

70. D. Miller & Effron 2010; Ryan Brown et al. 2011.

71. Merritt et al. 2012; Effron 2014; Thai, Hornsey, & Barlow 2016.

72. Merritt, Effron, & Monin 2010; Effron, Miller, & Monin 2012; Cascio & Plant 2015; Mullen & Monin 2016.

73. Interestingly, moral licensing seems to be a form of moral reasoning that is unique to capitalistic Western, highly educated, industrialized, rich, and democratic (WEIRD) countries. Others do not seem to think of morality as a ledger, where one can "even out" bad actions by performing good ones (in most other places, a bad act is still viewed as bad even if it was closely preceded or followed by good or anticipated good; prosocial behaviors do not entitle someone to engage in immoral behaviors). See Simbrunner & Schlegelmilch 2017.

74. Effron & Conway 2015; Rotella et al. 2023.

75. Perez et al. 2022.

76. Fink 2018.

77. Harkrider et al. 2013; Z. Rothschild et al. 2015; Z. Rothschild & Keefer 2017.

78. See Bandura 2016 for a deep exploration of moral disengagement (by the scholar who coined the term).

79. Krumm & Corning 2010; Kouchaki 2011; Meijers et al. 2019; R. Wang & Chan 2019.

80. Ashforth & Lange 2016; K. Newman & Brucks 2017; Ahmad, Klotz, & Bolino 2021.

81. Sullivan et al. 2012.

82. Z. Rothschild et al. 2013.

83. Ahmed 2004, 2006.

84. Moser 2019; N. Robinson 2019.

85. Jelani Cobb 2017; Fang 2017.

86. Kantor & Twohey 2017; Moniuszko & Kelly 2017.

87. Rosenberg 2019.

88. One particularly compelling additional example may be former religious and civil rights leader Jim Jones. See Shellenberger 2021, pp. 219–238, for a good overview of Jones and his ties to prominent left-aligned activists and politicians (from Harvey Milk and Jimmy Carter to Angela Davis and beyond)—along with a powerful description of how Jones's moral credentials as a civil rights champion enabled the exploitation and eventual mass murder that took place at Jonestown, committed primarily against people of color.

89. See Chibber 2022 for an excellent elaboration on this point.

90. Leifer 1992.

91. For more on this point, see David Scott 1999.

92. E.g., Chakroff et al. 2015; Rittenburg, Gladney, & Stephenson 2016; Haugh 2020; Farrow, Grolleau, & Mzoughi 2021.

93. E.g., Southwood 1978; Crenshaw 1989.

94. Hager 2017; Widra 2018.

95. Chetty et al. 2020.

96. Chetty et al. 2020.

97. Lareau 2011.

98. Derenocourt et al. 2022.

99. For a deeper exploration of these points, see al-Gharbi 2020c.

100. For more on this point, see Bright 2024.

101. E.g., James Scott 1999; Leonard 2016; Taleb 2018.

Conclusion

1. Owen, Videras, & Wu 2010; Schuldt & Pearson 2016. See also Pearson et al. 2018, fig. S8. The main body of the Pearson et al. article conflates respondents who "somewhat" identify with environmentalism with those who "definitely" do and fails to find major differences along the lines of race or education. However, disaggregating these responses, as the authors do in the supplemental materials, reveals the typical picture: even *among* liberals, highly educated and white Americans are more likely than others to say they are "definitely" environmentalists. And when stripped of controls for ideology, these patterns are even starker (because highly educated white people are far more likely than others to self-identify as "liberal," and liberals are overwhelmingly likely to identify as "environmentalists").

2. Fisher & Renaghan 2023. Dorceta Taylor (2014) shows that environmental advocacy organizations, agencies, and foundations are likewise composed almost exclusively of highly educated, relatively affluent white liberals.

3. E.g., Delmas & Burbano 2011; Maki & Raimi 2017; Lahsen & Ribot 2022; Raju, Boyd, & Otto 2022.

4. E.g., Paoletta 2023; Tyson, Funk, & Kennedy 2023.

5. Urban areas consume most of the food, energy, and manufactured goods produced in "flyover country"—and by proxy, the water used to produce those goods, the resources required to transport them, and so on. Those who are relatively well off within cities tend to consume a radically disproportionate (per capita) share of all the above (as compared with fellow urban denizens who are less wealthy). Yet the costs for this consumption are offloaded onto "others" (i.e., the people who live in flyover country), who are on the front lines of environmental degradation from

extraction, exposure to toxic materials and industrial waste from manufacturing, the physical risks and toll involved in resource extraction, manufacturing, agricultural work, and so on. It is nonurban areas that typically receive and process the enormous amounts of waste produced in cities as well. Put another way, in virtue of saying, thinking, and feeling the "correct" things, symbolic capitalists often feel entitled to condemn others who benefit far less from environmental devastation than they themselves do, and who also bear a hugely disproportionate share of the costs required for symbolic capitalists to enjoy the lifestyles they take for granted. For more on these points, see Lipschitz 2014; John Day & Hall 2016; Gustafson 2016; Dieter 2018; Roberts 2019.

6. E.g., M. Hall et al. 2018.

7. Brook, O'Brien, & Taylor 2020.

8. Guilluy 2019.

9. Muzergues 2019; Piketty 2021; Kitschelt & Rehm 2022.

10. Goodhart 2017.

11. Gibbs 2021a, 2021b.

12. Leroux 2019.

13. Leo 2021.

14. It may be tempting to attribute the global nature of the contemporary Great Awakening to the rise of digital technologies and so on. However, virtually all the previous Awokenings were also global in nature (e.g., Ehrenreich & Ehrenreich 1969). And it makes sense they would be. Insofar as these periods of unrest are driven by macroeconomic trends, one might expect that conditions that gave rise to an Awokening in the United States might have contemporaneous analogues in other WEIRD countries and beyond. Meanwhile, cultural syncretism and institutional isomorphism across the symbolic professions would be expected to lead symbolic capitalists in a broad range of contexts to channel their anxieties and engage in power struggles in broadly similar ways. Technological advances may have exacerbated some of these tendencies, but they did not produce the Great Awokenings, nor are they responsible for their globalized nature.

15. Foa et al. 2022, pp. 26–27.

16. Rozado 2023b.

17. Maharawal 2016.

18. Todd 2016.

19. BBC 2017; Smith-Spark 2017.

20. Smith, Wu, & Murphy 2020.

21. Kyeune 2022.

22. John 2022.

23. Onishi 2021.

24. Cusset 2008.

25. Hadot 1995.

26. G. Becker 1978; Jerolmack & Khan 2014; Taleb 2018.

27. G. Cohen 2001.

28. Khorsandi 2018.

29. Bejan 2022.

REFERENCES

AAUP (2023). "Preliminary 2022–23 Faculty Compensation Survey Results: Summary Tables and Explanation of Statistical Data." Washington, DC: American Association of University Professors. https://www.aaup.org/sites/default/files/AAUP-2023-SurveyTables.pdf.

Abad-Santoz, Alex (2018). "Nike's Colin Kaepernick Ad Sparked a Boycott—and Earned $6 Billion for Nike." Vox, 24 September.

Abbott, Andrew (1988). *The System of Professions: An Essay on the Division of Expert Labor.* Chicago: University of Chicago Press.

Abbott, Andrew (2016). *Processual Sociology.* Chicago: University of Chicago Press.

Abbott, Jared, et al. (2021). *Commonsense Solidarity: How a Working-Class Coalition Can Be Built, and Maintained.* Brooklyn, NY: Center for Working-Class Politics.

Abernathy, Penelope (2018). *The Expanding News Desert.* Chapel Hill: UNC Center Innovation and Sustainability in Local Media.

Abrahams, Jessica (2017). "Everything You Wanted to Know about Fourth Wave Feminism—but Were Afraid to Ask." *Prospect*, 14 August.

Abramowitz, Alan, & Steven Webster (2018). "Negative Partisanship: Why Americans Dislike Parties but Behave like Rabid Partisans." *Advances in Political Psychology* 39(S1): 119–135.

Abrams, Samuel (2016). "Professors Moved Left since the 1990s, the Rest of the Country Did Not." *Heterodox Academy*, 9 January.

Activist School (n.d.). "Challenging Activism (Symposium Three)." Accessed 27 November 2023. https://www.activistschool.org/challenging-activism-symposium-3.

Adichie, Chimamanda (2021). "It Is Obscene: A True Reflection in Three Parts." *Chimamanda Adichie*, 15 June. https://www.chimamanda.com/it-is-obscene-a-true-reflection-in-three-parts/.

Adler-Bell, Sam (2022a). "Do Democrats Really Want Amazon's Workers to Win?" *New York Magazine*, 8 April.

Adler-Bell, Sam (2022b). "The Liberal Obsession with 'Disinformation' Is Not Helping." *New York Magazine*, 20 May.

Adler-Bell, Sam (2022c). "Unlearning the Language of 'Wokeness.'" *New York Magazine*, 10 June.

Agoyo, Acee (2022). "Native Food Sovereignty Figure Admits No Tribal Connections." *Indianz*, 21 October.

Ahmad, M. Ghufran, Anthony Klotz, & Mark Bolino (2021). "Can Good Followers Create Unethical Leaders? How Follower Citizenship Leads to Leader Moral Licensing and Unethical Behavior." *Journal of Applied Psychology* 106(9): 1374–1390.

Ahmari, Sohrab, et al. (2019). "Against the Dead Consensus." *First Things*, 21 March.

Ahmed, Sara (2004). "Declarations of Whiteness: The Non-performativity of Anti-racism." *Borderlands* 3(2). https://webarchive.nla.gov.au/awa/20050616083826/http://www.borderlandsjournal.adelaide.edu.au/vol3no2_2004/ahmed_declarations.htm.

Ahmed, Sara (2006). "The Non-performativity of Anti-racism." *Meridians* 7(1): 104–126.

Akhtar, Allana (2019). "More Uber and Lyft Drivers Are Using the App to Fit Their Schedules, but Those Who Make It a Full-Time Job Are Barely Earning a Living Wage." *Business Insider*, 6 May.

Alba, Richard (2020). *The Great Demographic Illusion: Majority, Minority, and the Expansion of the American Mainstream*. Princeton, NJ: Princeton University Press.

Alba, Richard (2021). "The Surge of Young Americans from Minority-White Mixed Families & Its Significance for the Future." *Daedalus* 150(2): 199–214.

Alexander, Julia (2018). "The Yellow $: A Comprehensive History of Demonetization and YouTube's War with Creators." *Polygon*, 10 May.

Alexander, Scott (2014). "The Toxoplasma of Rage." *Slate Star Codex*, 17 December.

Alexander, Scott (2018). "Is Science Slowing Down?" *Slate Star Codex*, 26 November.

Alexander, Scott (2019). "The APA Meeting: A Photo Essay." *Slate Star Codex*, 22 May.

Allen, Jennifer, et al. (2020). "Evaluating the Fake News Problem at the Scale of the Information Ecosystem." *Science Advances* 6(14): eaay3539.

Altay, Sacha, & Alberto Acerbi (2023). "People Believe Misinformation Is a Threat Because They Assume Others Are Gullible." *New Media & Society*. https://doi.org/10.1177/146144 48231153379.

Alto, Alix, et al. (2022). "'I Put Liberal but LOL': Investigating Psychological Differences between Political Liberals and Leftists." PsyArXiv preprint. https://psyarxiv.com/3qgep/.

American Society of News Editors (n.d.). "How Diverse Are US Newsrooms?" *American Society of News Editors*. Accessed 1 December 2023. https://googletrends.github.io/asne2019/.

American Society of Plastic Surgeons (2021). *Plastic Surgery Statistics Report: 2020*. Arlington Heights, IL: American Society of Plastic Surgeons.

Amin, Vikesh, & Jason Fletcher (2022). "What Is Driving the Relationship between Height and Cognition? Evidence from Twins Early Development Study." *Economics and Human Biology* 47: 101174.

Amiri, Farnoush, et al. (2019). "How America's Top Newsrooms Recruit Interns from a Small Circle of Colleges." *Voices*, 2 August.

Amis, John, Johanna Mair, & Kamal Munir (2020). "The Organizational Reproduction of Inequality." *Academy of Management Annals* 14(1): 195–230.

Anderson, Cameron, John Hildreth, & Daron Sharps (2020). "The Possession of High Status Strengthens the Status Motive." *Personality and Social Psychology Bulletin* 46(12): 1712–1723.

Anderson, Galusha (1908). *The Story of a Border City during the Civil War*. Boston: Little, Brown. https://babel.hathitrust.org/cgi/pt?id=ucl.$b61718.

Anderson, Gary, & Jamie Grinberg (1998). "Educational Administration as a Disciplinary Practice: Appropriating Foucault's View of Power, Discourse and Method." *Educational Administration Quarterly* 34(3): 329–353.

Anderson, L. V. (2016). "White Women Sold Out the Sisterhood and the World by Voting for Trump." *Slate*, 9 November.

Anderson, Nick (2018). "Which Boxes to Check? College Hopefuls Weigh Race, Identity and Affirmative Action." *Washington Post*, 23 December.

Angwin, Julia, & Hannes Grassegger (2017). "Facebook's Secret Censorship Rules Protect White Men from Hate Speech but Not Black Children." *ProPublica*, 28 June.

Antman, Francisca, & Brian Duncan (2015). "Incentives to Identify: Racial Identity in the Age of Affirmative Action." *Review of Economics and Statistics* 97(3): 710–713.

Aponte, Claudia (2021). "Food Delivery Workers Toiling through Historic Flooding Call Skimpy Wages and Tips 'a Cruel Joke.'" *The City*, 2 September.

Appel, Markus, & Timo Gnambs (2022). "Women in Fiction: Bechdel-Wallace Test Results for the Highest-Grossing Movies of the Last Four Decades." *Psychology of Popular Media*. https://doi.org/10.1037/ppm0000436.

Appiah, Kwame (2018). *The Lies That Bind: Rethinking Identity*. New York: W. W. Norton.

Aronwitz, Nona (2017). "Meet the Woke Misogynist." *Fusion*, 12 March.

Arora, Ashish, et al. (2019). "Why the U.S. Innovation Ecosystem Is Slowing Down." *Harvard Business Review*, 26 November.

Arora, Ashish, et al. (2020). "The Changing Structure of American Innovation: Some Cautionary Remarks for Economic Growth." *Innovation Policy and the Economy* 20: 39–93.

Asher, Brad (1994). "The Professional Vision: Conflicts over Journalism Education, 1900–1955." *American Journalism* 11(4): 304–320.

Ashforth, Blake, & Donald Lange (2016). "Beware of Organizational Saints: How a Moral Self-Concept May Foster Immoral Behavior." In *Organizational Wrongdoing: Key Perspectives and New Directions*, ed. Donald Palmer, Kristin Smith-Crowe, & Royston Greenwood (pp. 305–336). Cambridge: Cambridge University Press.

Ashkenas, Jeremy, Haeyoun Park, & Adam Pearce (2017). "Even with Affirmative Action, Blacks and Hispanics Are More Underrepresented at Top Colleges than 35 Years Ago." *New York Times*, 24 August.

Ashok, Arvind (2021). "The Persistent Grip of Social Class on College Admissions." *New York Times*, 26 May.

Atir, Stav, Emily Rosennzweig, & David Dunning (2015). "When Knowledge Knows No Bounds: Self-Perceived Expertise Predicts Claims of Impossible Knowledge." *Psychological Science* 26(8): 1295–1303.

Atkinson, Mary, et al. (2021). *The Dynamics of Public Opinion*. Cambridge: Cambridge University Press.

Auerbach, Jerold (1977). *Unequal Justice: Lawyers and Social Change in Modern America*. Oxford: Oxford University Press.

Autor, David (2014). "Skills, Education and the Rise of Earnings Inequality among the 'Other 99 Percent.'" *Science* 344(6186): 843–851.

Auxier, Brooke, & Monica Anderson (2021). "Social Media Use in 2021." *Pew Research Center*, 7 April.

Avery, Jill, & Rachel Greenwald (2023). "A New Approach to Building Your Personal Brand." *Harvard Business Review* 101(3): 147–151.

Ayonrinde, Oyedeji (2020). "'Brain Fag': A Syndrome Associated with 'Overstudy' and Mental Exhaustion in 19th Century Britain." *International Review of Psychiatry* 32(5–6): 520–535.

Azoulay, Pierre, Christian Fons-Rosen, & Joshua Graff Zivin (2019). "Does Science Advance One Funeral at a Time?" *American Economic Review* 109(8): 2889–2920.

Bacon, Perry, Jr. (2018). "Can Conservatives Ever Trust a Tech Industry Staffed Mostly by Liberals?" *FiveThirtyEight*, 2 October.

Badger, Emily, Kevin Quealy, & Josh Katz (2021). "A Close-Up Picture of Partisan Segregation, among 180 Million Voters." *New York Times*, 17 March.

Badgett, Lee, Soon Kyu Choi, & Bianca Wilson (2019). *LGBT Poverty in the United States: A Study of Differences Between Sexual Orientation and Gender Identity Groups*. Los Angeles: UCLA Williams Institute.

Badiou, Alain (2013). *Ethics: An Essay on the Understanding of Evil*. New York: Verso.

Bagalini, Adwoa (2020). "Colorism: How Skin-Tone Bias Affects Racial Equality at Work." *World Economic Forum*, 26 August.

Baker, Andrew, et al. (2023). "Diversity Washing." ECGI Finance Working Papers 868/2023. https://www.ecgi.global/sites/default/files/Paper%3A%20Diversity%20Washing.pdf.

Bakker, Bert, Yphtach Lelkes, & Ariel Malka (2020). "Understanding Partisan Cue Receptivity: Tests of Predictions from the Bounded Rationality and Expressive Utility Perspectives." *Journal of Politics* 82(3): 1061–1077.

Bakunin, Mikhail (1987). *Statism and Anarchy*. Cambridge: Cambridge University Press.

Baldassarri, Delia, & Andrew Gelman (2008). "Partisans without Constraint: Political Polarization and Trends in American Public Opinion." *American Journal of Sociology* 114(2): 408–446.

Baldwin, Davarian (2021). *In the Shadow of the Ivory Tower: How Universities Are Plundering Cities*. New York: Bold Type Books.

Baldwin, James (1998). *Collected Essays*. New York: Library of America.

Ballentine, Claire, & Charlie Wells (2023). "Are You Rich?" *Bloomberg*, 14 August.

Ban, Carolyn, & Patricia Ingraham (1988). "Retaining Quality Federal Employees: Life After PACE." *Public Administration Review* 48(3): 708–718.

Bandura, Albert (2016). *Moral Disengagement: How People Do Harm and Live with Themselves.* New York: Worth.

Barbeau, Arthur, & Florette Henri (1996). *The Unknown Soldiers: African American Troops in World War I.* New York: Da Capo Press.

Barker, Eric (2017). "Should We Play It Safe and Do What We're Told If We Want to Succeed?" In *Barking up the Wrong Tree: The Surprising Science behind Why Everything You Know about Success Is (Mostly) Wrong* (pp. 7–31). New York: HarpersOne.

Barroso, Amanda, & Richard Fry (2021). "On Some Demographic Measures, People in Same-Sex Marriages Differ from Those in Opposite-Sex Marriages." *Pew Research Center*, 7 July.

Bartlett, Bruce (2020). "The Whiners Who Earn $200,000 and Complain They're Broke." *New Republic*, 20 July.

Bartlett, Tom (2017). "When a Theory Goes Viral." *Chronicle of Higher Education*, 21 May.

Bartlett, Tom (2022). "The Dredging." *Chronicle of Higher Education*, 7 January.

Baskin, Jon (2019). "Academia's Holy Warriors." *Chronicle of Higher Education*, 12 September.

Battistella, Edwin (2019). "The Not-So Ironic Evolution of the Term 'Politically Correct.'" *OUPblog*, 7 July.

Baudrillard, Jean (1995). *The Gulf War Did Not Take Place.* Bloomington: Indiana University Press.

Baum, Gary, & Katie Kilkenny (2021). "Inside the Hollywood Labor Rebellion: 'We Have Awoken a Sleeping Giant.'" *Hollywood Reporter*, 17 December.

Baumol, William, Alan Blinder, & Edward Wolff (2003). *Downsizing in America: Reality, Causes, and Consequences.* New York: Russell Sage Foundation.

Bayer, Patrick, & Kerwin Charles (2018). "Divergent Paths: A New Perspective on Earnings Differences between Black and White Men since 1940." *Quarterly Journal of Economics* 133(3): 1459–1501.

Bazelon, Emily (2022). "The Battle over Gender Therapy." *New York Times*, 15 June.

Bazelon, Lara (2022). "The ACLU Has Lost Its Way." *The Atlantic*, 10 May.

BBC (2017). "March for Science: Rallies Worldwide to Protest against Political Interference." *BBC News*, 22 April.

BBC (2022). "Jussie Smollett: A Complete Timeline from Actor's 2019 Arrest to Jail Time." *BBC Newsbeat*, 11 March.

Beard, Henry, & Christopher Cerf (1993). *The Official Politically Correct Dictionary and Handbook.* New York: Villard Books.

Beck, Julie (2016). "'Americanitis': The Disease of Living Too Fast." *The Atlantic*, 11 March.

Becker, Gary (1978). *The Economic Approach to Human Behavior.* Chicago: University of Chicago Press.

Becker, Lisa (2016). "Adjuncts Are Unionizing, but That Won't Fix What's Wrong in Higher Education." *Washington Post*, 6 June.

Behr, Thomas (2019). *Social Justice and Subsidiarity: Luigi Taparelli and the Origins of Modern Catholic Social Thought.* Washington, DC: Catholic University of America Press.

Beiner, Ronald (2021). "Dangerous Minds in Dangerous Times." *Thesis Eleven* 163(1): 29–42.

Bejan, Teresa (2022). "Just Give Me My Equality." *Boston Review*, 7 February.

Belkin, Douglas (2018). "Colleges Bend the Rules for More Students, Give Them Extra Help." *Wall Street Journal*, 24 May.

Belkin, Douglas (2021). "A Generation of American Men Give Up on College: 'I Just Feel Lost.'" *Wall Street Journal*, 6 September.

Belkin, Douglas, Jennifer Levitz, & Melissa Korn (2019). "Many More Students, Especially the Affluent, Get Extra Time to Take the SAT." *Wall Street Journal*, 21 May.

Bell, Alex, et al. (2019). "Who Becomes an Inventor in America? The Importance of Exposure to Innovation." *Quarterly Journal of Economics* 134(2): 647–713.

Bell, Daniel (1972). "The Cultural Contradictions of Capitalism." *Journal of Aesthetic Education* 6(1/2): 11–38.

Bell, Daniel (1976). *The Coming of Post-industrial Society: A Venture in Social Forecasting.* New York: Basic Books.

Beltran, Christina (2021). "To Understand Trump's Support, We Must Think in Terms of Multi-racial Whiteness." *Washington Post*, 15 January.

Benenson, Joyce (2022). "Human Females as a Dispersal-Egalitarian Species: A Hypothesis about Women and Status." *Adaptive Human Behavior and Physiology*. https://doi.org/10.1007/s40750-022-00191-x.

Benenson, Joyce, & Henry Markovits (2014). *Warriors and Worriers: The Survival of the Sexes.* Oxford: Oxford University Press.

Benenson, Joyce, & Henry Markovits (2023). "Levelling as a Female-Biased Competitive Tactic." *Evolutionary Psychological Science*. https://doi.org/10.1007/s40806-023-00355-2.

Benjamin, John (2018). "Business Class." *New Republic*, 14 May.

Benner, Chris, et al. (2020). "On-Demand and On-the-Edge: Ride-Hailing and Delivery Workers in San Francisco." *UC Santa Cruz Institute for Social Transformation*, 5 May.

Benner, Katie (2017). "A Backlash Builds against Sexual Harassment in Silicon Valley." *New York Times*, 3 July.

Bennett, Jessica (2022). "If Everything Is 'Trauma' Is Anything?" *New York Times*, 4 February.

Bennett, Lerone, Jr. (1964). *The Negro Mood and Other Essays.* Chicago: Johnson.

Bennett, Mark, & Victoria Plaut (2018). "Looking Criminal and the Presumption of Dangerous-ness: Afrocentric Facial Features, Skin Tone and Criminal Justice." *UC Davis Law Review* 51(3): 745–803.

Benn Michaels, Walter, & Adolph Reed Jr. (2019). "The Trouble with Disparity." *NonSite* 32.

Bensinger, Greg (2021). "The Rideshare Bubble Bursts." *New York Times*, 17 October.

Benson, Buster (2016). "You Are Almost Definitely Not Living in Reality Because Your Brain Doesn't Want You To." *Quartz*, 16 September.

Benson, Rodney, & Victor Pickard (2017). "The Slippery Slope of the Oligarchy Media Model." *The Conversation*, 10 August.

Beran, Michael (2021). *WASPS: The Splendors and Miseries of an American Aristocracy.* New York: Pegasus Books.

Berman, Russell (2021). "The Blue States That Make It Hardest to Vote." *The Atlantic*, 15 April.

Bernstein, Joseph (2021). "Bad News." *Harper's*, September.

Bertrams, Alex, & Ann Krispenz (2023). "Dark Ego Vehicle Principle: Narcissism as a Predictor of Anti-sexual Harassment Activism." *Current Psychology*. https://doi.org/10.1007/s12144-023-04591-4.

Bertrand, Marianne, Emir Kamenica, & Jessica Pan (2015). "Gender Identity and Relative Income within Households." *Quarterly Journal of Economics* 130(2): 571–614.

Bestvater, Sam, et al. (2022). *Politics on Twitter: One-Third of Tweets from U.S. Adults Are Political.* Washington, DC: Pew Research Center.

Bhattacharya, Jay, & Mikko Packalen (2020). "Stagnation and Scientific Incentives." NBER Working Paper 26752. https://doi.org/10.3386/w26752.

Biddle, Sam (2021). "Revealed: Facebook's Secret Blacklist of 'Dangerous Individuals and Organizations.'" *The Intercept*, 12 October.

Binder, Amy, Daniel Davis, & Nick Bloom (2015). "Career Funneling: How Elite Students Learn to Define and Desire 'Prestigious' Jobs." *Sociology of Education* 89(1): 20–39.

Binder, Matt (2022). "Parler, Truth Social Won't Change Much Now That Elon Musk Owns Twit-ter." *Mashable*, 29 October.

Birger, Jon (2015). *Date-onomics: How Dating Became a Lopsided Numbers Game.* New York: Workman.

Blair, Karen, & Rhea Hoskin (2019). "Transgender Exclusion from the World of Dating: Patterns of Acceptance and Rejection of Hypothetical Trans Dating Partners as a Function of Sexual and Gender Identity." *Journal of Social and Personal Relationships* 36(7): 2074–2095.

Blake, Aaron (2021). "The Electoral Demise of 'Defund the Police.'" *Washington Post,* 5 November.

Blanpied, William (2009). "Science Policy in the Early New Deal, and Its Impacts in the 1940s." *Federal History* 1: 9–24.

Bloemraad, Irene, et al. (2019). "Membership without Social Citizenship? Deservingness and Redistribution as Grounds for Equality." *Daedalus* 148(3): 73–104.

Blom, Rianne, Raoul Hennekam, & Damiaan Denys (2012). "Body Integrity Identity Disorder." *PLoS One* 7(4): e34702.

Bloom, Nicholas, et al. (2020). "Are Ideas Getting Harder to Find?" *American Economic Review* 110(4): 1104–1144.

Boar, Corina, & Danial Lashkari (2021). "Occupational Choice and the Intergenerational Mobility of Welfare." NBER Working Paper 29381. https://doi.org/10.3386/w29381.

Bolonik, Kera (2019). "The Most Gullible Man in Cambridge." *The Cut,* 23 July.

Bonica, Adam (2013). "Mapping the Ideological Marketplace." *American Journal of Political Science* 58(2): 367–386.

Bonica, Adam (2023). "Database on Ideology, Money in Politics and Elections: Public Version 3.1 [Computer file]. Stanford, CA: Stanford University Libraries. https://data.stanford.edu/dime.

Bonilla-Silva, Eduardo (2017). *Racism without Racists: Color-Blind Racism and the Persistence of Racial Inequality in America.* Lanham, MD: Rowman & Littlefield.

Bor, Alexander, & Michael Bang Petersen (2021). "The Psychology of Online Political Hostility: A Comprehensive, Cross-National Test of the Mismatch Theory." *American Political Science Review* 116(1): 1–18.

Borjas, George (2005). "The Labor-Market Impact of High-Skill Immigration." *American Economic Review* 95(2): 56–60.

Borowiecki, Karol, & Christian Dahl (2021). "What Makes an Artist? The Evolution and Clustering of Creative Activity in the U.S. since 1850." *Regional Science and Urban Economics* 86:103614.

Bose, Nandita (2019). "Amazon Dismisses Idea Automation Will Eliminate All Its Warehouse Jobs Soon." *Reuters,* 1 May.

Boskin, Joseph (1976). *Urban Racial Violence in the 20th Century.* Beverly Hills, CA: Glencoe Press.

Bottum, Joseph (2014). *An Anxious Age: The Post-Protestant Ethic and the Spirit of America.* New York: Crown.

Bound, John, et al. (2021). "The Globalization of Postsecondary Education: The Role of International Students in the U.S. Higher Education System." *Journal of Economic Perspectives* 35(1): 163–184.

Bourdieu, Pierre (1986). "The Forms of Capital." In *Handbook of Theory and Research for the Sociology of Education,* ed. J. Richardson (pp. 241–258). Westport, CT: Greenwood Press.

Bourdieu, Pierre (1987). *Distinction: A Social Critique of the Judgement of Taste.* Cambridge, MA: Harvard University Press.

Bourdieu, Pierre (1990). *Homo Academicus.* Palo Alto, CA: Stanford University Press.

Bourdieu, Pierre (1993a). *The Field of Cultural Production.* New York: Columbia University Press.

Bourdieu, Pierre (1993b). *Language and Symbolic Power.* Cambridge, MA: Harvard University Press.

Bourdieu, Pierre (1996). *The Rules of Art: Genesis and Structure of the Literary Field.* Palo Alto, CA: Stanford University Press.

Bourdieu, Pierre, & Jean-Claude Passeron (1990). *Reproduction in Education, Society and Culture.* 2nd ed. London: Sage.

Bowen, William, & Derek Bok (2000). *The Shape of the River: Long-Term Consequences of Considering Race in College and University Admissions.* Princeton, NJ: Princeton University Press.

Bowles, Samuel, & Herbert Gintis (2013). *A Cooperative Species: Human Reciprocity and Its Evolution.* Princeton, NJ: Princeton University Press.

Brenan, Megan (2019). "Record-High 56% of U.S. Women Prefer Working to Homemaking." *Gallup*, 24 October.

Brenan, Megan (2020). "Women Still Handle Main Household Tasks in U.S." *Gallup*, 29 January.

Brennan, Jason, & Christopher Freiman (2022). "Against Champagne Socialists." *Reason*, February.

Bright, Liam Kofi (2023). "White Psychodrama." *Journal of Political Philosophy* 31(2): 198–221.

Bright, Liam Kofi (2024). "DuBoisian Leadership through Standpoint Epistemology." *The Monist* 107(1): 82–97.

Brint, Steven (1994). *In an Age of Experts.* Princeton, NJ: Princeton University Press.

Brint, Steven, Michaela Curran, & Matthew Mahutga (2022). "Are U.S. Professionals and Managers More Left than Blue-Collar Workers? An Analysis of the General Social Survey, 1974 to 2018." *Socius* 8. https://doi.org/10.1177/23780231211068654.

Brint, Steven, & Sarah Yoshikawa (2017). "The Educational Backgrounds of American Business and Government Leaders: Inter-industry Variation in Recruitment from Elite Colleges and Graduate Programs." *Social Forces* 96(2): 561–590.

Brocic, Milos, & Andrew Miles (2021). "College and the 'Culture War': Assessing Higher Education's Influence on Moral Attitudes." *American Sociological Review.* https://doi.org/10.1177/00031224211041094.

Bromwich, Jonah, & Ezra Marcus (2020). "The Anonymous Professor Who Wasn't." *New York Times*, 4 August.

Brook, Orian, Dave O'Brien, & Mark Taylor (2020). *Culture Is Bad for You: Inequality in the Cultural and Creative Industries.* Manchester: Manchester University Press.

Brown, Anna (2019). "Bisexual Adults Are Far Less Likely than Gay Men and Lesbians to Be 'Out' to the People in Their Lives." *Pew Research Center*, 18 June.

Brown, Jacob, & Ryan Enos (2021). "The Measurement of Partisan Sorting for 180 Million Voters." *Nature Human Behaviour.* https://doi.org/10.1038/s41562-021-01066-z.

Brown, Kevin (2014). *Because of Our Success: The Changing Racial and Ethnic Ancestry of Blacks on Affirmative Action.* Durham, NC: Carolina Academic Press.

Brown, Lee (2021). "White Influencer 'Identifies as Korean' after Surgeries to Look like BTS Singer." *New York Post*, 28 June.

Brown, Nadia, Fernando Tormos-Aponte, & Janelle Wong (2024). "An Incomplete Recognition: An Analysis of Political Science Department Statements after the Murder of George Floyd." *American Political Science Review.* https://doi.org/10.1017/S0003055423001375.

Brown, Riana, & Maureen Craig (2020). "Intergroup Inequality Heightens Reports of Discrimination along Alternative Identity Dimensions." *Personality and Social Psychology Bulletin* 46(6): 869–884.

Brown, Ryan, et al. (2011). "Moral Credentialing and the Rationalization of Misconduct." *Ethics & Behavior* 21(1): 1–12.

Brubaker, Rogers (2018). *Trans: Gender and Race in an Age of Unsettled Identities.* Princeton, NJ: Princeton University Press.

Bryne, Alyson, & Julian Barling (2017). "When She Brings Home the Job Status: Wives' Job Status, Status Leakage, and Marital Instability." *Organization Science* 28(2): 177–377.

Buckley, Cara (2012). "The New Student Activism." *New York Times*, 19 January.

Burge, Ryan (2023). "No One Participates in Politics More than Atheists." *Graphs about Religion*, 16 May. https://www.graphsaboutreligion.com/p/no-one-participates-in-politics-more.

Burgess, Matthew, et al. (2021). "Prepare Developed Democracies for Long-Run Economic Slowdowns." *Nature Human Behaviour* 5: 1608–1621.

Burrows, Dan (2020). "Where Millionaires Live in America." *Kiplinger*, 22 October.

Bursztyn, Leonardo, Thomas Fujiwara, & Amanda Pallais (2017). "'Acting Wife': Marriage Market Incentives and Labor Market Investments." *American Economic Review* 107(11): 3288–3319.

Buss, David (2021). *When Men Behave Badly: The Hidden Roots of Sexual Deception, Harassment and Assault*. New York: Little, Brown Spark.

Buss, David, & David Schmitt (2019). "Mate Preferences and Their Behavioral Manifestations." *Annual Review of Psychology* 70: 77–110.

Buss, David, et al. (2020). "Human Status Criteria: Sex Differences and Similarities across 14 Nations." *Journal of Personality and Social Psychology* 119(5): 979–998.

Cahn, Naomi, & June Carbone (2011). *Red Families v. Blue Families: Legal Polarization and the Creation of Culture*. Oxford: Oxford University Press.

Callahan, David (2010). *Fortunes of Change: The Rise of the Liberal Rich and the Remaking of America*. Hoboken, NJ: John Wiley & Sons.

Callahan, David (2018). *The Givers: Power, Money and Philanthropy in a New Gilded Age*. New York: Vintage Press.

Campbell, Bradley, & Jason Manning (2014). "Microaggressions and Moral Cultures." *Comparative Sociology* 13(6): 692–726.

Campbell, Bradley, & Jason Manning (2018). *The Rise of Victimhood Culture: Microaggressions, Safe Spaces, and the New Culture Wars*. London: Palgrave Macmillan.

Campbell, David, Geoffrey Layman, & John Green (2020). *Secular Surge: A New Fault Line in American Politics*. Cambridge: Cambridge University Press.

Campbell, Olivia (2018). "The Historical Struggle to Rid Socialism of Sexism." *Smithsonian Magazine*, 12 July.

Cantor, Jonathan, et al. (2021). "Who Is (and Is Not) Receiving Telemedicine Care during the COVID-19 Pandemic." *American Journal of Preventative Medicine* 61(3): 434–438.

Caplan, Bryan (2018). *The Case against Education: Why the Education System Is a Waste of Time and Money*. Princeton, NJ: Princeton University Press.

Caputo, Marc, & Sabrina Rodriguez (2021). "Democrats Fall Flat with 'Latinx' Language." *Politico*, 6 December.

Carnes, Nicholas, & Noam Lupu (2016). "What Good Is a College Degree? Education and Leader Quality Reconsidered." *Journal of Politics* 78(1): 35–49.

Carnevale, Anthony, Nicole Smith, & Jeff Strohl (2010). *Help Wanted: Projections of Jobs and Education Requirements through 2018*. Washington, DC: Georgetown University Center on Education and the Workforce.

Carr, Terrence (2017). "A Critique of GDP per Capita as a Measure of Wellbeing." *EconPress*, 23 January.

Carrington, Michal, Detlev Zwick, & Benjamin Neville (2016). "The Ideology of the Ethical Consumer Gap." *Marketing Theory* 16(1): 21–38.

Carson, Clayborne (2001). *The Autobiography of Martin Luther King Jr*. New York: Warner Books.

Cartwright, Ashleigh (2022). "A Theory of Racialized Cultural Capital." *Sociological Inquiry* 92(2): 317–340.

Cartwright, Nancy (2021). "Rigour versus the Need for Evidential Diversity." *Synthese* 199: 13095–13119.

Cascio, Jessica, & Ashby Plant (2015). "Prospective Moral Licensing: Does Anticipating Good Later Allow You to Be Bad Now?" *Journal of Experimental Social Psychology* 56: 110–116.

Cashin, Sheryll (2021). *White Space, Black Hood: Opportunity Hoarding and Segregation in the Age of Inequality*. Boston: Beacon Press.

Cass, Oren (2021). "Woking 9 to 5." *American Compass*, 24 September.

Cass, Oren, & Richard Oyeniran (2022). "The False Promise of Good Jobs." *American Compass*, 17 February.

Castilla, Emilio, & Stephen Benard (2010). "The Paradox of Meritocracy in Organizations." *Administrative Science Quarterly* 55(4): 543–676.

Cauwels, Peter, & Didier Sornette (2022). "Are 'Flow of Ideas' and 'Research Productivity' in Secular Decline?" *Technological Forecasting and Social Change* 174: 121267.

Cava, Kody (2022). "NPR Is Not Your Friend." *Current Affairs*, 28 September.

Cernik, Lizzie (2021). "'I Feel Hurt That My Life Has Ended Up Here': The Women Who Are Involuntary Celibates." *The Guardian*, 18 October.

Chakroff, Aleskandr, et al. (2015). "An Indecent Proposal: The Dual Functions of Indirect Speech." *Cognitive Science* 39(1): 199–211.

Chan, Jason, Probal Mojumder, & Anindya Ghose (2019). "The Digital Sin City: An Empirical Study of Craigslist's Impact on Prostitution Trends." *Information Systems Research* 30(1): 219–238.

Chauncey, George (2019). *Gay New York: Gender, Urban Culture, and the Making of the Gay Male World, 1890–1940*. New York: Basic Books.

Chen, Carolyn (2022). *Work Pray Code: When Work Becomes Religion in Silicon Valley*. Princeton, NJ: Princeton University Press.

Chen, Shawna, & Russell Contreras (2021). "Newsrooms Reckon with Their Own Story on Race." *Axios*, 13 November.

Cherid, Maha (2021). "'Ain't Got Enough Money to Pay Me Respect': Blackfishing, Cultural Appropriation, and the Commodification of Blackness." *Cultural Studies* 21(5): 359–364.

Chetty, Raj, et al. (2017). "Mobility Report Cards: The Role of Colleges in Intergenerational Mobility." NBER Working Paper 23618. https://doi.org/10.3386/w23618.

Chetty, Raj, et al. (2020). "Race and Economic Opportunity in the United States: An Intergenerational Perspective." *Quarterly Journal of Economics* 135(2): 711–783.

Chiappori, Pierre-Andre, Bernard Salanie, & Yoram Weiss (2017). "Partner Choice, Investment in Children, and the Marital College Premium." *American Economic Review* 107(8): 2109–2167.

Chibber, Vivek (2022). *The Class Matrix: Social Theory after the Cultural Turn*. Cambridge, MA: Harvard University Press.

Childress, Clayton, et al. (2021). "Genres, Objects, and the Contemporary Expression of Higher-Status Tastes." *Sociological Science* 8: 230–264.

Chinoy, Sahil (2019). "What Happened to America's Center of Gravity?" *New York Times*, 26 June.

Chinoy, Sahil, et al. (2023). "Zero-Sum Thinking and the Roots of U.S. Political Divides." NBER Working Paper 31688. https://doi.org/10.3386/w31688.

Chiswick, Barry, & RaeAnn Robinson (2021). "Women at Work in the United States since 1860: An Analysis of Unreported Family Workers." *Explorations in Economic History* 82. https://doi.org/10.1016/j.eeh.2021.101406.

Chokal-Ingram, Vijay, & Matthew Hansen (2016). *Almost Black: The True Story of How I Got into Medical School by Pretending to Be Black*. Pennsauken, NJ: BookBaby.

Chomsky, Noam (2002). *Understanding Power*. New York: New Press.

Chong, Dennis, Jack Citrin, & Morris Levy (2022). "The Realignment of Political Tolerance in the United States." *Perspectives on Politics*. https://doi.org/10.1017/S1537592722002079.

Chronicle of Higher Education (2021a). "Colleges with the Fewest and Most Full-Time-Equivalent Students per Noninstructional Staff Member, 2018–19." *Chronicle of Higher Education*, 15 August.

Chronicle of Higher Education (2021b). "Undergraduates Registered as Students with Disabilities, Fall 2019." *Chronicle of Higher Education*, 15 August.

Chu, Johan, & James Evans (2021). "Slowed Canonical Progress in Large Fields of Science." *Proceedings of the National Academy of Sciences* 118(41). https://doi.org/10.1073/pnas.2021636118.

Clark, Cory, & Bo Winegard (2020). "Tribalism in War and Peace: The Nature and Evolution of Ideological Epistemology and Its Significance for Modern Social Science." *Psychological Inquiry* 31(1): 1–22.

Clark, Cory, & Bo Winegard (2022). "Sex and the Academy." *Quillette*, 8 October.

Clarke, Jessica (2015). "Identity and Form." *California Law Review* 103(4): 747–839.

Clizza, Chris (2021). "Nancy Pelosi's Stunningly Tone-Deaf Quote on George Floyd." *CNN*, 21 April.

Coaston, Jane (2018). "Nike Has Made Billions Selling Rebellion to Young People." *Vox*, 6 September.

Coates, Ta-Nehisi (2017). *We Were Eight Years in Power: An American Tragedy.* New York: One World.

Coates, Ta-Nehisi (2018). "I'm Not Black, I'm Kanye." *The Atlantic*, 7 May.

Cobb, James (2018). "Even Though He Is Revered Today, MLK Was Widely Disliked by the American Public When He Was Killed." *Smithsonian Magazine*, 4 April.

Cobb, Jelani (2017). "Harvey Weinstein, Bill Cosby, and the Cloak of Charity." *New Yorker*, 14 October.

Cohen, G. A. (2001). *If You're an Egalitarian, How Come You're So Rich?* Cambridge, MA: Harvard University Press.

Cohen, Patricia (2015). "Study Finds Local Taxes Hit Lower Wage Earners Harder." *New York Times*, 13 January.

Cohen, Rachel (2021). "The Democratic Dilemma on Dark Money." *American Prospect*, 2 December.

Cohen, Robert (1993). *When the Old Left Was Young: Student Radicals and America's First Mass Student Movement, 1929–1941.* Oxford: Oxford University Press.

Cohn, Jonathan (2012). "Blue States Are from Scandinavia, Red States Are from Guatemala." *New Republic*, 5 October.

Cohn, Nate (2021). "How Educational Differences Are Widening America's Political Rift." *New York Times*, 8 September.

Cohn, Nate (2022). "Poll Shows Tight Race for Control of Congress as Class Divide Widens." *New York Times*, 13 July.

Collins, Patricia Hill (2000). *Black Feminist Thought.* 2nd ed. Abington, UK: Taylor & Francis.

Collins, Randall (2019). *The Credential Society: An Historical Sociology of Education and Stratification.* New York: Columbia University Press.

Columbus, Louis (2018). "10 Charts That Will Change Your Perspective on Amazon Prime's Growth." *Forbes*, 4 March.

Combahee River Collective (1977). "Combahee River Collective Statement." https://americanstudies .yale.edu/sites/default/files/files/Keyword%20Coalition_Readings.pdf.

Compton, D'Lane, & Tristan Bridges (2019). "2018 GSS Update on the U.S. LGB Population." *Inequality by (Interior) Design*, 12 April. https://inequalitybyinteriordesign.wordpress.com /2019/04/12/2018-gss-update-on-the-u-s-lgb-population/.

Compton, Janice, & Robert Pollak (2007). "Why Are Power Couples Increasingly Concentrated in Large Metropolitan Areas?" *Journal of Labor Economics* 25(3): 475–512.

Conti, Allie (2019). "Rich Families Are Legally Separating from Their Kids to Pay Less for College." *Vice*, 30 July.

Contreras, Russell (2022). "Latino Groups Want to Do Away with 'Latinx.'" *Axios*, 4 January.

Cooley, Erin, et al. (2019). "Complex Intersections of Race and Class: Among Social Liberals, Learning about White Privilege Reduces Sympathy, Increases Blame, and Decreases External Attributions for White People Struggling with Poverty." *Journal of Experimental Psychology: General* 148(12): 2218–2228.

Cooper, Bertrand (2021). "Who Actually Gets to Create Black Pop Culture?" *Current Affairs*, 25 July.

Cooper, Preston (2021). "Is College Worth It? A Comprehensive Return on Investment Analysis." *Foundation for Research on Equal Opportunity*, 19 October.

Corner, Adam (2013). "Ad Naseum." *Aeon*, 21 November.

Cote, Stephanie, et al. (2015). "High Economic Inequality Leads Higher Income Individuals to Be Less Generous." *Proceedings of the National Academy of Sciences* 112(52): 15838–15843.

Cousin, Bruno, Shamus Khan, & Ashley Mears (2018). "Theoretical and Methodological Pathways for Research on Elites." *Socioeconomic Review* 16(2): 225–249.

Cowen, Tyler (2015). "Peter Thiel on Stagnation, Innovation and What Not to Name Your Company." *Conversations with Tyler*, 6 April.

Cowen, Tyler (2017). *The Complacent Class: The Self-Defeating Quest for the American Dream.* New York: St. Martin's Press.

Cox, Daniel (2022). "The Political Gender Gap Is Exploding." *American Storylines,* 9 June. https://storylines.substack.com/p/the-political-gender-gap-is-exploding.

Cox, Daniel (2023). *From Swiping to Sexting: The Enduring Gender Divide in American Dating and Relationships.* Washington, DC: Survey Center on American Life.

Cox, Daniel, et al. (2020). "Socially Distant: How Our Networks Define Our Politics." *Survey Center on American Life,* 30 September.

Cox, Kiana, & Khadijah Edwards (2022). *Black Americans Have a Clear Vision for Reducing Racism but Little Hope It Will Happen.* Washington, DC: Pew Research Center.

Cox, Kiana, & Christine Tamir (2022). *Race Is Central to Identity for Black Americans and Affects How They Connect with Each Other.* Washington, DC: Pew Research Center.

Creamer, John, et al. (2022). *Poverty in the United States: 2021.* Washington, DC: U.S. Census Bureau.

Crenshaw, Kimberlé (1989). "Demarginalizing the Intersection of Race and Sex: A Black Feminist Critique of Antidiscrimination Doctrine, Feminist Theory and Antiracist Politics." *University of Chicago Legal Forum* 1989(1): 139–167.

Crenshaw, Kimberlé (2017). "Kimberlé Crenshaw on Intersectionality, More than Two Decades Later." *Columbia Law News,* 8 June.

Crenshaw, Kimberlé, et al., eds. (1996). *Critical Race Theory: The Key Writings That Formed the Movement.* New York: New Press.

Crispin, Jessa (2018). "Incels Aren't Just Angry Young Men." *DAME,* 29 May.

Cunningham, Scott, & Todd Kendall (2011). "Prostitution, Technology and the Law: New Data and Directions." In *Research Handbook on the Economics of Family Law,* ed. Lloyd Cohen & Joshua Wright (pp. 221–270). Northampton, MA: Edward Elgar.

Cunningham, Scott, & Todd Kendall (2016). "Prostitution Labor Supply and Education." SSRN working paper. https://doi.org/10.2139/ssrn.1583510.

Currid-Halkett, Elizabeth (2018). *The Sum of Small Things: A Theory of the Aspirational Class.* Princeton, NJ: Princeton University Press.

Cusset, François (2008). *French Theory: How Foucault, Derrida, Deleuze & Co. Transformed the Intellectual Life of the United States.* Minneapolis: University of Minnesota Press.

Dai, J. Doris, et al. (2021). "#NotAllWhites: Liberal-Leaning White Americans Racially Disidentify and Increase Support for Racial Equity." *Personality and Social Psychology Bulletin* 47(11): 1612–1632.

Daminger, Allison (2020). "De-gendered Processes, Gendered Outcomes: How Egalitarian Couples Makes Sense of Non-egalitarian Household Practices." *American Sociological Review* 85(5): 806–829.

Dang, Sheila (2022). "Exclusive: Twitter Is Losing Its Most Active Users, Internal Documents Show." *Reuters,* 26 October.

Daniels, Alex, & Julian Wyllie (2019). "Henry Ford III Elected to Ford Foundation's Board of Trustees." *Chronicle of Philanthropy,* 22 February.

Dank, Meredith, et al. (2014). *Estimating the Size and Structure of the Underground Commercial Sex Economy in Eight Major U.S. Cities.* Washington, DC: Urban Institute.

Dashan, Natalia (2019). "The Real Problem at Yale Is Not Free Speech." *Palladium,* 5 August.

Dastin, Jeffrey (2019). "Exclusive: Amazon Rolls Out Machines That Pack Orders and Replace Jobs." *Reuters,* 13 May.

Davidson, Thomas, Debasmita Bhattacharya, & Ingmar Weber (2019). "Racial Bias in Hate Speech and Abusive Language Detection Datasets." In *Proceedings of the Third Workshop on Abusive Language Online* (pp. 25–35). Florence: Association for Computational Linguistics. https://doi.org/10.18653/v1/W19-3504.

Davis, Tyler, et al. (2017). "How America Gives, Data: Leaders, Laggards, Giving Opportunities and More." *Chronicle of Philanthropy*, 2 October.

Day, Jennifer (2019). "Among the Educated, Women Earn 74 Cents for Every Dollar Men Make." *U.S. Census Bureau*, 29 May.

Day, John, & Charles Hall (2016). "The Myth of Urban Self-Sufficiency." In *America's Most Sustainable Cities and Regions: Surviving the 21st Century Megatrends* (pp. 25–36). New York: Springer.

DeBoer, Fredrik (2021a). "Will BlackLivesMatter Fall into the Elephant's Graveyard of Social Movements?" *Freddie deBoer*, 4 October. https://freddiedeboer.substack.com/p/has-blacklivesmatter-fallen-into.

DeBoer, Fredrik (2021b). "You Can't Censor Away Extremism (or Any Other Problem)." *Freddie deBoer*, 11 May. https://freddiedeboer.substack.com/p/you-cant-censor-away-extremism-or.

DeBoer, Fredrik (2022a). "The Gentrification of Disability." *Freddie deBoer*, 23 May. https://freddiedeboer.substack.com/p/the-gentrification-of-disability.

DeBoer, Fredrik (2022b). "'Multiple Personality Disorder' Probably Doesn't Exist, and There Certainly Hasn't Been an Explosion of It among the Youth." *Freddie deBoer*, 22 April. https://freddiedeboer.substack.com/p/multiple-personality-disorder-probably.

de Brey, Cristobal, et al. (2019). *Status and Trends in the Education of Racial and Ethnic Groups 2018*. Washington, DC: National Center for Education Statistics.

Delmas, Magali, & Vanessa Burbano (2011). "The Drivers of Greeenwashing." *California Management Review* 54(1): 64–87.

Del Ray, Jason (2022). "Leaked Amazon Memo Warns the Company Is Running Out of People to Hire." *Recode*, 17 June.

Deneen, Patrick (2018). "The Ignoble Lie." *First Things*, April 2018.

Denning, Andrew, & Heidi Tworek (2023). *The Interwar World*. London: Routledge.

DePillis, Lydia (2018). "Watch How Amazon Spread across the U.S." *CNN*, 4 October.

Derenocourt, Ellora, et al. (2022). "Wealth of Two Nations: The U.S. Racial Wealth Gap, 1860–2020." NBER Working Paper 30101. https://doi.org/10.3386/w30101.

DeSilver, Drew (2020). "Before the Coronavirus, Telework Was an Optional Benefit, Mostly for the Affluent Few." *Pew Research Center*, 20 March.

Desmond, Matthew (2023). *Poverty, by America*. New York: Crown.

DiCorpo, Ryan (2019). "Georgetown Reparations Plan for Slaves Sold by University Draws Criticism from Students." *America*, 4 November.

Dieter, Cheryl (2018). *Estimated Use of Water in the United States in 2015*. Reston, VA: U.S. Geological Survey.

Dikotter, Frank (2016). *The Cultural Revolution: A People's History, 1962–1976*. New York: Bloomsbury.

Dill, Kathryn (2022). "People Are Quitting Full-Time Jobs for Contract Work—and Making Six Figures." *Wall Street Journal*, 15 March.

Ding, Jamie (2022). "Video Game Workers Found Their Voices in the Pandemic. Could Unions Be Next?" *Los Angeles Times*, 19 March.

Dixon, Vince (2018). "The Case against Tipping in America." *Eater*, 22 February.

Dobbin, Frank (2011). *Inventing Equal Opportunity*. Princeton, NJ: Princeton University Press.

Dobbin, Frank, & Alexandra Kalev (2016). "Why Diversity Programs Fail." *Harvard Business Review* 94(7): 52–60.

Dobbin, Frank, & Alexandra Kalev (2021). "The Civil Rights Revolution at Work: What Went Wrong." *Annual Review of Sociology* 47: 281–303.

Doctor, Ken (2016). "Did the Media Win the Election?" *Politico*, 15 November.

Doctor, Ken (2017). "Trump Bump Grows into Subscription Surge—and Not Just for the New York Times." *The Street*, 3 March.

Doherty, Carroll, et al. (2016). "A Wider Ideological Gap Between More and Less Educated Adults." *Pew Research Center*, 26 April.

Doherty, Carroll, et al. (2017). *The Partisan Divide on Political Values Grows Even Wider.* Washington, DC: Pew Research Center.

Doherty, Carroll, et al. (2020). "In Changing U.S. Electorate, Race and Education Remain Stark Dividing Lines." *Pew Research Center*, 2 June.

Doherty, Carroll, et al. (2021). "Beyond Red vs. Blue: The Political Typology." *Pew Research Center*, 9 November.

Donaldson, Jenyne, & Anita Bennett (2022). "Amber Heard's Domestic Violence Op-Ed Was Timed to 'Capitalize' on 'Aquaman' Publicity, Email Reveals." *The Wrap*, 28 April.

Donovan, Paul (2020). *Profit and Prejudice: The Luddites of the Fourth Industrial Revolution.* London: Routledge.

Dotti-Sani, Giulia, & Judith Treas (2016). "Educational Gradients in Parents' Child-Care Time across Countries, 1965–2012." *Journal of Marriage and Family* 78(4): 1083–1096.

Douek, Evelyn (2020). "The Rise of Content Cartels." *Knight First Amendment Institute at Columbia University*, 11 February.

Dougherty, Danny, et al. (2018). "Where Graduates Move after College." *Wall Street Journal*, 15 May.

Dourado, Eli (2020). "Notes on Technology in the 2020s." *Eli Dourado Blog*, 31 December. https://elidourado.com/blog/notes-on-technology-2020s/.

Downs, Anthony (1972). "Up and Down with Ecology: The 'Issue-Attention' Cycle." *Public Interest* 28: 38–50.

Drake, Bruce (2013). "Incarceration Gap Widens between Whites and Blacks." *Pew Research Center*, 6 September.

Drezner, Daniel (2017). *The Ideas Industry: How Pessimists, Partisans and Plutocrats Are Transforming the Marketplace of Ideas.* Oxford: Oxford University Press.

Drummond, Caitlin, & Baruch Fischhoff (2017). "Individuals with Greater Science Literacy and Education Have More Polarized Beliefs on Controversial Science Topics." *Proceedings of the National Academy of Sciences* 114(36): 9587–9592.

Drutman, Lee (2017). "Political Divisions in 2016 and Beyond." *Voter Study Group*, June.

Dur, Robert, & Max van Lent (2018). "Socially Useless Jobs." *Industrial Relations: A Journal of Economy and Society* 58(1): 3–16.

Durkheim, Emile (2008). "Book II: The Elementary Beliefs." In *The Elementary Forms of Religious Life*, trans. Joseph Swain (pp. 102–298). Mineola, NY: Dover.

Durrant, Russil (2024). "Addiction and Substance Abuse." In *The Oxford Handbook of Evolution and the Emotions*, ed. Laith al-Shawaf & Todd Shackelford. Oxford: Oxford University Press.

Dzieza, Josh (2021). "Revolt of the Delivery Workers." *Curbed*, 13 September.

Eagan, Eileen (1982). *Class, Culture, and the Classroom: The Student Peace Movement of the 1930s.* Philadelphia: Temple University Press.

The Economist (2019). "Socially Liberal Companies Really Do Contribute More to Democrats." *The Economist*, 29 August.

Edsall, Thomas (2018). "The Democrats' Gentrification Problem." *New York Times*, 19 April.

Edsall, Thomas (2022). "The Gender Gap Is Taking Us to Unexpected Places." *New York Times*, 12 January.

Edsall, Thomas (2023). *The Point of No Return: American Democracy at the Crossroads.* Princeton, NJ: Princeton University Press.

Effron, Daniel (2014). "Making Mountains of Morality from Molehills of Virtue: Threat Causes People to Overestimate Their Moral Credentials." *Personality and Social Psychology Bulletin* 40(8): 972–985.

Effron, Daniel, & Paul Conway (2015). "When Virtue Leads to Villainy: Advances in Research on Moral Self-Licensing." *Current Opinion in Psychology* 6: 32–35.

Effron, Daniel, Dale Miller, & Benoit Monin (2012). "Inventing Racist Roads Not Taken: The Licensing Effect of Immoral Counterfactual Behaviors." *Journal of Personality and Social Psychology* 103(6): 916–932.

Ehrenberg, John (2017). "What Can We Learn from Occupy's Failure?" *Palgrave Communications* 3: 17062.

Ehrenhalt, Alan (2018). "Why Some Cities Want Graffiti." *Governing*, 28 June.

Ehrenreich, Barbara (2020). *Fear of Falling: The Inner Life of the Middle Class*. New York: Twelve.

Ehrenreich, Barbara (2021). *Nickel and Dimed: On (Not) Getting by in America*. New York: Picador.

Ehrenreich, Barbara, & John Ehrenreich (1969). *Long March, Short Spring: The Student Uprising at Home and Abroad*. New York: Monthly Review Press.

Ehrenreich, Barbara, & John Ehrenreich (1977a). "The New Left: A Case Study in Professional-Managerial Class Radicalism." *Radical America* 11(3): 7–24. https://libcom.org/files/Rad%20America%20V11%20I3.pdf.

Ehrenreich, Barbara, & John Ehrenreich (1977b). "The Professional Managerial Class." *Radical America* 11(2): 7–32. https://library.brown.edu/pdfs/1125403552886481.pdf.

Einwohner, Rachel, & Elle Rochford (2019). "After the March: Using Instagram to Perform and Sustain the Women's March." *Sociological Forum* 34(S1): 1090–1111.

Eisgruber, Christopher (2020). "Letter from President Eisgruber on the University's Efforts to Combat Systemic Racism." *Princeton University Office of Communication*, 2 September.

Ellenberg, Jordan (2014). "The Summer's Most Unread Book Is . . ." *Wall Street Journal*, 3 July.

Ellis, Christopher, & James Stimson (2012). *Ideology in America*. Cambridge: Cambridge University Press.

Ember, Sydney (2020). "Bernie Sanders Predicted Revolution, Just Not This One." *New York Times*, 19 June.

England, Jason (2020). "Why Was It So Easy for Jessica Krug to Fool Everyone?" *Chronicle of Higher Education*, 2 October.

England, Paula (2010). "The Gender Revolution: Uneven and Stalled." *Gender & Society* 24(2): 149–166.

Englehardt, Andrew (2019). "The Race Politics Makes: Parties, Polarization and White Racial Attitudes." PhD dissertation, Vanderbilt University. https://ir.vanderbilt.edu/bitstream/handle/1803/12280/engelhardt_dissertation_v050319.pdf.

Englehardt, Andrew (2023). "Observational Equivalence in Explaining Attitude Change: Have White Racial Attitudes Genuinely Changed?" *American Journal of Political Science* 67(2): 411–425.

Enos, Ryan, & Eitan Hersh (2015). "Party Activists as Campaign Advertisers: The Ground Campaign as a Principal-Agent Problem." *American Political Science Review* 109(2): 252–278.

Espenshade, Thomas, & Alexandria Radford (2009). *No Longer Separate, Not Yet Equal: Race and Class in Elite College Admission and Campus Life*. Princeton, NJ: Princeton University Press.

Evans, C. Stephen (2022). "Kierkegaard on Faith, Doubt and Uncertainty." In *Faith, Hope and Love: The Theological Virtues and Their Opposites*, ed. Troy DuJardin & M. David Eckel (pp. 61–80). Cham, Switzerland: Springer.

Evans, Tim, & Natalia Contreras (2020). "Satchuel Cole, Leader in the Fight for Racial Equality in Indianapolis, Lied about Own Race." *Indy Star*, 18 September.

Evans, Will (2019). "Ruthless Quotas at Amazon Are Maiming Employees." *The Atlantic*, 25 November.

Eveleth, Rose (2014). "Academics Write Papers Arguing over How Many People Read (and Cite) Their Papers." *Smithsonian Magazine*, 25 March.

Evershed, Megan (2021). "How an Upper West Side Hotel Came to Embody the City's Failure on Homelessness." *New Republic*, 31 March.

Ewen, Stuart (2001). *Captains of Consciousness: Advertising and the Social Roots of Consumer Culture*. New York: Basic Books.

Eyal, Gil (2013). "For a Sociology of Expertise: The Social Origins of the Autism Epidemic." *American Journal of Sociology* 118(4): 863–907.

Eyal, Gil (2019). *The Crisis of Expertise.* Cambridge: Polity Press.

Fales, Melissa, et al. (2016). "Mating Markets and Bargaining Hands: Mate Preferences for Attractiveness and Resources in Two National U.S. Studies." *Personality and Individual Differences* 88: 78–87.

Falkenheim, Jaquelina, et al. (2021). *Doctorate Recipients from U.S. Universities 2020.* Alexandria, VA: National Center for Science and Engineering Statistics.

Fan, Jennifer (2019). "Woke Capital: The Role of Corporations in Social Movements." *Harvard Business Law Review* 9: 441–494.

Fang, Marina (2017). "How Harvey Weinstein Used His Liberal Politics to Cover Up His History of Sexual Abuse." *Huffington Post*, 6 December.

Farrow, Anne, Joel Lang, & Jennifer Frank (2006). *Complicity: How the North Promoted, Prolonged and Profited from Slavery.* New York: Ballantine Books.

Farrow, Katherine, Gilles Grolleau, & Noaufel Mzoughi (2021). "'Let's Call a Spade a Spade, Not a Gardening Tool': How Euphemisms Shape Moral Judgement in Corporate Social Responsibility Domains." *Journal of Business Research* 131: 254–267.

Fassin, Didier, & Richard Rechtman (2009). *The Empire of Trauma: An Inquiry into the Condition of Victimhood.* Princeton, NJ: Princeton University Press.

Ferwerda, Jeremy, et al. (2017). "Explaining Opposition to Refugee Resettlement: The Role of NIMBYism and Perceived Threats." *Science Advances* 3(9): e1700812.

Feyerabend, Paul (2010). *Against Method.* London: Verso.

Fickenscher, Lisa (2021). "NYC Law Would Force Delivery Apps to Cover Costs of Driver Accidents." *New York Post*, 8 November.

Fields, Barbara (1990). "Slavery, Race and Ideology in the United States of America." *New Left Review* 1(181): 95–118.

Fields, Karen, & Barbara Fields (2012). *Racecraft: The Soul of Inequality in American Life.* London: Verso.

Fingerhut, Adam (2011). "Straight Allies: What Predicts Homosexuals' Alliance with the LGBT Community?" *Journal of Applied Social Psychology* 41(9): 2230–2248.

Fink, Larry (2018). "A Sense of Purpose." *Harvard Law School Forum on Corporate Governance*, 17 January. https://corpgov.law.harvard.edu/2018/01/17/a-sense-of-purpose/.

Finkel, Eli (2019). "Highly-Educated Americans Paved the Way for Divorce—Then Embraced Marriage." *The Atlantic*, 8 January.

Finkel, Eli, et al. (2020). "Political Sectarianism in America." *Science* 370(6516): 533–536.

Fiorina, Morris (2016). "Has the American Public Polarized?" *Hoover Institution*, 14 September.

Fiorina, Morris (2017). *Unstable Majorities: Polarization, Party Sorting, and Political Stalemate.* Stanford, CA: Hoover Institution Press.

Fischer, Molly (2018). "The Great Awokening: What Happens to Culture in an Era of Identity Politics?" *New York Magazine*, 8 January.

Fischer, Sara (2021). "Media on the Mend." *Axios*, 15 June.

Fisher, Dana (2019). *American Resistance: From the Women's March to the Blue Wave.* New York: Columbia University Press.

Fisher, Dana, & Quinn Renaghan (2023). "Understanding the Growing Radical Flank of the Climate Movement as the World Burns." *Brookings*, 26 July.

Fisher, Dana, et al. (2019). "The Science of Contemporary Street Protest: New Efforts in the United States." *Science Advances* 5(10). https://doi.org/10.1126/sciadv.aaw5461.

Florida, Richard (2002). *The Rise of the Creative Class.* New York: Basic Books.

Florida, Richard (2017). *The New Urban Crisis: How Our Cities Are Increasing Inequality, Deepening Segregation, and Failing the Middle Class—and What We Can Do about It.* New York: Basic Books.

Florida, Richard (2018). "Why Is Your State Red or Blue? Look to the Dominant Occupational Class." *Bloomberg*, 28 November.

Florida, Richard (2019a). "Blue Collar and Service Workers Fare Better outside Superstar Cities." *CityLab*, 21 May.

Florida, Richard (2019b). "The Geography of Brain Drain in America." *CityLab*, 3 May.

Florida, Richard (2019c). *The Rise of the Creative Class: Updated Edition.* New York: Basic Books.

Flynn, D. J., Brendan Nyhan, & Jason Reifler (2017). "The Nature and Origins of Misperceptions: Understanding False and Unsupported Beliefs about Politics." *Political Psychology* 38(S1): 127–150.

Foa, Roberto, et al. (2022). *A World Divided: Russia, China and the West.* Cambridge: Center for the Future of Democracy.

Folke, Olle, & Johanna Rickne (2022). "Sexual Harassment and Gender Inequality in the Labor Market." *Quarterly Journal of Economics* 137(4): 2163–2212.

Folkerts, Jean (2014). "History of Journalism Education." *Journalism & Communication Monographs.* https://doi.org/10.1177/1522637914541379.

Forman, Laura (2020). "New California Law Could Spoil Some Growth for Food Delivery Platforms." *Wall Street Journal*, 26 December.

Forman-Katz, Naomi, & Mark Jurkowitz (2022). "U.S. Journalists Differ from the Public in Their Views of 'Bothsiderism' in Journalism." *Pew Research Center*, 13 July.

Foster, Jacob, Andrey Rzhetsky, & James Evans (2015). "Tradition and Innovation in Scientists' Research Strategies." *American Sociological Review* 80(5): 875–908.

Fowler, Bridget (2020). "Pierre Bourdieu on Social Transformation, with Particular Reference to Political and Symbolic Revolutions." *Theory and Society* 49: 439–463.

Fox, Justin (2018). "Government Work Has Been Going Out of Style." *Bloomberg*, 7 September.

Fox, Liana (2020). "The Supplemental Poverty Measure: 2019." *U.S. Census Bureau Report P60-272*, September.

FRA (2022). *Bias in Algorithms: Artificial Intelligence and Discrimination.* Geneva: European Union Agency for Fundamental Rights. https://fra.europa.eu/sites/default/files/fra_uploads/fra-2022-bias-in-algorithms_en.pdf.

Frank, Robert (2015). "Most Millionaires Say They're Middle Class." *CNBC*, 6 May.

Frank, Thomas (1997). *The Conquest of Cool: Business Culture, Counterculture and the Rise of Hip Consumerism.* Chicago: University of Chicago Press.

Franklin, Joshua (2022). "Stakeholder Capitalism Is 'Not Woke,' Says JPMorgan's Jamie Dimon." *Financial Times*, 2 June.

Freedman, Miriam (2003). "Disabling the SAT." *Education Next* 3(4). https://www.educationnext.org/disablingthesat/.

Freehan, Blair (2021). "What the F*ck Happened to Social Media Engagement in 2020?" *Rival IQ*, 13 July. https://www.rivaliq.com/blog/social-engagement-benchmark-trends-2020/.

Freeman, Jo (1976). "Trashing: The Dark Side of Sisterhood." *Ms.*, April. https://www.jofreeman.com/joreen/trashing.htm.

Freeman, Richard (1976). *The Overeducated American.* New York: Academic Press.

Frenette, Alexandre, Nathan Martin, & Steven Tepper (2018). "Oscillate Wildly: The Underacknowledged Prevalence, Predictors and Outcomes of Multi-disciplinary Arts Practice." *Cultural Trends* 27(5): 339–352.

Frenette, Alexandre, & Richard Ocejo (2018). "Sustaining Enchantment: How Cultural Workers Manage Precariousness and Routine." *Research in the Sociology of Work* 32: 35–60.

Friedman, Benjamin (2006). "The Moral Consequences of Economic Growth." *Society* 43(2): 15–22.

Friedman, Gillian (2021). "Jobless, Selling Nudes Online and Still Struggling." *New York Times*, 13 January.

Fry, Richard (2022a). "College Grads in the U.S. Tend to Partner with Each Other—Especially if Their Parents Also Graduated from College." *Pew Research Center*, 7 September.

Fry, Richard (2022b). "Young Women Are Out-Earning Young Men in Several U.S. Cities." *Pew Research Center*, 28 March.

Fu, Angela (2021). "Not Just a Wave, but a Movement: Journalists Unionize at Record Numbers." *Poynter*, 16 July.

Fuller, Joseph, et al. (2017). *Dismissed by Degrees*. New York: Accenture.

Furnas, Alexander, & Timothy LaPira (2024). "The People Think What I Think: False Consensus and Unelected Elite Misperception of Public Opinion." *American Journal of Political Science*. https://doi.org/10.1111/ajps.12833.

Galka, Max (2017). "America's Geography of Wealth: The Shrinking Urban Middle Class Visualized." *The Guardian*, 17 May.

Gallagher, Brenden (2019). "You Can't Eat Your Dreams. Hollywood Expects Assistants to Do Just That." *Talk Poverty*, 14 November.

Gallup (2023). "Abortion Trends by Party Identification." *Gallup.* https://news.gallup.com/poll/246278/abortion-trends-party.aspx.

Galston, William (2019). "How Race and Education Are Reshaping Ideology in the Democratic Party." *Brookings*, 19 February.

Gamerman, Amy (2020). "Luxury Developers Are Curating Their Condos with In-House Artists." *Wall Street Journal*, 1 April.

Ganzach, Yoav, & Yaacov Schul (2021). "Partisan Ideological Attitudes: Liberals Are Tolerant; the Intelligent Are Intolerant." *Journal of Personality and Social Psychology* 120(6): 1551–1566.

Garcia, Paola (2020). "Boycotting Hajj: Why Saudi Arabia Does Not Represent Islam." *Inside Arabia*, 10 February.

Gardner, Chelsea (2020). "Exploring the Role of Skin Tone among Low-Income Black College Students." *Inquiries Journal* 12(10).

Gauchat, Gordon (2012). "Politicization of Science in the Public Sphere: A Study of Public Trust in the United States, 1974 to 2010." *American Sociological Review* 77(2): 167–187.

Gavin, Lettie (1997). *American Women in World War I: They Also Served*. Boulder: University Press of Colorado.

GDELT Project (2018). "Mapping the Geography of Television News 2009–2018." *The GDELT Project Blog*, 18 November. https://blog.gdeltproject.org/mapping-the-geography-of-television-news-2009-2018/.

Ge, Suqin, Elliot Isaac, & Amalia Miller (2019). "Elite Schools and Opting In: Effects of College Selectivity on Career and Family Outcomes." NBER Working Paper 25215. https://doi.org/10.3386/w25315.

Geary, Daniel (2008). "'Becoming International Again': C. Wright Mills and the Emergence of a Global New Left, 1956–1962." *Journal of American History* 95(3): 710–736.

Gebre-Medhin, Ben, et al. (2022). "Application Essays and the Ritual Production of Merit in US Selective Admissions." *Poetics* 94: 101706.

Gelman, Andrew (2009). *Red State, Blue State, Rich State, Poor State: Why Americans Vote the Way They Do*. Princeton, NJ: Princeton University Press.

Gerson, Jacob, & Jeannie Suk (2016). "The Sex Bureaucracy." *California Law Review* 104(4): 881–948.

Ghaffary, Shirin, & Jason Del Rey (2020). "The Big Tech Antitrust Report Has One Big Conclusion: Amazon, Apple, Facebook and Google Are Anti-competitive." *Recode*, 6 October.

Al-Gharbi, Musa (2014). "Don't Think of the 'Islamic State' in Religious Terms." *Middle East Policy Council*, 31 October. Revised and expanded version. https://musaalgharbi.com/2014/10/31/yes-isis-is-islamic-but-it-really-really-doesnt-matter/.

Al-Gharbi, Musa (2016a). "Ammon Bundy Is Not a Terrorist: The Authorities Are Waiting Out the Militia—Just as They Should Do with Black Lives Matter Protesters." *Salon*, 9 January. Revised and updated version. https://musaalgharbi.com/2016/01/09/no-ammon-bundy-is-not-a-terrorist/.

Al-Gharbi, Musa (2016b). "From Political Liberalism to Para-liberalism: Epistemological Plural-ism, Cognitive Liberalism & Authentic Choice." *Comparative Philosophy* 7(2): 1–25.

Al-Gharbi, Musa (2016c). "How I Predicted Trump's Victory." *National Interest*, 14 November. Expanded version. https://musaalgharbi.com/2016/11/10/trumps-victory-not-surprising/.

Al-Gharbi, Musa (2016d). "The 1 Percent Wins Again: How Entrepreneurship—Supposedly the Cornerstone of American Society—Favors the Wealthy." *Salon*, 20 March. Revised and updated version. https://musaalgharbi.com/2016/03/20/myth-reality-american-entrepreneurship/.

Al-Gharbi, Musa (2018a). "DNA Is Irrelevant—Elizabeth Warren Is Simply Not Cherokee." *The Hill*, 19 October. Revised and updated version. https://musaalgharbi.com/2018/10/19/what-was -elizabeth-warren-thinking/.

Al-Gharbi, Musa (2018b). "Race and the Race for the White House: On Social Research in the Age of Trump." *American Sociologist* 49(4): 496–519. https://osf.io/preprints/socarxiv/n8bkh.

Al-Gharbi, Musa (2019a). "Actually Students Are Substantially Less Free than the General Public." *Heterodox Academy*, April. Revised and updated version. https://musaalgharbi.com/2019/04 /19/comparing-perceived-freedom-of-expression-on-campus-v-off/.

Al-Gharbi, Musa (2019b). "Seizing the Means of Knowledge Production." *Heterodox Academy*, 4 October. Revised and updated version. https://musaalgharbi.com/2019/10/04/reactionary -myopic-approaches-higher-ed-reform/.

Al-Gharbi, Musa (2020a). "Amy Cooper: The Paradox of the Shameless White Liberal." *Public Semi-nar*, 29 May. Revised and updated version. https://musaalgharbi.com/2020/05/29/karen -democrat/.

Al-Gharbi, Musa (2020b). "The Awokening Will Not Bring an End to the Nightmare." *Interfaith America*, 15 December. Revised and expanded version. https://musaalgharbi.com/2020/12 /15/great-awokening-racial-realities/.

Al-Gharbi, Musa (2020c). "Callosal Failure: One Hundred Years of Viewpoint Diversity Activism." *Heterodox Academy*, 14 January. Revised and updated version. https://musaalgharbi.com/2020 /01/14/positionality-homogeneity-social-research-holism/.

Al-Gharbi, Musa (2020d). "Democrats No Longer Have a Coalition." *The Nation*, 23 November.

Al-Gharbi, Musa (2020e). "Diversity-Related Training: What Is It Good For?" *Heterodox Acad-emy*, 16 September. Updated and expanded version. https://musaalgharbi.com/2020/09/16 /diversity-important-related-training-terrible/.

Al-Gharbi, Musa (2020f). "Partisans Agree Muslims Face Lots of Discrimination." *Interfaith Amer-ica*, 9 October. Revised and expanded version. https://musaalgharbi.com/2020/10/09/social -networks-shape-politics/2/.

Al-Gharbi, Musa (2020g). "Universities Run on Disposable Scholars." *Chronicle of Higher Educa-tion*, 5 May. Updated and expanded version. https://musaalgharbi.com/2020/05/01/disposable -scholars/.

Al-Gharbi, Musa (2020h). "Who Gets to Define What's Racist?" *Contexts*, 15 May. Revised and updated version. https://musaalgharbi.com/2020/05/15/definition-racist-actions-actors/.

Al-Gharbi, Musa (2021a). "Education, Social Elites, and Uneven Racial Progress." *Heterodox Acad-emy*, 17 February. Revised and updated version. https://musaalgharbi.com/2021/02/17/one -lifetime-black-americans-college/.

Al-Gharbi, Musa (2021b). "Difference and Repetition in the Viewpoint Diversity Space." *Heterodox Academy*, 27 February. Revised and updated version. https://musaalgharbi.com/2020/01/14 /positionality-homogeneity-social-research-holism/2/.

Al-Gharbi, Musa (2022). "First World Problems." *Reason*, 20 February. Revised and updated ver-sion. https://musaalgharbi.com/2022/02/20/asian-americans-loneliest-americans/.

Al-Gharbi, Musa (2023a). "Education as Privilege Laundering." *Inside Higher Ed*, 10 July. Expanded version available here. https://musaalgharbi.com/2023/07/10/education-and-privilege -laundering/.

Al-Gharbi, Musa (2023b). "The 'Great Awokening' of Scholarship May Be Ending." *Heterodox Academy*, 16 February. Updated version. https://musaalgharbi.com/2023/02/08/great-awokening-ending/2/.

Al-Gharbi, Musa (2023c). "How to Understand the Well-Being Gap between Liberals and Conservatives." *American Affairs*, 21 March. Expanded version. https://musaalgharbi.com/2023/03/21/ideological-gaps-mental-illness-well-being/.

Al-Gharbi, Musa (2023d). "How Well Do U.S. Faculty Reflect America? (Spoiler: Not Well)." *Heterodox Academy*, 24 January. Expanded version. https://musaalgharbi.com/2023/01/24/college-professors-representation-disparities/.

Al-Gharbi, Musa (2023e). "Woke-Ism Is Winding Down." *Compact*, 8 February. Revised and expanded version. https://musaalgharbi.com/2023/02/08/great-awokening-ending/.

Al-Gharbi, Musa (2023f). "Concerns about 'Leftist Indoctrination' in Higher Ed Are Inaccurate. But This Doesn't Make Them Unreasonable." *Heterodox Academy*, 29 June. Revised and expanded version. https://musaalgharbi.com/2020/02/06/surfacing-students-ideological-diversity/2/.

Al-Gharbi, Musa (2023g). "Free Speech Advocates Are Often Hypocrites. This Doesn't Make the Cause Less Important." *Reason*, 20 November. Revised and expanded version. https://musaalgharbi.com/2023/11/20/censorship-self-science-paper/4/.

Al-Gharbi, Musa (2024). "Misunderstanding Antisemitism in America." *Slow Boring*, 11 January. Revised and expanded version. https://musaalgharbi.com/2024/01/11/misunderstanding-antisemitism-america/.

Al-Gharbi, Musa, & Jonathan Haidt (2017). "It's Disadvantaged Groups That Suffer Most When Free Speech Is Curtailed on Campus." *The Atlantic*, 8 July. Revised and updated version. https://musaalgharbi.com/2017/07/08/progressives-vulnerable-groups-campus-free-speech-protections/.

Gibbs, Stephen (2021a). "Exclusive: Why This Document Could Change Racial Identity Politics at Aussie Universities Forever." *Daily Mail*, 17 July.

Gibbs, Stephen (2021b). "How White Aussies Who Pretend to Be Aboriginal Are Taking Over Universities and Stealing High-Paid Jobs Meant for Real Indigenous Australians—and Their Numbers Are Skyrocketing." *Daily Mail*, 9 July.

Gibson, Caitlin (2016). "How 'Politically Correct' Went from Compliment to Insult." *Washington Post*, 13 January.

Gibson, James, & Joseph Sutherland (2021). "Keeping Your Mouth Shut: Spiraling Self-Censorship in the United States." *SSRN*. https://doi.org/10.2139/ssrn.3647099.

Gilberstadt, Hannah, & Andrew Daniller (2020). "Liberals Make Up the Largest Share of Democratic Voters, But Their Growth Has Slowed in Recent Years." *Pew Research*, 17 January.

Gioia, Ted (2022). "Is Old Music Killing New Music?" *The Atlantic*, 23 January.

Girard, René (2001). *I See Satan Fall like Lightning*. Maryknoll, NY: Orbis Books.

Giridharadas, Anand (2018). *Winners Take All: The Elite Charade of Changing the World*. New York: Knopf.

Gitlin, Todd (1993). *The Sixties: Years of Hope, Days of Rage*. New York: Bantam Books.

Glancey, Tess (2021). "Fox News Digital Surpasses CNN in Total Multiplatform Minutes in March." *Businesswire*, 22 April.

Glasford, Demis (2022). "The Privileged Liberal Principle-Implementation Gap: How the Personal Behavior of Privileged Liberals Contributes to Social Inequality." *Journal of Applied Social Psychology* 52(9): 865–885.

Godlewski, Nina (2018). "Amazon Working Conditions: Urinating in Trash Cans, Shamed to Work Injured, List of Employee Complaints." *Newsweek*, 12 September.

Goffman, Erving (1983). "The Interaction Order: American Sociological Association 1982 Presidential Address." *American Sociological Review* 48(1): 1–17.

Goldberg, Zach (2020). "How the Media Led the Great Racial Awakening." *Tablet*, 4 August.

Goldberg, Zach (2022a). "Explaining Shifts in White Racial Liberalism: The Role of Collective Moral Emotions and Media Effects." PhD dissertation, Georgia State University. https://doi.org/10.57709/28976321.

Goldberg, Zach (2022b). "Is Defunding the Police a 'Luxury Belief'? Analyzing White vs. Nonwhite Democrats' Attitudes on Depolicing." *Manhattan Institute*, 8 September.

Goldberg, Zach (2023). *The Rise of College Educated Democrats.* New York: Manhattan Institute.

Golden, Lonnie (2015). "Irregular Work Scheduling and Its Consequences." *Economic Policy Institute*, 9 April.

Goldin, Claudia (2014). "A Grand Gender Convergence: Its Last Chapter." *American Economic Review* 104(4): 1091–1119.

Goldin, Claudia, & Lawrence Katz (2011). "Putting the 'Co' in Education: Timing, Reasons and Consequences of College Coeducation from 1835 to the Present." *Journal of Human Capital* 5(4): 377–417.

Goldstein, Dana, & Jugal Patel (2019). "Need Extra Time on Tests? It Helps to Have Cash." *New York Times*, 30 July.

Goldstein, Eric (2008). "The Great Wave: Eastern European Jewish Immigration to the United States, 1880–1924." In *The Columbia History of Jews and Judaism in America*, ed. Marc Raphael (pp. 70–92). New York: Columbia University Press.

Gonzalez, Christian (2019a). "Capitalist Critics on the Right." *City Journal*, 6 September.

Gonzalez, Christian (2019b). "The New Neocons." *Intercollegiate Studies Institute*, 4 June.

Gonzalez, Matt (2023). "Why Are DEI Roles Disappearing?" *SHRM*, 15 March.

Gonzalez-Barrera, Ana (2019). "Hispanics with Darker Skin Are More Likely to Experience Discrimination than Those with Lighter Skin." *Pew Research Center*, 2 July.

Goodhart, David (2017). *The Road to Somewhere: The Populist Revolt and the Future of Politics.* London: Hurst.

Goodman, Amy (2006). "Stephen Colbert's Blistering Performance Mocking Bush and the Press Goes Ignored by the Media." *Democracy Now*, 3 May.

Gordon, Rachel, Robert Crosnoe, & Xue Wang (2014). *Physical Attractiveness and the Accumulation of Social and Human Capital in Adolescence and Young Adulthood: Assets and Distractions.* New York: Wiley-Blackwell.

Gordon, Robert (2017). *The Rise and Fall of American Growth: The U.S. Standard of Living since the Civil War.* Princeton, NJ: Princeton University Press.

Gorski, Paul (2019a). "Fighting Racism, Battling Burnout: Causes of Activist Burnout in US Racial Justice Activists." *Ethnic and Racial Studies* 42(5): 667–687.

Gorski, Paul (2019b). "Racial Battle Fatigue and Activist Burnout in Racial Justice Activists of Color at Predominately White Colleges and Universities." *Race Ethnicity and Education* 22(1): 1–20.

Gorski, Paul, & Noura Erakat (2019). "Racism, Whiteness, and Burnout in Antiracism Movements: How White Racial Justice Activists Elevate Burnout in Racial Justice Activists of Color in the United States." *Ethnicities* 19(5): 784–808.

Gottfried, Jeffrey, et al. (2022). "Journalists Sense Turmoil in Their Industry amid Continued Passion for Their Work." *Pew Research Center*, 14 June.

Gottfried, Paul (2004). *Multiculturalism and the Politics of Guilt: Towards a Secular Theocracy.* Columbia: University of Missouri Press.

Gouldner, Alvin (1979). *The Future of Intellectuals and the Rise of the New Class.* New York: Palgrave.

Graeber, David (2019). *Bullshit Jobs: A Theory.* New York: Simon & Schuster.

Gramlich, John (2020). "Black Imprisonment Rate in the U.S. Has Fallen by a Third since 2006." *Pew Research Center*, 6 May.

Gramlich, John (2021). "10 Facts about Americans and Facebook." *Pew Research Center*, 1 June.

Grant, Alexandra, et al. (2020). "Detecting Feigned Symptoms of Depression, Anxiety, and ADHD, in College Students with the Structured Inventory of Malingered Symptomatology." *Applied Neuropsychology: Adult.* https://doi.org/10.1080/23279095.2020.1769097.

Grasso, Samantha (2017). "White Woman Undergoes Cosmetic Procedures to Make Herself 'Black.'" *Daily Dot*, 23 June.

Gray, Kurt, & Daniel Wegner (2009). "Moral Typecasting: Divergent Perceptions of Moral Agents and Moral Patients." *Journal of Personality and Social Psychology* 96(3): 505–520.

Green, Emma (2021). "Should Princeton Exist?" *The Atlantic*, 10 October.

Green, Jeff, et al. (2023). "Corporate America Promised to Hire a Lot More People of Color. It Actually Did." *Bloomberg*, 25 September.

Greenberg, Milton (2004). "How the GI Bill Changed Higher Education." *Chronicle of Higher Education*, 18 June.

Greene, Jay (2015). "Amazon More Diverse at Warehouses than in Professional Ranks." *Seattle Times*, 14 August.

Greenwood, Jeremy, et al. (2014). "Marry Your Like: Assortative Mating and Income Inequality." *American Economic Review* 104(5): 348–353.

Gregory, James (2005). *The Southern Diaspora: How the Great Migrations of Black and White Southerners Changed America*. Chapel Hill: University of North Carolina Press.

Greitemeyer, Tobias (2007). "What Do Men and Women Want in a Partner? Are Educated Partners Always More Desirable?" *Journal of Experimental Social Psychology* 43(2): 180–194.

Grieco, Elizabeth (2019). "For Many Rural Residents in U.S., Local News Media Mostly Don't Cover the Area Where They Live." *Pew Research Center*, 12 April.

Grigorenko, Elena, & Donna Lockery (2002). "Smart Is as Stupid Does: Exploring Bases of Erroneous Reasoning of Smart People regarding Learning and Other Disabilities." In *Why Smart People Can Be So Stupid*, ed. Robert Sternberg (pp. 159–186). New Haven, CT: Yale University Press.

Grim, Ryan (2022). "Elephant in the Zoom." *The Intercept*, 13 June.

Grinspan, Jon (2009). "'Young Men for War': The Wide Awakes and Lincoln's 1860 Presidential Campaign." *Journal of American History* 96(2): 357–378.

Grodach, Carl, Nicole Foster, & James Murdoch (2018). "Gentrification, Displacement and the Arts: Untangling the Relationship between Arts Industries and Place Change." *Urban Studies* 55(4): 807–825.

Gross, Neil, & Solon Simmons (2009). "The Religiosity of American College and University Professors." *Sociology of Religion* 70(2): 101–129.

Grossman, Matthew (2014). *Artists of the Possible: Governing Networks and American Policy Change since 1945*. Oxford: Oxford University Press.

Grossman, Matthew, & David Hopkins (2022). "The Politics of Policy Expertise: Democratic Deference and Republican Resentment." American Political Science Association working paper. http://matthewg.org/expertise.pdf.

Grosz, Michael, et al. (forthcoming). "A Meta-analytic Review of the Associations of Personality, Intelligence and Physical Size with Social Status." *Psychological Bulletin*. Preprint. https://osf.io/preprints/psyarxiv/73mf4.

Gruman, Galen (2020). "Women Do Better, Minorities Worse, When It Comes to the Tech Wage Gap." *Computerworld*, 21 October.

G'Sell, Eileen (2022). "What Do Women Really Deserve?" *Current Affairs*, 4 April.

Gu, Jackie (2020). "The Employees Who Gave Most to Trump and Biden." *Bloomberg*, 2 November.

Guay, Brian, & Christopher Johnston (2021). "Ideological Asymmetries and the Determinants of Politically Motivated Reasoning." *American Journal of Political Science*. https://doi.org/10.1111/ajps.12624.

Guerin, Daniel (1970). *Anarchism: From Theory to Practice*. New York: Monthly Review Press.

Guilluy, Christophe (2019). *Twilight of the Elites: Prosperity, Periphery and the Future of France*. New Haven, CT: Yale University Press.

Guo, Naijia, & Charles Leung (2021). "Do Elite Colleges Matter? The Impact on Entrepreneurship Decisions and Career Dynamics." *Quantitative Economics* 12(4): 1347–1397.

Gupta, Arun (2020). "Micah White Is the Ultimate Occupy Grifter." *Jacobin*, 30 January.

Gurley, Lauren (2021). "Amazon Drivers Are Instructed to Drive Recklessly to Meet Delivery Quotas." *Motherboard*, 6 May.

Gurri, Martin (2018). *Revolt of the Public*. 2nd ed. San Francisco: Stripe Press.

Gurwinder, Bhogal (2022). "The Perils of Audience Capture." *The Prism*, 30 June. https://gurwinder .substack.com/p/the-perils-of-audience-capture.

Gustafson, Sara (2016). "Growing Food for Growing Cities." *International Food Policy Research Institute*, 13 May.

Gutkin, Len (2019). "Anthony Kronman on the 'Aristocratic Ethos' in Higher Education." *Chronicle of Higher Education*, 12 July.

Gutkin, Len (2021). "The Sociologist Musa al-Gharbi on Empire, Islam and the Hypocritical Liberalism of Manhattan." *Chronicle of Higher Education*, 30 June.

Guzman, Gloria, & Melissa Kollar (2023). *Income in the United States: 2022*. P-60-279. Washington, DC: US Census Bureau. https://www.census.gov/content/dam/Census/library/publications /2023/demo/p60-279.pdf.

Haag, Matthew, & Winnie Hu (2019). "1.5 Million Packages a Day: The Internet Brings Chaos to N.Y. Streets." *New York Times*, 27 October.

Hadot, Pierre (1995). *Philosophy as a Way of Life: Spiritual Exercises from Socrates to Foucault*. Oxford: Wiley-Blackwell.

Hager, Eli (2017). "A Mass Incarceration Mystery." *The Marshall Project*, 15 December.

Hagey, Keach (2021). "Peter Theil, J.D. Vance Invest in Rumble Video Platform Popular on Political Right." *Wall Street Journal*, 19 May.

Hahl, Oliver, Ezra Zuckerman, & Minjae Kim (2021). "Why Elites Love Authentic Lowbrow Culture: Overcoming High-Status Denigration with Outsider Art." *American Sociological Review* 82(4): 828–856.

Haider, Asad (2020). "PMC Posturing." *Asad Haider (Substack)*, 29 July. https://asadhaider.substack .com/p/pmc-posturing.

Hall, Michael, et al. (2018). "Believing in Climate Change, but Not Behaving Sustainably: Evidence from a One-Year Longitudinal Study." *Journal of Environmental Psychology* 56: 55–62.

Hall, Stuart (1994). "Some 'Politically Incorrect' Pathways through PC." In *The War of the Words: The Political Correctness Debate*, ed. Sarah Durant (pp. 164–184). London: Virago Press.

Han, Hahrie, Elizabeth McKenna, & Michelle Oyakawa (2021). *Prisms of the People: Power and Organizing in Twenty-First-Century America*. Chicago: University of Chicago Press.

Hanania, Richard (2022a). "Why Do I Hate Pronouns More than Genocide?" *Hanania Newsletter*, 23 May.

Hanania, Richard (2022b). "Women's Tears Win in the Marketplace of Ideas." *Hanania Newsletter*, 7 February.

Hannon, Lance (2015). "White Colorism." *Social Currents* 2(1): 13–21.

Hannon, Lance, Robert DeFina, & Sarah Bruch (2013). "The Relationship between Skin Tone and School Suspension for African Americans." *Race and Social Problems* 5: 281–295.

Hansen, Eric, & Andrew Tyner (2019). "Educational Attainment and Social Norms of Voting." *Political Behavior*. https://doi.org/10.1007/s11109-019-09571-8.

Hanson, Gordon, & Chen Liu (2018). "High-Skilled Immigration and the Comparative Advantage of Foreign-Born Workers across U.S. Occupations." In *High-Skilled Migration to the United States and Its Economic Consequences*, ed. Gordon Hanson, William Kerr & Sarah Turner (pp. 7–40). Chicago: University of Chicago Press.

Harinam, Vincent (2021). "Mate Selection for Modernity." *Quillette*, 28 June.

Harkrider, Lauren, et al. (2013). "Threats to Moral Identity: Testing Effects of Incentives and Consequences of One's Actions on Moral Cleansing." *Ethics & Behavior* 23(2): 133–147.

Harmon, Amy (2021). "BIPOC or POC? Equity or Equality? The Debate over Language on the Left." *New York Times*, 1 November.

Harnett, Sam (2021). "Tech Workers Organizing Is Nothing New . . . but Them Actually Forming Unions Is." *KQED*, 2 June.

Harrington, Anne (2019). *Mind Fixers: Psychiatry's Troubled Search for the Biology of Mental Illness*. New York: W. W. Norton.

Harrington, Mary (2022). "The New Female Ascendency." *The Critic*, December/January.

Harris, Fred, & Adam Curtis (2018). "The Unmet Promise of Equality." *New York Times*, 28 February.

Harris, Johnny, & Binyamin Appelbaum (2021). "Blue States, You're the Problem." *New York Times*, 9 November.

Harrold, Mycah, Chadwick Miller, & Andrew Perkins (2023). "Pink Tasks: Feminists and Their Preferences for Premium Beauty Products." *Psychology & Marketing*. https://doi.org/10.1002/mar.21826.

Hartz, Andrew (2020). "'Splitting' and Identity Politics." *Heterodox Academy*, 18 February.

Harvey, David (2012). "The Urban Roots of Financial Crises: Reclaiming the City for Anti-capitalist Struggle." *Socialist Register* 48: 1–35.

Haskins, Caroline (2019). "Amazon's Home Security Company Is Turning Everyone into Cops." *Motherboard*, 7 February.

Haslam, Nick, et al. (2020). "Harm Inflation: Making Sense of Concept Creep." *European Review of Social Psychology* 31(1): 254–286.

Hassell, Hans, Matthew Miles, & Kevin Reuning (2021). "Does the Ideology of the Newsroom Affect the Provision of Media Slant?" *Political Communication* 39(2): 184–201.

Hatemi, Peter, & Rose McDermott (2016). "Give Me Attitudes." *Annual Review of Political Science* 19: 331–350.

Hatt, Laura (2016). "LBJ Wants Your GPA: The Vietnam Exam." *Harvard Crimson*, 23 May.

Haugh, Todd (2020). "Behavioral Ethics and Euphemisms." In *Encyclopedia of Business and Professional Ethics*, ed. Deborah Poff & Alex Michalos (pp. 1–4). Cham, Switzerland: Springer. https://link.springer.com/referenceworkentry/10.1007/978-3-319-23514-1_198-1.

Hawkins, Stephen, et al. (2018). "Progressive Activists." In *Hidden Tribes: A Study of America's Polarized Landscape* (pp. 29–31). New York: More in Common.

Hays, Nicholas (2013). "Fear and Loving in Social Hierarchy: Sex Differences in Preferences for Power versus Status." *Journal of Experimental Social Psychology* 49(6): 1130–1136.

Heap, Chad (2009). *Slumming: Sexual and Racial Encounters in American Nightlife, 1885–1940*. Chicago: University of Chicago Press.

Hebbelstrup, Stig, Mattias Osmundsen, & Michael Petersen (2022). "Political Resources and Online Political Hostility: How and Why Hostility Is More Prevalent among the Resourceful." PsyArXiv preprint. https://doi.org/10.31234/osf.io/tp93r.

Heilman, Madeline, & Brian Welle (2006). "Disadvantaged by Diversity? The Effects of Diversity Goals on Competence Perceptions." *Journal of Applied Social Psychology* 36(5): 1291–1319.

Henderson, Rob (2019a). "'Luxury Beliefs' Are the Latest Status Symbol for Rich Americans." *New York Post*, 17 August.

Henderson, Rob (2019b). "Thorstein Veblen's Theory of the Leisure Class—a Status Update." *Quillette*, 16 November.

Henderson, Rob (2022). "Luxury Beliefs Are Status Symbols." *Rob Henderson's Newsletter*, 12 June. https://robkhenderson.substack.com/p/status-symbols-and-the-struggle-for.

Hendrix, Michael (2017). *The Closing of the American City: A New Urban Agenda*. Washington, DC: American Enterprise Institute.

Henry, P. J., & Jamie Napier (2017). "Education Is Related to Greater Ideological Prejudice." *Public Opinion Quarterly* 81(4): 930–942.

Hernandez-Kent, Ana, & Lowell Ricketts (2022). "Educational Household Wealth Trends and Wealth Inequality." *Federal Reserve Bank of St. Louis*, 29 November.

Herndon, Astead, & Katie Glueck (2020). "Biden Apologizes for Saying Voters 'Ain't Black' If They're Considering Trump." *New York Times*, 22 May.

Hersh, Eitan (2020). *Politics Is for Power: How to Move beyond Political Hobbyism, Take Action, and Make Real Change*. New York: Scribner.

Hersh, Eitan, & Sarang Shah (2023a). "The Partisan Realignment of American Business: Evidence from a Survey of Corporate Leaders." Working paper, 1 August. https://www.eitanhersh.com/uploads/7/9/7/5/7975685/hersh_shah_business_realignment_080123_.pdf.

Hersh, Eitan, & Sarang Shah (2023b). "Who Wants Stakeholder Capitalism? Public and Elite Perceptions of the Role of Business in Politics." Working paper, 20 August. https://www.eitanhersh.com/uploads/7/9/7/5/7975685/hersh_shah_stakeholder_capitalism_082223.pdf.

Herzog, Katie (2020). "More and More People Identify as 'Queer.'" *The Stranger*, 19 February.

Herzog, Katie (2022). "How an Academic Grudge Turned into a #MeToo Panic." *Reason*, 14 March.

Hess, Frederick (2020). "Princeton's President Says His School Is Racist—So Betsy DeVos Launched an Investigation." *Forbes*, 21 September.

Heyward, Anna (2017). "Since Trump's Victory, Democratic Socialists of America Has Become a Budding Political Force." *Jacobin*, 21 December.

Hickman, Ben (2022). "Stop Doing the Work." *Compact*, 20 July.

Hilger, Nathaniel (2016). "Upward Mobility and Discrimination: The Case of Asian Americans." NBER Working Paper 22748. https://doi.org/10.3386/w22748.

Hill, Steven (2018). "Ridesharing versus Public Transit." *The American Prospect*, 27 March.

Hillstrom, Laurie (2010). *The Muckrackers and the Progressive Era*. Detroit: Omnigraphics.

Hirschman, Charles, & Elizabeth Mogford (2009). "Immigration and the American Industrial Revolution from 1880 to 1920." *Social Science Research* 38(4): 897–920.

Hirschman, Daniel (2021). "Rediscovering the 1%: Knowledge Infrastructures and Stylized Facts of Inequality." *American Journal of Sociology* 127(3): 739–786.

Hoff-Sommers, Christina (2015). *The War against Boys: How Misguided Policies Are Harming Our Young Men*. New York: Simon & Schuster.

Hogan, Thomas (2021). "Public Safety—If You Can Afford It." *City Journal*, 21 December.

Holcombe, Randall (1996). "The Growth of Federal Government in the 1920s." *Cato Journal* 16(2): 175–199.

Holder, Alex (2017). "Sex Doesn't Sell Anymore, Activism Does. And Don't the Big Brands Know It." *The Guardian*, 3 February.

Hollands, Thomas (2020). "The Economics of OnlyFans." *Xsrus*, 24 April. https://xsrus.com/the-economics-of-onlyfans.

Hollister, Sean (2021). "Amazon Apologizes for Lying about Pee—and Attempts to Shift Blame." *The Verge*, 3 April.

Holloway, Kali (2021). "Stop Telling Me Trust Fund Kids Are Financial Wizards." *Daily Beast*, 14 November.

hooks, bell (2000). *Feminist Theory: From Margin to Center*. Cambridge, MA: South End Press.

Hopcroft, Rosemary (2021). "High Income Men Have High Value as Long-Term Mates in the U.S.: Personal Income and the Probability of Marriage, Divorce, and Childbearing in the U.S." *Evolution and Human Behavior* 42(5): 409–417.

Hopkins, Daniel (2018). "All Politics Is National Because All Media Is National." *FiveThirtyEight*, 6 June.

Hopkins, Daniel, Eunji Kim, and Soojong Kim (2017). "Does Newspaper Coverage Influence or Reflect Public Perceptions of the Economy?" *Research & Politics* 4(4). https://doi.org/10.1177/2053168017737900.

Horace Mann School (n.d.). "Our School: Facts and Figures." Accessed 16 January 2024. https://www.horacemann.org/our-school/facts-figures.

Horan, Hubert (2019). "Uber's Path of Destruction." *American Affairs* 3(2): 108–133.

Horgan, John (2015). *The End of Science: Facing the Limits of Knowledge in the Twilight of the Scientific Age*. New York: Basic Books.

Horowitch, Rose (2024). "Skull and Bones and Equity and Inclusion." *The Atlantic*, 11 January.

Horowitz, Jonathan (2018). "Relative Education and the Advantage of a College Degree." *American Sociological Review* 83(4): 771–801.

Horowitz, Juliana, & Kim Parker (2023). "How Americans View Their Jobs." *Pew Research Center*, 30 March.

Hout, Michael (2021). "America's Liberal Social Climate and Trends: Change in 283 General Social Survey Variables between and within U.S. Birth Cohorts, 1972–2018." *Public Opinion Quarterly* 85(4): 1009–1049.

Howell, Junia, & Elizabeth Korver-Glenn (2021). "The Increasing Effect of Neighborhood Racial Composition on Housing Values, 1980–2015." *Social Problems* 68(4): 1051–1071.

Hsieh, Chang-Tai, et al. (2019). "The Allocation of Talent and U.S. Economic Growth." *Econometrica* 87(5): 1439–1474.

Hsu, Hua (2015). "When White Poets Pretend to Be Asian." *New Yorker*, 9 September.

Hubbs, Nadine (2014). *Rednecks, Queers and Country Music*. Berkeley: University of California Press.

Hughes, Adam (2017). "5 Facts about U.S. Political Donations." *Pew Research Center*, 17 May.

Hughes, Adam (2019). "A Small Group of Prolific Users Account for a Majority of Political Tweets Sent by U.S. Adults." *Pew Research Center*, 23 October.

Hughes, Bradley, et al. (2022). "Occupational Prestige: The Status Component of Socioeconomic Status." PsyArXiv preprint. https://doi.org/10.31234/osf.io/6qgxv.

Hughey, Matthew (2012a). "Stigma Allure and White Antiracist Identity Management." *Social Psychology Quarterly* 75(3): 219–241.

Hughey, Matthew (2012b). *White Bound: Nationalists, Antiracists, and the Shared Meanings of Race*. Palo Alto, CA: Stanford University Press.

Huizar, Laura (2019). "Exposing Wage Theft without Fear: States Must Protect Workers from Retaliation." *National Employment Law Project*, 24 June.

Hunt, Darnell, & Ana-Christina Ramon (2021a). *Hollywood Diversity Report 2021: Film*. Los Angeles: UCLA Institute for Research on Labor & Employment.

Hunt, Darnell, & Ana-Christina Ramon (2021b). *Hollywood Diversity Report 2021: Television*. Los Angeles: UCLA Institute for Research on Labor & Employment.

Hunter, Margaret (2007). "The Persistent Problem of Colorism: Skin Tone, Status and Inequality." *Sociology Compass* 1(1): 237–254.

Hunter, Tatum (2022). "Online Creators Are De Facto Therapists for Millions. It's Complicated." *Washington Post*, 29 August.

Hurst, Erik, Yona Rubinstein, & Kazuatsu Shimizu (2021). "Task-Based Discrimination." NBER Working Paper 29022. https://doi.org/10.3386/w29022.

Hyra, Derek (2017). *Race, Class, and Politics in the Cappuccino City*. Chicago: University of Chicago Press.

Iacurci, Greg (2021). "The Legacy of 2020: Riches for the Wealthy, Well Educated and Often White, Financial Pain for Others." *CNBC*, 1 January.

Illing, Sean (2021). "'Wokeness Is a Problem and Everyone Knows It.' James Carville on the State of Democratic Politics." *Vox*, 27 April.

Inglehart, Ronald (2018). "The Rise of Postmaterialist Values in the West and the World." In *Cultural Evolution: People's Motivations Are Changing, and Reshaping the World* (pp. 25–35). Cambridge: Cambridge University Press.

Inhorn, Marcia (2023). *Motherhood on Ice: The Mating Gap and Why Women Freeze Their Eggs*. New York: New York University Press.

Intelligent (2021). "34% of White College Students Lied about Their Race to Improve Chances of Admission, Financial Aid Benefits." *Intelligent*, 21 October.

Ip, Greg (2016). "Dwindling Gains in Science, Medicine and Technology Hold Back Growth; Is America Too Risk-Averse?" *Wall Street Journal*, 20 December.

Iqbal, Mansoor (2021). "Tinder Revenue and Usage Statistics 2021." *Business of Apps*, 17 March.

Iqbal, Nosheen (2019). "Woke Washing? How Brands like Gillette Turn Profits by Creating a Conscience." *The Guardian*, 19 January.

Irwin, Amos, & Betsy Pearl (2020). "The Community Responder Model." *Center for American Progress*, 28 October.

Isenberg, Nancy (2017). *White Trash: The 400-Year Untold History of Class in America*. New York: Penguin Books.

Jack, Anthony (2019). *The Privileged Poor: How Elite Colleges Are Failing Disadvantaged Students*. Cambridge, MA: Harvard University Press.

Jackson, Lauren (2019). *White Negroes: When Cornrows Were in Vogue . . . and Other Thoughts on Cultural Appropriation*. Boston: Beacon Press.

Jaffe, Eric (2014). "The Hidden Ways Urban Design Segregates the Poor." *Fast Company*, 12 August.

Jaffe, Sarah (2021). *Work Won't Love You Back: How Devotion to Our Jobs Keeps Us Exploited, Exhausted and Alone*. New York: Bold Type Books.

Jancar-Webster, Barbara (1978). *Women under Communism*. Baltimore: Johns Hopkins University Press.

Jansen, Charlotte (2019). "The Art Movements of the 2010s." *Artsy*, 18 January.

Jayaraman, Saru (2014). *Behind the Kitchen Door*. Ithaca, NY: ILR Press.

Jayaraman, Saru (2016). *Forked: A New Standard for American Dining*. Oxford: Oxford University Press.

Jeffery, Clara (2022). "What Pundits Don't Understand about the San Francisco Recall." *Mother Jones*, 16 February.

Jerolmack, Colin, & Shamus Khan (2014). "Talk Is Cheap: Ethnography and the Attitudinal Fallacy." *Sociological Methods and Research* 43(2): 178–209.

Jimenez-Moya, Gloria, et al. (2015). "By Any Means Necessary? When and Why Low Group Identification Paradoxically Predicts Radical Collective Action." *Journal of Social Issues* 71(3): 517–535.

John, Tara (2022). "The 'Anti-woke' Crusade Has Come to Europe. Its Effects Could Be Chilling." *CNN*, 7 January.

Johns, Joe, & Nicole Chavez (2021). "A Black Couple Had a White Friend Show Their Home and Its Appraisal Rose by Nearly Half a Million Dollars." *CNN*, 9 December.

Johnson, Matthew (2020). *Undermining Racial Justice: How One University Embraced Inclusion and Inequality*. Ithaca, NY: Cornell University Press.

Johnson, Scott (2019). "'Everybody's Doing It': Cheating Scandal Shows How Privileged Kids Fake Disability." *Hollywood Reporter*, 16 March.

Johnston, Christopher, Howard Lavine, & Christopher Federico (2017). *Open versus Closed: Personality, Identity, and the Politics of Redistribution*. Cambridge: Cambridge University Press.

Johnston, Taylor (2022). "The U.S. Labor Movement Is Popular, Prominent and Also Shrinking." *New York Times*, 25 January.

Jones, Jeffrey (2019). "Conservatives Greatly Outnumber Liberals in 19 U.S. States." *Gallup*, 22 February.

Jones, Jeffrey (2021a). "LGBT Identification Rises to 5.6% in Latest U.S. Estimate." *Gallup*, 24 February.

Jones, Jeffrey (2021b). "Socialism, Capitalism Ratings in U.S. Unchanged." *Gallup*, 6 December.

Jones, Jeffrey (2023). "U.S. LGBT Identification Steady at 7.2%." *Gallup*, 22 February.

Jones, Philip (2020). "Partisanship, Political Awareness, and Retrospective Evaluations, 1956–2016." *Political Behavior* 42: 1295–1317.

Jones, Philip (2023). "Political Awareness and the Identity-to-Politics Link in Public Opinion." *Journal of Politics*. https://doi.org/10.1086/723022.

Jonsson, Jan, et al. (2009). "Microclass Mobility: Social Reproduction in Four Countries." *American Journal of Sociology* 114(4): 977–1036.

Jordan, Jillian, & Maryam Kouchaki (2021). "Virtuous Victims." *Science Advances* 7(42). https://doi.org/10.1126/sciadv.abg5902.

Joslyn, Mark, & Donald Haider-Markel (2014). "Who Knows Best? Education, Partisanship, and Contested Facts." *Politics & Policy* 42(6): 919–947.

Judge, Timothy, Charlice Hurst, & Lauren Simon (2009). "Does It Pay to Be Smart, Attractive, or Confident (or All Three)? Relationships among General Mental Ability, Physical Attractiveness, Core Self-Evaluations, and Income." *Journal of Applied Psychology* 94(3): 742–755.

Kafka, Kyriaki, & Pantelis Kostis (2021). "Post-materialism and Economic Growth: Cultural Backlash, 1981–2019." *Journal of Comparative Economics* 49(4): 901–917.

Kahan, Dan (2013). "Ideology, Motivated Reasoning and Cognitive Reflection." *Judgment and Decision Making* 8(4): 407–424.

Kahan, Dan, & Jonathan Corbin (2016). "A Note on the Perverse Effects of Actively Open-Minded Thinking on Climate Change Polarization." *Research & Politics*. https://doi.org/10.1177/2053168016676705.

Kahan, Dan, et al. (2012). "The Polarizing Impact of Science Literacy and Numeracy on Perceived Climate Change Risks." *Nature Climate Change* 2: 732–735.

Kahan, Dan, et al. (2017). "Motivated Numeracy and Enlightened Self-Government." *Behavioral Public Policy* 1(1): 54–86.

Kalagher, Katherine (2014). "The Invasion of the Flapper: How the College Women of the 1920s Transformed the American College Experience." *Goodwin College Faculty Publications* 14. https://citeseerx.ist.psu.edu/viewdoc/download?doi=10.1.1.678.61&rep=rep1&type=pdf.

Kane, Matt, et al. (2013). *Where We Are on TV: 2012–2013 Season*. Los Angeles: GLAAD.

Kang, Jay (2019). "Where Does Affirmative Action Leave Asian Americans?" *New York Times*, 28 August.

Kantor, Jodi, & Megan Twohey (2017). "Harvey Weinstein Paid Off Sexual Harassment Accusers for Decades." *New York Times*, 5 October.

Kantor, Jodi, Karen Weise, & Grace Ashford (2021). "The Amazon That Customers Don't See." *New York Times*, 15 June.

Kantrowitz, Alex (2023). "The Elon Effect." *Slate*, 23 October.

Kapin, Allyson (2020). "Sexual Harassment in Silicon Valley: Still Rampant as Ever." *Forbes*, 15 September.

Kaplan, Richard (2002). *Politics and the American Press: The Rise of Objectivity, 1865–1920*. Cambridge: Cambridge University Press.

Karabel, Jerome (2006). *The Chosen: The Hidden History of Admission and Exclusion at Harvard, Yale and Princeton*. New York: Houghton Mifflin.

Karpinski, Ruth, et al. (2018). "High intelligence: A Risk Factor for Psychological and Physiological Overexcitabilities." *Intelligence* 66: 8–23.

Kassow, Samuel (1989). *Students, Professors and the State in Tsarist Russia*. Berkeley: University of California Press.

Katznelson, Ira (2006). *When Affirmative Action Was White: An Untold Story of Racial Inequality in Twentieth-Century America*. New York: W. W. Norton.

Kaufman, Scott (2020). "Unraveling the Mindset of Victimhood." *Scientific American MIND* 31(5): 14–18.

Kaufmann, Eric (2004). *The Rise and Fall of Anglo-America*. Cambridge, MA: Harvard University Press.

Kaufmann, Eric (2019). "Americans Are Divided by Their Views on Race, Not Race Itself." *New York Times*, 18 March.

Kaufmann, Eric (2021). "The Social Construction of Racism in the United States." *Manhattan Institute*, 7 April.

Kaufmann, Eric (2022). "Born This Way? The Rise of LGBT as a Social and Political Identity." *Center for the Study of Partisanship and Ideology*, 30 May.

Kaufmann, Eric (2023). "White Flight from Immigration? Attitudes to Diversity and White Residential Choice." *Social Science Quarterly*. https://doi.org/10.1111/ssqu.13268.

Kay, Katty (2018). "The Truth about False Assault Accusations by Women." *BBC News*, 18 September.

Kearney, Melissa (2023). *The Two-Parent Privilege: How Americans Stopped Getting Married and Started Falling Behind.* Chicago: University of Chicago Press.

Keeler, Jacqueline (2022). "Sacheen Littlefeather Was a Native American Icon. Her Sisters Say She Was an Ethnic Fraud." *San Francisco Chronicle*, 22 October.

Keister, Lisa, Sarah Thebaud, & Jill Yavorsky (2022). "Gender in the Elite." *Annual Review of Sociology* 48: 149–169.

Kenworthy, Lane, & Lindsay Owens (2012). *Political Attitudes, Public Opinion, and the Great Recession.* Stanford, CA: Stanford Center on Poverty and Inequality.

Khan, Matthew (2011). "Do Liberal Cities Limit New Housing Development? Evidence from California." *Journal of Urban Economics* 69(2): 223–228.

Khan, Shamus (2012a). "Elite Identities." *Identities: Global Studies in Culture and Power* 19(4): 477–484.

Khan, Shamus (2012b). "The Sociology of Elites." *Annual Review of Sociology* 38: 361–377.

Khan, Shamus (2015a). "The Counter-cyclical Character of the Elite." *Research in the Sociology of Organizations* 43: 81–103.

Khan, Shamus (2015b). "Not Born This Way." *Aeon*, 23 July.

Khan, Shamus (2016). "The Many Futures of Elite Research: A Comment on the Symposium." *Sociologica* 10(2). https://doi.org/10.2383/85294.

Khan, Shamus (2021a). "Capital Inequalities: Veblen, Bourdieu and the Weight of a Word." *Hedgehog Review*, Summer.

Khan, Shamus (2021b). *Privilege: The Making of an Adolescent Elite at St. Paul's School.* Princeton, NJ: Princeton University Press.

Khawaji, Fatemah (2022). "Characteristics of Culturally Inclusive Art Education Pedagogy: A Historical Document Analysis Study." PhD dissertation, Virginia Commonwealth University. https://scholarscompass.vcu.edu/cgi/viewcontent.cgi?article=8308&context=etd.

Khorsandi, Shaparak (2018). "As a Proud Champagne Socialist, I Know That Having Money Doesn't Have to Stop You Believing in Equality." *The Independent*, 2 November.

Khurana, Rakesh (2010). *From Higher Ends to Hired Hands: The Social Transformation of American Business Schools and the Unfulfilled Promise of Management as a Profession.* Princeton, NJ: Princeton University Press.

Kiefer, Peter, & Peter Savodnik (2022). "Hollywood's New Rules." *Common Sense*, 11 January. https://bariweiss.substack.com/p/hollywoods-new-rules.

Kiley, Kevin, & Stephen Vaisey (2020). "Measuring Stability and Change in Personal Culture Using Panel Data." *American Sociological Review* 85(3): 477–506.

Kim, ChangHwan, & Arthur Sakamoto (2014). "The Earnings of Less Educated Asian American Men: Educational Selectivity and the Model Minority image." *Social Problems* 61(2): 283–304.

Kim, Kyung Hee (2011). "The Creativity Crisis: The Decrease in Creative Thinking Scores on the Torrance Tests of Creative Thinking." *Creativity Research Journal* 23(4): 285–295.

Kinder, Donald, & Nathan Kalmoe (2017). *Neither Liberal Nor Conservative: Ideological Innocence in the American Public.* Chicago: University of Chicago Press.

King, Martin Luther, Jr. (1968). "The Role of the Behavioral Scientist in the Civil Rights Movement." *Journal of Social Issues* 24(1): 1–12.

King, Martin Luther, Jr. (2000). "Remaining Awake through a Great Revolution." In *A Knock at Midnight: Inspiration from the Great Sermons of Reverend Martin Luther King Jr.*, ed. Clayborne Carson & Peter Holloran (pp. 201–224). New York: Warner Books.

King, Martin Luther, Jr. (2005). "Remaining Awake through a Great Revolution." In *The Papers of Martin Luther King Jr.*, vol. 5, *Threshold of a New Decade, January 1959–December 1960*, ed. Clayborne Carson et al. (pp. 219–226). Berkeley: University of California Press.

King, Martin Luther, Jr. (2010). *Where Do We Go from Here: Chaos or Community?* Boston: Beacon.

Kingkade, Tyler, & Nigel Chiwaya (2021). "Schools Facing Critical Race Theory Battles Are Diversifying Rapidly, Analysis Finds." *NBC News*, 13 September.

Kipnis, Laura (2022). "Why Are Scholars Such Snitches?" *Chronicle of Higher Education*, 17 March.

Kirsch, Adam (2021). "Culture as Counterculture." *The New Criterion*, September.

Kirzinger, Ashley, et al. (2023). "Trans in America." *Kaiser Family Foundation*, March 24. https://www.kff.org/report-section/kff-the-washington-post-trans-survey-trans-in-america/.

Kitschelt, Herbert, & Philipp Rehm (2022). "Polarity Reversal: The Socioeconomic Reconfiguration of Partisan Support in Knowledge Societies." *Politics & Society*. https://doi.org/10.1177/00323292221100220.

Klawitter, Marieka (2015). "Meta-analysis of the Effects of Sexual Orientation on Earnings." *Industrial Relations* 54(1): 4–32.

Klein, Christopher (2020). "How Nixon's Presidency Became Increasingly Erratic after Kent State." *History*, 4 May.

Klein, Ezra (2016). "Ta-Nehisi Coates: 'I'm a Big Believer in Chaos.'" *Vox*, 19 December.

Klein, Ezra (2021). "California Is Making Liberals Squirm." *New York Times*, 11 February.

Klofstad, Casey, Rose McDermott, & Peter Hatemi (2012). "Do Bedroom Eyes Wear Political Glasses? The Role of Politics in Human Mate Attraction." *Evolution and Human Behavior* 33(2): 100–108.

Knight Foundation & Gallup (2022). *Media and Democracy: Unpacking America's Complex Views on the Digital Public Square*. Washington, DC: Gallup.

Knights, Ben (2010). *The Idea of Clerisy in the Nineteenth Century*. Cambridge: Cambridge University Press.

Kochhar, Rakesh, & Anthony Cilluffo (2018). "Income Inequality in the U.S. Is Rising Most Rapidly among Asians." *Pew Research Center*, 12 July.

Koo, Hyunjin, Paul Piff, & Azim Shariff (2022). "If I Could Do It, So Can They: Among the Rich, Those with Humbler Origins Are Less Sensitive to the Difficulties of the Poor." *Social Psychological and Personality Science*. https://doi.org/10.1177/19485506221098921.

Korn, Melissa, & Anthony DeBarros (2021). "Journalism Schools Leave Graduates with Hefty Student Loans." *Wall Street Journal*, 10 September.

Korn, Melissa, & Andrea Fuller (2021). "'Financially Hobbled for Life': The Elite Master's Degrees That Don't Pay Off." *Wall Street Journal*, 8 July.

Korn, Melissa, & Jennifer Levitz (2019). "Students Were Advised to Claim to Be Minorities in College-Admissions Scandal." *Wall Street Journal*, 19 May.

Korte, Gregory (2021). "Democrats' Tax-Hike Bet Relies on Their New $500,000-Plus Voters." *Bloomberg*, 19 April.

Koshet, Herbert (1976). "1975: Start of Recovery, Easing of Inflation and U.S. Tax Cuts." *New York Times*, 1 January.

Kosmin, Barry A., & Ariela Keysar (2009). *American Religious Identification Survey (ARIS 2008): Summary Report*. Hartford, CT: Program on Public Values, Trinity College.

Kouchaki, Maryam (2011). "Vicarious Moral Licensing: The Influence of Others' Past Moral Actions on Moral Behavior." *Journal of Personality and Social Psychology* 101(4): 702–715.

Kriss, Sam (2020). "White Skin, Black Squares." *Idiot Joy Showland*, 10 June.

Krumm, Angela, & Alexandra Corning (2010). "Who Believes Us When We Try to Conceal Our Prejudices? The Effectiveness of Moral Credentials with In-Groups versus Out-Groups." *Journal of Social Psychology* 148(6): 689–710.

Kucsera, John, & Gary Orfield (2014). *New York State's Extreme School Segregation: Inequality, Inaction and a Damaged Future*. Los Angeles: Civil Rights Project.

Kuhn, Thomas (1996). *The Structure of Scientific Revolutions*. Chicago: University of Chicago Press.

Kuppens, Toon, et al. (2018). "Educationism and the Irony of Meritocracy: Negative Attitudes of Higher Educated People towards the Less Educated." *Journal of Experimental Social Psychology* 76: 429–447.

Kuran, Timur (1997). *Private Truths, Public Lies: The Social Consequences of Preference Falsification*. Cambridge, MA: Harvard University Press.

Kuziemko, Ilyana, Nicolas Marx, & Suresh Naidu (2023). "'Compensate the Losers?' Economic Policy and Partisan Realignment in the U.S." NBER Working Paper 31794. https://doi.org/10.3386/w31794.

Kyeyune, Malcom (2022). "Wokeness, the Highest Stage of Managerialism." *City Journal*, Spring.

Labaree, David (2008). "An Uneasy Relationship: The History of Teacher Education in the University." In *Handbook of Research on Teacher Education*, ed. Marilyn Cochran-Smith et al. (pp. 290–306). London: Routledge.

LaBue, Anthony (1960). "Teacher Certification in the United States: A Brief History." *Journal of Teacher Education* 11(2): 147–172.

Lagos, Danya (2022). "Has There Been a Transgender Tipping Point? Gender Identification Differences in U.S. Cohorts Born between 1935 and 2001." *American Journal of Sociology* 128(1): 94–143.

Lahsen, Myanna, & Jesse Ribot (2022). "Politics of Attributing Extreme Events and Disasters to Climate Change." *WIREs Climate Change* 13(1): e750.

Lamont, Michele (2018). "Addressing Recognition Gaps: Destigmatization and the Reduction of Inequality." *American Sociological Review* 83(3): 419–444.

Lamont, Michele (2023). *Seeing Others: How Recognition Works—and How It Can Heal a Divided World*. New York: One Signal.

Laniyonu, Ayobami (2018). "Coffee Shops and Street Stops: Policing Practices in Gentrifying Neighborhoods." *Urban Affairs Review* 54(5): 898–930.

LaPorte, Nicole (2021). "Will Private Schools Survive the Culture Wars?" *Town & Country*, 27 August.

Lareau, Annette (2011). *Unequal Childhoods: Class, Race, and Family Life*. 2nd ed. Berkeley: University of California Press.

Lasch, Christopher (1996). *The Revolt of the Elites and the Betrayal of Democracy*. New York: W. W. Norton.

Lasch-Quinn, Elisabeth (2002). *Race Experts: How Racial Etiquette, Sensitivity Training, and New Age Therapy Hijacked the Civil Rights Revolution*. Lanham, MD: Rowman & Littlefield.

Latour, Bruno (1993). *We Have Never Been Modern*. Cambridge, MA: Harvard University Press.

Lauzen, Martha (2021a). *Boxed In: Women On Screen and behind the Scenes on Broadcast and Streaming Television in 2020–21*. San Diego, CA: Center for the Study of Women in Television & Film. https://womenintvfilm.sdsu.edu/wp-content/uploads/2021/09/2020-21_Boxed_In_Report.pdf.

Lauzen, Martha (2021b). *The Celluloid Ceiling: Behind-the-Scenes Employment of Women on the U.S. Films of 2020*. San Diego, CA: Center for the Study of Women in Television & Film. https://womenintvfilm.sdsu.edu/wp-content/uploads/2021/01/2020_Celluloid_Ceiling_Report.pdf.

Lazeron, Marvin (1998). "The Disappointments of Success: Higher Education after World War II." *Annals of the American Academy of Political and Social Science* 559: 64–76.

Le, Jane, et al. (2013). "Attitudes towards Healthy Eating: A Mediator of the Educational Level-Diet Relationship." *European Journal of Clinical Nutrition* 67: 808–814.

Leary, Mark, Katrina Jongman-Sereno, & Kate Diebels (2014). "The Pursuit of Status: A Self-Presentational Perspective on the Quest for Social Value." In *The Psychology of Status*, ed. Joey Cheng, Jessica Tracy & Cameron Anderson (pp. 159–178). New York: Springer.

Lecher, Colin (2019). "How Amazon Automatically Tracks and Fires Warehouse Workers for 'Productivity.'" *The Verge*, 25 April.

Lee, Dave, John Burn-Murdoch, & Alice Kantor (2020). "Sanders and Warren Scare Big Tech but Thrill Its Workers." *Financial Times*, 2 March.

Lee, Elizabeth (2021). "In U.S., Line between Politics, Entertainment Increasingly Blurred." *Voice of America*, 15 February.

Lee, John (2021). "Party Polarization and Trust in Science: What about Democrats?" *Socius* 7. https://doi.org/10.1177/23780231211010101.

Le Gales, Patrick, & Paul Pierson (2019). "'Superstar Cities' and the Generation of Durable Inequality." *Daedalus* 148(3): 46–72.

Legewie, Joscha, & Merlin Schaeffer (2016). "Contested Boundaries: Explaining Where Ethnoracial Diversity Provokes Neighborhood Conflict." *American Journal of Sociology* 122(1): 125–161.

Leiden, Warren, & David Neal (1990). "Highlights of the U.S. Immigration Act of 1990." *Fordham International Law Journal* 14(1): 328–339.

Leifer, Eric (1992). "Denying the Data: Learning from the Accomplished Sciences." *Sociological Forum* 7(2): 283–299.

Lemann, Nicholas (2000). *The Big Test: The Secret History of the American Meritocracy*. New York: Farrar, Straus and Giroux.

Leo, Geoff (2021). "Indigenous or Pretender?" *CBC News*, 27 October.

Leonard, Thomas (2016). *Illiberal Reforms: Race, Eugenics & American Economics in the Progressive Era*. Princeton, NJ: Princeton University Press.

Leonce, Tesa (2020). "The Inevitable Rise of Dual-Income Households and the Intertemporal Effects on Labor Markets." *Compensation and Benefits Review* 52(2): 64–76.

Leong, Nancy (2007). "Multiracial Identity and Affirmative Action." *Asian Pacific American Law Journal* 12(1): 1–34.

Leong, Nancy (2021). *Identity Capitalists: The Powerful Insiders Who Exploit Diversity to Maintain Inequality*. Palo Alto, CA: Stanford University Press.

Leonhardt, David (2024). "A Top College Reinstates the SAT." *New York Times*, 5 February.

Leopold, David (2018). "Marx, Engels and Some (Non-foundational) Arguments against Utopian Socialism." In *Reassessing Marx's Social and Political Philosophy*, ed. Jan Kandiyali (pp. 60–79). New York: Routledge.

Leroux, Darryl (2019). *Distorted Descent: White Claims to Indigenous Identity*. Winnipeg: University of Manitoba Press.

Leslie, Lisa, David Mayer, & David Kravitz (2014). "The Stigma of Affirmative Action: A Stereotyping-Based Theory and Meta-analytic Test of the Consequences for Performance." *Academy of Management Journal* 57(4): 964–989.

Lessing, Lawrence (2018). *America, Compromised*. Chicago: University of Chicago Press.

Levin, Sam (2015). "Racial Profiling via Nextdoor.com." *East Bay Express*, 7 October.

Levine, Arthur, & Keith Wilson (1979). "Student Activism in the 1970s: Transformation Not Decline." *Higher Education* 8(6): 627–640.

Levine, Ross, & Yona Rubinstein (2017). "Smart and Illicit: Who Becomes an Entrepreneur and Do They Earn More?" *Quarterly Journal of Economics* 132(2): 963–1018.

Levitz, Eric (2023). "Blaming 'Capitalism' Is Not an Alternative to Solving Problems." *New York Magazine*, 10 April.

Levy, David, & Sandra Peart (2008). "Thinking about Analytical Egalitarianism." *American Journal of Economics and Sociology* 67(3): 473–480.

Lewak, Doree (2018). "Rich Parents Are Using Doctor's Notes to Help Kids Cheat the SATs." *New York Post*, 2 May.

Lewis, Helen (2021). "The Identity Hoaxers." *The Atlantic*, 16 March.

Li, Diyi, & Cory Koedel (2017). "Representation and Salary Gaps by Race-Ethnicity and Gender at Selective Public Universities." *Educational Researcher* 46(7): 343–354.

Lichter, Daniel, Joseph Price, & Jeffrey Swigert (2019). "Mismatches in the Marriage Market." *Journal of Marriage and Family* 82(2): 796–809.

Liesen, Laurette (2017). "Feminist and Evolutionary Perspectives of Female-Female Competition, Status Seeking, and Social Network Formation." In *The Oxford Handbook of Women and Competition*, ed. Maryanne Fisher (pp. 71–88). Oxford: Oxford University Press.

Lind, Michael (2021). "The Importance of James Burnham." *Tablet*, 1 September.

Lindsey, Brink, & Steven Teles (2017). *The Captured Economy: How the Powerful Enrich Themselves, Slow Down Growth and Increase Inequality.* Oxford: Oxford University Press.

Lipschitz, Forbes (2014). "Not in My City: Rural America as Urban Dumping Ground." *Architecture_MPS* 6(1). https://doi.org/10.14324/111.444.amps.2014v6i2.001.

Lipset, Seymour, & Gary Marks (2000). *It Didn't Happen Here: Why Socialism Failed in the United States.* New York: W. W. Norton.

Littman, Julie (2021). "Grubhub Settles Lawsuit over Non-partnered Listings." *Restaurant Dive*, 21 April.

Liu, Catherine (2021). *Virtue Hoarders: The Case against the Professional Managerial Class.* Minneapolis: University of Minnesota Press.

Lizardo, Omar, & Dustin Stoltz (2018). "Max Weber's Ideal versus Material Interest Distinction Revisited." *European Journal of Social Theory* 21(1): 3–21.

Logan, Lewis, & Glenn Deane (2003). "Black Diversity in Metropolitan America." *Lewis Mumford Center for Comparative Urban and Regional Research*, 15 August.

Lohr, Steve (2017). "Where the STEM Jobs Are (and Where They Aren't)." *New York Times*, 1 November.

Lott, Eric (2006). *The Disappearing Liberal Intellectual.* New York: Basic Books.

Lu, Denise, et al. (2021). "Faces of Power: 80% Are White, Even as U.S. Becomes More Diverse." *New York Times*, 9 September.

Lu, Jackson, Richard Nisbett, & Michael Morris (2020). "Why East Asians but Not South Asians Are Underrepresented in Leadership Positions in the United States." *Proceedings of the National Academy of Sciences* 117(9): 4590–4600.

Lu, Yao, & Xiaoguang Li (2021). "Vertical Education–Occupation Mismatch and Wage Inequality by Race/Ethnicity and Nativity among Highly Educated US Workers." *Social Forces* 100(2): 706–737.

Lucier, Paul (2009). "The Professional and the Scientist in Nineteenth-Century America." *Isis* 100(4): 699–732.

Lufkin, Bryan (2021). "Why Do We Buy into the 'Cult' of Overwork?" *BBC*, 9 May.

Lurie, Julia (2015). "Just How Few Professors of Color Are at America's Top Colleges? Check Out These Charts." *Mother Jones*, 23 November.

Lutz, Jessie (1971). "The Chinese Student Movement of 1945–1949." *Journal of Asian Studies* 31(1): 89–110.

MacDonald, Heather (1996). "The Billions of Dollars That Made Things Worse." *City Journal*, Autumn.

MacDonald, Stuart (2023). "The Gaming of Citation and Authorship in Academic Journals: A Warning from Medicine." *Social Science Information*. https://doi.org/10.1177/0539 0184221142218.

MacGillis, Alec (2021). *Fulfillment: Winning and Losing in One-Click America.* New York: Farrar, Straus & Giroux.

MacLellan, Lila (2016). "Science Confirms Rich People Don't Really Notice You—or Your Problems." *Quartz*, 23 October.

MacMaster, Tom (2011). "Apology to Readers." *Gay Girl in Damascus*, 12 June. Archived version available through the Internet Archive Wayback Machine. https://web.archive.org/web/20110613142214/http://damascusgaygirl.blogspot.com/2011/06/apology-to-readers.html.

Madara, James (2021). "Reckoning with Medicine's History of Racism." *American Medical Association*, 17 February. https://www.ama-assn.org/about/leadership/reckoning-medicine-s-history-racism.

Magner, Erin (2019). "People Are Cooking Less than Ever Before—Here's Why We're Determined to Change That." *Well + Good*, 15 April.

Magness, Phil, & Michael Makovi (2022). "The Mainstreaming of Marx: Measuring the Effect of the Russian Revolution on Karl Marx's Influence." *Journal of Political Economy*. https://doi.org/10.1086/722933.

Maharawal, Manissa (2016). "Occupy Movements." In *The Wiley Blackwell Encyclopedia of Gender and Sexuality Studies*, ed. Nancy Naples et al. Hoboken, NJ: Wiley-Blackwell. https://doi.org/10.1002/9781118663219.wbegss203.

Mahdawi, Arwa (2018a). "Woke-Washing Brands Cash In on Social Justice. It's Lazy and Hypocritical." *The Guardian*, 10 August.

Mahdawi, Arwa (2018b). "Would You Live in a House without a Kitchen? You Might Have To." *The Guardian*, 24 June.

Mahtesian, Charlie, & Madi Alexander (2023). "'This Is a Really Big Deal': How College Towns Are Decimating the GOP." *Politico*, 21 July.

Maki, Alexander, & Kaitlin Raimi (2017). "Environmental Peer Persuasion: How Moral Exporting and Belief Superiority Relate to Efforts to Influence Others." *Journal of Environmental Psychology* 49: 18–29.

Malka, Ariel, Yphtach Lelkes, & Christopher Soto (2017). "Are Cultural and Economic Conservatism Positively Correlated? A Large Scale Cross-National Test." *British Journal of Political Science* 49(3): 1045–1069.

Malone, Clare (2023). "Hasan Minaj's 'Emotional Truths.'" *New Yorker*, 15 September.

Malone, Noreen (2022). "Did Jeff Zucker and Chris Cuomo Make Me Too a Weapon in Their Power Struggle?" *Slate*, 3 February.

Malone, Scott, & David Ingram (2016). "Despair and Introspection on the U.S. Coasts after Trump Win." *Reuters*, 9 November.

Mamakos, Michalis, & Eli Finkel (2023). "The Social Media Discourse of Engaged Partisans Is Toxic Even When Politics Are Irrelevant." *PNAS Nexus*. https://doi.org/10.1093/pnasnexus/pgad325.

Manduca, Robert (2018). "Income Inequalities and the Persistence of Racial Economic Disparities." *Sociological Science* 5: 182–205. https://doi.org/10.15195/v5.a8.

Manduca, Robert (2019). "The Contribution of National Income Inequality to Regional Economic Divergence." *Social Forces*. https://doi.org/10.1093/sf/soz013.

Mann, Marcus, & Cyrus Schleifer (2020). "Love the Science, Hate the Scientists: Conservative Identity Protects Belief in Science and Undermines Trust in Scientists." *Social Forces* 99(1): 305–332.

Mansfield, Edward, & Diana Mutz (2009). "Support for Free Trade: Self-Interest, Sociotropic Politics and Out-Group Anxiety." *International Organization* 63(3): 425–457.

Manstead, Antony (2018). "The Psychology of Social Class: How Socioeconomic Status Impacts Thought, Feelings and Behavior." *British Journal of Social Psychology* 57(2): 267–291.

Manza, Jeff, & Clem Brooks (1999). *Social Cleavages and Political Change: Voter Alignments and the U.S. Party Coalitions*. Oxford: Oxford University Press.

Marcos, Coral (2021). "A Neighborhood Watch to Keep New York's Delivery Workers Safe." *New York Times*, 12 October.

Marcus, Jon (2020). "More People with Bachelor's Degrees Go Back to School to Learn Skilled Trades." *Hechinger Report*, 20 November.

Markovits, Daniel (2020). "How McKinsey Destroyed the Middle Class." *The Atlantic*, 3 February.

Martin, Christopher (2019). *No Longer Newsworthy: How Mainstream Media Abandoned the Working Class*. Ithaca, NY: Cornell University Press.

Martins, Julia (2023). "Unmasking Imposter Syndrome." *Asana*, 20 April. https://asana.com/resources/impostor-syndrome.

Marx, Karl (1993). *Capital*. Vol. 3. London: Penguin Classics.

Marx, Karl (2015). *The 18th Brumaire of Louis Bonaparte*. New York: International Publishers.

Marx, Karl, & Friedrich Engels (1978). *The Marx-Engels Reader*. New York: W. W. Norton.

Mason, Liliana (2018). *Uncivil Agreement: How Politics Became Our Identity*. Chicago: University of Chicago Press.

Massey, Douglas, et al. (2007). "Black Immigrants and Black Natives Attending Selective Colleges and Universities in the United States." *American Journal of Education* 113(2): 243–271.

Massie, Victoria (2016). "White Women Benefit Most from Affirmative Action—and Are among Its Fiercest Opponents." *Vox*, 23 June.

Mastroianni, Adam (2022). "Pop Culture Has Become an Oligarchy." *Experimental History*, 2 May.

Mastroianni, Adam, & Jason Dana (2022). "Widespread Misperceptions of Long-Term Attitude Change." *Proceedings of the National Academy of Sciences* 119(11): e2107260119.

Matsa, Katerina (2017). "Buying Spree Brings More Local TV Stations to Fewer Big Companies." *Pew Research Center*, 11 May.

Matthews, Dylan (2015). "Woodrow Wilson Was Extremely Racist—Even by the Standards of His Time." *Vox*, 20 November.

Mattioli, Dana (2020). "How Amazon Wins: By Steamrolling Rivals and Partners." *Wall Street Journal*, 22 December.

Mattson, Greggor (2019). "The Stonewall Riots Didn't Start the Gay Rights Movement." *JSTOR Daily*, 12 June.

Mayer, Jane (2017). *Dark Money: The Hidden History of the Billionaires behind the Rise of the Radical Right*. New York: Anchor Books.

Mazrekaj, Deni, Kristof De Witte, & Sofie Cabus (2020). "School Outcomes of Children Raised by Same-Sex Parents: Evidence from Administrative Panel Data." *American Sociological Review* 85(5): 830–856.

McAdam, Doug, et al. (2005). "'There Will Be Fighting in the Streets': The Distorting Lens of Social Movement Theory." *Mobilization: An International Journal* 10(1): 1–18.

McCabe, Janice (2005). "What's in a Label? The Relationship between Feminist Self-Identification and 'Feminist' Attitudes among U.S. Women and Men." *Gender & Society* 19(4): 480–505.

McCall, Leslie (2013). *The Undeserving Rich: American Beliefs about Inequality, Opportunity and Redistribution*. Cambridge: Cambridge University Press.

McCann, Adam (2021). "Tax Burden by State." *Wallet Hub*, 31 March.

McCann, Adam (2023). "Most & Least Diverse States in America." *Wallet Hub*, 20 September.

McClain, Colleen (2021). "70% of U.S. Social Media Users Never or Rarely Post or Share about Political, Social Issues." *Pew Research Center*, 4 May.

McClain, Colleen, et al. (2021). *The Behaviors and Attitudes of U.S. Adults on Twitter*. Washington, DC: Pew Research Center.

McCready, Ryan (2016). "How Much Do Freelance Writers Actually Make?" *Venngage*, 10 June. https://venngage.com/blog/how-much-do-writers-make/.

McGerr, Michael (2005). *A Fierce Discontent: The Rise and Fall of the Progressive Movement in America, 1870–1920*. Oxford: Oxford University Press.

McGrady, Ryan, et al. (2023). "Dialing for Videos: A Random Sample of YouTube." *Journal of Quantitative Description: Digital Media* 3. https://doi.org/10.51685/jqd.2023.022.

McKinnish, Terra, Randall Walsh, & T. Kirk White (2010). "Who Gentrifies Low-Income Neighborhoods." *Journal of Urban Economics* 67(2): 180–193.

McLaughlin, Melinda, & Andrew Blake (2022). *Diversity in Ad Creative: Gender, Age, Race & Ethnicity Benchmarks, January 2019–October 2022*. Dedham, MA: Extreme Reach. https://extremereach.com/diversity-in-ad-creative/.

McPhail, Beverly (2004). "Setting the Record Straight: Social Work Is Not a Female-Dominated Profession." *Social Work* 49(2): 323–326.

McPherson, Miller, Lynn Smith-Lovin, & James Cook (2001). "Birds of a Feather: Homophily in Social Networks." *Annual Review of Sociology* 27: 415–444.

McWhorter, John (2021). "How 'Woke' Became an Insult." *New York Times*, 17 August.

Meijers, Markin, et al. (2019). "Taking Close Others' Environmental Behavior into Account When Striking the Moral Balance? Evidence for Vicarious Licensing, Not for Vicarious Cleansing." *Environment and Behavior* 51(9–10): 1027–1054.

Mejia, Paula (2021). "The Secret Life of H.G. Carrillo." *Rolling Stone*, 11 February.

Melby, Caleb (2021). "New York's Real Estate Tax Breaks Are Now a Rich-Kid Loophole." *Bloomberg*, 8 October.

Menand, Louis (2022). *The Free World: Art and Thought in the Cold War.* New York: Picador.

Mendlowitz, Hannah (2018). "In Support of Student Protests." *Yale Admissions Blog*, 23 February. https://admissions.yale.edu/bulldogs-blogs/hannah/2018/02/23/support-student-protests.

Menendian, Stephen, Samir Gambhir, & Arthur Gailes (2021). *The Roots of Structural Racism Project: Twenty-First Century Racial Residential Segregation in the United States.* Berkeley, CA: Othering & Belonging Institute.

Mercier, Hugo (2020). *Not Born Yesterday: The Science of Who We Trust and What We Believe.* Princeton, NJ: Princeton University Press.

Merritt, Anna, Daniel Effron, & Benoit Monin (2010). "Moral Self-Licensing: When Being Good Frees Us to Be Bad." *Social and Personality Compass* 4(5): 344–357.

Merritt, Anna, et al. (2012). "The Strategic Pursuit of Moral Credentials." *Journal of Experimental Social Psychology* 48(3): 774–777.

Merton, Robert (1972). "Insiders and Outsiders: A Chapter in the Sociology of Knowledge." *American Journal of Sociology* 78(1): 9–47.

Messer-Kruse, Timothy (2009). *The Yankee International: Marxism and the American Reform Tradition, 1848–1876.* Chapel Hill: University of North Carolina Press.

Milkman, Katherine, et al. (2021). "Megastudies Improve the Impact of Applied Behavioral Science." *Nature* 600: 478–483.

Milkman, Ruth, Stephanie Luce, & Penny Lewis (2013). *Changing the Subject: A Bottom-Up Account of Occupy Wall Street in New York City.* New York: Murphy Institute, City University of New York.

Miller, Claire (2017). "The Gender Pay Gap Is Largely Because of Motherhood." *New York Times*, 13 May.

Miller, Dale, & Daniel Effron (2010). "Psychological License: When It Is Needed and How It Functions." *Advances in Experimental Social Psychology* 43: 115–155.

Millot, Jim (2023). "Colleen Hoover Was Queen of 2022's Bestseller List." *Publishers Weekly*, 6 January.

Mills, C. Wright (1960). "Letter to the New Left." *New Left Review* 5. https://www.marxists.org/subject/humanism/mills-c-wright/letter-new-left.htm.

Mills, C. Wright (2000). *The Power Elite.* Oxford: Oxford University Press.

Miranda, Leticia (2018). "Amazon Sellers Say the Tech Giant Is Crushing Them with Competitive Pricing." *Buzzfeed News*, 13 June.

Mishel, Lawrence (2018). *Uber and the Labor Market.* Washington, DC: Economic Policy Institute.

Mitchell, Josh (2019). "The Long Road to the Student Debt Crisis." *Wall Street Journal*, 7 June.

Mitchell, Maurice (2022). "Building Resilient Organizations: Toward Joy and Durable Power in a Time of Crisis." *Convergence*, 29 November.

Mitchell, Stacy (2021). *Amazon's Toll Road: How the Tech Giant Funds Its Monopoly Empire by Exploiting Small Businesses.* Minneapolis: Institute for Local Self-Reliance.

Mitrana, Sam (2014). *The Rise of the Chicago Police Department: Class and Conflict, 1850–1894.* Champaign: University of Illinois Press.

Mittleman, Joel (2023). "Stable and Shifting Sexualities among American High School Students, 2015–2021." *Socius* 9. https://doi.org/10.1177/23780231231196012.

Mochkofsky, Graciela (2020). "Who Are You Calling Latinx?" *New Yorker*, 5 September.

Moench, Duncan (2018). "Anti-German Hysteria and the Making of the 'Liberal Society.'" *American Political Thought* 7(1): 86–123.

Moghe, Sonia (2022). "Legal Victory for Johnny Depp after He and Amber Heard Found Liable for Defamation." *CNN*, 1 June.

Molla, Rani (2018). "Tech Employees Are Much More Liberal than Their Employers—at Least as Far as the Candidates They Support." *Recode*, 31 October.

Molla, Rani (2022). "This Is Not Your Millennial's Job Market." *Vox*, 6 October.

Moniuszko, Sara, & Cara Kelly (2017). "Harvey Weinstein Scandal: A Complete List of the 87 Accusers." *USA Today*, 27 October.

Monk, Ellis, Jr. (2019). "The Color of Punishment: African Americans, Skin Tone, and the Criminal Justice System." *Ethnic and Racial Studies* 42(10): 1593–1612.

Monk, Ellis, Jr. (2021). "The Unceasing Significance of Colorism: Skin Tone Stratification in the United States." *Daedalus* 150(2): 76–90.

Monk, Ellis, Jr., Michael Esposito, & Hedwig Lee (2021). "Beholding Inequality: Race, Gender, and Returns to Physical Attractiveness in the United States." *American Journal of Sociology* 127(1): 194–241.

Monto, Martin, & Christine Milrod (2014). "Ordinary or Peculiar Men? Comparing the Customers of Prostitutes with a Nationally Representative Sample of Men." *International Journal of Offender Therapy and Comparative Criminology* 58(7): 802–820.

Moore, Anne Elizabeth (2007). *Unmarketable: Brandalism, Copyfighting, Mocketing, and the Erosion of Integrity*. New York: New Press.

Moore, Antonio (2018). "African Americans Are More than Just Africans in America." *Electronic Urban Report*, 9 June.

Moran, Marie (2015). *Identity and Capitalism*. London: Sage.

Morgan, Allison, et al. (2022). "The Socioeconomic Roots of Academic Faculty." *Nature Human Behaviour*. https://doi.org/10.1038/s41562-022-01425-4.

Morozov, Evgeny (2011). *The Net Delusion: The Dark Side of Internet Freedom*. New York: Public Affairs.

Morozov, Evgeny (2013). *To Save Everything, Click Here: The Folly of Technological Solutionism*. New York: Public Affairs.

Morris, Wesley (2018). "The Morality Wars." *New York Times*, 3 October.

Morse, Alison (2020). "The Dirty Truth behind Los Angeles' Garment Sector." *Re/Make*, 24 July.

Morton, Matthew, et al. (2018). *Missed Opportunities: LGBTQ Youth Homelessness in America*. Chicago: Chapin Hall at the University of Chicago.

Moser, Bob (2019). "The Reckoning of Morris Dees and the Southern Poverty Law Center." *New Yorker*, 21 March.

Moss, Emily, et al. (2020). "The Black-White Wealth Gap Left Black Households More Vulnerable." *Brookings*, 8 December.

Motta, Matthew (2018). "The Polarizing Effect of the March for Science on Attitudes toward Scientists." *PS: Political Science and Politics* 51(4): 782–787.

Mounk, Yascha (2020). "Stop Firing the Innocent." *The Atlantic*, 27 June.

Mukherjee, Roopali, & Sarah Banet-Weiser (2012). *Commodity Activism: Cultural Resistance in Neoliberal Times*. New York: New York University Press.

Mulder, Monique (2018). "Economic Inequality Drives Female Sexualization." *Proceedings of the National Academy of Sciences* 115(35): 8638–8660.

Mullen, Elizabeth, & Benoit Monin (2016). "Consistency versus Licensing Effects of Past Moral Behavior." *Annual Review of Psychology* 67: 363–385.

Musso, Mandi, & William Gouvier (2012). "'Why Is This So Hard?' A Review of Detection of Malingered ADHD in College Students." *Journal of Attention Disorders* 18(3): 186–201.

Muzergues, Thibault (2019). *The Great Class Shift: How New Social Class Structures Are Redefining Western Politics.* London: Routledge.

Myers, Ben (2016). "Where Are the Minority Professors?" *Chronicle of Higher Education*, 14 February.

Nair, Yasmin (2021). "AOC and the Weaponization of Trauma." *Yasmin Nair*, 27 February. https://yasminnair.com/aoc-and-the-weaponisation-of-trauma/.

Nair, Yasmin (2023). "On Hasan Minaj, Trauma Passports, and Immigrant Fictions." *Yasmin Nair*, 26 September. https://yasminnair.com/hasanminhaj/.

Nasar, Sylvia (1991). "Source of Jobs in 80's Fizzles in 90's." *New York Times*, 24 August.

National Center for Education Statistics (n.d.). "ACS-ED District Demographic Dashboard 2017–21." Accessed 7 December 2023. https://nces.ed.gov/Programs/Edge/ACSDashboard.

National Center for Education Statistics (2007). "College Enrollment and Enrollment Rates of Recent High School Completers, by Sex: 1960 through 2006." In *Digest of Education Statistics* (Table 191). https://nces.ed.gov/programs/digest/d07/tables/dt07_191.asp.

National Writers Union (2006). "Author Fired from Day Job Wins Settlement." Press release, 20 March. https://nwu.org/issues-we-care-about/freedom-of-expression/author-fired-from-day-job-wins-settlement/.

Naude, Wim (2019). "The Surprising Decline of Entrepreneurship and Innovation in the West." *The Conversation*, 8 October.

Nelson, Michael (1982). "A Short, Ironic History of American National Bureaucracy." *Journal of Politics* 44(3): 747–778.

Newall, Mallory, Charlie Rollason, & Sarah Feldman (2023). "Americans Divided on Whether 'Woke' Is a Compliment or Insult." *Ipsos*, 8 March.

Newman, Kevin, & Merrie Brucks (2017). "The Influence of Corporate Social Responsibility Efforts on the Moral Behavior of High Self-Brand Overlap Consumers." *Journal of Consumer Psychology* 28(2): 253–271.

Newman, Sandra (2017). "What Kind of Person Makes False Rape Accusations?" *Quartz*, 11 May.

Newport, Frank (2018). "In U.S., Estimate of LGBT Population Rises to 4.5%." *Gallup*, 22 May.

New York State Education Department (2023). "Nonpublic School Enrollment." Last updated 3 May 2023. http://www.p12.nysed.gov/irs/statistics/nonpublic/home.html.

Nielsen (2021). *Podcasting Today: Insights for Podcast Advertisers.* New York: Nielsen.

Nielson, Erik (2018). "If We Silence Hate Speech, Will We Silence Resistance?" *New York Times*, 9 August.

Nietfeld, Emi (2021). "After Working at Google, I'll Never Let Myself Love a Job Again." *New York Times*, 7 April.

Nietzsche, Friedrich (1956). *The Birth of Tragedy and the Genealogy of Morals.* New York: Anchor Books.

Nilforoshan, Hamed et al. (2023). "Human Mobility Networks Reveal Increased Segregation in Large Cities." *Nature* 624: 586–592.

Noah, Timothy (2023). "The Red State Brain Drain Isn't Coming. It's Happening Right Now." *New Republic*, 22 November.

Noe-Bustamante, Luis, Lauren Mora, & Mark Hugo Lopez (2020). "About One-in-Four U.S. Hispanics Have Heard of Latinx, but Just 3% Use It." *Pew Research Center*, 11 August.

Noelle-Neumann, Elisabeth (1993). *Spiral of Silence: Public Opinion—Our Social Skin.* 2nd ed. Chicago: University of Chicago Press.

Nolke, Ana-Isabel (2018). "Making Diversity Conform? An Intersectional, Longitudinal Analysis of LGBT-Specific Mainstream Media Advertisements." *Journal of Homosexuality* 65(2): 224–255.

Novak, William (2019). "The Progressive Idea of Democratic Administration." *University of Pennsylvania Law Review* 167(7): 1823–1848.

Noyes, Rich (2004). "The Liberal Media: Every Poll Shows Journalists Are More Liberal than the American Public—and the Public Knows It." *Media Research Center*, 30 June. http://archive.mrc.org/SpecialReports/2004/report063004_p1.asp.

O'Connor, Brendan (2018). "Confessions of a U.S. Postal Worker: We Deliver Amazon Packages until We Drop Dead." *Gen*, 31 October.

O'Connor, Sarah (2022). "Farewell to the Servant Economy." *Financial Times*, 14 June.

O'Donnell, James (2022). "How to Become a Billionaire: These Industries Have the Most People on the 2022 Forbes List." *Forbes*, 6 April.

Ogunwole, Stella, et al. (2021). "Population under Age 18 Declined Last Decade." *U.S. Census Bureau*, 12 August.

Ok, Ekin, et al. (2021). "Signaling Virtuous Victimhood as Indicators of Dark Triad Personalities." *Journal of Personality and Social Psychology* 120(6): 1634–1661.

Olds, Tim (2016). "The Long and Short of It: Eight Reasons Why Short Men Come Up Short." *The Conversation*, 21 March.

Olson, Keith (1973). "The G.I. Bill and Higher Education: Success and Surprise." *American Quarterly* 25(5): 596–610.

Onishi, Norimitsu (2021). "Will American Ideas Tear France Apart? Some of Its Leaders Think So." *New York Times*, 9 February.

OpenSecrets (2021). "Which Industries Are Giving the Most Money to PACs, Parties and Candidates?" https://www.opensecrets.org/elections-overview/industries?cycle=2020.

Orwell, George (1958). *The Road to Wigan Pier*. Orlando, FL: Harvest.

Orwell, George (1972). "The Freedom of the Press." *Times Literary Supplement*, 15 September. https://www.orwellfoundation.com/the-orwell-foundation/orwell/essays-and-other-works/the-freedom-of-the-press/.

Orwell, George (2005). *Why I Write*. New York: Penguin Books.

O'Sullivan, Feargus (2014). "The Pernicious Realities of 'Artwashing.'" *Bloomberg*, 24 June.

Owsal, Shiva (2021). "Faculty at American Universities: Becoming Increasingly Liberal?" *SSRN* preprint, 11 August. https://papers.ssrn.com/sol3/papers.cfm?abstract_id=3816971.

Owen, Ann, Julio Videras, & Stephen Wu (2010). "Identity and Environmentalism: The Influence of Community Characteristics." *Review of Social Economy* 68(4): 465–486.

Owen, Laura (2022). "A Large Portion of the Americans Who Will Pay for News Are Rich." *Neiman Lab*, 20 October.

Oyler, Lauren (2018). "What Do We Mean When We Call Art 'Necessary'?" *New York Times*, 8 May.

Page, Benjamin, Larry Bartels, & Jason Seawright (2013). "Democracy and the Policy Preferences of Wealthy Americans." *Perspectives on Politics* 11(1): 51–73.

Page, Scott (2019). *The Diversity Bonus: How Great Teams Pay Off in the Knowledge Economy*. Princeton, NJ: Princeton University Press.

Paglayan, Agustina (2022). "Education or Indoctrination: The Violent Origins of Public School Systems in an Era of State-Building." *American Political Science Review*. https://doi.org/10.1017/S0003055422000247.

Palmer, Annie (2021). "Amazon Warehouse Workers Injured at Higher Rates than Those at Rival Companies, Study Finds." *CNBC*, 1 June.

Panovka, Rebecca, & Kiara Barrow (2023). "'There's a Lot More That Needs to Be Done': An Interview with Barbara Smith." *The Drift*, Issue 9.

Paoletta, Kyle (2023). "The Incredible Disappearing Doomsday." *Harper's*, April.

Park, Gregory, et al. (2016). "Women Are Warmer but No Less Assertive than Men: Gender and Language on Facebook." *PLoS ONE* 11(5): e0155885.

Park, Michael, Erin Leahey, & Russell Funk (2023). "Papers and Patents Are Becoming Less Disruptive over Time." *Nature* 613: 138–144.

Parker, Gillian, et al. (2022). "Why Women Choose Divorce: An Evolutionary Perspective." *Current Opinion in Psychology* 43: 300–306.

Parker, Kim, & Renee Stepler (2017). "As U.S. Marriage Rate Hovers at 50%, Education Gap in Marital Status Widens." *Pew Research Center*, 14 September.

Parker, Kim, et al. (2015). "The American Family Today." In *Parenting in America: Outlook, Worries, Aspirations Are Strongly Linked to Financial Situation* (pp. 15–26). Washington, DC: Pew Research Center.

Patel, Eboo (2019). "Whom Do Activists of Color Speak For?" *Inside Higher Ed*, 2 April.

Patel, Vimal (2023). "Prominent Scholar Who Claimed to Be Native American Resigns." *New York Times*, 27 August.

Patton, Leslie (2019). "Food Delivery Boom Means Sandwiches Don't Come from Restaurants Now." *Bloomberg*, 15 May.

Paul, Kari, & Julie Carrie Wong (2020). "California Passes Prop 22 in a Major Victory for Uber and Lyft." *The Guardian*, 4 November.

Pearson, Adam, et al. (2018). "Diverse Segments of the U.S. Public Underestimate the Environmental Concerns of Minority and Low-Income Americans." *Proceedings of the National Academy of Sciences* 115(49): 12429–12434.

Peck, Emily (2022). "Big Labor Is Failing to Meet the Moment, Advocates Say." *Axios*, 14 April.

Peck, Timothy (2019). "What Happened to the SAT Adversity Score?" *College Vine*, 18 December.

Pennock, Lewis (2023). "Exclusive: Top American Universities Including Harvard and Yale Accused of Peddling 'Woke Hysteria' by Charging Thousands of Dollars for Politically-Charged Diversity, Equity and Inclusion Courses That Are 'Run by Activists.'" *Daily Mail*, 26 March.

Pereira, Norman, & Linda Pereira (2003). "Work Ethics and the Collapse of the Soviet Union." *Canadian Slavonic Papers* 45(1/2): 61–94.

Perez, Lucy, et al. (2022). "Does ESG Really Matter—and Why?" *McKinsey Quarterly* 58(4). https://www.mckinsey.com/capabilities/sustainability/our-insights/does-esg-really-matter-and-why.

Perl, Jed (2014). "Liberals Are Killing Art." *New Republic*, 4 August.

Perman, Stacy (2019). "Hollywood Assistants Who Suffered Poor Pay and Abuse Are Fighting Back." *Chicago Tribune*, 6 November.

Perrin, Andrew, & Sara Atske (2021). "About Three-in-Ten U.S. Adults Say They Are 'Almost Constantly' Online." *Pew Research Center*, 26 March.

Perry, Ruth (1992). "Historically Correct." *Women's Review of Books* 9(5): 15–16.

Perry, Samuel, Kenneth Frantz, & Joshua Grubbs (2021). "Who Identifies as Anti-racist? Racial Identity, Color-Blindness, and Generic Liberalism." *Socius* 7. https://doi.org/10.1177/23780231211052945.

Peterson, Hayley (2018). "Missing Wages, Grueling Shifts, and Bottles of Urine: The Disturbing Accounts of Amazon Delivery Drivers May Reveal the True Human Cost of 'Free' Shipping." *Business Insider*, 11 September.

Peterson, Holly (2017). "The Secret Code of Poor Mouth." *Town & Country*, 20 July.

Petrarca, Emilia (2021). "Before We Make Out, Wanna Dismantle Capitalism?" *The Cut*, 24 June.

Petrzela, Natalia (2019). "The Precarious Labor of the Fitpro." *Public Seminar*, 16 December.

Petrzela, Natalia (2020). "From Performance to Participation: The Origins of Fit Nation." *Transatlantica* 19(2). https://doi.org/10.4000/transatlantica.16318.

Pew Research Center (2021). "News Coverage Index Methodology." https://www.journalism.org/news_index_methodology/.

Pew Research Center (2023). "Newspapers Fact Sheet." 10 November. https://www.pewresearch.org/journalism/fact-sheet/newspapers/.

Phillips, L. Taylor, & Brian Lowery (2015). "The Hard-Knock Life? Whites Claim Hardships in Response to Racial Inequity." *Journal of Experimental Social Psychology* 61: 12–18.

Phillips, L. Taylor, & Brian Lowery (2018). "Herd Invisibility: The Psychology of Racial Privilege." *Current Directions in Psychological Science* 27(3): 156–162.

Phillips, L. Taylor, & Brian Lowery (2020). "I Ain't No Fortunate One: On the Motivated Denial of Class Privilege." *Journal of Personality and Social Psychology* 119(6): 1403–1422.

Piff, Paul, & Angela Robinson (2016). "Wealth Can Make Us Selfish and Stingy. Two Psychologists Explain Why." *World Economic Forum*, 5 October.

Piff, Paul, et al. (2010). "Having Less, Giving More: The Influence of Social Class on Prosocial Behavior." *Journal of Personality and Social Psychology* 99(5): 771–784.

Pike, Brian, & Adam Galinsky (2020). "Power Leads to Action Because It Releases the Psychological Brakes on Action." *Current Opinion in Psychology* 33: 91–94.

Piketty, Thomas (2021). "Brahmin Left vs Merchant Right: Rising Inequality and the Changing Structure of Political Conflict in France, the United States and the United Kingdom, 1948–2020." In *Political Cleavages and Social Inequalities: A Study of Fifty Democracies, 1948–2020*, ed. Amory Gethin, Clara Martinez-Toledano, & Thomas Piketty (pp. 85–135). Cambridge, MA: Harvard University Press.

Pinsker, Joe (2016). "The Financial Perks of Being Tall." *The Atlantic*, 18 May.

Pinsker, Joe (2018). "The Reason Many Ultrarich People Aren't Satisfied with Their Wealth." *The Atlantic*, 4 December.

Plank, Liz (2021). *For the Love of Men: From Toxic to a More Mindful Masculinity*. New York: Griffin.

Polanyi, Karl (2001). *The Great Transformation: The Political and Economic Origins of Our Time.* Boston: Beacon Press.

Portocarrero, Sandra (2023). "Racialized Expertise: The Consequences of Perceiving the Race of Workers as a Type of Expertise." *Academy of Management Proceedings* 2023(1). https://doi.org/10.5465/AMPROC.2023.1bp.

Portocarrero, Sandra (forthcoming). "Racialized Expertise: How the Race and Ethnicity of Workers Becomes an Essential Component of Workers' Status as Experts." *Administrative Science Quarterly.*

Portocarrero, Sandra, & James Carter (2022). "'But the Fellows Are Simply Diversity Hires!' How Organizational Contexts Influence Status Beliefs." *RSF: The Russell Sage Foundation Journal of Social Sciences* 8(7): 172–191.

Potts, Monica (2022). "Why Being Anti-science Is Now Part of Many Rural Americans' Identity." *FiveThirtyEight,* 25 April.

Powell, Michael (2021a). "Inside a Battle over Race, Class and Power at Smith College." *New York Times*, 24 February.

Powell, Michael (2021b). "New York's Private Schools Tackle White Privilege. It Has Not Been Easy." *New York Times*, 27 August.

Power, Nina (2022). *What Do Men Want? Masculinity and Its Discontents.* London: Allen Lane.

Praet, Stiene, et al. (2021). "What's Not to Like? Facebook Page Likes Reveal Limited Polarization in Lifestyle Preferences." *Political Communication* 39(3): 311–338.

Premack, Rachel (2019). "Truckers Say Amazon's New Logistics Empire Is Being Underpinned by Low, 'Ridiculous' Rates—and Some Are Refusing to Work for Them." *Business Insider*, 22 June.

Press, Alex (2021). "Gig Companies Are Bringing the Disastrous Prop 22 to a State Near You." *Jacobin*, 16 August.

Pret, Tobias, Eleanor Shaw, & Sarah Dodd (2016). "Painting the Full Picture: The Conversion of Economic, Cultural, Social and Symbolic Capital." *International Small Business Journal: Researching Entrepreneurship* 34(8): 1004–1027.

Prior, Markus (2013). "Media and Political Polarization." *Annual Review of Political Science* 16: 101–127.

Protzko, John, & Jonathan Schooler (2019). "Kids These Days: Why the Youth of Today Seem Lacking." *Science Advances* 5(10): eaav5916.

Putnam, Robert (2020). *The Upswing: How America Came Together a Century Ago and How We Can Do It Again.* New York: Simon & Schuster.

Qian, Yue (2016). "Gender Asymmetry in Educational and Income Assortative Marriage." *Journal of Marriage and Family* 79(2): 318–336.

al-Qudsi, Ismael (2023). "Are the Days of Organic Social Media Reach Over?" *Forbes*, 27 April.

Quealy, Kevin, & Eliza Shapiro (2019). "Some Students Get Extra Time for New York's Elite High School Entrance Exam. 42% Are White." *New York Times*, 17 June.

Quest Diagnostics (2023). "Industry Insights." *2023 Drug Testing Index.* https://www .questdiagnostics.com/content/dam/corporate/restricted/documents/employer-solutions /2023-drug-testing-index-and-industry-insights/Drug-Testing-Index---Industry-DTI-2023 -Tables-20230511.pdf.

Quillian, Lincoln, et al. (2017). "Meta-analysis of Field Experiments Shows No Change in Racial Discrimination in Hiring over Time." *Proceedings of the National Academy of Sciences* 114(41): 10870–10875.

Quintanilla, Victor, & Cheryl Kaiser (2016). "The Same-Actor Inference of Nondiscrimination: Moral Credentialing and the Psychological and Legal Licensing of Bias." *California Law Review* 104(1): 1–70.

Race Disparity Unit (2022). "Why We No Longer Use the Term 'BAME' in Government." *UK Ministry of Equalities*, 7 April. https://equalities.blog.gov.uk/2022/04/07/why-we-no-longer -use-the-term-bame-in-government/.

Raju, Emmanuel, Emily Boyd, & Friederike Otto (2022). "Stop Blaming the Climate for Disasters." *Nature Communications: Earth & Environment* 3. https://doi.org/10.1038/s43247-021 -00332-2.

Ramaswamy, Vivek (2021). *Woke Inc: Inside Corporate America's Social Justice Scam.* New York: Center Street.

Ransom, Tyler, & John Winters (2021). "Do Foreigners Crowd Natives Out of STEM Degrees and Occupations? Evidence from the US Immigration Act of 1990." *ILR Review* 74(2): 321–351.

Rasanen, Joona (2023). "Sexual Loneliness: A Neglected Public Health Problem." *Bioethics* 37(2): 101–102.

Rauch, Jonathan (2019). "Rethinking Polarization." *National Affairs* 41: 86–100.

Raz, Mical (2013). *What's Wrong with the Poor? Psychiatry, Race, and the War on Poverty.* Chapel Hill: University of North Carolina Press.

Reaves, Brian (2015). "Campus Law Enforcement: 2011–12." U.S. Bureau of Justice Statistics Report NCJ 248028. https://bjs.ojp.gov/content/pub/pdf/cle1112.pdf.

Redding, J. Saunders (1943). "Southern Awakening." *Negro Digest* 1(6): 41–46. https://archive.org /details/sim_black-world_1943-04_1_6/.

Reed, Adolph, Jr. (2000). *Class Notes: Posing as Politics and Other Thoughts on the American Scene.* New York: New Press.

Reed, Adolph, Jr. (2018). "Antiracism: A Neoliberal Alternative to the Left." *Dialectical Anthropology* 42: 105–115.

Reed, Adolph, Jr. (2022). "'Let Me Go Get My Big White Man': The Clientelist Foundation of Contemporary Antiracist Politics." *Nonsite* 39. https://nonsite.org/let-me-go-get-my-big-white -man/.

Reed, Touré (2020). "'Jess La Bombalera' and the Pathologies of Racial Authenticity." *Jacobin*, 6 September.

Reeden, Elizabeth (2020). "41% of Recent Grads Work in Jobs Not Requiring a Degree." *Inside Higher Ed*, 18 February.

Reeves, Richard (2002). *President Nixon: Alone in the White House.* New York: Simon & Schuster.

Reeves, Richard (2017a). *Dream Hoarders: How the American Upper Middle Class Is Leaving Everyone Else in the Dust, Why That Is a Problem, and What to Do about It.* Washington, DC: Brookings Institution Press.

Reeves, Richard (2017b). "'Exclusionary Zoning' Is Opportunity Hoarding by Upper Middle Class." *Brookings*, 24, May.

Reeves, Richard (2017c). "Stop Pretending You're Not Rich." *New York Times*, 10 June.

Reeves, Richard (2022). *Of Boys and Men: Why the Modern Male Is Struggling, Why It Matters, and What to Do about It*. Washington, DC: Brookings Institution Press.

Reeves, Richard, & Nathan Joo (2017). "White, Still: The American Upper Middle Class." *Brookings*, 4 October.

Reeves, Richard, & Christopher Pulliam (2020). "Middle Class Marriage Is Declining, and Likely Deepening Inequality." *Brookings*, 11 March.

Reilly, Wilfred (2019). *Hate Crime Hoax: How the Left Is Selling a Fake Race War*. Washington, DC: Regnery.

Rekker, Roderik (2021). "The Nature and Origins of Political Polarization over Science." *Public Understanding of Science* 30(4): 352–368.

Remler, Dahlia (2014). "Are 90% of Academic Papers Never Cited? Reviewing the Literature on Academic Citations." *LSE Impact Blog*, 23 April.

Renaud, Terence (2021). *New Lefts: The Making of a Radical Tradition*. Princeton, NJ: Princeton University Press.

Rensin, Emmett (2017). "Total Quality Revolution." *The Baffler*, September.

RePass, David (2008). "Searching for Voters along the Liberal-Conservative Continuum: The Infrequent Ideologue and the Missing Middle." *The Forum* 6(2): Article 5.

Reynolds, Tania, et al. (2023). "A Slim Majority: The Influence of Sex Ratio on Women's Body Dissatisfaction and Weight Loss Motivations." *Archives of Sexual Behavior.* https://doi.org/10.1007/s10508-023-02644-0.

Rich, Motoko (2008). "Gang Memoir, Turning Page, Is Pure Fiction." *New York Times*, 4 March.

Richter, Felix (2018). "Podcast Listeners Are Young, Educated and Affluent." *Statista*, 27 September. https://www.statista.com/chart/15609/podcast-audience-characteristics/.

Ridgeway, Cecilia L. (2019). *Status: Why Is It Everywhere? Why Does It Matter?* New York: Russell Sage Foundation.

Rigsby, Elliot (2016). "Understanding Exclusionary Zoning and Its Impact on Concentrated Poverty." *The Century Foundation*, 23 June.

Ritchie, Greg (2019). "Luxury Brands Are Taking Over the Street Art Scene." *Bloomberg*, 23 July.

Rittenburg, Terri, George Gladney, & Teresa Stephenson (2016). "The Effects of Euphemism Usage in Business Contexts." *Journal of Business Ethics* 137(2): 315–320.

Rivera, Lauren (2016). *Pedigree: How Elite Students Get Elite Jobs*. Princeton, NJ: Princeton University Press.

Rivero, Nicolas (2021). "The Tech Industry Is Leading a Record Boom in Mergers and Acquisitions." *Quartz*, 3 July.

Robbins, Liz (2014). "In Queens Court, Women in Prostitution Cases Are Seen as Victims." *New York Times*, 21 November.

Roberts, David (2019). "Cities Are Beginning to Own Up to the Climate Impacts of What They Consume." *Vox*, 1 July.

Robinson, Nathan (2018). "Maybe Taxi Drivers Don't Hate Progress, Maybe They Just Don't Want to Be Poor." *Current Affairs*, 2 March.

Robinson, Nathan (2019). "The Southern Poverty Law Center Is Everything That's Wrong with Liberalism." *Current Affairs*, 26 March.

Robinson, Simon (2005). "On the Beach with Dave Chappelle." *Time*, 15 May.

Robson, David (2019). *The Intelligence Trap: Why Smart People Make Dumb Mistakes*. New York: W. W. Norton.

Rockey, James (2014). "Who Is Left Wing and Who Just Thinks They Are?" University of Leicester Working Paper No. 9/23. https://www.le.ac.uk/economics/research/RePEc/lec/leecon/dp09-23.pdf.

Rodrigue, Edward, & Richard Reeves (2015). "Five Bleak Facts on Black Opportunity." *Brookings*, 15 January.

Rogers, Nick (2017). "Lenin's Misreading of Marx's Critique of the Gotha Programme." *Journal of Global Faultlines* 4(2): 95–109.

Romano, Aja (2020). "A History of 'Wokeness.'" *Vox*, 9 October.

Romeo, Jess (2021). "ADHD: The History of a Diagnosis." *JSTOR Daily*, 20 July.

Roose, Kevin (2021). "Farewell, Millennial Lifestyle Subsidy." *New York Times*, 8 June.

Rorty, Richard (1999). *Achieving Our Country*. Cambridge, MA: Harvard University Press.

Rose, Stephen (2020). *Squeezing the Middle Class: Income Trajectories from 1967 to 2016*. Washington, DC: Brookings Institution Press.

Rosenberg, Rebecca (2019). "Harvey Weinstein: I Deserve Pat on Back When It Comes to Women." *New York Post*, 15 December.

Rosenbloom, Nancy (1987). "Between Reform and Regulation: The Struggle over Film Censorship in Progressive America, 1909–1922." *Film History* 1(4): 307–325.

Rosenfeld, Michael (2017). "Who Wants the Breakup? Gender and Breakup in Heterosexual Couples." In *Social Networks and the Life Course: Integrating the Development of Human Lives and Social Relational Networks*, ed. Duane Alvin, Diane Felmlee, & Derek Kreager (pp. 221–243). New York: Springer.

Rosenfield, Kat (2019). "What Is #OwnVoices Doing to Our Books?" *Refinery 29*, 9 April.

Rosenfield, Kat (2022). "Sensitivity Readers Are the New Literary Gatekeepers." *Reason*, August/ September.

Rosenfield, Kat (2023). "The Lies of Trauma Merchants." *UnHerd*, 21 September.

Rosentiel, Tom, et al. (2021). *A New Way of Looking at Trust in the Media: Do Americans Share Journalism's Core Values?* Chicago: Media Insight Project.

Rosiak, Luke (2023). "Bloomberg Flubs Data for Bombshell Report That Only 6% of New Corporate Hires Are White." *Daily Wire*, 30 September.

Rossi, Enzo, & Olufemi Taiwo (2020). "What's New about Woke Racial Capitalism (and What Isn't)." *Spectre*, 18 December.

Rotella, Amanda, et al. (2023). "Observation Moderates the Moral Licensing Effect: A Meta-analytic Test of Interpersonal and Intrapsychic Mechanisms." PsyArXiv working paper. https://doi.org /10.31234/osf.io/tmhe9.

Roth, Philip, et al. (2021). "Organizational Political Affiliation and Job Seekers: If I Don't Identify with Your Party, Am I Still Attracted?" *Journal of Applied Psychology*. https://doi.org/10.1037 /apl0000932.

Rothschild, Neal (2021). "Young Dems More Likely to Despise the Other Party." *Axios*, 7 December.

Rothschild, Zachary, & Lucas Keefer (2017). "A Cleansing Fire: Moral Outrage Alleviates Guilt and Buffers Threats to One's Moral Identity." *Motivation and Emotion* 41: 209–229.

Rothschild, Zachary, et al. (2013). "Displacing Blame over the Ingroup's Harming of a Disadvantaged Group Can Fuel Moral Outrage at a Third-Party Scapegoat." *Journal of Experimental Social Psychology* 49(5): 898–906.

Rothschild, Zachary, et al. (2015). "Another's Punishment Cleanses the Self: Evidence for a Moral Cleansing Function of Punishing Transgressors." *Motivation and Emotion* 39: 722–741.

Rothwell, Jonathan (2019). *A Republic of Equals: A Manifesto for a Just Society*. Princeton, NJ: Princeton University Press.

Rothwell, Jonathan, & Steve Crabtree (2021). *How COVID-19 Affected the Quality of Work*. Washington, DC: Gallup.

Rozado, David (2022). "Themes in Academic Literature: Prejudice and Social Justice." *Academic Questions* 35(2). https://doi.org/10.51845/35.2.5.

Rozado, David (2023a). "Define Wokeness! Or How You Shall Know a Word by the Company It Keeps." *Rozado's Visual Analytics*, 24 March. https://davidrozado.substack.com/p/wo.

Rozado, David (2023b). "The Great Awokening as a Global Phenomenon." *arXiv*. https://doi.org /10.48550/arXiv.2304.01596.

Rozado, David, Musa al-Gharbi, & Jamin Halberstadt (2021a). "Our Research Shows the 'Great Awokening' Preceded Trump—and Outlasted Him." *Newsweek*, 7 September.

Rozado, David, Musa al-Gharbi, & Jamin Halberstadt (2021b). "Prevalence of Prejudice-Denoting Words in News Media Discourse: A Chronological Analysis." *Social Science Computer Review*. https://doi.org/10.1177/08944393211031452.

Rubinstein, Dana, & Azi Paybarah (2020). "N.Y.C. Was Once a Bastion of G.O.P. Moderates. Then Trump Came Along." *New York Times*, 17 October.

Rudder, Christian (2015). *Dataclysm: Love, Sex, Race, and Identity—What Our Online Lives Tell Us about Our Offline Selves*. New York: Crown.

Rufo, Christopher F. (2021). "We have successfully frozen their brand—'critical race theory'—into the public conversation and are steadily driving up negative perceptions." Twitter, 15 March, 3:15 p.m. https://twitter.com/realchrisrufo/status/1371540368714428416.

Rumore, Kori, & Jemal Brinson (2019). "The Jussie Smollett Incident: Minute-by-Minute of That Cold January Night." *Chicago Tribune*, 25 February.

Russell-Brown, Katheryn, & Vanessa Miller (2022). "Policing the Campus: History, Race and Law." *UF Faculty Law Publications* 1199.

Rustin, Baynard (1965). "From Protest to Politics: The Future of the Civil Rights Movement." *Commentary*, February. https://www.commentary.org/articles/bayard-rustin-2/from-protest-to-politics-the-future-of-the-civil-rights-movement/.

Rutenberg, Amy (2019). *Rough Draft: Cold War Military Manpower Policy and the Origins of Vietnam-Era Draft Resistance*. Ithaca, NY: Cornell University Press.

Rzhetsky, Andrey, et al. (2015). "Choosing Experiments to Accelerate Collective Discovery." *Proceedings of the National Academy of Sciences* 112(47): 14567–14574.

Saad, Lydia (2017). "Social Liberals Nearly Tie Social Conservatives in U.S." *Gallup*, 28 July.

Saad, Lydia (2020). "The U.S. Remained Center-Right, Ideologically, in 2019." *Gallup*, 9 January.

Saad, Nardine (2021). "Black Lives Matter Stands with Jussie Smollett after Verdict, but Don Lemon Does Not." *LA Times*, 10 December.

Sakamoto, Arthur, & ChangHwan Kim (2013). "The Economic Characteristics of Asian Americans in the 21st Century." In *The Economics of Inequality, Poverty and Discrimination in the 21st Century*, ed. Robert Rycroft (pp. 236–253). Santa Barbara, CA: Praeger.

Salam, Reihan (2018). "The Utility of White-Bashing." *The Atlantic*, 6 August.

Samaras, Thomas (2007). "Advantages of Taller Human Height." In *Human Body Size and the Laws of Scaling*, ed. Thomas Samaras (pp. 33–45). Hauppauge, NY: Nova Science Publishers.

Sanchez-Mora, Carlos (2022). "The 2022 Forbes 400 Self-Made Score: From Silver-Spooners to Bootstrappers." *Forbes*, 27 September.

Sap, Maarten, et al. (2019). "The Risk of Racial Bias in Hate Speech Detection." In *Proceedings of the 57th Annual Meeting of the Association for Computational Linguistics* (pp. 1668–1678). Florence: Association for Computational Linguistics. https://doi.org/10.18653/v1/P19-1163.

Sassen, Saskia (2009). "The Other Workers in the Advanced Corporate Economy." *Scholar & Feminist Online* 8(1). http://sfonline.barnard.edu/work/sassen_01.htm.

Sassen, Saskia (2018). *Cities in a World Economy*. New York: Sage.

Savage, Luke (2020). "Woke Capitalism Isn't Your Friend." *Jacobin*, 3 June.

Sawhill, Isabel, & Joanna Venator (2015). "Is There a Shortage of Marriageable Men?" *Brookings*, 22 September.

Scheeringa, Michael (2022). *The Trouble with Trauma: The Search to Discover How Beliefs Become Facts*. Las Vegas: Central Recovery Press.

Schemmel, Alec (2021). "Neighborhoods Continue to Hire Private Security to Clamp Down on Rampant Crime." *ABC News*, 15 December.

Schlegal, Ryan (2016). *Pennies for Progress: A Decade of Boom for Philanthropy, a Bust for Social Justice*. Washington, DC: National Committee for Responsive Philanthropy.

Schlessinger, Joel, Daniel Schlessinger, & Bernard Schlessinger (2010). "Prospective Demographic Study of Cosmetic Surgery Patients." *Journal of Clinical and Aesthetic Dermatology*. https://jcadonline.com/prospective-demographic-study-of-cosmetic-surgery-patients/.

Schlott, Rikki (2023). "Ivy League LGBTQ+ Numbers Soar and Students Point to Identity Politics." *New York Post*, 20 July.

Schmidt, Benjamin (2018). "The Humanities Are in Crisis." *The Atlantic*, 23 August.

Schmidt, Jeff (2001). *Disciplined Minds: A Critical Look at Salaried Professionals and the Soul-Battering System That Shapes Their Lives*. New York: Rowman & Littlefield.

Schmill, Stu (2022). "We Are Reinstating Our SAT/ACT Requirement for Future Admissions Cycles." *MIT Admissions Blog*, 28 March. https://mitadmissions.org/blogs/entry/we-are-reinstating-our-sat-act-requirement-for-future-admissions-cycles/.

Schneider, Leonid (2020). "BethAnn McLaughlin Affair: Now Also Research Fraud?" *For Better Science*, 9 August. https://forbetterscience.com/2020/08/09/bethann-mclaughlin-affair-now-also-research-fraud/.

Schoenmueller, Verena, Oded Netzer, & Florian Stahl (2022). "Polarized America: From Political Polarization to Preference Polarization." *Marketing Science* 42(1): 48–60.

Schoffstall, Joe (2022). "Top DEI Staff at Public Universities Pocket Massive Salaries as Experts Question Motives of Initiatives." *Fox News*, 30 March.

Scholes, Shaun, & David Bann (2018). "Education-Related Disparities in Reported Physical Activity during Leisure Time, Active Transportation, and Work among U.S. Adults: Reported Cross-Sectional Analysis from the National Health and Nutrition Examination Surveys, 2007–2016." *BMC Public Health* 18 (926). https://doi.org/10.1186/s12889-018-5857-z.

Schonfeld, Roger (2016). "Book Publishing: University Presses Adapt." *Nature* 540: 35–37.

Schor, Juliet (2020). *After the Gig: How the Sharing Economy Got Hijacked and How to Win It Back*. Oakland: University of California Press.

Schuessler, Jennifer (2017). "Princeton Digs Deep into Its Fraught Racial History." *New York Times*, 6 November.

Schuldt, Jonathan, & Adam Pearson (2016). "The Role of Race and Ethnicity in Climate Change Polarization: Evidence from a U.S. National Survey Experiment." *Climate Change* 136: 495–505.

Schulman, Sarah (2016). *Conflict Is Not Abuse: Overstating Harm, Community Responsibility, and the Duty of Repair*. Vancouver, BC: Arsenal Pulp Press.

Schulte, Gabriela (2021). "One-Third of Voters Identify as 'Woke.'" *The Hill*, 16 July.

Schwab, Tim (2020). "Journalism's Gates Keepers." *Columbia Journalism Review*, 21 August.

Schwarz, Alan (2013). "The Selling of Attention Deficit Disorder." *New York Times*, 14 December.

Schwarz, Alan (2015). "Workers Seeking Productivity in a Pill Are Abusing A.D.H.D. Drugs." *New York Times*, 18 April.

Scott, Daryl (1997). *Contempt and Pity: Social Policy and the Image of the Damaged Black Psyche, 1880–1996*. Chapel Hill: University of North Carolina Press.

Scott, David (1999). *Refashioning Futures: Criticism after Postcoloniality*. Princeton, NJ: Princeton University Press.

Scott, James (1999). *Seeing like a State: How Certain Schemes to Improve the Human Condition Have Failed*. New Haven, CT: Yale University Press.

Scott, James (2017). *Against the Grain: A Deep History of the Earliest States*. New Haven, CT: Yale University Press.

Sedlak, Michael, & Steven Schlossman (1986). *Who Will Teach? Historical Perspectives on the Changing Appeal of Teaching as a Profession*. Santa Monica, CA: RAND.

Seim, Josh, & Michael McCarthy (2023). "Classes without Labor: Three Critiques of Bourdieu." *Critical Sociology*. https://doi.org/10.1177/08969205231200898.

Sewell, Graham, & James Barker (2006). "Coercion versus Care: Using Irony to Make Sense of Organizational Surveillance." *Academy of Management Review* 31(4): 934–961.

Shafer, Jack, & Tucker Doherty (2017). "The Media Bubble Is Worse than You Think." *Politico*, May/June.

Shanahan, Ed (2019). "$27 Million for Reparations over Slave Ties Pledged by Seminary." *New York Times*, 21 October.

Sharkey, Patrick (2018). *Uneasy Peace: The Great Crime Decline, the Renewal of City Life, and the Next War on Violence*. New York: W. W. Norton.

Sharp, Elaine (2014). "Politics, Economics and Urban Policing: The Postindustrial City Thesis and Rival Explanations of Heightened Order Maintenance Policing." *Urban Affairs Review* 50(3): 340–365.

Sharp, Rachel (2021). "Ohio Private School Expels Students Because Their Moms Launched Campaign against Woke Curriculum and Critical Race Theory—but Principal Insists They Breached Contract Promising a 'Positive Relationship.'" *Daily Mail*, 2 July. https://www.dailymail.co .uk/news/article-9751209/Ohio-private-school-expels-students-MOMS-launched-campaign -against-woke-curriculum.html.

Sheehan, Patrick (2022). "The Paradox of Self-Help Expertise: How Unemployed Workers Become Professional Career Coaches." *American Journal of Sociology* 127(4): 1151–1182.

Shellenberger, Michael (2019). "The Real Reason They Behave Hypocritically on Climate Change Is Because They Want To." *Forbes*, 20 August.

Shellenberger, Michael (2021). *San Fransicko: Why Progressives Ruin Cities*. New York: Harper.

Shema, Hadas (2012). "On Self-Citation." *Scientific American*, 24 July.

Shenav, Na'ama (2021). "Lowering Standards to Wed? Spouse Quality, Marriage, and Labor Market Responses to the Gender Wage Gap." *Review of Economics and Statistics* 103(2): 265–279.

Sherman, Rachel (2017). *Uneasy Street: The Anxieties of Affluence*. Princeton, NJ: Princeton University Press.

Shin, Rachel (2023). "Elite College Students Are Doing It to Themselves." *The Atlantic*, 5 September.

Sibarium, Aaron (2021). "Why Private Schools Have Gone Woke." *Washington Free Beacon*, 28 July.

Siddiqui, Faiz, & Greg Bensinger (2019). "As IPO Soars, Can Uber and Lyft Survive Long Enough to Replace Their Drivers with Computers?" *Washington Post*, 29 March.

Silbert, Andrea, & Christy Dube (2021). *The Power Gap among Top Earners at America's Elite Universities*. Washington, DC: American Association of University Women.

Silver, Nate (2011). "The Geography of Occupy Wall Street (and Everywhere Else)." *FiveThirtyEight*, 17 October.

Silverman, Jacob (2021). "The Citizen App's Gamification of Vigilantism." *New Republic*, 15 June.

Simbrunner, Philipp, & Bodo Schlegelmilch (2017). "Moral Licensing: A Culture-Moderated Meta-analysis." *Management Review Quarterly* 67: 201–225.

Simon, Jonathan (2009). *Governing through Crime: How the War on Crime Transformed American Democracy and Created a Culture of Fear*. Oxford: Oxford University Press.

Singer, Allen (1989). "The Effect of the Vietnam War on Numbers of Medical School Applicants." *Academic Medicine* 64(10): 567–573.

Skrentny, John (2023). *Wasted Education: How We Fail Our Graduates in Science, Technology, Engineering and Math*. Chicago: University of Chicago Press.

Smirnov, Ivan, & Stefan Turner (2017). "Formation of Homophily in Academic Performance: Students Change Their Friends Rather than Performance." *PLoS ONE* 12(8): e0183473.

Smith, Aaron, & Monica Anderson (2017). "Automation in Everyday Life: 2. Americans' Attitudes towards a Future in Which Robots and Computers Can Do Many Human Jobs." *Pew Research Center*, 4 October.

Smith, Adam (2003). *The Wealth of Nations*. New York: Bantam Classics.

Smith, Andrea (1993). "For All Those Who Were Indian in a Former Life." In *Ecofeminism and the Sacred*, ed. Carol J. Adams (pp. 168–171). New York: Continuum.

Smith, Ben (2021). "The Misinformation Wars." *New York Times*, 28 November.

Smith, Christian (2014). *The Sacred Project of American Sociology*. Oxford: Oxford University Press.

Smith, Jeffrey, Miller McPherson, & Lynn Smith-Lovin (2014). "Social Distance in the United States: Sex, Race, Religion, Age, and Education Homophily among Confidants, 1985 to 2004." *American Sociological Review* 79(3): 432–456.

Smith, Savannah, Jiachuan Wu, & Joe Murphy (2020). "Map: George Floyd Protests around the World." *NBC News*, 9 June.

Smith, Serena (2020). "Have You Been 'Wokefished' while Dating? Here's How to Tell." *Vice*, 28 July.

Smith-Spark, Laura (2017). "Protesters Rally Worldwide in Solidarity with Washington March." *CNN*, 22 January.

SNCC Vine City Project (1966). *Black Power*. Atlanta: United States National Student Association. https://snccdigital.org/inside-sncc/policy-statements/atlanta-project-statement/.

Soave, Robby (2016). "Colleges Canceled Exams for Students Traumatized by Trump's Election." *Reason*, 10 November.

Soave, Robby (2019). "A Professor Tried to End a Flirty Email Exchange with a Young Woman. Then She Threatened to Blackmail Him." *Reason*, 10 December.

Sobo, Elisa, Michael Lambert, & Valerie Lambert (2021). "Land Acknowledgments Meant to Honor Indigenous People Too Often Do the Opposite—Erasing American Indians and Sanitizing History Instead." *The Conversation*, 7 October.

Sodd, Anthony (2016). "Street Art in the Office: The Story behind the Graffiti at 4 NYC Tech Companies." *Built in NYC*, 16 November.

Somin, Ilya (2016). *Democracy and Political Ignorance: Why Smaller Government Is Smarter*. Palo Alto, CA: Stanford University Press.

Sonnemaker, Tyler (2020). "Uber and Lyft Say the Battle over AB-5 Is about Preserving Flexibility for Part-Time Gig Workers. The Reality Is Their Businesses Have Become Dependent on Full-Time Drivers and They Can't Afford to Pay Them like Employees." *Business Insider*, 21 August.

Soper, Spencer (2021). "Fired by Bot: 'It's You against the Machine.'" *Bloomberg*, 28 June.

Sorens, Jason (2018). "The Effects of Housing Supply Restrictions on Partisan Geography." *Political Geography* 66: 44–56.

Southwood, Kenneth (1978). "Substantive Theory and Statistical Interaction: Five Methods." *American Journal of Sociology* 83(5): 1154–1203.

Sowell, Thomas (2005). *Affirmative Action around the World: An Empirical Study*. New Haven, CT: Yale University Press.

Sowell, Thomas (2009). *Intellectuals and Society*. New York: Basic Books.

Speri, Alice (2023). "Progressive Group Roiled by Accusations Diversity Leader Misrepresented Her Ethnic Background." *The Intercept*, 16 February.

Srinivasan, Amia (2018). "Does Anyone Have the Right to Sex?" *London Review of Books* 40(6).

Staiger, Matthew (2022). "The Intergenerational Transmission of Employers and Earnings of Young Workers." Harvard University Opportunity Insights working paper, December. https://matthewstaiger.github.io/matthewstaiger.com/The%20Intergenerational%20Transmission%20of%20Employers%20and%20the%20Earnings%20of%20Young%20Workers.pdf.

Stampnitzsky, Lisa (2013). *Disciplining Terror: How Experts Invented "Terrorism."* Cambridge: Cambridge University Press.

Stanley, Mattew, Christopher B. Neck, & Christopher P. Neck (2023). "Loyal Workers Are Selectively and Ironically Targeted for Exploitation." *Journal of Experimental Social Psychology* 106: 104442.

Stanovich, Keith (2021). *The Bias That Divides Us: The Science and Politics of MySide Thinking*. Cambridge, MA: MIT Press.

Staples, Vince (2015). "Lift Me Up." *Summertime '06*. New York: Def Jam Recordings.

Staples, Vince (2016). "War Ready." *Prima Donna*. New York: Def Jam Recordings.

Steadman, Olivia (2021). "OnlyFans Creators Say This Agency Trapped Them in Exploitative Contracts and Published Nudes without Consent." *Buzzfeed News*, 16 December.

Stebbins, Samuel (2018). "25 Richest Cities in America: Does Your Metro Area Make the Cut?" *USA Today*, 17 May.

Steinmetz-Jenkins, Daniel (2022). "Are We Still Fighting the Battles of the New Left?" *The Nation*, 15 March.

Stern, Ken (2013). "Why the Rich Don't Give to Charity." *The Atlantic*, April.

Stewart, Emily (2021). "You Should Be Suspicious of Benevolent Big Business." *Recode*, 27 May.

Stewart, James (2014). "When Media Mergers Limit More than Competition." *New York Times*, 25 July.

Stewart, Matthew (2018). "The 9.9% Is the New American Aristocracy." *The Atlantic*, June.

Stewart, Matthew (2021). *The 9.9 Percent: The New Aristocracy That Is Entrenching Inequality and Warping Our Culture.* New York: Simon & Schuster.

Stewart, Nikita (2020). "N.Y. Will Move Homeless Men from Liberal Neighborhood after Backlash." *New York Times*, 8 September.

Stimson, James (2015). *Tides of Consent: How Public Opinion Shapes American Politics.* 2nd ed. Cambridge: Cambridge University Press.

Stoet, Gijsbert, & David Geary (2018). "The Gender-Equality Paradox in Science, Technology, Engineering, and Mathematics Education." *Psychological Science* 29(4): 581–593.

Stoller, Matt (2019). *Goliath: The 100-Year War between Monopoly Power and Democracy.* New York: Simon & Schuster.

Stolper, Harold (2019). "New Neighbors and the Over-policing of Communities of Color." *Community Service Society*, 6 January. https://cssny.org/news/entry/New-Neighbors.

Stolzenberg, Ellen Bara, et al. (2019). *Undergraduate Teaching Faculty: The HERI Faculty Survey 2016–2017.* Los Angeles: Higher Education Research Institute, University of California, Los Angeles. https://www.heri.ucla.edu/monographs/HERI-FAC2017-monograph-expanded.pdf.

Storey, Ian (2018). "Political Firings of Left-Leaning Faculty—Academic Freedom Is Not a Partisan Issue." *Heterodox Academy*, 14 June.

Storme, Martin, Pinar Celik, & Nils Myszkowski (2021). "Creativity and Unethicality: A Systematic Review and Meta-analysis." *Psychology of Aesthetics, Creativity, and the Arts* 14(4): 664–672.

Stormquist, Shelton (2006). *Reinventing "the People": The Progressive Movement, the Class Problem, and the Origins of Modern Liberalism.* Champaign: University of Illinois Press.

Storr, Will (2021). *The Status Game: On Social Position and How We Use It.* London: William Collins.

Strategic Organizing Center (2022). *The Worst Mile: Production Pressure and the Injury Crisis in Amazon's Delivery System.* Washington, DC: Strategic Organizing Center. https://thesoc.org/what-we-do/the-worst-mile-production-pressure-and-the-injury-crisis-in-amazons-delivery-system/.

Streib, Jessi (2020). *Privilege Lost: Who Leaves the Upper Middle Class and How They Fall.* Oxford: Oxford University Press.

Strossen, Nadine (2018). *Hate: Why We Should Resist It with Free Speech, Not Censorship.* Oxford: Oxford University Press.

Subin, Samantha (2021). "Ford and Argo AI to Launch Self-Driving Cars with Lyft by the End of the Year." *CNBC*, 21 July.

Sullivan, Daniel et al. (2012). "Competitive Victimhood as a Response to Accusations of Ingroup Harm Doing." *Journal of Personality and Social Psychology* 102(4): 778–795.

Superti, Chiara (2015). "Popular Trust, Mistrust, and Approval: Measuring and Understanding Citizens' Attitudes toward Democratic Institutions." *Harvard University, Graduate School of Arts & Sciences*. https://doi.org/10.7910/DVN/CB3EKB.

Swanson, Carl (2017). "Is Political Art the Only Art That Matters Now?" *Vulture*, 21 April.

Syal, Rajeev (2022). "Why Did the Depp-Heard Libel Outcomes Differ in the US and UK?" *The Guardian*, 2 June.

Szetela, Adam (2021). "I'm a Democratic Socialist. But the DSA Has Lost Its Way." *Newsweek*, 1 August.

Taber, Charles, & Milton Lodge (2006). "Motivated Skepticism in the Evaluation of Political Beliefs." *American Journal of Political Science* 50(3): 755–769.

Tadepalli, Apoorva (2020). "The Rhetorical Weapons of Liberal Nimbyism." *New Republic*, 14 September.

Taibbi, Matt (2018). "Before the Media Lionized Martin Luther King Jr., They Denounced Him." *Rolling Stone*, 4 April.

Taiwo, Olufemi (2020a). "Being-in-the-Room Privilege: Elite Capture and Epistemic Deference." *The Philosopher* 108(4): 61–69.

Taiwo, Olufemi (2020b). "Identity Politics and Elite Capture." *Boston Review*, 7 May.

Taleb, Nassim (2016a). *Antifragile: Things That Gain from Disorder*. New York: Random House.

Taleb, Nassim (2016b). *The Black Swan: The Impact of the Highly Improbable*. New York: Random House.

Taleb, Nassim (2018). *Skin in the Game: Hidden Asymmetries in Daily Life*. New York: Random House.

Tamir, Christine (2021). "The Growing Diversity of Black America." *Pew Research Center*, 25 March.

Tamir, Christine, & Monica Anderson (2022). "One-in-Ten Black People Living in the U.S. Are Immigrants." *Pew Research Center*, 20 January.

Tannock, Stuart (2008). "The Problem of Education-Based Discrimination." *British Journal of Sociology of Education* 29(5): 439–449.

Tapper, Jake, Dan Morris, & Lara Setrakian (2006). "Does Loophole Give Rich Kids More Time on SAT?" *ABC News*, 30 March.

Taska, Bledi, et al. (2018). *The Permanent Detour: Underemployment's Long-Term Effects on the Careers of College Grads*. Boston: Burning Glass.

Tax Policy Center (2018). *Briefing Book: A Citizen's Guide to the Fascinating (though Often Complex) Elements of the Federal Tax System*. Washington, DC: Tax Policy Center.

Taylor, Ashley (2019). "The Complicated Issue of Transableism." *JSTOR Daily*, 17 August.

Taylor, Danielle (2019). "Male Couples Make Up Majority of Same-Sex Households in Large Cities but Not Nationwide." *U.S. Census Bureau*, 18 September.

Taylor, Dorceta (2014). *The State of Diversity in Environmental Organizations: Mainstream NGOs, Foundations, Government Agencies*. Washington, DC: Green 2.0. https://doi.org/10.13140/RG .2.2.34512.40962.

Taylor, Verta (1989). "Social Movement Continuity: The Women's Movement in Abeyance." *American Sociological Review* 54(5): 761–775.

Tetlock, Philip (2006). *Expert Political Judgment: How Good Is It? Can We Know?* Princeton, NJ: Princeton University Press.

Tetlock, Philip, & Dan Gardner (2016). *Superforecasting: The Art and Science of Prediction*. New York: Crown.

Thai, Michael, Matthew Hornsey, & Fiona Barlow (2016). "Friends with Moral Credentials: Minority Friendships Reduce Attributions of Racism for Majority Group Members Who Make Conceivably Racist Statements." *Social Psychological and Personality Science* 7(3): 272–280.

Thai, Michael, Morgana Lizzio-Wilson, & Hema Preya Selvanathan (2021). "Public Perceptions of Prejudice Research: The Double-Edged Sword Faced by Marginalized Group Researchers." *Journal of Experimental Social Psychology* 96: 104181.

Thelin, John (2021). *Going to College in the Sixties*. Baltimore: Johns Hopkins University Press.

32BJ SEIU et al. (2019). "Fired on a Whim: The Precarious Existence of NYC Fast-Food Workers." *National Employment Law Project*, 13 February.

Thomas, Kevin (2011). "Familial Influences on Poverty among Young Children in Black Immigrant, U.S.-Born Black, and Nonblack Immigrant Families." *Demography* 48(2): 437–460.

Thomas, Matthew (2021). "How the DeVos Family Made Grand Rapids Woke." *Vulgar Marxism*, 19 November. https://vulgarmarxism.substack.com/p/right-wing-money-is-fueling-both.

Thomas, Matthew (2022). "Professional Losers: The Transformation of the Democratic Electorate." *Vulgar Marxism*, 9 May. https://vulgarmarxism.substack.com/p/professional-losers-the-transformation.

Thompson, Derek (2022a). "The Millennial Urban Lifestyle Is About to Get More Expensive." *The Atlantic*, 15 October.

Thompson, Derek (2022b). "What Moneyball-for-Everything Has Done to American Culture." *The Atlantic*, 30 October.

Thorson, Mitchell, Janie Haseman, & Carlie Procell (2020). "Four Maps That Show How America Voted in the 2020 Election with Results by County, Number of Voters." *USA Today*, 10 November.

Ticona, Julia (2022). *Left to Our Own Devices: Coping with Insecure Work in a Digital Age*. Oxford: Oxford University Press.

Tilcsik, Andras, Michel Anteby, & Carly Knight (2015). "Concealable Stigma and Occupational Segregation: Toward a Theory of Gay and Lesbian Occupations." *Administrative Science Quarterly* 60(3): 446–481.

Tilton, Emily (2024). "'That's above My Paygrade': Woke Excuses for Ignorance." *Philosophers' Imprint*. https://doi.org/10.3998/phimp.2796.

Tkacik, Maureen (2020). "Restaurants Are Barely Surviving. Delivery Apps Will Kill Them." *Washington Post*, 29 May.

Tkacik, Moe (2020). "Rescuing Restaurants: How to Protect Restaurants, Workers, and Communities from Predatory Delivery App Corporations." *American Economic Liberties Project*, 18 September.

Todd, Emmanuel (2016). *Who Is Charlie? Xenophobia and the New Middle Class*. Cambridge: Polity Press.

Toloudi, Zenovia (2016). "Are We in the Midst of a Public Space Crisis?" *The Conversation*, 7 June.

Tompkins, Al (2021). "How Rush Limbaugh's Rise after the Gutting of the Fairness Doctrine Led to Today's Highly-Partisan Media." *Poynter*, 17 February.

Topaz, Chad, et al. (2022). "Race- and Gender-Based Under-representation of Creative Contributors: Art, Fashion, Film, and Music." *Humanities and Social Sciences Communications* 9: Article 221.

Torrez, Brittany, Cydney Dupree, & Michael Kraus (2024). "How Race Influences Perceptions of Objectivity and Hiring Preferences." *Journal of Experimental Social Psychology* 110. https://doi.org/10.1016/j.jesp.2023.104524.

Tosi, Justin, & Brandon Warmke (2020). *Grandstanding: The Use and Abuse of Moral Talk*. Oxford: Oxford University Press.

Townsend, Megan, et al. (2021a). *Studio Responsibility Index 2021*. Los Angeles: GLAAD Media Institute.

Townsend, Megan, et al. (2021b). *Where We Are on TV: 2020–2021*. Los Angeles: GLAAD Media Institute.

Tracy, Marc (2020). "News Media Outlets Have Been Ravaged by the Pandemic." *New York Times*, 10 April.

Traldi, Oliver (2018). "Campus Speech Debate: The Nightmare of the Nineties Is Alive." *Areo*, 14 May.

Trounstine, Jessica (2021). "The Production of Local Inequality: Race, Class and Land Use in American Cities." In *The American Political Economy: Politics, Markets and Power*, ed. Jacob Hacker et al. (pp. 158–180). Cambridge: Cambridge University Press.

Tuck, Eve, & K. Wayne Yang (2012). "Decolonization Is Not a Metaphor." *Decolonization: Indigeneity, Education & Society* 1(1): 1–40.

Turchin, Peter (2010). "Political Instability May Be a Contributor in the Coming Decade." *Nature* 463: 608.

Turchin, Peter (2012). "Dynamics of Political Instability in the United States, 1780–2010." *Journal of Peace Research* 49(4): 577–591.

Turchin, Peter (2023). *End Times: Elites, Counter-elites, and the Path of Political Disintegration*. New York: Penguin.

Turchin, Peter, & Andrey Korotayev (2020). "The 2010 Structural-Demographic Forecast for the 2010–2020 Decade: A Retrospective Assessment." *PLoS ONE* 15(8): e0237458.

Turchin, Peter, & Sergey Nefedov (2009). *Secular Cycles*. Princeton, NJ: Princeton University Press.

Tuvel, Rebecca (2021). "Changing Identities: Are Race and Gender Analogous?" *Blog of the APA*, 6 July.

Twenge, Jean (2023). *Generations: The Real Differences between Gen Z, Millennials, Gen X, Boomers, and Silents—and What They Mean for America's Future*. New York: Atria Books.

Twenge, Jean, Ryne Sherman, & Brooke Wells (2017). "Declines in Sexual Frequency among American Adults, 1989–2014." *Archives of Sexual Behavior* 46: 2389–2401.

Tyson, Alex, Cary Funk, & Brian Kennedy (2023). "What the Data Says about Americans' Views on Climate Change." *Pew Research Center*, 18 April.

UCLA Undergraduate Admission (n.d.). "First-Generation Applicants." Accessed 6 December 2023. https://admission.ucla.edu/apply/first-generation-applicants.

Ungar-Sargon, Batya (2022). "Is the Woke Cultural Agenda of Union Leaders Undermining Support for Unions?" *Outside Voices*, 14 April. https://outsidevoices.substack.com/p/is-the-woke-cultural-agenda-of-union.

Unger, Roberto (2019). *The Knowledge Economy*. London: Verso.

University of Pennsylvania (n.d.). "About Penn First Plus." Accessed 6 December 2023. https://pennfirstplus.upenn.edu/about-penn-first-plus/.

Urofsky, Melvin (2020). *The Affirmative Action Puzzle: A Living History from Reconstruction to Today*. New York: Pantheon Books.

U.S. Bureau of Economic Analysis (2021). "Annual Gross Domestic Product by State: 2020." *BEA .gov Tools: GDP and Personal Income Mapping*.

U.S. Bureau of Labor Statistics (2021b). "SNR01: Highest Rates for Total Cases: Injuries and Illnesses 2020." *Injuries, Illnesses, and Fatalities*. https://www.bls.gov/iif/nonfatal-injuries-and-illnesses-tables/supplemental-table-1-2020-national.xlsx.

U.S. Bureau of Labor Statistics (2023a). "Fastest Growing Occupations." *Occupational Outlook Handbook*. Last updated 6 September. https://www.bls.gov/ooh/fastest-growing.htm.

U.S. Bureau of Labor Statistics (2023b). "Household Data: Annual Averages—11. Employed Persons by Detailed Occupation, Sex, Race, and Hispanic or Latino Ethnicity." *Labor Force Statistics from the Current Population Survey*. Last updated 25 January. https://www.bls.gov/cps/cpsaat11.htm.

U.S. Bureau of Labor Statistics (2023c). "Household Data: Annual Averages—18. Employed Persons by Detailed Industry, Sex, Race, and Hispanic or Latino Ethnicity." *Labor Force Statistics from the Current Population Survey*. Last updated 25 January. https://www.bls.gov/cps/cpsaat18.htm.

U.S. Bureau of Labor Statistics (2023d). "Occupations with the Most Job Growth." *Employment Projections*. Last updated 6 September. https://www.bls.gov/emp/tables/occupations-most-job-growth.htm.

U.S. Census Bureau (2020a). "Annual Estimates of the Resident Population for the United States, Regions, States, and Puerto Rico: April 1, 2010 to July 1, 2019." https://www2.census.gov/programs-surveys/popest/tables/2010-2019/state/totals/nst-est2019-01.xlsx.

U.S. Census Bureau (2020b). "Gini Index of Income Inequality." In *2019: ACS 1 Year Estimated Detailed Tables*. New York: U.S. Census Bureau.

U.S. Census Bureau (2023). "Households by Type: 1940-Present." https://www.census.gov/data/tables/time-series/demo/families/households.html.

Useem, Jerry (2017). "Power Causes Brain Damage." *The Atlantic*, June/July.

U.S. Federal Reserve (2023). "Distribution of Household Wealth since 1989." *Board of Governors of the Federal Reserve System*. https://www.federalreserve.gov/releases/z1/dataviz/dfa/distribute/chart/.

Usher, Nikki (2021). *News for the Rich, White, and Blue: How Place and Power Distort American Journalism*. New York: Columbia University Press.

U.S. National Archives & Records Administration (2021). "Transcript of the Morrill Act (1862)." https://www.ourdocuments.gov/print_friendly.php?flash=true&page=transcript&doc=33&title=Transcript+of+Morrill+Act+%281862%29.

Uttaro, Carl (2020). "Millionaire Rankings by State through Year-End 2019." *Phoenix Wealth and Affluent Monitor*, April.

Vaisey, Stephen, & Kevin Kiley (2021). "A Model-Based Method for Detecting Persistent Cultural Change Using Panel Data." *Sociological Science* 8: 83–95.

Vaisey, Stephen, & Omar Lizardo (2016). "Cultural Fragmentation or Acquired Dispositions? A New Approach to Accounting for Patterns of Cultural Change." *Socius* 2. https://doi.org/10.1177/2378023116669726.

Vaisse, Justin (2009). "Was Irving Kristol a Neoconservative?" *Brookings*, 23 September.

van Kessel, Patrick, et al. (2018). "Detailed Tables: Where Americans Find Meaning in Life." *Pew Research Center*, 20 November.

van Ree, Eric (2019). "Marx and Engels' Theory of History: Making Sense of the Race Factor." *Journal of Political Ideologies* 24(1): 54–73.

Vasquez, Tina (2021). "The National Lawyers Guild's Former First 'Latina' President Is a White Woman." *Prism*, 7 January.

Verdant Labs (2017). "Democratic v. Republican Occupations." http://verdantlabs.com/politics_of_professions/.

Villadsen, Kaspar (2007). "Managing the Employee's Soul: Foucault Applied to Modern Management Technologies." *Cadernos EBAPE.BR* 5(1): 1–10.

Vincent, Lynne, & Maryam Kouchaki (2015). "Why Creative People Are More Likely to Be Dishonest." *Harvard Business Review*, 23 November.

Viren, Sarah (2020). "The Accusations Were Lies. But Could We Prove It?" *New York Times*, 18 March.

Viren, Sarah (2021). "The Native Scholar Who Wasn't." *New York Times*, 25 May.

Vitali, Stefania, James Glattfelder, & Stefano Battiston (2011). "The Network of Global Corporate Control." *PLoS ONE* 6(10): e25995.

Vobejda, Barbara (1989). "Relative Value of a College Degree Soared in 1980s." *Washington Post*, 3 May.

Vogel, Joseph (2018). "The Forgotten Baldwin." *Boston Review*, 14 May.

Vylomova, Ekaterina, Sean Murphy, & Nicholas Haslam (2019). "Evaluation of Semantic Change of Harm-Related Concepts in Psychology." In *Proceedings of the 1st International Workshop on Computational Approaches to Historical Language Change* (pp. 29–34). Florence: Association for Computational Linguistics. https://aclanthology.org/W19-4704/.

Wacquant, Loic (2022). "Resolving the Trouble with 'Race.'" *New Left Review* 133/134: 67–88.

Wacquant, Loic, & Pierre Bourdieu (1989). "For a Socio-analysis of Intellectuals: On 'Homo Academicus.'" *Berkeley Journal of Sociology* 34: 1–29.

Wade, Lisa (2018). *American Hookup: The New Culture of Sex on Campus*. New York: W. W. Norton.

Wadman, Meredith, & Ann Gibbons (2020). "Twitter Account of Embattled #MeTooSTEM Founder Suspended." *Science*, 3 August.

Wagner, Kate (2023). "You Can't Even Tell Who's Rich Anymore." *The Nation*, 24 March.

Wai, Jonathan, & Kaja Perina (2018). "Expertise in Journalism: Factors Shaping a Cognitive and Culturally Elite Profession." *Journal of Expertise* 1(1): 57–78.

Walker, Mason (2021). "U.S. Newsroom Employment Has Fallen 26% since 2008." *Pew Research Center*, 13 July.

Wang, Rong, & Darius Chan (2019). "Will You Forgive Your Supervisor's Wrongdoings? The Moral Licensing Effect of Ethical Leader Behaviors." *Frontiers in Psychology* 10: 484. https://doi.org/10.3389/fpsyg.2019.00484.

Wang, Wendy (2015). "The Link between a College Education and a Lasting Marriage." *Pew Research Center*, 4 December.

Wang, Yi-Chia, Moira Burke, & Robert Kraut (2013). "Gender, Topic, and Audience Response: An Analysis of User-Generated Content on Facebook." *Facebook Research*, 27 April.

Wang, Zhechen, Jolanda Jetten, & Niklas Steffens (2020). "The More You Have, the More You Want? Higher Social Class Predicts a Greater Desire for Wealth and Status." *European Journal of Social Psychology* 50(2): 360–375.

Wapman, K. Hunter, et al. (2022). "Quantifying Hierarchy Dynamics in U.S. Faculty Hiring and Retention." *Nature* 610: 120–127.

Ward, Ian (2021). "The Democrats' Privileged College-Kid Problem." *Politico*, 9 October.

Warikoo, Natasha (2016). *The Diversity Bargain and Other Dilemmas of Race, Admissions and Meritocracy at Elite Universities*. Chicago: University of Chicago Press.

Watkins, Ronald (2020). "Growing List of Universities Acknowledge Land Belonged to Native Americans." *College Post*, 27 November.

Watkins-Hayes, Celeste (2009). *The New Welfare Bureaucrats: Entanglements of Race, Class, and Policy Reform*. Chicago: University of Chicago Press.

Watters, Ethan (2011). *Crazy like Us: The Globalization of the American Psyche*. New York: Free Press.

Weatherby, Leif (2024). "The Misguided Idea That Universities Are Left-Wing Hotbeds." *Boston Globe*, 4 January.

Weaver, Velsa (2018). "Why White People Keep Calling the Cops on Black Americans." *Vox*, 29 May.

Webb, Michael (2020). "The Impact of Artificial Intelligence on the Labor Market." Working paper. https://www.michaelwebb.co/webb_ai.pdf.

Webb, Simon (2014). *The Suffragette Bombers: Britain's Forgotten Terrorists*. Barnsley, UK: Pen and Sword.

Weber, Max (1958). *From Max Weber: Essays in Sociology*. Ed. H. H. Gerth & C. Wright Mills. Oxford: Oxford University Press.

Weber, Max (2001). *The Protestant Ethic and the Spirit of Capitalism*. London: Routledge.

Weber, Max (2020). *Charisma and Disenchantment: The Vocation Lectures*. New York: New York Review of Books Classics.

Weeden, Jason, & Robert Kurzban (2014). *The Hidden Agenda of the Political Mind: How Self-Interest Shapes Our Opinions and Why We Won't Admit It*. Princeton, NJ: Princeton University Press.

Weeden, Kim (2002). "Why Do Some Occupations Pay More than Others? Social Closure and Earnings Inequality in the United States." *American Journal of Sociology* 108(1): 55–101.

Weeden, Kim, & David Grusky (2012). "The Three Worlds of Inequality." *American Journal of Sociology* 117(6): 1723–1785.

Weill, Kelly (2020). "White Male Prof Allegedly Posed as Woman of Color to Bully Women." *Daily Beast*, 6 October.

Weiner, Tim (2012). *Enemies: A History of the FBI*. New York: Random House.

Weis, Robert, & Sophie Bittner (2022). "College Students' Access to Academic Accommodations over Time: Evidence of a Matthew Effect in Higher Education." *Psychological Injury and Law* 15(3): 236–252.

Weise, Elizabeth, & Jessica Guynn (2014). "Black and Hispanic Computer Scientists Have Degrees from Top Universities, but Don't Get Hired in Tech." *USA Today*, 12 October.

Weiss, Bari (2021). "The Miseducation of America's Elites." *City Journal*, 9 March.

Weiss, Suzy (2022). "He Was a World-Renowned Cancer Researcher. Now He's Collecting Unemployment." *Common Sense*, 19 May. https://bariweiss.substack.com/p/he-was-a-world-renowned-cancer-researcher.

Wellmon, Chad (2016). *Organizing Enlightenment: Information Overload and the Invention of the Modern Research University*. Baltimore: Johns Hopkins University Press.

Wermund, Benjamin (2017). "How U.S. News College Rankings Promote Inequality on Campus." *Politico*, 10 September.

Weymouth, Lally (1978). "Foundation Woes, the Saga of Henry Ford II: Part Two." *New York Times*, 12 March.

Wezerek, Gus, Ryan Enos, & Jacob Brown (2021). "Do You Live in a Political Bubble?" *New York Times*, 3 May.

White, Aaron (2021). "Foucault! Five Leftist and Feminist Thinkers Also Inspiring the Far Right." *Open Democracy*, 8 September.

White, Micah (n.d.). Homepage. Accessed 27 November 2023. https://www.micahmwhite.com/.

Whiten, Andrew, & Richard Byrne (1997). *Machiavellian Intelligence II: Extensions and Evaluations*. Cambridge: Cambridge University Press.

Widra, Emily (2018). "Stark Racial Disparities in Murder Victimization Persist, Even as Overall Murder Rate Declines." *Prison Policy Initiative*, 3 May.

Wilkinson, Will (2021). "NIMBYism and the Externalities of Non-development." *Model Citizen*, 13 June. https://modelcitizen.substack.com/p/nimbyism-and-the-externalities-of.

Willer, Robb, Ko Kuwabara, & Michael Macy (2009). "The False Enforcement of Unpopular Norms." *American Journal of Sociology* 115(2): 451–490.

Williams, Aaron, & Armand Emamdjomeh (2018). "America Is More Diverse than Ever—but Still Segregated." *Washington Post*, 10 May.

Williams, Alex (2015). "Why Aren't There More Minority Journalists?" *Columbia Journalism Review*, 22 July.

Williams, Daniel (2022). "The Roots of Social Irrationality." *Open for Debate*, 17 October. https://blogs.cardiff.ac.uk/openfordebate/the-social-roots-of-irrationality/.

Williams, Raymond (1985). *Keywords: A Vocabulary of Culture and Society*. Oxford: Oxford University Press.

Williamson, Vanessa. (2019). "The Philanthropy Con." *Dissent*, Winter.

Willnat, Lars, David Weaver, & G. Cleveland Wilhoit (2017). *The American Journalist in the Digital Age: A Half-Century Perspective*. New York: Peter Lang.

Willnat, Lars, David Weaver, & G. Cleveland Wilhoit (2022). *The American Journalist under Attack: Key Findings*. Syracuse, NY: S. I. Newhouse School of Public Communications.

Wills, Matthew (2020). "Abolitionist 'Wide Awakes' Were Woke before 'Woke.'" *JSTOR Daily*, 29 June.

Wilmers, Nathan (2017). "Does Customer Demand Reproduce Inequality? High-Income Consumers, Vertical Differentiation, and Wage Structure." *American Journal of Sociology* 123(1): 178–231.

Wilmers, Nathan, & Letian Zhang (2022). "Values and Inequality: Prosocial Jobs and the College Wage Premium." *American Sociological Review* 87(3): 415–442.

Wilson, John (1995). *The Myth of Political Correctness: The Conservative Attack on Higher Education*. Durham, NC: Duke University Press.

Wilson, Valier, Ethan Miller, & Melat Kassa (2021). *Racial Representation in Professional Occupations: By the Numbers*. Washington, DC: Economic Policy Institute.

Wilson, William (1981). "Race, Class and Public Policy." *American Sociologist* 16(2): 125–134.

Wingfield, Tai, et al. (2021). *How Chief Diversity Officers Are Meeting the Challenges of Today and Tomorrow*. New York: United Minds. https://www.webershandwick.com//wp-content/uploads/2021/11/United-Minds_CDO_Study.pdf.

Winship, Scott, et al. (2021). *Long Shadows: The Black-White Gap in Multigenerational Poverty*. Washington, DC: Brookings Institution Press.

Wittgenstein, Ludwig (2009). *Philosophical Investigations*. Hoboken, NJ: Wiley-Blackwell.

Wlezien, Christopher, & Stuart Soroka (2023). "Media Reflect! Policy, the Public and the News." *American Political Science Review*. https://doi.org/10.1017/S0003055423000874.

Wodtke, Geoffry (2016). "Are Smart People Less Racist? Verbal Ability, Anti-Black Prejudice, and the Principle-Policy Paradox." *Social Problems* 63(1): 21–45.

Wojcik, Stefan, & Adam Hughes (2019). "Sizing Up Twitter Users." *Pew Research Center*, 24 April.

Wolf, Jonathan (2021). "Law Schools Are Building Another Giant Lawyer Bubble Destined to Burst in the Legal Job Market." *Above the Law*, 4 August.

Wolfe, Julia, et al. (2020). "Domestic Workers Chartbook." *Economic Policy Institute*, 14 May.

Wolfinger, Nicholas (2023). "Bisexual America." *Institute for Family Studies*, 5 June.

Wolters, Raymond (1975). *The New Negro on Campus: Black College Rebellions of the 1920s*. Princeton, NJ: Princeton University Press.

Wong, Alia (2023). "Why Are Colleges Offering Up More DEI Degrees? Demand for Diversity Expertise Is Growing." *USA Today*, 6 February.

Woodhouse, Leighton (2022). "They Questioned Gender-Affirming Care. Then Their Kids Were Kicked Out of School." *Common Sense*, 23 June.

Wright, Colin (2022). "I Got Thrown Off Etsy and PayPal for Expressing My Belief in Biological Reality." *Quillette*, 23 June.

Wu, Tim, & Stuart Thompson (2019). "The Roots of Big Tech Run Disturbingly Deep." *New York Times*, 7 June.

Wuest, Joanna (2022). "The Dead End of Corporate Activism." *Boston Review*, 18 May.

X, Malcolm (2020). *The End of White Supremacy: Four Speeches*. New York: Arcade Publishing.

Yam, Kimmy (2021). "Viral Images Show People of Color as Anti-Asian Perpetrators. That Misses the Big Picture." *NBC News*, 15 June.

Yang, Andrew (2018). *The War on Normal People: The Truth about America's Disappearing Jobs and Why Universal Basic Income Is Our Future*. New York: Hachette Books.

Yang, Yuan (2019). "Inside China's Crackdown on Young Marxists." *Financial Times*, 13 February.

Yarrow, Allison (2018). *90s Bitch: Media, Culture, and the Failed Promise of Gender Equality*. New York: Harper Perennial.

Yavorsky, Jill, Claire Kamp-Dush, & Sarah Schoppe-Sullivan (2015). "The Production of Inequality: The Gender Division of Labor across the Transition to Parenthood." *Journal of Marriage and Family* 77(3): 662–679.

Yglesias, Matthew (2018). "Why Criticism of Amazon Isn't Sticking." *Vox*, 11 December.

Yglesias, Matthew (2019). "The Great Awokening." *Vox*, 1 April.

Yglesias, Matthew (2020). "Why Elizabeth Warren Is Losing Even as White Professionals Love Her." *Vox*, 3 March.

Yglesias, Matthew (2022a). "Democrats' College Degree Divide." *Slow Boring*, 14 February.

Yglesias, Matthew (2022b). "The Misinformation Cope." *Slow Boring*, 20 April.

Yglesias, Matthew (2023). "Who Is Included by 'Inclusive' Language?" *Slow Boring*, 18 January.

Yglesias, Matthew, & Milan Singh (2022). "Democrats Have Changed a Lot since 2012." *Slow Boring*, 11 May.

Young, Julia (2015). *Mexican Exodus: Emigrants, Exiles, and Refugees of the Cristero War*. Oxford: Oxford University Press.

Young, Kevin (2017). *Bunk: The Rise of Hoaxes, Humbug, Plagiarists, Phonies, Post-facts, and Fake News*. Minneapolis: Graywolf Press.

Younis, Mohamed (2020). "Americans Want More, Not Less, Immigration for First Time." *Gallup*, 1 July. See survey crosstabs for breakdown by education.

Yudkin, Daniel, Stephen Hawkins, & Tim Dixon (2019). "The Perception Gap: How False Impressions Are Pulling Americans Apart." *More in Common*, June.

Zacher, Sam (2023). "Polarization of the Rich: The New Democrat Allegiance of Affluent Americans and the Politics of Redistribution." *Perspectives on Politics*. https://doi.org/10.1017/S1537592722003310.

Zeitz, Josh (2015). "When America Hated Catholics." *Politico*, 23 September.

Zetlin, Minda (2016). "It's Official: 'Brogrammer' Culture Is Driving Women Out of STEM Jobs." *Inc.*, 4 May.

Zhang, Baobao, & Allan Dafoe (2019). "Artificial Intelligence: American Attitudes and Trends." *Oxford Center for the Governance of AI*, January.

Zhang, Floyd (2023). "Political Endorsement by Nature and Trust in Scientific Expertise during COVID-19." *Nature Human Behaviour* 5: 1528–1534.

Zhang, Liang, Ronald Ehrenberg, & Ziangmin Liu (2021). "The Increasing Stratification of Faculty Employment at Colleges and Universities in the United States." *Advances in Industrial and Labor Relations* 26: 73–97.

Zimbardo, Philip, & Nikita Coulombe (2016). *Man Interrupted: Why Men Are Struggling & What We Can Do about It.* Newburyport, MA: Conari Press.

Zimmer, Ben (2017). "'Woke,' from a Sleepy Verb to a Badge of Awareness." *Wall Street Journal*, 14 April.

Zingher, Joshua (2022). "Diploma Divide: Educational Attainment and the Realignment of the American Electorate." *Political Research Quarterly* 75(2): 263–277.

Zinsmeister, Karl (2016). "Who Gives Most to Charity?" In *Almanac of American Philanthropy* (pp. 1169–1182). Washington, DC: Philanthropy Roundtable.

Zipperer, Ben, et al. (2022). "National Survey of Gig Workers Paints a Picture of Poor Working Conditions, Low Pay." *Economic Policy Institute*, 1 June.

Zucker, Kenneth (2017). "Epidemiology of Gender Dysphoria and Transgender Identity." *Sexual Health* 14(5): 404–411.

Zumoff, Jacob (2020). "The Left in the United States and the Decline of the Socialist Party of America, 1934–1935." *Labour/La Travail* 85: 165–198.

INDEX